To be encouraged to put one's own preaching into broad historical context, beginning with the apostles, is a rare treat. This is a book for all preachers and not only those who have a liking for church history. The various authors provide a comprehensive examination of the context and method of preaching through the ages. Those of us who preach—especially those who preach without a carefully examined philosophy of preaching or a constantly reviewed biblical hermeneutics—can only be enriched and encouraged by these studies.

> GRAEME L. GOLDSWORTHY, was lecturer in Old Testament
> and biblical theology at Moore Theological College

The apostle Paul commanded, "Preach the word." This book introduces some of the most influential preachers from the first through the eighteenth centuries and offers fascinating studies of how they responded to Paul's mandate with great diversity of doctrine and methodology.

> JOEL R. BEEKE, president, Puritan Reformed
> Theological Seminary, Grand Rapids, Michigan

What an incredible work. I was so impressed by the thoughtfulness and care the editors put into their selections. To have so many of Christian history's great preachers and teachers of God's Word sampled and collected in one location makes reading these volumes an incredible delight, not to mention an invaluable resource. If you want to be blessed by, and mentored by, some of the most anointed teachers in history, this great work is where to begin! I'm excited to add it to my library and hope every serious student of God's Word will do the same.

> J. D. GREEAR, pastor, The Summit Church, Raleigh-Durham, North Carolina

Paul said, "follow my example, as I follow the example of Christ." Discipleship always works best when the Christian life is modeled for others. The same truth also applies in preaching. My advice to preachers young and old is to stay committed to the Word and learn from those who preach well. Sitting at the feet of history's greatest preachers is a great honor that will enrich your soul, enliven your flock, and enhance your ministry. If this is your desire, then read this book. It tells the tales of history's greats and relates to you a legacy that will inspire you to, like Paul, "boldly ... proclaim the mysteries of the gospel."

> DR. TONY EVANS, senior pastor, Oak Cliff Bible
> Fellowship; president, The Urban Alternative

It is well-known that the Reformers and their heirs regarded faithful preaching of the Scriptures as a mark of a true church. In these two volumes we have a rich exploration of the way in which God has indeed blessed his people with such preaching ever since the apostolic era. Given the unique biographical focus of these essays, these two volumes also remind us that preaching is always mediated through distinct personalities, hence the differences in exegetically-sound preaching over the years. In sum, what we have here is a treasure trove for all who love the preaching of the Word and for all called to this central task in the church's life.

MICHAEL A. G. HAYKIN, Professor & Chair of Church History, The Southern Baptist Theological Seminary

"How did you learn to preach?" is one of the more frequent questions I'm asked. In addition to practice (trial and error!), I can honestly say that I learned much in terms both of what to do and not to do by studying great preachers from the past and present. Virtually all effective preachers will admit that in some sense they stand on the shoulders of someone who has preceded them, from whose method and style and understanding of Scripture they have drawn. That is certainly true of me. These volumes are a treasure trove of homiletical insights from the greatest of preachers in the history of the Christian church. It is a wonderful resource that I am extremely happy to recommend.

SAM STORMS, Bridgeway Church, Oklahoma City, Oklahoma

For most pastors—maybe for all—becoming a better preacher is a lifelong quest. And on that quest, few things are more beneficial than spending quality time with more gifted preachers. Reading *A Legacy of Preaching* affords an unprecedented opportunity for all kinds of pastors to learn from a legion of men and women who are widely regarded as among the best preachers in history, from Peter and Paul to Billy Graham and Gardner Taylor. Hearing their life stories, learning their homiletical theology, and listening to their gospel proclamation will help any pastor fulfill the high calling of preaching the gospel of Jesus Christ.

PHILIP RYKEN, president, Wheaton College

A *Legacy* OF PREACHING

VOLUME ONE

A *Legacy* OF PREACHING

VOLUME ONE

APOSTLES TO
THE REVIVALISTS

BENJAMIN K. FORREST, KEVIN L. KING,
BILL CURTIS, AND DWAYNE MILIONI

ZONDERVAN

A Legacy of Preaching, Volume One—Apostles to the Revivalists
Copyright © 2018 by Benjamin K. Forrest, Kevin L. King, and Dwayne Milioni

This title is also available as a Zondervan ebook.

Requests for information should be addressed to:
Zondervan, *3900 Sparks Dr. SE, Grand Rapids, Michigan 49546*

ISBN 978-0-310-53822-6

Cover design: LUCAS Art & Design
Cover photo: Michael D. Beckwith/Unsplash
Interior design: Kait Lamphere

Printed in the United States of America

18 19 20 21 22 23 24 25 26 27 28 /DHV/ 15 14 13 12 11 10 9 8 7 6 5 4 3 2 1

This book is dedicated to my wife, Lerisa—who (as it happens) is not a preacher—but she daily proclaims the glories of the Lord, with her life and love. Thank you!

BKF

This book is dedicated to my partner in life and ministry—Joy. Your name aptly describes our decades of serving together and the life I have been blessed to share with you! To Daylee, Walter, Sebastian, Solomon, Kevin, Sharin, and Julianna—you are gifts from the Father that have added immeasurably to my life. As the homiletical luminaries in this volume continue to illuminate the Word, may your lives continue to bear witness to the life-changing message of the gospel of Jesus Christ.

KLK

This book is dedicated to my wife, Lyla, who has always embraced my love of preachers and preaching. Thank you, dearest friend, for sharing this journey with me. I love you!

BC

This book is dedicated to Kay, my wife and dear sister in the faith, and to my students whom I desire to know preaching history so they will carry on the legacy.

DM

Contents

Part Three:

Part Four:

Abbreviations

AB	Anchor Bible
BECNT	Baker Exegetical Commentary on the New Testament
B. SOTAH	Tractate Sotah in the Babylonian Talmud
CO	*Ioannis Calvini Opera Quae Supersunt Omnia*
COR	*Ioannis Calvini Opera Omnia*
CPG	*Clavis Patrum Graecorum*. Edited by Maurice Geerard. 5 vols. Turnhout: Brepols, 1974–1987.
CTS	*Selected Works of John Calvin: Tracts*
DW	*Die detschen werke*
ET	English translation
FC	Fathers of the Church
HEX.	Hexameron, Basil of Caesarea
ICC	International Critical Commentary
JRELS	Journal of Religious Studies
MGHSS	*Monumenta Germaniae Historica Scriptores*
NICNT	New International Commentary on the New Testament
NIVAC	New International Version Application Commentary
OS	*Johannis Calvini Opera Selecta*
PG	Patrdogia Graeca
PNTC	Pillar New Testament Commentary
Q.	Question
R.	reign
SC	*Supplementa Calviniana*
T. SOTAH	Tractate Sotah in the Tosefta
WJE	The Works of Jonathan Edwards
Y. SHABBAT	Tractate Shabbat in the Jerusalem Talmud
ZECNT	Zondervan Exegetical Commentary of the New Testment

Foreword

At the heart of the Christian faith is a Savior who was a preacher. This stands in contrast to the gods of Olympus or the Roman pantheon whose interaction with mortals, when it happened at all, was transient, ephemeral, detached—like a circle touching a tangent. Zeus thundered, but he did not preach. Nor did the dying and rising savior gods of the mystery religions. There were ablutions and incantations and the babbling utterances of the Sibylline Oracles, but nothing that could rightly be called a sermon.

But when the divine Logos was made flesh (*egeneto sarx*), he embraced the full range of human pathos and human discourse: Jesus wept, and Jesus preached. Mark opened his account of the Christian story with this announcement, "Jesus came into Galilee, preaching the gospel" (Mark 1:14 KJV). Jesus himself declared that the very purpose of his mission on earth was to preach: "'I must proclaim the good news of the kingdom of God to the other towns also, *because that is why I was sent.*' And he kept on preaching . . . ." (Luke 4:43–44, emphasis added). The old liberal construal of this text was to say that Jesus came preaching the kingdom but what we got was the church. But that way of putting it is to deny the coinherence of the kingdom and the King, a title ascribed to Jesus Christ at several places in the New Testament (see John 12:15, 18:37; 1 Tim 6:13–16; Rev 17:14, 19:16). In the Gospels, Jesus not only proclaimed the kingdom, he was the bearer of it. Thus, from the beginning, the content of early Christian preaching was neither a new philosophical worldview nor a code of ethics to improve human behavior, but rather Jesus Christ himself: Jesus remembered in his words and deeds, Jesus crucified, buried, and risen from the dead, and Jesus yet to come again in glory— all of which is included in that earliest of Christian confessions, "Jesus is Lord!"

Early Christian proclaimers fanned out across the Roman Empire to engage in what Ephrem the Syrian called "the sweet preaching of the cross." The aim of such preachers was not merely to express their opinions or to provide entertainment to their listeners. No, they were in the vanguard of the *militia Christi*, and their preaching had an urgent eschatological motivation and thrust. It propelled redemptive history forward toward the consummation of all things. This is certainly how Matthew 24:14 has been understood, from the age of the apostles right down through the dawn of the modern ecumenical movement: "And this gospel of the kingdom will be preached in the whole world as a testimony to all nations, and then the end will come."

The end has not yet come, and so the preaching of the Gospel continues. It is done in many ways by countless voices in numerous settings—from tall-steeple cathedrals and mass meetings to small village churches and out-of-the-way Bible study groups that are forced to meet in hiding. Today's proclaimers often have access to media—radio, television, print, and the internet—that would have astounded the preachers covered in this volume. But in these and other ways, the gospel still goes forth, lives are transformed, and the church is renewed.

This volume tells the story of preaching through biography. The context, theology, and contributions of some of the most notable proclaimers in the history of the Christian movement are gathered here. It is a strong list but not an exhaustive one. What we do have in this volume is a distinctive account of preaching told through the lives of thirty of the most consequential proclaimers from the first 1800 years of the church.

The diversity and variety of witnesses is striking, but so are the common themes and single-minded passion that motivated these proclaimers. The Holy Scriptures—the charter documents of the Christian faith—are at the heart of their preaching, and the centrality of Jesus Christ shines through their sermons. We see here how preaching as a spiritual and ecclesial vocation shaped every aspect of the church's work: evangelism, theology, exegesis, worship, and witness. We also see how in different ages God has renewed the church through new forms of preaching—the monks, the mendicants, the mystics, the missionaries, the Reformers, and the awakeners—all of whom drew from the wellspring of the apostolic faith announced by the first proclaimers of the gospel.

One of Martin Luther's favorite verses from Saint Paul is Romans 10:17, "Faith comes from hearing the message, and the message is heard through the word about Christ . . . and how can they hear without someone preaching to them?" (Rom 10:17, 14). May God yet renew the church again through a new generation of faithful gospel proclaimers.

TIMOTHY GEORGE is the founding dean of Beeson Divinity School of Samford University and general editor of the *Reformation Commentary on Scripture*.

Acknowledgments

Ben, Kevin, and Dwayne would first like to thank all the contributing authors who gave of their time, study, and expertise. They pass along wisdom from the past for the training up of future preachers—who will eventually leave their own legacy of preaching. Most of these contributing authors responded to a random email from an unknown "colleague." Their gracious response made this project something that we hope will have a long-lasting impact on the field of preaching. We would also like to thank Sarah Funderburke for first seeing the potential in this book many years ago. Laura Sipple, Cheryl Job, and Heather Bradly, although connected to this project only for a short while, were extremely helpful—we appreciate your encouragement and assistance. A special thanks to Joshua Erb, Graduate Assistant extraordinaire, who worked behind the scenes on several occasions, looking up footnotes, editing bibliographical information, and becoming quite proficient in the history of preaching along the way.

We also must (and want to heartily) thank the entire team at Zondervan for bringing this project to fulfillment. Dr. Stan Gundry, Ryan Pazdur, Jesse Hillman, Josh Kessler, Kim Tanner, Jesse Welliver, and a host of others worked behind the scenes to bring this idea to fruition. Thank you for your assistance and friendship along the way. It is a great blessing to be considered Zondervan authors! Here, we would also like to thank Dr. Ed Hindson for encouraging us to submit this project to Zondervan in the first place. He is, and has been, a great advocate—and we appreciate his leadership!

I (Ben) would like to thank all the pastors and preachers who have influenced my life. There are too many to name individually, but (hopefully) you know who you are. The proclamation of the gospel from these many pulpits has contributed to my own understanding of the call to "preach the word" (2 Tim. 4:2). Specifically, I would like to thank Dr. Nathan Smith, and Heritage Baptist Church, for being an encouragement and an example of faithfulness to the biblical text. To my wife, Lerisa—thank you for being an example of a woman who "preaches" Christ with your life daily. Each morning when you get out of bed to meet with Jesus, you remind me of whose we are and where we want to invest our lives. To Reagan, Hudson, and Graham, look at the example set by your mother— and follow it! We love you and pray that your lives are committed to following Jesus. Share him with those you meet along the way; share with life and love, deed and word! To Will and Greg—thank you for being great examples, even as younger brothers. I will continue to pray that the church you plant in Seattle will "fearlessly make known the mystery of the gospel" (Eph. 6:19). Dad and Mom, thank you for training me up in the way I should go, for teaching me from Scripture, and encouraging me toward holiness. The fruit of your discipleship is reflected in all my work. To my students Landon, Sri, Josh, Patrick, AJ, Sean, and Torrey, hold high the Word of God. I am encouraged by your heart, passion, and desire to faithfully proclaim the gospel as good news. Lastly, I want to thank my coeditors—Kevin, Bill, and Dwayne. Thank you for your friendship and mentorship. I look up to you and appreciate the ways you have let me partner with you in ministry.

I (Kevin) would like to thank Ben Forrest, whose inspiration, creativity, and persistence brought this project from its inception to its completion. It has been a great pleasure to work alongside you these few years at Liberty University. I thank God for your leadership and friendship. I also want to thank my two other coeditors, Bill Curtis and Dwayne Milioni. Your expertise and passion for preaching and preachers is contagious. You push me to greater exploration in the field as I try just to "keep up." To Joy—my girlfriend and wife of over thirty-three years. It was in church we first met and it is in the church we serve together. I do appreciate the weekly sermon critiques that you provide between the services. Your desire to see my preaching improve pushes me to strive for excellence, as I am privileged each week to preach the "incomparable riches of his grace, expressed in his kindness to us in Christ Jesus" (Eph 2:7). To my children—Daylee (and her husband Wal Ter and son Sebastian), Kevin Jr. (and his wife Sharin), and Julianna. You are a great blessing to me and I rejoice to see your commitment to our Savior as you serve in his church. To my students—I am privileged to share in your journey. As I have had the occasion to share with you what has been shared with me, I await with great anticipation and expectation that the world will one day say of you as you step out into service of our King, they have been with Jesus (Acts 4:13). This book is a continuation of our conversation on preaching. Preach the Word!

I (Bill) would like to thank my coeditors for their work on this project. Ben, Dwayne, and Kevin made this a journey that was both enriching and enjoyable.

I would also like to thank the elders at Cornerstone Baptist Church, Darlington, South Carolina, for their ongoing support of my investment in academia. Despite the heavy load of my pastoral ministry, they encourage me to teach and to write. What a blessing to shepherd God's church with these men! Finally, I would like to thank my amazing wife, Lyla, for her patience and sacrifice. She makes countless sacrifices so that I can fulfill God's calling through the proclamation of the Word and the production of works that strive to bring him glory.

I (Dwayne) would like to thank my wife, Kay, for her love, devotion, and sacrifice of time while writing and editing this project. I would also like to thank the elders and pastoral staff of Open Door Church in Raleigh for their encouragement. Finally, thanks to the faculty and administration of Southeastern Baptist Theological Seminary, who allow me to teach History of Preaching courses to graduate and PhD students. I hope this volume may benefit my students and many others in the decades to follow.

About the Authors

JONATHAN J. ARMSTRONG (PhD, Fordham University) is Associate Professor of Bible and Theology at Moody Bible Institute–Spokane. He has also served as a postdoctoral researcher at the Friedrich-Alexander-Universität Erlangen-Nürnberg in Germany and has lectured at Wycliffe Hall as a full member of the theology faculty of the University of Oxford. Jonathan is also the founder and president of Aqueduct Project, a nonprofit corporation dedicated to creating access to transformative theological education for the entire global community.

DAVID R. BECK (PhD, Duke University) is Associate Dean of Biblical Studies and Professor of New Testament and Greek at Southeastern Baptist Theological Seminary in Wake Forest, North Carolina. He has pastored several churches and is the author of *The Discipleship Paradigm: Readers and Anonymous Characters in the Fourth Gospel*, "Whom Jesus Loved: Anonymity and Identity. Belief and Witness in the Fourth Gospel" in *Characters and Characterization in the Gospel of John*, and is the coeditor of *Rethinking the Synoptic Problem* with David Alan Black.

BYARD BENNETT (PhD, University of Toronto) is Professor of Historical and Philosophical Theology at Grand Rapids Theological Seminary.

BILL CURTIS (PhD, Southeastern Baptist Theological Seminary) is Assistant Professor of Homiletics at Southeastern Baptist Theological Seminary and pastor of Cornerstone Baptist Church in Darlington, South Carolina. His newest book is *Gypsy Smith: The Forgotten Evangelist*.

G. R. EVANS (PhD, DLitt, Oxford; LittD, Cambridge) is Professor Emeritus of Medieval Theology and Intellectual History at the University of Cambridge and was British Academy Research Reader in Theology from 1986 to 1988. She has written on a wide range of medieval authors including Augustine, Anselm, and Bernard of Clairvaux.

DANIEL FĂRCAŞ (PhD, University of Paris-Sorbonne) is an Instructor of Theology at Liberty University, Rawlings School of Divinity. He has completed his dissertation at the Sorbonne on Meister Eckhart and Albertus Magnus, as well as two postdoctoral research fellowships, one on Paul Ricœur, at the Institut Protestant de Théologie, in Paris (France), and the other on Meister Eckhart, at Babeş-Bolyai University, in Romania.

PAUL A. HARTOG (PhD, Loyola University Chicago) is Professor of Christian Thought at Faith Baptist Theological Seminary. He has published extensively on early Christianity.

W. ROSS HASTINGS (PhD, Queen's University, Ontario; PhD St. Andrews University, Scotland) is the Sangwoo Youtong Chee Associate Professor of Theology at Regent College in Vancouver, British Colombia. His research interests include Trinitarian theology, pastoral theology, and the theology of Jonathan Edwards.

ELIZABETH HOARE (PhD, University of Durham) is a Tutor in Spiritual Formation and Dean for Women at Wycliffe Hall, University of Oxford. Her doctoral research focused on the impact of the Reformation on the Tudor royal household.

TIMOTHY D. HOLDER (PhD, University of Kentucky) is a Professor of History at Walters State and an adjunct professor of History at Toccoa Falls College. He is the author or coauthor of over a dozen books.

MARK A. HOWELL (PhD, Southeastern Baptist Theological Seminary) is Pastor of Hunters Glen Baptist Church in Plano, Texas.

KEVIN L. KING (PhD, University of Pretoria; DMin, Southern Baptist Theological Seminary) is Professor of Homiletics and Historical Theology at Liberty Baptist Theological Seminary and pastor of Palestine Baptist Church, Huddleston, Virginia.

MARTIN I. KLAUBER (PhD, University of Wisconsin) is Affiliate Professor of Church History at Trinity Evangelical Divinity School and Adjunct Professor of Church History at Liberty University. His specialty and publications largely revolve around the areas of Reformation and Post-Reformation History. His publications include *Between Reformed Scholasticism and Pan-Protestantism: Jean-Alphonse Turretin (1671–1737) and Enlightened Orthodoxy at the Academy of Geneva, The Great Commission: Evangelicals and the History of World Missions*, and *The Theology of the French Reformed Church: From Henry IV to the Edict of Nantes* published by Reformation Heritage Books.

HENRY M. KNAPP (PhD, Calvin College) is Pastor of Adult Nurture and Discipleship at First Presbyterian Church in Beaver, Pennsylvania. His dissertation research was focused on the Theology of John Owen.

ROBERT KOLB (PhD, University of Wisconsin-Madison) is Missions Professor of Systematic Theology Emeritus at Concordia Seminary. Kolb served as associate editor (1973–1994) and coeditor (1995–1997) of *The Sixteenth Century Journal* and is still coeditor, with A. R. Victor Raj, of *Missio Apostolica* (since 1996). He was a member of the Commission on Theology and Church Relations of The Lutheran Church—Missouri Synod (1984–1992) and its chair (1990–1992). He served as president of the Sixteenth Century Studies Conference (1981–1982) and the Society for Reformation Research (1994–1996). Since 1993, he has been a member of the Continuation Committee of the International Congress for Luther Research.

ANTHONY N. S. LANE (DD [by publications], University of Oxford) is Professor of Historical Theology at the London School of Theology. Since 1992, he has been a member of the Presidium of the International Congress on Calvin Research. He is the author of a number of books, including *Calvin and Bernard of Clairvaux, John Calvin: Student of the Church Fathers,* and *A Reader's Guide to Calvin's Institutes.*

GERALD R. MCDERMOTT (PhD, University of Iowa) is the Anglican Chair of Divinity at Beeson Divinity School. His academic research focus has been threefold: Jonathan Edwards, Christian understandings of other religions, and the meaning of Israel. McDermott has produced six books on Edwards; his *Theology of Jonathan Edwards* (coauthored with Michael McClymond) won Christianity Today's 2013 award for Top Book in Theology/Ethics. McDermott has written, cowritten, or edited numerous books and scores of articles. His most recent books are *Famous Stutterers* and *Israel Matters.* Before coming to Beeson, he was the Jordan-Trexler Professor of Religion at Roanoke College.

LARRY STEVEN MCDONALD (PhD, Southeastern Baptist Theological Seminary; DMin, Reformed Theological Seminary) is the Dean, Director of Doctor of Ministry Studies, and Professor of Christian Spirituality at North Greenville University's Graduate School of Christian Ministry. He is a member of the International John Bunyan Society, the Evangelical Theological Society, and the Tyndale Fellowship. He also wrote *The Merging of Theology and Spirituality* and coedited/contributed to *A Passion for the Great Commission.*

TIMOTHY MCKNIGHT (PhD, The Southern Baptist Theological Seminary) is Assistant Professor of Christian Studies at Anderson University.

DWAYNE MILIONI (PhD, Southeastern Baptist Theological Seminary) is Assistant Professor of Preaching and Coordinator of the PhD in Preaching at Southeastern Baptist Theological Seminary. He is also lead pastor of Open Door Church in Raleigh, North Carolina, and serves as board chairman for the Pillar Church Planting Network.

JONATHAN MORGAN (PhD, Marquette University) is Associate Professor of Theology at Indiana Wesleyan University and an ordained minister in the Wesleyan Church. He has published articles in several scholarly journals including *Pro Ecclesia, Evangelical Quarterly, St. Vladimir's Theological Quarterly,* and the *Journal for the Study of the Pseudepigrapha.*

MICHAEL PASQUARELLO III (PhD, University of North Carolina at Chapel Hill) is Beeson Professor of Methodist Divinity and Director of The Robert Smith Jr. Preaching Institute, Beeson Divinity School, Samford University, Birmingham, Alabama. His most recent homiletical publications include *John Wesley: A Preaching Life* (Abingdon, 2010), *The Beauty of Preaching* (Eerdmans, forthcoming), and *Dietrich Bonhoeffer and a Theology of the Preaching Life* (Baylor University Press, 2017).

STEPHEN PRESLEY (PhD, University of St. Andrews) is Associate Professor of Church History and Director of the Center for Early Christian Studies at Southwestern Baptist Theological Seminary. He is the author of *The Intertextual Reception of Genesis 1–3 in Irenaeus of Lyons* (Brill, 2015), as well as many other essays and articles on various topics in patristic theology and exegesis.

ERIC ROWE (PhD, University of Notre Dame) has focused his academic research on interplay between New Testament and Early Christianity focusing on the oral transmission of the apostles' teachings throughout the period prior to the writing of the books of the New Testament. He also teaches adjunctively for Grace College and Seminary (Winona Lake, Indiana), Moody Bible Institute (Chicago, Illinois), and the University of Notre Dame.

W. BRIAN SHELTON (PhD, Saint Louis University) is Provost and Professor of Theology and Church History at Toccoa Falls College. He has published principally on Christianity in the west, including *Martyrdom from Exegesis in Hippolytus: An Early Church Presbyter's Commentary on Daniel* (Paternoster, 2008), "Irenaeus" in *Shapers of Christian Orthodoxy* (InterVarsity Press, 2010), and *Quest for the Historical Apostles: Tracing their Lives and Legacies* (Baker, 2018).

CORNELIU C. SIMUȚ (PhD, Aberdeen, the United Kingdom; ThD, University of Tilburg, the Netherlands; Dr. Habil, the Reformed Theological University of Debrecen, Hungary; DD, University of Pretoria, South Africa) is Professor of Historical and Systematic Theology at Emanuel University of Oradea, Romania, and Associate Research Fellow in Dogmatic Theology at the University of Pretoria as well as a Research Supervisor at Union School of Theology, formerly Wales Evangelical School of Theology, the United Kingdom. He is also the Editor-in-Chief of *Perichoresis*, the theological journal of Emanuel University, published by Emanuel University Press in conjunction with De Gruyter Open and occasionally Refo500.

EDWARD L. SMITHER (PhD, University of Wales Trinity Saint David; PhD, University of Pretoria) is Professor of Intercultural Studies and Dean of the School of Intercultural Studies at Columbia International University and the author of *Augustine as Mentor: A Model for Preparing Spiritual Leaders, Brazilian Evangelical Missions in the Arab World,* and translator of François Decret's *Early Christianity in North Africa.*

SIMON VIBERT (DMin, Reformed Theological Seminary) was Vice Principal and Director of the School of Preaching at Wycliffe Hall, Oxford. Currently he is Vicar of Christ Church, Virginia Water, England.

WILLIAM C. WATSON (PhD, University of California, Riverside) is Professor of Modern History at Colorado Christian University. His research interests focus on the seventeenth and eighteenth centuries and he is the author of *Dispensationalism before Darby.*

SCOTT A. WENIG (PhD, University of Colorado, Boulder) is the Haddon W. Robinson Chair of Biblical Preaching and Professor of Applied Theology at Denver Seminary.

Introduction

Preach the word; be prepared in season and out of season (2 Tim 4:2). This book is about the seasons of preaching history and the preachers who proclaimed the eternal riches of God's grace and truth. Our goal is to present a historical, theological, and methodological introduction to the history of preaching. This approach to the history of preaching is one of this volume's unique markers. Instead of teaching the history of preaching from a perspective of movements and eras, our goal is to aid the reader in the exploration of preaching history, with a biographical and theological examination of its most important preachers. Therefore, each contributing author will tell the story of a preacher in history, allowing these preachers from the past to come alive and instruct us about their lives, theologies, and methods of preaching.

Our intent is not to focus *only* on the history of preaching as a past event, but to consider how to best move forward in our own pulpits and in the training of future preachers. To accomplish this goal, we have looked backward in order to explore how theology intersects with and informs the practice of preaching *in context*. By telling the stories of these preachers, we provide a stage for understanding how their theology informed their practice and how they methodized the task of approaching the Scriptures for the proclamation of the gospel. It will be readily evident that preachers throughout history have approached this differently. Some preachers have a very robust theology *of* preaching, while others, instead, have a theology *for* preaching.

This book details how great pulpiteers in history have approached their task of preaching as pastor-theologians. Much of the challenge in teaching students is not just what to know, but how to communicate what they have learned, in a way that is understood by their audience. This book doesn't teach *how* biblical preaching is done, but demonstrates how it *has* been done.

Our hope is that this approach will yield fruit for present and future preachers as they formulate their own understanding of how to be a theologian from the pulpit. There has been a great legacy of research in the area of the history of preaching. It is our goal to stand upon the shoulders of this research, much like the figures in this book have stood on the shoulders of the preachers who have gone before them.

CHOOSING THE PREACHERS

Choosing which preachers to include for a book such as this is an imperfect process, and some readers may be disappointed about who was left out. When this project was birthed over breakfast at Cracker Barrel, we only had a vague notion about whom to include. A later discussion over lunchtime pizza gave our list more clarity, but it was still not perfect. Our final product is still lacking, but it is an attempt to give a voice to those whose impact must certainly be remembered and those with a unique methodology or theological perspective on preaching that we believed was significant enough to include. We hope readers will commit to researching those important preachers who were not included and yet deserve a place among those who have preached from some of history's most influential pulpits.

ORGANIZATION OF TEXT

This book follows the great preachers of history. Each chapter has been written by a different author who is a scholar of the particular preacher. We left room for each author to express his own voice while maintaining consistency throughout the book. Each chapter will start with the "historical background" of the preacher. The length and scope of the biographical sections vary based on how much background information is needed to clarify their social and ministerial context. Next, each author will explore theological aspects of the preacher's approach to preaching. Sectional divisions vary slightly. But the essence of each will articulate what aspects of theology concerned the preacher and will identify either the preacher's theology *of* preaching or their theology *for* preaching. Then there will be an analysis of the preacher's methodology. Some preachers were very strict in their methodology while others more loose and extemporaneous. The final section will explore the preacher's overall contribution to the field of preaching along with a sermon excerpt from the preacher, so readers can hear the voice of the preacher in their own words.

OUR CHALLENGE

Our challenge to readers is threefold, and there is a nuance in our challenge to you, depending on why you have come to this book.

If you are an inquisitive pastor wanting to look back at the pulpiteers of history, then our hope for you is that you will find comradery and encouragement in the strengths of these preachers. We also hope you find solidarity as you recognize (perhaps very intimately) their challenges. As a pastor, at some point in your ministry, you will find yourself in a situation where looking back just may help you to move forward. As you look back on these pulpiteers, we hope you see their resolve, their commitment to the ministry of the Word, and their pursuit *for* the church. As you see these, we hope you will be refreshed and encouraged to press in and press on in your calling.

If you find yourself reading this book as a student, we hope you will find several heroes, or at least examples to imitate. Just as George Whitefield was inspired by Matthew Henry, and John Piper has been inspired by Jonathan Edwards, we hope you will find an example and hero for yourself. No preacher is perfect and what is written here is not hagiography, but in most cases it is deferential. Do not look to anyone but Christ to find the perfect role model for ministry, but look to these preachers who sought to follow Christ, love his bride—the church— and preach the Word. Let this be how you read this book: recognize your own imperfections and learn from those who have gone before you.

Lastly, if you are reading this book as you prepare to teach in the field of homiletics, history, or practical theology—we hope you will enjoy these chapters and the research your colleagues have provided. For those you disciple in ministry, encourage them to be students of the Word. Inspire them to see the practices of history's greats and learn from their dedicated study as they approach the task of sermon preparation. Challenge them with the reality that sermon preparation is never done—that life is constantly preparing us for the next sermon. Prod them with examples from your own life about the challenges and joys of drinking the Word personally and sharing it with a thirsty flock. For those you disciple in the classroom, urge them to compare those in history with those we are familiar with today. Embolden them with a vision that places the proclamation of the gospel at the summit of seminary preparation. Share with them stories about your own heroes of the pulpit. Your hero may be in this book, or may be a pastor barely known to history. This is important because you will likely have students who will go on to have ministries that make a visible impact, while others will remain largely unseen until eternity. Let them know both of these epitaphs are to be celebrated. Do not set before students the goal that to be remembered is to leave a legacy, but let them see faithfulness to the gospel through the proclamation of Christ is what counts when considering *a legacy of preaching!*

Soli Deo Gloria!

Benjamin K. Forrest
Kevin L. King
Bill Curtis
Dwayne Milioni

PART *One*

Preaching in the Early Church and among the Patristic Fathers

The history of the Christian church has been shaped by preaching as early as the apostles. Biblical preaching played a central role in the regular gatherings of the early church (Acts 2:42). The apostles were set aside from the responsibilities of a growing church to focus on prayer and preaching (Acts 6:3–4). **Peter** modeled biblical preaching by using the Old Testament Scriptures to reveal the centrality of Jesus Christ in God's plan to redeem his people (Acts 2:14–36). As a missionary, **Paul** utilized preaching as his means for spreading the gospel throughout the known world. Paul's proclamation was doctrinal and apologetic, arguing for the resurrection and appealing for believers to live resurrected lives (Col 3:1–3). Paul passed on the legacy of preaching to his disciples, exhorting them to "Preach the word" and entrust other faithful people to do likewise (2 Tim 2:2; 4:2).

Beyond the biblical era, the early church was marked by the preaching of the church fathers (second–fifth centuries). Initially, they modeled the missionary preaching of Paul amidst periods of severe persecution by Rome. Preaching Christ's return was common among those suffering from persecution and martyrdom. As churches became established, catechismal or instructional preaching was added for new believers. There remained a strong affiliation to the Old Testament up through the second century. Soon, settled churches began to develop liturgy. The *Didache* understood preaching and teaching to be the central component of worship. **Melito of Sardis** (d. ca. 190) gracefully preached how the Jewish Passover has been fulfilled by Jesus Christ. **Origen** (ca. 185–254) offered an allegorical approach to preaching that would model a preaching method for Western Christendom against the grammatical-historical preaching found in the East led by **John Chrysostom** (349–407).

The Edict of Milan (AD 313) legalized Christianity, which radically altered preaching. The church was infused with non- and novice believers. Heresies were introduced and preaching often took the form of rational appeal to the truth about Jesus Christ. As time went on, sacramentalism, especially the Eucharist, would replace preaching as the center of Christian worship. **Ephrem the Syrian** (ca. 303–373) wrote sermons about Christ in verse. **Basil of Caesarea** (330–379) was an influential preacher and theologian who supported the high Christology of the Nicene Creed (AD 325) and saw the preacher as the "mouthpiece of Christ." Of all the church fathers, the preaching and writing of **Augustine** (354–430) may have the strongest legacy on the church up through the Reformation. His preaching captivated congregations in North Africa and he wrote *On Christian Doctrine,* which was the first book formally describing the interplay of hermeneutics and homiletics.

Paul
Proclaiming Christ Crucified

ERIC ROWE

The apostle Paul was, for a time, a highly esteemed and educated Jewish rabbi who persecuted other Jews who believed that Jesus was the Messiah. Then he himself was called by Jesus to preach the very faith he had opposed. From that moment on, Paul's life revolved around preaching the gospel of Jesus's death and resurrection, expounding doctrines that revolved around that central truth, and exhorting other believers to live in the life of the risen Christ.

HISTORICAL BACKGROUND

The preaching ministry of the apostle Paul spanned roughly the middle third of the first century AD. His greatest influence on the church today is through his letters, which comprise a major part of the New Testament. However, according to both his own testimony in those letters and the portrayal of him in the book of Acts, his primary vocation was not one of writing, but preaching. The following survey of the surviving evidence will both establish that fact and describe the nature and content of his preaching.

Throughout Paul's epistles he writes with confidence that his audiences will accept his words, coming as they do from him, as supremely authoritative on all matters he addresses. The fact that these letters remain for us to this day in the New Testament is evidence that they were accepted as Paul insisted they be. Paul's foundation of authority came through the power God exhibited in Paul's ministry of traveling the world and preaching a message he called *the gospel*. Paul repeatedly harkens back to the trust he established through his preaching as the basis on which the apostolic authority of his letters should be trusted (1 Cor 1:17; 2:1–5; 3:5–6; 4:14–16; 9:1, 13–18; 15:1–11; 2 Cor 3:1–2, 12; 5:12; 10:13–16; 13:10; Gal 1:8–11; 3:1; 4:12–16; Phil 2:12; 1 Thess 1:5–2:16; 2 Thess 2:5; 3:10). Even in his letter to the Romans, his magnum opus, written to an audience whom he had not yet visited, Paul speaks as though his letter to them is a stopgap measure designed to meet their need for doctrinal guidance until he is able to do what he really wants to do for them, which is to preach the gospel in person (Rom 1:11–15; 15:22–24, 32; 16:25). Paul reiterates in his own words throughout his epistles that his defining ministry is preaching: "Christ did not send me to baptize, but to preach the gospel" (1 Cor 1:17); "Woe to me if I do not preach the gospel" (1 Cor 9:16); "This grace was given to me: to preach" (Eph 3:8); "I was appointed a herald and an apostle" (1 Tim 2:7; 2 Tim 1:11). After Paul's conversion to faith in Christ, his reputation among the Judean Christians changed from being infamous for persecuting their faith to being famous as a preacher of it (Gal 1:23). The book of Acts paints the same portrait of Paul, as the preacher. Consider Litfin's summary of this evidence:

> We may begin by noting the centrality of public speaking to Paul's ministry in Acts. Immediately upon his conversion (Acts 9:1–19) Paul begins to preach (Acts 9:20, *kēryssō*). When Barnabas commends him to the Jerusalem apostles, it is for his bold speaking (*parrēsiazomai*, Acts 9:27), which the new convert enthusiastically continues (Acts 9:28). After Paul is sent out on his initial missionary journey by the Holy Spirit in Acts 13:4, the first reference to the activity of proclamation (*katangellō*) occurs immediately (Acts 13:5). From this point on proclamation is the most persistent element in the account of Paul's missionary activity. Whether the term is *euangelizō, kēryssō, katangellō, peithō, parrēsiazomai, dialegō, martyreō, diamartyromai, paradidōmi,* or *didaskō,* and whether the audience is large or small, formal or informal, indoors or out of doors, preaching remains at the center of Paul's ministry. Hence we are unsurprised when the final verse of Acts leaves Paul "proclaiming [*kērussō*] the kingdom of God and teaching [*didaskō*] about the Lord Jesus Christ with all boldness" (Acts 28:31).[1]

Paul's preaching left a powerful impression not only on those who believed his message, but also a wide variety of ideological opponents, who often felt threatened enough by him to go to great lengths to silence and contradict him. The existence of such strong opposition is a testament to Paul's fame and infamy as a preacher. One such group, whom Paul calls *the circumcision,* apparently followed him from city to city seeking to undermine his teachings (Gal 2:12; 3:1; 4:9, 17, 21; Phil 3:2; Col 4:11; Titus 1:10). It may be this or another group whose charges Paul addresses in 2 Corinthians, where both the content and the manner of Paul's preaching are explicit objects of their scorn (2 Cor 10:7, 10; 11:6).

---

1. Duane Litfin, *Paul's Theology of Preaching: The Apostle's Challenge to the Art of Persuassion in Ancient Corinth,* rev. ed. (Downer's Grove, IL: InterVarsity, 2015), 328. The transliterated Greek words in this quote were presented in Greek by Litfin. Scripture quotations are from the English Standard Version.

Paul's fame was not limited to his fellow Jews. Major political players around the Roman Empire took notice of Paul's preaching, sometimes admiring, but more often fearing it as subverting the people's allegiance to the emperor. Sergius Paulus, a proconsul of Cyprus in the 40s AD, was one of Paul's converts, and some evidence suggests that this resulted in several generations of Christians in what was then a very important family in Pisidian Antioch (Acts 13:12).[2] In AD 51, Paul was also brought before the judgment seat of Gallio, proconsul of Achaia, who took little interest in Paul's message, but unexpectedly so from the vantage point of those who brought the charges (Acts 18:12–14). According to Acts, controversy about what Paul taught in his preaching was a major factor in instigating the riot in Jerusalem that resulted in his arrest and ensuing multiyear imprisonment (Acts 21:27–28). As Acts recounts the ordeal, multiple major political figures took an interest (albeit generally negatively) in this famous preacher Paul's message, including a commander of a thousand soldiers (Claudias Lysias), the Jewish high priest (Ananias) along with other local Jewish elders, two governors of Judea (Felix and Festus), and the client king of nearby territories under Rome (Herod Agrippa), who was not obligated to participate in the trial but who did so because, as he said, "I would like to hear this man myself" (Acts 25:22). At one point, Felix too, along with his wife Drusilla, made a special extrajudicial inquiry of Paul so that he could explain his teachings more in depth to them (Acts 24:24–27). Festus, though wholly opposed to Paul's beliefs, was nonetheless impressed by his learning (Acts 26:24).

This general picture of Paul's fame and infamy given in Acts is corroborated by his epistles, several of which are sent from prison (Eph 6:20; Phil 1:7; Col 4:18; 2 Tim 2:9; Phlm 13). And even earlier than those prison epistles were probably written, Paul wrote that he had received multiple beatings and imprisonments from both Jewish and gentile authorities (2 Cor 11:23–25). All on account of his being a "minister of Christ," a label he applies to himself as a preacher (Rom 15:16).

THEOLOGY OF PREACHING

We have less direct knowledge of the content of Paul's preaching than we might expect, when we consider how much preaching he did. The quotations of his sermons in Acts are probably significantly abridged versions that preserve for us only a tiny fraction of his oratory *opera omnia*.[3] Nevertheless, between those records

---

2. William Ramsay, *The Bearing of Recent Discoveries on the Trustworthiness of the New Testament* (London: Hodder & Stoughton, 1926), 154–55; G. L. Cheesman, "The Family of the Caristanii at Antioch in Pisidia," *JRelS* 3.2 (1913): 261–66; Steven Mitchell, *Anatolia*, 2 vols. (Oxford: Clarendon, 1993), 1:151, 2:7.

3. See below, fn. 13.

and a number of clues scattered throughout his epistles, much can be deduced about Paul's sermons.

For starters, when Paul refers to his preaching, he often uses shorthand expressions to encapsulate the totality of the message. These include that he preached "the gospel" (Rom 1:9, 15; 15:19, 20; 16:25; 1 Cor 1:17; 9:16, 18; 15:1; 2 Cor 10:16; 11:4, 7; Gal 1:8, 9, 11; 2:2; 3:8; 4:13; Phil 4:15); he preached "Jesus Christ" (Rom 16:25; 1 Cor 15:12; 2 Cor 1:19; 11:4; Phil 1:15; Col 1:28); he preached "Christ Jesus as Lord" (2 Cor 4:5); he preached "the unfathomable riches of Christ" (Eph 3:8); he preached "Christ crucified" (1 Cor 1:23); he preached "the word/message concerning faith" (Rom 10:8); he preached "the word/message of God" (Col 1:25); he preached simply "the word/message" (1 Cor 15:2; 2 Tim 4:2); he preached "foolishness" (1 Cor 1:21); he preached "the faith he once tried to destroy" (Gal 1:23). Without using the verb "preach" he also refers to his message as "the word/message of the cross" (1 Cor 1:18); "God's wisdom, a mystery that has been hidden" (1 Cor 2:7); and other variations of "the mystery" (Eph 6:19; Col 1:26–27; 2:2; 4:3).

We can conclude from these phrases that all of Paul's preaching revolved around Jesus Christ, most importantly a message about his death on the cross and ensuing resurrection, which is to be accepted by faith, and which Paul calls "the gospel," meaning "good news." Paul's clearest summary of this gospel is 1 Corinthians 15:1–11, an important enough passage for this subject to quote in full:

> Now, brothers and sisters, I want to remind you of the gospel I preached to you, which you received and on which you have taken your stand. By this gospel you are saved, if you hold firmly to the word I preached to you. Otherwise, you have believed in vain.
>
> For what I received I passed on to you as of first importance: that Christ died for our sins according to the Scriptures, that he was buried, that he was raised on the third day according to the Scriptures, and that he appeared to Cephas, and then to the Twelve. After that, he appeared to more than five hundred of the brothers and sisters at the same time, most of whom are still living, though some have fallen asleep. Then he appeared to James, then to all the apostles, and last of all he appeared to me also, as to one abnormally born.
>
> For I am the least of the apostles and do not even deserve to be called an apostle, because I persecuted the church of God. But by the grace of God I am what I am, and his grace to me was not without effect. No, I worked harder than all of them—yet not I, but the grace of God that was with me.

Whether, then, it is I or they, this is what we preach, and this is what you believed.[4]

According to Paul, this gospel not only formed the center of his own preaching, but also that of all the other apostles, especially Peter. This is supported by the book of Acts, wherein Luke frequently recounts how Christianity was introduced to new audiences and quotes in summary form what the apostles told them (esp. Acts 2:22–36; 3:12–26; 4:8–12; 7:51–56; 10:34–43; 13:16–41; and 17:2–3). Although varying slightly in some details, all these passages emphasize that Jesus is the Messiah (or Christ) and Lord, that he died for sins, that he rose again, that he was seen by eyewitnesses, and that all of this fulfills the prophetic Scriptures of what Christians today call the Old Testament. Scholars typically call this formulaic summarization of the apostles' preaching the *kerygma*, from the Greek word meaning "preaching."[5] Two of these *kerygma* passages in Acts refer to Paul's preaching of the gospel (13:16–41; 17:2–3). While the similarity between Paul's preaching and Peter's is probably what is most apparent,[6] Paul's own voice can be recognized in his preaching, such as in 13:39, where Paul proclaims that everyone who believes in Jesus is freed from the law of Moses.[7] Notably, the four canonical gospels are essentially expanded versions of this *kerygma*, focusing as they do on the death and resurrection of Jesus. Indeed, Acts 10:34–43, which is an account of Peter's preaching could well serve as an outline for the gospel of Mark, which early Christian tradition says to have been Mark's recollection of the preaching of Peter.[8]

We should not conclude from Paul's references to his preaching of the gospel that this brief message was all he ever preached, or that other matters comprised a small or insignificant part of his preaching. But we would be safe in concluding that this gospel proclamation was the center around which all his other preaching revolved. As we shall see, he preached many other things as well, but he preached all of these things as support for the gospel, corollaries to it, or inferences drawn

---

4. Cf. Rom 1:1–5.

5. See especially C. H. Dodd, *The Apostolic Preaching and its Developments,* repr. (New York: Harper & Row, 1964).

6. See especially their similar treatments of Psalm 16 in Acts 2:25–32 and 13:34–37. Paul never makes this argument in his epistles. Similarly, in his epistles Paul never mentions John the Baptist, although Acts informs us that he did in his gospel preaching, much like Peter (Acts 10:37–38; 13:24–25). In his epistles, Paul only once mentions Pilate by name (1 Tim 6:13), and rarely emphasizes Jesus's lineage from David (Rom 1:3–4), both of which also factored into the *kerygma* he and Peter both preached (Acts 2:30; 13:23).

7. Cf. Rom 6:14; 7:6; Gal 2:19; 3:11–14, 23–25. Notice also how, in the midst of these same verses, Paul draws attention to the law's curse of anyone hung on a pole, as Jesus was (Gal 3:13), to which he also alludes in Acts 13:29.

8. Papias, quoted by Eusebius (*Ecclesiastical History* 3.39.14–15), hereafter *Hist. eccl.*; Irenaeus (*Against Heresies* 3.1.1); Tertullian (*Against Marcion* 4.5); Origen, quoted by Eusebius (*Hist. eccl.* 6.25.5).

from it. Thus, he can refer to what he preaches about practical Christian living as conduct "worthy of the gospel" (Phil 1:27; cf. 1 Tim 1:11). To any audience concerning any subject—whether his philosophy of history, things to come, marriage, divorce, wealth, poverty, politics, persecution, culture, death, friendship, love, or any other matter—Paul's preaching was oriented around the gospel. As Dennis Johnson says, "[Paul] prods us toward the goal of perfection not by moving our gaze away from Jesus to other issues but by driving our exploration deeper into Christ, who is the manifold wisdom of God."[9]

Johnson makes that remark in a helpful study on Paul's theology of preaching as presented in Colossians 1:27–2:4.[10] There, as he does so often, Paul laconically states that the content of his preaching is *him*, i.e. Jesus, Col 1:28.[11] In the same verse, Paul then mentions two tasks in this preaching: "admonishing and teaching everyone with all wisdom," which aptly summarizes a range of preaching from the initial proclamation of the gospel to an unbelieving audience to training of mature Christians.[12] He concludes this verse with his statement of purpose for all such preaching, which is, "that we may present everyone fully mature in Christ." Paul considers his role in this mission as one with cosmic significance, a stewardship given by God to fill up what is lacking in Christ's afflictions (vv. 24–25). And the means by which Paul accomplishes his mission is nothing less than Christ's own energy, which works powerfully within Paul (v. 29).

As said, gaining detailed knowledge of Paul's preaching on the full spectrum of topics through which everyone is to be brought to maturity in Christ is challenging. Acts records some of his speeches. However, some of these are defense speeches in his trials (Acts 22:1–21; 24:10–21; 26:4–23), and others are strictly evangelistic (13:16–41; 17:22–31). Acts often alludes to his preaching and teaching directed toward believers, but the only passage in Acts that presents the content of such teaching is Acts 20:17–38. When Acts does quote evangelistic sermons, it seemingly does so in an abbreviated manner with the resulting abridgements being at most partially composed by Paul and partially by Luke as he puts into words the gist of what Paul said. In Acts 2:40, Luke indicates that he has abbreviated Peter's sermon, and it is therefore likely that he does so for all speeches in Acts.[13]

---

9. Dennis Johnson, *Him We Proclaim: Preaching Christ from All the Scriptures* (Phillipsburg, NJ: P & R, 2007), 67–68.

10. Ibid., 63–97.

11. In this context the shorthand "Him" is synonymous with the previous shorthand in v. 25, "the word of God."

12. In other words, these tasks include, "proclamation, explanation, and application." Johnson, *Him We Proclaim*, 95.

13. See Craig Keener, *Acts: An Exegetical Commentary*, 4 vols. (Grand Rapids: Baker, 2012–15), 1:258–319.

On the other hand, it is not clear how much Paul's epistles resemble his orally delivered sermons. His epistles generally presuppose that his audience has already been exposed to a regimen of preaching delivered by him or someone else—a regimen that was fairly consistent from one church to another. The epistles themselves primarily address pressing issues unique to their original audiences, pointing to more general principles only in that context. However, throughout these epistles, various details refer back to Paul's and others' earlier oral preaching and combine to provide more information about that preaching than might be expected.

Additionally, one Pauline epistle in particular, Romans, shows significant signs of recycled material that Paul had previously delivered orally. As David Aune writes, "The body of Romans is so complex that it seems obvious that Paul must have worked and reworked the material found here many times in many different teaching, preaching, and debating situations."[14] Moreover, Romans reads like a *logos protreptikos*, or "speech of exhortation," which, according to Greco-Roman rhetorical classifications, was a speech designed to persuade people to adopt a particular way of life. Not only does its content patently conform to such a purpose, but its structure also consists of the three basic parts of such a speech: a negative presentation of the rejected way of life (1:16–4:25), a positive presentation of the author's favored alternative (5:1–8:39), and an exhortation to the audience (12:1–15:14).[15] Finally, throughout Romans, Paul uses the technique of speech in character, such as when he puts words into the mouth of an imaginary interlocutor and then resumes his own persona to answer that imaginary person (3:1–9, 27–31; 4:1–3, 9–10; 6:1–3, 15–16; 7:7, 13; 9:14, 19–20). Such a technique lends itself to oral delivery, where the preacher can indicate the change in persona via voice and gestures.[16] Fortunately, the evidence in Romans, the allusions to prior orally delivered teaching throughout Paul's epistles, and the sermons in Acts, in many respects all corroborate one another in what they tell us about the methods, content, and philosophy of Paul's preaching.

As previously mentioned, the gospel itself provided the foundation for all the content of Paul's preaching and teaching, and he had this in common with the other apostles and brothers of the Lord (1 Cor 15:1–11). Building on this foundation, Paul and his cohorts often spent an extended time teaching new converts (Acts 18:7; 19:8–9; 20:20). Not only the gospel, but also much of this entire

14. David Aune, *The Westminster Dictionary of New Testament and Early Christian Literature and Rhetoric* (Louisville: Westminster John Knox, 2003), 430.

15. Ibid., 430–31.

16. See Stanley Stowers, *A Rereading of Romans: Justice, Jews, and Gentiles* (New Haven: Yale University Press, 1994), 16–21.

course of instruction apparently followed a formula that Paul had in common with the other apostles and the missionaries aligned with them. When Paul writes to the Roman Christians, with whom he has no prior personal background, he is able to assume a great deal about what they know about baptism and the spiritual consequences of justification by faith in Jesus Christ (e.g. Rom 6:3, 6, 9, 16; 13:11). And he alludes to a "pattern of teaching" which had been committed to them (Rom 6:17). From other clues in Paul's epistles and the rest of the New Testament, we can infer that this pattern of teaching also included instructions for observing the Lord's Supper (1 Cor 11:23–26), passing on the teachings which Jesus had given during his earthly ministry (Rom 12:14; 13:8–10; 1 Cor 7:10; 9:14; 13:2), instructions for Christian living (1 Thess 4:1–2; 2 Thess 3:6), eschatology (1 Cor 16:22[17]; 1 Thess 5:1), the divine and human natures of Jesus Christ, and the doctrine of Holy Spirit, among other things.[18]

Just as the gospel was the uniting theme of Paul's preaching, so also was the constant appeal to the authority of the Scriptures, which, in the earliest period of apostolic preaching, consisted solely of what we now call the Old Testament. Indeed, this constant reliance on the Scriptures was part of the gospel itself. Paul says, "according to the Scriptures," twice in his recitation of the gospel formula in 1 Corinthians 15:3–4. Along with mention of the death and resurrection of Jesus, appeal to the Old Testament Scriptures is one of the few elements that appear in every *kerygma* passage in Acts without exception. And constant appeal to the Scriptures throughout the book of Romans is one of the most important features of the letter. Paul indicates this importance of the Scriptures in his thesis statement (Rom 1:17), his opening words (1:2), and his closing words (16:26), and quotes the Old Testament over sixty times throughout the letter.

METHODOLOGY FOR PREACHING

A flourishing area of research concerning Paul's preaching since the 1990s has been the question of his reliance on techniques prescribed by ancient rhetoricians. Most of this research has been focused on rhetorical analysis of his epistles.[19] The results have been mixed. However, at least some of his epistles seem to conform

---

17. The fact that the expression *Maranatha* is Aramaic indicates that this slogan, which Paul had apparently passed on to the Greek-speaking former pagans of Corinth, must have originated earlier among Judean believers in Jesus and attained enough of a cliché status there to continue on in its original language among those who did not speak it.

18. See the discussion of the early oral transmission of all these doctrines in A. M. Hunter, *Paul and His Predecessors*, rev. ed. (London: SCM, 1961).

19. See, for example, Hans Dieter Betz, *Galatians* (Minneapolis: Fortress, 1989); and Margaret Mitchell, *Paul and the Rhetoric of Reconciliation: An Exegetical Investigation of the Language and Composition of 1 Corinthians* (Louisville: Westminster John Knox, 1993).

closely enough to certain rhetorical conventions to support the conclusion that Paul was influenced by the rhetoricians, even if only indirectly.[20] Similarly, Paul's speeches in Acts conform in varying degrees to the requirements of Greco-Roman rhetoric.[21] Among the speeches that we call sermons (as opposed to his forensic speeches), Paul's speech in Acts 17:22–31 conforms especially well to a form called *deliberative* (that is, speeches aimed at convincing an audience to do something). Dr. Philip E. Satterthwaite shows this deliberative structure with the following outline: "proem (v. 22, seeking to secure audience goodwill); narration (v. 23a, giving background); division (again a single proposition: I will tell you of this god you worship as unknown, v. 23b); demonstration (God as incomparably greater than idols, vv. 24–29); peroration (vv. 30–31).[22] It is not unlikely that Paul's rabbinical studies under Gamaliel would have included at least some exposure to Greek rhetoric. Rabban Simeon said the following about his father, Gamaliel II, who flourished around the beginning of the second century AD and was the grandson of the Gamaliel who taught Paul: "There were a thousand young men in my father's house, five hundred of whom studied the Law, while the other five hundred studied Greek wisdom."[23]

However, we still encounter the problem of extrapolating from the style of Luke's summary presentations of Paul's speeches in Acts and Paul's writing style exhibited in his epistles, to Paul's preaching style in full sermons—the transcripts of which we do not have. Duane Litfin has helpfully called attention to another important piece of data: Paul's theological explanation of his preaching style, especially in the opening chapters of 1 Corinthians.[24] Paul seems to say that when he preaches, he does not try to conform to the requirements of the rhetoricians, that his preaching style differs from that of his opponents in this respect, that his preaching style also differed from his writing style, and that others noticed this and criticized him for these things (1 Cor 2:1–5; 2 Cor 10:10). In light of all of the evidence available, a balanced conclusion is probably warranted. Paul probably did not put much emphasis on conforming his sermons to the rhetorical expectations of other highly educated people, but he most likely exhibited some level of conformity just by force of habit.

---

20. Aune, *Westminster Dictionary of New Testament and Early Christian Literature and Rhetoric*, 342–44.

21. Bruce Winter, "Official Proceedings and the Forensic Speeches in Acts 24–26," in vol. 1 of *The Book of Acts in Its Ancient Literary Setting*, ed. Bruce W. Winter and Andrew D. Clarke (Grand Rapids: Eerdmans, 1993), 305–35; and Philip E. Satterthwaite, "Acts against the Background of Classical Rhetoric," in *Ibid.*, 337–79.

22. Satterthwaite, "Acts against the Background of Classical Rhetoric," 360.

23. B. Sotah 49b and parallels (cf. t. Sotah 15:8, and y. Shabbat 6:1, 7d and parallels). See Saul Lieberman, *Greek in Jewish Palestine* (Philadelphia: Jewish Publication Society, 1942), especially p. 20.

24. Litfin, *Paul's Theology*, 31–53.

What Paul deliberately avoided was not so much oratory excellence, but the attitude and values of the sophists, a professional class of itinerant teachers who promoted themselves for fame and fortune.[25] In contrast to them, Paul refused to allow adherents of his doctrines to call themselves by his name; they were to identify with Christ, not Paul (1 Cor 1:12–13; 3:21–23).[26] Similarly, Paul foreswore his right to be paid for his preaching, although he undoubtedly could have made a comfortable living from it (Acts 20:33–34; 1 Cor 4:12; 9:6–18; 1 Thess 2:9; 2 Thess 3:8).

CONTRIBUTIONS TO PREACHING

Paul teaches modern preachers several concepts. First, their sermons should at all points appeal to the authority of Scripture. In this respect, Paul's own methods probably cannot be emulated completely. After all, no modern preachers can appeal to their own apostolic authority like Paul could. Nor do modern preachers have firsthand access to the original orally delivered apostolic "pattern of teaching" (Rom 6:17), or access to the collaboration between the apostles in its development (Acts 15:6–29; Gal. 1:18–19; 2:2), or to the instruction Jesus gave the eleven in preparation for their mission (Luke 24:44–49; Acts 2:1–2). However, they do have secondhand access to all these things through the writings of the apostles and their cohorts in the New Testament. They also have the very same Old Testament Scriptures on which Paul and his allies took their stand. And they have the Holy Spirit, by whom the energy of Christ worked powerfully in Paul's preaching (Col 1:29). In light of these things, the modern preacher would do well to practice an expository method of preaching, setting forth and explaining the apostolic writings which comprise the New Testament as our most reliable witnesses to Paul's *kerygma*, together with the Scriptures to which Paul appealed in that *kerygma*, which comprise our Old Testament. In so doing, Paul's guidance in that method would remind them to point to Christ on every page, not only in the New Testament, but also the Old, and to make that focus on Christ the foundation on which all other appeals are built.[27] Self-help for the sake of the self will not find a

25. Bruce Winter, *Paul and Philo among the Sophists,* 2nd ed. (Grand Rapids: Eerdmans, 2002), 1–13.

26. See the discussion of this in Eric Rowe, "Called by the Name of the Lord: Early Uses of the Names and Titles of Jesus in Identifying His Followers," (PhD diss., University of Notre Dame, 2012), 81–85.

27. A number of works in recent decades, especially in Reformed circles, have brought renewed attention to the need for preachers to preach Christ from the Old Testament. See, for example, Johnson, *Him We Proclaim*; Edmund Clowney, *Preaching Christ in All of Scripture* (Wheaton, IL: Crossway, 2003); Graeme Goldsworthy, *Preaching the Whole Bible as Christian Scripture* (Grand Rapids: Eerdmans, 2000); and Sidney Greidanus, *Preaching Christ from the Old Testament: A Contemporary Hermeneutical Method* (Grand Rapids: Eerdmans, 1999). This concern to see Jesus in the Old Testament is sometimes presented in terms of a distinction between a christocentric approach, which sees Christ as the heart of the Bible's message at all stages of its unfolding

place in such sermons. To be sure, there will be ample opportunities for practical instruction, but always with the aim of maturity in Christ. Finally, to make Christ increase, the preachers themselves will find that they must decrease. Cults of personality around preachers and partisan alignment of lay people around one over against another can never be the preacher's aim; and indeed, when they appear, require correction and renewed focus on the one person whose name Christians bear, whom churches learn, and preachers proclaim—Jesus Christ, the Lord.

CONCLUSION

By way of conclusion, we look at the foregoing observations concerning Paul's theology and practice of preaching in a sample sermon of his. In Acts 20:18–38, Paul addresses the Ephesian elders as fellow preachers. He reminds them how he "served the Lord with great humility and with tears and in the midst of severe testing" (v. 19), "declared both to Jews and Greeks that they must turn to God in repentance and have faith in our Lord Jesus" (v. 21), declared "the whole will of God" (v. 27), and coveted no one's "silver or gold or clothing" (v. 33). Paul commended the Ephesian elders follow his example (v. 35). The modern preacher is also encouraged to follow in the footsteps of Paul.

As seen in this passage and the Pastoral Epistles, part of Paul's preaching ministry was the deputizing of other preachers to proclaim the same gospel he proclaimed, and to ensure that this ministry of preaching would continue until Christ's return. This baton has been passed through the centuries to the preachers today, who have a charge to keep. Preachers who carry this baton have already been shown the way to do so by Paul. They would be wise to imitate his self-effacing style, never showing off or pursuing personal glory, but always putting Christ crucified at the center of their message, and relating every other theme back to that one.

Finally, Paul's sermon in Acts 20 allows us to return to the two questions of how much we can extrapolate from Paul's letters and how much weight we can place on Luke's abbreviated versions of Paul's sermons in Acts. For it turns out that the parallels between Acts 20:17–38 and Paul's letters are remarkable,

---

throughout the Old and New Testaments, and a christotelic approach, which sees Christ as the ultimate goal toward which Old Testament revelation was always moving but not always explicitly so. These approaches are not necessarily mutually contradictory, and to the extent that they can be, it is outside the scope of this article to adjudicate between them. A christocentric approach to the Old Testament comports well with the Pauline evidence. However, a christotelic approach is not necessarily excluded, provided that whenever preachers do not identify Jesus directly within any given Old Testament passage, they still show how the passage contributes to the overarching goal of the Old Testament to point to him and to Christian beliefs and practices that revolve around him.

especially the letters that were similar to this sermon in audience and purpose, the Pastoral Epistles.[28] A critic might counter that these parallels are likely due to either the pastorals (often thought to be pseudonymous) drawing on Acts or vice versa. However, this is highly unlikely because of one striking contrast: in Acts 20:25 (cf. v. 38) Paul predicts that he will never see the Ephesians again, but in 1 Timothy 1:3 we learn that Paul must have been wrong about that, since at some time after his Roman imprisonment at the end of Acts, he again had a ministry in Ephesus, at which time he left Timothy there. This discrepancy could not have been tolerable to Luke if he himself had composed this sermon in light of 1 Timothy, nor to a pseudonymous author of 1 Timothy if he had composed that letter in light of Acts 20.[29]

Sermon Excerpt

Acts 20:18–38

When they arrived, he said to them: "You know how I lived the whole time I was with you, from the first day I came into the province of Asia. I served the Lord with great humility and with tears and in the midst of severe testing by the plots of my Jewish opponents.[30] You know that I have not hesitated to preach anything that would be helpful to you but have taught you publicly and from house to house.[31] I have declared to both Jews and Greeks[32] that they must turn to God in repentance and have faith in our Lord Jesus.

"And now, compelled by the Spirit, I am going to Jerusalem, not knowing what will happen to me there. I only know that in every city the Holy Spirit warns me that prison and hardships are facing me.[33]

"However, I consider my life worth nothing to me; my only aim is to finish the race and complete the task the Lord Jesus has given me—the task of testifying to the good news of God's grace.[34]

---

28. William D. Mounce, *Pastoral Epistles* (Nashville: Thomas Nelson, 2000), lii-liii. The most significant parallels Mounce draws are indicated below in footnotes as they appear in the sermon.

29. Keener, *Acts*, 1:3024–25.

30. In 1 Timothy and Titus Paul battles a heresy of what he calls "Jewish myths" (Tit 1:14).

31. Paul's opponents in 2 Timothy 3:6 also exert their influence in households.

32. In 1 Tim 2:1-7 Paul sees a need to emphasize once again that believers ought to pray for all, including Gentiles, and that God's saving grace is extended to them.

33. Paul instructs Timothy to harbor this same expectation for himself (2 Tim 1:8).

34. The pastorals also show Paul's preoccupation with his task of preaching the Gospel, next to which all else, including his sufferings pale in importance (1 Tim 1:12-17; 2 Tim 1:12-16; 4:6-8).

"Now I know that none of you among whom I have gone about preaching the kingdom will ever see me again. Therefore, I declare to you today that I am innocent of the blood of any of you. For I have not hesitated to proclaim to you the whole will of God.[35]

"Keep watch over yourselves and all the flock of which the Holy Spirit has made you overseers. Be shepherds of the church of God,[36] which he bought with his own blood.[37]

"I know that after I leave, savage wolves will come in among you you,[38] and will not spare the flock. Even from your own number men will arise and distort the truth in order to draw away disciples after them. So be on your guard! Remember that for three years I never stopped warning each of you night and day with tears.[39]

"Now I commit you to God and to the word of his grace, which can build you up and give you an inheritance among all those who are sanctified.[40] I have not coveted anyone's silver or gold or clothing. You yourselves know that these hands of mine have supplied my own needs and the needs of my companions. In everything I did, I showed you that by this kind of hard work we must help the weak, remembering the words the Lord Jesus himself said: 'It is more blessed to give than to receive.'"[41]

When Paul had finished speaking, he knelt down with all of them and prayed. They all wept as they embraced him and kissed him. What grieved them most was his statement that they would never see his face again. Then they accompanied him to the ship. ♦

BIBLIOGRAPHY

Aune, David. *The Westminster Dictionary of New Testament and Early Christian Literature and Rhetoric.* Louisville: Westminster John Knox, 2003.

Betz, Hans Dieter. *Galatians.* Minneapolis: Fortress, 1989.

Bruce, F. F. *The Speeches in Acts.* London: Tyndale, 1942.

Cheesman, George L. "The Family of the Caristanii at Antioch in Pisidia." *Journal of Religious Studies* 3.2 (1913): 261–66.

---

35. Paul similarly defends himself in 1 Tim 1:1, 12-17, implying opposition like what he predicts in Acts 20:29-30.

36. Cf. 1 Tim 3:1-7, 15.

37. Cf. 1 Tim 2:5-6.

38. Likewise, Paul's opponents in the pastorals had come from within the church (1 Tim 4:1; Tit 1:11).

39. 1 Timothy reflects the situation of well-established churches with structured leadership and bylaws, such as one would expect in a city where Paul had spent so much time (1 Tim 5:9, 17, 19).

40. In 1 Tim 4:16, as here, the solution to the threats Paul, Timothy, and the elders faced was to be found in the Gospel.

41. Contrast this with the greed of Paul's opponents in 1 Tim 6:5.

Dibelius, Martin. *The Book of Acts: Form, Style, and Theology*. Trans. by Mary Ling and Paul Schuber. London: SCM, 1956.

Dodd, C. H. *The Apostolic Preaching and Its Developments*. Reprint. New York: Harper & Row, 1964.

Given, Mark D. *Paul's True Rhetoric: Ambiguity, Cunning, and Deception in Greece and Rome*. Harrisburg: Trinity, 2001.

Hansen, G. Walter. "Rhetorical Criticism." Pages 822–26 in *Dictionary of Paul and His Letters*. Edited by Gerald F. Hawthorne, Ralph P. Martin, and Daniel G. Reid. Downer's Grove, IL: InterVarsity Press, 1993.

Hawthorne, Gerald F., Ralph P. Martin, and Daniel G. Reid, eds. *Dictionary of Paul and His Letters*. Downers Grove, IL: InterVarsity Press, 1993.

Hunter, Archibald M. *Paul and His Predecessors*. Rev. and enl. ed. London: SCM, 1961.

Johnson, Dennis. *Him We Proclaim: Preaching Christ from All the Scriptures*. Phillipsburg, NJ: P & R, 2007.

Keener, Craig S. *Acts: An Exegetical Commentary*. 4 vols. Grand Rapids: Baker Academic, 2012–2015.

Lieberman, Saul. *Greek in Jewish Palestine*. Philadelphia: Jewish Publication Society, 1942)

Litfin, Duane. *Paul's Theology of Preaching: The Apostle's Challenge to the Art of Persuassion in Ancient Corinth*. Rev. and enl. ed. Downers Grove, IL: InterVarsity Press, 2015.

Mahlerbe, Abraham J. *Moral Exhortation: A Greco-Roman Sourcebook*. Philadelphia: Westminster, 1986.

Mitchell, Margaret. *Paul and the Rhetoric of Reconciliation: An Exegetical Investigation of the Language and Composition of 1 Corinthians*. Louisville: Westminster John Knox, 1993.

Mitchell, Steven. *Anatolia*. 2 vols. Oxford: Clarendon, 1993.

Mounce, Robert H. "Preaching, Kerygma." Pages 735–37 in *Dictionary of Paul and His Letters*. Edited by Gerald F. Hawthorne, Ralph P. Martin, and Daniel G. Reid. Downers Grove, IL: InterVarsity Press, 1993.

Nock, Arthur Darby. *St. Paul*. New York: Harper & Row, 1938.

Olbricht, Thomas H., and Jerry L. Sumney, eds. *Paul and Pathos*. Atlanta: Society of Biblical Literature, 2001.

Ramsay, William. *The Bearing of Recent Discoveries on the Trustworthiness of the New Testament*. London: Hodder & Stoughton, 1926.

Rowe, Eric. *Called by the Name of the Lord: Early Uses of Names and Titles of Jesus in Identifying His Followers*. Unpublished PhD diss., University of Notre Dame, 2012.

Sampley, J. Paul, and Peter Lampe, eds. *Paul and Rhetoric*. New York: T&T Clark, 2010.

Satterthwaite, Philip E. "Acts against the Background of Classical Rhetoric." Pages 337–79 in *The Book of Acts in Its Ancient Literary Setting*. Edited by Bruce W. Winter and Andrew D. Clarke. Vol. 1 of *The Book of Acts in Its First Century Setting*. Edited by Bruce Winter. Grand Rapids: Eerdmans, 1993.

Stowers, Stanley. *A Rereading of Romans: Justice, Jews, and Gentiles*. New Haven: Yale University Press, 1994.

Van Bruggen, Jakob. *Paul: Pioneer for Israel's Messiah*. Phillipsburg, NJ: P&R, 2005.

Winter, Bruce W. "Official Proceedings and the Forensic Speeches in Acts 24–26." Pages 305–35 in *The Book of Acts in Its Ancient Literary Setting*. Edited by Bruce W. Winter and Andrew D. Clarke. Vol. 1 of *The Book of Acts in Its First Century Setting*. Edited by Bruce Winter. Grand Rapids: Eerdmans, 1993.

_____. "Rhetoric." Pages 820–22 in *Dictionary of Paul and His Letters*. Edited by Gerald F. Hawthorne, Ralph P. Martin, and Daniel G. Reid. Downers Grove, IL: InterVarsity Press, 1993.

_____. *Paul and Philo Among the Sophists: Alexandrian and Corinthian Responses to a Julio-Claudian Movement*. 2nd ed. Grand Rapids: Eerdmans, 2002.

Winter, Bruce W. and Andrew D. Clarke. *The Book of Acts in Its Ancient Literary Setting*. Vol. 1 of *The Book of Acts in Its First Century Setting*. Edited by Bruce W. Winter. Grand Rapids: Eerdmans, 1993.

Wright, N. T. *Paul and the Faithfulness of God*. 2 vols. Minneapolis: Fortress, 2013.

Peter

Proclaiming the Gospel in the Power of the Spirit

DAVID R. BECK

It was the Cambridge scholar F. J. Foakes-Jackson who, in the title of his 1927 monograph, stressed the extraordinary importance and prominence of the apostle Peter in the early church and in the New Testament with the designation "Prince of Apostles."[1] In the Gospel narratives, he is the designated spokesman of the twelve. In Acts, he is the first among them to publicly proclaim the gospel. This recognition of Peter's role and function in the biblical narratives does not obscure his human failings. But in spite of those failings, through the experience of God's transforming grace, he was shaped and equipped for his role as the outspoken leader of the apostles, the first to preach the gospel of God's saving grace to his covenant people, and the recipient of the revelation that the good news of God's offer of salvation through Jesus the Messiah was also for the nations.

HISTORICAL BACKGROUND

As a preacher, Simon Peter had the unique perspective of one who was an eyewitness to events which led to the message he proclaimed. Among the disciples, he had the unique position of being in the inner circle, the designated spokesman, and the one who, after his confession at Caesarea Philippi, Jesus singled out as the apostolic embodiment of the confessional rock upon which he would build his church. Peter not only witnessed Jesus walking on water, he joined him. He not only witnessed Jesus's healings, his own mother-in-law was the recipient of the Master's power to restore health. He not only heard Jesus was risen, he was the first to enter the tomb and see its vacancy for himself.

But Peter's eyewitness experience was not all triumph and glory. He was the one who, after confessing Jesus as the Christ, rebuked him for his talk of suffering

---

1. See F. J. Foakes-Jackson, *Peter, Prince of Apostles: A Study in the History and Tradition of Christianity* (New York: Doran, 1927).

and death. When privileged to witness a foretaste of Jesus's eternal glory, Peter tried to capture and contain it in booths made by human hands. And after pledging his undying fealty to Jesus and following him into the high priest's courtyard, he denied even knowing him. According to C. Richard Wells, these failures were not a hindrance to his development into the leading apostolic spokesman, but just the opposite. They were what necessitated his own repentance and restoration, which was required for the development of his preaching, since "the most authentic preaching will always be mediated through the most genuinely transformative life experience."[2]

Peter was the recipient of a special restoration and commissioning encounter with Jesus, assuring him that God's mantle of service had not been removed from him. The content of his call and ministry was identified as tending, nurturing, and feeding God's flock. First at Pentecost, then repeated in the pages of Acts, Peter, empowered by the Holy Spirit, was the first to proclaim the gospel to the people who witnessed the manifestation of God's presence and power, and also to the very authorities instrumental in placing Jesus on the cross. Furthermore, it was Peter to whom God gave direct revelation of the all-encompassing reach of the gospel, Jew and gentile alike.

However, it was not his mediatory role reconciling Jew and gentile as recipients of God's saving grace that made Peter the leading apostolic authority. Martin Hengle has rightly refuted this claim, noting instead that it was his "powerful, Spirit filled proclamation during a most threatening situation right from the beginning" that placed him in this role.[3]

The eyewitness character of Peter's calling, the apostolic office of his ministry, and the time in which he ministered were all unique. He witnessed the cruelty of Jesus's trial and execution on the cross and experienced the despair of the uncertain days that followed, the unspeakable joy of encountering the risen Savior, and the initial empowerment of the Holy Spirit which fell upon the church like a "blowing of a violent wind" (Acts 2:2).

Historical Sources for Peter's Preaching

The task of identifying Peter's theology of preaching and his methodology becomes one of historiography. Unlike noted preachers of later centuries, the question that must be asked is from what material do we derive our understanding of Peter's preaching? In the book of Acts, we have multiple accounts of Peter's preaching to crowds, as well as his addresses to both his accusers and to the church

---

2. C. Richard Wells and A. Boyd Luter, *Inspired Preaching: A Survey of Preaching Found in the New Testament* (Nashville: Broadman & Holman, 2002), 66.

3. Martin Hengel, *Saint Peter: The Underestimated Apostle* (Grand Rapids: Eerdmans, 2010), 34.

(Acts 10, 15). But what we do *not* have are transcripts of his exact words on any of those occasions. Instead, we are provided with brief summaries, translated into Greek by Luke, of what were certainly much longer discourses.[4] We do also have two epistles he wrote, but are they sources for knowledge of Peter's preaching? A further question arises concerning the gospel of Mark. According to tradition, Mark's gospel is based on Peter's preaching of the gospel in Rome. But for the historiographical task at hand, it must be asked: is this assessment accurate?

The identification of Mark's gospel as a recorded summary of Peter's preaching is as ancient as the first century witness Papias, preserved in the writings of the fourth-century historian Eusebius. Papias declared that Peter's hearers in Rome were not content with their memory of his preaching, but urged Mark "to leave them a written statement of the teaching given them verbally."[5] While many have discounted the testimony of the early church on gospel origins, a recent but cautious reexamination of this question by Helen K. Bond concludes: "a Petrine link to Mark's Gospel is not as self-evidently impossible as many critical scholars suppose."[6] It is appropriate to view the second gospel as at least representative of the preaching of Peter.

The New Testament includes two letters that bear Peter's name. As with many New Testament letters, some modern scholars have disputed the authenticity of both of these letters as being genuinely written by the apostle Peter. In the case of 1 Peter, those who are skeptical of Petrine authorship must stand in the face of the unanimous affirmation of the earliest church in its acceptance of this letter as genuine.[7] However, with 2 Peter, there was ancient doubt concerning its authenticity. Eusebius places it among the "disputed books, which are nevertheless known to most."[8] It is worth noting, however, that this is *not* the "spurious" category he reserves for books he knows are not Scripture (e.g. the Acts of Paul, the Shepherd of Hermas, etc.). And every book he placed in the "disputed" list (James, Jude, 2 John, and 3 John) came to be recognized as canonical, their writing inspired by God and superintended by the Holy Spirit.[9]

But are epistles legitimate source material for the preaching of a New Testament personage? In a work that reminds us of both the oral and aural nature

---

4. Darrel L. Bock, *Acts,* BECNT (Grand Rapids: Baker Academic, 2007), 145.

5. Eusebius, *Hist. eccl.* 2.15.1.

6. Helen K. Bond, "Was Peter Behind Mark's Gospel?" in *Peter in Early Christianity,* ed. Helen K. Bond and Larry W. Hurtado (Grand Rapids: Eerdmans, 2015), 60. C.f. Richard Bauckham, *Jesus and the Eyewitnesses: The Gospels as Eyewitness Testimony* (Grand Rapids: Eerdmans, 2006), 170–80.

7. Markus Bockmuehl, *Simon Peter in Scripture and Memory: The New Testament Apostle in the Early Church* (Grand Rapids: Baker Academic, 2012), 126.

8. Eusebius, *Hist. eccl.* 3.25.1. For a recent thorough examination of the evidence, see Gene L. Green, *Jude & 2 Peter,* BECNT (Grand Rapids: Baker Academic, 2008), 139–50.

9. Eusebius, *Hist. eccl.* 3.25.2.

of first-century culture in general, and the earliest church and its reception of Scripture in particular, C. Richard Wells identifies these letters as "inspired incarnational preaching,"[10] and as such, they will be considered source material for the assessment of the preaching of the apostle Peter.

Peter's Preaching in Acts

The first recorded exhortation of Peter in the book of Acts occurs in the context of the pre-Pentecost upper room prayer gathering in 1:15–22. He addressed the fledgling community of faith concerning the circumstances in which they found themselves after Jesus's departure and the practical need for replacing Judas. His primary emphasis was the sovereignty of God in the fulfillment of his purposes. He followed Jesus's example by interpreting Scripture to show recent events as the fulfillment of what God had already declared.[11] In the practical qualifications for fulfilling the apostolic vacancy, he asserted the necessity of one who was an eyewitness to all that Jesus did, in order to give credible proclamation of His resurrection as Lord and Christ.[12] Here in Peter's admonition to the church, prior to the choosing of Matthias as a replacement for Judas, Peter's influential leadership and role as authoritative spokesperson is evidenced. His emphasis in this brief excerpt was on the inevitability of the fulfillment of Scripture—the Old Testament read through the hermeneutical lens of Jesus, the Messiah.[13]

Peter's next recorded exhortation is his opportunistic presentation of the gospel of Jesus the Christ that followed the outpouring of the Holy Spirit at Pentecost in Acts 2:14–40. Here we see the same emphasis on God's sovereignty and the fulfillment of Scripture. But with the change in audience to nonbelievers, there is an added emphasis on the accomplishment of God's salvific purposes through Jesus the Nazarene. Again this fulfillment is seen as the interpretation of present events through God's prophetic Word. Peter identified the phenomenon his audience had witnessed, the outpouring of the Spirit with its accompanying visible manifestations, as an indication of the arrival of the eschaton as prophesied by Joel.[14]

After this eschatological declaration, Peter turned to the person of Jesus, identifying him by his hometown (the Nazarene). He confronted the crowd with the knowledge that they themselves possessed as eyewitnesses to God's supernatural attestation of him. He assured them that the events of Jesus's death, and their

---

10. Wells and Luter, *Inspired Preaching*, 60.
11. David G. Peterson, *The Acts of the Apostles*, PNTC (Grand Rapids: Eerdmans, 2009), 120.
12. Bock, *Acts*, 88.
13. Larry R. Helyer, *The Life and Witness of Peter* (Downers Grove, IL: IVP Academic, 2012), 70.
14. Craig S. Keener, *Acts: An Exegetical Commentary*, 4 vols. (Grand Rapids: Baker Academic, 2012–2015), 1:877–78.

culpability in it, were not of human origin, but bore witness to the sovereign plan of God. He further declared that God raised Jesus from the dead. Then he turned again to the Scriptures that both he and his audience knew to be God's truth to demonstrate God's prophetic foretelling of Jesus's resurrection. Peter then boldly declared that Jesus is risen, that he is exalted at the Father's right hand, and that he is both Lord (a title for Yahweh in Palestinian Judaism), reigning over salvation, and also Messiah (God's anointed king coming to save his people).[15] In this detailed explanation of the events surrounding Jesus's death, resurrection, and exaltation as well as the outpouring of the Holy Spirit, Peter's interpretation of the fulfillment of Joel's prophecy was to convince his listeners that "Jesus is the Lord upon whom one is to call for salvation."[16]

The response to Peter's proclamation was a heartfelt conviction that led to an outcry—people seeking the means of salvation. This gospel presentation was not yet the universal appeal it became. It was initially targeted at Jews, calling them to salvation.[17] The prerequisite for their salvation was repentance. This would have been a familiar concept to faithful first-century Jews, and they would have understood it as a call to turn from sin and embrace God's reign by accepting the Lordship of Jesus as King.[18] The Jews are called to full participation within the community of believers, initiated through baptism and their public identification with Christ and his church. Jesus, the Messiah, had to be acknowledged as the baptismal authority. Part of their repentance entailed rejecting the open hostility directed toward God's incarnational presence in Jesus "whom you crucified," and fully embracing him as "both Lord and Messiah" (Acts 2:36), as revealed in his preceding Psalms citations.[19] They are then assured that they too will be participants in the outpouring of the Holy Spirit upon the church, the effects of which they have just seen for themselves.

In Acts 2:40, Luke recorded a concluding summary of this sermon that informs us that what immediately preceded was not a sermon manuscript nor a recorded transcript. Instead, in what has been termed "a reporter's stock device,"[20] the reader is provided an abbreviated summary of a much longer exhortation, translated into the native Greek of Luke's readership. But it is nonetheless an accurate depiction of the central thrust of Peter's message, as well as a normative

---

15. Bock, *Acts*, 136.
16. John Kilgallen, "'With Many Other Words' (Acts 2,40): Theological Assumptions in Peter's Pentecost Speech," *Biblica* 83:1 (2002): 76.
17. Ben Witherington, *The Acts of the Apostles: A Socio-Rhetorical Commentary* (Grand Rapids: Eerdmans, 1998), 141.
18. Keener, *Acts*, 1:973–74.
19. Peterson, *The Acts of the Apostles*, 152.
20. C. K. Barrett, *Acts*, vol. 1, ICC (Edinburgh: T&T Clark, 1994), 156.

example of what followed and would continue to follow. With "many other words" Peter urged them to abandon their eternally destructive rejection of the Messiah whom God sent to save them.[21]

Peter's next recorded sermon was prompted by the healing of the lame beggar. The man sat in the temple gate and sought a monetary pittance to temporarily meet his physical needs. What he received instead was a supernatural physical restoration that transformed his whole life. He would no longer need to depend on the pity and sense of duty of the people entering the place of worship from which his contaminating presence was forbidden (Acts 3:1–8).

When the surrounding crowds expressed their amazement, their admiration was directed toward Peter and John for the accomplishment of this miraculous transformation. Peter quickly corrected them. He informed them it was not he and John who healed, but the God of their fathers, whose glory was manifested in Jesus. This was the same Jesus they had disowned, rejected, and delivered to Pilate to be put to death, and instead favored the release of a murderer (Acts 3:13–16). As in his sermon at Pentecost, Peter rapidly moved to the correct interpretation of the present circumstances as a manifestation of the power of God, their God who was known by their fathers Abraham, Isaac, and Jacob. The healing was done by the God of their fathers, working through the authority of his Son, their Messiah, Jesus.[22] Peter turned once again to the Scriptures, which both he and his hearers recognized as God's authoritative Word. He details in Acts 3:22–25 how the sufferings of Christ were part of God's predetermined plan to accomplish his salvation, as prophesied by Moses and the prophets.[23] Again Peter urged his listeners to repent, have their sins forgiven, and experience God's salvation.

Unlike at Pentecost, Peter and John were not present to witness the response to their proclamation, as they were interrupted and hauled off to prison by the temple guard. But as with Peter's previous sermon in chapter two, the response was remarkable. The salvation of five thousand men is recorded, implying a much greater number since in their first-century culture it is reasonable to assume that their households would have followed their lead.[24]

Peter's address before the council in Acts 4 is a continuation of his proclamation in chapter 3. The same miraculous healing prompted the inquiry. Again Peter is identified as being empowered by God, not speaking from his own authority or

---

21. Eckhard J. Schnabel, *Acts,* ZECNT (Grand Rapids: Zondervan, 2012), 106–7.
22. Bock, *Acts,* 168.
23. F. F. Bruce, *The Acts of the Apostles: The Greek Text with Introduction and Commentary,* 3rd ed. (Grand Rapids: Eerdmans, 1990), 146.
24. Keener, *Acts,* 1134.

ability. He immediately turned to the issue at hand: Jesus the Messiah, rejected by them, but vindicated by God through the resurrection, as the only means by which anyone can experience God's salvation. Peter once more cited the Scriptures as the authoritative truth concerning God's salvific plan accomplished and fulfilled in Jesus, the Messiah, specifically referencing Psalm 118. In these first three sermons recorded in the early chapters of the book of Acts, Peter consistently proclaimed God's predetermined plan of salvation shown in the law, the prophets, and the writings and accomplished through Jesus, the Messiah.[25]

The council's response to Peter's proclamation recorded in Acts 4:13–22 was not the same positive coming to faith that was seen at Pentecost and the healing of the lame man. But even in their rejection of the message, the council's response reveals much. They admitted that God had acted powerfully in this healing. And they recognized that the presence of Jesus had empowered the words spoken by Peter, despite Peter's lack of formal training. But they were threatened by such bold proclamation and forbid it to continue. However, they were incapable of stopping the proclamation of the availability of God's salvation exclusively through Jesus, God's risen, reigning, Anointed One. The council's rejection of the power of God left them powerless and stripped them of any genuine authority as God's representatives.[26] In the face of their threats, Peter and John openly defied them. And the church responded to their cease and desist order with a prayer for boldness to continue doing what they had been ordered not to. It was a prayer God answered with an outpouring of his Spirit that emboldened the church to continue their outspoken proclamation of his truth (4:31).

The next time the apostles appear before the Sanhedrin is in Acts 5 and is a continuation of the story begun in chapter 3. In response to the apostles' defiance, the high priest and the council had them arrested. However, they were miraculously released and given the divine directive to go back and continue doing precisely what they had been arrested for doing, preaching the "all about this new life" in Jesus (5:20). When arrested yet again and confronted with their defiance, Peter again spoke as their representative, in a brief passage where Luke succinctly summarizes the salient points that drive the apostolic preaching: (1) We must obey God; (2) the One you crucified, God has raised, exalted, and made him Savior; (3) we, together with the Holy Spirit, bear witness to God's truth (5:29–32).

The last reported evangelistic sermon of Peter is in Acts 10 when he proclaimed the gospel to Cornelius and his fellow gentiles. A special revelation from

---

25. Paul A. Himes, "Peter and the Prophetic Word: The Theology of Prophecy Traced through Peter's Sermons and Epistles," *Bulletin for Biblical Research* 21, no. 2 (2011): 232–33.

26. Bock, *Acts*, 199.

God was needed for Peter to overcome his deeply entrenched Judaic sensibilities concerning the contamination of gentile contact. Having corrected the homage that was initially given to him upon his arrival, Peter heard Cornelius recount how he too had received a special revelation that prompted him to send for Peter. Peter then preached the gospel for the first time to gentiles. In this proclamation he demonstrated that as a preacher, he was open to God's correction.[27]

The content of his sermon again focused on Jesus and the recent events concerning him. He summarized Jesus's ministry as anointed by God, empowered by the Holy Spirit, and overcoming the oppression of Satan in the lives of those he healed (10:38). Peter next recounted Jesus's death on the cross and his resurrection by God's power, verified by eyewitnesses—those with whom he had spoken and eaten. Peter declared that his preaching mission was a divine imperative to proclaim Jesus as "judge of the living and the dead" (10:42). He again referenced the Old Testament prophets as those who bear witness to the salvation offered through Jesus's name to those who believe in him.

The response on this occasion occurred before Peter was finished, again demonstrating that salvation is a sovereign activity of God, not within human control. After witnessing the Spirit's outpouring, manifested through tongues, exactly as they themselves experienced in Acts 2, Peter and those with him acknowledged the inclusiveness of God's offer of salvation to those not a part of his original covenant people, and baptized them in the name of Jesus.[28]

Twice more in Acts, extended discourses by Peter are recorded—in chapters 11 and 15. Both times, instead of being gospel proclamations to unbelievers, they address the church on the issue of the inclusion of gentiles in God's community of faith. Peter declares that gentiles do not need to be initiated into God's covenant through circumcision in adherence to the law of Moses. It could be argued that these are not sermons, but they are an account of the leaders of the church proclaiming and applying God's revealed truth to a contemporary and controversial situation facing the church.[29] Many preachers today would agree that is very much like what they do from the pulpit on a regular basis.

Peter's teaching in chapter 11 was especially revealing and transparent. He gave a detailed account of God's revelation to him, and its convicting work in his life. It showed Peter his error in thinking that gentiles apart from observance of the law were outside the sphere of God's salvation. He recounted the vision he received, the arrival of those seeking him, and his proclamation of the gospel to the gentiles in Cornelius's house. He then reminded them of the words of

---

27. Ajith Fernando, *Acts,* NIVAC (Grand Rapids: Zondervan, 1998), 323.
28. Schnabel, *Acts,* 505.
29. John B. Polhill, *Acts,* New American Commentary (Nashville: Broadman & Holman, 1992), 327.

Jesus, and asked how anyone could "stand in God's way" (11:17) by refusing those whom God had already included in his Holy Spirit baptism.

Despite this, in Acts 15 the same issue was still unresolved in the hearts of many Jewish believers. While the leading spokesman on this occasion was James, Peter reiterated what he had already stated in chapter 11. His emphasis was completely on the sovereignty of God.[30] God chose to send the gospel to the gentiles by means of Peter, and God testified to their salvation by giving them his Spirit. Refusing to acknowledge this equates to putting God to the test and denying his grace (15:7–11).

In summation, several characteristics of Peter's preaching in Acts are notable. The foremost feature in all his sermons/speeches was the person of Jesus and his identity as the Christ, the Jewish Messiah. At the forefront of this proclamation was the recognition of Jesus's death as God's predetermined plan to accomplish the salvation of his people, the overturning of death through Jesus's resurrection, and Jesus's current exalted reign at the Father's right hand. All of this was foretold by God through the Scriptures, properly understood through a christological hermeneutic.

Echoes of Peter's Preaching: The Gospel of Mark

Although the connection between Peter's eyewitness testimony and the gospel of Mark comes to us from the testimony of Papias in the earliest days of the church through Eusebius, most scholars today discount this notion.[31] However, that consensus has recently been challenged. Martin Hengel is one example of recent scholarly support for a Petrine connection with the second gospel, arguing that Peter is the "empowered guarantor of the traditions about Jesus" and those traditions "lie behind the second gospel."[32] As Helen Bond has suggested, once the connection between Peter and the gospel of Mark is established, then it becomes logical to explore the possibility of Peter as the source of Mark's theology.[33]

While an in-depth analysis of the gospel of Mark is beyond the scope of this study, a brief analysis will show that it shares much in common with the theological emphases already observed in Peter's recorded sermons. Both are christologically focused, declare the salvific purpose of Jesus's death, proclaim the truth of his resurrection and exaltation, all which had been prophetically foretold in the Scriptures.

---

30. John A. McIntosh, "'For It Seemed Good to the Holy Spirit,' Acts 15:28: How Did the Members of the Jerusalem Council Know This?" *Reformed Theological Review* 61, no. 3 (December 2002): 145.

31. For a summary of these arguments see Joel Marcus, *Mark 1–8: A New Translation with Introduction*, AB vol. 2 (New York: Doubleday, 2000), 21–24.

32. Hengel, *Saint Peter*, 101.

33. Bond, "Was Peter Behind Mark's Gospel?," 61. C.f. Bauckham, *Jesus and the Eyewitnesses*, 170–80.

The gospel of Mark is well known for its emphasis on the passion narrative, which constitutes approximately half of the gospel's content. After a fast-paced narration of Jesus's ministry, notable for its frequent transitional phrase "and immediately," the gospel slows down for the narrative hinge pin of 8:25–10:52, which includes three passion predictions of Jesus. This then leads into the passion narrative itself, which comprises chapters 11 through 16, where the narrative pace slows dramatically. This literary plan led to the often-repeated characterization by Martin Kähler over a century ago that Mark is a passion narrative with an extended introduction.[34] The resulting emphasis on Jesus's crucifixion and resurrection parallels Peter's emphasis in Acts. William Lane notes the similarities between Mark's gospel and Peter's sermon in Acts 10:36–41.[35] Lane shows the remarkable parallels between Mark chapters one through sixteen and Peter's words in Acts. These include the verbal parallels such as, "Jesus the Messiah," "good news," and the reference to God's anointing Jesus with the Holy Spirit, narrated in Mark at Jesus's baptism when the Spirit descends upon him like a dove. Lane points out that the summary statement of Jesus's ministry in Acts 10:38 is a concise and accurate summary of Jesus's Galilean ministry in Mark 1:16–10:52: "He went around doing good and healing all who were under the power of the devil, because God was with him." He then notes that Peter's words in Acts 10:39–40 would serve appropriately as outline headings for Mark chapters 11–16. "And we are his witnesses of all the things He did both in the land of the Jews and in Jerusalem (Mark 11–14). They also put Him to death by hanging Him on a cross (Mark 15). God raised Him from the dead on the third day and granted that He become visible" (Mark 16).[36] Lane concludes, "The content of Mark's gospel is as kerygmatic as the outline, and provides added support to the tradition linking the written account with the apostolic preaching."[37]

Homeletical Letters: 1 and 2 Peter

While some have characterized Peter's epistles as sermonic letters or homilies, Wells and Luter go further still, arguing that in contrast to our experience of the New Testament as a collection of written documents, they were something more than that in the first-century context. The recorded words would have been spoken aloud by the author as he visualized his hearers, regardless of his use of a recording secretary.[38] They note that New Testament letters were

34. Martin Kähler, *The So-Called Historical Jesus and the Historic Biblical Christ*, trans. Carl E. Braaten (Philadelphia: Fortress, 1964), 80 n.11.

35. William Lane, *The Gospel According to Mark*, NICNT (Grand Rapids: Eerdmans, 1974), 10–11.

36. Ibid., 11.

37. Ibid.

38. Wells and Luter, *Inspired Preaching*, xii.

public communications, and meant to be heard communally, not read privately in silence. They posit a communication model consisting of an author who spoke his words while composing, perhaps having them recorded by a secretary, entrusted for delivery to a courier, who may well have been the designated public reader. In the case of the courier who was also the reader, the author would have in all probability "rehearsed" the public reading so that intended emphases and into-nation would be accurately communicated. If the reader was someone other than the courier, the courier would have "coached" the recipient to ensure an accurate hearing for the letter.[39]

Whether one is completely convinced by all the details of this communi-cation scenario, it is almost certainly closer to the first-century reality than the author-text-reader communication model normally conceived in the twenty-first century. By characterizing 1 and 2 Peter as "incarnational preaching," Wells is saying that the life experiences of Simon Peter as follower of Jesus—a disciple absorbing his teaching—and his own awareness of his catastrophic failure and graceful restoration are what formed and shaped the theological content of his apostolic preaching expressed in these letters.[40]

The content of 1 Peter contains the same emphases noted in his sermons from Acts. Just as he did with Jesus's betrayal and death, Peter acknowledged the sovereignty and foreknowledge of God in the circumstances of these *scattered aliens* who walk in this world as strangers and outcasts (1:1–2, 20). He intro-duced his letter with a fresh reminder of the gospel, the death and resurrection of Jesus, the work of the Holy Spirit, and looking forward to the living hope of an imperishable inheritance (1:2–4).[41]

Chapters 2 and 3 illustrate Peter's christological hermeneutic that allowed him to properly interpret the Old Testament, citing from Isaiah, Hosea, and the Psalms. As in his exhortation to the church in Acts 1, 11, and 15, Peter applied God's revelation in the Old Testament Scripture and the life and teachings of Christ to his readers' present circumstances. Their identification with Christ both marked them as "foreigners and exiles" (2:11) and necessitated that they live in a manner so as to exemplify God's character in their daily lives as a testimony before the world in which they walked, but to which they did not belong.[42]

As his exhortation closes, Peter specifically addressed those called by God to proclaim his truth. He insisted this calling always be exercised in the reverent awe produced by an awareness of God. It is his word being spoken, his service

---

39. Ibid., 19–22.
40. Ibid., 68–69.
41. Peter H. Davids, *The First Epistle of Peter,* NICNT (Grand Rapids: Eerdmans, 1990), 52.
42. Karen H. Jobes, *1 Peter,* BECNT (Grand Rapids: Baker Academic, 2005), 171–72.

being given, his strength that enables, and his glory that is sought (4:11). The fulfillment of this by those who preach the gospel is only possible through utter dependence upon him. Peter continued in this vein in chapter 5, as he specified how his fellow elders should fulfill their commission to shepherd God's flock. It must be willingly and eagerly, not forced, or with material gain as the goal. The leader's life is to be an example of walking faithfully with God, never "lording it over" anyone (5:2–3). The necessary character traits are humility, utter dependence upon God, resisting temptation, standing firm in the faith, and accepting suffering for his name's sake (5:6–10). This is the faithful character required of those called by God, especially those shepherds called to preach his word.[43]

In 2 Peter, the apostle began with the foundation of the saving grace of God made available through the gospel (1:1–3). Peter's primary focus in this letter was the false teachers who could lead the flock astray. He once more returned to his experience with the incarnate Christ to lay the foundation of his argument (1:16–18), then moved to the reliability and certainty of God's revealed word (1:19–21).

Just as when addressing the legalists in Acts 15, who mimicked his own earlier false understanding of the necessity of law-keeping for salvation, Peter stressed the importance of accepting God's revealed truth and rejecting anything opposed to it. He declared Scripture to be God's prophetic word, with no human origin (1:20–21). In contrast, the false teaching was destructive and misleading, denying Christ himself (2:1).

Next, Peter turned to the problem of the scoffers who mocked believers that anticipated Christ's return. The mockers are the ones who were misled. The certainty of Christ's return is guaranteed by both the authors of Scriptures—"the holy prophets"—and the command of Jesus himself, proclaimed by the apostles (3:1–4).

Wells finds six "incarnational themes" in 1 and 2 Peter that flow out of Peter's own life experience with Jesus. First is the experience of regeneration, birthed to a salvation that gives a living, certain hope; second is a life permeated with humility; third is the usefulness of a steadfast life upon which and with which God builds his habitation. The fourth theme Wells identifies is faithfully walking in the way of the cross. This means accepting the suffering that is the norm for those faithfully living for Christ. Fifth is the primary ministry of shepherding the flock God has entrusted to his appointed leaders. The sixth and final theme is the transformative power of God's word proclaimed.[44]

---

43. Timothy S. Laniak, *Shepherds after My Own Heart: Pastoral Traditions and Leadership in the Bible*, vol. 20, New Studies in Biblical Theology, ed. D. A. Carson (Downers Grove, IL: InterVarsity Press, 2006), 234.

44. Wells and Luter, *Inspired Preaching*, 69–74.

THEOLOGY OF PREACHING

Luke's narrative record of Peter's sermons, Mark's gospel produced from the content of Peter's preaching, and the letters Peter wrote as authoritative substitutes for his personal proclamation reveal much about Peter's understanding of the task of preaching. For Peter, preaching was a divine mandate. He did not preach because of the personal satisfaction he derived from it, nor the accolades he received for it. Peter preached because he never lost sight of the command his Lord had given him at his restoration recorded in John 21. He was to feed the sheep God had assigned to his care. He did not preach because someone required him to, he did not preach because of any compensation he received, he preached because he could not do otherwise. It was God's imperative for his life, as he told the Jewish council in Jerusalem, "we cannot help speaking about what we have seen and heard" (Acts 4:20). After being flogged and ordered to stop preaching in Jesus's name, instead of being outraged at the injustice of the punishment to which they were subjected, they rejoiced because "they had been counted worthy of suffering disgrace for the Name" (Acts 5:41) and "never stopped teaching and proclaiming the good news that Jesus is the Messiah" (5:42).[45]

A second reality revealed in these New Testament sermons is that for Peter, there was only one message to preach: the good news of God's salvation foretold throughout Scripture. This salvation was made available through the atoning death of God's Son, Jesus, who was both the Messiah of the Jews and Lord and Savior of all the earth, raised by God, and now reigning at his Father's right hand.[46] Those who will repent and believe, receive forgiveness and salvation, and are given "new birth into a living hope" (1 Pet 1:3) through the power of the Holy Spirit. That is the gospel. Peter Hans Bayer captures well the essence of Peter's proclamation: he was a Christ-centered "prophetic preacher of repentance."[47] As Acts 1, 11, and 15 and 1 and 2 Peter clearly demonstrate, this gospel has practical and necessary implications and application for every circumstance and facet of our individual lives and the life of the church.

A final observation on Peter's theological underpinnings for the task of preaching is Peter's recognition of the sovereignty of God in every aspect of the task. Peter knew that the effectiveness of preaching is dependent upon the presence and power of a sovereign God. In his theocentric presentation of the gospel in 1 Peter, Peter clearly proclaimed God as Lord, sovereign over

---

45. Keener, *Acts*, 1:1242–44.
46. Helyer, *The Life and Witness of Peter*, 129–31.
47. Hans F. Bayer, "The Preaching of Peter in Acts," in *Witness to the Gospel: The Theology of Acts*, ed. I. Howard Marshall and David Peterson (Grand Rapids: Eerdmans, 1998), 262.

all.[48] When the church prayed in response to the council's threats in Acts 4, they asked not only for boldness on their part, but for God to tangibly demonstrate his power and presence to authenticate their proclamation (4:30). They understood the ingathering of new believers on these occasions not in terms of the success of their evangelistic efforts, but as the work of the Lord, who "added to their number daily those who were being saved" (Acts 2:47).

METHODOLOGY FOR PREACHING

In analyzing Peter's preaching methodology, several notable features are observed. The first is that for Peter, preaching was not a matter of human effort, but a divinely inspired activity. In his address to the 120 in the upper room, the statement immediately preceding his address is that they were united in devoting themselves to prayer (Acts 1:14). In Acts 2, the Holy Spirit has just been poured out on the church with the visible manifestation of God's presence and power. At the healing of the lame man, the first issue Peter addressed with the amazed crowd is the source of the power they have just witnessed. It was not Peter and John themselves, but the power that comes from faith in the name of Jesus (3:12–16). His proclamation before the Jewish council in chapter 4 is prefaced with the declaration, "Peter, filled with the Holy Spirit, said to them . . ." (4:8). In chapter 10, prior to Peter's encounter with Cornelius, he had withdrawn to pray, when God communicated directly with him in a vision. And when the emissaries from Cornelius arrive, the Holy Spirit told Peter to go with them (10:9–20). When Peter addressed the church in Acts 11 and 15, he did not try to reason with them concerning the inclusion of the gentiles. His focus was completely on God's power poured out visibly upon gentiles, just as it was with the Jewish believers at Pentecost. Peter's preaching was an extension of the manifestation of the presence and power of God on his Spirit-filled church.

Peter's preaching was also opportunistic. He proclaimed the gospel in response to the people's amazement at God's manifested presence and power—including the tongues heard at Pentecost and the healing of the lame man. And when Peter bragged, "I have never eaten anything impure or unclean," (10:14) God corrected him and prompted him to travel to the house of a gentile to proclaim the gospel, stay under his roof, and share fellowship at his table (10:48–11:3). For Peter and the early church, evangelistic proclamation was not a scheduled event, but a response to those who witnessed the presence and power of the living God working in the believers' daily lives.

---

48. Joel B. Green, *1 Peter,* Two Horizons New Testament Commentary (Grand Rapids: Eerdmans, 2007), 203–4.

Scripture was the foundation for Peter's proclamation. The revelation of the incarnational presence of God in the person of Jesus of Nazareth was not a new truth, but a fulfillment of what God had already declared. Peter had the conviction that Scripture is God's authoritative revelation and can only properly be interpreted christologically.

A final observation on Peter's preaching methods is the importance of correct application of Scripture and of the gospel to every circumstance that arises. Living lives devoted to God, rooted in Scripture, and surrendered to the living presence of the Holy Spirit serves to correct our misunderstandings and to overturn the failure to perceive what God is doing. Peter accepted that corrective himself, on a rooftop in Joppa, and he boldly called for such correction when confronting false teachers in his written exhortations.

CONTRIBUTIONS TO PREACHING

The response to Peter's preaching in Acts, carefully portrayed by Luke, revealed that it was not the preacher's persuasive speech or winsome personality that drew people into God's family; it is the power of God through the conviction of the Holy Spirit. The ingathering statements indicate the sovereignty of God in the process of salvation, "And the Lord added to their number daily." (2:47). In Acts 3, the five thousand coming to faith occurs after Peter and John are gone, having been hauled off to prison. On the first proclamation of the gospel to gentiles in Acts 10, it was God who initiated their salvation. This was evidenced by the Holy Spirit falling upon Cornelius and those listening with him with the same visible manifestation as experienced by Peter and the Jewish believers at Pentecost. This occurred "while Peter was still speaking" (10:44) and without him extending any kind of evangelistic appeal.

In the events leading up to Peter's proclamation of the gospel to Cornelius and his fellow gentiles, and in the content of that proclamation, Peter evinced the humility that permitted God to correct his interpretation and application of God's revelation. He overcame his inherent prejudices and fully embraced God's truth revealed to him by the Holy Spirit, even when it went against everything he had been taught and believed about how God does and should act. This is the same humility and total dependency upon God toward which he exhorts his fellow elders in 1 Peter 5.

Peter's foundational preaching in the earliest days of the church provides the model for preaching to every generation. It must be practiced in the power of the Holy Spirit, as the natural outflow of a life lived for and empowered by the presence of God, humbly submitted fully to him. It must be authentically proclaimed by one who has first personally come under the convicting power of God's truth and also responded in repentance and received God's forgiveness. And the message must always be Christ-centered, gospel focused, rooted in Scripture, and relevantly applied to contemporary circumstances. The response to such preaching is in the hands of a sovereign God, and all the glory is his.

Sermon Excerpt
Acts 10:34–43

I now realize how true it is that God does not show favoritism but accepts from every nation the one who fears him and does what is right. You know the message God sent to the people of Israel, announcing the good news of peace through Jesus Christ, who is Lord of all. You know what has happened throughout the province of Judea, beginning in Galilee after the baptism that John preached—how God anointed Jesus of Nazareth with the Holy Spirit and power, and how he went around doing good and healing all who were under the power of the devil, because God was with him.

We are witnesses of everything he did in the country of the Jews and in Jerusalem. They killed him by hanging him on a cross, but God raised him from the dead on the third day and caused him to be seen. He was not seen by all the people, but by witnesses whom God had already chosen—by us who ate and drank with him after he rose from the dead. He commanded us to preach to the people and to testify that he is the one whom God appointed as judge of the living and the dead. All the prophets testify about him that everyone who believes in him receives forgiveness of sins through his name. ◆

BIBLIOGRAPHY

Barrett, C. K. *Acts*. 2 vols. International Critical Commentary. Edinburgh: T&T Clark, 1994–1998.

Bauckham, Richard. *Jesus and the Eyewitnesses: The Gospels as Eyewitness Testimony*. Grand Rapids: Eerdmans, 2006.

Bayer, Hans F. "The Preaching of Peter in Acts," Pages 257–74 in *Witness to the Gospel: The Theology of Acts*. Edited by I. Howard Marshall and David Peterson. Grand Rapids: Eerdmans, 1998.

Bock, Darrel L. *Acts*. Baker Exegetical Commentary on the New Testament. Grand Rapids, Baker Academic, 2007.

Bockmuehl, Markus. *Simon Peter in Scripture and Memory: The New Testament Apostle in the Early Church*. Grand Rapids: Baker Academic, 2012.

Bond, Helen K. and Larry W. Hurtado, eds. *Peter in Early Christianity*. Grand Rapids: Eerdmans, 2015.

Bruce, F. F. *The Acts of the Apostles: The Greek Text with Introduction and Commentary*, 3rd ed. Grand Rapids: Eerdmans, 1990.

Davids, Peter H. *The First Epistle of Peter*. The New International Commentary on the New Testament. Grand Rapids: Eerdmans, 1990.

Eusebius. *Ecclesiastical History*. Trans. by Kirsopp Lake. 2 vols. Loeb Classical Library. Cambridge: Harvard University Press, 1926.

Fernando, Ajith. *Acts*. NIV Application Commentary. Grand Rapids: Zondervan, 1998.

Foakes-Jackson, F. J. *Peter, Prince of Apostles: A Study in the History and Tradition of Christianity*. New York: George H. Doran, 1927.

Green, Gene L. *Jude & 2 Peter*. Baker Exegetical Commentary on the New Testament. Grand Rapids: Baker Academic, 2008.

Green, Joel B. *1 Peter*. The Two Horizons New Testament Commentary. Grand Rapids: Eerdmans, 2007.

Helyer, Larry R. *The Life and Witness of Peter*. Downers Grove, IL: InterVarsity Press Academic, 2012.

Hengel, Martin. *Saint Peter: The Underestimated Apostle*. Grand Rapids: Eerdmans, 2010.

Himes, Paul A. "Peter and the Prophetic Word: The Theology of Prophecy Traced through Peter's Sermons and Epistles." *Bulletin for Biblical Research* 21, no. 2 (2011): 227–43.

Jobes, Karen H. *1 Peter*. Baker Exegetical Commentary on the New Testament. Grand Rapids: Baker Academic, 2005.

Kähler, Martin. *The So-Called Historical Jesus and the Historic Biblical Christ*. Trans. by Carl E. Braaten. Philadelphia: Fortress, 1964.

Keener, Craig S. *Acts: An Exegetical Commentary*. 4 vols. Grand Rapids: Baker Academic, 2012–2015.

Kilgallen, John J. "'With Many Other Words' (Acts 2,40): Theological Assumptions in Peter's Pentecost Speech," *Biblica* 83, no. 1 (2002): 76.

Lane, William. *The Gospel According to Mark*. New International Commentary on the New Testament. Grand Rapids: Eerdmans, 1974.

Laniak, Timothy S. *Shepherds After My Own Heart: Pastoral Traditions and Leadership in the Bible*. New Studies in Biblical Theology 20. Edited by D. A. Carson. Downers Grove, IL: InterVarsity Press, 2006.

Marcus, Joel. *Mark 1–8*. The Anchor Bible. New York: Doubleday, 2000.

McIntosh, John A. "'For It Seemed Good to the Holy Spirit,' Acts 15:28: How Did the Members of the Jerusalem Council Know This?" *The Reformed Theological Review* 61, no. 3 (December 2002): 131–47.

Peterson, David G. *The Acts of the Apostles*. Pillar New Testament Commentary. Grand Rapids: Eerdmans, 2009.

Polhill, John B. *Acts*. New American Commentary. Nashville: Broadman & Holman, 1992.

Schnabel, Eckhard, J. *Acts*. Zondervan Exegetical Commentary on the New Testament. Grand Rapids: Zondervan, 2012.

Wells, C. Richard, and A. Boyd Luter. *Inspired Preaching, A Survey of Preaching Found in the New Testament*. Nashville: Broadman & Holman, 2002.

Witherington, Ben. *The Acts of the Apostles: A Socio-Rhetorical Commentary*. Grand Rapids: Eerdmans, 1998.

Melito of Sardis
Proclaiming Christ the Lamb

PAUL A. HARTOG

S. MELITO, BISHOP of SARDIS.

S. MELITO.

Melito (d. ca. 190) was a second-century Christian leader in Sardis in Asia Minor. According to the church historian Eusebius, Melito was a well-respected bishop and the author of many works—nearly all of which are now lost. In 1940, Melito's homiletic material captivated patristic scholarship through the publication of his newly identified work, *On the Pascha*. The sermon reflects on Exodus 12, focuses on Jesus as the sacrificial Lamb prefigured by Passover, insists on the deity and humanity of Christ, and is characterized by vivid typology and rhetorical polish. Melito's cultivated oratory was probably influenced by the "Asianic" style of the Second Sophistic.

HISTORICAL BACKGROUND

We know neither the exact date of Melito's birth nor of his death.[1] At the end of the second century, Polycrates, bishop of Ephesus, wrote a letter to Victor of Rome. Polycrates presented a case for the historic Asian tradition of keeping Pascha (the origins of Easter) on the fourteenth of Nisan, aligned with Passover in the Jewish calendar. In ecclesiastical history, this custom was known as "Quartodecimanism" ("fourteenthism"). Although this tradition was opposed by Victor of Rome and was later condemned by the Council of Nicaea in AD 325, it was a common tradition in second-century Asia Minor. To buttress his case, Polycrates listed various church leaders of Asia Minor ("great lights of the church of Asia") who had kept this custom, the most notable including the Apostle Philip and his daughters, the Beloved John, and Polycarp of Smyrna.

Within this list, Polycrates mentioned "Melito the eunuch who governed entirely in the Holy Spirit, who lies at Sardis awaiting the visitation from the

---

1. Richard C. White, *Melito of Sardis, Sermon "On the Passover": A New English Translation with Introduction and Commentary*, Lexington Theological Seminary Library Occasional Studies (Lexington: Lexington Theological Seminary Library, 1976), 4.

heavens when he shall be raised from the dead."[2] This is the first reference to Melito in extant Christian literature, and it relates Melito's residence (Sardis), his reputable and prophetic character (one who was led in the Spirit), his status as a "eunuch" (probably a reference to a celibate chastity dedicated to religious purposes), and his internment awaiting the future resurrection.[3] The context of the reference also reminds us of a fourth attribute of Melito: his "Quartodeciman" practice of the Pascha. Some scholars wish to deduce from the nature of Polycrates's list that Melito was Jewish, and that he had recently passed away when Polycrates wrote his letter (perhaps providing us with an approximate date of 190 for Melito's death).[4]

One may probably assume that Melito was the "bishop" of Sardis,[5] without necessarily importing later connotations of the term.[6] Sardis lay in the Roman province of Asia Minor, and its Christian community was addressed in the biblical book of Revelation (Rev 3:1–6). Archaeologists have unearthed a sizable Jewish synagogue in Sardis, one of the largest Roman-era synagogues yet discovered. Alteration of the building into a synagogue took place after the second century, but literary evidence reveals that a Jewish community resided in Sardis in Melito's time (cf. Rev 3:1–6).[7] In Melito's era, the fledgling Christian community "lived in the shadow of the large and influential Jewish community."[8]

Eusebius of Caesarea, the early church historian, informs us that Melito made a trip to Palestine in order to determine the contents of the Hebrew Scriptures.[9] His task was to ascertain "the recognized sacred writings of the Old

---

2. Eusebius, *Hist. eccl.* 5.24.

3. Alistair Stewart-Sykes, *Melito of Sardis: On Pascha, with the Fragments of Melito and Other Material Related to the Quartodecimans* (Crestwood, NY: St. Vladimir's Seminary Press, 2001), 2–9; Richard C. White, "Melito of Sardis—An Ancient Worthy Reappears," *Lexington Theological Quarterly* 14 (1979): 7–10. On such celibacy, see Matt 19:11–12.

4. Alistair Stewart-Sykes, *The Lamb's High Feast: Melito's Peri Pascha and the Quartodeciman Paschal Liturgy at Sardis*, Supplements to Vigiliae Christianae 42 (Leiden: Brill, 1998), 2–3. Stewart-Sykes, *Melito of Sardis*, 3. Cf. Richard Bauckham, "Papias and Polycrates on the Origin of the Fourth Gospel," *Journal of Theological Studies*, 44 (1993): 24–69.

5. *Hist. eccl.* 4.26.1.

6. Stewart-Sykes, *Melito of Sardis*, 4; denied by Pierre Nautin, *Lettres et écrivains chrétiens des IIe et IIIe siècles* (Paris: Éditions du Cerf, 1961), 71–74; but affirmed by Othmar Perler, *Méliton de Sardes: Sur la Pâque et fragments: Introduction, texte critique, traduction et notes* (Paris: Éditions du Cerf, 2008), 7–9. Lieu cites Eusebius's calling Melito a "bishop" and reasons, "but there is no other evidence to support this, and it may have been supposition" (Judith Lieu, "Melito of Sardis," *Expository Times* 110 [1998]: 43).

7. Cf. Lynn H. Cohick, *The Peri Pascha Attributed to Melito of Sardis: Setting, Purpose, and Sources*, Brown Judaic Studies 327 (Providence: Brown University, 2000), 5.

8. Robert L. Wilken, "Melito, the Jewish Community at Sardis, and the Sacrifice of Isaac," *Theological Studies* 37 (1976): 56.

9. Zuntz maintained that *On Pascha* was preached in Palestine (Günther Zuntz, "On the Opening Sentence of Melito's Paschal Homily," *Harvard Theological Review* 36 [1943]: 315). Most scholars assume that the homily was delivered in Sardis. Cohick, however, believes that "nothing in the homily itself points unequivocally to Sardis," and therefore a Sardis milieu is "precarious at best" and should not be treated as a "given" or as the basis of interpretation (Cohick, *Peri Pascha*, 31, 85).

Covenant."[10] Eusebius and Anastasius listed numerous works of Melito,[11] which Stuart Hall has emended to a list of twenty-two works.[12] Scholars have sifted through numerous fragments attributed to Melito, in an attempt to separate the genuine from the spurious.[13] Eusebius provided two illustrative excerpts, one from Melito's *Apology* and another from his *Extracts* (*Eclogues*), a six-volume collection of Old Testament materials (*Hist. eccl.* 4. 26.10, 13). Melito's *Apology*, officially addressed to Marcus Aurelius (r. 161–180), was widely influential.[14]

The character of Melito and the subject of Paschal observance (the beginnings of Easter observance) come together in his one extant sermon, *On the Pascha*.[15] Eusebius of Caesarea mentioned Melito's "two books on the Pascha" but seemingly without directly quoting from their contents.[16] Anastasius Sinaiticus (a seventh-century author), however, provided a short excerpt from a work of Melito he called *On the Passion* (apparently a somewhat muddled reference to our *On the Pascha*). An additional passage in Eusebius suggests that Clement of Alexandria (who flourished around AD 200) knew of Melito's work, citing it in his own book on the topic (i.e., Clement's own *On Pascha* borrowed from Melito's *On Pascha*).[17] By inferring from the evidence found within the patristic literature, scholars tend to date *On Pascha* around the 160s, though a "precise" or "exact" date cannot be fixed with certainty.[18]

---

10. Eusebius, *Hist. eccl.* 4.26.12. Lieu comments, "If these are indeed his own words he becomes the first to use the term 'Old Testament' of the Jewish scriptures" (Lieu, "Melito of Sardis," 43). Melito's list parallels the Hebrew Scriptures and the Protestant Old Testament, with the exception of Esther being omitted.

11. Eusebius, *Hist. eccl.* 4.26.2

12. Stuart George Hall, *Melito of Sardis: On Pascha and Fragments* (Oxford: Clarendon, 1979), xiii-xvii. Eusebius probably interacted with copies of Melito's works at the library of Caesarea (White, "Melito of Sardis—An Ancient Worthy Reappears," 10). Eusebius lists sixteen to eighteen works, depending on one's interpretation of his wording (Campbell Bonner, *The Homily on the Passion by Melito Bishop of Sardis, with Some Fragments of the Apocryphal Ezekiel* (Philadelphia: University of Pennsylvania Press, 1940), 4; Michel Testuz, *Papyrus Bodmer XIII: Méliton de Sardes, Homélie sur la Pâque, Manuscrit du IIIe siècle* (Geneva: Bibliotheca Bodmeriana, 1960), 8.

13. See Hall, *Melito of Sardis*, xviii-xxxix. Bonner has entertained the hypothesis that Melito wrote chapters 11 and 12 of the *Epistle to Diognetus* (Bonner, *Homily on the Passion*, 61).

14. White, *Melito of Sardis*, 6.

15. Three introductory texts in English containing a full translation are Hall, *Melito of Sardis*; Stewart-Sykes, *Melito of Sardis*; White, *Melito of Sardis*.

16. Eusebius refers to "the two books On the Pascha," which could refer to two separate works or (more likely) a two-part, single work (see Hall, *Melito of Sardis*, xix-xxii). Nevertheless, Pseutonkas argued that the second book of Melito *On Pascha* referenced by Eusebius is actually Pseudo-Chrysostom VI. See Vasileios S. Pseutonkas, Μελίτωνος Σάρδεων "Τα περί του Πάσχα δύο," Analekta Blatadon 8 (Thessalonica: Patriarchikon Hidryma Paterikōn Meletōn, 1971). The chronological notation found in Eusebius, *Hist. eccl.* 4.26.3, purportedly taken from "the beginning" of Melito's *On Pascha*, appears to be a chronological note at the head of a manuscript (Stewart-Sykes, *Lamb's High Feast*, 120).

17. Eusebius, *Hist. eccl.* 6.13.9., accompanied by a comparison of VI.13.3, 9 with IV.26.2–3. The nature of the connection between "the two books on the Pascha" (or one of the two) in IV.26.2 and our available text is not certain, however.

18. Hall, *Melito of Sardis*, xii, xxii; Perler, *Méliton de Sardes*, 123–24; Stewart-Sykes, *Lamb's High Feast*, 2; J. Ligon Duncan III, "The Covenant Idea in Melito of Sardis: An Introduction and Survey," *Presbyterion* 28 (2002): 27 n.65. Eusebius states that the beginning of *On the Pascha* was written while Servillius Paulus

On Pascha was lost to the modern world until less than a century ago.[19] In 1932, Frederic Kenyon described a fourth-century codex containing unidentified homiletic material, along with chapters from the *Book of Enoch*.[20] Some leaves of the codex were kept in the Chester Beatty collection of the British Museum, while others resided at the University of Michigan. By 1936, Campbell Bonner solved the mystery by identifying the homiletic material as a work of Melito of Sardis (which he titled *On the Passion*), and he published his findings in 1940.[21] Bonner made his case for the identification and title of the work by comparing the known excerpt in Anastasius Sinaiticus with a parallel passage in the Beatty-Michigan text, and he also collated extant Greek, Coptic, and Syriac fragments.[22] By 1960, Michel Testuz had published a Greek manuscript from the Bodmer collection bearing the title "Melito's *On the Pascha*," which filled in the lacunae of the Beatty-Michigan Codex (including the missing conclusion).[23] The puzzle pieces of the work's accepted title and full Greek text had finally come together.[24] Additional Latin, Coptic, Syriac, and Georgian discoveries soon followed.[25]

The value of the textual identification of Melito's *On Pascha* has been inestimable—a serendipitous treasure of early Christian homiletic material.[26] Writing in 1960, F. L. Cross even called the homily "the most important addition to patristic literature in the present century."[27] Sixteen years later, Richard White declared that *On Pascha* "offers new information about preaching in the second century and markedly alters the picture of that activity."[28] "Further," added White, "it provides important witness concerning hermeneutical, theological and

---

was proconsul of Asia (Eusebius, *Hist. eccl.* 4.26.3), perhaps a reference to Sergius Paulus (see Stewart-Sykes, *Lamb's High Feast*, 155–57).

19. White, "Melito of Sardis—An Ancient Worthy Reappears," 6–18. Fragmentary copies of the homily were identified from Syriac, Greek, and Coptic sources in the late 1800s and early 1900s (see the overview in White, *Melito of Sardis*, 7–8). The Bonner discovery described here proved that all the fragments came from the same work.

20. The codex has now been tagged as fourth-century, although previously thought to have been fifth-century. The manuscript is also the only manuscript witness to the *Apocryphon of Ezekiel* (cf. Clement of Alexandria, *Paedagogus*, I.9.84).

21. Bonner, *Homily on the Passion*. Cf. Testuz, *Papyrus Bodmer XIII*, 17.

22. The particular excerpt found in Anastasius was "God suffered under an Israelitish hand" (cf. Melito, *On Pascha*, 96). In 1855, William Cureton had discovered similar material in an untitled Syriac fragment ascribed to Melito ("God put to death; the king of Israel slain by an Israelitish hand"). See White, *Melito of Sardis*, 7.

23. Testuz, *Papyrus Bodmer XIII*.

24. This is not to deny that lingering doubts may exist among some scholars (see Cohick, *Peri Pascha*).

25. The Latin work is an epitome of the homily. See Henry Chadwick, "A Latin Epitome of Melito's Homily on the Passion," *Journal of Theological Studies* 11 (1960): 76–80.

26. The discovery has allowed historians of early Christianity to balance out the homiletic work of *2 Clement*, another second-century text (Andrew Michael Manis, "Melito of Sardis: Hermeneutic and Context," *Greek Orthodox Theological Review* 32 [1987]: 387; Richard C. White, "Melito of Sardis: Earliest Christian Orator?" *Lexington Theological Quarterly* 2 [1967]: 82, 91). See Wyatt Aaron Graham, "The Passover of the Church: Melito of Sardis on the Church and Israel's Exodus in *Peri Pascha*," *Fides et humilitas* 2 (2015): 5.

27. F. L. Cross, *The Early Christian Fathers* (London: Duckworth, 1960), 104.

28. White, *Melito of Sardis*, 1; White, "Melito of Sardis—An Ancient Worthy Reappears," 16–17.

liturgical concerns in the late second century."[29] Melito's "sermon" or "homily" reflects its liturgical context, the Paschal celebration.[30] It has even been called "the earliest Christian Easter sermon" we have.[31]

THEOLOGY OF PREACHING

The theme of *On Pascha* is the suffering, death, and resurrection of Christ as a deliverance of humanity, with the Passover serving as a prefiguration of his passion.[32] The homily suggests an indebtedness to the Jewish Passover recitation (the "Haggadah"), but with a distinctively Christian character.[33] Some have argued that chapters 46–105 especially reflect a haggadic character.[34] Alistair Stewart-Sykes agrees with this conclusion, noting further that "the first half is fundamentally a diēgēma [narrative], and that the second part is described as a kataskeuē [confirmation or construction]; both are hymnic in tone and form."[35] Although the work probably originated as a homily, it may have become a liturgical act in context.[36] Several scholars have argued that *On Pascha* uses baptismal terminology ("sealed," "illuminated," etc.), implying that the rite of baptism also took place in the originating church service.[37] Nevertheless, the work never uses the

---

29. White, *Melito of Sardis*, 2.

30. Stewart-Sykes argues that the piece is not a "sermon" but "a liturgical text, a speech which accompanies and effects a liturgical event" (Stewart-Sykes, *Melito of Sardis*, 15). Contrast White, *Melito of Sardis*, 11, reasoning that the work can "properly be called a 'sermon.'" Perler discussed the options of "homily" and *praeconium* (Perler, *Méliton de Sardes*, 24–26; cf. Stewart-Sykes, *Lamb's High Feast*, 132). For a complete discussion of the genre of *On Pascha* (including the further alternatives of haggadah, diatribe, epideixis, rhetorical history, allegory, targum, ligurgical hymn, and midrash), see Stewart-Sykes, *Lamb's High Feast*, 55–113. Stewart-Sykes maintains that at least part of *On Pascha* could be classified as hymnic (Stewart-Sykes, *Lamb's High Feast*, 127); see also E. J. Wellesz, "Melito's Homily on the Passion, an Investigation into the Sources of Byzantine Hymnography," *Journal of Theological Studies* 44 (1943): 41–52. In any case, Melito likely influenced the development of early Christian liturgy; see Perler, *Méliton de Sardes*, 26–28.

31. As reflected in the subtitle of Josef Blank, *Meliton von Sardes: Vom Passa, Die älteste christliche Osterpredigt*, Sophia 3 (Frieburg im Breisgau: Lambertus-Verlag, 1963). Stewart-Sykes maintains that at least part of *On Pascha* could be classified as hymnic (Stewart-Sykes, *Lamb's High Feast*, 127); see also Wellesz, "Melito's Homily on the Passion," 41–52.

32. Lynn Cohick, "Melito of Sardis's *Peri Pascha* and Its Intertextuality," in *Intertextuality in the Second Century*, ed. D. Jeffrey Bingham and Clayton N. Jefford, Bible in Ancient Christianity 11 (Leiden: Brill, 2016), 126–49; White, "Melito of Sardis: Earliest Christian Orator?," 88.

33. Hall, *Melito of Sardis*, xxvi–xxvii; Stewart-Sykes, *Lamb's High Feast*, 7.

34. Stuart G. Hall, "Melito in the Light of the Passover Haggadah," *Journal of Theological Studies* 22 (1971): 29–46; cf. Manis, "Melito of Sardis," 391–92; Stewart-Sykes, *Lamb's High Feast*, 113.

35. Stewart-Sykes, *Lamb's High Feast*, 130. For a critique of Stewart-Sykes's interpretation, see Cohick, "Melito of Sardis's *Peri Pascha*," 128.

36. Stewart-Sykes, *Lamb's High Feast*, 136. Stewart-Sykes calls *On Pascha* "the most ancient Christian liturgy known to us in its completeness" (Stewart-Sykes, *Lamb's High Feast*, 206).

37. Josef B. Blank, *Meliton von Sardes: Vom Passa, Die älteste christliche Osterpredigt*, Sophia 3 (Frieburg im Breisgau: Lambertus-Verlag, 1963); Hall, *Melito of Sardis*, 9 n.5; Gabriel Racle, "Perspectives christologiques de l'Homélie Pascale de Méliton de Sardes," *Studia Patristica* 9 (1966): 263–69. Perler maintained that *On Pascha* reflected a Paschal baptism (Perler, *Méliton de Sardes*, 144–45, 172–73, 204–7).

word *baptisma* or its cognates.[38] Raniero Cantalamessa and Gerald Hawthorne have therefore expressed caution or dissent from such baptismal interpretations.[39] In any case, the address may have been initially delivered at a Paschal Vigil, perhaps the night of a Quartodeciman Paschal celebration.[40]

According to Hall, Melito's homily quotes directly from Genesis, Exodus, Deuteronomy, Psalms, Isaiah, and Jeremiah, and clearly alludes to other Hebrew Scripture texts.[41] *On Pascha* also reflects knowledge of Matthew, John, Revelation, and perhaps Luke-Acts and some epistles.[42] Only Old Testament passages are formulaically quoted and referred to as "Scripture." The use of the biblical texts themselves is complicated by the possible use of "derivative" sources in various instances, including catechetical materials, liturgical materials, paraenetic materials, anthologies, catenae, logia, oral traditions, and memory.[43] Because of its specific topic, *On Pascha* is primarily derived from the narrative of the first Passover, situated within Israel's escape from Egypt. The introductory sentence of the extant text affirms, "The Scripture of the exodus of the Hebrews has been read, and the words of the mystery have been declared" (*On Pascha* 1).[44] Therefore, there are multiple echoes and allusions to the book of Exodus (centered in Ex 12:1–20).[45] As Hall notes, *On Pascha* demonstrates "that the reading of Exodus 12 was from an early date part of the Christian Paschal observance."[46] There are also echoes of New Testament materials, and Melito's substance and tenor

---

38. See Gerald F. Hawthorne, "Christian Baptism and the Contribution of Melito of Sardis Reconsidered," in *Studies in New Testament and Early Christian Literature*, ed. David E. Aune (Leiden: Brill, 1972), 243.

39. Raniero Cantalamessa, *L'omelia "In S. Pascha" dello Pseudo-Ippolito di Rome*, Pubblicazioni dell'Università Cattolica del Sacro Cuore, Contributi III, Scienze filologiche e letteratura 16 (Milano: Vita et pensiero, 1967), 282–333; Hawthorne, "Christian Baptism," 241–51.

40. Frankie J. Melton Jr., "Preaching and Melito's Use of Greco-Roman Rhetoric," *Bibliotheca Sacra* 167 (2010): 465. See, however, Cohick, *Peri Pascha*, 30.

41. Cohick, "Melito of Sardis's *Peri Pascha*," 144; Hall, *Melito of Sardis*, xl. According to Hall, Melito seems to have used the Wisdom of Solomon as well.

42. Hall, *Melito of Sardis*, xli. Hall also finds some affinities with the Acts of Peter, the Acts of John, and especially the Gospel of Peter (ibid., xlii). See Bonner, *Homily on the Passion*, 36–41; White, "Melito of Sardis—An Ancient Worthy Reappears," 16.

43. Cohick, *Peri Pascha*, 105–13, 139–46. "The theory that the author of [*Peri Pascha*] used derivative-biblical sources helps develop a picture of early Christian hermeneutics and interpretations of Jesus informed by readings of Jewish Scriptures" (Cohick, *Peri Pascha*, 144).

44. English translations of *On Pascha* throughout come from Stewart-Sykes, *Melito of Sardis*. See Campbell Bonner, "A Supplementary Note on the Opening of Melito's Homily," *Harvard Theological Review* 36 (1943): 317–19; Thomas Forsyth Torrance, "Dramatic Proclamation of the Gospel: Homily on the Passion by Melito of Sardis," *Greek Orthodox Theological Review* 37 (1992): 149; Testuz, *Bodmer Papyri XIII*, 18. Zuntz and Angerstorfer translated the opening sentence as an indication that the Exodus account had been read in the Hebrew language (Zuntz, "On the Opening Sentence," 298–315; Ingeborg Angerstorfer, "Melito und das Judentum," PhD diss., University of Regensburg, 1985, 37–47).

45. Manis, "Melito of Sardis," 390; Cohick, *Peri Pascha*, 92–95.

46. Hall, *Melito of Sardis*, xxvi. Cf. Pseudo-Hippolytus, *In sanctum pascha*. Cohick notes that "Passover celebrations discussed in the Mishnah do not develop from Exod 12" (Cohick, "Meltio of Sardis's *Peri Pascha*," 128).

especially resemble the Johannine tradition.[47] As a homily rooted in the Passover event, *On Pascha* naturally focuses upon redemptive history and the mighty acts of God.[48]

At the heart of Melito's sermon is a christological focus.[49] As Stewart Sykes remarks, "At the center of the Christian faith stands Christ, and Christ is at the center of the faith proclaimed, lived and celebrated by Melito."[50] Christ is the focus of redemption. According to the bishop of Sardis, Jesus Christ was proclaimed by the Hebrew prophets and was prefigured in the events of Hebrew history.[51] While Melito refers to Jesus Christ as *Theos* on five occasions, he predominantly calls him *Kurios*.[52] Bonner characterized Melito's Christology as a "naïve modalism."[53] For instance, Melito uses the title "Father" of Jesus Christ (yet compare Isa. 9:6). However, the label "christocentric monotheism" might serve as a more apropos designation.[54] Melito's multiple doxologies are very christocentric (*On Pascha*, 10, 45, 65, 105). And he espouses the preexistence of Christ and the incarnation through the Virgin Mary (*On Pascha*, 70–71).

Melito's "high Christology" crescendos in the thundering declaration that "God has been murdered" (*On Pascha* 96). Melito is not reflecting systematic thought upon the *communicatio idiomatum* but presenting an exclamation similar to the apostle Paul's, that the "rulers of this age" crucified "the Lord of glory" (1 Cor. 2:8). Melito's Christology is fundamentally founded upon a belief in the deity of Jesus Christ, as well as his historical humanity.[55] This theological foundation is patent to readers of the text.[56] As one comments, "In Melito's theology, everything hinges on the nature of Christ as both God and man."[57] Another states that Melito "holds indeed with sure grasp the central mystery, that God and man are united in Christ who is both God and Man."[58] An anonymous,

---

47. Stewart-Sykes, *Melito of Sardis*, 26.

48. John Hainsworth, "The Force of the Mystery: Anamnesis and Exegesis in Melito's *Peri Pascha*," *St. Vladimir's Theological Quarterly* 46 (2002): 107–46.

49. Perler, *Méliton de Sardes*, 32–42.

50. Stewart-Sykes, *Melito of Sardis*, 28.

51. Manis, "Melito of Sardis," 394–95.

52. Donald F. Winslow, "The Polemical Christology of Melito of Sardis," *Studia Patristica* 17 (1982): 767.

53. Bonner, *Homily on the Passion*, 27–28; White, "Melito of Sardis—An Ancient Worthy Reappears," 15; Winslow, "Polemical Christology of Melito of Sardis," 767.

54. Hall, *Melito of Sardis*, xliii.

55. Of course, the explicit use of "orthodox" in this context would be anachronistic. Cantalamessa characterized Melito's Christology as "anti-gnostic" (Raniero Cantalamessa, "Méliton de Sardes: Une christologie antignostique du II siècle," *Revue des sciences religieuses* 37 [1963]: 1–26). Cf. Cohick, *Peri Pascha*, 80–81. According to Cohick, *On Pascha* carries an "anti-docetic message" (Cohick, "Melito of Sardis's *Peri Pascha*," 134.

56. White, *Melito of Sardis*, 5.

57. Torrance, "Dramatic Proclamation of the Gospel," 155.

58. Stuart G. Hall, "The Christology of Melito: A Misrepresentation Exposed," *Studia Patristica* 13 (1975): 168.

third-century text known as *The Little Labyrinth* encapsulated Melito's works as "proclaiming Christ, God and Man."[59] On the other hand, the christological language and tenor of *On Pascha* is not as refined as the conciliar theology of Late Antiquity.[60] One cannot anachronistically demand postconciliar theological refinement of the bishop of Sardis.[61] Melito spoke of Christ "with an authentically second-century voice."[62] As Hall declares, "We may relieve him of the duty to pioneer the Chalcedonian doctrine in its subtle precision."[63]

Even the eschatology of *On Pascha* is very christocentric, where "Christ is Lord of all history, past, present, and future."[64] Polycrates may reflect Melito's own eschatological views by stating that he lay buried in Sardis, "awaiting the visitation from heaven when he shall rise from the dead."[65] Melito's pneutmatology has been described as "rudimentary."[66] Soteriologically, Melito preached an accomplished redemption, "complete in Christ's death and resurrection, which illumine the mystery, interpret what was parabolic, make plain what was veiled."[67]

Melito's homily speaks of each human as a body and soul "marvelously knit together" (*On Pascha* 55).[68] But the fall of Adam "unraveled" this unity (*On Pascha* 55). The bishop "goes deeply into the fall of Adam" in order to demonstrate the necessity of Christ's redemptive work.[69] "All flesh fell under sin, and every body under death, and every soul was plucked from its dwelling of flesh, and that which was taken from the dust was reduced to dust" (*On Pascha* 55).[70]

A regrettable trait of *On Pascha* is its anti-Jewish tenor.[71] Using a "caustic, satirical style," the homily "bitterly assails" the Jews, charging them with the death of Jesus.[72] Melito's vituperative rhetoric has been characterized as the

---

59. As found in Eusebius, *Hist. eccl.* 5.28.5.

60. White, *Melito of Sardis*, 5.

61. Stewart-Sykes, *Melito of Sardis*, 29.

62. Hall, "Christology of Melito," 168.

63. Ibid.

64. Hall, *Melito of Sardis*, xlv.

65. As found in Eusebius, *Hist. eccl.* 5.24.2–6. A chiliastic group known as the *Melitani* perhaps derived their views from Melito (see Hall, *Melito of Sardis*, xii). Some claimed that the Melitonians followed Melito in teaching that the body and not the soul was made in the *imago Dei* (White, *Melito of Sardis*, 5).

66. Bonner, *Homily on the Passion*, 28.

67. White, "Melito of Sardis—An Ancient Worthy Reappears," 14.

68. Cf. *On Pascha* 47. Origen, followed by Gennadius, claimed that Melito taught a form of divine corporealism. But the substance and foundation of the claim are debated (see Hall, *Melito of Sardis*, xii).

69. Cornelius van der Waal, *Het Pascha van onze Verlossing* (Johannesburg: De Jong, 1979), 236.

70. Stewart-Sykes, *Melito of Sardis*, 52.

71. See K. W. Noakes, "Melito of Sardis and the Jews," *Studia Patristica* 13 (1975): 244–49; Cohick, "Melito of Sardis's *Peri Pascha*," 143. For varying assessments, see Eric Werner, "Melito of Sardis," *Hebrew Union College Annual* 37 (1966): 191–210; Hall, "Melito in the Light of the Passover Haggadah"; S. G. Wilson, "Melito and Israel," in *Separation and Polemic*, vol. 2 of *Anti-Judaism in Early Christianity*, ed. S. G. Wilson (Waterloo, ON: Wilfrid Laurier University Press, 1986), 81–102.

72. Wilken, "Melito, the Jewish Community at Sardis," 56–57. Cf. Winslow, "Polemical Christology

original charge of "deicide" (murder of God), an accusation frequently and at times violently leveled against Jews through the centuries.[73] While reading his invective, however, one should remember Melito's likely Jewish background as well as the religious context (the Jewish-Christian tensions in Sardis).[74] Melito's rancor could be attributed to a social/political motive, a religious/theological motive, or a self-definitional motive.[75]

Jewish Christian tensions probably fell along a spectrum of approaches, so that beyond a competition with or *against* "Judaism" there were probably struggles *within* the Christian community concerning self-identity.[76] Interestingly, the discourse never uses the term "Jews" but only "Israel" and "the people."[77] This usage may draw attention to Jews of biblical times, and away from Melito's contemporary Jews.[78] Also, one recalls the Quartodeciman nature of Melito's ministry, a movement condemned by other early Christians as being "too Jewish."[79] Perhaps Melito felt compelled to distance himself from the Jewish community precisely because of their similar practices.[80] Thus, the interpreter is faced with the irony of a "very Jewish" homily (and homilist), yet one "anti-Jewish" in tenor. "Moreover," reminds Judith Lieu, "some allowance must be made for Melito's rhetorical style, which to the modern reader often sounds overblown and extravagant."[81]

METHODOLOGY FOR PREACHING

The doxology in chapter 45 straightforwardly divides Melito's *On Pascha* in half.[82] The shift from the Passover account to Christ's passion in chapter 45 is the homily's climax.[83] Hall structurally outlines the homily as follows:

of Melito of Sardis," 772.

73. White, *Melito of Sardis*, 15. Some have compared Melito with the *improperia*, the anti-Jewish reproaches in the Eastern and Western Good Friday liturgies (Werner, "Melito of Sardes," 201, 210).

74. See van der Waal, *Het Pascha van onze Verlossing*, 236–37; Wilken, "Melito, the Jewish Community at Sardis," 53–69; Noakes, "Melito of Sardis," 245–46. Theoretically, a Jewish threat may have been "perceived" without presenting a "real" threat (Cohick, *Peri Pascha*, 72). Cohick reasons, "Judaism was allegedly a threat for several possible reasons: (1) it was a force itself, (2) it was too similar to the homily's Quartodeciman beliefs, (3) our homilist was Jewish, or (4) some in the congregation were Jewish" (Cohick, *Peri Pascha*, 76).

75. These three categorizations are taken from Cohick, *Peri Pascha*, 64.

76. Cohick, *Peri Pascha*, 2, 7, 152. Some have posited "Judaizing" disputes. See Zuntz, "On the Opening Sentence," 313; Manis "Melito of Sardis," 400–401.

77. Noakes, "Melito of Sardis," 248; Lieu, "Melito of Sardis," 45; Cohick, *Peri Pascha*, 61, 149, 153; Lynn Cohick, "Melito of Sardis's *Peri Pascha* and Its 'Israel,'" *Harvard Theological Review* 91 (1998): 351–72.

78. Cohick, *Peri Pascha*, 87.

79. Ibid., 74.

80. Stewart-Sykes, *Melito of Sardis*, 27. He adds, "On the Jewish side, moreover, there appears to have been some attempt to put a distance between themselves and Quartodeciman Christians."

81. Lieu, "Melito of Sardis," 45.

82. According to Stewart-Sykes, each half can be further subdivided by the other doxologies in chapters 10 and 65 (Stewart-Sykes, *Lamb's High Feast*, 124).

83. Cohick, "Melito of Sardis's *Peri Pascha*," 129.

I. Book I: The Paschal narrative and its interpretation
   A. Prologue: The mystery of the Pascha, 1–10
   B. The Paschal events anticipate the gospel, 11–45
II. Book II: The meaning of the Pascha
   A. What constitutes the Pascha? 46–65
   B. The Lord's coming and saving work, 66–105[84]

In all likelihood, Melito's homily was originally composed in Greek.[85] The style of *On Pascha* reflects a bold vitality, both in form and effect.[86] The style is both lyrical and poetical, and at times even extravagant.[87] The marvels of redemption, the sorrows of the cross, and the triumph of the resurrection come to life in the discourse. Melito employed highly polished rhetoric in *On Pascha*.[88] In fact, Tertullian referenced Melito's *elegans et declamatorium ingenium* ("sophisticated and oratorical ingenuity").[89] Albert Wifstrand reasoned that "Melito forms his sentences in a very close accordance with a certain Greek rhetorical style of his age."[90] His oratory has been compared with "the Asianic school" and the "Second Sophistic" in particular, a rhetorical movement that flourished in second-century Asia Minor.[91] Lynn Cohick maintains that Melito represented a "developing homiletic tradition."[92] In White's assessment, the homily is characterized by an eloquence designed "to persuade, to move, to actuate (not simply to inform) the listener."[93]

Scholars have identified sundry rhetorical devices within the sermon. Bonner discussed the homily's employment of anaphora, antitheses, exclamations,

---

84. Hall's full outline is found in Hall, *Melito of Sardis*, xxii–xxiii.

85. Cf. Paul E. Kahle, "Was Melito's Homily on the Passion Originally Written in Syriac?" *Journal of Theological Studies* 44 (1943): 52–56. Kahle's theory of a Syriac original has been near universally abandoned (J. Smit Sibinga, "Melito of Sardis: The Artist and His Text," *Vigiliae Christianae* 24 [1970]: 96 n.37). See, however, Eric Werner, "Melito of Sardes, the First Poet of Deicide," *Hebrew Union College Annual* 37 [1966]: 200, 202). Cf. also Campbell Bonner, "The Text of Melito's Homily," *Vigiliae Christianae* 3 (1949): 183.

86. White, *Melito of Sardis*, 2. Cf. Testuz, *Bodmer Papyrus XIII*, 20.

87. Thomas K. Carroll, *Preaching the Word*, Message of the Fathers of the Church 11 (Wilmington: Michael Glazier, 1984), 36–37.

88. Hillyer H. Straton, "Melito of Sardis, Preacher Extraordinary," *Anglican Theological Review* 29 (1947): 169.

89. Jerome, *De viris illustribus*, 24. Tertullian's *Apology* was probably influenced by his reading of Melito (White, "Melito of Sardis: Earliest Christian Orator?," 91).

90. Albert Wifstrand, "The Homily of Melito on the Passion," *Vigiliae Christianae* 2 (1948): 213.

91. Carroll, *Preaching the Word*, 34–37; Sibinga, "Melito of Sardis," 85; Wifstrand, "Homily of Melito," 201–23; Robert M. Grant, "Melito of Sardis on Baptism," *Vigiliae Christianae* 4 (1950): 34; Thomas Halton, "Stylistic Device in Melito, *Peri Pascha*," in *Kyriakon*, vol. 1, ed. by Patrick Granfield and Josef A. Jungmann (Münster: Aschendorff, 1970), 249–55; Laurence Broadhurst, "Melito of Sardis, the Second Sophistic, and 'Israel,'" in *Rhetoric and Reality in Early Christianities*, ed. Willi Braun (Waterloo, ON: Wilfrid Laurier University Press, 2005), 57–59. Cf. White, *Melito of Sardis*, 12; Hall, *Melito of Sardis*, xix; Cohick, "Melito of Sardis's *Peri Pascha*," 136–37.

92. Cohick, *Peri Pascha*, 47.

93. White, *Melito of Sardis*, 2.

first-person declarations, oxymorons, parallelisms, questions, and repetition.[94] White and Wifstrand added the use of alliteration, cadence, rhyme, and isocolon (sentences composed of parts equivalent in length, rhyme, and structure).[95] Stewart-Sykes has discussed the use of homoiarcton (adjacent lines beginning in the same way), homoeoteleuton (adjacent lines ending in the same way), paronomasia (the same or similar word used with different meanings for rhetorical effect), and asyndeton (a series of related clauses listed together with conjunctions omitted).[96] Frankie Melton has examined Melito's use of such classical rhetorical features as antithesis, ecphrasis, erotesis, apostrophe, antistrophe, parallelism, prosopopoeia, pusma, isocolon, anaphora, and aitiologia.[97] Such rhetorical phenomena reflect an orator who gave attention to detail.[98]

Beyond these specific oratorical devices, the structural outline of *On Pascha* has also been considered rhetorically. Stewart-Sykes provides the following rhetorical analysis:

> *Propositio*: The scripture has been read, and in the paschal celebration we can come to realize how it is fulfilled. *Narratio*: The firstborn of the Egyptians died horribly whilst Israel was liberated. The liberation of Israel is the experience of the Christian through the commemoration of the death of Christ. *Probatio*: The whole was the result of Adam's disgrace, as we remember the history of humankind in need of salvation. *Peroratio*: Yet the messiah came, and comes to us. In the murder of Christ by Israel, repeating their slaughter of the lamb, is the triumph of God, which in its proclamation is a present reality for us as we celebrate.[99]

Melito's most fundamental rhetorical stratagem is the use of typology.[100] According to Melito, the Old Testament contained wondrous wisdom for the Christian believer, and the typological method is his means "by which the riddle is understood."[101] Melito's typology, however, was not one that discarded

---

94. Bonner, *Homily on the Passion*, 20–27. Cf. Hall, *Melito of Sardis*, xxiii.

95. White, *Melito of Sardis*, 3; Wifstrand, "Homily of Melito," 14. Werner refers to Melito's "isosyllabisms" (Werner, "Melito of Sardis, the First Poet of Deicide," 202, 204).

96. Stewart-Sykes, *Melito of Sardis*, 14–17.

97. Melton, "Preaching and Melito's Use of Greco-Roman Rhetoric," 475–80. Melton adds, "Other examples of Melito's use of rhetoric, some only recognizable in Greek, are homoeoteleuton, polysyndeton, alliteration, syllabic parallelism, metaphor, climax, chiasmus, synonymia, and paronomasia" (480).

98. Sibinga, "Melito of Sardis," 87. Sibinga's article arithmetically analyzes Melito's rhetorical and literary techniques.

99. Stewart-Sykes, *Melito of Sardis*, 21–22.

100. Perler, *Méliton de Sardes*, 29–32; Manis, "Melito of Sardis," 394–98; Cohick, "Melito of Sardis's *Peri Pascha*," 132–34.

101. Stewart-Sykes, *Melito of Sardis*, 33.

historical events, but one that unfolded their true meaning.[102] The events of the Old Testament remained historically significant, even as the redemptive history of Exodus prefigured full redemption in Christ in the gospel. Melito's typology is shaped by the term *mystery*, which appears seventeen times (all within chapters 1–65).[103] In Henry Knapp's examination of Melito's methodology, the typological stratagem of *On Pascha* manifests a threefold emphasis: "(1) the inherent importance of the type; (2) the escalation of the reality over the type, and (3) the eventual displacement of the type by the foreshadowed reality."[104]

Melito directly labels the Exodus events as *typoi* ("types") which have been fulfilled in the work of Jesus. According to White, "the ancient events are linked powerfully, not just symbolically, to the work that Christ will later fully actualize."[105] The *parabolai* (comparisons) arising from the Hebrew Scriptures point to the words and deeds of Christ in the gospel.[106] The Old Testament events were *prokentēma* ("advance sketches") foreshadowing the full truths of Christ.[107] Therefore, notes Hall, "Israel gives way to the Church, the law to the Gospel, the earthly Jerusalem to the heavenly, the paschal lamb to Christ."[108] Old Testament figures exhibited the coming Christ, who was "murdered in Abel, tied up in Isaac, exiled in Jacob" (*On Pascha* 69).[109] In a sense, "everything in the Old Testament is embraced in Jesus Christ."[110] Most fundamental, however, Jesus is the sacrificed Lamb, prefigured by the unblemished Passover Lamb (cf. 1 Cor 5:6–8; 1 Pet 1:19; Isa 53:7), and his blood upon the cross was prefigured by the blood upon the doorposts (*On Pascha* 14–15, 31–344).[111] For Melito, the Christ event is the *alēthinos* ("true") reality foreshadowed by the "types."

Beyond the use of typology, a second stratagem that weaves its way throughout the homily is the use of antithetical language. Melito repeatedly contrasts "the

---

102. Manis, "Melito of Sardis," 396.

103. Cohick, "Melito of Sardis's *Peri Pascha*," 133–34; Dragoş-Andrei Giulea, "Seeing Christ through Scriptures as the Paschal Celebration: Exegesis as Mystery Performance in the Paschal Writings of Melito, Pseudo-Hippolytus, and Origen," *Orientalia Christiana Periodica* 74 (2008): 27–47.

104. Henry M. Knapp, "Melito's Use of Scripture in *Peri Pascha*," *Vigiliae Christianae* 54 (2000): 368.

105. White, *Melito of Sardis*, 14. White actually has "ancients events [sic]." For a unique take on the symbolism, see Jean Pierre Laurant, *La clef du symbolisme de Méliton de Sardes* (Paris: Éditions de la Maisnie, 1979).

106. Cohick, "Melito of Sardis's *Peri Pascha*," 131.

107. White, *Melito of Sardis*, 13; van der Waal, *Het Pascha van onze Verlossing*, 236. See also John 1:17. Cf. Paul Corby Finney, "Prokentēma: An Architectural Model in Melito?," in Ἀναθήματα ἑορτικά, ed. Thomas F. Mathews, Joseph D. Alchermes, Helen C. Evans, and Thelma K. Thomas (Mainz: Philipp von Zabern, 2009), 158–59; Cohick, "Melito of Sardis's *Peri Pascha*," 127.

108. Hall, *Melito of Sardis*, xl. Cf. Cohick, *Peri Pascha*, 151.

109. Cf. *On Pascha* 59.

110. Hall, *Melito of Sardis*, xli. Melito clearly was no Marcionite, considering his continuity between the works of God in the Old Testament with the redemptive works of the gospel (ibid.). See also White, *Melito of Sardis*, 5; Cohick, *Peri Pascha*, 81–85.

111. White, *Melito of Sardis*, 14–15. Cf. Irenaeus, *Adv. haer.* IV.20.1.

old and new, temporal and eternal, terrestrial and celestial, mortal and immortal."[112] He also highlights prosopopeial language, as when he declares, "'It is I,' says the Christ. 'So come all families of people, adulterated with sin, and receive forgiveness of sins. For I am your freedom. I am the Passover of salvation, I am the lamb slaughtered for you, I am your ransom, I am your life, I am your light, I am your salvation, I am your resurrection, I am your King'" (*On Pascha* 102–103).[113]

As Frankie Melton explains, "Melito did not merely interpret the scriptural text. He also gave extensive consideration to his words, the construction of his sentences, the use of word pictures, and the use of verbal ornamentation in general." Melton adds, "He wanted his peroration to be beautiful and pleasing to the ear. He did not want to merely dump information on his audience; he also sought to arrest their attention and interest and thereby to encourage them to appreciate and apply the truth."[114] "It is a complex work," reasons Stewart-Sykes, "containing in itself a number of forms, and a number of functions, as well as simultaneously being a product of Hebrew tradition and Hellenistic culture."[115]

CONTRIBUTIONS TO PREACHING

While Melito was influenced by Justin Martyr (and perhaps Athenagoras), he made singular contributions in the history of Christian preaching.[116] Melito's sermon has been called "the earliest known Christian use of rhetoric in preaching."[117] The discovery of *On Pascha* refuted the theory that Christian preaching did not become elaborately rhetorical until the third century, with the likes of Hippolytus and Origen.[118] Some have claimed that Melito introduced flowery and extravagant oratory into early Christian preaching.[119] Bonner opined, "It is to be feared that Melito is partly responsible for the impassioned, decorated, wearisomely repetitious style that is characteristic of church oratory in the Byzantine age."[120]

One wonders what the apostle Paul would have made of Melito's eloquent oratory, based on the discussion and assessment of oratorical rhetoric in 1 Cor

---

112. White, *Melito of Sardis*, 14.

113. Prosopopoeia is a figure of speech in which an absent or imaginary person is presented as speaking and/or acting. Stewart-Sykes suggests that the use of prosopopoeia is actually prophetic, in the case of Melito (Stewart-Sykes, *Lamb's High Feast*, 13–14, 201–02).

114. Melton, "Preaching and Melito's Use of Greco-Roman Rhetoric," 480.

115. Stewart-Sykes, *Lamb's High Feast*, 206.

116. See Hall, *Melito of Sardis*, xxviii.

117. White, "Melito of Sardis: Earliest Christian Orator?," 82.

118. Bonner, *Homily on the Passion*, 57; White, *Melito of Sardis*, 12–13. Straton maintains that both Hippolytus and Origen were influenced by Melito (Straton, "Melito of Sardis, Preacher Extraordinary," 170).

119. See Carroll, *Preaching the Word*, 35; Hall, *Melito of Sardis*, xxiii-xxiv.

120. Bonner, *Homily on the Passion*, 27.

1–2.[121] Nevertheless, we may infer that Melito did not believe his homiletical power resided in rhetorical prowess. His focus was always the primacy of the Christian message, so that "rhetoric is at its service and is never an end in itself."[122] In fact, other patristic authors mention Melito's prophetic reputation. Jerome (borrowing from Tertullian) refers to Melito's "fine oratorical genius," but quickly adds that he was "reputed by many of us to be a prophet."[123]

From *On Pascha* we learn the possibility and power of combining refined rhetoric and vivid imagery with the narratives of Scripture. Melito exemplifies a skillful mastery of elegant phrasing and polished cadence. He deftly weaves the use of antithesis, paradox, alliteration, first-person characterization, and emotive language into his typological sermon. Melito also illustrates the potency of christocentric preaching, including the stratagem of the preacher speaking on behalf of Christ in the first person through direct appeal, beckoning the hearer to respond.

CONCLUSION

Melito's homily has been praised for a character "as balanced and ingenious as any work of great art."[124] Hillyer Straton claimed if Melito's other works "maintained the high standard of this message, he surely would be classified among the outstanding Christian preachers of all time."[125] We may perhaps lament the fact that we do not possess more homiletic materials from this gifted minister of the Word. But we can also rejoice in his exemplary sermon that has become available. Through the modern discovery of *On Pascha*, his homiletical beacon still shines.

Sermon Excerpt

On the Pascha 100–104[126]

The Lord clothed himself with humanity,
and with the suffering on behalf of the suffering one,
and bound on behalf of the one constrained,
and judged on behalf of the one convicted,

---

121. Cf. White, *Melito of Sardis*, 11.
122. Carroll, *Preaching the Word*, 37.
123. Jerome, *De viris illustribus* 24.
124. Sibinga, "Melito of Sardis," 104.
125. Straton, "Melito of Sardis, Preacher Extraordinary," 168.
126. Excerpt from Stewart-Sykes, *Melito of Sardis*, 65–66. I have capitalized the word *father* throughout this excerpt.

and buried on behalf of the one entombed,
rose from the dead and cried out aloud:
"Who takes issue with me? Let him stand before me.
I set free the condemned.
I gave life to the dead.
I raise up the entombed.
Who will contradict me?"
"It is I", says the Christ,
"I am he who destroys death,
and triumphs over the enemy,
and crushes Hades,
and binds the strong man,
and bears humanity off to the heavenly heights."
"It is I," says the Christ.
"So come all families of people,
adulterated with sin,
and receive forgiveness of sins.
For I am your freedom.
I am the Passover of salvation,
I am the lamb slaughtered for you,
I am your ransom,
I am your life,
I am your light,
I am your salvation,
I am your resurrection,
I am your King.
I shall raise you up by my right hand,
I will lead you to the heights of heaven,
there shall I show you the everlasting Father."
He it is who made the heaven and the earth,
and formed humanity in the beginning,
who was proclaimed through the law and the prophets,
who took flesh from a virgin,
who was hung on a tree,
who was buried in earth,
who was raised from the dead,
and ascended to the heights of heaven,

who sits at the right hand of the Father,
who has the power to save all things,
through whom the Father acted from the beginning and for ever. ♦

BIBLIOGRAPHY

Angerstorfer, Ingeborg. "Melito und das Judentum." PhD diss., University of Regensburg, 1985.

Bauckham, Richard. "Papias and Polycrates on the Origin of the Fourth Gospel." *Journal of Theological Studies* 44 (1993): 24–69.

Blank, Josef. *Meliton von Sardes: Vom Passa, Die älteste christliche Osterpredigt.* Sophia 3. Frieburg im Breisgau: Lambertus-Verlag, 1963.

Bonner, Campbell. *The Homily on the Passion by Melito Bishop of Sardis, with Some Fragments of the Apocryphal Ezekiel.* Philadelphia: University of Pennsylvania Press, 1940.

_____. "A Supplementary Note on the Opening of Melito's Homily." *Harvard Theological Review* 36 (1943): 317–19.

_____. "The Text of Melito's Homily." *Vigiliae Christianae* 3 (1949): 184–85.

Broadhurst, Laurence. "Melito of Sardis, the Second Sophistic, and 'Israel.'" Pages 57–59 in *Rhetoric and Reality in Early Christianities.* Edited by Willi Braun. Waterloo, Ontario: Wilfrid Laurier University Press, 2005.

Cantalamessa, Raniero. "Méliton de Sardes: Une christologie antignostique du II siècle." *Revue des sciences religieuses* 37 (1963): 1–26.

_____. *L'omelia "In S. Pascha" dello Pseudo-Ippolito di Rome.* Publicazioni dell'Università Cattolica del Sacro Cuore, Contributi III, Scienze filologiche e letteratura 16. Milano: Vita et pensiero, 1967.

Carroll, Thomas K. *Preaching the Word.* Message of the Fathers of the Church 11. Wilmington: Michael Glazier, 1984.

Chadwick, Henry. "A Latin Epitome of Melito's Homily on the Passion." *Journal of Theological Studies* 11 (1960): 76–80.

Cohick, Lynn. "Melito of Sardis's *Peri Pascha* and Its Intertextuality." Pages 126–49 in *Intertextuality in the Second Century.* Edited by D. Jeffrey Bingham and Clayton N. Jefford. Bible in Ancient Christianity 11. Leiden: Brill, 2016.

_____. "Melito of Sardis's *Peri Pascha* and Its 'Israel.'" *Harvard Theological Review* 91 (1998): 351–72.

_____. *The Peri Pascha Attributed to Melito of Sardis: Setting, Purpose, and Sources.* Brown Judaic Studies 327. Providence: Brown Judaic Studies, 2000.

Cross, F. L. *The Early Christian Fathers.* London: Duckworth, 1960.

Duncan, J. Ligon, III. "The Covenant Idea in Melito of Sardis: An Introduction and Survey." *Presbyterion* 28 (2002): 12–33.

Eusebius. *Ecclesiastical History.* Trans. by Kirsopp Lake. 2 vols. Loeb Classical Library. Cambridge: Harvard University Press, 1926.

Finney, Paul Corby. "Prokentēma: An Architectural Model in Melito?" Pages 158–59 in Ἀναθήματα ἑορτικά. Edited by Thomas F. Mathews, Joseph D. Alchermes, Helen C. Evans, and Thelma K. Thomas. Mainz: Philipp von Zabern, 2009.

Giulea, Dragoş-Andrei. "Seeing Christ through Scriptures as the Paschal Celebration: Exegesis as Mystery Performance in the Paschal Writings of Melito, Pseudo-Hippolytus, and Origen." *Orientalia Christiana Periodica* 74 (2008): 27–47.

Graham, Wyatt Aaron. "The Passover of the Church: Melito of Sardis on the Church and Israel's Exodus in *Peri Pascha.*" *Fides et humilitas* 2 (2015): 4–24.

Grant, Robert M. "Melito of Sardis on Baptism." *Vigiliae Christianae* 4 (1950): 33–36.

Hainsworth, John. "The Force of the Mystery: Anamnesis and Exegesis in Melito's *Peri Pascha.*" *St. Vladimir's Theological Quarterly* 46 (2002): 107–46.

Hall, Stuart George. "The Christology of Melito: A Misrepresentation Exposed." *Studia Patristica* 13 (1975): 154–68.

_____. "Melito in the Light of the Passover Haggadah." *Journal of Theological Studies* 22 (1971): 29–46.

_____. *Melito of Sardis: On Pascha and Fragments.* Oxford: Clarendon, 1979.

Halton, Thomas. "Stylistic Device in Melito, *Peri Pascha*." Pages 249–55 in *Kyriakon*. Vol. 1. Edited by Patrick Granfield and Josef A. Jungmann. Münster: Aschendorff, 1970.

Hawthorne, Gerald F. "Christian Baptism and the Contribution of Melito of Sardis Reconsidered." Pages 241–51 in *Studies in New Testament and Early Christian Literature*. Edited by David E. Aune. Leiden: Brill, 1972.

———. "Melito of Sardis: His Rhetoric and Theology." PhD diss., University of Chicago, 1969.

Kahle, Paul E. "Was Melito's Homily on the Passion Originally Written in Syriac?" *Journal of Theological Studies* 44 (1943): 52–56.

Knapp, Henry M. "Melito's Use of Scripture in *Peri Pascha*: Second-Century Typology." *Vigiliae Christianae* 54 (2000): 343–74.

Kraabel, A. T. "Melito the Bishop and the Synagogue at Sardis: Text and Context." Pages 77–85 in *Studies Presented to George M. A. Hanfmann*. Edited by David Gordon Mitten, John Griffiths Pedley, and Jane Ayer Scott. Cambridge: Fogg Art Museum, 1971.

Laurant, Jean Pierre. *La clef du symbolisme de Méliton de Sardes*. Paris: Éditions de la Maisnie, 1979.

Lieu, Judith. "Melito of Sardis." *Expository Times* 110 (1998): 43–46.

Lohse, Bernhard. *Die Passa-Homilie des Bischofs Meliton von Sardes*. Textus Minores 24. Leiden: Brill, 1958.

Manis, Andrew Michael. "Melito of Sardis: Hermeneutic and Context." *Greek Orthodox Theological Review* 32 (1987): 387–401.

Melton, Frankie J., Jr. "Preaching and Melito's Use of Greco-Roman Rhetoric." *Bibliotheca Sacra* 167 (2010): 460–80.

Nautin, Pierre. *Le dossier d'Hippolyte et de Méliton dans les florilèges dogmatiques et chez les historiens modernes*. Patristica 1. Paris: Éditions du Cerf, 1953.

———. *Lettres et écrivains chrétiens des IIe et IIIe siècles*. Paris: Éditions du Cerf, 1961.

Noakes, K. W. "Melito of Sardis and the Jews." *Studia Patristica* 13 (1975): 244–49.

Perler, Othmar. *Méliton de Sardes: Sur la Pâque et fragments: Introduction, texte critique, traduction et notes*. Paris: Éditions du Cerf, 2008.

Pseutonkas, Vasileios S. Μελίτωνος Σάρδεων "Τα περί του Πάσχα δύο." Analekta Blatadōn 8. Thessalonica: Patriarchikon Hidryma Paterikōn Meletōn, 1971.

Racle, Gabriel. "Perspectives christologiques de l'Homélie Pascale de Méliton de Sardes." *Studia Patristica* 9 (1966): 263–69.

Sibinga, J. Smit. "Melito of Sardis: The Artist and His Text." *Vigiliae Christianae* 24 (1970): 81–104.

Stewart-Sykes, Alistair. *The Lamb's High Feast: Melito's Peri Pascha and the Quartodeciman Paschal Liturgy at Sardis*. Supplements to Vigiliae Christianae 42. Leiden: Brill, 1998.

———. *Melito of Sardis: On Pascha, with the Fragments of Melito and Other Material Related to the Quartodecimans*. Crestwood, NY: St. Vladimir's Seminary Press, 2001.

Straton, Hillyer H. "Melito of Sardis, Preacher Extraordinary." *Anglican Theological Review* 29 (1947): 167–70.

Testuz, Michel. *Papyrus Bodmer XIII: Méliton de Sardes, Homélie sur la Pâque, Manuscrit du IIIe siècle*. Geneva: Bibliotheca Bodmeriana, 1960.

Torrance, Thomas Forsyth. "Dramatic Proclamation of the Gospel: Homily on the Passion by Melito of Sardis." *Greek Orthodox Theological Review* 37 (1992): 147–63.

Van der Waal, Cornelius. *Het Pascha van onze Verlossing*. Johannesburg: De Jong, 1979.

Wellesz, E. J. "Melito's Homily on the Passion: An Investigation into the Sources of Byzantine Hymnography." *Journal of Theological Studies* 44 (1943): 41–52.

Werner, Eric. "Melito of Sardes, the First Poet of Deicide." *Hebrew Union College Annual* 37 (1966): 191–210.

White, Richard C. "Melito of Sardis—An Ancient Worthy Reappears." *Lexington Theological Quarterly* 14 (1979): 6–18.

———. "Melito of Sardis: Earliest Christian Orator?" *Lexington Theological Quarterly* 2 (1967): 82–91.

———. *Melito of Sardis, Sermon "On the Passover": A New English Translation with Introduction and Commentary*. Lexington Theological Seminary Library Occasional Studies. Lexington: Lexington Theological Seminary Library, 1976.

Wifstrand, Albert. "The Homily of Melito on the Passion." *Vigiliae Christianae* 2 (1948): 201–23.

Wilken, Robert L. "Melito, the Jewish Community at Sardis, and the Sacrifice of Isaac." *Theological Studies* 37 (1976): 53–69.

Wilson, S. G. "Melito and Israel." Pages 81–102 in *Separation and Polemic*. Vol. 2 of *Anti-Judaism in Early Christianity*. Edited by S. G. Wilson. Waterloo, Ontario: Wilfrid Laurier University Press, 1986.

Winslow, Donald F. "The Polemical Christology of Melito of Sardis." *Studia Patristica* 17 (1982): 765–76.

Zuntz, Günther. "On the Opening Sentence of Melito's Paschal Homily." *Harvard Theological Review* 36 (1943): 299–315.

Origen of Alexandria

Preaching as Spiritual Edification

STEPHEN O. PRESLEY

A look at Origen (ca. 185–254) offers the first glimpse of the preacher at work in the early church. According to Origen, the purpose of preaching was spiritual edification. He saw the church as a community of the faithful, at various stages of growth in sanctification, and the preaching of the Word was an essential means to guide their spiritual lives. This focus on spiritual transformation often led Origen to search the details of the text and make observations that might seem unconvincing to the modern mind. But his example of dedication to the study and preaching of the Scriptures has continued to influence the church throughout Christian history.

HISTORICAL BACKGROUND

In the history of preaching, Origen stands out as one of the church's first great Bible interpreters and preachers.[1] There is a scattering of sermons and homilies that predate Origen, but his works offer the first comprehensive picture of a preacher applying his task in the service of the church.[2] There is little doubt, however, that Origen was a controversial figure. Ultimately, he was condemned as a heretic at the Council of Constantinople in AD 553 for some of his more speculative views. But in his day, Origen drew creatively from Neoplatonic thought and regularly enjoyed engaging the intellectual elites with the truth of Scripture. His contribution to the church and historical theology has been hotly debated throughout the Christian tradition.

Origen did not set out to be a preacher, nor did he make preaching his life goal. In fact, he did not begin preaching until late in his career. But he took the task and calling seriously. After all, he considered the study of the Scriptures

---

1. Hugh T. Kerr, *Preaching in the Early Church* (New York: Revell, 1942), 110.
2. Hughes Oliphant Old, *The Reading and Preaching of the Scriptures in the Worship of the Christian Church: Volume 1, The Biblical Period* (Grand Rapids: Eerdmans, 1998), 306.

the highest of all pursuits.[3] For Origen, the main purpose of the sermon was to instruct, convict, and prepare God's people for sanctification. Origen believed that preaching accomplished very little if it did not edify the hearers. He believed the preacher should explain the Scripture and equip the faithful in their daily struggle with sin. This intention led Origen to search the details of the text and make spiritual and allegorical observations that are often unconvincing. Nevertheless, Origen remains the greatest preacher of the third century, and his sermons are the best collection of homilies from the first three centuries of the church.

Origen was born around AD 185 in Alexandria, Egypt, as the eldest of seven children.[4] He was raised in a Christian family with devout parents and he received his training in Greek thought and the Scriptures from his father, Leonides. His father, a man of sincere faith, was martyred in AD 202 during the persecution of Christians at the hands of Septimus Severus. The memory of his father's sacrifice continued to inspire Origen throughout his life. Even in his later years, it was not uncommon for him to mention his father in discussions on martyrdom.[5] Origen was most at home in Alexandria, a melting pot of Hellenistic culture and philosophy, as well as one of the most important cultural centers of the Roman Empire. From Origen's earliest days it was evident he had an aptitude for learning and teaching. To support his family, Origen established an academy dedicated to training Christian philosophers. He began writing and teaching and gained notoriety for the publication of several theological treatises and biblical commentaries.

While Origen's life and work were centered in Alexandria, he often utilized the bustling seaport to visit churches in Rome, Antioch, Caesarea, and Athens. On one visit to Caesarea in AD 215, Theoctistus, the bishop of Caesarea, requested that the renowned Bible scholar deliver a sermon to his church. Origen's sermon caused a stir, especially with Demetrius, his bishop back home in Alexandria. Demetrius denounced this decision to have Origen deliver a homily and argued that the duties of preaching should be reserved for ordained clergy.[6] Origen, though brilliant, was only a layman. In a move to circumvent Demetrius's charges, Origen consented to ordination in Palestine, which only frustrated

---

3. Origen famously exhorts his young catechumen Gregory to study the Scriptures diligently, saying, "Do you then, my son, diligently apply yourself to the reading of the sacred Scriptures? Apply yourself, I say. For we who read the things of God need much application, lest we should say or think anything too rashly about them." Origen, "A Letter of Origen to Gregory," in *Ante-Nicene Fathers*, Volume 4, ed. Alexander Roberts and James Donaldson (Peabody, MA: Hendrickson, 2004), 394.

4. For a summary of Origen's life, see *Eusebius' Ecclesiastical History*, trans. C. F. Cruse (Peabody, MA: Hendrickson, 1998), 6.1–36. Hereafter *Hist. eccl.*

5. *Hom. Ezech.*, 4.8, *Hom. Judic.* 7.12, and *Hom. Num.* 10.2.1.

6. For the letter from Theoctistus and Alexander to Demetrius defending their decision see: *Eccl. Hist.* 6.19.17–18.

Demetrius more. After this incident, Origen realized his gifts would be of better use elsewhere, so he moved from Alexandria to Caesarea around AD 232 when he was about forty-seven years old.

During his initial years in Caesarea, Origen continued several writing projects he had begun in Alexandria.[7] These years were also punctuated by the persecution of Maximinius (AD 235–38), which certainly challenged the resolve of his congregation. After the persecution subsided sometime around AD 239, Theoctistus turned over the preaching duties to Origen and he preached more or less daily from around AD 239–44. There is little doubt that the recent persecutions from Maximinus loomed large in the collective memory of the congregation. This is evidenced in the emphasis on sanctification in Origen's preaching and the way he prepared the congregation to suffer for the gospel.

In general, however, Origen set his aim at two groups that regularly challenged his congregation in the broader culture: Jews and Gnostics. Caesarea boasted a significant Jewish population and his sermons suggest regular interactions with Jews and their reading of Scripture.[8] He often accused the Jews of adhering only to the literal sense of the Scriptures and not recognizing the spiritual significance. Heine reasons that this is why Origen's sermons show a greater dependence on Paul's writings, especially his discussions of the relationship between Jews and gentiles.[9] There are other heretical groups that also garner Origen's attention in his sermons, especially Valentinus, Basilides, and Marcion.[10] For example, in his first *Homily on Luke*, Origen discusses the opening verses of Luke's gospel that mention how many have tried to draw up an account of the life of Christ. Origen suggests that these verses indicate that while the church has four gospels, the heretics have many.[11] He even names several of these heretical gospels, including the *Gospel to the Egyptians* and the *Gospel of Thomas*, and considers them spurious.

Origen was able to remain dedicated to his preaching duties thanks to the financial assistance of a wealthy supporter named Ambrosius. Eventually, and reluctantly, Origen also allowed Ambrosius to pay for a number of stenographers to transcribe his sermons.[12] Origen's homilies were often brief and

---

7. Heine identifies four "transitional texts:" *Comm. Gen.*, *Comm. Jo.*, *Prayer*, and *Exhortation to Martyrdom*. Ronald E. Heine, "Origen and a Hermeneutic for Spirituality," *Stone-Campbell Journal* 14 (Spring 2011): 169.

8. Heine, *Origen*, 173. For examples of interactions with Jews, see: *Hom. Ps.* 1.1, *Hom. Judic.* 8.1, and *Hom. Jer.* 19.12.

9. Heine, *Origen*, 176.

10. For some examples of references to one or more of these heretics, see: *Hom. Exod.* 3.2, *Hom. Num.* 9.1.3, 12.2, *Hom. Josh.* 7.7, 12.3, *Hom. Jer.* 10.5.1, 17.2.1, *Hom. Ezech.* 2.5, 7.4, 8.2, *Hom. Lc.* 29.4, 31.3. See also discussion in Peter W. Martens, *Origen and Scripture: The Contours of the Exegetical Life* (Oxford: Oxford University Press, 2012), 111.

11. *Hom. Lc.* 1.2.

12. *Hist. eccl.* 6.36.

extemporaneous, which likely explains his reluctance to have them recorded. His regular preaching duties ended after Decius came to power and the church experienced the first empire-wide persecution. Origen was imprisoned and tortured in AD 250, but the emperor died before he was killed. He was released from prison physically broken, and he eventually died in AD 254 at the age of sixty-nine.

While the exact number of homilies Origen preached is unknown, there is a healthy collection of nearly two hundred extant sermons. Most are preserved in Latin translations by Rufinus and Jerome, though a selection of homilies on Jeremiah and one sermon on 1 Samuel 28 survive in Greek. The majority are sermon collections on select Old Testament books including: sixteen sermons on Genesis, thirteen on Exodus, sixteen on Leviticus, twenty-eight on Numbers, twenty-six on Joshua, nine on Judges, one on 1 Samuel, nine on Psalms, two on Songs, nine on Isaiah, fourteen on Jeremiah, and nineteen on Ezekiel.[13] His thirty-nine homilies on Luke are the only surviving sermons on the New Testament.[14] This collection of homilies provides a solid basis to study his theology and methodology of preaching.

THEOLOGY OF PREACHING

Any discussion of Origen's theology of preaching must begin with his general hermeneutical approach. Origen's interpretation of Scripture is highly controversial since he often appeals to a spiritual or allegorical sense of the text. Origen was certainly a product of his time and place in Christian history and while his interpretations are not always convincing or congruent with the received apostolic hermeneutic, he was a devoted preacher and exegete, and many in the ancient world found his interpretation intriguing and edifying. The most straightforward articulation of Origen's hermeneutical method is found in his theological treatise titled, *On First Principles*. In this text, Origen famously compared biblical interpretation to the threefold aspect of the human person, saying:

> The right way, therefore, as it appears to us, of approaching the scriptures and gathering their meaning, is the following, which is extracted from the writings themselves. . . . One must therefore portray the meaning of the sacred writings in a threefold way upon one's own soul, so that the simple man may be edified by what we may call the flesh of the scripture, this name being given to the obvious interpretation; while the man who has made

---

13. For a comprehensive list of Origen's homilies, both extant and lost, see: Pierre Nautin, *Origène: Sa vie et son oeuvre* (Paris: Beauchesne, 1977), 253–60.

14. This does not include the various sermon fragments found in other early Christian writings.

some progress may be edified by its soul, as it were; and the man who is perfect ... this man may be edified by the spiritual law, which has a "shadow of the good things to come" [Heb 10:1]. For just as man consists of body, soul, and spirit, so in the same way does the scripture, which has been prepared by God to be given for man's salvation.[15]

Just as the human person is composed of three elements (body, soul, and spirit), so any interpretation of Scripture must account for the multiple senses present in written word. There is always an obvious literal sense for the "simple man" that forms the body and the most basic historical meaning of the text. The faithful interpreter, however, will make "some progress" in sanctification in order to grasp the spiritual sense of the text found among those who are "perfect" (cf. 1 Cor 2:6–7).

It is easy, however, to get caught up in Origen's discussion of the senses of Scripture and miss the larger point that threads them together: the emphasis on "edification" mentioned repeatedly in the passage.[16] Notice as the interpreter moves progressively through the various senses of Scripture, each stage builds up the reader or hearer. For Origen, biblical interpretation and edification are necessarily interconnected. The good biblical interpreter did not stand outside the text, but entered into the drama of salvation and "only those who had made some moral progress on the itinerary of the Christian faith could interpret the Scriptures well."[17]

For Origen, the application of this method of biblical interpretation was nowhere more important that in the homily. The preacher progressed in personal virtues and regularly exhorted the faithful toward sanctification through the spiritual sense. Edification and sanctification, for Origen, were the goal of biblical interpretation in general and preaching in particular.

This hermeneutical method depends on a doctrine of inspiration that elevates the Word of God as sacred and holy and regularly invokes the Spirit for the ongoing work of illumination of the meaning of the text. Beyond this, Origen had no detailed methodology, but instead utilized a variety of rhetorical and hermeneutical strategies derived from his Greco-Roman education and the patterns of the apostolic exegesis he discovered in the New Testament writings. Whatever allegorical or typological methods he applied, Origen would determine the right reading of a text by attending to the divine intention expressed in the passage, while relying on prayer, Christian virtue, and the church's rule of faith.

---

15. *On First Principles*, 4.2.4.

16. Martens, *Origen and Scripture*, 197. See also Karen Jo Torjesen, *Hermeneutical Procedure and Theological Method in Origen's Exegesis* (New York: Walter De Gruyter, 1986), 43, 47–48.

17. Martens, *Origen and Scripture*, 161. Torjesen, *Hermeneutical Procedure*, 29–32.

When Origen applied this hermeneutical theory to his preaching, the heart of his preaching was dedicated to the theme of the Christian's spiritual journey. For Origen, members of his congregation lived in various stages of the Christian life, from conversion (or preconversion/pagan) to the mature believer anticipating entrance into the kingdom of God. The role of preaching was to equip the people of God through the proclamation of divine revelation, to make progress in sanctification. In his sermons, unlike his commentaries, he did not always address every grammatical or linguistic aspect of the text, nor commit time to detailing technical issues of translation. Instead, he routinely drew on the images and metaphors of the biblical text in order to portray this journey and exhort the faithful in the church to continue striving against sin in pursuit of the holy life. A fine example of this is his homily on Numbers 33 that identifies the summary of the stages of Israel's journey from Egypt to the crossing of the Jordan and entering the promised land as distinct stages of the spiritual life moving from bondage to sin, to conversion, to progressive sanctification, and at last to entrance into the kingdom of God. In a brief summary of his general reading of this passage, Origen writes:

> [T]he stages [of the journey of Israel in Num 33] point to the progress of the soul when placed in this life, which, after its conversion from a pagan life, it follows not so much Moses as the law of God, and not so much Aaron as that priest who remains forever. Before it comes to perfection, it dwells in the wilderness, where, of course, it is trained in the commandments of the Lord and where its faith is tested by temptations. And when it conquers one temptation and its faith has been proven by it, from there it goes to another one; and it passes as it were from one stage to another; and then, when it prevails over the things that have happened and endures them faithfully, it moves on to another stage. And thus, the progress through each of the temptations of life and faith will be said to have stages in which increases in virtues are acquired one by one, and what is written is fulfilled: "They will go from virtue to virtue," [Ps 84:7] until the soul reaches its final end, or rather, the highest degree of the virtues, and it crosses the river of God and receives the promised inheritance.[18]

In Origen's spiritual reading of Numbers 33, he exhorted his hearers to continue to make progress in sanctification throughout the stages of the Christian journey, like Israel did in their journey from Egypt to the promised land.

---

18. *Hom. Num.* 27.5.2.

This growth in sanctification included both the moral and theological convictions of faith described by Christian virtue and Christian faith. He viewed his congregation as caught in the torrent of a depraved world with all it vices and sensualities. Whatever the cost and regardless of distractions, the preacher must preach the Word of God for the edification of the faithful. In another sermon, Origen compared the nature of exhortation to the image of fire that both burns and gives light.[19] In a similar way, the preacher of the Word should seek to edify believers through reproving them by the Word of God that burns and consoling them with the truth of the Scripture that enlightens. A good sermon, therefore, should provide the pain of conviction and the encouragement to lead the sinner back to God.

Finally, and above all, the preacher must be personally committed to this goal of growth in sanctification. Origen touched on this topic in his homily on Numbers 25 where the leaders of the nation of Israel are seduced by the daughters of Moab. The Lord called Moses to execute them and in his reflection on this judgment, Origen speculated that the leader's failure to rebuke and warn the people about their sins resulted in their judgment.[20] According to Origen, the preacher should lead the congregation in sanctification and continually exemplify the holy life.

METHODOLOGY FOR PREACHING

Despite the attention he gives to a theory of interpretation, Origen does not develop a specific homiletical theory. Instead, in Origen we find the contours of Christian preaching fashioned through the practice itself. Origen's sermons were delivered in the traditional setting of an early Christian worship service. In one sermon, he implied that before he preached he was seated with the clergy at the front of the sanctuary and some even graciously paid their respects as they entered.[21]

Based on a variety of ancient sources, Nautin provided the most convincing reconstruction of the ancient worship services at the time of Origen.[22] There were two separate types of services with different sets of Scripture readings and, therefore, different kinds of texts to preach. The regular weekly morning service was a non-Eucharist gathering that lasted about an hour and included an extended reading from the Old Testament, typically two or three chapters. He often

---

19. *Hom. Exod.* 13.4.
20. *Hom. Num.* 20.4.1.
21. *Hom. Josh.* 10.3.
22. Nautin, *Origène*, 389–409. See also Heine, Origen, 171–72. Origen, *Homilies on Genesis and Exodus*, 19–22. Old raises some important questions about Nautin's summary, but his criticisms are unsubstantiated and Nautin's study remains the best treatment of the topic. Old, *The Reading and Preaching*, 341–49.

referred to the reading in the opening lines of his homily.[23] The Scripture reading was the basis for the homily and the preacher normally selected a pericope from the larger portion of Scripture read aloud. These services were supplemented with Eucharist services held every Sunday, Wednesday, and Friday evening. During the Eucharist services, three Scripture passages were read, including a text from the Old Testament, a gospel passage, and a text from the New Testament epistles. Unlike his Old Testament sermons, Origen's homilies on Luke are so brief that there was time for a short homily after each of the three Scripture readings. Following this cycle, the church would read through the whole canon in a three-year period and consequently a faithful preacher would also preach through the whole Bible in that same time. Based on cross-references between the sermons, Nautin believes that Origen began preaching through the Psalms and Wisdom Literature. He then moved to the Prophetic Literature and finished with the Historical Books.[24] If this is correct, then the sermon on Psalm 36 would be close to the time when he began preaching in Caesarea.

Turning to the actual process of preaching, the pericope read during the service was normally the basis for the homily. Thus, his sermons worked consecutively through a text of Scripture based on the daily reading. Following this preaching model, Origen was never burdened to create new preaching series or develop his own topical arrangements of sermons. Instead, he simply selected a smaller portion from the chapters read, which was ample for his homilies. At one point in his homilies on Numbers, Origen offers an eloquent defense for why he only comments on a portion of a larger reading, saying:

> Many things have been read aloud for us simultaneously, and neither our time restraints nor the greatness of the mysteries permit us to speak about all these things. It is permitted, however, to pick a few little flowers from the vast fields and to pluck, not as much as the field grows in abundance, but as much as suffices to catch the fragrance. It is just as when someone comes to a spring. He does not need to draw all that the deep reservoir pours forth, but as much as soothes the mouths of those parched with thirst. Otherwise, what more than a due measure of health-giving water is consumed, it may become harmful to the one drinking.[25]

There were occasions when he deviated from this reading cycle to cover a particularly important passage read on a previous day. For example, in his homilies

---

23. For example, see: *Hom. Num.* 2.1.1, 4.1.1, 6.1.1.
24. Nautin, *Origène,* 22.
25. *Hom. Num.* 6.1.1.

on Numbers, he deviates from preaching the daily readings to give several sermons on Balaam's oracles.[26] Origen writes: "Although the order of readings that are being read aloud requires that we speak about the things that the lector has expounded, nevertheless since some of the brothers are instead requesting that the things written about the prophecy of Balaam be brought forth into the words of discussion, I have thought it fair to satisfy the desires of the hearers more than the order of the readings."[27]

This quote also points out how Origen would often preach contemporaneously based on the desires of his hearers. In another famous example of this, he preached a sermon on the Witch of Endor in 1 Samuel 28 at the behest of the bishop. In the opening statement of the sermon, Origen alludes to the fact that all of 1 Samuel 25–28 was read during the service, which was too long to discuss. He asked the bishop which pericope he wanted him to preach, and the bishop replied that he wanted the one about the Witch.[28]

Before he began his sermon, Origen offered a prayer for illumination to understand the Scriptures. He also petitioned the people to recall the passage read during the service and encouraged them to pray for their own understanding. For example, in his sermon on the blessings promised to Abraham after he demonstrated his faith by sacrificing Isaac in Genesis 22, Origen appeared overwhelmed by the significance of the passage and its theological implications. He compared his attempt at preaching to a small ship within the vast ocean of God's revelation. He requested the prayers of the people to have the favorable wind of the Spirit to steer him through the Word, saying:

> The further we progress in reading, the greater grows the accumulation of mysteries for us. And just as if someone should embark on the sea borne by a small boat, as long as he is near land he has little fear. But, when he has advanced little by little into the deep and has begun either to be lifted on high by the swelling waves or brought down to the depths by the same gaping waves then truly great fear and terror permeate his mind because he has entrusted a small craft to such immense waves. So also we seem to have suffered, who, small in merits and slight in ability, dare to enter so vast a sea of mysteries. But if by your prayers the Lord should see fit to give us a favorable breeze of his Holy Sprit we shall enter the port of salvation with a favorable passage of the word.[29]

---

26. *Hom. Num.* 15.1.1. Cf. *Hom. Num.* 21.1.1.
27. *Hom. Num.*15.1.1.
28. *Hom. 1Reg.* 1.1–3.
29. *Hom. Gen.* 9.1. cf. *Hom. Gen.* 3.5.

Origen also requests prayer when commenting on a difficult portion of the Old Testament. In his sermon on the priestly clothing in Leviticus 7, he confesses the difficulty in finding edification in these passages and petitions the church for their prayers as he handles this difficult text, saying, "We must strive to explain these things not by the power of human thinking but by prayers and supplications poured out to God. In this likewise, we stand in need of your aid, that God, Father of the Word, may give us the word 'in the opening of our mouth' that we can consider the wonders of the Law."[30] These kinds of prayers for the Spirit to give understanding were an essential part of his theology of preaching that influenced his methodology.

When he began preaching, Origen's sermons moved sequentially verse by verse through the text, giving special attention to any important words or concepts that related directly to the spiritual life of the faithful. Origen was concerned about substance over style, but this does not mean his sermons lacked any sentimentality. His purpose was not to awe the crowd with his oratory skills, but to offer clear and lucid prose that directed the faithful toward the understanding of the divine revelation before them. Origen applied the tools of textual exposition and biblical cross-references. As he taught, he relied on the Spirit, and his mind was actively engaged in drawing together the vast ocean of biblical texts to comment on the passage before him. The excerpt of his homily on Numbers 33 provided at the end of this essay gives a taste of his mastery of the biblical witness and theological integration of passages from across the Scriptures. Even in this one brief example, he cited a variety of texts, including passages from Exodus, Numbers, Psalms, Luke, Ephesians, and 1 John.[31] This kind of intertextual Scripture networking was a hallmark of patristic biblical interpretation and preaching. The mechanics of Origen's exegesis borrow all the technical features of ancient Christian hermeneutical strategies, including: cross-references, catchwords, allegory, typology, prophecy-fulfillment, and so on. Some of these strategies were determined by the type of biblical literature he was preaching. Many of these interpretive strategies were also learned from his interest in Second Temple Jewish sources and the patterns of New Testament interpretation of the Old. Generally speaking, the application of these methods were bound by the church's rule of faith and directed toward the spiritual edification of the faithful.

Origen was never apprehensive about interpreting any portion of Scripture. He believed firmly in the inspiration of all of Scripture, so everything was of

---

30. *Hom. Lev.* 6.1.
31. See the excerpt from Origen's homily on Num 33 (*Hom. Num.* 27.7.7) at the conclusion of this essay.

value. As he was preaching consecutively through texts, he was forced to handle even the difficult and obscure passages. For example, after hearing a reading on the rebellion of Korah and the sprouting of Aaron's rod in in Numbers 16–17, Origen remarks, "With God, as it is granted that he is to be understood, there is nothing that is not beneficial, there is nothing pointless, but even the things that seem alienating to the people worthy of rejection are found to play some necessary role."[32]

Regarding the congregation present at the services, the morning service was for anyone, including precatechumens, catechumens, and the rest of the congregation. Origen's sermons often transitioned to second person when he addressed his congregation individually or collectively. In this way, his preaching had a very personal or conversational feel. At times he spoke to the catechumens.[33] At other times he spoke directly to the priests, whom he believed had a higher calling of sanctification.[34] Some members of the church were wealthy enough to own personal copies of the Scriptures. There is evidence that some of these parishioners even challenged his reading and brought charges against his interpretations.[35]

At other times, Origen admonished the people for their spiritual apathy. He confronted their regular practices of indulging in superstitions, participating in the games and pagan celebrations, and general moral laxity.[36] There are reports that his congregation included a mixed audience that occasionally walked out before the sermon started, attended only on special holidays or feast days, or gossiped and sat in the back of the church near the catechumens.[37] In one sermon, while commenting on Genesis 21 and Abraham's joy at the birth of Isaac, Origen expressed his frustrations with some of their practices, saying:

> But I fear that the Church is still bearing sons in sadness and sorrow. Or does it not cause her sadness and sorrow when you do not gather to hear the word of God? And scarcely on feast days do you proceed to the Church, and you do this not so much from a desire for the word as from a fondness for the festival and to obtain, in a certain manner, common relaxation. . . . You spend most of this time, no rather, almost all of it in mundane occupations; you pass some of it in the marketplace, some in business; one has time for

---

32. *Hom. Num.*, 9.1.1.
33. For example, see: *Hom. Josh.* 9.9, *Hom. Jer.* 27.3, *Hom. Lc.* 7.8.
34. *Hom. Josh.* 7.6; *Hom. Lev.* 5.8, 6.6, 7.1; *Hom. Jer.* 11.3, *Hom. Ezech.* 5.4, 9.2.
35. *Hom. Gen.* 13.3. For further discussion of Origen's interaction with his congregation, see: Heine, *Origen*, 179–83.
36. For example, see; *Hom. Josh.* 26.2, *Hom. Josh.* 10.1.
37. *Hom. Exod.* 8.3, *Hom. Num.* 5.1, *Hom. Lev.* 9.5,7,9.

the country, another for lawsuits, and no one or very few have time to hear the word of God. Even when you are present and placed in the Church you are not attentive, but you waste your time on common everyday stories; you turn your backs to the word of God or to the divine readings.[38]

Origen had little patience for those who were not dedicated to Christian life and serious about sanctification. His complaints resounded with the common theme that Christians were only interested in attending church on important holidays, which is certainly a common complaint even today!

Finally, most of Origen's homilies end with the invocation to stand and pray.[39] He usually concluded with a prayer that was taken from one of the doxologies in the New Testament epistles; most often 1 Peter 4:11: "To him be the glory and the power for ever and ever. Amen."[40] Coupled with this doxology, as they departed, the church was generally admonished to apply some aspect of the Word to their lives.

CONTRIBUTIONS TO PREACHING

Origen's contribution to the history of preaching is significant, even if it is controversial. He certainly read the text with a passion that produced some imaginative interpretations. In spite of his shortcomings, Origen's preaching shaped the trajectory and methodology of preaching for much of the patristic period. Preaching, for Origen, was biblical from beginning to end. He had no other concept of preaching besides preaching through particular texts of Scripture and explaining the meaning of passages within the contours of the entire biblical narrative. At the same time, the primary goal of preaching was spiritual edification. This means that preaching should not only stir the heart, but also challenge the mind as every Christian strives daily to grow in sanctification. Origen also believed that the sermon should begin and end with prayer for the Spirit's guidance in interpretation and that the life of the preacher must exemplify the content of the sermon in the pursuit of the holy life. All of these features of Origen's preaching flow together to construct his theology and methodology of preaching. His stature as a theologian and his dedication to biblical interpretation position him as a pivotal figure in the history of preaching in the church.

---

38. *Hom. Gen.* 10.1.

39. *Hom. Lc.* 12.6, 36.3, and 39.7.

40. For examples of his closing doxology with allusions to 1 Pet 4:11, see: *Hom. Num.* 1.3.7, 2.2.5, 3.4.2, 4.3.4, 5.3.5, 9.9.2. Other texts cited in his doxologies include: 1 Pet 5:11, Gal 1:5, and Rom 1:25. See: *Hom. Num.* 6.4.2, 7.6.3, 8.1.9, and 19.4.6.

Sermon Excerpt

On the Stages of the Spiritual Journey in Numbers 33[41]

It says: "And Moses wrote down their starting places and their stages by the Word of the Lord" [Num 33:2]. He wrote them down, then, "by the Word of the Lord" so that when we read them and see how many starting places and stages lie ahead of us on the journey that leads to the kingdom, we may prepare ourselves for this way and, by considering the journey that lies ahead of us, we may not allow the time of our life to be wasted by laziness and negligence. Otherwise, while we linger in the vanities of the world and take delight in each of the sensations that come to our sight or hearing or even to touch, smell, and taste, the days may slip by, the time may pass and we shall not find any opportunity for completing the journey that lies ahead, and we may faint while only halfway there. And it will come to pass to us what is reported of certain ones who were unable to reach the destination, but their "limbs fell in the desert" [Heb 3:17]. Thus, we are making a journey, and the reason we have come into this world is so that we may pass "from virtue to virtue" [Ps 84:7], not to remain on the earth for earthly things, like the man who said: "I will pull down my barns and build larger ones, and I will say to my soul: Soul, you have many good things laid up for many years, eat, drink, and be merry" [Luke 12:18–19]. Otherwise, the Lord may say to us, as he said to him: "Fool! This night your soul will be taken from you" [Luke 12:20]. He did not say "this day," but "this night." For he is destroyed at night like the firstborn of the Egyptians [Exod 12:29], as one who "loved the world" [1 John 2:15] and its darkness and who belonged to "the rulers of the darkness of this world" [Eph 6:12]. Not this world is called darkness and night, because of those who live in ignorance and do not accept the light of truth. But those who are like this do not set out "from Rameses," nor do they pass on "to Succoth" [Num 33:3, 5]. ♦

BIBLIOGRAPHY

Danielou, Jean. *Origen*. Trans. by Walter Mitchell. New York: Sheed & Ward, 1955.

Eusebius' Ecclesiastical History. Trans. by C. F. Cruse. Peabody, MA: Hendrickson, 1998.

Heine, Ronald E. "Origen and a Hermeneutic for Spirituality," *Stone-Campbell Journal* 14 (Spring 2011): 67–79.

_____. *Origen: Scholarship in the Service of the Church*. Oxford: Oxford University Press, 2010.

---

41. *Hom. Num.* 27.7.7.

Holliday, Lisa. "From Alexandria to Caesarea: Reassessing Origen's Appointment to the Presbyterate," *Numen* 58 (2011): 674–96.

Jacobsen, Anders-Christian. "Conversion to Christian Philosophy—the case of Origen's School in Caesarea," *Zeitschrift für Antikes Christentum* 16 (2012): 145–57.

Kerr, Hugh T. *Preaching in the Early Church*. New York: Revell, 1942.

Lienhard, S. J. "Origen as Homilist," Pages 36–52 in *Preaching in the Patristic Age: Studies in Honor of Walter J. Burghardt, S. J.* Edited by David G. Hunter. New York: Paulist, 1989.

Martens, Peter W. *Origen and Scripture: The Contours of the Exegetical Life.* Oxford: Oxford University Press, 2012.

Nautin, Pierre. *Origène: Sa vie et son oeuvre.* Paris: Beauchesne, 1977.

Nodes, Daniel J. "Allegory and Spiritual Observance in Origen's Discussions of the Sabbath." Pages 130–46 in *Origen of Alexandria: His World and His Legacy.* Edited by Charles Kannengiesser and William L. Petersen. Notre Dame: University of Notre Dame Press, 1988.

Old, Hughes Oliphant. *The Biblical Period.* Vol. 1 of *The Reading and Preaching of the Scriptures in the Worship of the Christian Church.* Grand Rapids: Eerdmans, 1998.

Origen, "A Letter of Origen to Gregory." Pages 393–94 in *Ante-Nicene Fathers.* Volume 4. Edited by Alexander Roberts and James Donaldson. Peabody, MA: Hendrickson, 2004.

————. *Homilies 1–14 on Ezekiel.* Trans. by Thomas P. Scheck. New York: Newman, 2010.

————. *Homilies on Genesis and Exodus.* Trans. by Ronald E. Heine. Washington, DC: Catholic University of America Press, 1982.

————. *Homilies on Jeremiah and Homily on 1 Kings 28.* Trans. by John Clark Smith. Washington, DC: Catholic University of America Press, 1998.

————. *Homilies on Joshua.* Trans. by Barbara J. Bruce. Edited by Cynthia White. Washington, DC: Catholic University of America Press, 2002.

————. *Homilies on Judges.* Trans. by Elizabeth Ann Dively Lauro. Washington, DC: Catholic University of America Press, 2010.

————. *Homilies on Leviticus 1–16.* Trans. by Gary Wayne Barkley. Washington, DC: Catholic University of America Press, 1990.

————. *Homilies on Luke.* Trans. by Joseph T. Lienhard, S.J. Washington, DC: Catholic University of America Press, 1996.

————. *Homilies on Numbers.* Trans. by Thomas P Scheck. Edited by Christopher A. Hall. Downers Grove, IL: InterVarsity Press Academic, 2009.

————. *On First Principles.* Trans. by G. W. Butterworth. Gloucester, MA: Peter Smith, 1973.

————. *The Song of Songs Commentary and Homilies.* Trans. by R. P. Lawson. New York: Newman, 1957.

Sheerin, Daniel. "The Role of Prayer in Origen's Homilies." Pages 200–14 in *Origen of Alexandria: His World and His Legacy.* Edited by Charles Kannengiesser and William L. Petersen. Notre Dame: University of Notre Dame Press, 1988.

Torjesen, Karen Jo. *Hermeneutical Procedure and Theological Method in Origen's Exegesis.* New York: Walter De Gruyter, 1986.

Ephrem the Syrian

Preaching Christ through Poetry and Paradox

JONATHAN J. ARMSTRONG

Syriac—a Semitic language similar to the Aramaic that Jesus spoke—acted as the *lingua franca* of Mesopotamia and Syria during the fourth century of the Christian era, and to this day continues to be the liturgical language of the Syrian Orthodox Church, the Church of the East, and the Marionite Church. The Syriac doctrinal hymns and sermons in poem by Ephrem the Syrian (ca. 303–373) circulated far and wide in antiquity and were in part responsible for Syriac's rise as one of the principle theological languages of the first millennium. Modern scholars agree in their assessment of Ephrem as the most important Syrian Father and the greatest poet of the patristic era. For centuries, Ephrem's symbolic and iconographic approach to theology has astounded readers for its capacity to convey even the most difficult concepts across linguistic and cultural barriers. In the context of our world—unified in an unprecedented way by technology but acutely divided by seemingly irresolvable worldview differences—there is a great deal we can learn from Ephrem about communicating Christian dogma through universally accessible word pictures.

HISTORICAL CONTEXT

Ephrem[1] was born in Nisibis—modern-day Nusaybin, Turkey, along the Turkish-Syrian[2] border some 285 miles inland from the Mediterranean

---

1. For those interested in reading further in St. Ephrem the Syrian, I would recommend Sebastian Brock's translation of *Hymns on Paradise* (Crestwood, NY: St. Vladimir's Seminary Press, 1990); Sidney Griffith's *Faith Adoring the Mystery: Reading the Bible with St. Ephraem the Syrian* (Milwaukee: Marquette University Press, 1997) also provides an excellent introduction to Ephrem's exegesis. Regarding Ephrem, F. Rilliet said he was "unquestionably the most important of the Syrian Fathers and the greatest poet of the patristic era" ("Ephrem the Syrian," in *Encyclopedia of Ancient Christianity*, ed. Di Berardino [Downers Grove, IL: IVP Academic, 2014], 1:810). In the oft-cited judgment of Robert Murray, Ephrem is "the greatest poet of the patristic age and, perhaps, the only *theologian-poet* to rank beside Dante" ("Ephrem Syrus," *A Catholic Dictionary of Theology* [Nashville: Nelson, 1967], 2:222). The admiration of Ephrem from antiquity continues into the modern period, and in 1920, Pope Benedict XV declared Ephrem to be a doctor of the Roman Catholic Church.

2. Sebastian Brock, "Introduction to Syriac Studies," in *Horizons in Semitic Studies*, ed. J. H. Eaton (University of Birmingham, 1980), 30–33. Like biblical Hebrew, Syriac has twenty-two consonants and is

Sea.[3] Lying on the border area between the Roman and Parthian Empires, Nisibis had exchanged hands repeatedly between Roman and Parthian rule in the centuries prior to Ephrem's lifetime. Although an ancient biography of Ephrem has survived to the present day, many of the details of this otherwise promising source are ostensibly false, and the historical events of Ephrem's life are known only in outline form.[4] The Syriac *Vita* claims that Ephrem's father was a pagan priest, but some of the lines from Ephrem's own poems have convinced scholars that Ephrem's parents were in fact Christian: "I was born in the path of truth," Ephrem writes, "your truth was with me in my youth, your faithfulness is with my old age."[5] Ephrem grew up under the leadership of Bishop Jacob of Nisibis (d. 338), and it was under Bishop Jacob's leadership that Ephrem served as a deacon and also as a catechetical teacher in Nisibis. Bishop Jacob is remembered in church history as one of the 318 council fathers who attended the First Council of Nicaea in 325. The *Vita* also portrays Ephrem as an Egyptian-style monk, but scholars have generally concluded that this tradition is hagiographical rather than historical. Sebastian Brock, former Reader in Syriac Studies at the University of Oxford and renowned scholar of the Christian East, concludes: "Ephrem probably only came across tributaries of Egyptian monasticism right at the end of his life during his last years at Edessa."[6]

The city of Nisibis was triumphant in three sieges against the Persians—in 338, 346, and 350. In 363, Julian the Apostate died while campaigning against the Persians, and Julian's successor, Jovian, surrendered Nisibis to the Persians.[7] In the wake of this loss, Ephrem—along with the other citizens of Nisibis—was forced to relocate some 130 miles due west to Edessa, where he lived until the end of his life less than a decade later. At the time, Edessa was renowned as the first kingdom to convert to Christianity, for an imperially sanctioned church had been established in Edessa well over a century before Constantine declared

---

written right-to-left. Syriac is the language of the *Peshitta*, the translation of the Hebrew Old Testament and the Greek New Testament. The *Peshitta* remains today one of the principal sources for text critical decisions in modern translations of the Bible.

3. For an overview of the origins of the church in Syria, see Samuel Hugh Moffett, *A History of Christianity in Asia* (Maryknoll, NY: Orbis, 1998), 1:45–90.

4. Joseph P. Amar, *The Syriac Vita Tradition of Ephrem the Syrian*, in *Corpus Scriptorum Christianorum Orientalium* (Leuven: Peeters, 2001). Arthur Vööbus was the first modern scholar to analyze critically the biographical sources concerning Ephrem and to begin to assemble a historical account of Ephrem's life and his authentic literary corpus (*Literary Critical and Historical Studies in Ephrem the Syrian* [Stockholm: ETSE, 1958]).

5. *Hymns against the Heresies*, 26; *Hymns on Virginity*, 37. Quoted from Brock's introduction in *Hymns on Paradise*, 9.

6. Ibid., 25.

7. In *Hymns against Julian*, 2 and 3, Ephrem concludes that Nisibis had been captured by the Persians in order to teach the people the dangers of idolatry. Ephrem witnessed with his own eyes as Julian the Apostate's lifeless corpse was paraded into the city of Nisibis when the Persians proclaimed victory over the city.

Christianity to be a licit religion in the Roman Empire by the Edict of Milan in 313. Eusebius records the incredible story of how King Abgar, afflicted with a terrible disease, wrote a letter to Jesus of Nazareth, requesting that he come to Edessa and heal him. In Eusebius's narrative, Jesus responds by letter, praising King Abgar for his faith and promising to send one of his disciples to heal him after the ascension.[8] While modern scholars view Eusebius's report as credulous, there can be no doubt this tradition circulated broadly during Ephrem's day and that the city of Edessa perceived itself as a center of Christianity with a long and illustrious history.

Sometime after arriving in Edessa, Ephrem founded a school which became known as the "School of the Persians," as many of the teachers and students who populated the school during its first year were refugees from Persia.[9] The Bible commentaries Ephrem produced were used as standard textbooks until the time of Theodore of Mopsuestia (d. 428). Because of its suspected Nestorian leanings, the school languished after Nestorius's condemnation at the Council of Ephesus in 433 and was finally closed by Emperor Zeno in 489. However, prior to the closure, the director of the school at the time, Narsai, traveled to Nisibis along with a number of his pupils and founded the school of Nisibis, and so Ephrem came to play a significant although indirect role in shaping the school founded in his hometown of Nisibis.[10] Ephrem was renowned in the fourth-century Christian world for the beauty of his theological poetry; no other ancient Syriac writer achieved such acclaim among Greek and Latin Christian readers. Jerome, who could be a very harsh critic of those whose literary style he deemed deficient, writes of Ephrem: "Even in translation I could recognize the acuteness of his sublime genius."[11] In Ephrem's literary corpus, scholars count over four hundred hymns, three biblical commentaries, and several homilies.[12]

---

8. Eusebius, *Hist. eccl.*, 1.13. For a careful evaluation of the historicity of Eusebius's report, see Sebastian Brock, "Eusebius and Syriac Christianity," in *Eusebius, Christianity and Judaism*, ed. H. W. Attridge and G. Hatta (Detroit: Wayne State University Press, 1992), 212–34.

9. Alfeyev of Podolsk, "Theological Education in the Christian East: First to Sixth Centuries," in *Abba: The Tradition of Orthodoxy in the West*, eds. John Behr, Andrew Louth, and Dimitri Conomos (Crestwood, NY: St. Vladimir's Seminary Press, 2003), 55. Contrariwise, Han J. W. Drijvers had argued that Ephrem did not found the school of Edessa and that the school at Edessa dates back into the second century ("The School of Edessa: Greek Learning and Local Culture," in *Centres of Learning: Learning and Location in Pre-Modern Europe and the Near East*, eds. Jan Willem Drijvers and A. A. MacDonald [Leiden: Brill, 1995], 58).

10. Arthur Vööbus dates the departure of Narsai and his colleagues from Edessa to sometime after 471 AD (*History of the School of Nisibis* [Louvain: Secrétariat du Corpus SCO, 1965], 41). This monograph is the single best source for further information on the School of Nisibis and is still frequently cited in the literature.

11. Jerome, *Vir. Ill.*, 115.2 (*On Illustrious Men*, trans. Thomas P. Halton [Washington, DC: Catholic University of America Press, 1999], 100:149). See also Sozomen's lavish praise in *Hist. eccl.*, 3.16.

12. St. Ephrem the Syrian, *The Hymns on Faith*, trans. Jeffrey T. Wickes, vol. 130 in *Fathers of the Church* (Washington, DC: Catholic University of America Press, 2015), 4. Ephrem's works have come down to us in three genres: *madrāšê* (hymns), *mêmrê* (homilies in verse), and *pûšāqâ* or *turgāmâ* (commentaries).

THEOLOGY OF PREACHING

At the heart of Ephrem's theology is the concept of the "luminous eye": God reveals himself in both Scripture and nature, and both are filled with symbols that express divinely inspired truth. But it requires a spiritual or "luminous" eye to recognize these truths.[13] Ephrem's chief concern, whether in his preaching specifically or in his theological writing generally, is to set before his audience the revelatory symbols of Scripture and nature and to exposit their meaning with artistry and insight. In *Hymns on Paradise*, Ephrem describes how Scripture and nature serve as fonts of God's revelation:

> In his book Moses
> described the creation of the natural world,
> so that both Nature and Scripture
> might bear witness to the Creator:
> Nature, through man's use of it,
> Scripture, through his reading of it.
> These are the witnesses
> which reach everywhere,
> they are to be found at all times,
> present at every hour,
> confuting the unbeliever
> who defames the Creator.[14]

In one of his most enduring word pictures, Ephrem describes precisely how this theology of symbol works: "The eye and the mind traveled over the lines as over a bridge, and entered together the story of Paradise. The eye as it read transported the mind; in return the mind, too, gave the eye rest from its reading, for when the book had been read the eye had rest, but the mind was engaged."[15] For Ephrem, the key to understanding the words and stories of Scripture was to discover the allegories that lead the reader into spiritual contemplation of God. In relating his own experience of entering into this spiritual contemplation of God, Ephrem writes this concerning Scripture: "Its verses and lines spread out

---

13. Sebastian Brock explains: "Everything is imbued with significance, but, although this meaning is objectively present (St. Ephrem calls it 'the hidden power,' or 'meaning,' *ḥayla kasya*), it requires the eye of faith on the part of each individual to penetrate both inward and beyond the outer material reality in order to perceive the relationship, sacramental in character, between the exterior physical and interior spiritual realm" (*Hymns on Paradise*, 39).

14. Brock, *Hymns on Paradise* 5.2, 102–3.

15. Brock, *Hymns on Paradise* 5.4, 103). See also *Hymns on Faith*, 15.10, 86.16 (FC 130:141, 396).

their arms to welcome me; the first rushed out and kissed me."[16] The first three chapters of Genesis have oriented Christian theological reflection for centuries, not least in the appeal of the Reformed tradition to the salvation-historical triad of creation, fall, and redemption as the framework for systematic theology. In a similar fashion, Ephrem sees in the first three chapters of Genesis the blueprint for his entire theological system. They act as an allegory, Ephrem affirms, welcoming the reader into paradise, which is the contemplation of God: "The story of Paradise, it lifted me up and transported me from the bosom of the book to the very bosom of Paradise."[17]

In Brock's measured judgment, "if a label is required, 'symbolic theology' would be the least inappropriate designation of Ephrem's approach."[18] It is through the set of symbols bequeathed to the church through tradition that the Christian imagination perceives divine revelation in both Scripture and nature: "The keys of doctrine which unlock all of Scripture's books, have opened up before my eyes the book of creation."[19] It is clear that, whereas in Protestant theology it is the words of Scripture themselves that are the essence of God's revelation, for Ephrem (and, subsequently, the Christian East) the words of Scripture are only entry points into the symbols of divine revelation: "Scripture brought me to the gate of Paradise, and the mind, which is spiritual, stood in amazement and wonder as it entered."[20] Ephrem then relates that, as he began to enter Paradise in his mind—that is, as he began to perceive the allegories portrayed in the symbols of Scripture—his intellect was inundated with the majesty of God's revelation, "as the senses were no longer able to contain its treasures . . . or take in its beauties so as to describe them in words."[21] The impossibility of language to convey the fullness of God's revealed truths drives Ephrem to appeal to paradox almost incessantly. God's revelation overwhelms the structures of language, and we can bear witness to God's revelation only by pointing toward a series of transcendent but logically inconsistent word pictures. The result of Ephrem's theological method is the discovery of God's revelation everywhere and the consequent quest to worship God in every experience. As Brock writes, Ephrem's approach produces "the total invasion of theology into ordinary, everyday life, cultivating an

---

16. Brock, *Hymns on Paradise* 5.3, 103.

17. Ibid.

18. "The Poet as Theologian," *Sobornost* 7 (1977): 243. Brock explains that Ephrem's approach to theology is one of "paradox and symbolism, and for this purpose poetry proves a far more suitable vehicle than prose, seeing that poetry is much better capable of sustaining the essential dynamism and fluidity that is characteristic of this sort of approach to theology" (*The Luminous Eye: The Spiritual World Vision of Saint Ephrem*, rev. ed. [Kalamazoo, MI: Cistercian, 1992], 24).

19. Brock, *Hymns on Paradise* 6.1, 108.

20. Brock, *Hymns on Paradise* 6.2, 109.

21. Ibid.

attitude of praise and wonder that allows the Holy Spirit to bring about in each one of us the kingdom of God."[22]

Although paradoxes bring with them logical inconsistences, paradoxes are not defined by their logical inconsistences but by the truth that their parts communicate when independently considered.[23] Rather than seeking to resolve paradoxes, Ephrem passionately pursues them, knowing it is in the contemplation of the unfathomable mysteries of God that we experience God's revelation most intimately. For Ephrem, the cross is the source and foundation of all theological paradoxes, and it is the cross that sheds light on all other paradoxes in God's revealed stories in Scripture:

> The First-born put on the weapons of the Deceitful One
> so that with the weapons that killed He might, conversely, give life.
> By the wood with which he killed us, we were delivered;
> By the wine that maddened us, we became modest.[24]

It is through the cross that Jesus gives life; it is through the wine of the Eucharist that Christians come to see beyond sensible reality and are brought to true sobriety. Ephrem's sheer ability to sustain such intricate, beautiful, and profound verse, page after page, has elicited acclamation from readers for centuries. Ephrem exults: "As again he dwelt in His mother's womb, in His womb dwells all creation. Mute He was as a babe, yet He gave to all creation all His commands."[25] Mary can say to her infant son in Ephrem's fifth *Hymn on the Nativity*: "I am servant of Your divinity, but I am also mother of Your humanity, [my] Lord and [my] son."[26] In christological statements that parallel those of other Eastern Church Fathers, Ephrem writes: "Today the Deity imprinted itself on humanity, so that humanity might also be cut into the seal of Deity," and again: "He descended and became one of us that we might become heavenly."[27]

---

22. Brock, "The Poet as Theologian," 249.

23. Brock summarizes: "The difference between these two approaches, Hellenic and Semitic, can be well illustrated if one visualizes a circle with a point in the center, where the point represents the object of theological enquiry; the philosophical tradition of theology will seek to define, to set *horoi*, 'boundaries' or 'definitions,' to this central point, whereas St Ephrem's Semitic approach through his poetry will provide a series of paradoxical statements situated as it were at opposite points on the circumference of the circle: the central point is left undefined, but something of its nature can be inferred by joining up the various opposite points around the circumference" (*Hymns on Paradise*, 40).

24. Kathleen E. McVey, trans., "Hymns on the Nativity 4" in *Ephrem the Syrian: Hymns* (New York: Paulist Press, 1989), 98.

25. Ibid., 100.

26. McVey, "Hymns on the Nativity 5" in *Ephrem*, 109.

27. McVey, "Hymns on the Nativity 1, 3" in *Ephrem*, 74, 87. Irenaeus of Lyons formulates this paradoxical truth in this way: "The Word of God, our Lord Jesus Christ . . . through His transcendent love, become what we are, that He might bring us to be even what He is Himself" (*Haer.*, 5. preface [*ANF* 1:526]). Athanasius

Paradox is not merely a literary device in the hands of Ephrem; it is the very fabric of the revealed Christian message concerning God's plan of salvation for sinners through the death and resurrection of his incarnate Son. For Ephrem, the theological reflection that motivates his every poem or prose work is the pursuit of seeing Christ in everything:

> Never have mortal minds touched him.
> Who has a hand of fire and a finger of spirit
> To explore him in the presence of his hiddenness?
> Revealed knowledge has not understood
> That Luminous One who is inside and outside of all.
> His is the knowledge within our knowledge.
> He is the life of the soul which dwells within us . . . .
> Who will not give thanks to that one more hidden than all,
> Who revealed himself more than all![28]

Christ, as the revelation of God to humanity, is the sacrament that is communicated in all of God's creative and providential activities; absolutely nothing exists that does not reflect at some level God's character and being. Ephrem can only burst out in an ecstatic pitch: "In sacrifices you are slain. In a meal, you are eaten. . . . All of you, my Lord, in everything!"[29]

METHODOLOGY FOR PREACHING

There is an intensely scriptural character to Ephrem's work. He writes in the first of the *Hymns on the Nativity*: "From your treasury, my Lord, let us fetch from the treasures of your Scriptures."[30] Ephrem clearly believed in the polyvalence of Scripture. For Ephrem, it is the task of the interpreter to separate out and analyze the various layers of the sacred text. Ephrem writes in his *Commentary on the Diatessaron*: "If there were [only] one meaning for the words [of Scripture], the first interpreter would find it, and all other listeners would have neither the toil of seeking nor the pleasure of finding. But every word of our Lord has its own image, and each image has many members, and each member possesses its own species

---

of Alexandria adds: "He, indeed, assumed humanity that we might become God" (*On the Incarnation*, 54 [Crestwood, NY: St. Vladimir's Seminary Press, 2002], 93). Gregory of Nazianzus echoes this same tradition: "For that which He has not assumed He has not healed; but that which is united to His Godhead is also saved" (*Epistulae*, 101 [*NPNF*, second series, 7:440]).

28. *Hymns on Faith*, 19.4–7 (FC 130:152).
29. Ibid., 6.5 (FC 130:92).
30. McVey, "Hymns on the Nativity 1" in *Ephrem*, 66.

and form. Each person hears in accordance with his capacity, and it is interpreted in accordance with what has been given to him."[31]

Ephrem's primary interest in Scripture is not an exposition of the literal meaning of the text, but, as is standard in the hermeneutics of the Church Fathers, Ephrem is concerned to decipher the allegorical meaning of the text. At the conclusion of his *Commentary on Genesis*, Ephrem states that he had spoken of the literal meaning of Jacob's blessings up to that point but that he would then write about the spiritual sense of these blessings. Ephrem then proceeds to interpret almost every key word in the text as an allegory for the church, the gospel, and the apostles. Reuben, whom Jacob curses, is Adam, who is cursed by God, but as Reuben's curse was reversed by Moses (Ephrem does not explain), so the curse of Adam is reversed by Jesus in the resurrection; Issachar is a type of Christ, who *"bowed his shoulder* [Gen 49:15] to the cross and became the one who paid off the debt."[32] Some of Ephrem's conclusions seem unnaturally adjusted to make sense of this gospel-focused hermeneutic, such as interpreting the forty thousand robbers of Gad—mentioned only in the Peshitta version of Genesis 49:19—as the apostles and their disciples who journeyed to every corner of the earth to steal back, as it were, the nations that the devil had taken captive. *"Benjamin is a ravenous wolf*' [Gen 49:27] [refers to] Paul," Ephrem explains, "who was a wolf to the wolves and snatched all souls away from the evil one."[33] The symbols that Ephrem seeks in his allegorical interpretations are controlled by the underlying themes of Christ and the church.

Ephrem is explicit in his appeals to Old Testament saints as types of Christ and writes concerning the resurrection: "Types for you were both Daniel and Lazarus: the one in the den that the peoples sealed, and the other in the grave that the people opened."[34] This is a standard feature of Ephrem's poetry: he muses on the motifs operating within the biblical narrative, and once he has identified the symbol set at play, he then proceeds to weave a christological tapestry from the various allegorical threads he pulls from the passage. Invariably, Ephrem finds a way that the symbol set in an Old Testament passage points to a New Testament account of Christ. Typology, therefore, fulfills the logic of Ephrem's theology; the theological answers Ephrem seeks are discovered in symbols. Ephrem exhorts his readers to see Christ everywhere in Scripture: "Again, toward whomever you wish to incline Scripture, he, too, will be proved unable to fulfill its histories in

---

31. Carmel McCarthy, *Saint Ephrem's Commentary on Tatian's Diatessaron* (Oxford University Press on behalf of the University of Manchester, 2000), 139; quoted from Griffith, *Faith Adoring the Mystery*, 32.

32. *Commentary on Genesis*, 43.5 (FC 91:210).

33. Ibid., 43.11 (FC 91:211).

34. McVey, "Hymns on the Nativity 10.4" in *Ephrem*, 129.

himself. For it is Christ who perfects its symbols by His cross, its types by His body, its adornments by His beauty, and all of it by all of Him!"[35]

The fact that Ephrem is interested primarily in the allegorical rather than the historical sense of the text is evident in his readiness to add curious details to the narrative. Following a common Jewish legend, Ephrem elaborates that it was extremely hot on the day that Pharoah's daughter went to bathe and found Moses. Because she had leprosy, Ephrem explains, she went to the river in order to seek relief from her suffering.[36] The story is further "improved" by the detail that Pharaoh's daughter was barren and so, upon finding Moses, she concluded that the gods had granted her wish for a child. Ephrem allows his theological emphasis to overwhelm the plain reading of Scripture when he paraphrases God's response to Moses from Exodus 4:11–12: "You will become great by that which makes you small, so that you will become an eloquent prophet for the God who is silent. I will be with your mouth, not to loosen your tongue or improve your answers, but so that something better might result from the sound of your stammering."[37] However, as we read in the text of Scripture, God's instruction to Moses had been that he would aid Moses in speaking, not that he would bring success from Moses's failing speech. While at times Ephrem's willingness to rework the literal meaning of the text seems harmless and can even yield edifying reflections, at times his exegesis clearly runs amok. In retelling the story of the woman at the well from John 4, Ephrem concludes that the woman had been married to five husbands because each of her husbands had passed away one after another before the marriage could be consummated. Ephrem imagines that the woman remarried only because it was shameful for a woman not to be married in her culture, but that she had remained a virgin through each of these marriages. Most dangerous in this bizarre revision of the gospel story is that the mercy and forgiveness of Jesus is totally lost—Ephrem is adamant that the woman must have still been a virgin, for otherwise Jesus would have immediately perceived her lewdness and refused to associate with her.[38] Ephrem eisegetes his own theological agenda about chastity into John 4, and in so doing seems to entirely bypass the meaning the Evangelist intended.

Ephrem's homilies have an extraordinary capacity for dogmatic exposition. In the *Homily on Our Lord*, which is the only surviving example from his corpus of a homily that is not in poem form, Ephrem gives some of his clearest teachings

35. McVey, "*Hymns on Virginity 9*" in *Ephrem*, 303.

36. *Commentary on Exodus*, 2.2 (FC 91:226). See Louis Ginzberg, *The Legends of the Jews*, trans. Henrietta Szold (Philadelphia: Jewish Publication Society of America, 1913), 2:266.

37. *Commentary on Exodus*, 4.2 (FC 91:234).

38. McVey, "Hymns on Virginity 22" in *Ephrem*, 356.

on Trinitarian and christological orthodoxy. The homily opens with a string of intensely paradoxical statements, including the following: "The Only-Begotten journeyed from the God-head and resided in a virgin, so that through physical birth the Only-Begotten would become a brother to many. And he journeyed from Sheol and resided in the kingdom, to tread a path from Sheol, which cheats everyone, to the kingdom, which rewards everyone."[39] These paradoxes, for Ephrem, are not contradictions that defeat the meaningfulness of the doctrines presented but are static words that reflect the dynamic and transformative nature of God's redemptive work, bringing lost humanity to paradise and into union with the Creator. These paradoxical ideas are best communicated in pictorial language. Ephrem's appeal to poetic forms in no way lessens his ability to address serious doctrinal matters. In the *Hymns on Faith*, Ephrem can write: "The sun's shining is no younger than [the sun itself], and there is no time when it was not. [Though] its light is second and its heat is third, they are neither less than it, nor are they the same as it."[40] Turned in the skilled hand of Ephrem, this analogy becomes a gem of almost endless theological meaning. While the sun is a heavenly body far removed from the earth, its light and heat are things experienced on earth. And so the Father is also transcendent and unknown except as the Son and Spirit reveal him to us.[41] As the sun ripens fruit, so the Holy Spirit matures believers.[42] Nonetheless, Ephrem seems to have little patience for the sophistry of the Greeks and their perpetual Trinitarian debates. Ephrem appeals to the image of Uzzah, who attempted to steady the Ark of the Covenant and was struck dead (see 2 Samuel 6:7). Ephrem writes: "Do not think that the faith, which steadies those cast down, is about to fall. Do not steady the faith like Uzzah, lest it destroy you in anger."[43] In his preaching, Ephrem seeks to communicate the truth of Scripture not in a way that is entangled by Greek philosophy but rather that is unfettered by the Spirit to perceive the meaning of the text immediately and unpretentiously: "Blessed is the one, my Lord, who has become worthy of believing simply."[44]

Ephrem's poetic sense is not limited to words alone. Ephrem experiments with poetic structures as well. The sixth of the *Hymns on Faith* is an acrostic, which surprisingly ends with the stanza on the letter *yod* rather than continuing

---

39. *Homily on Our Lord*, 2 (FC 91:273–274).

40. *Hymns on Faith*, 40.1 (FC 130:225). Ephrem explains elsewhere that, in this analogy, the Father is like the sun, the Son like the light of the sun, and the Holy Spirit is like the heat from the sun (ibid., 73.1 [FC 130:349]).

41. Ibid., 73.12 (FC 130:350).

42. Ibid., 74:9 (FC 130:353).

43. Ibid., 8.11 (FC 130:109–110).

44. Ibid., 3.3 (FC 130:68).

through the entire Syriac alphabet. The reader at first experiences perplexity at suddenly reaching the end of the poem, but the final words of the hymn make it clear that Ephrem's break from traditional acrostic form is entirely purposeful. The last stanza reads:

> O Jesus, glorious name!
> Hidden bridge for crossing
> From death to life!
> To you I have arrived and stood—
> By a *yod*—your letter—I am kept back.
> Be a bridge for my word,
> So that it might cross to your truth.
> Let your love serve as a bridge for your servant—
> In you I will cross to your Father.
> I will cross over and say, "Blessed is he
> Who has softened his strength through his Child!"[45]

In concluding the poem at the letter *yod*, Ephrem is communicating his unwillingness to enter into theological speculation beyond the revelation of Jesus, whose name is the first word in this stanza. Jesus represents the final truth that Ephrem pursues. In all of his allegorical interpretations—which modern readers may regard as whimsical and undisciplined—Ephrem's only professed goal is to find the spiritual elements that bring us to God through Jesus Christ. Ephrem exhorts the reader to pursue the symbols in creation and Scripture into the contemplation of God: "Be not lazy, O mind! Build bridges of the Spirit and cross over to your Creator!"[46] Jesus is the symbol through which God reveals his sacramental grace, his grace in the real world; Jesus is the bridge over which we cross to God and eternal life. Ephrem's assumed task in his homilies and hymns is to awaken the reader to God's revelation and to call the reader to eternal life in Christ.

CONTRIBUTIONS TO PREACHING

Saint Ephrem the Syrian stands as one of the most celebrated figures of the ancient church, not only in the East but also in the West. So famous was Ephrem among non-Syriac readers that he inspired an enormous corpus of pseudepigraphical

---

45. Ibid., 6.17 (FC 130:97–98).
46. Ibid., 75.21 (FC 130:358).

literature in Greek.[47] Ephrem's theology is communicated not through syllogisms but through a cornucopia of symbols—symbols mined from reflection on the metaphors in Scripture; symbols that elucidate pictorially the facets of the truths scattered throughout the sacred text. Ephrem's theology does not lend itself to argument; it is difficult to argue with a series of word pictures and paradoxes. The great strength of this form of preaching is its memorability and persuasiveness. Ephrem translated the technicalities of Nicene orthodoxy into something that people could remember and sing! In addition to its compelling force, Ephrem's poetic preaching also has a power to draw the listener directly into worship. Those who listen actively to this form of preaching find themselves in the act of worshiping God, for the preacher has already translated doctrine into confessions of the heart and declarations of emotion. Perhaps the most significant limitation of this form of preaching is the rarity of finding, in one person, equal giftedness in poetry and preaching. There is a simple reason that no other poet-preacher in Christian antiquity rose to the level of fame as Ephrem: none achieved the same virtuosity in theology and rhyme.

Ephrem's exact technique is perhaps not something modern preachers will be able to emulate; few will begin to preach in couplets! However, a careful study of the rich theology Ephrem communicates through his expertly crafted word pictures can inspire us to choose beautiful and significant mental images to frame theological truths. Ephrem's writing reflects little of the forcefulness of Roman law or the technicality of Greek philosophy. Rather, Ephrem calls his reader to plunge into the mystery and paradox of God's activity within humanity. With unparalleled skill and confidence, Ephrem invites us to experience God through reflection on beauty. Ephrem's homilies and biblical commentaries are bejeweled with eloquent symbols, and Ephrem brings these symbols before us not merely for purposes of illustration; these symbols represent the animating logic of Ephrem's theology. It may at first seem counterintuitive that theology can be expressed in the form of a poem, but anyone who has meditated through the Psalms or reflected on the hymns of Charles Wesley knows that poetry can be not only a memorable medium for communicating theological truth but in fact a precise instrument for mirroring the intricacies of certain biblical doctrines. Evagrius of Pontus once wrote: "If you are a theologian, you will pray in truth; if you pray in truth, you will be a theologian."[48] Prayer is not pure syllogism; prayer is a dialogue

---

47. Sebastian Brock comments wryly: "In Greek as in Syriac, Ephrem soon suffered the consequences of popularity by having numerous works attributed to him which he had never written" ("The Changing Faces of St. Ephrem as Read in the West," in *Abba: The Tradition of Orthodoxy in the West*, 66).

48. Quoted from Brock, "The Poet as Theologian," 243.

with the divine. Ephrem models for us a way of doing theology that begins to resemble the dynamics and ecstasy of prayer.

Jacob of Sarug characterized Ephrem as "a marvelous rhetor . . . who could include a thousand subjects in a single speech."[49] Sebastian Brock also praises Ephrem's method of preaching for its power to overcome virtually all boundaries:

> St. Ephrem's mode of theological discussion, essentially Biblical and Semitic in character, thus stands in sharp contrast to the dogmatizing approach which, under the influence of Hellenistic philosophy, has characterized much of the Christian theology with which we are today familiar. Indeed it is precisely because Ephrem's theology is not tied to a particular cultural or philosophical background, but rather operates by means of imagery and symbolism which are basic to all human experience, that this theological vision, as expressed in his hymns, has a freshness and immediacy today that few other theological works from the early Christian period can hope to achieve.[50]

And yet, Ephrem viewed his poems and compositions as attending to concerns in his congregation. Ephrem sees his writings as setting up walls of protection for the people of God: "O Lord, may the works of your herdsman not be defrauded; I will not then have troubled your sheep, but as far as I was able, I will have kept the wolves away from them, and I will have built, as far as I was capable, enclosures of hymns for the lambs of your flock."[51] In this way, we can see how spiritually insightful and pastorally practical Ephrem's approach can be.

Sermon Excerpt

Hymns on Paradise[52]

Listen further
and learn
how lamps with thousands of rays
can exist in a single house,
how ten thousand scents

---

49. Quoted from Griffith, *Faith Adoring the Mystery*, 6.
50. Brock, *Hymns on Paradise*, 40.
51. Quoted from Griffith, *Faith Adoring the Mystery*, 9.
52. Brock, *Hymns on Paradise* 6.9–10, 13–15; 105–08.

can exist in a single blossom;
though they exist within a small space,
they have ample room
to disport themselves.
So it is with Paradise:
though it is full of spiritual beings,
it is amply spacious for their disportment.
Again, thoughts,
infinite in number, dwell
even in the small space of the heart,
yet they have ample room;
they neither constrict each other,
nor are they constricted there.
How much more will Paradise
the glorious
suffice for the spiritual beings
that are so refined in substance
that even thoughts
cannot touch them! . . .
I was in wonder as I crossed
The borders of Paradise
at how well-being, as though a companion,
turned round and remained behind.
And when I reached the shore of earth,
the mother of thorns,
I encountered all kinds
of pain and suffering.
I learned how, compared to Paradise,
our abode is but a dungeon;
yet the prisoners within it
weep when they leave it!
I was amazed at how even infants
weep as they leave the womb—
weeping because they come out
from darkness into light
and from suffocation they issue forth
into this world!

Likewise death, too,

is for the world

a symbol of birth,

and yet people weep because they are born

out of this world, the mother of suffering,

into the Garden of splendors.

Have pity on me,

O Lord of Paradise,

And if it is not possible for me

To enter Your Paradise,

grant that I may graze

outside, by its enclosure;

within, let there be spread

the table for the "diligent,"

but may the fruits within its enclosure

drop outside like the "crumbs"

for sinners, so that, through Your grace,

they may live! ♦

BIBLIOGRAPHY

Amar, Joseph P. *The Syriac Vita Tradition of Ephrem the Syrian.* In *Corpus Scriptorum Christianorum Orientalium.* Leuven: Peeters, 2001.

Athanasius of Alexandria. *On the Incarnation.* Trans. by John Behr. Crestwood, NY: St. Vladimir's Seminary Press, 2002.

Brock, Sebastian. "Eusebius and Syriac Christianity." Pages 212–34 in *Eusebius, Christianity and Judaism.* Edited by H. W. Attridge and G. Hatta. Detroit: Wayne State University Press, 1992.

_____, trans. *Hymns on Paradise.* Crestwood, NY: St. Vladimir's Seminary Press, 1990.

_____. "Introduction to Syriac Studies." Pages 1–33 in *Horizons in Semitic Studies.* Edited by J. H. Eaton. Birmingham: University of Birmingham, 1980.

_____. "The Changing Faces of St. Ephrem as Read in the West." Pages 65–80 in *Abba: The Tradition of Orthodoxy in the West.* Edited by John Behr, Andrew Louth, and Dimitri Conomos. Crestwood, NY: St. Vladimir's Seminary Press, 2003.

_____. *The Luminous Eye: The Spiritual World Vision of Saint Ephrem.* Rev. ed. Kalamazoo, MI: Cistercian, 1992.

_____. "The Poet as Theologian." *Sobornost* 7 (1977): 243–50.

Drijvers, Han J. W. "The School of Edessa: Greek Learning and Local Culture." Pages 49–59 in *Centres of Learning: Learning and Location in Pre-Modern Europe and the Near East.* Edited by Jan Willem Drijvers and A. A. MacDonald. Leiden: Brill, 1995.

Ephrem the Syrian. *The Hymns on Faith.* Trans. by Jeffrey T. Wickes. FC 130. Washington, DC: Catholic University of America Press, 2015.

_____. *Selected Prose Works.* Trans. by Edward G. Matthews Jr. and Joseph P. Amar. Edited by Kathleen McVey. FC 91. Washington, DC: Catholic University of America Press, 1994.

Ginzberg, Louis. *The Legends of the Jews.* Trans. by Henrietta Szold. Philadelphia: Jewish Publication Society of America, 1913.

Griffith, Sidney. *Faith Adoring the Mystery: Reading the Bible with St. Ephraem the Syrian*. Milwaukee: Marquette University Press, 1997.

Hilarion (Alfeyev) of Podolsk. "Theological Education in the Christian East: First to Sixth Centuries." In *Abba: The Tradition of Orthodoxy in the West*. Edited by John Behr, Andrew Louth, and Dimitri Conomos. Crestwood, NY: St. Vladimir's Seminary Press, 2003.

Jerome. *On Illustrious Men*. Trans. by Thomas P. Halton. FC 100. Washington, DC: Catholic University of America Press, 1999.

McVey, Kathleen E., trans. *Ephrem the Syrian: Hymns*. New York: Paulist, 1989.

Moffett, Samuel Hugh. *A History of Christianity in Asia*. Maryknoll, NY: Orbis Books, 1998.

Murray, Robert. "Ephrem Syrus." In *A Catholic Dictionary of Theology*. Nashville: Thomas Nelson, 1967.

Rilliet, F. "Ephrem the Syrian." In *Encyclopedia of Ancient Christianity*. Edited by Di Berardino. Downers Grove, IL: IVP Academic, 2014.

Vööbus, Arthur. *History of the School of Nisibis*. Louvain: Secrétariat du Corpus SCO, 1965.

_____. *Literary, Critical and Historical Studies in Ephrem the Syrian*. Stockholm: ETSE, 1958.

Basil of Caesarea
The Preacher as the Mouthpiece of Christ

JONATHAN MORGAN

Basil of Caesarea (330–379) was one of the most influential figures of the patristic era. Known as one of the Cappadocian fathers (along with his younger brother, Gregory of Nyssa, and their friend Gregory of Nazianzus), Basil made profound contributions to the theological development of the church, particularly concerning the person of Christ and the divinity of the Holy Spirit. Given his role, it is fitting that the first two ecumenical councils, focused as they were on Christology and Pneumatology, serve as bookends to Basil's life and career. Perhaps equal to Basil's contribution to the church's doctrine is his influence on Christian monasticism. In spite of his wealthy family and a promising career in rhetoric, Basil took up the ascetic life and became one of its most influential proponents. His celebrated *Rules* were profoundly influential in shaping later monastic communities. But beyond his reputation as theologian and ascetic, Basil is known for his preaching.

HISTORICAL BACKGROUND

Basil of Caesarea is no ordinary figure in Christian history. As one of the four Eastern "doctors of the church," he played a pivotal role in shaping the theological trajectory of the fourth century. A brilliant thinker, Basil was also practical. For him, the activity of one's mind was secondary in importance to how one lived.[1] As such, he wed together a keen intellect, extraordinary communication skills, integrity of character, and a call to live out Christian virtue. Of Basil's versatility, one scholar has noted: "Basil's accomplishments were manifold: he wrote instructions for monastic communities; he organized relief for victims of poverty and famine in Caesarea; he corresponded with major ecclesiastical and political figures as far apart as Alexandria and Rome; and, in letters, sermons, and theological treatises, he provided a snapshot of Christian doctrine in its formative period."[2]

---

1. Philip Rousseau, *Basil of Caesarea* (Berkeley: University of California Press, 1994), 27.
2. Andrew Radde-Gallwitz, *Basil of Caesarea: A Guide to His Life and Doctrine* (Eugene, OR: Cascade, 2012), 6.

Basil was born around 330, just five years after Nicaea and less than twenty years since the Edict of Milan which gave Christianity a status of legitimacy in the Roman Empire. His family was of the wealthy and socially well-connected class in Cappadocia (the central region in modern-day Turkey) with a rich heritage in the Christian community. His paternal grandparents had survived the persecution of Emperor Maximinus Daia. His parents were devout Christians who were known for their piety and virtue. They made sure to give their children a rich Christian upbringing.[3] Though Basil learned the Scriptures and Christian teachings at home, he received a traditional education, reading classical literature and learning the art of rhetoric.[4] When Basil was in his twenties, he travelled to Athens for more advanced studies, following the way of *paideia*, that is, cultural formation through the intellectual life.[5] According to his friend Gregory of Nazianzus, who had studied with him in Athens, Basil left the city after a few years to enter "a more perfect life," beyond what secular learning could offer.[6] Though he would always retain and often utilize much of what he had learned from his classical training for the edification of the church, Basil decided to devote himself to virtue and the study of Scripture within an ascetic context.

After a time of touring the Mediterranean to observe others living the monastic life, Basil went to Caesarea and was baptized. It was on account of his baptism that Basil renounced his career ambitions in rhetoric and dedicated himself to emulating the ascetics he had visited in the deserts. Eventually, Basil returned home near his family estate and cleared a place of solitude for himself and others to join him near the Iris River in order to pursue the Christian disciplines and biblical virtues. Within a few years, Basil would become a well-known mentor and guide to those aspiring after the monastic life throughout Caesarea. Many of his homilies, in addition to his celebrated works such as the *Morals, Longer Responses,* and *Shorter Responses* express Basil's vision for pursuing holiness within community.

While he had been a priest since at least 365, Basil became bishop of Caesarea in 370, a position he would hold for the rest of his life. Though he had become a

---

3. Aside from Basil, four of his siblings are known in Christian history. His younger brother, Gregory of Nyssa, is celebrated as one of the fourth century's most gifted theologians and prolific writers, and came to be known as one of the three Cappadocian Fathers. Their older sister, Macrina, is celebrated for her exceptional piety and wisdom as conveyed through Gregory's *Life of Macrina* and *On the Soul and the Resurrection.* Less well known, but nonetheless noteworthy are Naucratius, an ascetic who cared for the elderly, and Peter, bishop of Sebasteia. For a brief but helpful summary of Basil's family, see Radde-Gallwitz, *Basil of Caesarea,* 22–24.

4. Basil's father was also trained in rhetoric. This may, in part, account for the value Basil's family placed on classical education.

5. Rousseau, *Basil of Caesarea,* 28.

6. Gregory of Nazianzus, *Oration 43.24,* trans. Leo McCauley. FC 22 (New York: Fathers of the Church, Inc., 1953), 48.

public figure with all the responsibilities of church administration, Basil continued to receive questions from ascetics throughout the region.[7] He spent a good deal of time responding to inquiries about how to live the disciplined life, showing that while he was no longer an ascetic in physical circumstance, he was certainly one in spirit. In Basil's view, ascetic Christianity was genuine Christianity. There was no distinction between monks and "ordinary" Christians.[8] Throughout his ministry, Basil was celebrated for his excellent preaching. His sermons convey a zeal for knowing the Scriptures and living a life set apart from the world.

As with the other celebrated preachers in this series, we will explore and evaluate Basil of Caesarea's theology, method, and contributions to preaching. To do so we will draw on important homilies in Basil's corpus, as well as other writings in which he discussed the essentials of the vocation of preaching, the character of those who preach, and the characteristics of effective preaching.

THEOLOGY OF PREACHING

Basil's theology of preaching shares an interdependent relationship with his view of Scripture. He affirmed the nearly universal conviction among early Christians that Scripture is the inspired, unerring Word of God. The Bible, for Basil, was set apart from all other literature not only in its content, but also in its style and goals. In the first homily of his celebrated *Hexameron*, he affirms that the Scriptures are "the words of truth expressed not in the persuasive language of human wisdom, but in the teachings of the Spirit, whose end is not praise from those hearing, but the salvation of those taught."[9] He insists that the totality of Scripture is inspired and useful for the teaching and correction of its readers (or hearers), and that none of its words, "even as much as a syllable," is insignificant.[10] Teaching the Scriptures, therefore, is not a casual task, since the minister is expressing the very revelation of God. Basil's high view of Scripture, however, does not mean he endorses a naïve fundamentalism or wooden literalism in deciphering the meaning of the texts. He knew that, like all texts, the Scriptures must be interpreted with a spirit of humility and wisdom and through the lens of sound doctrine.

Thankfully, Basil's voluminous literary corpus, including sermons, letters, theological treatises, and other writings, makes it possible to determine his philosophy and method of Scriptural interpretation. Especially insightful

---

7. Radde-Gallwitz, *Basil of Caesarea*, 36.
8. Ibid., 38.
9. *Hex.* 1.1, 4–5.
10. *Hex.* 6.11, 101.

are Basil's remarks on the various methods of interpretation prevalent in his day, and how one should go about interpreting particular passages. On some occasions, for example, Basil favors a literal rendering of Scripture while criticizing the use of allegory. Allegory was an ancient literary tool used by many interpreters of the early church to uncover a hidden spiritual meaning that was not obvious from the plain, literal sense.[11] Some thinkers made heavy use of allegory[12] while others shied away.[13] Regardless, most biblical interpreters of the patristic period affirmed two basic senses (or layers) of meaning within the Scriptures, the literal and spiritual.[14] Though Basil acknowledged a spiritual sense within the Scriptures, and sometimes used allegory to uncover it, he often preferred a more literal reading.[15] Indeed, some texts, Basil confesses, need to be accepted "simply and without curiosity, following the meaning of Scripture."[16] In his ninth homily on the *Hexameron,* he is even more forceful concerning the abuses of allegory:

> I know the laws of allegory, although I did not invent them of myself, but have met them in the works of others. Those who do not admit the common meaning of the Scriptures say that water is not water, but some other nature, and they explain a plant and a fish according to their opinion. They describe also the production of reptiles and wild animals, changing it according to their own notions, just like the dream interpreters, who interpret for their own ends the appearances in their dreams. When I hear

---

11. For much of Christian history, particularly throughout the patristic and Medieval periods, biblical interpreters assumed that Scripture conveyed multiple layers of meaning. Thinkers such as Origen espoused three (literal, moral, spiritual) while writers like John Cassian affirmed four (literal, moral (or tropological), allegorical, anagogical). Most, at any rate, believed that divine revelation was not restricted to historical narrative or propositions. This is certainly true of Basil. See Hildebrand, *St. Basil the Great,* 55.

12. For example, see Origen. Note that Origen did not invent allegory. Allegory was a common way for Greek writers to interpret difficult passages of the poet Homer. Jewish exegetes such as Philo, a contemporary of Christ, made use of allegory to interpret the Pentateuch. Origen did, however, help popularize the use of allegory among Christian exegetes. For a fine study on the influence of Origen's hermeneutics on Basil, see Peter Martens, "Interpreting Attentively: The Ascetic Character of Biblical Exegesis according to Origen and Basil of Caesarea," in *Origeniana Octava: Origen and the Alexandrian Tradition,* vol. 2 (2003): 1115–1121.

13. For example, note the so-called "Antiochenes," Diodore of Tarsus and Theodore of Mopsuestia.

14. The "literal sense" was considered the plain, historical meaning, while the "spiritual sense" was broad and included all figurative interpretations including moral, allegorical, etc. Students interested in biblical exegesis in the early church should consult Manlio Simonetti, *Biblical Interpretation in the Early Church* (Edinburgh: T&T Clark, 1994); Frances Young, *Biblical Interpretation and the Formation of Christian Culture* (Cambridge: University Press, 1997); John O'Keefe and R. R. Reno, *Sanctified Vision: An Introduction to Early Christian Interpretation of the Bible* (Baltimore: Johns Hopkins, 2005); Lewis Ayres, " 'There's Fire in that Rain': On Reading the Letter and Reading Allegorically," in *Modern Theology* 28.4 (2012): 616–34.

15. Hildebrand, *St. Basil the Great,* 52–56. Hildebrand notes that Basil may have been influenced by his correspondence with Diodore, known for his preference for the literal, historical meaning of Scripture over tendencies to spiritualize the text.

16. *Hex.* 2.5, 29. It should be noted, however, that in this example, Basil is not discounting figurative or allegorical explanations in general, but for the specific interpretation of Genesis 1:2.

"grass," I think of grass, and in the same manner I understand everything as it is said, a plant, a fish, a wild animal, and an ox. "Indeed, I am not ashamed of the gospel."[17]

Basil's positive affirmation of the literal sense of Scripture may have been due, in part, to his focus on the practical needs of his hearers. Basil had little patience for theological abstractions or ethereal profundity (even though his theological sophistication is beyond dispute). Instead, he was interested in giving his hearers something they could understand and apply to their daily lives.[18] In one of his sermons, Basil admitted that the church gathered "does not expect a lecture on paradoxical concepts but seeks the resolution of problems with a view to edification."[19] Therefore, it is not surprising that Basil sometimes favored a more "straightforward" rather than figurative reading of the biblical text insofar as the plain sense often avoids more speculative interpretations, and is geared more toward practical appropriation.

At the same time, Basil was willing to employ allegory and other methods of interpretation when he deemed appropriate. A good example is his *Homily on Psalm 28* (LXX) where Basil noted that the occasion for the Psalm was the completion of the tabernacle. He then connected the occasion with verse one, citing the commandments to bring the offspring of rams as well as to bring glory and honor to the Lord.[20] After a brief consideration of the historical background and meaning of the passage, Basil encouraged his hearers to have a mindset which "contemplates the sublime and makes the law familiar to us through a meaning which is noble and fitted to the divine Scripture."[21] Basil went on to suggest that,

---

17. *Hex.* 9.1, 135. See further on in this same section where Basil warns against those who, through allegorical interpretations, "bestow on the Scripture a dignity of their own imagining."

18. Mark DelCogliano, "Introduction," in *St. Basil the Great: On Christian Doctrine and Practice* (Crestwood, NY: St. Vladimir's Seminary Press, 2012), 18–19. Cf. Nonna Verna Harrison, "Introduction," in *On Fasting and Feasts,* trans. Mark DelCogliano and Susan R. Holman (Crestwood, NY: St. Vladimir's Seminary Press, 2013), 29. Harris observes that Basil is "a profound theologian and biblical interpreter, but his concerns are always practical. And he took the lead in living by what he believed and teaching others to do the same." Richard Lim argues that Basil's decision to use or even criticize allegory was influenced by the level of sophistication among his hearers. Commenting on Basil's criticism and muted use of allegory in the *Hexaemeron,* Lim claims that "Basil is not categorically rejecting the allegorical method *per se,* but that, instead, he is warning his specific, and largely unsophisticated, audience not to abandon the literal meaning of scriptures in favor of more arcane spiritual meanings." See his "The Politics of Interpretation in Basil of Caesarea's *Hexaëmeron,*" in *Vigiliae Christianae* 44 (1990): 362.

19. *On the Origin of Humanity, Discourse 2* in Nonna Verna Harrison, *St. Basil the Great: On the Human Condition,* vol. 30 of *Popular Patristics Series.* (Crestwood, NY: St. Vladimir's Seminary Press, 2005), 8, 55. This homily and one other (*Discourse 1*) are believed to be the final two homilies appended to Basil's *Hexaemeron.* However, scholars debate whether these two homilies are from Basil's pen.

20. The LXX of 28:1 reads, "Bring to the Lord, sons of God, bring to the Lord offspring of rams, bring to the Lord glory and honor."

21. *Hom. Ps. 28* 1, 193. Interpreting a text according to its "fittingness" or "suitability" for the divine was a common trope among the fathers which often justified a spiritual interpretation of difficult passages over a

according to the spiritual meaning of the text, the tabernacle is not limited to a physical structure, and rams are not meant to indicate male sheep. Instead, the "tabernacle" represents human bodies, and the "completion of the tabernacle" represents the end of life for which we are to be prepared. We prepare ourselves (our "tabernacles") through godly works which bring "glory and honor" to the Lord. In turn, we will participate in glory and honor as our eternal reward. Likewise, the rams indicate the leaders of the church who guide the Lord's flock into the nourishment of the Holy Spirit and sound doctrine and keep them safe from evil snares.[22]

Basil employed other interpretive strategies as well, such as word association,[23] and was fond of drawing out moral lessons from biblical passages.[24] He was also comfortable with bringing the best science and cosmology of his day to bear on his interpretation of the Bible. At the same time, Basil steered clear of extremes: he was not interested in speculative flights of fancy or exegetical free-for-alls, nor did he allow human wisdom to trump or detract from divine wisdom.[25] Instead, his goal was to arrive at God's truth, revealed explicitly or implicitly, in the Bible. Therefore, one of his primary purposes of his theological exegesis was to point the hearer of the Scripture to Christ. A powerful example of his christological interpretation of Scripture is his *Homily on Psalm 44* where Basil deduced from the Psalm the doctrines of the incarnation and resurrection, as well as the narrative of Christ's baptism. In doing so, Basil followed the general patristic practice of seeing Christ on every page of Scripture.

For Basil, preachers of the gospel must not only know and reverence the Scriptures, but also understand how to interpret them. Preachers must recognize that divine revelation is deep and profound, though often packaged in simple language. As such, preachers should recognize both the literal and, when appropriate, spiritual meaning of the text. While Basil cautioned against idiosyncratic interpretations, he believed that as long as the derived meaning leads one to Christ

---

literal one. For example, passages depicting God in anthropomorphic terms called for a theological, rather than a literal, understanding, because such passages intend to teach something deeper (and everyone knows that God does not have a literal hand!). For an excellent study on this patristic axiom for the interpretation of Scripture, see Mark Sheridan, *Language for God in Patristic Tradition* (Downers Grove, IL: IVP Academic, 2015).

22. *Hom. Ps. 28* 1–2, 193–195.

23. The technique of "word association" occurs when the interpreter focuses on a key word from a passage, then scours the Scriptures to find more instances where that same word is used. The way the word is used in other texts informs its meaning in the text at hand. Basil does this on a number of occasions (e.g., his interpretation of "waters" in *Hom. Ps. 28* 4, 201–202). On patristic uses of associative strategies, see O'Keefe and Reno, *Sanctified Vision*, 63–68.

24. See especially his eighth homily of his *Hexameron*, where he offers a multitude of moral lessons one can learn from observing creation. The "moral" sense of Scripture was made popular among Christian exegetes by Origen.

25. For example, see *Hex.* 1.10, where he encourages the faithful to "let the simplicity of faith be stronger than the deductions of reason."

and the pursuit of holiness, the interpretation is acceptable. Thus, preachers must be grounded in sound doctrine and the wisdom that comes from the Holy Spirit in order to rightly divide the Word of Truth.

METHODOLOGY FOR PREACHING

Modern scholarship has witnessed recent translations of Basil's homilies, suggesting a growing interest in Basil as a preacher and in the form and substance of his sermons.[26] His methodology focused both on the character of the preacher and the proper goals and outcomes of the preaching.

The Required Character of the Preacher

Throughout his writings Basil discussed the quality of character one must have in order to preach the gospel. His *Morals, Shorter Rules,* and *Longer Rules* provided structures for the burgeoning monastic movement spreading throughout the Christian landscape. In the first of these works,[27] particularly rule seventy, we find a concentrated and penetrating analysis of the kind of person a preacher should be.[28] First, Basil indicated that a preacher is one who surrenders his will and agenda to God. Submission of this kind is marked by humility and dependence on God's leading and equipping. A preacher knows better than to rely on his own intelligence, intuition, training, or gifts. In his *Morals* 70.26, Basil admonished that "we should not think that we achieve success in preaching through our own devices, but we should rely entirely on God."[29] Even the timing and location for ministry is not for the preacher to decide. Basil claimed that no one should undertake to preach on his own initiative, but "wait for the time acceptable to God" and the assigned place for ministry.[30] Basil warned that, once engaged in the ministry of proclamation, preachers should resist using human devices that aggrandize oratorical skills, since this tends to obscure the grace of

---

26. There are forty-nine extant homilies on various topics in Basil's corpus. Recent English translations of collections of Basil's homilies include *St. Basil the Great: On Fasting and Feasting,* trans. Susan Holman and Mark DelCogliano; *St. Basil the Great: On Christian Doctrine and Practice,* trans. Mark DelCogliano; *St. Basil the Great: On the Human Condition,* trans. Nonna Verna Harrison. Basil's very important *Hexameron,* a series of nine homilies on creation, as well as thirteen of his homilies on the Psalms are published in *St. Basil: Exegetic Homilies,* translated by Agnes Way, FC 46 (Washington, DC: Catholic University of America Press, 1963).

27. References to the *Morals* are taken from M. Wagner's English translation in *Saint Basil: Ascetical Works,* FC 9 (New York: Fathers of the Church, Inc., 1950). The Greek edition is found in Migne's *Patrologia Graeca* 31, 700–888.

28. For an excellent summary of Basil's concept of preaching and the character of the preacher, with special reference to the material found in his *Moralia,* see Fedwick, *The Church and the Charisma of Leadership in Basil of Caesarea,* 77–100.

29. *Morals* 70.26, 180.

30. Ibid., 70.2, 164.

God and draw attention to the person speaking.[31] Attempts to impress crowds with smooth rhetoric are often driven by self-interest. Instead, preachers must abandon all forms of flattery and any desire for attention and instead act as if "speaking for the glory of God in his very presence."[32] Doing so provides a powerful antidote to vainglory. By glorifying God in his sermons, the preacher himself fades into the background and becomes the "lips of Christ."[33]

Second, preachers must be faithful in declaring "all the precepts of the Lord."[34] As tempting as it may be to soften the message to please hearers, Basil offered a stark warning: "They who, to please their listeners, neglect to give a frank presentation of the will of God become the slaves of those they would please and abandon service of God."[35] Basil insisted that preachers have a responsibility to proclaim the gospel in its fullness—the pleasant precepts as well as the hard teachings—even if the result is persecution and death.[36] This means that those who preach the gospel must be equipped with boldness and courage, recognizing that the ministry of proclamation can be a costly one. Further, faithfulness to the gospel means that the preacher has a role in helping preserve the church's identity. The church possesses history, culture, traditions, customs, and vocabulary that has characterized it from the beginning, and has distinguished it through the ages from other cultures, both religious and secular.[37] Basil was interested in preserving the doctrines and practices entrusted to the church rather than being innovative or original. He cared about, as Radde-Gallwitz puts it, "the public, shared language of the church—the grammar of its prayer, liturgy, and faith."[38] Preachers, then, are not called to be idiosyncratic or novel; they are called to guide the church faithfully, according to its scriptural mission and identity.

---

31. Ibid., 70.25, 179. It is important to note that Basil is not arguing for abandoning education for an anti-intellectualism. Any cursory reading of Basil's works reveals a deep, carefully trained mind at work, familiar with the philosophies and cultural thought forms of his day. However, having been trained in rhetoric in Athens from some of the world's best teachers, Basil seems to have been turned off by the hollow pursuits of vainglory through oratory. As Rousseau observes, in spite of Basil's classical training, he only allowed a limited degree of traditional skills to shape his sermons. He believed Christianity had its own traditions and rules for public speaking. Sermons were to spur hearers on to imitation and change in conduct, not to impress them with lofty speech. See Rousseau, *Basil of Caesarea*, 46–47.

32. *Morals* 70.22, 176.

33. *Homily On Psalm 44*, 283.

34. *Morals* 70.5, 166.

35. Ibid., 70.29, 181.

36. Ibid., 70.12, 170: "That all should be summoned to the hearing of the Gospel, that the Word must be preached with all candor, that the truth must be upheld even at the cost of opposition and persecution of whatever sort, unto death."

37. Paul Fedwick, *The Church and the Charisma of Leadership* (Toronto: Pontifical Institute of Mediaeval Studies, 1979), 93. Cf. Basil's *On the Holy Spirit* 7.16 for an example of his determination to maintain vocabulary and patterns of speech consistent with the Christian generations before him.

38. Radde-Gallwitz, *Basil of Caesarea*, 13.

Third, a preacher's lifestyle must be consistent with their message. Basil charged that the "preacher of the Word" must be "a model of every virtue by first practicing what he teaches."[39] For Basil, there was an unbreakable link between doctrine and practice. As Fedwick observes, Basil would have considered absurd the Augustinian notion of an abstract truth that is not necessarily expressed in one's conduct. If one who preaches the gospel does not live out what he preaches, that person is like an actor—one person on stage, but another person in real life. Those who proclaim the truth must exemplify the truth so that the hearers may experience the truth.[40]

Finally, Basil instructs that a preacher of the gospel must be endowed with love for their people. The love of a pastor shows itself through compassion for their flock in all circumstances.[41] Preachers must make themselves available to their people, striving to meet their needs and visiting them whenever appropriate.[42] Basil also directed that preachers should be especially attentive toward anyone who is "suffering distress of soul."[43] With these various instructions, Basil made clear that the priority of the preacher is the people of the church. Therefore, love, submission, faithfulness, and consistency are the hallmarks of a preacher's character, according to St. Basil.

The Goals of Preaching

Like most preachers, Basil sought to accomplish a number of aims through his preaching: encouraging his people to faithful living, helping them understand the meaning of Scripture, challenging them to a deeper understanding of God, and spurring them on to maturity. For the sake of convenience, however, it might be useful to group Basil's goals for preaching under two overarching categories: *doxology* and *discipleship*. That is, Basil contoured the style and content of his sermons in such a way that his hearers would be drawn into both worship and the pursuit of holiness.

While Basil often called his hearers to stand in awe of God, his exhortations to worship were especially common in his sermons on creation. He taught that the purpose of preaching on creation—from great celestial bodies to the tiniest of insects—was to point us to the glory and splendor of God.[44] In his *Homily on*

---

39. *Morals* 70.9, 168.
40. Fedwick, *The Church and the Charisma of Leadership*, 88. Cf. Basil sums up this sentiment well in his *Homily on Psalm 44* 17.11, 293: "But I believe that the spiritual garment is woven when the attendant action is interwoven with the word of doctrine."
41. *Morals* 70.18, 173–74.
42. Ibid., 70.16–17, 172–73.
43. Ibid., 19. 174–75.
44. *Hex.* 6.11, 103. For example, Basil declares that "in comparison with the Creator, the sun and moon possess the reason of a gnat or an ant. Truly, it is not possible to attain a worthy view of the God of the universe

Psalm 33 Basil proclaimed, "The deeper one penetrates into the reasons for which things in existence were made and are governed, the more he contemplates the magnificence of the Lord and, as far as lies in him, magnifies the Lord."[45]

Basil especially highlighted God's providence, creativity, power, and goodness in creation. He insisted that nothing that exists has come about by chance, and that nothing happens at random. God is omniscient and sovereign over every parcel of creation, and governs all activities—both good and bad—toward his desired ends.[46] Basil contended that when believers really ponder the intricacy and beauty of creation, it will engender amazement. Indeed, even when we consider insignificant parts of human anatomy, such as the eyebrow, "the whole day would not be sufficient" to speak of them.[47] Almost anticipating Anselm's famous dictum about God,[48] Basil exclaimed, "He is incomprehensible in greatness. Consider what a great thing is, and add to the greatness more than you have conceived, and to the more add more, and be persuaded that your thought does not reach boundless things."[49] In other words, when we study God's self-communication through what he has made, we will discover he is incomparably great. But Basil did not reduce the picture of God to mere power and glory; he emphasized the goodness of God through what he has made. In his sermon commemorating the martyr Julitta, he offered this doxology: "For our sake it rains, the sun shines, there are mountains and plains, and he has prepared for us places of shelter in the mountains even up to the highest peak. The rivers flow for our use, springs bubble up, the sea is open to us for trade, the mines for treasures. All that we enjoy, bestowed on us in all creation, we have around us through the rich and marvelous good of the creator."[50]

These few examples from Basil's reflections on creation demonstrate his concern to draw his hearers into the worship of God.

Basil was equally concerned to build up and encourage his flock in the pursuit of holiness. In his *Moralia*, Basil declared that the preacher's goal is to lead each of their congregants to perfection and full maturity in Christ while fostering conviction of sin in those who are disobedient.[51] Basil was an ascetic and honored the monastic way of life as the best means of attaining godliness.

---

from these things, but to be led on by them, as also by each of the tiniest of plants and animals to some slight and faint impression of Him."

45. *Hom Ps. 33* 16.3, 252–53.

46. *Hom. Ps. 32* 15.3, 232.

47. *On the Origin of Man, Discourse Two* 17, 64.

48. In his *Proslogion* 15, Anselm famously states that God is "that than which a greater cannot be thought."

49. *On the Origin of Man, Discourse One* 5, 34.

50. *On the Martyr Julitta* 6, 118 in *St. Basil the Great: On Fasting and Feasting.*

51. *Moralia* 70.30, 181 and 80.13, 200.

And though some of Basil's hearers would have been monks, he does not make a distinction between ordinary Christians and "super" Christians. Neither are there two distinct sets of ethics. Rather, his intention was that *all* Christians should take up ascetical practices in order to strive for perfection, though that might look differently among his many hearers. As Nonna Harrison observes, Basil believed Christians are called to a "radical reorientation and transformation in their mode of existence." Though he taught this to his monastic communities, "he really intended it for everyone and sought to reform the whole of society along these lines."[52] Regardless of the various vocations of the members of his flock, Basil urged his hearers to become "like God" insofar as one can reflect God's character of love and virtue.[53] After all, Basil noted, being like God, as far as that is possible, is what Christianity is all about for lay, monk, and clergy alike.[54]

Basil's exhortations to godliness were ubiquitous. Space does not permit a litany of examples, but his two homilies on 1 Thessalonians 5:17 are representative of his emphasis.[55] In these two complementary sermons, Basil explored the implications of Paul's commands to "rejoice always, pray continually, and give thanks in all circumstances" (1 Thess 5:16–18). Basil challenged two basic objections that implied living out these commands is impossible. The first objection runs thus: insofar as we are surrounded by a multitude of sorrows, sicknesses, tragedies, and trials, how is it possible to rejoice and give thanks in *all* circumstances? Who can rejoice in the loss of a child or the loss of reputation or the onslaught of persecution? The second objection asks whether it is physically possible to offer up verbal prayers at all times. Without ducking behind ambiguous language or mealymouthed platitudes, Basil faced these objections head-on.

First, Basil warned that anyone who suggests it is impossible to carry out a biblical commandment is guilty of blasphemy. If a commandment comes from God, it is possible to obey it.[56] Second, giving way to sorrow and grief in the face of hardship is proof that one is living according to the flesh. By contrast, Basil pressed, the "perfect soul" that desires the Creator over created things can "rejoice here and now in a beauty, joy, and delight not shaken by the twists and turns of sinful desire." The losses and setbacks that cause sadness for those who delight

52. Nonna Verna Harrison, "Introduction" to *St. Basil the Great: On the Human Condition*, 29. Cf. Fedwick, *The Church and the Charisma of Leadership*, 97.

53. *On the Origin of Humanity, Discourse One* 17, 44. Basil here is commenting on Jesus's command in Matt 5:48: "Be perfect, therefore, as your heavenly Father is perfect."

54. *On the Origin of Humanity, Discourse One* 17, 45. Basil asks rhetorically, "What is Christianity?" Then he answers his own question: "Likeness to God as far as is possible for human nature."

55. The two homilies, contained in *Saint Basil the Great: On Fasting and Feasting*, are titled *On Giving Thanks* and *On the Martyr Julitta*. In the second homily Basil celebrates the testimony of Julitta with a few remarks, then goes on to finish what he began in the first homily; teasing out the implications of 1 Thess 5:17.

56. *On Giving Thanks* 1, 97–98.

in the flesh will strengthen the joy of those who have put to death fleshly desires and bear the death of Christ in their lives.[57] Third, Christians can rejoice no matter what because of the eternal joy set before us. Basil did not say we must give *thanks* that a terrible event has occurred, but if we "set present suffering against future good" we will remain firm and steadfast in the face of disturbance.[58] This does not mean, however, that Christians cannot weep or express emotions—Basil was not a Stoic. Rather, Christians must express themselves in moderation. Jesus wept, Basil noted, but Jesus's example was to curb the passions among those who express them immoderately.[59]

Finally, Basil taught that to "pray without ceasing" does not mean we must physically mouth prayers twenty-four hours a day. Rather, it describes a lifestyle of praise, worship, dependence, and the sustained pursuit of virtue. Basil told his hearers to thank God for clothing when getting dressed, strength when eating a meal, the sun that gives its light during the day, and fire that illumines the evening.[60] Beyond frequent, impromptu prayers throughout the day, Basil taught that prayer encompasses all of life: "So then, you will pray without ceasing when you offer prayer that is not restricted to words but also uniting it with God in all that you do in life. Indeed, your life should become an unceasing and uninterrupted prayer."[61]

For Basil, preaching was neither intellectually ponderous nor aimless. Rather, preaching the gospel was shaped by specific outcomes. Basil exemplified proper goals of preaching in his own sermons. According to Basil, preaching involves drawing hearers to worship God and to pursue holiness that resembles God's character.

CONTRIBUTIONS TO PREACHING

From what we can gather from Basil's sermons and other writings, he offered several strategies for effective preaching through both instruction and his own example as a preacher. First, Basil observed that the word of God is sometimes hard to grasp. For the benefit of hearers, therefore, sermons should be brief yet substantive, concise, and easy to remember.[62] Basil had no room for dense verbiage or long-windedness that obscures the Word of God.

---

57. Ibid., 2, 98–99.

58. Ibid., 3,100; 7, 107.

59. Ibid., 5, 102–03. Cf. *On the Martyr Barlaam* in Ibid., 1, 131, where Basil observes that while the Old Testament figures wept aloud and wore sackcloth and ashes, Christians now celebrate the death of a saint with a party. "For the nature of grief has been reversed by the cross."

60. *On the Martyr Julitta* 3, 112.

61. Ibid., 4, 113.

62. *Homily on the Words "Be Attentive to Yourself"* 1 in *St. Basil the Great: On the Human Condition*, 93.

Second, Basil's sermons contain a striking degree of authenticity and genuine concern for connecting with his congregation. He exuded a humble, down-to-earth posture toward his people who were made up of diverse classes and occupations. Many in his flock were poor, and not a few were catechumens.[63] His sermons are seasoned with illustrations from regular, workaday life, geared to assist his hearers in understanding the biblical or theological point at hand. Basil can be refreshing to read, in that despite the depth and complexity of many of his topics, he did not get lost in ethereal speculations or theological abstractions, nor did he shy away from asking hard questions about the text he was discussing.[64] As Rousseau observes, Basil's "address was direct . . . and carries more conviction than the ruminations of his brother Gregory."[65] He was a man who knew his people and gave them what they needed.

This brief description of Basil's method of preaching reveals the value of connecting with one's audience. This means that preachers have to understand the daily joys, struggles, and questions of their parishoners. Further, sermons should be short and to the point in order to keep people's attention. This does not mean that sermons should be simplistic and shallow, however. Basil exemplified well that sermons can be down to earth and easy to remember while containing powerful theological substance.

CONCLUSION

Basil taught that those who preach the gospel are the "lips of Christ."[66] As the lips of Christ, preachers must possess virtuous character consistent with the virtues they preach. They must submit to God and the work of the church without any desire for personal accolades. Preachers must also understand the Scriptures and know how to unpack them for their hearers. The wise preacher, according to Basil, knows that the Bible is not one-dimensional, but is a spiritual work that weaves together several layers of meaning. Most important, the text points to Jesus Christ. Thus, to preach the Scriptures is to preach Christ. Further, Basil models how preaching should aim for both doxology and discipleship. Biblical preaching draws hearers to deeper worship of God and a passion for becoming more like God. Finally, effective preaching connects with those who listen. Sermons should not be long-winded or contain burdensome language, but should

---

63. Fedwick, *The Church and the Charisma of Leadership*, 7.

64. For example, see his *Homily Explaining that God is not the Cause of Evil* in Harrison, *St. Basil the Great: On the Human Condition*, 65–80.

65. Rousseau, *Basil of Caesarea*, xiii.

66. *Hom. Ps. 44* 4, 283.

be digestible and easy to understand. Yet sermons should never be superficial or trite. The one who proclaims the gospel must give his hearers doctrinal substance while crafting his discourse to a level that all can grasp. Throughout his sermons and other writings, Basil revealed a compelling theology of preaching. So celebrated was Basil as a preacher in his own day, that some of his sermons became templates for other preachers who would copy or adapt them to their own circumstances.[67] One may not agree with all of Basil's views, let alone use his sermons as models, but the example of this fourth-century theologian, ascetic, and preacher of Caesarea is worthy of admiration and emulation for those who minister in the church today.

Sermon Excerpt
On the Origin of Humanity[68]

In what sense are we according to the image of God? Let us purify ourselves of an ill-informed heart, and uneducated conception about God. If we came into being according to the image of God, they say, God is of the same shape as ourselves; there are eyes in God and ears, a head, hands, a behind on which to sit—for it says in Scripture that God sits—feet with which to walk. So is God not like this? Put away from your heart unseemly fantasies. Expel from your reason things not in accord with the greatness of God. God is without structure and simple. Do not imagine a shape in regard to him. Do not diminish the Great One in a Jewish way. Do not enclose God in bodily concepts, nor circumscribe him according to your mind. He is incomprehensible in greatness. Consider what a great thing is, and add to the greatness more than you have conceived, and to the more add more, and be persuaded that your thought does not reach boundless things. Do not conceive a shape; God is understood from his power, from the simplicity of his nature, not greatness in size. He is everywhere and surpasses all; and he is intangible, invisible, who indeed escapes your grasp. He is not circumscribed by size, nor encompassed by a shape, nor measured by power, nor enclosed by time, nor bounded by limits. Nothing is with God as it is with us. ✦

---

67. Susan Holman, "Introduction" in *St. Basil the Great: Feasting and Fasting*, translated by Susan Holman and Mark DelCogliano (Crestwood, NY: St. Vladimir's Seminary Press, 2013), 15.
68. *On the Origin of Humanity, Discourse 1.*

BIBLIOGRAPHY

Primary Sources and Translations

Defarrari, Roy Joseph, and Martin R. P. McGuire. *Basil: Letters*. Pages 190, 215, 243, and 270 in Loeb Classical Library. Cambridge: Harvard University Press, 1926–1934.

DelCogliano, Mark. *St. Basil the Great: On Christian Doctrine and Practice*. Vol. 47 of *Popular Patristics Series*. Crestwood, NY: St. Vladimir's Seminary Press, 2012.

DelCogliano, Mark, and Andre Radde-Gallwitz. *St. Basil of Caesarea: Against Eunomius*. Vol. 122 of FC. Washintgton, DC: Catholic University of America Press, 2011.

Harrison, Nonna Verna, trans. *St. Basil the Great: On the Human Condition*. Vol. 30 of *Popular Patristics Series*. Crestwood, NY: St. Vladimir's Seminary Press, 2005.

Hildebrand, Stephen. *St. Basil the Great: On the Holy Spirit*. Vol 42 in *Popular Patristics Series*. Crestwood, NY: St. Vladimir's Seminary Press, 2011.

Holman, Susan, and Mark DelCogliano, trans. *St. Basil the Great: On Fasting and Feasting*. Vol. 50 in *Popular Patristics Series*. Crestwood, NY: St. Vladimir's Seminary Press, 2013.

Migne, J.-P. *Patrologia Graeca* 29–32. Paris: J.-P. Migne, 1857; repr. Paris: Garnier, 1886; Turnhout: Brepols, 1959–1961.

Schroeder, C. Paul. *St. Basil the Great: On Social Justice*. Vol. 38 in *Popular Patristics Series*. Crestwood, NY: St. Vladimir's Seminary Press, 2009.

Wagner, M. Monica. *Saint Basil: Ascetical Works*. FC 9. New York: The Fathers of the Church, Inc., 1950.

Way, Agnes Clare. *Saint Basil: Letters*. Volume 1 (1–185). FC 13. New York: The Fathers of the Church, Inc., 1951.

_____. *Saint Basil: Letters*. Volume 2 (186–368). FC 28. New York: The Fathers of the Church, Inc., 1955.

_____. *Saint Basil: Exegetic Homilies*. FC 46. Washington, DC: Catholic University of America Press, 1963.

Studies

Ayres, Lewis. *Nicaea and its Legacy: An Approach to Fourth-Century Trinitarian Theology*. Oxford: Oxford University Press, 2004.

Bardy, Gustave. "L'homélie de saint Basile Adversus eos qui calumniantur nos." *Recherches de science religieuse* 16 (1926): 21–28.

DelCogliano, Mark. "Tradition and Polemic in Basil of Caesarea's Homily on the Theophany." *Vigiliae Christianae* 65 (2011): 30–55.

Fedwick, Paul. *The Church and the Charisma of Leadership in Basil of Caesarea*. Toronto: Pontifical Institute of Mediaeval Studies, 1979.

Fedwick, Paul, ed. *Basil of Caesarea: Christian, Humanist, Ascetic*. A Sixteen-Hundredth Anniversary Symposium. 2 vols. Toronto: The Pontifical Institute of Mediaeval Studies, 1981.

Hildrebrand, Stephen M. *Basil of Caesarea*. Grand Rapids: Baker Academic, 2014.

_____. *The Trinitarian Theology of Basil of Caesarea: A Synthesis of Greek Thought and Biblical Truth*. Washington, DC: Catholic University of America Press, 2007.

Leeman, Johan. "Martyr, Monk and Victor of Paganism: An Analysis of Basil of Caesarea's Panegyrical Sermon on Gordius." Pages 45–78 in *More than a Memory: The Discourse of Martyrdom and the Construction of Christian Identity in the History of Christianity*. Edited by Gert Partoens, Geert Roskam, and Toon Van Houdt. Leuven: Peeters, 2004.

Lim, Richard. "The Politics of Interpretation in Basil of Caesarea's *Hexameron*." *Vigiliae Christianae* 44 (1990): 351–70.

Marti, H. "Rufinus' Translation of St. Basil's Sermon on Fasting." *Studia Patristica* 16 (1985): 418–22.

Martens, Peter. "Interpreting Attentively: The Ascetic Character of Biblical Exegesis According to Origen and Basil of Caesarea." *Origeniana Octava: Origen and the Alexandrian Tradition*, vol. 2. (2003): 1115–21.

Radde-Gallwitz, Andrew. *Basil of Caesarea: A Guide to His Life and Doctrine*. Eugene, OR: Cascade, 2012.

Rousseau, Philip. *Basil of Caesarea*. Berkeley: University of California Press, 1994.

Sesboüé, Bernard. *Saint Basil et la Trinité: Un acte théologique au IVe siècle*. Paris: Descleé, 1998.

Silvas, Anna M. "The Emergence of Basil's Social Doctrine." Pages 133–76 in *Prayer and Spirituality in the Early Church*. Vol. 5 of *Poverty and Riches*. Edited by Geoffrey D. Dunn, David Luckensmeyer, and Lawrence Cross. Strathfield, Australia: St. Pauls Publication, 2009.

Smith, Richard Travers. *St. Basil the Great*. The Fathers for English Readers. London: Society for Promoting Christian Knowledge, 1879.

Van Dam, Raymond. *Becoming Christian: The Conversion of Roman Cappadocia*. Philadelphia: University of Pennsylvania Press, 2003.

John Chrysostom
Golden-Mouthed Preacher

PAUL A. HARTOG

John Chrysostom (ca. 349–407) ministered as a bishop in Antioch and Constantinople, where he became famous for his oratorical skills. He was trained in classical rhetoric, and his eloquence posthumously won him the epithet of "Chrysostom" or "Golden-Mouthed." He boldly called for distinctive Christian living and piety, and he denounced the abuses of the wealthy and powerful. His direct preaching eventually raised the ire of the imperial family, and he was deposed and died in exile. His moral commitment, liturgical refinement, and biblical commentary still remain influential. But his claim to fame remains his powerful oratory.

HISTORICAL BACKGROUND

John Chrysostom was a contemporary of the Cappadocians (Basil of Caesarea, Gregory of Nyssa, and Gregory of Nazianzus), and his ministry flourished during the so-called "golden age of early Christian literature."[1] According to Yngve Brilioth, "The history of the ancient church does not present a more thrilling life story."[2] John was born in Antioch on the Orontes, in the province of Syria, probably around AD 349.[3] His father was a civil servant in the Roman military government but passed away while John was still an infant. Anthusa, John's saintly mother, had him educated in the literary and oratorical traditions of Greek culture; John studied under Libanius, a distinguished rhetorician of the period.[4] An ancient

1. Hendrik F. Stander, "Fourth-and Fifth-Century Homilists on the Ascension of Christ," in *The Early Church in Its Context*, eds. Abraham J. Malherbe, Frederick W. Norris, and James W. Thompson (Leiden: Brill, 1998), 271.

2. Yngve Brilioth, *A Brief History of Preaching*, trans. Karl E. Mattson (Philadelphia: Fortress, 1986), 31.

3. J. H. W. G. Liebeschuetz, *Ambrose and John Chrysostom: Clerics between Desert and Empire* (Oxford: Oxford University Press, 2011), 124–25. His birthdate cannot be nailed down with exactitude (see Toivo Harjunpaa, "St. John Chrysostom in the Light of His Catechetical and Baptismal Homilies," *Lutheran Quarterly* 29 (1977): 168–69.

4. Jaclyn LaRae Maxwell, *Christianization and Communication in Late Antiquity: John Chrysostom and His Congregation in Antioch* (Cambridge: Cambridge University Press, 2006), 60. The ecclesiastical historian

testimony cites Libanius declaring that John ought to have been his successor "had not the Christians stolen him from us."[5]

John, however, sensed another calling. He was baptized in 368, and he may have served as an aide to Meletius bishop of Antioch, for three years.[6] Around this time John committed himself to ascetic living, including wearing a habit, remaining celibate, abstaining from meat and wine, and devoting himself to prayer.[7] John was made an ecclesiastical *lector* ("reader") at the age of twenty-three, but he refused to join the priesthood. Instead, he was tutored by an aged monk, lived for a time in monastic seclusion, and then resided for two years as a hermit in a cave on Mount Silpios. He committed himself to constant communion with God and to the memorization of both the Old and New Testaments.[8] The rigor of his ascetic lifestyle broke his health, however, and he returned to Antioch a few years later. John was named to the diaconate in 381, and five years later he was ordained to the priesthood (in AD 386).[9] His ministry among the churches of Antioch flourished over the next decade, and his congregation reveled in his splendid and powerful eloquence.

In 397, John was snatched from Antioch and taken to Constantinople, where he was named the new bishop. There he supported mission work among the Goths in the Balkans, including a Gothic translation of the Bible. His preaching engaged and enraptured the townspeople, but his ascetic tendencies met with opposition among the wealthy and powerful. He castigated the luxuries of the rich and influential, urging them to help the poor rather than spending money on lavish clothing and opulent living. His pointed preaching offended the Empress Eudoxia. At one point he even insinuated that she was a contemporary parallel to Jezebel.

Conflict erupted when John welcomed four Egyptian monks who had been opposed by Theophilus, the patriarch of Alexandria. Women of the imperial court, political leaders, and powerful clerics formed a coalition in opposition to John. Five years into his Constantinopolitan ministry, John was deposed and exiled, but was quickly recalled and reinstated after an earthquake and rioting. When renewed rioting broke out shortly after, on Easter Eve in 404, the situation escalated. Mobs invaded churches and desecrated them, and the emperor

---

Socrates adds that Chrysostom also studied philosophy under Andragathius (see Liebeschuetz, *Ambrose and John Chrysostom*, 118).

5. Quoted in O. C. Edwards Jr., *A History of Preaching*, vol. 1 (Nashville: Abingdon, 2004), 73; Jonathan Hustler, *Making the Words Acceptable: The Shape of the Sermon in Christian History* (London: Epworth, 2009), 29.

6. Liebeschuetz, *Ambrose and John Chrysostom*, 117.

7. Edwards, *History of Preaching*, 74. Socrates and Sozomen mention that Chrysostom and two friends received ascetic schooling under Diodorus and Carterius (see Liebeschuetz, *Ambrose and John Chrysostom*, 127–28).

8. Hustler, *Making the Words Acceptable*, 21.

9. Liebeschuetz argues that ecclesiastical politics in Antioch may have delayed Chrysostom's ordination to the priesthood (Liebeschuetz, *Ambrose and John Chrysostom*, 132).

published another order of exile. While being transported to a more remote location, John died on September 14, 407, at the age of fifty-eight.

John's remains were returned to the city of Constantinople a few decades later, where they were interned in the Church of the Apostles. By the sixth century, the epithet of "Chrysostom" ("Golden-Mouthed") had been attached to John's name.[10] Over the years, multiple biographies were disseminated. One *Vita* describes John Chrysostom as: "The blessed preacher and exegete and driver of the apostolic and orthodox faith, who taught fasting, proclaimed asceticism, rejected arrogance, praised humility, persuaded people to abandon the theaters and Olympic games and rush to the churches, and to forget lewd and dissolute songs in favor of learning by heart psalms and hymns and God's word."[11]

Over a thousand authentic works of Chrysostom survive, and more than a thousand more have been erroneously credited to him.[12] The delineation of "authentic" sermons is still not absolute, as the textual status of various homilies remains questionable (including the presence of both lacunae and interpolations).[13] The greater part of the extant Chrysostomic corpus consists of homilies.[14] In fact, more of his sermons survive than of any other church father.[15] A Greek Orthodox liturgy that is still in use is attributed to him and named after him.[16] Chrysostom's "enduring popularity is remarkable."[17]

CONTEXTS OF PREACHING

Chrysostom was "closely attuned to his listeners and their world," and he was "willing and able to adapt his teaching to them."[18] His audience in Antioch met in a large octagonal edifice. In Constantinople, the congregation assembled in a

---

10. Wendy Mayer, "John Chrysostom," in *The Wiley Blackwell Companion to Patristics*, ed. Ken Parry (Chichester: Wiley Blackwell, 2015), 141.

11. *V. Joh.* 74. As quoted in Mayer, "John Chrysostom," 148.

12. Mayer, "John Chrysostom," 141; Wendy Mayer, "John Chrysostom: Extraordinary Preacher, Ordinary Audience," in *Preacher and Audience: Studies in Early Christian and Byzantine Homiletics*, ed. Mary Cunningham and Pauline Allen (Leiden: Brill, 1998), 107.

13. Robert C. Hill, "St. John Chrysostom as Biblical Commentator: Six Homilies on Isaiah 6," *St. Vladimir's Theological Quarterly* 47 (2003): 307; Mayer, "John Chrysostom: Extraordinary Preacher," 108–9. See Nikolai Lipatov-Chicherin, "Preaching as the Audience Heard It: Unedited Transcripts of Patristic Homilies," *Studia Patristica* (2013): 277–97.

14. Catherine Broc-Schmezer, "Théologie et philosophie en predication: Le cas de Jean Chrysostome," *Revue de sciences philosophiques et theologiques* 97 (2013): 188.

15. Hustler, *Making the Words Acceptable*, 22.

16. Mayer, "John Chrysostom," 141. See Jean-Noël Guinot, "Prédication et liturgie chez Saint Jean Chrysostome," in *Prédication et liturgie au Moyen Âge*, edited by Nicole Bériou and Franco Morenzoni (Turnhout: Brepols, 2008), 53–77.

17. Mayer, "John Chrysostom," 142.

18. David M. Rylaarsdam, *John Chrysostom on Divine Pedagogy: The Coherence of His Theology and Preaching* (Oxford: Oxford University Press, 2014), 228.

magnificent Episcopal church.[19] His Constantinopolitan congregation included Greek, Syriac, Latin, and Gothic speakers, as reflected in their Psalm singing.[20] The socio-cultural environment in both cities was "politically turbulent," and assemblies in both localities were beset by schism, including the Arian-Nicene controversies.[21] As Robert Wilken notes, the urban context remained "a competitive religious environment, in which the loyalties and allegiances of Christians were constantly shifting."[22] Wendy Mayer reasons that Chrysostom's faction was not "necessarily dominant" in either city.[23]

At times, Chrysostom commented on the size of his audience, and how the makeup of the congregation would affect his sermon that day.[24] Motivations for attendance were undoubtedly mixed, including personal piety but also the popularity of Chrysostom's preaching, a dissatisfaction with other preachers in town, the desire to meet with friends or patrons or clients, the intent to make business connections or discuss politics, and the aspiration simply to be seen by others.[25] Some attendees made no claim to Christian belief.[26] But the congregation also included the devout, whom Chrysostom praised for their enthusiasm.[27]

Historians still dispute the socio-economic demographics of Chrysostom's congregations.[28] Chrysostom himself estimated that 10 percent of his Antiochene congregation came from the wealthy class and another 10 percent came from the poor, with the remainder living in between the extremes.[29] Chrysostom accordingly declared that his audience consisted of the wealthy and powerful, as well as slaves.[30] His sermons also mention "tradesmen, artisans, merchants and

---

19. David Dunn-Wilson, "John Chrysostom," in *A Mirror for the Church: Preaching in the First Five Centuries* (Grand Rapids: Eerdmans, 2005), 107.

20. Mayer, "John Chrysostom: Extraordinary Preacher," 125.

21. Dunn-Wilson, "John Chrysostom," 114; Liebeschuetz, *Ambrose and John Chrysostom*, 131–32. See Thomas Karmann, "Johannes Chrysostomus und der Neunizänismus: Eine Spurensuche in ausgewählten Predigten des antiochenischen Presbyters," *Sacris Erudiri* 51 (2012): 79–107.

22. Robert L. Wilken, *John Chrysostom and the Jews: Rhetoric and Reality in the Late 4th Century* (Berkeley: University of California Press, 1983), 30.

23. Mayer, "John Chrysostom: Extraordinary Preacher," 117.

24. Ibid., 132. There is no way of calculating exact numbers (Aideen M. Hartney, *John Chrysostom and the Transformation of the City* [London: Duckworth, 2004], 48).

25. Mayer, "John Chrysostom: Extraordinary Preacher," 133–34; Maxwell, *Christianization and Communication*, 108.

26. Hustler, *Making the Words Acceptable*, 20.

27. Maxwell, *Christianization and Communication*, 108.

28. Mayer, "John Chrysostom: Extraordinary Preacher," 116. See also Wendy Mayer, "Who Came to Hear John Chrysostom Preach?" *Ephemerides Theologicae Lovanienses* 76 (2000): 73–87.

29. Maxwell, *Christianization and Communication*, 69. See Aideen M. Hartney, "Men, Women and Money—John Chrysostom and the Transformation of the City." *Studia Patristica* (2001): 527–34; Wendy Mayer, "The Audience(s) for Patristic Social Teaching: A Case Study," in *Reading Patristic Texts on Social Ethics: Issues and Challenges for Twenty-First-Century Christian Social Thought*, eds. Johan Leemans, Brian J. Matz, and Johan Verstraeten (Washington, DC: Catholic University of America Press, 2011), 85–99.

30. Dunn-Wilson, "John Chrysostom," 102. See Chris L. De Wet, *Preaching Bondage: John Chrysostom and the Discourse of Slavery in Early Christianity* (Oakland: University of California Press, 2015); Maxwell, *Christianization and Communication*, 76–78.

laborers, shopkeepers, cooks and blacksmiths, shoemakers, plowmen, dyers, braziers, and soldiers."[31]

His congregants came from "a variety of educational backgrounds," but most of Chrysostom's hearers were less educated than he was.[32] However, he possessed a "rare ability to make the finer points of Christian doctrine" accessible to the less educated, delivering messages that were comprehensible to his hearers.[33] Sometimes, however, he lamented that his audience's lack of progress in Christian training prohibited him from going as deep as he wished.[34] Accordingly, he encouraged the more capable to be patient as he repeated or simplified concepts for others.[35] For instance, he remarked, "For those able to pay close attention, what has been said is already clear, just from my reading it. But since it is fitting for us to be concerned for all people . . . let me unveil the meaning of what I said more clearly and repeat the same words again."[36] He also recognized the inherent difficulties of discussing technical theological terms. "Therefore, I often avoid meddling with the results of this type of reasoning, because most people would not be able to follow these arguments."[37]

Weather conditions as well as special events in the city could affect church turnout.[38] Chrysostom often criticized his congregants for their irregular church attendance and for their preference for the theater and games.[39] He claimed they could memorize the lyrics of the theater or remember trivia about political leaders and events but could not retain his messages.[40] It is hard to know, however, whether Chrysostom's rhetoric reflects habitual practice or hyperbole for the sake of underscoring a rhetorical ideal.[41]

One of Chrysostom's pastoral concerns was the seriousness of worship.[42] He viewed worship as *sacrificium laudis* (a sacrifice of praise).[43] A normal service

31. Dunn-Wilson, "John Chrysotom," 102.

32. Maxwell, *Christianization and Communication*, 42, 90.

33. Hustler, *Making the Words Acceptable*, 21; Maxwell, *Christianization and Communication*, 67. See Peter Charles Moore, "Plain Talk with A Gilt Edge: An Exploration of the Relationship between 'Plain' Biblical Exposition and Persuasion in Chrysostom and Calvin," *Westminster Theological Journal* 73 (2011): 351–58.

34. Maxwell, *Christianization and Communication*, 98.

35. Ibid., 96.

36. *Hom. Gen.* 18.5. Quoted in Maxwell, *Christianization and Communication*, 97.

37. *Hom. Jo.* 4.2. Quoted in Maxwell, *Christianization and Communication*, 97.

38. Mayer, "John Chrysostom: Extraordinary Preacher," 130–31.

39. Dunn-Wilson, "John Chrysostom," 105. Although many attended both church and theater, pastoral objections to the latter included the sensuous female dancers and the male actors performing as females (Maxwell, *Christianization and Communication*, 52).

40. See Maxwell, *Christianization and Communication*, 42, 95. He emphasized the importance of memorization (Maxwell, *Christianization and Communication*, 104–7).

41. Mayer, "John Chrysostom: Extraordinary Preacher," 106.

42. Robert Taft, "St. John Chrysostom, Preacher Committed to the Seriousness of Worship," in *The Serious Business of Worship*, eds. Melanie C. Ross and Simon Jones (London: T&T Clark, 2010), 13–21; Liebeschuetz, *Ambrose and John Chrysostom*, 195.

43. Geoffrey Wainwright, "Preaching as Worship," *Greek Orthodox Theological Review* 28 (1983): 329.

included opening prayers, Scripture reading, and a homily in the first half, followed by the Eucharist in the second half. His homilies always ended with a brief prayer and a doxology.[44] In between the two halves of the service, the catechumens were instructed to leave, as they had not yet been initiated into the church's divine mysteries through baptism.[45] Chrysostom was not the only minister to preach to his congregation, and more than one preacher might homilize during a given service, especially on feast days and significant liturgical festivals.[46]

Chrysostom's sermons mention the audience breaking out in applause, outbursts, laughter, grumbling, shouts, and jeers.[47] He decried the chattering, joking, and even pick-pocketing that occurred during the services.[48] He contended, "The church is not a place of conversation but of teaching."[49] At the least, he insisted, congregants should remain quiet so as not to disturb others who were trying to pay attention.[50] He retorted that if his audience wished to act as if they were going to the bath or forum, "It would be better to stay at home."[51] He also lamented diversions during the services, even exhorting his congregants to focus instead of being distracted by the servant lighting the lamps.[52]

THEOLOGY OF PREACHING

Chrysostom's theology for preaching was grounded in his use of Scripture and was reflected in his homiletic themes. Thematically, he often returned to topics that highlighted Christian distinctiveness, including holy living, ascetic piety, and the proper approaches to material wealth and social recognition.

Use of Scripture in Preaching

Chrysostom insisted that all pastoral duties have one goal: "the glory of God and the upbuilding of the Church."[53] He delivered sermons based on biblical

---

44. Thomas K. Carroll, *Preaching the Word*, Message of the Fathers of the Church 11 (Wilmington: Michael Glazier, 1984), 120.

45. Hartney, *John Chrysostom and the Transformation of the City*, 33.

46. Mayer, "John Chrysostom: Extraordinary Preacher," 125–26. See Wendy Mayer, "At Constantinople, How Often Did John Chrysostom Preach?: Addressing Assumptions about the Workload of a Bishop," *Sacris Erudiri* 40 (2001): 83–105.

47. Mayer, "John Chrysostom: Extraordinary Preacher," 132; Taft, "St. John Chrysostom," 14.

48. Mayer, "John Chrysostom: Extraordinary Preacher," 132–33; Taft, "St. John Chrysostom," 16. Sextons placed placards along the church walls in Antioch, warning attendees about thieves who might rob their money pouches (Abe Attrep, "The Teacher and His Teachings: Chrysostom's Homiletic Approach as Seen in Commentaries on the Gospel of John," *St. Vladimir's Theological Quarterly* 38 [1994]: 293).

49. *Hom. 1 Cor.* 36.5–6. Quoted in Taft, "St. John Chrysostom," 16.

50. Maxwell, *Christianization and Communication*, 109.

51. *Hom. Act.* 29.3. Quoted in Taft, "St. John Chrysostom," 16.

52. Hustler, *Making the Words Acceptable*, 23.

53. Chrysostom, *On the Priesthood* 6.5. Quoted in Wainwright, "Preaching as Worship," 326.

books, homilies on saints' days and festivals, and treatises on Christian living. His homiletical corpus also includes catechetical and baptismal homilies.[54] Even in his topical sermons and initiatory homilies, Chrysostom's biblical rootedness remains evident.[55] He sometimes combined topical and expository approaches.[56] Panayiotis Papageorgiou insists that Chrysostom is *"par excellence* a preacher whose every thought springs forth from a biblical injunction or theme."[57] Chrysostom's twelve extant initiatory homilies purposed to change behavior through Scripture-based catechesis, and thus simply took scriptural authority for granted.[58] He expected his hearers to learn biblical materials, and he complained that some of them knew the names of race-horses better than the names of the churches the apostle Paul addressed in his epistles.[59]

Chrysostom was indeed a homilist and orator, but also a pastor and biblical commentator.[60] Behind Chrysostom's oratory stood careful biblical exegesis, which was based on "minute explanation of the texts."[61] Such exact precision in exegesis was known as *akribeia*.[62] His biblical homilies were sometimes structured in series or miniseries, although the exact provenance and nature of specific "series" have been debated.[63] Some of the sermon "series" may have been collated by editors or copyists, even though they were not originally preached in succession. Nevertheless, his habit was to deliver expository messages, often preaching sequentially through Bible books.[64] These expository sermons were

54. Harjunpaa, "St. John Chrysostom"; Pamela Jackson, "John Chrysostom's Use of Scripture in Initiatory Preaching," *Greek Orthodox Theological Review* 35 (1990): 345–66.

55. On Chrysostom's famous *Homilies on the Statues,* see David G. Hunter, "Preaching and Propaganda in Fourth Century Antioch: John Chrysostom's Homilies on the Statues," in *Preaching in the Patristic Age,* ed. David G. Hunter (New York: Paulist, 1989), 119–38; Frans Van de Paverd, *St. John Chrysostom, the Homilies on the Statues: An Introduction,* Orientalia Christiana Analecta 239 (Rome: Institutum Studiorum Orientalium, 1991).

56. Hustler, *Making the Words Acceptable,* 31; Jackson, "John Chrysostom's Use of Scripture," 345.

57. Panayiotis Papageorgiou, "The Paschal Catechetical Homily of St. John Chrysostom: A Rhetorical and Contextual Study," *Greek Orthodox Theological Review* 43 (1998): 95.

58. Jackson, "John Chrysostom's Use of Scripture," 348, 350.

59. Wainwright, "Preaching as Worship," 331–32.

60. Robert C. Hill, "St. John Chrysostom: Preacher on the Old Testament," *Greek Orthodox Theological Review* 46 (2001): 268.

61. Anne Marie Malingrey, as quoted in Thomas R. McKibbens, "The Exegesis of John Chrysostom: Homilies on the Gospels," *Expository Times* 93 (1982): 264–70.

62. Robert C. Hill, *"Akribeia:* A Principle of Chrysostom's Exegesis," *Colloquium* 14 (1981): 32–36.

63. Broc-Shmezer, "Théologie et philosophie en predication," 196–97, 199–202; Wendy Mayer, *The Homilies of St. John Chrysostom: Provenance. Reshaping the Foundations,* Orientalia Christiana Analecta 273 (Rome: Institutum Patristicum Orientalium Studiorum, 2005); Allen and Mayer have cautioned against reconstructions of Chrysostomic expositional series (and their provenance) that go beyond the direct evidence. See Pauline Allen and Wendy Mayer, "Chrysostom and the Preaching of Homilies in Series: A Re-Examination of the Fifteen Homilies in Epistulam ad Philippenses (*CPG* 4432)," *Vigiliae Christianae* 49 (1995): 271; Pauline Allen and Wendy Mayer, "Chrysostom and the Preaching of Homilies in Series: A New Approach to the Twelve Homilies in *epistulam ad Colossenses* (*CPG* 4433)," *Christiana Periodica* 60 (1994): 21–39; See also Hartney, *John Chrysostom and the Transformation of the City,* 41–42.

64. Hartney, *John Chrysostom and the Transformation of the City,* 41.

thus structured by the method of *lectio continua*, with a new sermon resuming where the previous one had ended.[65] Many of his homilies commence with a short summary of the previous message.[66] His exposition worked its way through biblical passages, offering explanatory comments.[67]

Chrysostom was less enthusiastic for allegorical interpretation than many of his contemporaries.[68] He did not entirely avoid typology, however, and made use of it as a sermon enhancement.[69] He believed that conversion, faith, and prayer were necessary for the proper understanding of Scripture.[70] Moreover, he assumed a responsible preacher would spend time in private study, preparing for his sermons.[71] He believed the preacher's responsibilities centered on explaining the Word of God and inculcating Christian habits.[72]

Chrysostom's sermons were commonly structured by introduction, then exegesis, then application to everyday life.[73] Thomas Carroll summarizes, "For Chrysostom, preaching was essentially the interpretation of a text from scripture and its application to a particular congregation."[74] The Word, vivified by the Spirit, must be applied in the present situation and to the issues of the day.[75] For this reason, the congregation should pray for the preacher and invoke the Spirit's empowerment.[76] Moreover, preachers are responsible to obey the same Word they preach, and they must give account for their ministry.[77]

THEMES IN PREACHING

Chrysostom addressed both personal ethics and public issues. Several themes weave their way through his sermons, which return to timely topics, no matter how much it "wearies him" or "disgusts his hearers."[78] In Robert Hill's estimation, common themes included "almsgiving, riches and extravagance, the dangers

65. Hustler, *Making the Words Acceptable*, 24.
66. Maxwell, *Christianization and Communication*, 92.
67. Hustler, *Making the Words Acceptable*, 25.
68. Edwards, *History of Preaching*, 73; James W. Cox, "'Eloquent . . . , Mighty in the Scriptures' Biblical Preachers from Chrysostom to Thielicke," *Review & Expositor* 72 (1975): 190.
69. Carroll, *Preaching the Word*, 116.
70. Wainwright, "Preaching as Worship," 330.
71. Ibid., 331.
72. Liebeschuetz, *Ambrose and John Chrysostom*, 185, 190.
73. Dunn-Wilson, "John Chrysostom," 112. "While the form is not invariable, these sermons are often in three parts with an introduction, a central exposition, and a closing exhortation" (Hustler, *Making the Words Acceptable*, 32).
74. Carroll, *Preaching the Word*, 114.
75. Wainwright, "Preaching as Worship," 333–34.
76. Ibid., 333.
77. Ibid., 336.
78. *Hom. Act.* 29. Quoted in Dunn-Wilson, "John Chrysostom," 108.

of the theatre and other secular amusements, disorder in church, hospitality, sloth and indifference."[79]

Wealth and Poverty

According to Aideen Hartney, "We can safely say that the concern with wealth was the great theme of all Chrysostom's preaching."[80] In David Dunn-Wilson's estimation, "Of all the ethical subjects treated in his sermons, it is to the theme of affluence and poverty that Chrysostom returns most frequently."[81] Chrysostom manifested an intense passion for the poor, and he acknowledged that he was "forever preaching about almsgiving."[82] Chrysostom tended to criticize the *nouveau riche* for their "fraudulent, aristocratic airs."[83] He was unafraid to confront the wealthy and powerful and to excommunicate the unrepentant, "be he prince, be he even a crowned head."[84] He rebuked ruthless estate owners and pitiless usurers.[85] And he condemned extravagant apparel and fine jewelry;[86] he criticized female parishioners who attended services in clothes more suited for a dance or court gala than for church worship.[87] When he castigated the silver chamberpots of wealthy women, he recognized that addressing such an earthy topic might upset some hearers.[88]

Ascetic Piety

Chrysostom declared to his congregation, "If I see you living in piety, I have all that I wish."[89] He constantly denounced drunkenness and swearing.[90] He also frequently attacked the theatrical entertainment of the day. The "filthy songs" of the theater are like "swine grunting on a dunghill," and the immoral plots "pluck up chastity by the foundations and encourage crime."[91] He berated his listeners who could not repeat a single psalm yet could belt out the lewd

---

79. Hill, "St. John Chrysostom," 282.

80. Hartney, *John Chrysostom and the Transformation of the City*, 44.

81. Dunn-Wilson, "John Chrysostom," 116. For examples, see Catherine P. Roth and David Anderson, eds., *St. John Chrysostom: On Wealth and Poverty* (Crestwood, NY: St. Vladimir's Seminary Press, 1984); Francine Cardman, "Poverty and Wealth as Theater: John Chrysostom's Homilies on Lazarus and the Rich Man," in *Wealth and Poverty in Early Church and Society* (Grand Rapids: Baker Academic, 2008), 159–75.

82. *Hom. Matt.* 88; *Hom. 1 Cor.* 43. See Dunn-Wilson, "John Chrysostom," 117; Gus George Christo, ed., *St. John Chrysostom on Repentance and Almsgiving*, FC 96 (Washington, DC: Catholic University of America Press, 1998).

83. Dunn-Wilson, "John Chrysostom," 102.

84. *Hom. Act.* 8. Quoted in Dunn-Wilson, "John Chrysostom," 107.

85. Dunn-Wilson, "John Chrysostom," 110.

86. Hartney, *John Chrysostom and the Transformation of the City*, 43.

87. Ibid., 44.

88. *Hom. Col.* VII. Quoted in Hartney, *John Chrysostom and the Transformation of the City*, 39.

89. *On the Statues* VI.19. Quoted in Dunn-Wilson, "John Chrysostom," 111.

90. Dunn-Wilson, "John Chrysostom," 114–15.

91. As quoted in Dunn-Wilson, "John Chrysostom," 115.

songs of the day.[92] But what especially peeved the bishop was when his congregants missed church for the sake of attending the theater and "the devil's show."[93] He charged, "The theater is a constant temptation; yet no one hesitates to go there nor remains away from it; no one alleges lack of time."[94]

He criticized those who followed after their favorite actors in the theaters and their favorite horses in the races.[95] Perhaps he even felt a sense of responsibility to hold the attention of churchgoers so that they would not be sidetracked by such worldly amusement.[96] Hartney reasons that Chrysostom "became adept at preaching exciting or well-polished sermons—especially on the days when he found his congregation diminished by some more secular attraction."[97] He hoped that "word would spread to those who had stayed away that they had missed a virtuoso performance, therefore encouraging them to be more diligent in their attendance, if only to appreciate his golden tongue."[98]

Christian Distinctiveness

In the post-Constantinian era, the boundaries between Christianity and paganism and between piety and superstition were becoming blurred.[99] In this context of compromise, Chrysostom insisted upon a distinctive Christian ethos. He spoke of a Christian transformation of habit leading to virtuous living.[100] He believed that Christians should reflect a moral distinctiveness in everyday living, including "their patterns of thought, their food, their clothes, their speech, their laughter."[101] Yet the laity were not called to cultural isolation. He declared, "I do not make it a law that you are to occupy the mountains and the deserts, but to be good and considerate and chaste, dwelling in the midst of the city."[102]

Many of Chrysostom's moral topics were "stock subjects," even in pagan moral treatises.[103] He assumed his hearers were capable of performing everything God required of them.[104] In fact, he could suffer from a moralism that

92. Dunn-Wilson, "John Chrysostom," 109.

93. *Hom. Evil Comes of Sloth* 1. Quoted in Dunn-Wilson, "John Chrysostom," 115.

94. *Inscrip. Altar.* Quoted in Carroll, *Preaching the Word*, 111.

95. *Contra ludos et theatra I.* Quoted in Hartney, *John Chrysostom and the Transformation of the City*, 48.

96. Hartney, *John Chrysostom and the Transformation of the City*, 51.

97. Ibid., 48.

98. Ibid.

99. Dunn-Wilson, "John Chrysostom," 106.

100. Jaclyn LaRae Maxwell, "Lay Piety in the Sermons of John Chrysostom," in *Byzantine Christianity*, vol. 3 of *A People's History of Christianity*, ed. Derek Krueger (Minneapolis: Fortress, 2006), 21.

101. Maxwell, "Lay Piety in the Sermons of John Chrysostom," 21.

102. *Hom. Matt.*7. Quoted in Maxwell, "Lay Piety in the Sermons of John Chrysostom," 29.

103. Maxwell, "Lay Piety in the Sermons of John Chrysostom," 20.

104. Liebeschuetz, *Ambrose and John Chrysostom*, 194. See Frances M. Young, "God's Word Proclaimed: The Homiletics of Grace and Demand in John Chrysostom and John Wesley," in *Orthodox and Wesleyan Scriptural Understanding and Practice*, ed. S. T. Kimbrough Jr. (Crestwood, NY: St. Vladimir's Seminary

emphasized the imperatives of changed behavior in a manner that overshadowed the indicatives of the gospel.[105] He did remind those who claimed weakness of will that "we have God *working with us* and *acting with us.*"[106] Yet the very fact that Chrysostom returned to certain themes implies he sensed the need to do so. Jaclyn LaRae Maxwell muses, "The congregation sometimes accepted and sometimes rejected the demands of the preacher, and this determined how they would live their lives, how their preacher could progress with his teachings, and ultimately how their society was Christianized."[107] It was inevitable, however, that his rigid sense of "Christian distinctiveness and purity" would earn him some "bitter and powerful enemies."[108]

METHODOLOGY FOR PREACHING

Public orators of the era were known for their "loud voices, gestures, and eye-catching appearance."[109] By contrast, Chrysostom is described as small of stature and emaciated, with a large and balding head, and a straggly beard and piercing eyes.[110] Yet his "personal charisma" was undeniable.[111] And he loved preaching, which he found invigorating. He declared, "When I begin to speak, weariness disappears; when I begin to teach, fatigue too disappears."[112] He could at times be "blunt-spoken, ill-tempered and harsh."[113] His candid and outspoken nature obviously affected his preaching style.[114] A later biographer describes the congregation's amazement that Chrysostom could preach with skill and polish without even a scrap of paper for scribbled notes.[115] He could at times preach entirely extemporaneously.[116] Chrysostom's style has been called "forthright, entertaining, and accessible."[117]

Press, 2005), 137–48; Peter C. Moore, "Chrysostom's Concept of γνώμη: How 'Chosen Life's Orientation' Undergirds Chrysostom's Strategy in Preaching," *Studia Patristica* 67 (2013): 351–58.

105. See Iain R. Torrance, "'God the Physician': Ecclesiology, Sin and Forgiveness in the Preaching of St. John Chrysostom," *Greek Orthodox Theological Review* 44 (1999): 173; Joel Pless, "Seven Pulpit Paradigms from the Prince of Preachers: John Chrysostom," *Wisconsin Lutheran Quarterly* 95 (1998): 193–96.

106. As quoted in Torrance, "'God the Physician,'" 171; italics original.

107. Maxwell, "Lay Piety in the Sermons of John Chrysostom," 38.

108. Dunn-Wilson, "John Chrysostom," 106.

109. Maxwell, *Christianization and Communication*, 44.

110. Dunn-Wilson, "John Chrysostom," 107.

111. Mayer, "John Chrysostom," 142.

112. As quoted in Carl A. Volz, "The Genius of Chrysostom's Preaching," *Christian History* 13 (1994): 24.

113. J. N. D. Kelly, *Golden Mouth: The Story of John Chrysostom—Ascetic, Preacher, Bishop* (Ithaca, NY: Cornell University Press, 1995), 222.

114. Hartney, *John Chrysostom and the Transformation of the City*, 47.

115. Ibid., 40.

116. Hustler, *Making the Words Acceptable*, 23.

117. Mayer, "John Chrysostom," 142. See Donald Heet, "Preaching: Entertaining or Entertainment?," in *Religion as Entertainment*, ed. C. K. Robertson (New York: Lang, 2002), 67–78.

Chrysostom's rhetorical training received under Libanius of Antioch continued with him, affecting his sermonic structure, content, and delivery.[118] At the same time, Chrysostom avoided a "slavish obedience to oratorical rules."[119] As a result, his style both resembled classical eloquence in some respects and differed markedly in others.[120] Chrysostom employed antithesis, comparison, metaphor, and rhetorical questions.[121] He also incorporated diatribe, stock phrasing, ring composition, and the personification of narrative characters.[122] Furthermore, he used *panaphora* (repetition), *reductio ad absurdum* (reduction to absurdity), and especially *ekphrasis* (vivid word-painting, bringing imagery to life).[123]

David Rylaarsdam explains that Chrysostom was "engaged in a complex process of image-making, image-breaking, and image-relocation."[124] Thus Chrysostom's preaching was "a factory of images," incorporating both biblical images and images from daily life.[125] He commonly used language and metaphors adopted from popular culture, even while inverting the culture's values.[126] Common sources included athletic, military, and nuptial imagery.[127] His use of accessible examples from daily life led to "relevant and vivid" illustrative material.[128] He drew verbal pictures of paupers sleeping in the furnace ashes outside the baths, gladiators drowning their sorrows in the taverns, and the wealthy gorging themselves at lavish feasts until their bowels ached.[129] His sermons are so conversant with the everyday life of his parishioners that they have become a goldmine for socio-cultural historians.

Rylaarsdam has argued that Chrysostom varied his preaching in three ways. First, he mixed sublime theology with elementary teaching. Second, he included pragmatic concessions within his strong ethical teachings. And third, he modulated the tone of his rhetoric.[130] His tone varied from severe to gentle, with the consistent goal of edifying listeners.[131] Both praise and condemnation were rhetorical tools in his pedagogical toolbox.[132] He sought to find the right timing in

---

118. Pauline Allen and Wendy Mayer, *John Chrysostom* (New York: Routledge, 2000), 27. See also Liebeschuetz, *Ambrose and John Chrysostom*, 127.

119. Dunn-Wilson, "John Chrysostom," 108.

120. P. J. Ryan, "Chrysostom: A Derived Stylist?" *Vigiliae Christianae* 36 (1982): 5.

121. Jackson, "John Chrysostom's Use of Scripture," 360, 365.

122. Hartney, *John Chrysostom and the Transformation of the City*, 47.

123. Dunn-Wilson, "John Chrysostom," 108.

124. Rylaarsdam, *John Chrysostom on Divine Pedagogy*, 229.

125. Ibid.

126. Ibid., 254–61.

127. Jackson, "John Chrysostom's Use of Scripture," 361, 363.

128. Dunn-Wilson, "John Chrysostom," 109.

129. Ibid.

130. Rylaarsdam, *John Chrysostom on Divine Pedagogy*, 270–74.

131. Ibid., 231.

132. Maxwell, *Christianization and Communication*, 109. See David M. Rylaarsdam, "Painful Preaching:

his delivery, as well as the right level of information.[133] He was neither a morally strident sophist nor an anti-intellectual populist.[134]

Chrysostom expected his audience to engage actively in the understanding and application of his preaching. He encouraged independent Bible reading and private study among his hearers, in order to reinforce his public messages.[135] He promoted the reading of Scripture with "earnest prayer" by the laypeople, "studying the prescribed passages before coming to worship and, afterward, reviewing the passages again with their families in the light of the sermons they have heard."[136] He also espoused family psalm singing (especially after meals), prayer at home, reflection upon the day's sins before bedtime, and regular almsgiving.[137] Even illiterate laypersons could "speak with a voice clearer than a trumpet" and thereby "win others by their lives."[138]

Chrysostom declared that "excellence in preaching should not be measured by the length of the sermon but by the interest of the congregation."[139] He knew that sometimes he was losing his audience's attention. At one point, he exclaimed, "But come now, rouse yourselves, as though I were just beginning my discourse, and pay attention to me with fresh minds. I would like to break off the discourse, but it will not allow me."[140] He implored, "But now do not become drowsy."[141] His messages refer to his hearers yawning, shuffling their feet, and expressing boredom on their countenances.[142] His homilies also mention churchgoers complaining aloud if he spoke too long on a topic.[143] He also received other specific criticisms, including spending too much time on his introductions.[144] Some acknowledged that he was a fine preacher but critiqued him for failing to visit his people.[145]

Chrysostom was concerned that the audience at times praised him for his rhetoric alone, and not for the content of his message. He lamented that many hearers did not change their day-to-day living, and many continued to find

John Chrysostom and the Philosophical Tradition of Guiding Souls," *Studia Patristica* 41 (2006): 463–68; Jaclyn LaRae Maxwell, "Pedagogical Methods in John Chrysostom's Preaching," *Studia Patristica* 41 (2006): 445–50.

133. Maxwell, *Christianization and Communication*, 92.

134. Rylaarsdam, *John Chrysostom on Divine Pedagogy*, 284. Jackson compared Chrysostom to the Second Sophistic (Jackson, "John Chrysostom's Use of Scripture," 354, 360).

135. Maxwell, *Christianization and Communication*, 115.

136. Dunn-Wilson, "John Chrysostom," 111. See Chrysostom, *Hom. Jo.* 21.1; 11.1; *Hom. Matt.* 5.1.

137. Liebeschuetz, *Ambrose and John Chrysostom*, 195. See Roth and Anderson, eds., *St. John Chrysostom*.

138. *Hom. Statues* 6.19; *Hom. 1 Cor.* 3.9. Quoted in Dunn-Wilson, "John Chrysostom," 111.

139. *Rule of Demons* 1.1. Quoted in Carroll, *Preaching the Word*, 126.

140. *Hom. Eph.* VII. Quoted in Hartney, *John Chrysostom and the Transformation of the City*, 38.

141. Ibid., 39.

142. Hartney, *John Chrysostom and the Transformation of the City*, 49.

143. Ibid.

144. Mayer, "John Chrysostom: Extraordinary Preacher," 130.

145. Wainwright, "Preaching as Worship," 334.

chariot racing more exciting than worship services.[146] He stated, "For the public are accustomed to listen not for profit, but for pleasure, sitting like critics of tragedies, and of musical entertainments."[147] Though he recognized that his hearers would sometimes admire his skillful oratory or polished rhetoric rather than his calls for life-transformation.[148] As Hartney explains, "They cheered when an argument was nicely phrased, enjoyed the vivid imagery employed by someone such as Chrysostom, and demanded a polished performance every week."[149]

Undoubtedly, audience members compared the performances of preachers and actors, and their applause in church sounded "disturbingly similar" to that of the theater, in Chrysostom's view.[150] He responded that his hearers would do better to heed his exhortations than to applaud them.[151] "What is the benefit of this applause to me, or what does the praise and fuss profit me? It will be my praise if you transmute all my words into deeds."[152] He therefore reminded his hearers that the church is not a theater for the sake of amusement, and he "deplored the practice of applauding the word of God."[153] At times, however, the more he upbraided his audience for applauding him, the more they applauded.[154] As Maxwell surmises, "Chrysostom emphasized that a preacher should say what was necessary rather than what would make him popular among the laity, and above all should try not to be affected by applause or lack thereof."[155] He therefore condemned preachers who bowed to popular pressure, "acting a preposterous and pitiable part, that they may please, and be applauded and depart with praise."[156]

Of course, not all of Chrysostom's sermons were deemed successful. Repetition was inevitable, and at times, he belabored his points.[157] Chrysostom also recognized that his hearers did not always follow his train of thought. But in one instance he claimed their confusion was due to their ignorance of Scripture and not to his speaking style.[158] Chrysostom realistically knew he would not reach every audience member, nor were visible results typically instantaneous.[159]

---

146. Liebeschuetz, *Ambrose and John Chrysostom*, 204.
147. *Sac.* 5.1. Quoted in Hartney, *John Chrysostom and the Transformation of the City*, 38–39.
148. *Hom. 1 Cor.* XIII. Quoted in Hartney, *John Chrysostom and the Transformation of the City*, 38.
149. Hartney, *John Chrysostom and the Transformation of the City*, 49–50.
150. Maxwell, *Christianization and Communication*, 54.
151. See Taft, "St. John Chrysostom," 14.
152. *Hom. Statues* II.4. Quoted in Carroll, *Preaching the Word*, 103–04.
153. See Cox, "'Eloquent,'" 190.
154. Ryan, "Chrysostom," 12.
155. Maxwell, *Christianization and Communication*, 62.
156. *Hom. Act.* 14. Quoted in Dunn-Wilson, "John Chrysostom," 108.
157. Ryan, "Chrysostom," 12.
158. *Hom. 1 Cor.* XXXIV. See Hartney, *John Chrysostom and the Transformation of the City*, 46.
159. Maxwell, *Christianization and Communication*, 110.

He lamented, "My work is like that of a man who is trying to clean a piece of ground into which a muddy stream is constantly flowing."[160] Yet he found satisfaction if even one hearer, including a slave, was moved toward faith or proper behavior.[161]

CONTRIBUTIONS TO PREACHING

Chrysostom authored the first known treatise on ecclesiastical ministry, titled *On the Priesthood*.[162] This work emphasized the maturity of character required to shepherd a flock, including the mastery of passions.[163] Rather than functioning as a homiletical textbook or a handbook of methodology, however, the resource serves more as a spiritual survival manual.[164] *On the Priesthood* concentrates more on the qualities of a preacher than the techniques of preaching.[165] He exhorted preachers to "apply the Word powerfully."[166] Quality preaching "does not come by nature but by study," he insisted, and the preservation of the gift of preaching requires "constant application and exercise."[167] In particular, Chrysostom soars as a model of biblical memorization, and his scriptural knowledge "powered his preaching to great heights."[168]

Doctrinal precision was key. He declared, "Let a man's diction be beggarly, and his verbal composition simple and artless, but do not let him be inadequate in the knowledge and careful statement of doctrine."[169] For Chrysostom, however, the recommended training of a pastor included more than just biblical and theological studies. For him, a classical education "was considered well-nigh essential for anyone hoping to be responsible for a congregation of immortal souls."[170] At the same time, Chrysostom denounced plagiarism, explaining that

---

160. As quoted in Kevin Dale Miller, "Did You Know? Little-Known and Remarkable Facts about John Chrysostom," *Christian History* 13 (1994): 2.

161. Maxwell, *Christianization and Communication*, 110.

162. In his *De viris illustribus*, Jerome stated, "Chrysostom is said to have composed many books, of which I have read only *On the Priesthood*" (*De viris illustribus* 129; as cited in Liebeschuetz, *Ambrose and John Chrysostom*, 123). See Neville Graham and T. Allen Moxon, eds., *St. John Chrysostom: Six Books on the Priesthood* (Crestwood, NY: St. Vladimir's Seminary Press, 1977).

163. See Joseph J. Allen, "The Relations of Shepherd and Flock," in *The Ministry of the Church: The Image of Pastoral Care* (Crestwood, NY: St. Vladimir's Seminary Press, 1986), 101–2. Allen recommends that Chrysostom's work should be read by everyone interested in pastoral ministry (Allen, *Ministry of the Church*, 115).

164. Dunn-Wilson, "John Chrysostom," 118.

165. Carroll, *Preaching the Word*, 98.

166. *Sac.* 4.3ff. Quoted in Dunn-Wilson, "John Chrysostom," 118.

167. *Sac.* 5.5. Quoted in Dunn-Wilson, "John Chrysostom," 118.

168. Robert A. Krupp, "Golden Tongue & Iron Will," *Christian History* 13 (1994): 7, 9.

169. *Hom. 1 Cor.* IV.6. Quoted in Carroll, *Preaching the Word*, 99.

170. Hartney, *John Chrysostom and the Transformation of the City*, 37.

the audience will condemn a preacher who weaves into his sermon "any part of other men's work," condemning him as if he were a robber.[171] He also insisted that one should develop homiletical skills, such as the avoidance of "stumbling, stopping short and blushing."[172]

Chrysostom warned that audiences may fawn over great orators, but they also tend to be fickle and may soon turn on the preacher (who may subsequently suffer catcalls and jeers).[173] An audience-pleasing preacher who has a passion for human praise "aims to speak more for the pleasure than the profit of his hearers."[174] Such a preacher may devolve into a mere entertainer. "That is the price he pays for rounds of applause."[175] Even idolized preachers may soon be forgotten has-beens, as crowds follow the latest and greatest.[176] Therefore, pastors must cultivate "indifference to praise," because those who "enter upon the trial of preaching, longing for applause" may only be greeted with heartache and pain in the end.[177]

Above all, the preacher must labor in his preaching so as to please God, seeking only his approval.[178] Preaching is a stewardship from God. "For this reason," explained Chrysostom, "the preacher must proclaim the divine word or sow the seed whether anyone listens to him or not, for God has entrusted to Him his treasures and will demand a reckoning. Thus I have reproached you, reprimanded you, prayed for you, and admonished you."[179] This attitude created an admirable fearlessness within the great "Golden-Mouthed" preacher. Without compromise, he upheld the "courage of his convictions."[180] In his final homily, he exclaimed, "What am I to fear? Is it death? Life to me means Christ and death is gain. Is it exile? The earth and everything it holds belongs to the Lord. Is it loss of property? I brought nothing into this world and I will bring nothing out of it. I have only contempt for the world and its ways and I scorn its honours."[181] Chrysostom's last recorded words were "Glory to God for all things! Amen."[182]

---

171. *Sac.* 5.1. Quoted in Dunn-Wilson, "John Chrysostom," 118–19.
172. *Sac.* 5.3, 7. Quoted in Dunn-Wilson, "John Chrysostom," 119.
173. See Dunn-Wilson, "John Chrysostom," 119.
174. *Sac.* 5.2. Quoted in Carroll, *Preaching the Word*, 100.
175. Ibid., 101.
176. See Dunn-Wilson, "John Chrysostom," 119.
177. *Sac.* 5.4. Quoted in Dunn-Wilson, "John Chrysostom," 119. See Richard Lischer, "Temptations of Greatness / John Chrysostom," in *The Company of Preachers: Wisdom on Preaching, Augustine to the Present* (Grand Rapids: Eerdmans, 2002), 57–63.
178. *Sac.* 5.3, 7. See Dunn-Wilson, "John Chrysostom," 119.
179. *On Anna* 5.1. Quoted in Carroll, *Preaching the Word*, 114.
180. Kallistos Ware, "More than a Great Preacher," *Christian History* 13 (1994): 38.
181. As quoted in Carroll, *Preaching the Word*, 127.
182. As quoted in Dunn-Wilson, "John Chrysostom," 120.

CONCLUSION

John Chrysostom's preaching was "without equal," and his career marks "a landmark in the history of preaching."[183] He has been called "the greatest pulpit orator and commentator of the Greek Church."[184] He has also been praised as "the greatest preacher of the early church."[185] He has even been labeled the "Demosthenes of Christian oratory."[186] But the influence of the "Golden-Mouthed" preacher goes beyond his powerful rhetoric. The liturgy he refined has been in continuous use since his day. His biblical commentary, especially on New Testament books, still informs critical commentaries.[187] Furthermore, his resolute commitment to his ideals and moral convictions continues to serve as an admirable example to follow in the midst of moral compromise and the abuse of power.

Sermon Excerpt

Second Homily on Eutropius 2–4[188]

"The grass withers and the flower fades; but the word of God abides forever."[189] Have you seen the insignificance of human affairs? Have you seen the frailty of power? Have you seen the wealth which I always called a runaway and not a runaway only, but also a murderer? For it not only deserts those who possess it, but also slaughters them . . . Why do you court wealth which can never be held fast? Do you desire to court it? Do you desire to hold it fast? Do not bury it but give it into the hands of the poor. For wealth is a wild beast. If it be tightly held it runs away; if it be let loose it remains where it is. "For," it is said, "he has dispersed abroad and given to the poor; his righteousness remains forever."[190] Disperse it then that it may remain with you; bury it not lest it run away. Where is wealth? I would gladly enquire of those who have departed. Now I say these

---

183. Volz, "Genius of Chrysostom's Preaching," 26; Hustler, *Making the Words Acceptable*, 20. For seven exemplary paradigms, see Pless, "Seven Pulpit Paradigms," 191–209.

184. Philip Schaff, ed., *Saint Chrysostom: On the Priesthood; Ascetic Treatises; Select Homilies and Letters; Homilies on the Statues*, vol. 9 of *Nicene and Post-Nicene Fathers* Series I (Grand Rapids: Eerdmans, 1956), 5.

185. O. C. Edwards, as quoted in Dunn-Wilson, "John Chrysostom," 118.

186. See Harjunpaa, "St. John Chrysostom," 170.

187. Hill, "St. John Chrysostom," 283.

188. English translation adapted from W. R. W. Stephens, trans., "Two Homilies on Eutropius," in vol. 9 of *NPNF* I, 350.

189. Isaiah 40:8.

190. Psalm 112:9.

things not by way of reproach, God forbid, nor by way of irritating old sores, but as endeavoring to secure a haven for you out of the shipwreck of others. . . . Well I do fasten upon the rich: or rather not the rich, but those who make a bad use of their riches. For I am continually saying that I do not attack the character of the rich person, but of the rapacious. A rich person is one thing, a rapacious person is another: an affluent person is one thing, a covetous person is another. Make clear distinctions, and do not confuse things which are different. Are you a rich man? I forbid you not. Are you a rapacious man? I denounce you. Do you have property of your own? Enjoy it. Do you take the property of others? I will not hold my peace. Would you stone me for this? I am ready to shed my blood, only I forbid your sin. I heed not hatred, I heed not conflict. One thing only do I heed, the advancement of my hearers. The rich are my children, and the poor also are my children. The same womb has travailed with both, both are the offspring of the same labor pangs. . . . Let him who wills cast me off, let him who wills stone me, let him who wills hate me: for the plots of enemies are the pledges to me of crowns of victory, and the number of my rewards will be as the number of my wounds. So then I fear not an enemy's plots. One thing only do I fear, which is sin. If no one convicts me of sin, then let the whole world make war upon me. For this kind of war only renders me more prosperous. Thus also do I wish to teach you a lesson. Fear not the devices of a potentate, but fear the power of sin. ♦

BIBLIOGRAPHY

Allen, Joseph J. "The Relations of Shepherd and Flock." Pages 97–124 in *The Ministry of the Church: The Image of Pastoral Care.* Crestwood, NY: St. Vladimir's Seminary Press, 1986.

Allen, Pauline, and Wendy Mayer. "Chrysostom and the Preaching of Homilies in Series: A New Approach to the Twelve Homilies *in epistulam ad Colossenses* (CPG 4433)." *Christiana Periodica* 60 (1994): 21–39.

_____. "Chrysostom and the Preaching of Homilies in Series: A Re-Examination of the Fifteen Homilies *in Epistulam ad Philippenses* (CPG 4432)." *Vigiliae Christianae* 49 (1995): 270–89.

_____. *John Chrysostom.* New York: Routledge, 2000.

Attrep, Abe. "The Teacher and His Teachings: Chrysostom's Homiletic Approach as Seen in Commentaries on the Gospel of John." *St. Vladimir's Theological Quarterly* 38 (1994): 293–301.

Brilioth, Yngve. *A Brief History of Preaching.* Trans. by Karl E. Mattson. Philadelphia: Fortress, 1986.

Broc-Schmezer, Catherine. "Théologie et philosophie en predication: Le cas de Jean Chrysostome." *Revue de sciences philosophiques et theologiques* 97 (2013): 187–212.

Cardman, Francine. "Poverty and Wealth as Theater: John Chrysostom's Homilies on Lazarus and the Rich Man." Pages 159–75 in *Wealth and Poverty in Early Church and Society.* Grand Rapids: Baker Academic, 2008.

Carroll, Thomas K. *Preaching the Word.* Message of the Fathers of the Church 11. Wilmington: Michael Glazier, 1984.

Christo, Gus George, ed. *St. John Chrysostom on Repentance and Almsgiving.* Fathers of the Church 96. Washington, DC: Catholic University of America Press, 1998.

Cox, James W. "'Eloquent . . . , Mighty in the Scriptures': Biblical Preachers from Chrysostom to Thielicke." *Review & Expositor* 72 (1975): 189–201.

De Wet, Chris L. *Preaching Bondage: John Chrysostom and the Discourse of Slavery in Early Christianity.* Oakland: University of California Press, 2015.

Dunn-Wilson, David. "John Chrysostom." Pages 102–120 in *A Mirror for the Church: Preaching in the First Five Centuries.* Grand Rapids: Eerdmans, 2005.

Edwards, O. C., Jr. *A History of Preaching.* Vol. 1. Nashville: Abingdon, 2004.

Graham, Neville, and T. Allen Moxon, eds. *St. John Chrysostom: Six Books on the Priesthood.* Crestwood, NY: St. Vladimir's Seminary Press, 1977.

Guinot, Jean-Noël. "Prédication et liturgie chez Saint Jean Chrysostome." Pages 53–77 in *Prédication et liturgie au Moyen Âge.* Edited by Nicole Bériou and Franco Morenzoni. Turnhout: Brepols, 2008.

Harjunpaa, Toivo. "St. John Chrysostom in the Light of His Catechetical and Baptismal Homilies." *Lutheran Quarterly* 29 (1977): 167–95.

Hartney, Aideen M. *John Chrysostom and the Transformation of the City.* London: Duckworth, 2004.

――――. "Men, Women and Money—John Chrysostom and the Transformation of the City." *Studia Patristica* (2001): 527–34.

Heet, Donald. "Preaching: Entertaining or Entertainment?" Pages 67–78 in *Religion as Entertainment.* Edited by C. K. Robertson. New York: Peter Lang, 2002.

Hill, Robert C. "*Akribeia*: A Principle of Chrysostom's Exegesis." *Colloquium* 14 (1981): 32–36.

――――. "St. John Chrysostom as Biblical Commentator: Six Homilies on Isaiah 6." *St. Vladimir's Theological Quarterly* 47 (2003): 307–22.

――――. "St. John Chrysostom: Preacher on the Old Testament." *Greek Orthodox Theological Review* 46 (2001): 267–86.

Hunter, David G. "Preaching and Propaganda in Fourth Century Antioch: John Chrysostom's Homilies on the Statues." Pages 119–38 in *Preaching in the Patristic Age.* Edited by David G. Hunter. New York: Paulist, 1989.

Hustler, Jonathan. *Making the Words Acceptable: The Shape of the Sermon in Christian History.* London: Epworth, 2009.

Jackson, Pamela. "John Chrysostom's Use of Scripture in Initiatory Preaching." *Greek Orthodox Theological Review* 35 (1990): 345–66.

Karmann, Thomas. "Johannes Chrysostomus und der Neunizänismus: Eine Spurensuche in ausgewählten Predigten des antiochenischen Presbyters." *Sacris Erudiri* 51 (2012): 79–107.

Kelly, J. N. D. *Golden Mouth: The Story of John Chrysostom—Ascetic, Preacher, Bishop.* Ithaca, NY: Cornell University Press, 1995.

Krupp, Robert A. "Golden Tongue & Iron Will." *Christian History* 13 (1994): 6–11.

Liebeschuetz, J. H. W. G. *Ambrose and John Chrysostom: Clerics between Desert and Empire.* Oxford: Oxford University Press, 2011.

Lipatov-Chicherin, Nikolai. "Preaching as the Audience Heard It: Unedited Transcripts of Patristic Homilies." *Studia Patristica* (2013): 277–97.

Lischer, Richard. "Temptations of Greatness/John Chrysostom." Pages 57–63 in *The Company of Preachers: Wisdom on Preaching, Augustine to the Present.* Grand Rapids: Eerdmans, 2002.

Maxwell, Jaclyn LaRae. *Christianization and Communication in Late Antiquity: John Chrysostom and His Congregation in Antioch.* Cambridge: Cambridge University Press, 2006.

――――. "Lay Piety in the Sermons of John Chrysostom." Pages 19–38, 223–25 in *Byzantine Christianity.* Vol. 3 of *A People's History of Christianity.* Edited by Derek Krueger. Minneapolis: Fortress, 2006.

――――. "Pedagogical Methods in John Chrysostom's Preaching." *Studia Patristica* 41 (2006): 445–50.

Mayer, Wendy. "At Constantinople, How Often Did John Chrysostom Preach?: Addressing Assumptions about the Workload of a Bishop." *Sacris Erudiri* 40 (2001): 83–105.

――――. "The Audience(s) for Patristic Social Teaching: A Case Study." Pages 85–99 in *Reading Patristic Texts on Social Ethics: Issues and Challenges for Twenty-First-Century Christian Social Thought.* Edited by Johan Leemans, Brian J. Matz, and Johan Verstraeten. Washington, DC: Catholic University of America Press, 2011.

――――. *The Homilies of St. John Chrysostom: Provenance. Reshaping the Foundations.* Orientalia Christiana Analecta 273. Rome: Institutum Patristicum Orientalium Studiorum, 2005.

――――. "John Chrysostom." Pages 141–54 in *The Wiley Blackwell Companion to Patristics.* Edited by Ken Parry. Chichester: Wiley-Blackwell, 2015.

――――. "John Chrysostom: Extraordinary Preacher, Ordinary Audience." Pages 105–37 in *Preacher and Audience: Studies in Early Christian and Byzantine Homiletics.* Edited by Mary Cunningham and Pauline Allen. Leiden: Brill, 1998.

_____. "Who Came to Hear John Chrysostom Preach?" *Ephemerides Theologicae Lovanienses* 76 (2000): 73–87.

McKibbens, Thomas R. "The Exegesis of John Chrysostom: Homilies on the Gospels." *Expository Times* 93 (1982): 264–70.

Miller, Kevin Dale. "Did You Know? Little-Known and Remarkable Facts about John Chrysostom." *Christian History* 13 (1994), 2–3.

Moore, Peter C. "Chrysostom's Concept of γνώμη: How 'Chosen Life's Orientation' Undergirds Chrysostom's Strategy in Preaching." *Studia Patristica* 67 (2013): 351–58.

_____. "Plain Talk with A Gilt Edge: An Exploration of the Relationship between 'Plain' Biblical Exposition and Persuasion in Chrysostom and Calvin." *Westminster Theological Journal* 73 (2011): 351–58.

Papageorgiou, Panayiotis. "The Paschal Catechetical Homily of St. John Chrysostom: A Rhetorical and Contextual Study." *Greek Orthodox Theological Review* 43 (1998): 93–104.

Pless, Joel. "Seven Pulpit Paradigms from the Prince of Preachers: John Chrysostom." *Wisconsin Lutheran Quarterly* 95 (1998): 191–209.

Roth, Catherine P., ed. *St. John Chrysostom: On Wealth and Poverty*. Crestwood, NY: St. Vladimir's Seminary Press, 1984.

Roth, Catherine P., and David Anderson, eds. *St. John Chrysostom: On Marriage and Family Life*. Crestwood, NY: St. Vladimir's Seminary Press, 1986.

Ryan, P. J. "Chrysostom: A Derived Stylist?" *Vigiliae Christianae* 36 (1982): 5–14.

Rylaarsdam, David M. *John Chrysostom on Divine Pedagogy: The Coherence of His Theology and Preaching*. Oxford: Oxford University Press, 2014.

_____. "Painful Preaching: John Chrysostom and the Philosophical Tradition of Guiding Souls." *Studia Patristica* 41 (2006): 463–68.

Schaff, Philip, ed. *Saint Chrysostom: On the Priesthood; Ascetic Treatises; Select Homilies and Letters; Homilies on the Statues*. Vol 9 of *Nicene and Post-Nicene Fathers* Series I. Grand Rapids: Eerdmans, 1956.

Stander, Hendrik F. "Fourth- and Fifth-Century Homilists on the Ascension of Christ." Pages 268–86 in *The Early Church in Its Context*. Edited by Abraham J. Malherbe, Frederick W. Norris, and James W. Thompson. Leiden: Brill, 1998.

Taft, Robert. "St. John Chrysostom, Preacher Committed to the Seriousness of Worship." Pages 13–21 in *The Serious Business of Worship*. Edited by Melanie C. Ross and Simon Jones. London: T&T Clark, 2010.

Torrance, Iain R. "'God the Physician': Ecclesiology, Sin and Forgiveness in the Preaching of St. John Chrysostom." *Greek Orthodox Theological Review* 44 (1999): 163–76.

Van de Paverd, Frans. *St. John Chrysostom, the Homilies on the Statues: An Introduction*. Orientalia Christiana Analecta 239. Rome: Institutum Studiorum Orientalium, 1991.

Volz, Carl A. "The Genius of Chrysostom's Preaching." *Christian History* 13 (1994): 24–26.

Ware, Kallistos. "More than a Great Preacher." *Christian History* 13 (1994): 36–38.

Wainwright, Geoffrey. "Preaching as Worship." *Greek Orthodox Theological Review* 28 (1983): 325–336.

Wilken, Robert L. *John Chrysostom and the Jews: Rhetoric and Reality in the Late 4th Century*. Berkeley: University of California Press, 1983.

Young, Frances M. "God's Word Proclaimed: The Homiletics of Grace and Demand in John Chrysostom and John Wesley." Pages 137–48 in *Orthodox and Wesleyan Scriptural Understanding and Practice*. Edited by S. T. Kimbrough Jr. Crestwood, NY: St. Vladimir's Seminary Press, 2005.

Augustine of Hippo
Agape-Driven, Christocentric Preaching

EDWARD L. SMITHER

"When I set out the Holy Scriptures for you, it's as though I were breaking open bread for you. You the hungry, come, get it . . .
What you eat, I eat. What you live on, I live on. We have in heaven a storehouse, for from it comes the Word of God."[1] These words very much captured Augustine's approach to preaching; he fed on the bread of God's Word and then he broke that bread for his congregation so they would be nourished as well. Following his conversion, Augustine (354–430) was enamored with the Scriptures and spent the last forty years of his life studying them, writing about them, and communicating them to others through preaching and teaching.

HISTORICAL BACKGROUND

Aurelius Augustinus was born in 354 in Tagaste (modern Souk Ahras, Algeria)—a small, insignificant town in Roman Africa. Though ethnically Punic-Berber, Augustine was culturally Roman and spoke only Latin. His father Patricius, a functionary in the local Roman administration at Tagaste, was an adherent to the traditional Roman deities, though he converted to Christianity at the end of his life. Augustine's mother Monica was a committed Christian who informally instructed her son in the Scriptures during Augustine's formative years. Though his parents differed on religious views for much of his growing-up years, they both agreed the key to Augustine's future was education, and they sacrificed to send him away to study. Eventually, Augustine completed his studies in rhetoric (communication) in Carthage, after which he taught the art of speaking in Carthage, Rome, and eventually Milan.

---

1. Augustine, *Sermon* 95.1 cited in William Harmless, *Augustine in His Own Words* (Washington, DC: Catholic University Press of America, 2010), 127.

While in Milan, Augustine, who had been a hearer or novice in the Manichean sect for nine years, came under the influence of Bishop Ambrose's (337–397) preaching and was converted to Christianity in late 386. He was baptized on Easter of the following year. Resolved to renounce the world and serve God, Augustine resigned his teaching post in Milan and returned to Tagaste in 388, intending to live out his days in the "holy leisure" (*otium sanctum*) of study, prayer, and contemplation.

Augustine's life course changed drastically in 391 when he agreed to be ordained as a priest at the church in Hippo (modern Annaba) in response to the urging of Valerius, the church's aging bishop. In 395, Augustine was ordained as cobishop of Hippo and then in 396 or 397, he became the church's sole bishop when Valerius passed away. Though Augustine's intent had been to pursue a life of monastic withdrawal in community with like-minded friends, he took the call to ministry seriously, and he remained Hippo's bishop until his death in 430. That said, Augustine continued to live as a monk while serving as a priest and bishop. He established a monastery in Hippo upon his ordination in 391, and when he became bishop, he turned the bishop's house into a monastery for the clergy. In this way, Augustine joined the ranks of a growing group of fourth- and fifth-century monk-bishops that included the likes of Basil of Caesarea (330–379) and John Chrysostom (349–407).

Today, Augustine is largely remembered and studied as a philosopher and theologian, although others have explored the significance of his pastoral ministry as well. Arguably his greatest legacy was his writings, which included some 117 books and over 250 letters.[2] His surviving works also include a corpus of about one thousand sermons, which will be the focus of this essay.

THEOLOGY OF PREACHING

Augustine was an active participant at the councils of Hippo (393) and Carthage (397), two fourth-century venues where the books of the canonical Scriptures were affirmed.[3] Augustine believed the canonical Scriptures were inspired, authoritative, and the basis for sound doctrine. In fact, he often used the terms canonical Scriptures and sound doctrine interchangeably.[4] Practically speaking,

---

2. For a concise list see "Augustine's Works," in Allen Fitzgerald, *Augustine through the Ages* (Grand Rapids: Eerdmans, 1999), xxxv-il. Cf. Possidius, *Life of Saint Augustine,* ed. John E. Rotelle (Villanova, PA: Augustinian Press, 1988), 11.5.

3. See his discussion of the canon in Augustine, *Teaching Christianity* 2.8.13.

4. Cf. Edward L. Smither, *Augustine as Mentor: A Model for Preparing Spiritual Leaders* (Nashville: B & H Academic, 2008), 238–44.

the Scriptures were the basis for his preaching in the worship assembly and also for his instruction of new believers.

Augustine was quite concerned with interpreting the Scriptures faithfully, and his hermeneutics were characterized by a number of values and principles, which are largely found in his work *Teaching Christianity (On Christian Doctrine)*. In terms of values, Augustine insisted that the preacher must first be spiritually prepared before beginning to study the Scriptures. He writes, "First of all, then, it is necessary that we should be led by the fear of God to seek the knowledge of His will . . . Next it is necessary to have our hearts subdued by piety, and not to run in the face of Holy Scripture."[5] In addition to this spiritual foundation, Augustine emphasized the use of certain tools in interpretation. For example, he commended knowledge of biblical languages (Hebrew and Greek) and also biblical geography, natural history, chronology, numbers, science, history, and philosophy.[6] One of the most striking aspects of Augustine's hermeneutics was the value of love. That is, the impetus for exegesis and its outcomes should be loving God and loving neighbor. Augustine went so far as to argue that even if a passage was misinterpreted, if love resulted, then it was an acceptable use of Scripture. He wrote: "Whoever, then, thinks that he understands the Holy Scriptures, or any part of them, but puts such an interpretation upon them as does not tend to build up this twofold love of God and our neighbor, does not yet understand them as he ought."[7] Augustine's warning—one very relevant for today—is clear: we have not truly understood the Bible until we have applied it in such a way that our love for God and neighbor is evident. In short, Augustine's hermeneutics were *agape*-driven.

Regarding his hermeneutical principles, Augustine was first persuaded that Scripture interprets Scripture. He believed that the Bible ultimately had one divine author and that there was continuity between the Old and New Testament. Asserting that we interpret the obscure in light of the clear, he added, "Now from the places where the sense in which they are used is more manifest we must gather the sense in which they are to be understood in obscure passages."[8] If clarity was still lacking, Augustine added that interpretive help could come through the rule of faith; the manner in which the church had been interpreting the Bible and summarizing it through creedal statements since the apostolic period. Defined by Bryan Litfin as "a confessional formula . . . that summarized orthodox beliefs

---

5. Augustine, *Teaching Christianity* 2.7.9. Unless otherwise indicated, all translations of Augustine's writings are from the *Works of Saint Augustine* series (Hyde Park, NY: New City, 1990–1997).

6. Ibid., 2.16.

7. Ibid., 1.36.

8. Ibid., 3.26.

about the actions of God and Christ in the world,"[9] in Augustine's day, the rule of faith was best articulated through the Nicene Creed.[10]

Augustine is also remembered for his allegorical interpretation of Scripture. He believed that in each text there was a literal meaning, a moral meaning, and most important, a hidden spiritual meaning. Augustine was certainly not alone in this approach to Scripture; Eastern fathers, such as Clement (d. 200) and Origen (185–254) and Western pastors, like Ambrose and Gregory the Great (540–604), interpreted Scripture in this way. In fact, it was Ambrose's allegorical exegesis that attracted Augustine to the Scriptures, and ultimately the gospel, in Milan. Augustine believed that allegory was necessary because the fall had marred people's ability to apprehend the Scriptures.[11] Also, like other church fathers, Augustine was certainly influenced by neo-Platonic philosophy, which rejected the idea of God having humanlike qualities or emotions like anger. So a text referring to the "arm of the Lord" or God's wrath in general must have another spiritual interpretation. One final benefit of allegory for Augustine was that it allowed the preacher to reach multiple interpretations of a single passage of Scripture. Though Augustine embraced allegorical readings of Scripture, at times, he opted for a more literal hermeneutic. For instance, after writing allegorical commentaries on Genesis (*On Genesis Against the Manicheans* and in Books 11–13 of his *Confessions*), he later produced a *Literal Commentary on Genesis.*

A final key principle of Augustine's hermeneutics was that Scripture should be interpreted in a christocentric manner. His presupposition was that the overall narrative of Scripture was oriented toward Christ and his saving work at the cross and that much of Scripture referred to Christ, even if it was not explicit. Hence, for Augustine, every passage of Scripture ought to be read in light of Christ's person and work. Relatedly, Augustine was convinced that Christians grew in their faith because ultimately, Christ was the church's great Teacher. Augustine expressed this well in *Sermon* 301A: "Now just when I speak to you from this elevated place [in the basilica], that does not mean that I am your teacher. That One—Christ—is the Teacher of us all, the One whose professorial chair sits above all the heavens. Under that One we come together, convening as a single school. And you and I—we are fellow students. But I'm here to advise you, just the way older students tend to do."[12]

---

9. Bryan Litfin, "Learning from Patristic Use of the Rule of Faith," in *The Contemporary Church and the Early Church,* ed. Paul A. Hartog (Eugene, OR: Pickwick, 2010), 79.

10. Augustine, *Teaching Christianity* 3.2.2.

11. Ibid., 2.1.1.

12. Augustine, *Sermon* 301A cited in Harmless, *Augustine in His Own Words,* 162.

MINISTRY OF PREACHING

As we seek to gain insight into Augustine's approach to and values for preaching, let us first offer a brief summary word on his preaching corpus and then pose three broad questions: (1) where did Augustine preach, (2) what were his occasions for preaching, and (3) what characterized his preaching style?

The surviving corpus of Augustine's sermons contains some one thousand messages that have been preserved in commentaries, treatises, and sermons.[13] However, based on what we know of his weekly preaching schedule, which typically included multiple sermons, what remains is merely a fraction of what he actually preached. One historian has estimated that Augustine probably preached eight thousand sermons during his lifetime.[14] His surviving sermons included over 124 sermons on John's gospel, later published as the *Tractates on John's Gospel*, and another ten on the first letter of John. Augustine also preached at least one sermon on each of the Psalms, and these were published separately as his *Exposition on the Psalms*. Augustine's largest group of sermons, also referred to as "Sermons to the People," included 548 messages collected from Augustine's weekly preaching in Hippo and elsewhere. In the last few decades, Augustine's surviving corpus of sermons has grown, as twenty-six sermons were discovered in 1980 and another eight were found in 2008.[15]

Context of Preaching

Augustine's preaching career began in Hippo shortly after his ordination as a priest in 391. In fact, one of the reasons Augustine was recruited by Bishop Valerius was because of Augustine's skills as an orator and because Valerius was not a native Latin speaker and struggled with the task of preaching. While the idea of having an assistant pastor involved in preaching may not seem strange to the modern reader, in the fourth-century African church, priests were forbidden from preaching due to the negative impact of the Alexandrian priest Arius (ca. 256–336), who had spread his heresy while tasked with preaching in Egypt. Valerius was not only unafraid of inviting controversy by going against this established African church practice, he also seemed to have an eye for talent and potential, especially when it benefited the faithful of Hippo.[16]

As a priest and later a bishop, most of Augustine's sermons were given to

---

13. See Daniel E. Doyle, "Introduction to Augustine's Preaching," in Boniface Ramsey, ed. *Saint Augustine: Essential Sermons* (Hyde Park, NY: New City, 2007), 10.

14. Harmless, *Augustine in His Own Words*, 124 n.8.

15. Harmless, *Augustine in His Own Words*, 124–25; also Eric Rebillard, "Sermones," in Fitzgerald, *Augustine through the Ages*, 773–92.

16. Cf. Smither, *Augustine as Mentor*, 111–24.

his congregation at Hippo. His primary preaching venue was Hippo's Basilica of Peace, which, at forty-one yards long and twenty yards wide, was one of the largest church facilities in North Africa. Some scholars have estimated that the basilica could hold as many as five hundred people, because the building had no pews and the people stood for the liturgy and the sermon. Many African churches in this period were constructed in a similar manner. As the people stood, the preacher sat on a special seat *(cathedra)* on an elevated apse. Flanked by priests, deacons, and others involved in leading the worship assembly, Augustine and other African preachers gave their sermons sitting down.[17]

Though the majority of his sermons were delivered at Hippo, Augustine preached at least 153 of his surviving sermons in eight other cities between 393 and 424. Most of these sermons were preached in Carthage when Augustine was there for one of the many African church councils that took place. Augustine was also invited to preach in other African churches, particularly those pastored by his former disciples from Hippo who had been set apart to ministries of their own. For instance, while preaching in a church in Bulla Regia in 399, Augustine jokingly told the congregation that their bishop "retained me, ordered me, pleaded with me, and forced me to speak with you."[18]

Occasions for Preaching

Like many other bishops in the fourth and fifth centuries, Augustine's preaching schedule followed the church year, so there are many surviving sermons preached during Holy Week, Easter, Pentecost, and Christmas. Also, Augustine preached special sermons on the feast days of saints, such as the African martyrs Perpetua and Felicitas (March 7) and Bishop Cyprian of Carthage (September 14).[19] In fact, when Augustine's "Sermons to the People" corpus was first compiled in the thirteenth and fourteenth centuries, it was organized around the church calendar.[20] As noted above, Augustine also preached extended series on John's gospel and probably the Psalms, as well as theologically oriented sermons against the Donatists and Pelagians.

Though no liturgical manual indicating a precise order of service has survived, we do know there were at least two parts to a worship assembly—a first part that was open to seekers and those not yet baptized, and a second part, which

---

17. See Augustine, *Sermon* 95.2; also Harmless, *Augustine in His Own Words,* 122–23.

18. Augustine, *Letter* 84.1; cf. Smither, *Augustine as Mentor,* 128–29, 208.

19. For more on Augustine's sermons commemorating Cyprian, see Edward L. Smither, "'To Emulate and Imitate': Possidus' *Life of Augustine* as a Fifth-Century Discipleship Tool," *Southwestern Journal of Theology* 50:2 (Spring 2008): 153–55.

20. Cf. Doyle, "Introduction to Augustine's Preaching," in Ramsey, ed. *Saint Augustine: Essential Sermons,* 11.

featured the Eucharist, that was only open to baptized believers. As Augustine's sermons were given in the first part, his messages were aimed at a broad audience who had very different levels of spiritual interest.

Outside of Holy Week, Augustine did not appear to preach from a fixed lectionary of biblical texts; however, there were typically four readings in a service: one from the Old Testament, one from the New, another from a Pauline epistle, and also a Psalm. As most believers in Hippo did not bring a personal Bible to church, the readings were sung by a lector—typically a teenage boy with a clear singing voice who was probably a member of Augustine's clerical monastery.[21] Finally, in addition to Sunday worship assemblies, Augustine also led a daily service in Hippo for members of the monastery as well as the believing community, so he actually preached several times during a given week.

METHODOLOGY FOR PREACHING

Augustine would often begin his sermons by referring back to the Scripture passages just read by the lector, and then he would ask the congregation to pray for him as he began the task of preaching.[22] Beyond this, what characterized his approach to preaching and his overall style?

First, Augustine's messages were saturated with Scripture. Beginning with references to the texts read by the lector, "Augustine's preaching can be described as a veritable medley of scriptural citations woven effortlessly throughout his homilies with the frequent and near seamless insertion of psalm verse."[23] Commenting on Augustine's conviction that sermons must be rich in biblical and theological content, Harmless adds, "First-time readers of Augustine are struck by his deep biblicism. Every page, every paragraph, is threaded with biblical quotations, biblical allusions, biblical images. Augustine did more than comment on the Bible: he *spoke* Bible, making its words his words."[24]

Of course, Augustine's favorite subject within Scripture was Jesus. Because of his noted hermeneutical values, his sermons were quite christocentric. Over one thousand times in his surviving corpus of sermons, he quoted or referred to the *logos* passage of John 1:1–14—more than any other preacher in the early church. Throughout other sermons, he made regular references to Christ as the Great Physician or the True Teacher.[25]

---

21. Ibid., 14.
22. Ibid., 15; see for example, Augustine, *Sermon* 153.1.
23. Doyle, "Introduction to Augustine's Preaching," in Ramsey, ed. *Saint Augustine: Essential Sermons,* 15.
24. Harmless, *Augustine in His Own Words,* 156.
25. Doyle, "Introduction to Augustine's Preaching," in Ramsey, ed. *Saint Augustine: Essential Sermons,* 13.

Augustine preached in a fourth- and fifth-century African church context that was quite oral, and even a bit rowdy, which is something stenographers copying his sermons could not always capture. The modern reader can also easily miss this when reading Augustine's sermons silently. Some of his sermons lasted more than two hours—something ancient listeners embraced, especially if the speaker was a skilled orator. Though Augustine prepared thoroughly to preach through prayer and study, his sermons were not drafted out, and he seemed quite free to improvise and even interact with his spirited congregation.[26]

Having been trained in the ancient art of rhetoric, Augustine put all those skills to work in his preaching. In *Teaching Christianity,* he defended this practice by asserting, "Since the art of rhetoric is about persuading people to things . . . who would dare say that the defenders of truth should stand their ground unarmed against falsehood?" He added that the "capacity for eloquence . . . is available" to those preaching God's Word.[27] Following Cicero's classic model of rhetoric, Augustine believed that the preacher's job was to teach (*docere*), delight (*delectare*), and to persuade (*flectere*).[28] He also referred to different styles of speaking available to a preacher, which he described as subdued, grand, and moderate. Augustine wrote, "Now in the subdued style, he persuades us that what he says is true; in the grand style, he persuades us to do what we know we should be doing but are not doing. But in the moderate style, he persuades us that he is speaking beautifully and elegantly."[29] While defending the use of rhetorical strategies in preaching, he was clear that eloquence was not the desired end but that changed lives were. He added: "The very reason we teach is that it be acted on, it is useless simply to persuade people about the truth of what we are talking about, and useless simply to entertain them by the way we speak, if what is said is not acted upon."[30]

As Augustine employed specific rhetorical strategies in his preaching, his key value was connecting with and engaging his audience. It is interesting to observe that his Carthage sermons were much more academic in content and appealed to a more educated, cosmopolitan audience. On the other hand, his Hippo sermons were simpler, and he used agricultural illustrations to connect biblical truths with daily life in the smaller town of Hippo and the rural context of Numidia. Frederick Van der Meer affirms, "In the pulpit he never used language that was above his

26. Ibid., 10–11, 13–15; see also Harmless, *Augustine in His Own Words,* 124; Augustine, *Sermon 96*; Augustine, *Teaching Christianity* 4.15.32.

27. Augustine, *Teaching Christianity* 4.2.3.

28. Doyle, "Introduction to Augustine's Preaching," in Ramsey, ed. *Saint Augustine: Essential Sermons,* 18.

29. Augustine, *Teaching Christianity* 4.13.29.

30. Ibid.

hearers' heads, but always chose his words in such a fashion that everyone would understand him."[31]

Augustine preached in a conversational and dialogical style. Addressing his hearers as "brothers and sisters" or "dearly beloved," he spoke to them directly in the second person ("you") and, at times, he called them to attention by saying "listen to me." He also posed questions to the audience in a highly interactive manner and even engaged in fake dialogues with biblical characters to illuminate the text he was preaching.[32] He often used humor and even sarcasm to make a point. He used repetition, tongue twisters, and rhymes to engage the audience.[33] For example, the rhyming in *Sermon* 220 makes his preaching sound like an ancient rap song:

> *Pro peccatoribus iustum* (the righteous for sinners)
> *Pro servis Dominum* (the master for slaves)
> *Pro captivis liberum* (the free for captives)
> *Pro aegrotis medicum* (the doctor for the sick).[34]

By employing these rhetorical approaches in his preaching, Augustine demonstrated that he preferred clarity and simplicity, to help his congregation grasp what he was teaching.[35]

CONTRIBUTIONS TO PREACHING

While many remember Augustine as a great philosopher or theologian, the aim of this chapter was to present Augustine at work in his "day job"—pastoring the church at Hippo, in which his primary task was preaching. His disciple and fellow bishop Possidius of Calama wrote that the ones who benefited most from Augustine's life and ministry were those "who were able to hear him speaking in church and see him there present."[36]

Although he known for his writing, Augustine's primary occupation as a bishop in Hippo was preaching. His preaching was driven by a love for the

---

31. Frederick Van der Meer, *Augustine the Bishop,* trans. B. Battershaw and G. R. Lamb (London: Sheed & Ward, 1961), 258.

32. Augustine, *Teaching Christianity* 4.10.25; also Doyle, "Introduction to Augustine's Preaching," in Ramsey, ed. *Saint Augustine: Essential Sermons,* 17.

33. Ibid., 17–19. For an example of tongue twisters, see Augustine, *Tractates on the Gospel of John* 5; for repetition, see Augustine, *Sermon* 212.

34. Cited in Harmless, *Augustine in His Own Words,* 132.

35. Doyle, "Introduction to Augustine's Preaching," in Ramsey, ed. *Saint Augustine: Essential Sermons,* 19.

36. Possidus, *The Life of Saint Augustine* 31.1. All translations are from Possidius, *The Life of Saint Augustine.*

Scriptures as he literally "spoke Bible." His approach to Scripture was shaped by a clear hermeneutic in which his chief values were a christocentric focus and love for God and neighbor as the desired outcomes. In terms of style, Augustine made no apologies for employing the skills of rhetoric to persuade his hearers so that, ultimately, they would experience transformation in the journey of faith. Augustine's preaching offers much for modern ministers to reflect upon and emulate today.

Sermon Excerpt

Sermon 188.1 (at Christmas)[37]

The Son of God: Now if we set about the great task of praising him as he exists with the Father—equal to and co-eternal with the Father, the One in whom all things, visible and invisible, in heaven and on earth, were established, God and Word of God, Life and Light of humanity—it is no wonder that no human thinking, no words, can suffice. For how can our tongues rightly praise the One whom our hearts do not yet have the health and vigor to see? For it is in our hearts that he put the eyes He can be seen with—if wrongdoing be purged, if weakness be healed—and so we may come to be those blessed clean-of-heart, "for they shall see God" (Mt. 5:8). It's no wonder, I say, we cannot find words that we might speak about the one Word [of God] who spoke us into being and about whom we seek to say something. For our minds may form words like these, pondered over and uttered forth, but our minds were themselves formed by the Word. Nor does a human being make words in the same way human beings are made by the Word, because the Father did not beget His one and only Word in the same way He made all things through the Word. For God begot God, but the Begetter and the Begotten are together one God. God certainly made the world; the world, however, passes away while God endures. And so these things that were made did not make themselves, but by no one was God made, the One whom by all things were made. It is no wonder, then, that a human being [like me], a creature in the midst of it all, cannot explain the Word through Whom all things were made. ♦

---

37. Augustine, *Sermon* 188.1 cited in Harmless, *Augustine in His Own Words*, 128.

BIBLIOGRAPHY

Augustine. *Sermons. Works of Saint Augustine, Part III, Volumes 1–11.* Trans. by Edmund Hill. Hyde Park, NY: New City, 1990–1997.

_____. *Teaching Christianity. Works of Saint Augustine.* Trans. by Edmund Hill. Hyde Park, NY: New City, 1996.

Doyle, Daniel E. "Introduction to Augustine's Preaching." Pages 9–22 in *Saint Augustine: Essential Sermons.* Edited by Boniface Ramsey. Hyde Park, NY: New City, 2007.

Fitzgerald, Allan. *Augustine through the Ages: An Encyclopedia.* Grand Rapids: Eerdmans, 1999.

Harmless, William. ed. *Augustine in His Own Words.* Washington, DC: Catholic University of America Press, 2010.

Liftin, Bryan, "Learning from Patristic Use of the Rule of Faith," Pages 76–99 in *The Contemporary Church and the Early Church: Case Studies in Ressourcement.* Edited by Paul A. Hartog. Eugene, OR: Pickwick, 2010.

Possidius. *Life of Augustine.* Edited by John E. Rotelle. Villanova, PA: Augustinian Press, 1988.

Smither, Edward L. *Augustine as Mentor: A Model for Preparing Spiritual Leaders.* Nashville: B & H Academic, 2008.

_____. "'To Emulate and Imitate': Possidus' *Life of Augustine* as a Fifth-Century Discipleship Tool," *Southwestern Journal of Theology* 50:2 (Spring 2008): 146–68.

Van der Meer, Frederick. *Augustine the Bishop. Church and Society at the Dawn of the Middle Ages.* Trans. by B. Battershaw and G. R. Lamb. London: Sheed & Ward, 1961.

PART *Two*

Preaching in the Medieval Ages

It would be a great mistake to pass from the end of the patristic era and run straight to the Reformation. To consent to the caricature of the medieval era as the "Dark Ages" would be an error of the worst sort and a misreading of the importance of the preaching of the medieval period.

Hughes Oliphant Old offers five characteristics that assist us in framing the preaching of the Middle Ages.[1] The first characteristic is variety. The Middle Ages span a thousand years. The period was notably different from what preceded and what followed it. The variety of the preaching mirrors, in some respects, the variety of the topography, the architecture, the cultures, and the centuries in which the preaching took place. This variety produced preachers such as **Bernard of Clarivaux** (1090–1153), who preached during the Second Crusade to foster a love and devotion to God.

A second characteristic of the preaching of this period was the increasing difficulty of biblical interpretation. With the fall of the Roman Empire and the barbarian invasions, it did not take long for the illiteracy rate to rise among the laity and clergy. As this problem became more widespread and standard, the development of the liturgy and liturgical calendar became the means of addressing the crisis. The liturgy became the context in which the Scriptures were read and preached, in lieu of the historical context in which they were written. Gradually the reading and preaching of the Scriptures took a back seat to liturgical symbols. It was this that the Franciscans and Dominicans took particular pains to rectify.

A third characteristic of the medieval preaching was the dominance of the liturgical calendar. Whereas in patristic preaching, expository preaching moved

---

1. Hughes Oliphant Old, *The Reading and Preaching of the Scriptures in the Worship of the Christian Church, Volume 3: The Medieval Church* (Grand Rapids: Eerdmans, 1999), Kindle edition, introduction.

from one biblical book to another, medieval preaching followed the liturgical calendar and texts were read in light of the calendar. This became the dominant form of preaching, intended to instruct the faithful in the faith. **Gregory the Great** (ca. 540–604) devised a lectionary in order to provide structure and maintain a certain level of biblical instruction at the Mass as a correction to the illiterate state of many parish priests. The church calendar became the organizing principle for sermons.

The fourth characteristic of medieval preaching was spiritual catechism. Spiritual catechism was developed in the monasteries to deepen the commitment and spiritual vitality of the monastic orders. The Franciscans and Dominicans specialized in a type of revival preaching (to use an anachronistic term) as they attempted to deepen the devotional life of the laity. **Francis of Assisi** (1181/2–1226) and **Bonaventure** (1221–1274) represented the Franciscan preaching order, understood their ministry as a preaching ministry, and emphasized a recovery of the Word in their preaching as a work of the Holy Spirit. **Meister Eckhart** (ca. 1260–1329) and **Johannes Tauler** (ca. 1300–1361) were mystical theologians and preachers of the Dominican Order.

The fifth characteristic was the development of the sermon outline. The sermon became formalized for ease of memory for the preacher and made it easier for the listener to follow along. Introductions were elaborate and colorful and the conclusions were designed to move and "affect" the listeners. The *exempla* (sermon illustration) became an art form unto itself. The friars were masterful at developing sermon illustrations that would hold the attention of their listener.

The medieval ages ended with the Protestant Reformation in 1517, but there were forerunners to this reformation. The chapter concludes with **John Huss** (1369–1415), a Bohemian who inspired Luther, and **Girolamo Savonarola** (1452–1498), a friar who preached against the opulence of his time with an apocalyptic voice and a call toward repentance. These two preachers, in different ways, call for reform and demonstrate the prophetic element in medieval preaching.

Gregory the Great

The Art of Arts as the Health of Souls

W. BRIAN SHELTON

S·GREGORIVS·I·MAGNVS·ROMANVS

Gregory the Great (ca. 540–604) stands tall on the landscape of Christian preaching because of his role and influence as the bishop of Rome. Few historical individuals exemplify the paradox of a high administrative office and the humble office of preaching simultaneously. His life is characterized by personal tension between service and contemplation, leadership and inwardness, and empire management with local congregational passion. His preaching legacy includes a memorable *Pastoral Rule* written to fellow clergy that instructs, charges, and demands the fulfillment of responsibility of the office of shepherd, especially through informed preaching. This *Rule* became a standard for pastors in the West for generations, while still providing instruction and conviction for the importance of a well-prepared, intelligent, and scriptural sermon that is needed in churches today.

HISTORICAL BACKGROUND

Gregory the Great (540–604) has long been seen as a pivotal figure at the juncture between the patristic and medieval eras. His ministry and influence embody both eras, providing a closing chapter to the church fathers and an opening chapter to the medieval papacy. The patristic style of his preaching with its medieval context of application is one quality among several that offer continuity between eras. The paradigm of his thinking is still premodern in thought, and understanding this era is important for understanding its preaching. At the same time, this transitional figure bridged two periods of church history by using the office of the bishopric of Rome to elevate piety, theological thinking, the monastic way of life, and ecclesiastical emergence over the life of the church.

The story of Gregory the Great begins with the renunciation of great personal wealth to become a monk. His parents were a wealthy couple of senatorial rank who seem to have displayed a life of Christian devotion. Serving as *perfectus urbi* in Rome, Gregory retired in 574 from public service as the highest-ranking official in Rome's civilian sector of administration when he committed himself to monastic endeavors. As a monk, he was appointed ambassador of the Roman bishop in Constantinople (578–585). After returning to Rome, he showed his experienced administrative abilities early on by founding St. Andrews monastery on the Caelian hill of Rome and six other monasteries in Sicily. He introduced the Benedictine rule to his monasteries, including committing members to the study of Scripture and preparing the church fathers to preach to the church community. The role of the minister as preacher was an important value that shaped Gregory's writings, primarily designing a training ministry for the monastic community members that was then projected onto the larger church of the Roman Empire. Drobner remarks, "He thereby augmented his secular education with an equally sound theological one, which was to be of benefit to him in managing his later office."[1]

The year 590 began with flood, famine, and plague in Rome. The death of Pope Pelagius II found Gregory amidst a ministry to the suffering of the city. The recognition of his mercy led to his election as bishop of Rome, a role in which he would serve for fourteen years until his death in 604. Gregory was reluctant to accept the position, but his motives seem to be pure: he longed for the *via contemplativa* of the monastic life over the service of *via activa* in the administration of the Office of the Holy See.[2] By AD 594, Gregory of Tours records that Gregory "wanted very much to avoid the highest honor, lest as a result of his being elected the worldly pomp which he had renounced should invade once more his public life."[3] Yet, he accepted the role, and his longing for the spiritual exercises did not seem to interfere with his administrative duties. Rather, the administrative duties gave opportunity to promote spiritual values through his influence.

One particular event seems to have shaped his call to the bishopric. Church tradition recounts how Gregory confronted the death effects of the plague in Rome by leading the city's church members to march around the city in appeal to God for mercy. While approaching the Castel Sant'Angelo, Gregory had a vision of the archangel Michael atop the edifice with his sword sheathed. It was taken as a sign of God's mercy against the plague.[4]

---

1. Hubertus R Drobner, *The Fathers of the Church: A Comprehensive Introduction* (Peabody, MA: Hendrickson, 2007), 512.

2. Ibid., 512, 519.

3. Gregory of Tours, *The History of the Franks* X.1 (New York: Penguin Books, 1974), 544.

4. For a treatment of the veracity of the vision, see Louis Schwartz, "What Rome Owes to the Lombards: Devotion to Saint Michael in Early Medieval Italy and the Riddle of Castel Sant'Angelo," International Congress for Medieval Studies Session 429, Western Michigan University, Kalamazoo, MI, May 10–13, 2012. He suggests the legend became fixated on the historical landscape of Rome just before the plague in the thirteenth century and in the efforts to strengthen the activities of Michael the archangel.

As bishop of Rome, Gregory saw himself as *servus sevorum dei*, "servant of the servants of God."[5] At the same time, his able administration, from England to Spain to the Rhine to North Africa, filled a power vacuum that had emerged in the West as the imperial power seat moved eastward to Constantinople as the capital of the Roman Empire. When the Lombard invasion pressured the Italian peninsula, Gregory, as a symbolic defender of the faith, negotiated settlements with the Lombard King Agilulf to protect Rome in 591 and 595. Not only was temporal intercessor an inherited charge for Gregory, but also the execution of spiritual authority across the church in the West. Gregory expanded the power of the Roman bishop as he exercised episcopal care over Europe and Africa and watched his able administration consolidate a union among churches. As a missions-minded administrator, Gregory was able to bring Spain under his authority when Recared, the Visigothic ruler, renounced Arianism for orthodoxy in 589. By sending a missionary named Augustine to Britain in 597, Gregory was instrumental in winning the English to Christ.[6] Along with Ambrose, Augustine, and Jerome, Gregory has been named one of the four great doctors of the church.[7] His ministry of the Word through preaching contributes to this legacy.

As an ordained monk, Gregory insisted that, of all roles in society one might play, the art of arts is the health of souls: *ars artium est regimen animarum*.[8] For that generation, the role of a parish priest or a monk in ministry to local community was a high calling. The role of bishop of Rome was no different; this administrative post was a role requiring the perpetuation of personal monasticism and of ecclesiastical values, such as preaching, sacraments, liturgy, and pastoral care. The result was that a spiritually dedicated monk took on the highest position of power, wielding authority for genuine spiritual reasons. For example, the liturgy was enhanced by his Gregorian chants, sung in a stately and solemn monotone that is chanted by monks during the Mass. Earl Cairns recognizes a medieval

---

5. Gregory applies this title to himself in letters, such as in his salutation of Epistle 1.1 to "All the Bishops of Ravenna."

6. The popular story goes that when he had visited the Roman Forum one day and saw the blond Angles on the slave block, he inquired about their race before remarking, "They have faces of angels and should be coheirs with angels in heaven." He inquired about their provenance to learn they were of Deira, saying, "They shall be saved from God's ire and call upon the name of Christ." He learned the name of their king to be Aelia and commented, "Then Alleluia must be sung in their land." From this incident that led to Gregory's commissioning of Augustine to Britain, the king of Kent was won for the faith.

7. Drobner lays out five areas of attention that lead to this moniker: (1) Gregory reorganized the Roman *curia* and administration under his leadership; (2) he showed responsibility for the representation of the Western church to the Eastern empire; (3) he showed responsibility for political and physical protection against the Lombards; (4) he brought Brits, Gauls, Franks, and North Africans into unity of the church; and (5) he wrote works that permanently shaped the ecclesiastical theology of the church, so that liturgy and chants he did not author would bear his name. Drobner, *Fathers of the Church*, 513–15.

8. Gregory, *Pastoral Rule* 1.1; *NPNF*², vol. 12b, p.1. The phrase finds its origin in Gregory of Nazianzen's *Oration* 2.

character to Gregory's theological positions, such as a softening of Augustine's teaching on predestination, the upholding of purgatory, giving credence to both scriptural inspiration and tradition, and attention to the invocation of saints. Also noting Gregory's emphasis on good works and his understanding of the Eucharist as being transubstantiated into Christ's actual body and blood during each celebration of the sacrament, Cairns concludes that "medieval theology bore the stamp of Gregory's thought."[9]

THEOLOGY OF PREACHING

Preaching is at the heart of Gregory's ministry and his legacy. Demacopoulos remarks, "Following in a pedagogical tradition with both Greco-Roman and Christian antecedents, Gregory was deeply committed to the idea that individuals benefit from the insights and advice of their spiritual leaders."[10]

Paradox of Power and Preaching

One joy of studying Gregory is the profound paradox that he personally embodies. It might be surprising that the most powerful figure in the West would speak perpetually of the power of the preacher and promote the homily as the art of arts. As a monk who modeled humility and simplicity, he ascended to the papacy and perpetuated this art. Besides preaching, he wrote to a range of recipients through letters and treatises about preaching, from bishops to simple clerics. Evans says about Gregory's dedication, "Preaching is, in his view, so fundamentally the function of the successors of the apostles that it is only by preaching that they can fulfill Christ's two precepts; to love God and to love one's neighbor, within the terms of their office."[11]

Scholars recognize that the *Pastoral Rule* "explained the supreme office of a bishop in preaching."[12] Drobner cites what he calls "an oft repeated opinion: What Benedict's Rule was to the monks of the Middle Ages, the Pastoral Rule of Gregory the Great was to the clergy of the world,"[13] becoming required reading for pastors throughout the medieval period. This work was written as a training manual for clergy and shows a range of public and private issues for ministers to consider. This office of preaching is entered in paradox, Gregory intimated early in the work, recognizing that some were called to the office of preacher

---

9. Earl E. Cairns, *Christianity through the Centuries* (Grand Rapids: Zondervan, 1990), 163.

10. George E. Demacopoulos, *Gregory the Great: Ascetic, Pastor, and First Man of Rome* (Notre Dame: University of Notre Dame Press, 2015), 57.

11. G. R. Evans, *The Thought of Gregory the Great* (New York: Cambridge University Press, 1986), 80.

12. Margaret Deanesly, *A History of the Medieval Church 590–1500* (London: Methuen, 1969), 27.

13. Drobner, *Fathers of the Church*, 518.

through desire, while others are drawn by compulsion; both are valid callings. While Isaiah declared, "Send me" (Isa 6:8), Jeremiah insisted, "I do not know how to speak" (Jer 1:6). Meanwhile, Moses was "unwilling to be set over so great a multitude, and yet obeyed."[14] As the preacher who would later be considered the first modern pope, Gregory paradoxically saw preaching as a divine and humble undertaking, while himself serving as the most powerful figure in the Western empire.

Gregory provides examples to illustrate how individual devotion and obedience augment one's authority and the effects of one's preaching. In his *Dialogues*, Gregory tells of a monk Equitius who "was not in holy orders, yet travelled about from one place to another preaching the gospel most zealously." This monk is an example of how "the deed depends on the gift, and not on the deed."[15] Another figure, Albinus, functioned as an itinerant preacher, whereby he "opened the fountain of the Scriptures and watered the fields of men's minds."[16] In both cases, the gift of preaching transcended the ordained office of pastor because of the Word's powerful impression on the faith of God's people.

In his *Moralia in Job*, Gregory states: "The church is called adult when being wedded to the Word of God . . . .by the office of preaching she is with young in the conception of children."[17] The paradoxical wedding together of personal spiritual priorities and public church service created a more genuine, motivated, and committed individual in Gregory, who serves as a model for contemporary preachers today. The duty of preaching is a calling, not unlike our call to salvation in which ministry and service to others shape our understanding of that calling. Preaching should be pure, not manipulative; personal, not inhuman; and professional, not casual. The preacher finds a calling anchored in personal faith, in which spiritual values are relevant to all. Gregory is personally torn between the contemplative life and the sphere of public service, so his preaching understandably possesses this same duality.

Themes of Repentance and Judgment

Personal and corporate spiritual responsibility is also a fundamental principle in the preaching themes of Gregory. His preaching and correspondence to

---

14. Gregory, *Pastoral Rule* 1.7. Likewise, there are two precepts of charity: love of God and love of neighbor, illustrated by Jeremiah and Isaiah respectively.

15. Gregory, *Dialogues* 1.4, trans. Odo John Zimmerman (New York: Fathers of the Church, 1959).

16. Ibid.

17. Kevin L. Hester, *Eschatology and Pain in St Gregory the Great: The Christological Synthesis of Gregory's Morals on the Book of Job*, Studies in Christian History and Thought (Milton Keynes: Paternoster, 2007), 37; *Moralia in Job* excerpts contained in Kevin L. Hester, *Eschatology and Pain in St. Gregory the Great: The Christological Synthesis of Gregory's Morals on the Book of Job*. Studies in Christian History and Thought. (Milton Keynes: Paternoster, 2007), 19.12.19.

preachers boldly confront the worst of circumstances with the hope of inciting an obedient response. Repentance entails suffering and obedience, both personal and corporate, which are the obligation of every Christian and every church.

For example, his address to the Roman people during the plague includes the remarks: "Our present trial must open the way to our conversion. The afflictions which we suffer must soften the hardness of our hearts."[18] Likewise, the reason for their illness in the plague is in part due to their unrepentant behavior. Judgment against this behavior finds support in the Old Testament prophets sent to Israel: "Our fellow-citizens are not taken from us one at a time, for they are being bustled off in droves. . . . we must pass in review all those things which we ought not to have done, and we must weep as we think of our trespasses."[19] Here, judgment comes from lack of repentance, but repentance also assuages judgment. Von Hagel states: "Repentance was depicted negatively: 'Repentance means both bewailing the evil deeds we have committed, and not committing again what we have bewailed.' Christians must put behind them their past sins and not return to them. This repentance has numerous benefits: it purges the heart, consumes sins, and cleans stains. The penitential life, for Gregory, was not passive and detrimental, but active and beneficial."[20]

Whether the suffering is individual for believers or corporate for the church, repentance is required. The repentance and prayer of the individual unites with others to direct the church in larger repentance. Hester illuminates the fact that the pastoral task of preaching for Gregory is a "practical ramification of the coming end of the world."[21] Gregory calls for repentance in the earthly present because of the consequence of the heavenly future. Preaching and repentance are inseparable and even more akin than some people would enjoy. However, sinful circumstances and pastoral responsibility combine to necessitate preaching about suffering and the eternal consequence of ungodliness. Von Hagel insists, "This homiliarium of Gregory continues to serve to this day as an eschatological signpost for all preachers who follow him chronologically and are concerned with the care of souls."[22] This theme of repentance is linked to another theme of consequence: judgment.

While churches have always preached Christian living to church members, certain themes fall into obscurity, and eschatology is certainly one of these.

---

18. Gregory the Great, "Address to the People" in Gregory of Tours, *History of the Franks* X.1: 544.

19. Ibid., 545.

20. Thomas Von Hagel, "A Preaching of Repentance: The *Forty Gospel Homilies* of Gregory the Great," *Homiletic* 31 (2006): 5. The "bewailed" quote is taken from Sermon 34, *Forty Gospel Homilies*, 294. The "benefits" finds reference in Sermon 22, p. 171; Sermon 30, p. 243, and Sermon 34, p. 294.

21. Hester, *Eschatology and Pain*, 36.

22. Von Hagel, "Preaching of Repentance," 10.

Perhaps its prevalence in antiquity is greater because death is a marginalized topic in our generation, except for the occasions of terminal illness, fatal accidents, and funerals. Death then diminishes on our landscapes as we return to Christian living. Not so for antiquity, especially for Gregory the Great. He seems to relish in the imminence of judgment and this comfort means his sermons regularly touch on consequences to sin, both temporal and eternal.

Kevin Hester describes the unique way Gregory lays out "four distinct phases of preaching in the church in an elaborate allegory of the life of a matron," stemming from his exposition on the book of Job.[23] In its earliest phase, the church is like a young girl, too immature to feed on its preaching, which can be viewed as the pre-Pentecost church. In its second phase, the church is like a woman in maturity, who is "in full figure and capable of nurturing her children with milk from the Word of God." The church is "married to the Word of God" and "by the office of preaching she is pregnant with the conception of children, with whom by exhorting she travails, whom by converting she brings forth." In its third phase, the present church, who "has grown old because of sin, beyond the age of child-bearing," discovers that, "its efforts in preaching find little effect." The church has become "weak and does not have the strength to bring forth children by preaching." Now, "the church must remember the days of her past fruitfulness, when she truly served the Lord." Finally, in its fourth phase, the church preaches in a way befitting the last days. "Like aged Sarah bringing forth Isaac, the church will once again bear great fruit." Additionally, "at the very end of times, she is empowered with a mighty efficacy of preaching." This eschatological component helps explain Gregory's preaching and missionary sending enterprises. Preaching will continue in the tribulation to come, and preachers will cease when Christ is manifest and the opportunity for repentance, which is the primary goal of preaching, ends.[24]

Spiritual activities thus exist in the shadow of judgment. Hester remarks: "The church must strive daily through preaching and prayer to draw those poor ones back into its ranks."[25] It is the duty of every Christian, including those entrusted with spiritual leadership, to participate in a spiritual verve that blesses the church and honors God. Hester elaborates: "What we find in all of Gregory's eschatological passages in the *Moralia* is a real expectancy, a motivation for the spiritual life, and an awareness that the kingdom is already present in the

---

23. The material cited in this section is drawn from Hester, *Eschatology and Pain*, 37–38; *Moralia in Job* 19.12.19.

24. Hester, *Eschatology and Pain*, 38; *Moralia* 31.10.37.

25. Hester, *Eschatology and Pain*, 53.

church."[26] Gregory understood preaching to be a global task, sending preaching bishops to the church and missionaries to remote fringes of the known world. This was, in part, due to the impending judgment that expresses itself in the present and that looms on the horizon of the future. Preachers today can benefit from seeing how an eschatological vision shaped Gregory's sermons, preaching clear messages about consequences in ways that motivated the church.

The united themes of repentance and judgment could cast a bleak tone to the legacy of Gregory the Great's preaching. However, the next theme of healing is the counter side of suffering. Repentance in the face of judgment provides opportunity for both temporal and eschatological healing.

Theme of Healing

When one visits the monastery of St. Gregory the Great on the Caelian hill in Rome, the courtyard of the entrance to the church depicts the contribution of the saint in murals of his life. One shows Gregory carrying a suffering body during the plague at the scene of Castel Sant'Angelo. The inscription reads, "The plague goes far from the city. Michael is over the region. Gregory heals a young woman."[27] Such a profile highlights the physical healing that underscores his ministry of spiritual healing.

Such depictions on Gregory's monastery bring realization of his own life to the sermons he delivered. The legends of Gregory embody his own claim that *ars artium est regimen animarum*: "the art of arts is the health of souls." Just as the preacher should model care for others in his life, the preacher must also proclaim this same hope. McGrath-Merkle depicts Gregory the Great as a preacher whose aim is curative, like a physician. She observes how the healing theme of Gregory the Great can assist the church today: "An appropriation of the best of Gregory could aid the priesthood now in such crisis. A return to Gregory's long-lost icon of the 'physician of the heart' could support a theology of pastoral identity closer to that of the apostolic age, with a pastoral spirituality of compassion centered in the sacrament of Reconciliation and a charism-oriented life focused on community rather than on individual self-development. This would ground and simplify pastoral identity so as to make it a joyful vocation rather than a toilsome burden inflated with false expectations."[28]

This characteristic of pastoral sensitivity leads us to a final theme in Gregory's preaching: the identity of the preacher.

---

26. Ibid.

27. *It procul urbe lues. Michael supereminet aree. Gregorius supplet virginis.*

28. Clare McGrath-Merkle, "Gregory the Great's Metaphor of the Physician of the Heart as a Model for Pastoral Identity," *Journal of Religious Health* 50 (2011): 386.

Identity of the Preacher

Gregory writes as one acutely aware of how self-reflection and self-realization are instrumental for the role of pastor, including preaching. His writings have a sense of existentialism, the deep stamp of one called to preach who overcame the temptation to elude a higher calling against his own selfish will. Duty characterizes his exhortations in preaching; obligation fills the text and subtext of his incitement to other pastors. His words emphasize with paraenetic angst the responsibility to preach honestly, theologically, and intentionally. Thomas Oden has depicted Gregory as "a model of pastoral leadership to answer the crisis of identity facing pastors."[29]

As a result, Gregory's sermons, letters, and treatises provide a message to the contemporary pastor grappling with identity. His preaching takes on a deeper life, capable of addressing the most critical of issues in the lives of his congregants. From the *Pastoral Rule* alone, he teaches how learning and mastering the art of preaching is not easy (1.1–2), the work of one's office competes with the personal spiritual life (1.4), the preacher should beware that simple sins pass themselves off as virtues (2.10), the preacher should meditate on the Word (2.11), and pride and lust of praise should be watched by a preacher (4.1). These observations surround the person of the preacher, who has a responsibility to personal purity for the sake of service through preaching.

METHODOLOGY FOR PREACHING

Two main methodological qualities are evidentially important for understanding the nature of Gregory's preaching. The obligation of a homiletician to show good oratory requires devotion to preparation and style. The interpretation of Scripture requires an appreciation of the historical meaning of the text and a sensitivity to the spiritual sense. The pastor can then express the interpretation in allegory. Both of these hallmarks of patristic preaching contribute to the health of a soul who hears the preaching of a pastor.

The Obligation of Good Oratory

For Gregory, conviction lies behind the responsibility of preaching. His personal vocation, his sense of duty to the office of bishopric, and perhaps the tug from a contemplative life to a public life combined to require the preparation and delivery of worthy sermons for a congregation or other clergy. "It is necessary that the good which is displayed in the life of the pastor should also be

---

29. Ibid., 375.

propagated by his speech."[30] This responsibility manifested itself in style, strategy, and confrontation.

First, Gregory understood style to be an essential quality of preaching and even a responsibility to the hearers of the Word. In antiquity, public speaking was an art. G. R. Evans remarks, "Preaching was a lively and even theatrical business in the late Roman world." Gregory was no exception, "His preaching retains an air of the live delivery of ideas, filled out and explored before the audience as they occur to the preacher."[31] Although the rhetorical value of a sermon was not its most important component, it was of complementary importance; it could buttress the sermon for effectiveness and show the worthiness of the material. For this bishop, like others, the oratory of a sermon was a craft. Gregory of Tours reports in his *History of the Franks* about Gregory the Great, "He was so skilled in grammar, dialectic, and rhetoric that he was held second to none in the entire city."[32]

This attention to style was not, for Gregory, a matter of showmanship or performance. Instead, it seems to stem from personal conviction of the great importance of preaching. After all, "every preacher should give forth a sound more by his deeds than by his words, and rather by good living imprint footsteps for men to follow than by speaking shew them the way to walk in." This living gospel leads Gregory to the comparison of a cock arousing people from their slumber, "whom the Lord in his manner of speech takes to represent a good preacher."[33]

Evans describes how a solid sermon was both an ancient value for public speaking combined with a Christian value of the preaching of the Word: "Gregory's anxieties over structure and orderliness and his consciousness of the art of composition" are "a rhetorician's concerns, adapted to Christian purposes."[34] When Evans describes oratory as "subordinate to the exegetical purpose" in the context of potential biblical contradictions, there is recognition that "in every part of Scripture the author speaks at the prompting of the same Spirit, and that the Holy Spirit cannot contradict itself."[35] Moorhead recognizes this oratory element as a partner to the significance of Scripture, remarking: "But Gregory did not merely use the concepts of the ancient world to express his situation; his intellectual practices and concerns were often very traditional. The writing of exegetical commentaries on important texts had been a feature of the intellectual life for centuries."[36]

---

30. Gregory, *Pastoral Rule*, preface; *NPNF*², vol. 12b, p. 1.

31. Evans, *Thought of Gregory*, 75.

32. Gregory of Tours, *History of the Franks* X.1, p. 544.

33. Gregory, *Pastoral Rule*, 3.40.

34. Evans, *Thought of Gregory*, 77. Similarly, Gregory showed meticulous care to the recording of his sermons as an entirely other quality for consideration.

35. Evans, *Thought of Gregory*, 78–79.

36. John Moorhead, *Gregory the Great,* The Early Church Fathers (New York: Routledge, 2005), 18.

Second, Gregory had a strategy in his approach to preaching: the recipients of the sermon should be instructed effectively and tactically. The sermons needed to engage the hearer in a way that motivated them to kingdom work. Moorhead says, "In the situation Gregory found himself in, the task of the preacher was not so much to preach doctrine, for the battle to get people to believe had been largely won, as to get them to do better."[37]

His strategic approach to preaching finds characterization in a fascinating "audience intelligence" about the congregation in the third book of the *Pastoral Rule*. One section contains thirty-six unique instructions regarding different types of sermon hearers and how they are to be admonished differently. "Admonish" here has the tone of "caution" more than "reprove" or "rebuke." By identifying the type of sermon hearer, Gregory illustrates the diversity of one's audience, which in turn requires a strategic diversity of hortatory styles. For example, there is "wisdom in addressing the whole in a larger audience" (3.36), versus "wisdom in addressing individual needs in a larger audience" (3.37). There is "wisdom in addressing greater sins and not lesser sins" (3.38). Additionally, there is "wisdom in withholding deep things" (3.39).

Third, confrontation is a feature that is used by Gregory without fear. With such a strategic approach described above, the preacher can more effectively confront the congregation with the Word of the Lord. Moorhead says, "Gregory thought of the Bible as a letter sent by God to humankind, which people able to do so should not neglect to read passionately."[38] There is a methodology here not to cater nor to soften the power of exhortation, but to furnish and to strengthen it. The urgency of the material preached and the urgency to live it out are kept in tension with the ability to do so. Grace is essential to the ability to live the Christian life, such as explained by Gregory in the *Pastoral Rule*: "But because none in adversity can without the help of God's grace stand: and unless the same merciful father, who sendeth punishment, giveth also patience."[39]

However, this confrontation does not desert the strategy of effective and motivational preaching. Moorhead further says, "When he preached doctrine, Gregory took care to pitch his message at an appropriate level, in the belief that, when holy preachers saw that hearers were unable to receive the word of Christ's divinity, they should descend to the words of his incarnation alone."[40]

---

37. Moorhead, *Gregory the Great*, 29.

38. Ibid., 19.

39. Gregory, *Dialogues* 4.10. Baasten remarks for Gregory, "All the responsibility for the soul's renewed prowess must be laid upon God freely coming to an underserving soul." Matthew Baasten, *Pride According to Gregory the Great: A Study of the Moralia*, vol. 7 of *Studies in Bible and Early Christianity* (Lewiston, NY: Mellen, 1986), 93.

40. Moorhead, *Gregory the Great*, 29.

Furthermore, Moorhead describes how Gregory saw a "complex relationship" in which the reading of Scripture nourished the individual along his or her own spiritual progression. On Ezekiel, Gregory remarks, "Have you made progress in the active life? It walks with you. Have you made progress to an unchanging, constant spirit? It stands with you. Have you arrived, through the grace of God, at a life of contemplation? It flies with you."[41] The application calls to whomever would receive it, to the depth that each individual is able to receive it. The diversity of spiritual maturity infused within a given sermon is varied, with a human sensitivity for various applications for various spiritual maturities. Moorhead summarizes this quality: "His insight can be unnerving, and no reader will be under any illusion as to the difficulty of living in a manner which would have pleased him. But one cannot help feeling that the territory he describes is known from his own experience and inhabited by him, and that his demands are possible."[42]

Interpretation of Scripture

Gregory is a premier example of preaching multiple senses of biblical interpretation. His tradition involves a threefold meaning of scriptural interpretation: the literal, allegorical, and moral. While not discarding the literal sense, he ultimately works most passionately and assuredly in the allegorical realm. He instructs interpreters to proceed in steps from the bottom to the top of a ladder: "First we lay the historical foundations; next . . . we erect a fabric of the mind . . . the typical sense; and then, as the last step, we cover the edifice with color."[43] A single word might have multiple meanings, just as an entire passage might. Contemporary readers should understand that this allegory became the basis for confrontation and application for the church, not outside the boundaries of biblical application. Von Hagel remarks, "The motivation behind this hermeneutic style was not rhetorical splendor or exegetical novelty or even theological brilliance, but rather, care for souls."[44]

Meaningful interpretation, for Gregory, stemmed from his own dedication to the contemplation of Scripture. Contemplation of Scripture was a means for understanding God's will individually, and expounding Scripture was a means for God's will to be communicated corporately. John Moorhead describes Gregory's conviction: "Gregory believed a promise had been made: God would come through the pages of his testament, which had been appropriately described as a shady and thickly covered mountain, because it is made dark by the dense obscurities of

---

41. Ibid., 19; Gregory, *Homilies on Ezekiel* 1.7.16.
42. Moorhead, *Gregory the Great*, 89.
43. Evans, *Thought of Gregory*, 88; *Homilies on Ezekiel* 1.10.1.
44. Von Hagel, "Preaching of Repentance," 3.

allegory."[45] In fact, the process of interpretation that leads to preaching is part of the Christian's journey to knowing God and understanding Scripture. Moorhead posits: "In Gregory's eyes its very obscurity was a source of pleasure."[46] In his homilies from the Song, he remarks: "For allegory supplies the soul separated far from God with a kind of mechanism by which it is raised to God. By means of dark sayings in whose words a person can understand something of his own, he can understand what is not his to understand, and by earthly words he can be raised above the earth. Therefore, through means which are not alien to our way of understanding, that which is beyond our understanding can be known."[47]

The self-identified hermeneutical methodology of Gregory is laid out in his *Homily* 40 on Luke 16, the rich man and Lazarus. In opening instruction for hearing the sermon, he remarks:

> In the words of holy Scripture, dearly beloved, we must first attend to the literal truth, and then seek to understand the spiritual allegory. The fruit of allegory is easily plucked when it is rooted in truth through the literal meaning. But since the allegorical meaning builds up faith, and literal meaning morals, I who am not speaking to you who believe by God's inspiration, think it appropriate to transpose this normal order. You who already have strong faith should first hear something briefly of the allegorical meaning, and I will keep for the end of my explanation the indispensable moral teaching derived from the literal meaning. Frequently it happens that what is heard last is best remembered. Therefore I will run through the allegorical meaning quickly so as to come more swiftly to the breadth of moral teaching.[48]

Exegesis and homiletics combine to secure and promote the instruction of God for believers. This process has an end that is eschatological for Gregory, so that language about heavenly rewards is a positive motivator for individual and congregational obedience. On his *Homilies to the Song of Songs*, Gregory explains this methodology of *allegory through allegory* of the text itself: "We must seek out the more interior meaning in these bodily, exterior words and, through speaking of the body, ourselves be taken, as it were, out of the body. We must come to this sacred marriage-feast of the bride and bridegroom dressed in a wedding gown, that is, with the understanding which comes from interior chastity; this is

---

45. Moorhead, *Gregory the Great*, 19; *Moralia* 33.1.2.

46. Moorhead, *Gregory the Great*, 19.

47. Gregory, *Exposition of the Song of Songs* 2, trans. Denys Turner, *Eros and Allegory: Medieval Exegesis of the Song of Songs* (Kalamazoo, MI: Cistercian, 1995), 217.

48. Gregory, *Homily* 40 in *Forty Gospel Homilies*, 371. For a comprehensive treatment of Gregory's biblical exegesis, see Charles Kannengiesser, *Handbook of Patristic Exegesis*, vol. 2 (Leiden: Brill, 2004), 1336–68.

necessary."[49] Christman remarks, "'The very obscurity of God's speech is beneficial because it forces one to tirelessly seek out Scripture's message, and the more
wearying the search, the sweeter the reward."[50]

Perhaps his greatest contribution to biblical interpretation that illustrates
his preaching is seen in his large *Moralia in Job*. Here, the themes of judgment,
repentance, and healing thrive. The biblical Job is a model for Christian suffering
and offers a wealth of application for Gregory. Although Job is a literal figure, he
morally represents human suffering and allegorically represents Christ's suffering. Drobner remarks: "With the assistance of the angels and the preaching of the
church's shepherds, the person's way to God leads through the temptations of the
devil to a knowledge of self, yielding first of all the fruit of humility, purity of life,
fear of God, and remorse and thus rendering effective Christ's redemptive act for
the individual person."[51]

CONTRIBUTIONS TO PREACHING

No church father receives the title of "doctor" without a permanent contribution
to the welfare of the church. Each doctor of the church donated a legacy of sermons, ministering to congregations from the Scriptures and from the pulpit on
their own contemporary church issues. Standing at the crossroads of the ancient
and medieval churches, Gregory's life and ministry accompanied his premier
preaching, personally embodying the archetypal strong individual in the service
of the church. In the case of Gregory, his personal humility merges with a position of power, his attention to the distillation of the gospel remains in focus, and
his exhortation to the church takes on distinctives that are special to his era.

Attention to the preaching of Gregory as preacher is overdue. O. C. Edwards
declares, "The neglect of the importance of preaching in the thought of Gregory
is extraordinary." For example, he cites that in his writing, forms of *praedicare*
occur over 3,300 times.[52] For Gregory, the sermon was central to the vocation
of shepherding. His contributions to the legacy of preaching might be summed
up by his emphasis on Scripture as the source of human exhortation, in his dedication to excellence, and his recognition of personal calling and obedience as a
complement to the sermon.

---

49. Gregory, *Exposition of the Song of Songs* 4; Turner, *Eros and Allegory*, 220.

50. Angela Russell Christman, *"What Did Ezekiel See?" Christian Exegesis of Ezekiel's Vision of the
Chariot from Irenaeus to Gregory the Great*, vol. 4 of *Bible in Ancient Christianity* (Boston: Brill, 200), 158;
Gregory, *Homilies on Ezekiel* 1.6.1.

51. Drobner, *Fathers of the Church*, 517. Different understandings of Scripture can be found in the
elaboration by Gregory in *Moralia* 20.1.1.

52. O. C. Edwards Jr., "Preaching in the Thought of Gregory the Great," *Homiletic* 18.2 (1993): 5.

Scripture as the Source for Human Exhortation

The preaching of Gregory shows great effort to apply the full sense of Scripture in methodical and diverse fashion. While the era does not shy away from a spiritual interpretation that finds resource in the historical sense, the more obvious importance lies in the nature of the Word to feed the flock of the shepherd. The character of a Christian is central to Gregory's exhortations: obedience, repentance, and healing are biblical precepts that await each hearer of a sermon. It is the power of God that works on the human heart, but an apathetic church will see judgment, even as the barbarians threatened Italy's welfare. His extant sermons are like biblical commentaries, expounding the Scripture for the life of the church. "Throughout Scripture God speaks to us only for this purpose, that He may lead us to the love of Himself and of our neighbor."[53]

Dedication to Excellence

The monk Gregory became administrator of the Western church because of his gifting, and the power of his organization translated to his sermons and to Roman church culture across Europe. Preaching was a chief responsibility of a shepherd, and the office was obliged to provide excellent preaching to the people of God. In his *History of the Franks*, Gregory of Tours describes how Gregory the Great's skill was unrivaled in Rome. Gregory the Great's address to the people as an "exhortation to do penance" focused on suffering, reliance on God, prayers for mercy and compassion, participation in litanies, condemnation, and repentance of sin. At the tragic but miraculous AD 590 event at Castel Sant'Angelo, Gregory of Tours says, "The Pope never stopped preaching to the people" despite a supposed archangel appearance and eighty dropping dead, "nor did the people pause in their prayers."[54]

Style was an expression of the excellence that should characterize preaching. Evans remarks, "The preacher of the late antique world took his style from the orator."[55] Like Jerome, Tertullian, or even Justin, the technique of delivery was a craft to offer credibility to the message with its emphasis on fluency and persuasiveness.

Personal Calling and Obedience

Gregory was a deep individual. His biography is one of humble service in an office toward which he did not aspire, but was divinely called. "Humanity" is

53. F. Holmes Dudden, *Gregory the Great: His Place in History and Thought*, vol. 2 (Eugene, OR: Wipf & Stock, 2004), 310; Gregory, *Homilies on Ezekiel* 1.10, 14.

54. Gregory of Tours, *History of the Franks*, 56–74.

55. Evans, *Thought of Gregory*, 75.

an unintentional quality that finds expressions in Gregory's sermons, as sermon preparation and delivery stemmed from his calling to foster obedience within the flock. Personal spiritual disciplines, dedication to the study of the Word, and investment in sermon writing are high priorities for the preacher to be effective. Demacopoulos remarks, "Indeed, Gregory's praise for 'active contemplation' exists in every genre of his surviving corpus."[56] The effect on the congregation was the work of the Holy Spirit but delivered by the human steward. The *Pastoral Rule* functioned to guide the preacher in understanding their personal calling and living a personal life of obedience as a complement to the prepared sermon. The results are sober and convicting sermons, direct address to sin, accompanied by the threat of consequence and judgment. Still, to study Gregory's sermons is to study the voice of a man who was transparent, genuine, passionate, and focused on exhorting the people of God.

So, the preaching of Gregory perpetuates the gospel and his legacy awaits our study. The advantage of viewing Gregory as preacher, Edwards says, is "to have the past reconstructed more accurately" with preaching at the core of the ministry of the church in late antiquity. More importantly, "From the perspective of ecumenical Christian doctrine, there is the advantage of rediscovering among the Fathers an understanding of Christian life that is at once truly Catholic and truly Evangelical."[57]

Sermon Excerpt

Gospel Homily 19[58]

The Lord follows his preachers. Preaching comes first, and then the Lord comes to the dwelling places of our hearts; words of exhortation precede, and by means of them Truth is received by hearts. This is why Isaiah addresses preachers, "Prepare the way of the Lord, make straight the pathways of our God!" And the psalmist says, "Make a way for him who rises in the West." The Lord He rose in the West, because by rising he trampled underfoot the death he bore. We make a way for him who rises in the West, then, when we preach his glory to your hearts, so that he himself, coming afterwards, may enlighten them by the presence of his love.

---

56. Demacopoulos, *Gregory the Great*, 78.
57. Edwards, "Preaching," 6–7.
58. Gregory the Great, *Gospel Homily* 19; *Forty Gospel Homilies*, trans. David Hurst, (Kalamazoo, MI: Cistercian, 1990), 134–35, 136, 148.

A person who undertakes the office of preaching should not cause evils but rather suffer them. By his gentleness he may allay the anger of the violent, and being himself wounded by ill-treatment from others, he may heal the wounds of sinners. If his zeal for rectitude ever demands that he show anger against those subject to him, let his passion be the result of love and not of cruelty, then he many show proper regard for discipline externally, and love inwardly, with a father's devotion, towards those whom he reproves outwardly as if he were attacking them.

Let us imagine that day of accounting when the Judge will come and demand a reckoning from the servants to whom he entrusted his talents. We will see him in dreadful majesty, among choirs of angels and archangels. In that great examination the multitude of the elect and the condemned will be led forth, and it will be revealed what each one has done . . . .Let us fear these things, my friends; let our apostolate really correspond to our outward actions. Let us reflect daily on the forgiveness of our sins, lest our life, through which almighty God daily frees others, remain bound by sin. Let us constantly consider what we are, let us ponder our occupation, let us ponder the burden we have taken on. Let us have daily with ourselves the reckoning we are to have with our Judge. ◆

BIBLIOGRAPHY

Primary Sources

Gregory the Great. "Address to the People." Gregory of Tours, *History of the Franks*. New York: Penguin Books, 1974.

_____. *The Book of Pastoral Rule*. Trans. by George Demacopoulos. Crestwood, NY: St. Vladimir's Seminary Press, 2007.

_____. *Dialogues*. Trans. by Odo John Zimmerman. New York: Fathers of the Church, 1959.

_____. *Exposition of the Song of Songs*. Trans. Denys Turner. Contained in Denys Turner, *Eros and Allegory: Medieval Exegesis of the Song of Songs*. Kalamazoo, MI: Cistercian, 1995.

_____. *Forty Gospel Homilies*. Trans. and intro. by David Hurst. Kalamazoo, MI: Cistercian, 1990.

_____. *Moralia in Job*. Excerpts contained in Kevin L. Hester, *Eschatology and Pain in St. Gregory the Great: The Christological Synthesis of Gregory's Morals on the Book of Job*. Studies in Christian History and Thought. Milton Keynes: Paternoster, 2007.

_____. *Pastoral Rule. Nicene and Post-Nicene Fathers of the Christian Church*, Second Series, Vol. XII. Trans. and intro. by James Barmby. Grand Rapids: Eerdmans, 1997.

_____. *Register of the Epistles. Nicene and Post-Nicene Fathers of the Christian Church*, Second Series, Vol. XII. Trans. and intro. by James Barmby. Grand Rapids: Eerdmans, 1997.

Gregory of Tours. *History of the Franks*. New York: Penguin Books, 1974.

Secondary Sources

Baasten, Matthew. *Pride According to Gregory the Great: A Study of the Moralia*. Vol. 7 of *Studies in Bible and Early Christianity*. Lewiston, NY: Mellen, 1986.

Cairnes, Earl E. *Christianity through the Centuries*. Grand Rapids: Zondervan, 1990.

Christman, Angela Russell. *"What Did Ezekiel See?" Christian Exegesis of Ezekiel's Vision of the Chariot from Irenaeus to Gregory the Great.* Vol. 4 of *The Bible in Ancient Christianity*. Boston: Brill, 2005.

Deanesly, Margaret. *A History of the Medieval Church 590–1500*. London: Routledge, 1969.

Demacopoulos, George E. *Gregory the Great: Ascetic, Pastor, and First Man of Rome*. Notre Dame: University of Notre Dame Press, 2015.

Drobner, Hubertus R. *The Fathers of the Church: A Comprehensive Introduction*. Peabody, MA: Hendrickson, 2007.

Dudden, F. Holmes. *Gregory the Great: His Place in History and Thought*. 2 vols. Eugene, OR: Wipf & Stock, 2004.

Edwards, O. C., Jr. "Preaching in the Thought of Gregory the Great." *Homiletic* 18.2 (1993): 5–8.

Evans, G. R. *The Thought of Gregory the Great*. New York: Cambridge University Press, 1986.

Hester, Kevin L. *Eschatology and Pain in St Gregory the Great: The Christological Synthesis of Gregory's Morals on the Book of Job*. Studies in Christian History and Thought. Milton Keynes: Paternoster, 2007.

Kannengiesser, Charles. *Handbook of Patristic Exegesis*. Vol. 2 of *The Bible in Ancient Christianity*. Leiden: Brill, 2004.

McGrath-Merkle, Clare. "Gregory the Great's Metaphor of the Physician of the Heart as a Model for Pastoral Identity. *Journal of Religious Health* 50 (2011): 374–88.

Moorhead, John. *Gregory the Great*. The Early Church Fathers. New York: Routledge, 2005.

Schwartz, Louis. "What Rome Owes to the Lombards: Devotion to Saint Michael in Early Medieval Italy and the Riddle of Castel Sant'Angelo." International Congress for Medieval Studies, Session 429. Western Michigan University, Kalamazoo, MI, May 10–13, 2012.

Von Hagel, Thomas. "A Preaching of Repentance: The *Forty Gospel Homilies* of Gregory the Great." *Homiletic* 31 (2006): 1–10.

Bernard of Clairvaux

Preaching to Foster a Love and Devotion to God

ELIZABETH HOARE

Bernard of Clairvaux (1090–1153) was one of the most dynamic leaders of the church in the first half of the twelfth century. He was a man of contradictions: as a monk he was bound by the vow of stability and was devoted to his monks, yet he traversed Europe in the service of the church; as a representative of the Prince of Peace he brought about reconciliation between numerous warring parties, yet he was no stranger to controversy, and his reputation remains so to this day. He was a man filled with immense energy which he expended on his order and the wider church, yet he was dogged by ill-health throughout his life, some of it brought about by his extreme ascetic practices. He preached about the love of God and yearned for his presence, but he also preached during the Second Crusade to liberate the Holy Land and its sacred sites, which led to violence and destruction on a horrific scale. He was both contemplative and activist by temperament.

HISTORICAL BACKGROUND

"The theologian of the Cistercian life" is an extravagant claim to make of any single individual,[1] but Bernard of Clairvaux attracted extreme reactions during his own lifetime and ever since. He was adored and loathed by those who encountered him then and is revered by some and demonized by others today. Bernard was born in 1090 in Fontaine-les-Dijon, France, and in 1112, he entered the monastery of Citeaux, where St. Stephen Harding was abbot. Citeaux had been founded in 1098 when Robert of Molesme took twelve monks there to establish a new monastery, the purpose of which was to follow rigorously the Rule of St. Benedict.[2] Bernard was formed here and then sent out to found a new monastery near

---

1. Jean Leclercq, quoted by Basil Pennington in Bernard McGinn, John Meyendorff and Jean Leclercq, eds., *Origins to the Twelfth Century*, vol. 1 of *Christian Spirituality* (London: SCM, 1985), 204.
2. Cf. Louis Lekai, *The Cistercians: Ideals and Reality* (Kent, OH: Kent State University Press, 1977)

Aube, called Clairvaux, the Valley of Light. From here, he became the most pow-erful propagator of Cistercian reform, and during his thirty-eight years as abbot, he founded sixty-five new Cistercian monasteries while still governing his own community. Bernard's insights into human nature were forged in the monastery, where he came to understand firsthand what it meant to experience the grace of God that healed and made whole our humanity.[3]

Though a cloistered monk by calling, Bernard did not stay confined to his monastery but took a central place on the stage of history, especially when his spiritual son became Pope Eugene III. Already instrumental in healing the papal schism of 1130 when the anti-pope Anacletus II was elected, Bernard was recruited by Eugene to offer support for the Second Crusade. The First Crusade had led to the establishment of a feudal kingdom of Frankish barons in the Holy Land, but in 1144, the Muslims captured the Christian outpost of Edessa. The Franks first appealed for help to Byzantium but with no result, so the following year they appealed to the Pope, through King Louis VII of France. Eugene turned to the oratory skills and persuasive powers of his mentor to rally the support of the Christian nations of Europe to liberate Edessa.

During this season of his ministry, Bernard's influence expanded and his fiery preaching became a voice for truth and righteousness. He criticized the laxity of the French royal abbey of St. Denis, interfered in the appointment of an immoral priest to a Spanish see, rebuked the French king when he expelled the bishop of Paris for putting regular canons into his cathedral, and he called to account various nobles for their cruel treatment of peasants. He confuted heretics and arbitrated in spiritual and secular disputes. He also helped draw up the rule of the Templars and of the English Gilbertine order. Throughout his life Bernard wrote or dictated letters and other works and seemed to have ceaseless energy. He exchanged copious correspondence with people all over Europe and he wrote with intense theological and emotional passion. His correspondence, along with his sermons—especially the eighty-six sermons on the Song of Songs—represent clearly his entire spirituality. He believed that in the monastic life, and especially through the practice of *lectio divina*, one could reach out for the presence of God. Michael Casey summarized Bernard's overriding message as desire for God,

---

for the best historical study of the order. For a well-illustrated overview of monasticism and its influence on Europe in the Middle Ages, cf. Christopher Brooke, *The Monastic World: 1000–1300* (New York: Random House, 1974).

3. Several medieval titles on Bernard exist, though they are not biographies in the modern sense. Cf. *St. Bernard of Clairvaux: The Story of His Life as Recorded in the Vita Prima Bernardi by Certain of His Contemporaries, William of St. Thierry, Arnold of Bonnevaux, Geoffrey and Philip of Clairvaux, and Odo of Deuil* (trans. Geoffrey Webb and Adrian Walker; London: Mowbrays, 1960); William of St. Thierry, *Bernard of Clairvaux*, vol. 1 of *Early Biographies*, trans. Martinus Cawley (Lafayette, OR: Guadalupe Translations, 2000).

reform and discipline in the church, and love.[4] Bernard possessed great personal charisma and was deeply loved by his monks. He drew many wayward clerics back to a more faithful way of life, and even those with whom he disputed were eventually won over when they met him in person. It is ironic that Bernard left the cloister to make such an impact on the world, both in view of his own desire and his advice to others. In 1143, he wrote to his friend Peter the Venerable, Abbot of Cluny: "I have decided to stay in my monastery and not go out, except once a year for the general chapter of Abbots at Citeaux. Here, supported by your prayers and consoled by your good will, I shall remain for the few days that are left to me in which to fight until the time comes for me to be relieved at my post."[5]

Bernard was canonized by Pope Alexander III in 1174 and in 1830 he was declared a Doctor of the Church. In 1953, Pope Pius XII issued the encyclical *Doctor Mellifluus*, referring to Bernard's teaching as flowing with honey or as sweet as honey. While his advocacy of the Second Crusade was anything but sweet, his teaching on the love of God struck another note, that of "the spiritual peace distilled in the silence of the monastic life."[6] Isaac of Stella, a contemporary fellow Cistercian commented on his life that "we have seen a man that had something super-human."[7]

THEOLOGY OF PREACHING

The depth of Bernard's spirituality and passion is clearly evident in his sermons and demonstrates the theological framework that drove his worldview. What follows concentrates on the sermons he wrote on the Song of Songs as illustrative of the best of Bernard's theology and methodology. Here we see a man passionately in love with God and these sermons focus on the experiential relationship between God and humanity. For Bernard, the best context to foster devotion to God was the monastery, "the school of Christ" as the Rule of St. Benedict called it, a conviction that shaped both his theology and his methodology.

Love of God

Bernard was preoccupied in his writings with the analysis of Christian love, describing the Christian's journey from fearful distance to loving intimacy.[8] In his

---

4. Cf. Michael Casey, "Reading St. Bernard: The Man, the Medium and the Message," in *A Companion to Bernard of Clairvaux*, ed. B. P. McGuire (Leiden: Brill, 2011), 62–107.

5. Bruno Scott James, trans., *The Letters of Saint Bernard of Clairvaux* (London: Burns & Oates, 1953), 375.

6. Thomas Merton, *The Last of the Fathers* (London: The Catholic Book Club, 1954), 12.

7. Isaac of Stella, Sermon 52.15. Quoted in Michael Casey, "Reading St. Bernard," 82, n.50.

8. Cf. Michael Casey, "Reading St. Bernard," 99.

emphasis on love, Bernard was typical of his age but his series of sermons on the Song of Songs became his particular vehicle for exploring this journey: "'Let him kiss me with the kisses of his mouth.' Today we shall read from the book of our experience. Turn your minds inwardly upon yourselves and let each of you examine your own conscience in regard to the things that we shall talk about."[9] So began the third sermon on the Song of Songs in which he distinguished between the successive stages of kissing Christ's feet, his hands, and his mouth. This kiss of the feet is marked by fear and penitence, like that of the sinful woman in the gospels, lying prostrate and awaiting Christ's words of forgiveness. The second stage was the kiss of his hand, which would cleanse them from their stains and lift them up. Having reached these stages, the one desiring God might be bold enough to seek after even higher things, and venture to lift their eyes to Christ's face "for the purpose not only to adore, but (I say it with fear and trembling) to kiss his lips, because the Spirit before us is Christ the Lord, to whom being united in a holy kiss, we are by his marvellous [sic] condescension made to be one spirit with him."[10] Bernard's sermons on Song of Songs were imitated by many other writers who made him their model. Devotion to the sacred humanity of Jesus shines through these sermons which combined his speculative genius and his considerable spiritual power.[11]

Union with God

To be in union with God was the goal of the mystical life. Bernard used the images of mixing of water in wine and the heating of iron in the fire to explain what he meant by union. It was not the loss of one's self, because "Thy will be done" continues to be the pure prayer of love, which is the response by one subject to another. Nor was it the embrace of equals, for "My beloved is mine and I am his" expresses a mutual love between two persons, but in that love is seen the supreme happiness of the one and the wonderful condescension of the other.[12] In the Cistercian "school of Christ" there was no distinction between the Word of God and Christ himself and Bernard used the two interchangeably. He also depended on the Trinity as his guiding principle in speaking of God and his relationship with human beings. For example, in Sermon 8 he quoted Matthew 11:27, "No one knows the Son except the Father, and no one knows the Father

---

9. Bernard of Clairvaux, *Sermons on the Song of Songs*, in *Sancti Bernardi Opera*, 8 vols., eds., Jean Leclercq, C. H. Talbot, and Henri M. Rochais (Rome: Editiones Cisterciensis, 1957–1977), *sermon* 3. From here on out this will be referred to by *On the Song of Songs*, followed by the sermon number.

10. *On the Song of Songs*, sermon 3.

11. Cf. further on Bernard's concentration on the person of Jesus in his preaching in Michael Casey, "Bernard's Biblical Mysticism: Approaching sc74," *Studies in Spirituality* 4 (1994): 12–30.

12. *On the Song of Songs*, sermon 47.

except the Son and those to whom the Son chooses to reveal him." Going on, he explained, "But the bride has no doubt that if he wills to grant this knowledge to any, it will be to her. Therefore she prays boldly that this may be given to her—that is, the Holy Spirit—in whom the Son and the Father are revealed."[13] Union with God was the goal of Christian mysticism and Bernard's preaching beautifully exemplifies this heartfelt desire to be at one with God.

Humility

One of the key themes in Bernard's outlook was humility. His first major written work was *De gradibus humiliates et superbiae (Concerning the steps of humility and pride)*, a treatise describing twelve degrees of spiritual progress beginning with pride and ending with true humility. Theologically, he regarded human beings as being simultaneously wretched and exalted. Those who live proper, humble Christian lives will experience restoration of the image and likeness of God in the next life, while those who persevere in contemplative prayer may receive fleeting glimpses of this union in this life also. This is made possible by the supreme humility of Jesus who took on human flesh for the sake of our salvation. Bernard also placed humility at the center of another written work, *De diligendo Deo (On loving God)* in which he focuses on four degrees of love: to love oneself for one's own sake; to love God for one's own sake; to love God for God's sake and to love oneself completely for God's sake. The final stage here is a rarely reached mystical state of being in union with God. By loving ourselves for God's sake we show true love for God in an unlimited way. We are created by God; the return to him is learning to love in complete humility. Thus God's love is able to permeate and direct all our human loving.

For Bernard, free will (which for him meant free consent) met God's grace, which led to a love that produced good fruit in human beings. It had to begin with humility that in turn led to three steps towards freedom to love God: first, the absence of compulsion to sin, (*libertas a necessitate*); next, the possibility of choosing, even to sin, (*libertas a peccato*); and finally, the inability to sin (*posse non peccare*). The final stage is only reached in heaven, and the entire movement is made possible only by the love of God.

METHODOLOGY FOR PREACHING

It was said of Bernard that when he preached, the power of his words made people seek after the religious life such that "mothers hid their sons from him, wives

---

13. *On the Song of Songs*, Sermon 8.

their husbands and companions their friends, and inevitably someone would return to Clairvaux with him to embrace the monastic life."[14] He combined a fluent command of the Latin language with a fervent passion that gave him huge powers of expression, yet all his works were forged in monastic silence.[15] Bernard wrote to foster love for and devotion to God among his monastic brothers who were committed to a distinctive way of life involving rigorous asceticism. The Cistercians were a strict Benedictine reform that planted communities of monks in secluded places.[16] Bernard was specifically addressing those who were either students, secular clergy, or monks, and he firmly believed they had taken the straight way, the narrow road that leads to life: "The instructions that I address to you my brothers, will differ from those I would address to those outside in the world, at least, the manner would be different . . . .it is Paul's method of teaching . . . a more nourishing diet to those who are enlightened spiritually."[17] Monks were the ideal guides to enable the rest of humanity to realize their longing for God. Those called to teach, like Bernard, asked for prayers that they may receive from God what they were called to give. As guardians of the faith, they had the responsibility of loving God and their neighbor: "As such my brothers, if through an abundant spread of food we are found to be the true house of the great *Paterfamilias*, if through sanctification the temple of God, if the city of the mighty King through the common of a shared life, if the bride of the immortal bridegroom through delighted love, I think that there is no reason for me to hesitate to proclaim ourselves to be the solemnity."[18]

Writing and Preaching

While the majority of monastic sermons were preached, it was not possible to write them all down exactly as they were uttered. Thus, we have far more extant sermons which were originally written as outlines rather than verbatim records of what was actually said. Bernard is known to have written around 330 sermons; there are some full transcripts, but most were transmitted in the form of *sententiae* or resumes.[19] It is also likely that Bernard used the genre of the sermon to craft his meditations for his monks as the sermons on the Song of Songs indicate by their length, their complexity in refuting error, their polished Latin cadences, the way

---

14. As quoted in Margaret Deanesly, *A History of the Medieval Church: 590–1500,* 9th ed. (London: Routledge, 1969), 121.

15. Cf. G. R. Evans, *Bernard of Clairvaux* (Oxford: Oxford University Press, 2000), 5.

16. Cf. Brooke, *The Monastic World*, ch 9.

17. *On the Song of Songs*, sermon 1.

18. Bernard of Clairvaux, "For the Dedication of a Church" in *Sermons for the Autumn Season* (Collegeville, MN: Liturgical, 2016), 209. From here on out this will be referred to by *Sermons for the Autumn Season*, followed by the sermon number.

19. See Jean Leclercq, "Introduction" in Bernard of Clairvaux, *On the Song of Songs*, 4.

one meditation links to the next, and the deeply personal nature of the author's self-disclosure. During this time, sermons mined the Bible to aid the monks in contemplation, and Bernard's sermons were no exception. Michael Casey describes how the monks were accustomed to listening to conferences or short discourses, especially in chapter, which were "free-ranging reflections drawn from the whole Bible combined with other readings from 'the book of experience.'" Casey describes these sermons as "liturgical discourses."[20] Bernard commenced writing them in 1136 and was still revising them when he died in 1153. His teaching was inspired by a combination of his study of the Bible, the writings of the church fathers, and his personal mystical experiences of God. Bernard revived the theology of desire from the writings of Origen and Gregory and was influenced by the hermeneutical methods of interpretation adopted by the early fathers, which persisted into the Middle Ages. He wrote in twelfth-century Latin, which is not easy to translate. Leclercq wrote: "It was unthinkable for ancient and medieval writers not to base their composition on fixed rules and models appropriate to their purpose. It is those that determine the literary genre."[21]

Scripture

The Bible was viewed as a mirror, a source of self-knowledge and guidance. Thus it was the moral or tropological sense of Scripture that received the most attention.[22] Bernard's sermons are saturated with the Bible, with scarcely a line without some reference to it. Often the text simply sets out the theme, yet he still quotes it liberally, alludes to it, and borrows its style and vocabulary. The sermons on the Song of Songs in particular illustrate a lifetime of fruitful study, teaching, meditation and rewriting, all flowing into each other and flowing out in lucid prose.

The monastic approach to Scripture was nurtured through the practice of *lectio divina,* the daily diet of prayer and meditation wherein the monks chewed on the Word of God, reading it devotionally so that reading became prayer itself. The extent to which this process shaped the lives and output of those who practiced it was commented on by Bernard's friend John of Salisbury, who said, "He was so saturated in the Holy Scriptures that he could fully expound every subject in the words of the prophets and apostles. For he had made their speech his own and could hardly converse or preach or write a letter, except in the language of

---

20. McGuire, *A Companion to Bernard of Clairvaux*, 5.
21. Cf. Jean Leclercq, *The Love of Learning and the Desire for God: A Study of Monastic Culture*, 3rd ed. (New York: Fordham University Press, 1982). See pages 153–90 for a full discussion of the way literary genres constituted an important contribution of medieval monasticism to the culture of the time.
22. Cf. Casey, "Reading St. Bernard," 86.

Scripture."[23] In the same way, Bernard's treatises invited his readers to taste and savor the Word of God to strengthen the contemplative life of prayer and union with God, and his many references and allusions needed no explanation. Examples like pilgrimage and ladders going up and down are frequent metaphors that illustrate the journey of human life returning to God from exile. Metaphors for the relationship between human beings and God are bridal, spousal, and maternal ones. In one of his sermons on the Song of Songs, he heaped up the metaphors to describe the relationship between Christ and his beloved, pointing out that the Lord "delights in transforming himself from one charming guise to another in the beloved's presence. Thus he is a bashful bridegroom, a physician with oil and ointments, a traveler with his bride and her maidens, a wealthy father of a family 'with bread and enough to spare' and a magnificent and powerful king."[24]

Tradition

Bernard followed the exegetical methods of Origen and Augustine, favoring allegory out of the fourfold practice of the literal, allegorical, tropological, and anagogical meanings. Origen wrote a ten-volume work on the Song of Songs from 240 to 245, interpreting the book as an allegory in which the church is the Bride and Christ the Bridegroom, and this remained the classical interpretation to Bernard and beyond. Bernard's contribution was to harness human desire to draw the human soul towards God. In his spirituality, Bernard used concrete images and adopted an affective tone in his preaching, and the Song of Songs was the perfect text for this practice.

He wrote: "As for us, in the commentary of mystical and sacred words, let us proceed with caution and simplicity. Let us model ourselves on Scripture which expresses the wisdom hidden in mystery in our own words: when Scripture portrays God for us it suggests Him in terms of our own feelings. The invisible and hidden realities of God which are of such great price are rendered accessible to human minds, vessels, as it were of little worth, by means of comparisons taken from the realities we know through our senses. Let us also adopt the usage of this chaste language."[25]

Earthly affections have a real part to play in the soul's search for God: "What they do not know from experience, let them believe so that one day, by virtue of their faith, they may reap the harvest of experience ... We must add that the soul which knows this by experience has fuller and more blessed knowledge."[26]

---

23. Quoted in Casey, "Reading St. Bernard," 89.
24. *On the Song of Songs*, sermon 31.6–7.
25. *On the Song of Songs*, sermon 74.2.
26. *On the Song of Songs*, sermon 84.7.

Experience

Regarding experience, it is important to understand the historical context in which Bernard was situated. Experience had played a significant role in patristic theology and continued to do so in the monastic theology of the medieval West. Writers and preachers like Bernard did not separate spiritual or mystical theology from what they thought of as theology proper.[27] The rise of scholastic theology in the first half of the twelfth century led to a clash with Peter Abelard, especially over speculation and where it tended. Bernard's vehement attack on Abelard, however, did not mean he set devotion and experience over and above theology. Bernard was himself an able theologian, as his sermons amply demonstrate in language befitting the subject of love and devotion.[28] As the great historian of medieval monasticism, Dom David Knowles stated that Bernard was "a speculative theologian of wide reading and great intellectual power; a literary genius of the first order, the greatest master of language in the Middle Ages."[29] The greatest difference between the scholastics and the monastics was in the importance that the latter placed on the experience of union with God. "We search in a worthier manner, we discover with greater facility through prayer than through disputation [*orando quam disputando*]."[30]

As many authors on Bernard point out, his watchword was not *Credo ut intelligam* (I believe in order to understand) but *Credo ut experiar* (I believe in order to experience). Bernard himself did not define what he meant by experience, but his sermons demonstrate it as broad: embedded in desire, delight, love, awe, wonder, and anticipation. Above all, it was existentially present in Christ.[31] Three partners weave together like a dance in these sermons: Bernard's personal experience of God's love, the text of the Song of Songs, and an appeal to the experience of his readers.[32] The central image of the Bride is both the individual person and the church. The affection of the Bride for the Bridegroom is the gift of the Holy Spirit. The Spirit acts in a twofold direction: by infusion of the graces necessary for spiritual growth and by effusion of these graces from the recipient to the neighbor.[33] The Song of Songs is the expression of both desire and fulfilment. It is a song and a

---

27. See Leclercq, *The Love of Learning*, 191–235; Bernard Lonergan, *Method in Theology* (New York: Herder & Herder, 1972), 138–40.

28. Cf. for example his dogmatic treatise, *On Grace and Free Choice*. For a thorough study of his theology, cf. Evans, *Bernard of Clairvaux*.

29. David Knowles, *The Evolution of Medieval Thought* (Toronto: Vintage Books/Random House, 1962), 147.

30. *De consideratio* 5.32. Quoted in Leclercq, *The Love of Learning*, 211.

31. Kilian McDonnell, "Spirit and Experience in Bernard of Clairvaux," *Theological Studies* 58 (1997): 3–18.

32. William Loyd Allen, "Bernard of Clairvaux's Sermons on the Song of Songs: Why They Matter," *Review and Expositor* 105 (Summer 2008): 403–16.

33. *On the Song of Songs*, sermon 18.6.

love song—"we listen to it with our whole being and we sing it in our own hearts" as Leclercq says.[34] It both accompanies and sustains the progress of faith. Bernard himself never grew tired of emphasizing the importance of the Christian's ultimate goal: "A canticle of this kind, fervour alone can teach; it can be learned only through experience. Those who have experienced it will recognize this. Those who have not experienced it, may they burn with desire not so much to know as to experience."[35]

It has been commented that for those of us who read Saint Bernard's sermons today, "dispositions similar to those of the original audience are required: openness, docility, and a willingness to be converted."[36]

Liturgical Sermons

Turning to other examples of his preaching, Bernard's liturgical sermons were very carefully edited over time as he selected, rewrote, and ordered them to follow the liturgical year. Wim Verbaal has shown how Bernard seems to have changed the principles by which he organized his sermon material.[37] The guiding principle was how the human soul in its threefold capacities of reason, will, and memory, can be delivered from its captivity to sin. Verbaal discerns a linear and moral narrative structure to the sermons, as well as a circular or repetitive one. The result is a collection of 128 sermons which Bernard arranged in four blocks; they explore reason, will, and memory to show how a Christian soul grows towards maturity. Movement is central to the way the sermons are organized: ascending and descending, following the Word and being fruitful, growth using agricultural imagery including sowing and reaping. The main focus of the moment is of heavenly descent and human elevation to Christ. For example, he takes the ascension of Jesus and treats it as the complement of his descent to the world. Humankind must ascend in grace but only after descending in humility. The Autumn series of sermons began with a group of sermons about Mary, which includes one of Bernard's most famous images, equating her with an aqueduct. "The celestial artery descended through an aqueduct, not exhibiting the full measure of the fount but just a steady rain of grace upon our thirsty hearts, to one more, to another less. Truly that aqueduct is full so that others may take of its fullness, but not the full measure itself."[38]

Another theme in this liturgical series of sermons is that of building heaven on earth. Bernard employed an architectural image to explore the building of the

---

34. Leclercq, *The Love of Learning*, 5.

35. "*Sermo in nativitate Beatae Virginis Mariae,*" in *Sermons for the Autumn Season*, 72.

36. Casey, "Reading St. Bernard," 90.

37. In introduction to *Sermons for the Autumn Season*, ix-lxvi.

38. "*Sermo in nativitate Beatae Virginis Mariae,*" in *Sermons for the Autumn Season*, 72.

heavenly Jerusalem on earth. Human beings are the house of God he says, God's Temple and God's Bride. Sermons on the saints are included because they are already part of the New Jerusalem in heaven and remembering them makes us share in their lives. Here desire and longing come into play, for they nurture the looking ahead to belonging to the heavenly world with those who have reached their goal. As Verbaal puts it: "All movement coincides in memory's longing for what lies ahead."[39]

CONTRIBUTIONS TO PREACHING

Bernard is an important reminder and an example *par excellence* of the premodern style of preaching on the biblical text. He accepted that there were multiple meanings to be found in Scripture, which enabled him to draw out the relationship between God and his people, whether Israel, the church, or the individual soul. Renewed interest in the allegorical method means Bernard's sermons demand further study.[40] The Song of Songs was the most frequently chosen biblical text for sermons, while today it is one of the least likely to be chosen.[41] That alone suggests the need for closer investigation of what Bernard had to say about this beautiful piece of biblical literature.

Thomas Merton pointed out that Bernard's devotion to the humanity of Christ expressed in his preaching led to the formation of a new school of spirituality, the *Devotio Moderna*.[42] The principle of this school was the imitation of Christ, something Bernard drew attention to again and again in his preaching, to show how doctrine and experience come together in the love of God revealed in Jesus Christ. He led the way in expressing the emotional depths of devotion to Christ in his earthly sufferings. He was not anti-intellectual but he recognized that without experience of God, all knowledge was futile: "I am far from saying that the knowledge of literature is to be despised, for it provides culture and skill. But the knowledge of God and of one's self must come first, for they are essential to salvation . . . Know yourself and you will have a wholesome fear of God. Know God and you will also love God."[43] Bernard recognized that knowledge for knowledge's sake is antithetical to Christian faith, which continues to be relevant for preaching today.

---

39. In introduction of *Sermons for the Autumn Season*, xxxix.
40. For example, see Duncan Robertson, "The Experience of Reading: Bernard of Clairvaux 'Sermons on the Song of Songs,'" *Religion and Literature* 19, no. 1 (Spring 1987): 1–20.
41. J. Paul Tanner, "The History of Interpretation of the Song of Songs," *Bibliotheca Sacra* 154, no. 613 (1997): 23–46.
42. Merton, *The Last of the Fathers*, 9.
43. *On the Song of Songs*, sermon 37.1.

The Cistercian Order produced the greatest volume of devotional literature in the twelfth century and it was Bernard who gave it a theological background and a doctrinal stability and consistency. It was a literature full of warmth and intimacy requiring a greater amount of solitude and self-knowledge, but it was as much about the awareness of the Savior as it was about the self. Richard Southern credits Bernard with writing Latin capable of influencing the taste and practice of his own and succeeding generations: "He was the first to make Latin a capacious language for the thoughts of the twelfth century."[44] Part of this was due to the way he exploited biblical imagery.

It is difficult to reconcile Bernard's preaching of the Second Crusade with his later sermons on the Song of Songs and their focus on the love of God. If Bernard was as naive as he was bellicose in his attitude to the Crusade, the overriding principle of order and divine authority lay behind his obedience to the papal request to advocate it through preaching. His weaknesses as a man are a reminder of the contradictions of sinful humanity, however mellifluous their proclamation.

Merton noted that Saint Bernard's huge personality seems to have been too big for history to perceive him as one single person, so he has been celebrated in fragmentary ways: his piety, his leadership of his order, his political involvement, and his writings. To set his preaching in context, we need to take into account all these facets of his life to see a more integrated picture of what he stood for in his own time, as well as in the judgment of history. It is important to resist the temptation to say that the man who preached the Crusade was not the real Bernard. Merton regarded the power of his warlike attitude in the same light as his zeal for God. Moreover, Bernard did not understand the spiritual life in the same individualistic way we do today, which is another reason to consider his legacy. Union with God was not a personal subjective matter, but one shared by the whole church, the mystical body of Christ. Furthermore, the interior life could not be separate from the exterior visible order that reflects God's purposes in the world and gives assurance of salvation. "The last of the fathers" was revered for a considerable time following his death not only by medieval figures like Dante, but also the Reformers who quoted him repeatedly and the Puritans who referred to his writings as frequently as those of Saint Augustine. Bernard's influence for good was enormous, and his appearance as the wise spiritual guide in Dante's *Paradiso* is no accident. His eloquent Latin, his insights into the place of experience in the spiritual life, and his energetic defense of doctrinal orthodoxy are all bound up in his preaching.

---

44. Richard Southern, *The Making of the Middle Ages* (London: Hutchinson, 1967), 205. Southern charts the change in focus in spirituality in the century from 1050 to 1150, with St. Anselm as the dominating influence in the first half and St. Bernard in the second.

Sermon Excerpt
The Kiss of the Mouth[45]

You too, if you would make prudent progress in your studies of the mysteries of the faith, would do well to remember the Wise Man's advice: "Do not try to understand things that are too difficult for you, or try to discover what is beyond your powers." These are occasions when you must walk by the Spirit and not according to your personal opinions, for the Spirit teaches not by sharpening curiosity but by inspiring charity. And hence the bride, when seeking him whom her heart loves, quite properly does not put her trust in mere human prudence, nor yield to the inane conceits of human curiosity. She asks rather for a kiss, that is she calls upon the Holy Spirit by whom she is simultaneously awarded with the choice repast of knowledge and the seasoning of grace. How true it is that the knowledge imparted in the kiss is lovingly received, since the kiss is love's own token. But knowledge which leads to self-importance, since it is devoid of love, cannot be the fruit of the kiss. Even those who have a zeal for God, but not according to knowledge, may not for any reason lay claim to that kiss. For the favour of the kiss bears with it a twofold gift, the light of knowledge and the fervour of devotion. He is in truth the Spirit of wisdom and insight, who, like the bee carrying its burden of wax and honey, is fully equipped with the power both of kindling the light of knowledge and infusing the delicious nurture of grace. Two kinds of people therefore may not consider themselves to have been gifted with the kiss, those who know the truth without loving it, and those who love it without understanding it; from which we conclude that this kiss leaves room neither for ignorance nor for lukewarmness.

So therefore, let the bride about to receive the twofold grace of this most holy kiss set her two lips in readiness, her reason for the gift of insight, her will for that of wisdom, so that overflowing with joy in the fullness of this kiss, she may be privileged to hear the words: "Your lips are moist with grace, for God has blessed you forever." ♦

---

45. *Sermons on the Song of Songs*, sermon 8.

BIBLIOGRAPHY

Primary Sources

Bernard of Clairvaux. *Sermons on the Song of Songs* in *Sancti Bernardi Opera*. 8 vols. Edited by Jean Leclercq, C. H. Talbot, and Henri M. Rochais. Rome: Editiones Cisterciensis, 1957–1977.

_____. *Magnificat: Homilies in Praise of the Blessed Virgin Mary*. Trans. by M. B. Said and G. Perigo. Cistercian Fathers Series. Kalamazoo, MI: Cistercian, 1979.

_____. *Sermons on Conversion: On Conversion, a Sermon to Clerics and Lenten Sermons on the Psalm "He Who Dwells."* Trans. by M. B. Said. Cistercian Fathers Series. Kalamazoo, MI: Cistercian, 1981.

_____. *Sermons for the Autumn Season*. Trans. by Irene Edmonds. Rev. by Mark A. Scott. Cistercian Fathers Series. Collegeville, MN: Liturgical, 2016.

_____. *On Grace and Free Choice*. Trans. by Daniel O'Donovan. Kalamazoo, MI: Cistercian, 1988.

_____. *Bernard of Clairvaux: Selected Works*. Classics of Western Spirituality. Trans. by G. R. Evans. New York: Paulist, 1987.

Webb, Geoffrey and Adrian Walker, trans. *St. Bernard of Clairvaux: The Story of His Life as Recorded in the Vita Prima Bernardi by Certain of His Contemporaries, William of St. Thierry, Arnold of Bonnevaux, Geoffrey and Philip of Clairvaux, and Odo of Deuil*. London: Mowbrays, 1960.

Secondary Sources

Allen, William Loyd. "Bernard of Clairvaux's Sermons on the Song of Songs: Why They Matter." *Review and Expositor* 105 (Summer 2008): 403–16.

Brooke, Christopher. *The Monastic World: 1000–1300* (New York: Random House, 1974).

Casey, Michael. "Bernard's Biblical Mysticism: Approaching SC 74" *Studies in Spirituality* 4 (1994): 12–30.

_____. "The Book of Experience: The Western Monastic Art of Lectio Divina." *Eye of the heart* 2 (2008): 5–31.

_____. "Reading St. Bernard: The Man, the Medium and the Message." Pages 62–107 in *A Companion to Bernard of Clairvaux*. Edited by Brian Patrick McGuire. Leiden: Brill, 2011.

Cawley, Martinus. *Bernard of Clairvaux*. Early Biographies. Lafayette, OR: Guadalupe Translations, 2000.

Deanesly, Margaret. *A History of the Medieval Church, 590–1500*. London: Methuen, 1962.

Evans, G. R. *The Mind of St Bernard of Clairvaux*. Oxford: Clarendon, 1983.

_____. *Bernard of Clairvaux*. Oxford: Oxford University Press, 2000.

Gilson, Etienne. *The Mystical Theology of Saint Bernard*. Trans. by A. H. C. Downes. London: Sheed & Ward, 1958.

James, Bruno Scott, trans. *The Letters of Saint Bernard of Clairvaux*. London: Burns & Oates, 1953.

Knowles, David. *The Evolution of Medieval Thought*. Toronto: Random House, 1962.

Leclercq, Jean. "The Exposition and Exegesis of Scripture: From Gregory the Great to St Bernard." Pages 183–96 in *The Cambridge History of the Bible: The West from the Fathers to the Reformation*. Edited by Geoffrey Lampe. Cambridge: Cambridge University Press, 1969.

_____. *The Love of Learning and the Desire for God: A Study of Monastic Culture*. 3rd ed. New York: Fordham University Press, 1982.

Lekai, Louis Julius. *The Cistercians Ideals and Reality*. Kent, OH: Kent State University Press, 1977.

Lonergan, Bernard. *Method in Theology*. New York: Herder & Herder, 1972.

McGinn, Bernard, John Meyendorff, and Jean Leclercq, eds. *Christian Spirituality: Origins to the Twelfth Century*. London: SCM, 1985.

McGuire, B. P. *A Companion to Bernard of Clairvaux*. Leiden: Brill, 2011.

McDonnell, Kilian. "Spirit and Experience in Bernard of Clairvaux." *Theological Studies* 58 (1997): 3–18.

Merton, Thomas. *The Last of the Fathers*. London: The Catholic Book Club, 1954.

Norris, Richard A., Jr., ed. and trans. *The Song of Songs Interpreted by Early Christian and Medieval Commentators*. Grand Rapids: Eerdmans, 2003.

Robertson, Duncan. "The Experience of Reading: Bernard of Clairvaux 'Sermons on the Song of Songs.'" *Religion and Literature* 19, no.1 (Spring 1987): 1–20.

Southern, Richard. *The Making of the Middle Ages*. London: Hutchinson, 1967.

Tanner, J. Paul. "The History of Interpretation of the Song of Songs." *Bibliotheca Sacra* 154, no. 613 (1997): 23–46.

Vancard, E. *Vie de saint Bernard, abbe de Clairvaux*. 2 vols. 1895. Repr., Paris: Lecoffre, 1927.

Ward, Benedicta, ed. *The Influence of St Bernard: Anglican Essays with an Introduction by Jean Leclerq*. Oxford: SLG, 1976.

Williams, Rowan. *The Wound of Knowledge: Christian Spirituality from the New Testament to St. John of the Cross*. Rev. ed. London: Darton, Longman & Todd, 1990.

Francis of Assisi

Using Words and Life to Preach the Gospel

TIMOTHY D. HOLDER

Even in a book of great preachers, Saint Francis of Assisi (1181/2–1226) stands out as an extraordinary man. Biographer Adrian House said Francis was one of the three preeminent figures in medieval Europe, along with Pope Innocent III and Emperor Frederick II. Interestingly, House compares Francis to a pope and an emperor, men who held enormous institutional power.[1] Who was Francis—a poor beggar and itinerant preacher—to be considered among such men? Arguably, he was the most noteworthy of them. The man who famously prayed, "Lord, make me an instrument of Your peace," wielded more power than the men who could make war. Literally hundreds upon hundreds of authors have written books and articles about Francis. What made Francis so extraordinary? Inspired by the Holy Spirit, the man had one of the most counterintuitive approaches in history. He preached peace in a remarkably violent period, he gained influence despite embracing poverty, and he wielded considerable power in spite of submitting to every authority over him. He preached the gospel, and he lived it. Because he did both so dramatically, the people responded.

---

1. See Adrian House, *Francis of Assisi* (Mahwah, NJ: Hidden Spring, 2001), 294. This high estimation of Francis, however, is not unique to his biographer. Historian Patrick J. Geary describes him as "the most important religious figure of the thirteenth century" [Patrick J. Geary, *Readings in Medieval History* (Lewiston, NY: Broadview, 1989), 486]; Norman F. Cantor calls Francis "the favorite saint of the medieval middle class" [Norman F. Cantor, *The Medieval Reader* (New York: Harper Perennial, 1994), 61]; John R. H. Moorman points out that in addition to being a courageous and inspiring leader, Francis was also a poet and "the first to write verse in any modern language" [John R. H. Moorman, *Saint Francis of Assisi* (Chicago: Franciscan Herald, 1963), ix]; Leonardo Boff describes him as achieving "an admirable accord between *Logos* and *Pathos*, between *Logos* and *Eros*." Furthermore, Boff believes, "Sigmund Freud would have recognized that Francis was perhaps someone who carried the expression of love the farthest, who was able to relate to the strangest things" [Leonardo Boff, *Saint Francis* (New York: Crossroad, 1982), 19]; Harry Eskew and Hugh T. McElrath, hymnologists discussing Francis because of his authorship of the hymn "All Creatures of our God and King," credit Francis with having "the most remarkable personality of the early thirteenth century." These two authors also consider Francis to be one of the "giants" in church history alongside such men as Martin Luther, John Calvin, John Wesley, and a handful of others [Harry Eskew and Hugh T. McElrath, *Sing with Understanding* (Nashville: Church Street, 1995), 94, 279]. "Lord, make me an instrument of Your peace" is part of a famous prayer of St. Francis, "Make Me an Instrument of Your Peace," [Donald Spoto, *Reluctant Saint* (New York: Penguin Compass, 2003) xviii].

191

HISTORICAL BACKGROUND

Francis was one of the most influential individuals in medieval Europe. He was born in 1181 or 1182 in Assisi, Italy, to the family of a well-to-do merchant. Wealthy, popular, and charismatic, Francis enjoyed a comfortable and carefree life of self-indulgence, but circumstances early in his adult life left him a changed man. During 1202, Assisi and neighboring towns gathered a force to fight the Perugians. Francis was captured in the battle, and it was his love for the finer things that saved his life. His armor and equipment were so fancy that his enemies decided to hold him for ransom rather than kill him.[2]

Getting captured in battle and locked up with other prisoners in a dungeon did little to quench Francis's spirit. He had a natural optimism and cheerfulness despite his circumstances. One significant way the experience did impact him is that it changed the object of his ambition. Instead of pursuing the life of a wealthy merchant like his father, Francis decided to become a great warrior after hearing one of his fellow prisoners talk about the excitement of being a knight. Francis bragged to another prisoner, "You may think me foolish, but one day the whole world will come to respect me."[3]

After a year's confinement, Francis and his comrades were returned home in 1203. At first, Francis returned to a life of lavish parties, which he enjoyed throwing for himself and his friends.[4] But within a few years, Francis turned his back on his family's wealth and comfort.[5] A pivotal event in this decision occurred in 1205. He was walking back from a business errand for his father when he stopped in a run-down church to rest. There in San Damiano, Francis felt Christ was telling him to rebuild the church.[6] Francis was a changed man after that day. Instead of living for carnal pleasures or military glory, Francis spent the rest of his life rebuilding the church in one sense of the meaning or another.

A pilgrimage to Jerusalem in 1206 reinforced the new direction in life for Francis.[7] Francis left home with little more than a second-rate cloak and belt made of rope that he appropriated from a scarecrow. At first, Francis contented himself with fixing church buildings in disrepair. On February 24, 1209, though, he heard Scripture read from Matthew 10 and committed himself to a life of poverty and preaching the gospel. It was hard to attack his sincerity—the man sought no personal gain, walking around barefoot and spreading the good news.

---

2. House, *Francis of Assisi,* 39–44.
3. Ibid., 44–45.
4. Ibid., 47–48.
5. John J. Delaney, *Pocket Dictionary of Saints* (Garden City, NY: Image Books, 1983), 195.
6. Spoto, *Reluctant Saint,* 44.
7. Delaney, *Pocket Dictionary of Saints,* 195.

He attracted followers and a new order of monks was formed in 1210 with other orders to follow. Men and women both decided to take the vow, and many of them were drawn from the small medieval middle class. One result of this was that Francis, despite his disinterest in intellectual pursuits, created orders filled with some highly educated people with a love and respect for learning.[8] This resulted in tensions within the Franciscan orders, which will be described later.

Francis founded his second order in San Damiano when a woman named Clare rejected an arranged marriage and, at great physical risk from her family, pledged her loyalty to the movement Francis started. Clare and a handful of other women started a community of nuns committed to the same priorities as Francis.[9]

The third order was made up of men and women who likewise were inspired by Francis. They followed his guidance on issues of love, fraternity, and humility, even if for one reason or another they could not give up all their possessions and follow him into the ministry.[10]

In 1219, Francis decided to intervene in the Crusade-era tensions between Muslims and Christians in the Middle East. Francis traveled to Egypt and his humility and piety earned him an audience with Sultan al-Kamil. Francis offered to prove the validity of his faith by undergoing a trial by fire, but the sultan rejected this. The sultan also refused Francis's offer of a lengthy and public discussion on their faiths. When the sultan offered Francis many gifts, it was Francis's turn to decline the offer.[11] Francis was polite, but he was not so polite that he would disregard his vow of poverty. Francis had gone to Egypt to promote peace and make converts, and though he did not do the latter, the former came about because of other developments, all of which are not relevant to this work. What is relevant is that Francis, with his curious blend of optimism and humility, made a bold effort to spread peace.

Possibly the most distinctive aspect of this preacher was his personality, more so than his theology or his preaching. The romantic notions that at one point prompted his desire to be a knight were channeled into his ministry. As C. W. Previte-Orton put it, "To him, Lady Poverty was a mistress of his heart; he was a minstrel of the Lord." He was an ascetic, but not the gloomy or condemning kind. He urged his followers to be cheerful and display a chivalrous courtesy to everyone they encountered.[12]

---

8. Cantor, *The Medieval Reader*, 61.

9. House, *Francis of Assisi*, 132–37.

10. Michael de la Bedoyere, *Francis: A Biography of the Saint of Assisi* (New York: Harper & Row, 1962), 231–32.

11. Steven Runciman, *A History of the Crusades Volume III: The Kingdom of Acre and the Later Crusades* (Cambridge: Cambridge University Press, 1987), 159–60.

12. C. W. Previte-Orton, *The Shorter Cambridge Medieval History 2* (Cambridge: Cambridge University Press, 1983), 670.

For all his humility, Francis was still a decisive and proactive leader. He composed his "Testament," shortly before his death. In it, he outlined the philosophy and requirements of his orders, and he wrote that his followers were "bound by obedience not to add to these words or to take from them."[13] How many dynamic religious leaders have had followers who twisted their teachings? Francis at least attempted to guard against this, though he was not totally successful.

According to historians Paul R. Spickard and Kevin M. Cragg, "Francis was a dramatic, charismatic leader, but he lacked organizational skills." His admonitions to own nothing were spiritually inspiring, but impractical. As the order grew, group ownership of property was allowed and educational opportunities were encouraged. Francis and a minority of his followers resisted these changes, but their resistance was futile. By the fourteenth century, this minority group was declared heretical and wiped out by the church.[14]

There is a fairly popular belief that late in life Francis was afflicted miraculously with the stigmata (wounds similar to those Christ suffered during his torture and execution on the Cross). The story goes that Francis's life so resembled that of Christ that the monk was blessed to become that much more like the Savior.[15] There are no stories of miraculously-generated stigmata forming on someone's body before this, but there have been over three hundred documented claims since the death of Francis on October 3, 1226.[16]

Two years after he died, Francis was canonized as a saint by Gregory IX. Ironically, given Francis's sincere and long-lasting commitment to poverty, less than twenty-five years after his death, a great church was built in his honor at Assisi. Shortly thereafter, the Renaissance artist Giotto was brought into this church to create frescoes commemorating the life of Francis. Francis would have been appalled at all the honor and expense directed at him.[17]

THEOLOGY OF PREACHING

One popular quip about preaching, frequently attributed to Francis, is that preachers should "Preach the Gospel every day, and [then] use words if necessary." While there is something to commend here about the emphasis on the life of the preacher as a tool for communicating the gospel, there is no evidence

---

13. Brian Tierney, *The Middle Ages Volume I: Sources of Medieval History* (New York: McGraw-Hill, 1992), 272.

14. Paul R. Spickard and Kevin M. Cragg, *A Global History of Christians: How Everyday Believers Experienced Their World* (Grand Rapids: Baker Academic, 1994), 93.

15. Ibid., 92–93.

16. House, *Saint Francis of Assisi*, 259.

17. Jane Dillenberger, *Style and Content in Christian Art* (London: SCM, 1986), 85.

Francis ever said this.[18] It is important to recognize this because, while he does commend the importance of living well, it contradicts the gospel message to which Francis was so committed. Living virtuously gives credibility to our spoken words, but teaching people to act nicer through our example will not save their souls, and this was the concern of Francis. He recognized that salvation only came through an understanding and submission to the truth of Christ and his offer of grace told in the communication of the gospel. Thus, Francis used words to proclaim the truth, as is made clear, for example, in his *Rule* of 1221 where he describes the role Christ plays in salvation.[19] Given all the legends about how Francis preached to animals, does it make sense that he would have neglected to preach to people? Part Nine of *The Rule* was addressed specifically to the preachers in his order.[20]

The theology of Francis was gospel-driven. Church historian Bruce L. Shelley summarizes Francis's *Rule* for his followers as having three major components: Christ's call for believers to take up their crosses, Jesus's challenge to the rich young ruler, and the Great Commission.[21] *The Rule of Saint Francis of Assisi* was formalized three years before his death. Parts one, four, and five of this brief, twelve-part document admonished the members of his orders to remain above reproach by staying poor, humble, and hardworking.[22] It must be acknowledged that *The Rule*[23] focuses much more on orthopraxy than orthodoxy. Francis is more specific about how his followers should walk humbly before the people they encounter than he is about "the holy Gospel of our Lord Jesus Christ," which he references in Part 12, but does not define.[24]

Francis was not an advocate of education. Historian John H. Mundy maintains that "Francis of Assisi thought little of letters," because "the living example of apostolic poverty" was a strong enough message to stand on its own.[25] There was a downside to Francis's thinking, though. As historians Spickard and Cragg describe the problem, it would be difficult for the Franciscans to keep their message pure and preach against heresy if they were unable to study the finer points of Catholic orthodoxy. Studying and preparing for such battles was difficult since they were not allowed to own books.[26] Besides, according to Mundy, "What most

18. Ed Stetzer, "Preach the Gospel, and Since It's Necessary, Use Words," *The Christian Post.* 26 June 2012. http://www.christianpost.com/news/preach-the-gospel-and-since-its-necessary-use-words-77231/

19. Paul Sabatier, *Life of St. Francis of Assisi* (New York: Scribner's Sons, 1920), 255–56.

20. House, *Francis of Assisi*, 305–06.

21. Bruce L. Shelley, *Church History in Plain Language* (Dallas: Word, 1982), 231.

22. Geary, *Readings in Medieval History*, 486–87.

23. House, *Francis of Assisi*, 301–7.

24. Ibid., 307.

25. John H. Mundy, *Europe in the High Middle Ages: 1150–1309* (New York: Basic Books, Inc. 1973), 297.

26. Spickard and Cragg, *A Global History of Christians*, 93.

of [the laity] wanted were the preaching, sacramental, burial, and charitable services the [Franciscan] order could offer."[27] After the death of Francis, some of his followers turned to intellectual pursuits, as they and the Dominicans rivaled and then surpassed the academic quality of medieval universities.[28] There was a difference, however, in the direction of the two orders. The Dominicans devoted themselves to collaborative efforts to produce and/or revise important theological works. The Franciscans were more oriented towards studying languages, physics, firsthand knowledge, and independent thinking.[29]

According to Brian Tierney, "Francis saw all created things as good and beautiful because God had made them so."[30] Jane Dillenberger elaborates on this theme by explaining that "Francis saw all life as harmonious and knew no barriers between the natural world and man."[31] Thus, Francis's outlook on the world as a good gift from God runs counter to the negative, gloomy outlook of some preachers through the ages. One can gain a sense of both Francis's theology and his perception of the connectedness of all of creation in his most famous hymn, "All Creatures of our God and King."

> All creatures of our God and King
> Lift up your voice and with us sing
> Alleluia, Alleluia!
> Thou burning sun with golden beam
> Thou silver moon with softer gleam
>
> O praise Him, O praise Him
> Alleluia, Alleluia, Alleluia!

Lest one wonder if Francis is guilty of some kind of animism in his theology, it should be noted that Luke 19 refers to rocks crying out in worship of Christ. Psalm 19 declares that the heavens tell of the glory of God, though admittedly the Psalmist is not referring to literal speech. Francis is not plowing new ground here; he is building on a tradition long established in Scripture.

One thing that distinguished Francis from other wandering preachers is that he did not criticize the church. Instead, he communicated in an extraordinarily humble manner. As followers amassed, Francis sought the Pope's blessing

---

27. Mundy, *Europe in the High Middle Ages*, 571.
28. Previte-Orton, *The Shorter Cambridge Medieval History 2*, 675.
29. Ibid., 675–76.
30. Tierney, *The Middle Ages Volume I*, 272.
31. Dillenberger, *Style and Content in Christian Art*, 173.

for his first order, the Brothers Minor (also known as the Lesser Brothers).[32] The Catholic Church tended to be skeptical of these religious startups because such groups tended to be idealistic and independent, which led them to assume responsibilities that church officials wanted to keep for themselves. Also, these groups had a tendency to be critical of the institutional church, but because Francis was not interested in such things, he was able to win over many skeptics.[33] Still, it does not mean that such approval was easily achieved. In the words of Leonardo Boff, Francis "was much more than a 'yes-man' and conformist; he was a radical revolutionary and at the same time lived obedience in a heroic manner."[34] Francis might have been the first person in history to start a movement as a submissive revolutionary.[35] It sounds oxymoronic, yet Francis accomplished it.

Pope Innocent III officially approved of Francis's first order in 1210. Francis makes it clear in his "Testament," which he composed in 1226 shortly before he died, that he was a servant of the Catholic Church. He said regarding priests, "I desire to fear, love, and honor them and all others as my masters." Furthermore, he continued, "I do not wish to consider sin in them, for in them I see the Son of God and they are my masters."[36] Part of the reason Francis had such reverence for the priestly class was because of their authority over the Eucharist.[37]

One could argue that Francis should have cared more about accountability among Catholic officials, but one cannot help but wonder if his loving humility might have had a greater impact for good in the Catholic Church than would otherwise have been the case. Accountability is a necessity, but there are, as Paul writes, different parts of the Body; and we are not all called to play the same role.

METHODOLOGY FOR PREACHING

In Part Nine of the *Rule of Saint Francis of Assisi*, he gave his followers specific instructions regarding their preaching. Sermons were supposed to be evenhanded and short, providing information on "vices and virtues, punishment and glory," and featuring a "briefness of discourse." Brevity was expected, according to

---

32. The term "friars" comes from the Latin word *fratres*, which means "brothers." Spickard and Cragg, *A Global History of Christians*, 92.

33. House, *Francis of Assisi*, 97–98.

34. Boff, *Saint Francis*, 112.

35. Some might argue that Mohandas Gandhi belongs in this category too, but Gandhi wanted to frustrate and drive out British authority. He was a passive revolutionary, but he was not submissive to British authority.

36. The above quotations are from a translation of the "Testament" by Paschal Robinson and excerpted in Tierney, *The Middle Ages Volume I*, 270.

37. Tierney, *The Middle Ages Volume I*, 270–71.

Francis, because "the words were brief which the Lord spoke upon the earth."[38] Evenhanded sermons would present a change of pace to both prosperity preachers and those who preach jeremiads every week. Short sermons would also present a challenge to many modern pulpiteers.

Francis contributed to a significant change in orthopraxy in the Catholic Church. Up to this point, the parish system and the monastic orders were oriented towards a rural culture, but the growth of cities in central and western Europe would require a different system—one that accommodated city life.[39] Francis and those who followed him were able to handle this changing dynamic because their order had so little infrastructure. Their vow of poverty left them with few logistical concerns as circumstances changed.

That said, Francis did not make it easy for others to participate in his mission. In his "Testament" he wrote that "those who came to take this life upon themselves gave to the poor all that they might have."[40] Again, though, this was not a veiled swipe at the wealth of the church or the rulers of his day. In the words of Ray C. Petry, there was "no attack upon existing institutions, no discrimination between rich and poor, no conscious attempt at social reformation in and of itself, no plan of political upheaval or economic revolution."[41]

Spickard and Cragg describe Francis and his followers as street preachers. The popular impression of the Franciscans as poor beggars is accurate only to a point: they were supposed to work to support themselves with the essentials. If they earned extra, they were expected to give it away. If they did not earn enough, begging was acceptable.[42] They were not supposed to be full-time beggars, but neither were they supposed to store up for themselves treasures on earth. Their number one emphasis was to be preaching, and specifically, they were to preach the gospel.

The Franciscans were mindful of not only their message, but their audiences as well. Because so much of their earliest preaching was in informal settings, so too was their delivery. Franciscans preached in the vernacular languages of the locals, rather than sticking with the Latin language still present in formal church services.[43] The Franciscan churches that were eventually built were laid out with the congregation in mind, whereas other orders were housed in buildings where processionals and related liturgical considerations were prioritized.[44]

---

38. Geary, *Readings in Medieval History*, 488.
39. Spickard and Cragg, *A Global History of Christians*, 92.
40. Tierney, *The Middle Ages Volume I*, 271.
41. Ray C. Petry, *Francis of Assisi: Apostle of Poverty* (New York: AMS, 1964), 23.
42. Tierney, *The Middle Ages Volume I*, 271.
43. Cantor, *The Medieval Reader*, 61.
44. Previte-Orton, *The Shorter Cambridge Medieval History 2*, 676.

CONTRIBUTIONS TO PREACHING

Francis and the earliest monks in his order tended to relate their preaching to things pertaining to everyday life, in contrast to the Dominicans who tended to be more highly educated and preached about great leaders from ancient times.[45] Famously, part of Francis's appreciation of and focus on everyday life included an emphasis on God's creation. This contributed to such legends as the one about Francis convincing a wolf to repent for killing sheep and stories of Francis preaching to birds.[46] More credence is given to the account by some of Francis's contemporaries that he once remarked, "All men ought to give a good meal to our brothers the oxen and asses on Christmas Eve."[47] Some people might be tempted to dismiss the stories as silly and/or Francis as strange, but Spickard and Cragg see something significant in this. Francis was combatting the reemergence of Gnosticism by stressing the importance of the material world.[48]

Leonardo Boff points out that Francis started his ministry as "a lay person and wanted to remain such to evangelize the laity who were pastorally abandoned, above all the poor." Later, Francis was ordained, but his only goal with this was to "be able to preach with greater liberty, since there was a conciliar prohibition that disallowed the preaching by lay people on doctrinal matters."[49] Many in the ministry throughout the ages have been cocooned in a Christian subculture. Francis operated outside this barrier.

Francis had a global outlook. As Bruce L. Shelley puts it, "Almost from the start, Francis' vision was for the world." Demonstrating his point, Shelley points out Francis's visits to Syria, Morocco, Egypt, and Palestine.[50] In an age of great tensions between Muslims and Christians, these travels by Francis are noteworthy, especially considering he was not leading an army; he was simply communicating peace and the gospel.[51]

---

45. Ibid.

46. Such accounts are found in the thirteenth century work "The Little Flowers of St. Francis." Cantor, *The Medieval Reader*, 61–67. Of course, using a term like "legends" begs the question, "Did Francis not really preach to birds?" When one tries to find a sermon by the man, this is often the first one that comes up. Did he preach to birds, or was this story totally fabricated? Is it possible that his friends discovered him practicing a sermon alone one day and a story spun out of the incident that the birds were his only audience? After the story gained a life of its own, is it possible that a sermon text was inserted later by a reteller of the tale? It is impossible to say definitively.

47. House, *Francis of Assisi*, 251.

48. Spickard and Cragg, *A Global History of Christians*, 92.

49. Boff, *Saint Francis*, 115.

50. Shelley, *Church History in Plain Language*, 231.

51. Certainly, when it comes to relations between the Muslim world and the Christian world, there are political and military questions that come into play, but in a book about and for preachers, the focus is pretty narrowly defined. What can Christian preachers do regarding Muslims? Francis's situation was unique. He could have encountered other Muslims with a different disposition toward a Christian monk, so we should

CONCLUSION

As impressive as Francis was, he had his flaws. Donald Spoto, one of his many biographers, notes that Francis was so trusting, so willing to see the best in everyone, that he was not always able to see their personal weaknesses. This was Spoto's explanation for why Francis allowed Elias Bombarone to get so close to him that Elias was chosen to be Francis's successor. Once Francis passed and Elias succeeded him, the new leader became consumed with wealth and power. He ruled like a tyrant before he was not only expelled from the Franciscan order but excommunicated as well.[52]

Norman F. Cantor credits Francis and his Franciscans with helping to establish middle-class culture, especially middle-class religiosity, in the medieval period.[53] Francis biographer Michael de la Bedoyere elaborates on this theme by explaining that Francis's third order, those men and women who took a vow to follow his teachings but continued on in their everyday lives rather than taking up the cloth, contributed to a social revolution. Such beliefs and behaviors based on love, fraternity, and fellowship helped to end some of the cruelties of the feudal system, promoting liberty and justice instead.[54] Francis aspired to help Christians change their culture, which is certainly on the agenda of many modern preachers today.

Francis is a significant figure and role model for preachers because of his willingness—his passion—to reject worldly wealth and power and the temporary security they provide. Francis initially rejected a life of money and influence, but over time he was offered it again, as he became a virtual celebrity in the medieval world. But Francis stayed true to his calling. He continued to do what he had advocated since the beginning of his career in the ministry; he turned away from the potential fortune he could have made as a famous preacher, and he refused the trappings of power by continuing to submit to the Catholic Church. Whether or not the medieval church deserved his devotion is not the point; the point is that he maintained a humble spirit. The humility of Saint Francis of Assisi in his life and in his preaching is inspiring. His peace and hope did not come from financial security or serene world affairs. He lived a precarious existence in a dangerous world, but he found hope and joy in the Lord. This was his sermon to the world, and it is timeless.

---

not draw too much from his specific set of circumstances. But this aspect of his story is too important to be ignored.

52. Spoto, *Reluctant Saint*, 119.
53. Cantor, *The Medieval Reader*, 62.
54. De la Bedoyere, *Francis*, 233.

Sermon Excerpt

No One Should Boast in Himself but Rather Glory in the Cross of the Lord[55]

1. Be conscious, O man, of the wondrous state in which the Lord God has placed you, for He created you and formed you to the image of His beloved Son according to the body, and to His likeness according to the spirit (cf. Gen 1:26). 2. And [yet] all the creatures under heaven, each according to its nature, serve, know, and obey their Creator better than you. 3. And even the demons did not crucify Him, but you together with them have crucified Him and crucify Him even now by delighting in vices and sins.

4. In what then can you glory? 5. For if you were so subtle and wise that you had all knowledge (cf. 1 Cor 13:2) and knew how to interpret all tongues (cf. 1 Cor 12:28) and minutely investigate [the course of] the heavenly bodies, in all these things you could not glory. 6. For one demon knew more about the things of earth than all men together, even if there may have been someone who received from the Lord a special knowledge of the highest wisdom. 7. Likewise, even if you were more handsome and richer than everyone else and even if you performed wonders such as driving out demons, all these things would be an obstacle to you and none of them would belong to you nor could you glory in any of these things. 8. But in this we can glory: in our infirmities (cf. 2 Cor 12:5) and bearing daily the holy cross of our Lord Jesus Christ (cf. Luke 14:27). ♦

BIBLIOGRAPHY

Assisi, Francis, and Clare of Assisi. *Francis and Clare: The Complete Works*, The Classics of Western Spirituality. Trans. by Regis J. Armstrong and Ignatius C. Brady. Mahwah, NJ: Paulist, 1986.

Boff, Leonado. *Saint Francis: A Model for Human Liberation.* Trans. John W. Diercksmeier. New York: Crossroad, 1982.

Cantor, Norman F. *The Medieval Reader.* New York: Harper Perennial, 1994.

De la Bedoyere, Michael. *Francis: A Biography of the Saint of Assisi.* New York: Harper & Row, 1962.

Delaney, John J. *Pocket Dictionary of Saints.* Garden City, NY: Image Books, 1983.

Dillenberger, Jane. *Style and Content in Christian Art.* London: SCM, 1986.

Eskew, Harry, and Hugh T. McElrath. *Sing with Understanding: An Introduction to Christian Hymnology*, 2nd ed. Nashville: Church Street, 1995.

Geary, Patrick J. *Readings in Medieval History.* Lewiston, NY: Broadview, 1989.

House, Adrian. *Francis of Assisi: A Revolutionary Life.* Mahwah, NJ: Hidden Spring, 2001.

---

55. *Francis and Clare: The Complete Works,* The Classics of Western Spirituality, trans. Regis J. Armstrong and Ignatius C. Brady (Mahwah, NJ: Paulist, 1986), 29.

Munday, John H. *Europe in the High Middle Ages: 1150–1309*. New York: Basic Books, Inc., 1973.

Moorman, John R. H. *Saint Francis of Assisi*. Chicago: Franciscan Herald, 1963.

Petry, Ray C. *Francis of Assisi: Apostle of Poverty*. New York: AMS, 1964.

Previte-Orton, C. W. *The Shorter Cambridge Medieval History 2*. Cambridge: Cambridge University Press, 1983.

Runciman, Steven. *A History of the Crusades Volume III: The Kingdom of Acre and the Later Crusades*. Cambridge: Cambridge University Press, 1987.

Sabatier, Paul. *Life of St. Francis of Assisi*. New York: Scribner's Sons, 1920.

Shelley, Bruce L. *Church History in Plain Language*. Dallas: Word, 1982.

Spickard, Paul R. and Kevin M. Cragg. *A Global History of Christians: How Everyday Believers Experienced Their World*. Grand Rapids: Baker Academic, 1994.

Spoto, Donald. *Reluctant Saint: The Life of Francis of Assisi*. New York: Penguin Compass, 2003.

Smith, John Holland. *Francis of Assisi*. New York: Scribner's Sons, 1972.

Stetzer, Ed. "Preach the Gospel, and Since it is Necessary, Use Words." Posted June 26, 2012. *The Christian Post*. http://www.christianpost.com/news/preach-the-gospel-and-since-its-necessary-use-words-77231/

Tierney, Brian. *The Middle Ages Volume I: Sources of Medieval History*. New York: McGraw-Hill, 1992.

Saint Bonaventure

Franciscan Friar

G. R. EVANS

Bonaventure (1221–1274) was both a typical and an atypical preacher of his times. He was one of the first generations of Franciscan friars and one of the first students in the newly-invented universities of Europe. As a Franciscan, he had an education that was designed, first and foremost, to train him to preach to ordinary people about how to live a good Christian life. But it was also a formal training that involved the study of manuals about the "art of preaching." Then he was made the leader of his order and found himself with heavy administrative and political responsibilities. He went on preaching all his life and never lost sight of that first calling to bring Christ to local people.

HISTORICAL BACKGROUND

Bonaventure's parents, Giovanni di Fidanza and Maria Ritella, brought up their family at Bagnorea in Tuscany. He was baptized as Giovanni, after his father, who was probably a physician.[1] We do not know why Giovanni was attracted to the idea of becoming a Franciscan friar. It was still quite a new and fashionable career choice for a pious young man. The life of a friar combined the chance of getting a university education with a commitment to a new style of religious life in which preaching was central. While monks lived in the cloister, usually in houses built in the countryside, friars, known as "mendicants," lived an urban life, bringing them closer to the people to whom they were called to preach the gospel.

Giovanni, who would take the name Bonaventure when he became a friar, was able to choose between two main "orders" of this innovative way of life, the Franciscans and the Dominicans. The Dominicans, who took their name from

---

1. Two helpful introductions to Bonaventure are J. Guy Bourgerol, *Introduction to the Works of Bonaventure* (Patterson, NJ: St. Anthony Guild Press, 1964) and Ewert Cousins, *Bonaventure,* The Classics of Western Spirituality (New York: Paulist, 1978).

their founder Dominic (1170–1221), provided proper training for preachers so that they could persuade the heretics in the south of France and northern Spain to return to the mainstream church and the true faith. [2]

The Franciscans were founded by Francis of Assisi (1181/2–1226), Bonaventure's fellow Italian. Francis had originally embarked on a military career and expected to follow his father into the family business. However, in 1207, while at church, the figure of Christ on the cross spoke to him and called him to a new way of life. He was to return to a life of apostolic poverty in which he and his followers would live in the utmost simplicity, as Christ had taught his disciples to do, preaching the gospel wherever they went.[3]

Pope Innocent III approved Francis's new religious order in 1209 and it grew rapidly. By the time he died in 1226, there were several thousand Franciscan friars, and despite Francis's own reluctance to encourage too much academic ambition, they were addressing the need for a proper education for their members so that they could preach to a high standard.

Bonaventure joined the Franciscans in the late 1230s or early 1240s as an adolescent or young adult, and it was probably then that he began his serious education. Each friary had a *lector*, or in-house teacher, able to provide new friars with a good basic education to equip them to preach the gospel.

Educational Pursuits

The Franciscans, perhaps sensing his ability, sent Bonaventure to the Franciscan house in Paris as a university student. This was a practice that had developed from the introduction of the *lectores* and the development of their syllabus. Each province now ran a *studium generale*, a higher-level school, to teach the more intellectually promising recruits. The most advanced of these schools were located in the university towns of Oxford, Paris, and Cambridge, so students could hear university lectures and participate in academic life. Universities themselves were an innovation only a generation old. Paris had one of the first. By the time Bonaventure arrived, the presence of a growing community of students was visibly bolstering the local economy and transforming the city. It had acquired a city wall and paved streets and new houses for wealthy residents, and the cathedral of Notre Dame was in the process of being completed.

Although the timeline is not clear, it seems likely that Bonaventure would have arrived in the order and possibly to study in Paris as early as 1238, still in his late teens (the later date of his arrival would have been, 1242/1243). In either

2. Guy Bedouelle, *Saint Dominic: The Grace of the Word* (San Francisco: Ignatius, 1995).
3. Augustine Thompson, *Francis of Assisi: A New Biography* (Ithaca, NY: Cornell University Press, 2012).

case, his first task as a student was to complete his undergraduate degree in the arts. The syllabus comprised the basic subjects of grammar, logic, and rhetoric, with the four classical mathematical subjects (arithmetic, music, geometry, and astronomy) studied more cursorily. In addition to these, new textbooks of philosophy were added, since the scientific and philosophical writings of Aristotle were now available in Latin translations. During this course of studies, Bonaventure would have been continuing the requirements to complete his novitiate as a friar. This meant spending the required time learning the rules and the way of life before taking his final vows of obedience.

The friar-students had to take the same examinations as the "seculars" in order to become Masters of Arts and full, lifelong members of the *universitas* (the term is simply the Latin for "guild" and the governance structure was the same as that of a contemporary guild of goldsmiths or fishmongers). To gain a degree (*gradus*, from which we get the modern English "graduate") he had to satisfy the Masters in a *viva voce* examination. Higher degrees or doctorates in one of the three "higher degree" subjects of law, medicine, and theology were then open to him, and he began on the long course in theology. These were not "research degrees," but taught courses taking many years of study.

Relations between the friars and the "secular" Masters were rarely comfortable, because the seculars resented the friars. They were proving to be high-powered and ambitious to take over senior positions and control in the university, because the higher education of their friars was now a fundamental requisite within the Franciscan (and Dominican) order. There were energetic disputes about the sequence in which the course should proceed. The friars, who were anxious to get to the subject of theology as quickly as possible, did not necessarily want to follow the progression of the arts course before their theological study. Naturally, the theologians claimed they could cover the more elementary arts material, especially as the arts touched on theological topics.

As a result of such academic squabbles, both Bonaventure and Thomas Aquinas, one of the outstanding young Dominicans at the university, had to wait for three years after they had completed the requirements for the theology degree. Finally, the Pope intervened in 1257, and they were able to graduate.

The universities, with their competitive academic climate, attracted leading scholars and theologians; the Franciscans and Dominicans provided some of the best, so Bonaventure certainly had the best tuition available. Alexander of Hales (ca. 1185–1245) held the Franciscan "Chair." Bonaventure wrote of him as his "Master" and "father" and saw himself as trying to continue his work. Next, John of la Rochelle took over the professorship while Bonaventure was a student.

Bonaventure's own lecturing began, as did that of every aspiring Master of Theology, with lecture-commentaries on the *Sentences* of Peter Lombard (c.1096–1160). This was a textbook, at first highly controversial, which was adopted by the universities of Europe throughout the Middle Ages, because it offered a comprehensive survey of systematic theology, with quotations which enabled the student to compare the views on disputed points of such early Christian authors as Augustine of Hippo, Jerome, Gregory the Great, and the Venerable Bede. A lecturer would take his listeners through the text, familiarizing them with the historic and contemporary disputes on the theological ramifications of these arguments.

Ecclesiastical Leadership

In 1257, Bonaventure was elected minister general of the Francisans, and the focus of his work had to change. He did not cease to have responsibilities as a theologian, however. His university experience was invaluable to him in this new role. As minister general he had to be able to deal with some sophisticated theological disputes. High levels of academic achievement meant that some members of the order became prominent theologians and some of those were highly controversial. Roger Bacon (ca. 1214–1292) was one of these. In 1254, Gerard of Borgo San Donnino had published his *Introductorius in Evangelium æternum* (*An Introduction to the Eternal Gospel*). Many viewed this work as heretical. In 1260, the General Chapter of the Order held at Narbonne promulgated a decree prohibiting the publication of any work by a member of the order, without permission, though this was rescinded in 1266 in Bacon's case.

Bonaventure faced other problems when he took charge of the order as minister general. One was the consequence of a deep division in the order that had emerged when Francis died. Some (the "Spirituals") wanted to remain faithful to the simplicity of his vision and take the requirement of poverty seriously, not only as individuals but also as an order. Most (the "Conventuals") said this was not practical and saw the need for the acquisition of property if the order was to survive. An enormous controversy began, engaging the wider church. The claim that Jesus's instructions were not to be taken at their face value and there was nothing wrong with amassing wealth was hard to swallow. A working compromise was proposed by which property could be regarded as for "use" rather than as being owned, but that prompted extensive academic controversy. As the century went on and the "Spirituals" and "Conventuals" acquired their labels, it also became apparent that among the "Spirituals" were extremists who might prove to be heretical. They caused offense to the ecclesiastical authorities because they challenged vested interests, and they attracted to themselves even more radical and revolutionary fringe groups.

As minister general, Bonaventure had to take a position on this controversy between the two groups. The topic must have been of special interest to him, because in 1256, he had presided over an academic disputation in Paris on *Disputed Questions on Evangelical Perfection*. He took the side of the defenders of poverty, against arguments from some of the secular masters, notably William of Saint-Amour (1200–1272), but he did so moderately, restating what he understood to be Francis's vision. Papal bulls were already in force, relaxing the rule of poverty in part. The Franciscan General Chapter had already refused to obey these and Bonaventure made no change to this decision. He was prepared to make allowances to meet the needs of students in Franciscan houses and in the universities.

Bonaventure's ideas about Francis and his intentions for the order were eventually set out in his own book on the subject. In 1266, Bonaventure wrote *Legenda Maior* (the *Life of Francis*). The General Chapter of the order approved this text as a replacement for all previous attempts, and it was arranged that every Franciscan house should have its copy. The instruction was clearly followed, because a very large number of copies survive.[4]

Bonaventure was evidently seen as a promising man. The high regard in which he was held can be gauged by the fact that he was seen as a candidate for a bishopric in 1265. The Pope wanted to make him Archbishop of York, but he refused. He did accept Gregory X's decision to make him a cardinal in 1273, and that same year he agreed to be Bishop of Albano, which led to his resignation as minister general of the Franciscans in May 1274.

Late in his life, Bonaventure became involved in one of the attempts made to mend the schism of 1054 that divided Greek and Latin Christians. He attended the Council of Lyons in 1274 as a cardinal-bishop. The Greek representatives included Germanus, bishop of Nicaea, and a representative of the Byzantine emperor. Ecumenical agreement was envisaged in the late medieval centuries, at least in the West, in terms of persuading Christians in the schism from Rome to agree with Rome's views and position. The Greeks duly accepted (it was reported) the primacy of the Bishop of Rome over the Greek churches' Patriarchates and the Roman position on other points of doctrinal disagreement. Union was declared, an oath taken, and a joint Mass celebrated. The creed was sung in Latin and Greek with the controversial *filioque* clause included, although the Greeks had not been required to add it to their own creed. However, the local Greek bishops would not accept the agreement. Bonaventure never learned of this failure. He died suddenly, eight days after the union had been agreed to.

---

4. Christopher M. Cullen, *Bonaventure* (Oxford: Oxford University Press, 2006) gives an outline of the background to Bonaventure's life.

THEOLOGY OF PREACHING

Bonaventure preached within a tradition which carried a recognized and implicit theology of preaching. In formal training of clergy, a university teacher would lecture on the set texts of the theology course line by line, bringing to bear their opinions on the text so as to illuminate it, and as appropriate, offering supplementary quotations from the Early Church Fathers. Then, the teacher would preside over formal *disputations* at which particularly knotty and complex problems of interpretation would be discussed, again marshalling quotations from the fathers for and against a particular view. The Master presiding would then "determine" the question, once again providing a supportive text. Theological preaching of this era was approached in the same analytical way, testing theological positions with its support—using Scripture and the Early Church Fathers as substantiating authorities.

Bonaventure also inherited a tradition of pastoral preaching that had developed from the end of the twelfth century into the "art of preaching," which had a theological purpose that went beyond literal to the allegorical, moral, and prophetic interpretations of a text. Popular sermons especially took trouble to offer practical "moral" lessons which ordinary people with no theological training could take to heart.

In addition to Bonaventure's pastoral preaching, he also preached to enrich the spirituality of his listeners. From his own special, personal calling, he sought to encourage his listeners to find themselves uplifted toward God, experiencing the divine presence at a level where the spelling out of the theology vanished into "knowing God."

METHODOLOGY FOR PREACHING

At one level, Bonaventure was an "academic" preacher trained in the elaborate formal preaching conventions of his time and well able to impress the audience at a "university sermon." But there is good evidence that he preached "popular" sermons too, addressed to ordinary people and using homely examples and illustrations to clarify the meaning of the Scripture texts. (Sometimes a preacher in Latin would rely on a translator to convey what he was saying to his listeners in their own language).

All his life Bonaventure invested in the task of preaching; this was central to his calling as a Franciscan. However, medieval sermons present special difficulties in reconstructing how they sounded and how effective they were. By now the "art of preaching" involved several formal expectations. It was one of three medieval "rhetorical arts" that had been developed with appropriate technical requirements since the end of the eleventh century, borrowing heavily from the rhetorical rules of the ancient world where every educated Greek or Roman was expected to be able to make a speech for political, forensic, or eulogistic purposes.

The first of the rhetorical arts, the "art of letter writing" *(ars dictaminis),* had emerged at the end of the eleventh century to meet a need for properly trained notaries and letter writers to staff the civil services of Europe. They were trained in early "business schools" like the one at Bologna. The art of letter writing taught proper rules for greeting a correspondent *(salutatio),* the framework for a letter, and how to vary the cadence of sentences to please the ear and persuade the recipient to warm to what the letter said. Then during the twelfth century came the "art of poetry" *(ars poetriae).* Manuals for the training of poets emphasized ways of organizing the narrative and the choice of an appropriate style.

Toward the end of the twelfth century emerged the "art of preaching" *(ars praedicandi).* This was designed to meet the needs of the audience of a "university sermon," but it could be adapted for popular sermons too. The thirteenth century friars produced a variety of preaching aids, such as collections of *exempla,* or illustrations and packaged arguments, which could be brought into use as required. Dictionaries of key words in the Bible were compiled, bringing together texts using a given word in the Latin Vulgate, so the sermon could explore the teaching of Scripture as it was associated with that word.

The practical preacher was taught by the "art of preaching" manuals to begin by choosing a text of Scripture. They would then divide the lessons to be learned into three sections. Each of those should be subdivided further into more threes. The threes must then be expounded one at a time, with close reference to the text of Scripture at every point. Bonaventure's surviving sermons in written form keep closely to this pattern. As for popular preaching in the language of ordinary people, when that happened it was recorded in Latin, and it is hard to say how the preacher managed to reach out to an audience which had no Latin and no formal education.

CONTRIBUTIONS TO PREACHING

Bonaventure's surviving writings fill several modern printed volumes. Every medieval preacher preached on Scripture. Similarly, every medieval preacher thought he was explaining and defending the teaching of Scripture as he preached, though naturally they did not all see its truths in the same way. No doubt Bonaventure took seriously the Franciscan calling to personal humility, but it is common for medieval writers to use the "modesty topos," claiming to be unworthy, when sometimes they are really boasting.

Faithfulness to the Word for the Life of the Preacher

Some of Bonaventure's writings reflect his "university" work. Apart from his commentary on the *Sentences,* some Scriptural commentaries survive: on Saint Luke, Ecclesiastes, Wisdom, and on the Gospel of Saint John. Commentary of this sort derived from lecturing, literally *lectio,* when a lecturer "read" the text with his students, explaining difficult words and giving opinions with reference to earlier Christian authorities where a portion of the text raised a theological question. It was all very academic and traditional, though individual lecturers brought their own insights and might press their personal interpretations against those of other Masters and earlier authorities.

A disputation—a university activity prompted by questions arising during lectures—was an advanced exercise for students, and one in which they would need to show their proficiency in their degree examination. This disputation could also be a display piece presided over by a Master. Records of some of Bonaventure's *Disputed Questions* survive, including his *Disputed Questions on Evangelical Perfection,* which are concerned with the contemporary debates about poverty, and, probably from the time when he was completing his doctorate in theology, the *Disputed Questions on the Knowledge of Christ.* At the time, it was fashionable to debate about the different ways in which the incarnate Christ might know things, as God and as Man. The *Disputed Questions on the Mystery of the Trinity* includes a discussion of the long-standing debates on proofs for the existence of God.

Within the Franciscans' own houses and in the university at large it was common to hold *collationes* or "conferences." The Dominican Jordan of Saxony (c.1190–1237) had adapted this monastic tradition, found in the early Christian centuries, for use on Sundays and special feast days. Anyone with a degree or studying for a degree could attend, and secretaries took notes of the discussion that were later approved by the Master who had led it. The *collatio* could even be used by secular authorities when they needed a matter to be authoritatively settled by "the University," employing its academic experts. Louis IX, king of France, took advantage of this possibility in an attempt to settle the disturbance caused by one of the secular Masters at Paris, William of Saint-Amour, who had written a book *De Antichristo* in 1254, attacking the mendicants and calling them followers of Antichrist. Thomas Aquinas and Thomas of York, as well as Bonaventure, obliged with *collationes,* and the pope was able to formally condemn William of Saint-Amour's position in 1256.

In 1267, Bonaventure's own "conferences" on the *Collations on the Ten Commandments* allowed him to explore a contemporary controversy arising out of the impossibility of reconciling Aristotle's view that the world is eternal with the story told in Genesis. His *Collations on the Seven Gifts* were given in 1268.

He also gave a series of *Collations on the Six Days*. It is possible to get the flavor of these seminars from the polished text that has come down to us. Bonaventure begins with the qualities required of "hearers of divine knowledge of which Christ is the centre." Christ's people, who form the church, live in harmony and unity, according to divine law and in peace, praising God.[5] Thus, he sets the scene and the atmosphere for an exploration of the story of the creation in Genesis.

Bonaventure also wrote original works on spiritual theology, intended to help Franciscans and others on what he evidently saw as a spiritual journey. Of these, the most famous is *The Mind's Journey to God*. This was written after a retreat in 1259, soon after Bonaventure became minister general; it was in the very area where Francis had received the stigmata in 1224.

Among his spiritual writings there is also a *Soliloquy on the Four Spiritual Exercises*, *The Tree of Life*, and *The Triple Way*. For beginners in theology, he composed a brief aid to the main points of Christian theology, which he based on Scripture. He added a work (whose authenticity has been questioned) on the problem of understanding how a training in the liberal arts might equip the Christian to understand the faith, entitled, *Reduction of the Arts to Theology*.

Of Bonaventure's sermons, several collections survive.[6] His secretary of the moment carefully kept copies of his sermons. We have the advantage, not common with medieval preachers, of knowing who some of his secretaries were and what they thought about their role. Marc of Montefeltro was secretary to several ministers general. The historian Salimbene de Adam said in his *Chronicle* that Marc was a good *dictator* and composed various letters.[7] Salimbene also said that this secretary was especially fond of Bonaventure (*in tantum dilexit*). Bonaventure noted that on one occasion when he was preaching to some clergy, this secretary went to him and tried to prompt him to preach more in the fiery spirit of Ecclesiasticus 22:24 and make them cry. Others could have done the same if they wanted to possess copies of his sermons, but it is not easy now to reconstruct the trail of such recordings.

One sermon series was preached on Sundays through the year, probably in the early 1250s, though not necessarily as a set or in a single year, in the form in which we have them now.[8] The Sunday sermons were probably compiled later

---

5. First Collation 1.2, *Collations on the Six Days (Collationes in Hexaemeron)*, trans. José de Vinck (Paterson, NJ: St. Anthony Guild Press, 1969), 1.

6. The Quaracchi edition of the *Opera Omnia* also has sermons in vols. V. 329–579 = reportatio of *Collationes de decem praeceptis* and VI.239–42.

7. *Cronica fratris Salimbene de Adam*, ed. O. Holder-Eger, MGHSS 32 (Hannover/Leipzig 1905–13), 307–08.

8. *Sermones dominicales*, ed. J. G. Bougerol, Bibliotheca Franciscana Scholastica Medii Aevi (Grottaferrata, 1977).

and made into a corpus or collection.[9] These *Sermones dominicales* can be dated plausibly as separate entities given in different years in different places. The manuscript tradition preserves some versions as miscellaneous and some as a set.[10]

Another collection of sermons can be reconstructed: one preached for feast days and saints' days and for other occasions.[11] In some cases it is even possible to show when a sermon was actually delivered. For example, the sermon on "The Word was made flesh" (John 1:14) was given in Paris in the Friars' Church as a university sermon.[12] Sermons 2 and 4 were given on the same day, but "to the people" and not just to the friars.[13] For some feasts, several sermons survive; for example, three for Epiphany, beginning with reflections on *Ubi est qui natus est rex Iudaeorum* (Matt 2:2) and encouraging the hearers of the sermon to be "seekers after wisdom."[14] There is an introductory *prothema* that discusses the four kinds of people who are unsuited to this searching (*inhabilia*), the light-minded, pleasure-seeking, impious, and wicked, each with subkinds to be discussed.

The Necessity of Humility in the Life of the Preacher

The *prothema* was a sermon prologue, and it noted that the preacher is unworthy and should aim at a *captatio benevolentiae*, which is an attempt to win the goodwill of the hearers and include a call for the grace of the Holy Spirit. For Bonaventure, this was much more than a sermonic convention. Bonaventure concludes his own prologue by admitting that we all suffer from many failings, and he actively sought to engage his audience in the pursuit of personal humility. In this text, Bonaventure's personal piety and profound commitment to his preacher's calling as a friar shines through. Still devoutly drawn to the example of the man who was his own inspiration as a Franciscan preacher, Bonaventure preached on the life of Saint Francis and the lessons to be learned from it.[15] For example, on one St. Francis Day, Bonaventure took a text from Haggai 2:24 about the way the Lord chose his servant for particular tasks.[16] This gave him the theme: the characteristics of Francis that made him the right choice for his calling. He was humble (*humilis*) so as to be able to despise the good things of this

---

9. *Sermons de diversis*, ed. J. G. Bougerol, vol. 1 (Paris: Bougerol publisher Éditions franciscaines, 1993), 7.

10. *Sermones dominicales*, ed. J. G. Bougerol, Bibliotheca Franciscana Scholastica Medii Aevi (Grottaferrata, 1977), 31.

11. *Sermons de diversis*, ed. J. G. Bougerol, 2 vols. (Paris: Bougerol publisher Éditions franciscaines, 1993).

12. Sermon 3, *Verbum caro factum est* in *Sermons de diversis*, vol. 1, ed. J. G. Bougerol (Paris: Bougerol publisher Éditions franciscaines, 1993), 33.

13. *Sermons de diversis*, vol. 1, 34.

14. *Sermons de diversis*, vol. 1, 180 ff.

15. *Sermons de diversis*, vol. 1, 36.

16. Sermon I on Haggai 2.24, 4 October, St Francis' day, *Sermons de diversis*, vol. 2, ed. J. G. Bougerol (Paris: Bougerol publisher Éditions franciscaines, 1993), 742.

world, manly (*virilis*) in mortification of the flesh and rejection of its pleasures, and obedient to God's commandments, and so God chose him.[17] In a separate sermon on Saint Francis, Bonaventure took Isaiah 42 as his text. The story went that Pacificus, who was the first to take the order and its Franciscan mission into France, was praying with Francis one day, fell asleep, and had a vision. He saw the heavens open and a beautiful cathedral in the sky and asked whose it was. He was told in his dream that it was reserved for Francis because of his humility. When he woke up he asked Francis what he thought of himself. Francis said he thought he was the greatest sinner in the world.

CONCLUSION

From the written records that survive, it should be apparent that, as a preacher, Bonaventure was conventional in giving shape and direction to his words. He kept close to the Scripture, as did all his contemporaries, dividing his points neatly into twos and threes. Much harder to reconstruct are the tone of voice, the use of gesture, and the skills of delivery which were strongly felt to be appropriate to a "rhetorical art." The conventions in Bonaventure's sermons are obvious, but something of their vividness and the passion and sensitivity of Bonaventure's delivery can perhaps be glimpsed.

Sermon Excerpt

The Perfection of Life[18]

"Happy the man whom you instruct, O LORD, whome by your law you teach" (Ps 94.12). No one, admittedly, is to be esteemed wise save only him who is taught by the unction of the Spirit. This is why the Prophet David says that he alone is truly happy and wise whose mind the Lord instructs, and whose soul he teaches by his law. For the law of the Lord is the only law without stain, the only blameless law, the only one that converts souls to salvation (Ps 18.8 ff). Now, the teaching or the knowledge of this law is to be sought, not so much externally in its letter, but rather through a devout movement of the mind. It is to be longed for in spirit

---

17. Ibid., 744–47.

18. Sermon-treatise on the perfection of life, addressed to sisters, Mystical Opuscula, *The Works of Bonaventure*, trans. José de Vinckt (Paterson, NJ: St. Anthony Guild Press, 1960), 209–10.

and in power (1 Thessalonians 1.5), so as to let him teach interiorly who alone can change the exterior harshness of the law into inner sweetness.

The law of the Lord teaches us what to do and what to avoid, what to believe and what to pray for, what to desire and what to fear; it teaches us to be immaculate and blameless, to fulfil our promises and weep for our sins, to despise the things of the world and reject the things of the flesh; finally, it teaches us to turn with our whole heart, our whole soul, our whole mind, to Jesus Christ alone (Matthew 22.37). ◆

BIBLIOGRAPHY

Bedouelle, Guy. *Saint Dominic: The Grace of the Word*. San Francisco: Ignatius, 1995.

Bourgerol, J. Guy. *Introduction to the Works of Bonaventure*. Patterson, NJ: St. Anthony Guild Press, 1964.

Cousins, Ewert. *Bonaventure*. The Classics of Western Spirituality. New York: Paulist, 1978.

Cullen, Christopher M. *Bonaventure*. Oxford: Oxford University Press, 2006.

"First Collation 1.2." In *Collations on the Six Days (Collationes in Hexaemeron)*. Trans. by José de Vinck. Paterson, NJ: St. Anthony Guild Press, 1969.

Opera Omnia. vols. 329–579. reportatio of *Collationes de decem praeceptis* and VI.239–42.

Cronica fratris Salimbene de Adam. Edited by O. Holder-Eger. MGHSS 32 (Hannover/Leipzig 1905–13), 307–8.

Sermones dominicales. Edited by J. G. Bougerol. Bibliotheca Franciscana Scholastica Medii Aevi (Grottaferrata, 1977).

Sermons de diversis. Edited by J. G. Bougerol. 2 vol. Paris: Bougerol publisher Éditions franciscaines, 1993.

"Sermon-treatise on the perfection of life, addressed to sisters, Mystical Opuscula." Pages 209–10 in *The Works of Bonaventure*. Trans. by José de Vinckt. Paterson, NJ: St. Anthony Guild Press, 1960.

Thompson, Augustine. *Francis of Assisi: A New Biography*. Ithaca, NY: Cornell University Press, 2012.

Meister Eckhart
Preaching the Inexpressible God

DANIEL FĂRCAȘ

Meister Eckhart (ca. 1260–1329), a Dominican friar, was a mystical theologian concerned with preaching God in his transcendence as qualitatively different than his creation. While pulled between the scholasticism of the thirteenth century and the mysticism of the fourteenth century, he sought to preach and care for his congregation. For Eckhart, knowing God equals becoming one with God, in an ecstatic vision. As God cannot be fully grasped by human understanding, a true theologian should challenge human logic using imaginative preaching, full of symbols and paradoxes—a duty Eckhard pursued as he invited his listeners to a personal encounter with God through his preaching.

HISTORICAL BACKGROUND

Born ca. 1260, at Hochheim, in Thuringia, Germany, Eckhart became a Dominican monk in 1275. This was one year before the death of Thomas Aquinas, the most important Dominican of that time. Beginning in 1280, Eckhart studied at the Dominican *studium generale* in Cologne, where he likely met Albert the Great, who was one of the major figures of the Dominican order. Between 1293 and 1294, Eckhart read Peter Lombard's *Sentences*, which was, at that time, required for all those who stood to earn the title of master of theology at the University of Paris. There is one extant lesson from Eckhart's commentary on Lombard's *Sentences*.[1] Between 1294 and 1298, Eckhart was prior of the Erfurt Dominicans and vicar general of the Dominicans from Thuringia. He taught at the University of Paris between 1302 and 1303, where three of his *Parisian Questions* were publicly disputed. In 1303, he became the provincial of Saxony for the Dominican order until 1311. During this season, he founded three convents at Braunschweig, Dortmund, and Gröningen.[2] A couple years later, Eckhart started

---

1. Alessandra Beccarisi, "Eckhart's Latin Works," in *A Companion to Meister Eckhart* (Leiden: Brill, 2013), 86.
2. Alain de Libera, *Eckhart, Suso Tauler ou la divinisation de l'homme* (Paris: Seuil, 1996), 33.

to take spiritual care of the beguines, who were women yearning for a higher spiritual life, living in religious communities without taking lifelong religious vows. It was during this season of his ministry that a number of his more famous sermons were preached. During this time he also wrote a number of treatises (e.g., *The Book of Divine Consolation*). He left Strasbourg and the ministry there in 1323 or 1324 because he was suspected of heresy. From there he returned to Cologne to teach at the Dominican *studium generale*.

Eckhart died in 1327, striving to defend himself against accusations of heresy that had been formulated against him in 1325. The process ended in 1329, after Eckhart's death, with the condemnation of a number of his theses.[3] Eckhart was one of the first theologians to write both in the official ecclesiastical Latin and in the vernacular German. Both a scholar and a pastor, Eckhart was considered by his contemporaries a "master of reading" (*lesemeister*), as well as a "master of living" (*lebemeister*). He was both a man of theory and of praxis, and he lived his life between his duties in the academy and the pastorate.

Scholastic and Mystic Pastor

Educated as a theologian in the second part of the thirteenth century, Eckhart was more than a theologian—he was a man of the church who was close to people, in spite of his ecclesiastical positions and academic calling. The Dominican order to which he belonged was also known as the order of the preachers, because their purpose was to teach, preach the gospel, and defend the faith. In fact, the Dominicans were a significant presence at the University of Paris in the thirteenth century. As a Dominican monk, Eckhart was educated in the intellectual spirit of thirteenth century scholasticism, represented by some major theologians, including his Dominican fellows Albert the Great and Thomas Aquinas. Eckhart considered himself indebted to the two scholastic doctors of the church; the thirteenth century scholasticism and fourteenth century mysticism are intertwined in his writings. While Christian scholasticism focuses on modeling the Christian worldview based on using speculative methods and concepts of Greek philosophy, mysticism focuses more on the ecstatic experience of the soul in relation to God or even union with God. With Eckhart, there is no clear separation of the two—he is both a schoolman and a mystic. Indeed, Meister Eckhart is a speculative mystic, as he uses philosophical concepts to explain the mystical union. An important number of his writings—including some German treatises

---

3. For these biographical data, see: Alain de Libera, *La mystique rhénane d'Albert le Grand à Maître Eckhart* (Paris: Seuil, 1994); Libera, *Eckhart*; Anastasia Wendlinder, *Speaking of God in Thomas Aquinas and Meister Eckhart: Beyond Analogy* (Burlington, VT: Ashgate, 2014), 56–58; Kurt Flasch, *Meister Eckhart: Philosoph des Christentums* (München: Beck, 2010), 17–18.

and sermons—reflect Eckhart's genuine interest in pastoral care. Of course, it would be wrong to contrast Eckhart's academic writings and his pastoral sermons and treatises in a contextual vacuum. The difference between the two categories is more stylistic than theological. Eckhart's scholasticism is inherently mystical and his mysticism relies on his training in scholasticism. His presence in academia and his pastoral care are not in contradiction with each other, and this is one of the reasons for which Eckhart's case is fascinating.

Ministry of the Written and Spoken Word

One of Eckhart's sermons on Mary and Martha argued that Christians should partake of both a contemplative life (Mary) and an active life (Martha), and this twofold pursuit rang true for the mystic as well.[4] These dual pursuits influenced Eckhart's preaching, both his Latin sermons for the academy, and his German sermons for beguines and for the unlearned audience in general. A quick look at Eckhart's life reveals alternating periods when he taught in the academy and periods when he took care of his flock. At that time, different Christian religious movements—including the beguine movement—emerged in the Western church, which constituted a real challenge for the clergy. It seems that throughout his ministry, Eckhart was in charge of seventy-five Dominican nun convents in the area of Alsace and Switzerland and about eighty-five beguine convents in the area of Strasbourg.[5] Most of Eckhart's German treatises are pastoral writings. For instance, *The Book of the Divine Comfort* is considered a pastoral letter addressed to Queen Agnes of Hungary. *The Nobleman*, sometimes considered a part of the previous treatise, is a brief pastoral sermon demonstrating that Eckhart's treatises and sermons share a consistent theological framework whether they are presented in the written or spoken word. In both instances, he is concerned with the pastoral care and spiritual edification of those he shepherds.

PHILOSOPHICAL BACKGROUND

At the crossroads of the thirteenth and fourteenth centuries, preaching was reinvented in Western Europe. The emergence of German mysticism and its intersection with scholarly tradition by some of its representatives generated an extremely interesting and controversial theology coupled with a new manner of preaching.

The background of Eckhart's preaching is framed by different shifts in the theological debates of his time. One of them is the status of the intellect—both

---

4. Meister Eckhart, *Sermon 86* (McGinn, 2009, no. 9:83).
5. de Libera, *Eckhart*, 13.

the human and divine. Another controversy was over the hierarchy of the powers of the human soul. The Christian medieval image of the human soul was impacted by Plato's psychology, developed in dialogues such as *Phaidros, Phaidon* and *The Republic*, as well as by Aristotle's theory of the soul from *On the Soul*. The consensus of the Middle Ages was that the two most important powers of the soul were the intellect and the will. But, therein lies the question: which one should rank as the highest human faculty? This question caused a continual dispute between the Dominican and the Franciscan chairs at the University of Paris. According to the Dominicans, the intellect ranked as the highest power of the soul, because it was considered the *imago dei* in man—the image of God—the Logos. Humans are endowed with reason, marking a major difference between humans and animals. On the contrary, according to the Franciscans, the highest power of the soul was the will, because it is will that generates love. Eckhart's theology is a *mystical* one, and his mysticism is an *intellectual* one. This means that unity with God takes place in the intellect. God as Logos is intellect and so is the human soul.

A more sensitive aspect of the debate over the intellect included the Parisian Averroism, represented by philosophers who gathered at the faculty of arts of the University of Paris. The faculty of arts was the lower faculty of the university, as all students were supposed to learn in this faculty before enrolling at one of the three higher faculties: theology, canon law, and medicine. In fact, the "artists" were philosophers, such as Siger of Brabant and Boethius of Dacia—two of the major professors of the thirteenth century faculty of arts. One of their major philosophical theses was the "unity of the intellect" (monopsychism, i.e. the contention that only one intellect manifests itself in every human being and this is a divine intellect). While Eckhart was not an Averroist, there are some Averroist echoes in Eckhart's mysticism in the way he understood the mystical unity of human intellect and the Godhead.[6]

Another shift concerned the different unofficial spiritual movements of the time that impacted theology. The emergence of the feminine beguine movement highly preoccupied the church hierarchy. This movement emerged in different areas of the Low Countries and extended into the Germanic area. Meister Eckhart was assigned to preach to the beguines in the Strasbourg area, and this is where a large number of Eckhart's German sermons were preached.

The doctrinal debate between Dominican and Franciscans and the debate with the philosophers of the faculty of arts, as well as the beguine movement,

---

6. Kurt Flasch, *Meister Eckhart: Die Geburt der Deutschen 'Mystik' aus dem Geist der arabischen Philosophie* (München: Beck, 2008); Hans Daiber, *Islamic Thought in the Dialogue of Cultures: A Historical and Bibliographical Survey* (Leiden: Brill, 2012), 211.

all worked as a catalyst of a new approach in theology and preaching. This is how Eckhart's theology was possible.

THEOLOGY OF PREACHING

While Eckhart's theological corpus of writings is not as extensive as that of Aquinas, Albert the Great, or Bonaventure, it varies in its purposes, intended recipients, literary genres, language usage and style.[7]

A Threefold, Theological Organization

Eckhart imagined his own theological work as a system—a threefold system, which incorporates his so-called "work of propositions," a "work of questions," and a "work of commentaries."[8]

The Work of Propositions

The work of propositions was supposed to include more than a thousand theses defined in fourteen treatises (on being and nonbeing, on the One and the multiple, on the truth and the false, on the good and the bad, on God as the Supreme Being and on nothingness, etc.). It seems that the work of propositions was supposed to deal with basic philosophical terms or with pairs of philosophical terms on which the propositions were based.

The Work of Questions

The work of questions should be understood in the context of the so-called "disputed questions"—questions disputed between two different theologians. In the thirteenth century the disputed questions had become an academic duty at the University of Paris. They dealt with both philosophical and dogmatic issues. Also, different dogmatic treatises of that time were sometimes a list of theological questions, including pros and cons, as well as the author's proposed solution of the question. (This was the case of Aquinas's *Summa Theologiae*, which consists in

---

7. The critical edition of Eckhart's works, currently in use, is the Kohlhammer edition (ongoing edition, since 1958). By its structure and partitions, it clearly reflects Eckhart's scholarly readers and his flock he cared for. This edition includes the German works (*Die deutschen werke*, abbreviated DW) and the Latin works (*Die lateinischen werke*, abreviated LW). Most of Eckhart's sermons are written in German and they can be found in DW I, DW II, DW III, DW IV,1, DW IV,2 (a number of almost 130 German sermons). The authenticity of these sermons faces scrutinizing debate. The most reliable are the sermons included in the DW I (German sermons 1 to 24). The Latin sermons have been published in the LW IV (Latin sermons I to LVI). We should also mention the Easter Sermon of 1294 and the sermon on the feast day of St. Augustine (LW V). An English translation of Eckhart's German sermons is available. It includes 97 German sermons translated by Maurice O'C Walshe (translation revised by Bernard McGinn).

8. Meister Eckhart, *Prologus generalis* in *Opus tripartitum*, n. 3–6, LW I (Stuttgart: Kohnhammer), 149:3–151:12.

such a series of questions Aquinas strives to answer.) Eckhart's work includes only five questions dealing with different theological or philosophical issues.

The Work of Commentaries

The third section of the Eckhartian corpus is the work of commentaries. This includes both Eckhart's biblical commentaries on canonical (Genesis, Exodus, Song of Songs, Gospel of John) and noncanonical (Wisdom of Solomon, Ecclesiasticus) biblical books. An important part of these works are his corresponding sermons.[9] Commentaries and sermons were classified by Eckhart himself as two different subsections of the "work of commentaries." It is obvious that biblical commentaries of the thirteenth and fourteenth centuries were not yet exegetical commentaries in the thorough modern meaning of the word. Nevertheless, it is also clear that, in classifying commentaries and sermons together, Eckhart had a sense of the relationship between Bible reading and preaching. It is clear that, according to Eckhart, both commentaries and preaching belong to a larger system.

Mystical Theology

Eckhart was a mystic. Mysticism in the thirteenth and fourteenth centuries intended to correct the rigorous and dry scholasticism of the past. Nevertheless, it would be erroneous to think that Eckhart's mysticism had nothing to do with thirteenth century scholasticism. Eckhart is both a scholastic philosopher and a mystical theologian, and there is no consequential distinction between Eckhart's mystical writings and his scholastic ones. Eckhart's philosophy is full of Christian mysticism and his mysticism is amazingly philosophical. This is a particularity of Eckhart and of some other Rheno-Flemish mystics, such as Dietrich of Freiberg, Jan van Ruusbroek, Berthold of Moosburg, etc. In other words, Eckhart puts scholasticism in the service of mysticism.

Mysticism usually emerged as a reaction to the academic theology, and its implicit purpose is to make revelation accessible to the average parishioner. While scholasticism strived to reconcile Greek philosophy and logic with the biblical message—a useful initiative in itself, but somehow irrelevant for the ordinary people—the different forms of mysticism of the thirteenth and fourteenth centuries strived to bring revelation to the streets. While scholasticism intended to offer a solid philosophical foundation to theology, mysticism intended to offer an authentic Christian experience. As a result, thirteenth- and fourteenth-century

---

9. Eckhart's sermons include German and Latin sermons. In this paper, we will focus on Eckhart's German sermons, which are the result of Eckhart's pastoral activity. Also, the German corpus of sermons includes all the major concepts of Eckhart's theology.

mysticism brought a spiritual revival within the Roman Catholic Church. As the unschooled became interested in spirituality, they became involved in spiritual life and practiced spiritual disciplines. The mystical union with God is an audacious concept. Nevertheless, it should be interpreted in its spiritual and historical setting, namely as a call to average people to pursue a personal encounter with God.

While mysticism can be understood as a reaction to academic theology, a specific feature of the Rhineland mysticism is that it did not oppose scholasticism. On the contrary, it strived to use the intellectual accomplishments of thirteenth-century scholasticism to support mystical ideas resulting in a symbiotic relationship between scholasticism and mysticism. Two instruments were used to accomplish this goal: (1) the use of vernacular languages in writing and preaching and (2) purposeful engagement of the ordinary lay individuals that make up the body of the church. As a major representative of the Rhineland mysticism, Eckhart used both of these tools.

Hallmark Concepts of Preaching

Eckhart's German sermons are the most influential part of his corpus of writings. His theology is best understood through his sermons preached to noneducated audiences. In these sermons several themes reoccur, which gives us insight into Eckhartian thinking.

Synderesis: *The Divinity of the Intellect*

One of the major themes of the Eckhartian mystical preaching is that of *synderesis*. Eckhart defines it as, "A power in the soul which alone is free. I call it the guardian of the spirit, sometimes I have called it a light of the spirit, sometimes I have said that it is a little spark."[10] This little spark of the soul is associated with the intellect. While for his Dominican fellows the intellect personifies the image of God in man as the sign of the Creator in his creature, Eckhart suggests more: a part of the intellect remains uncreated, so it is divine. Eckhart speaks of the birth of the eternal God in the human soul: "in this same power God ever bears His only-begotten Son as truly as in Himself."[11] The fact that, by its upper

---

10. Meister Eckhart, *Sermon 2* in *The Complete Mystical Works of Meister Eckhart*, trans. Maurice O'C Walshe, ed. Bernard McGinn (New York: Crossroad, 2009), no. 8:80. For the little spark of the soul, see also *Sermon 9* (McGinn, 2009, no. 67:343). On this concept, see also E.-H. Wéber, "La petite Étincelle et le Fond de l'âme," ed. Émilie Zum Brunn, *Voici Maître Eckhart* (Grenoble: Jérôme Million, 1998), 105–18. For more information on the history of the concept of *synderesis*, see Denise N. Baker, "The Structure of the Soul and the 'Godly Wylle' in Julian of Norwich's *Showings*," in *The Medieval Mystical Tradition. Exeter Symposium VII*, ed. E. A Jones (Cambridge: Brewer, 2004), 37–49.

11. Meister Eckhart, *Sermon 2* (McGinn, 2009, no. 8:80).

part, which is the intellect, the soul is akin to God (or that God is akin to the soul) offers the conceptual basis for the mystical union of man with God, as well as for the theory of deification of man. The doctrine of deification is a patristic one found in Eastern-Orthodox theology. According to certain Greek fathers of the church, such as Athanasius, God became human in order that humans might become God.[12] What this means for Athanasius is not that people become ontologically God, in essence or being, but instead describes the salvific relation between God and people. In a different century, and in the context of Eckhart's own writings, this statement becomes controversial. While this approach could be worrisome for the theologian, Eckhart certainly sought to motivate his audience to a personal experience of spiritual realities, rather than to contradict orthodox theology. Eckhart likely assumed the position of the preacher and played against the dogmatic theologian who speaks *ex cathedra*. One should also notice that Eckhart's writings are full of metaphors, similes, oxymorons, and paradoxes. These are important stylistic considerations for what he says and how he says it throughout his preaching; thus, these literary devices held in contrast to his explanation should be understood together. Eckhart's whole system is made up of major oppositions which call into question its internal coherence. (For instance, in different texts, Being and God are identified, in other texts, God is defined as Nothingness, and so opposed to the being of the created things.) In fact, Eckhart's philosophy is a dialectical one, made up of apparent contradictions. Eckhart strove to express, in a shocking way, the human need of identifying with Christ and of becoming more like Christ. The stylistic and rhetorical aspects, rather than precision, are distinctive features of mystical preaching. Any debate in Eckhart's orthodoxy should be understood in his historical and theological setting. In studying Eckhart, one should not strive to justify Eckhart or his orthodoxy (which remains a questionable matter), but identify his contribution to the history of Christian spirituality. And, of course, his contribution to the way we preach the gospel.

Uncreatable: Soul, Time, and Eternity

A related concept is that of *uncreatable*. In its higher part, the soul is uncreated and uncreatable.[13] This is another controversial concept, condemned by the *In agro dominico* bull, given by the Pope John XXII in 1329.[14] This doctrine teaches that God meets the soul in eternity and, conversely, the soul meets God in eternity. This thesis is controversial because it could be interpreted as an influ-

---

12. Athanasius of Alexandria, *De Incarnatione Verbi Dei*, 54, PG 25, 192B.
13. Eckhart, *Sermon 10* (McGinn, 2009, no. 66:338).
14. *In agro dominico*, n. 65, LW V, 599:91–82 (McGinn, 2009: 28).

ence of Plato's preexistence of the soul. Again, this meeting between God and the soul in eternity should be understood in its mystical context. The mystical theologian strives to show that the divine mysteries *do not* fit into the human understanding. While the systematic theologian takes into account the temporal succession of time, the mystical theologian places himself into God's eternity. As to the question of whether the human intellect is created or not, Eckhart would say the human soul is uncreated. He seems to lack interest in the created world, including temporality (which is also part of the created world).

Detachment

The mystical union with God is possible by what Eckhart calls "detachment." In fact, one of his German mystical treatises is named *On Detachment*. Detachment reflects perfect humility, which exists "in the destruction of the self, and between perfect detachment and nothing, 'no thing' can exist."[15] Detachment means abandoning being for nothingness. This ontological terminology might surprise the reader, but Eckhart places in opposition the "being" of created things to the "nothingness" of God. In this philosophical sense, God is "No Thing," because he is not created. The mystical concept of detachment works in the framework of the opposition between God and creature. The hierarchical image of the world, professed by scholasticism, contended the existence of God as the Supreme Being from which a multilevel created world originated, with realities that have more or less being. Some of Eckhart's texts reflect this hierarchical image of the world, but Eckhart's mystical innovation is found in his texts that firmly oppose creature and God as being and nonbeing or nothingness. "God works beyond being, in breadth, where He can move, and He works in nonbeing."[16] Somehow surprisingly, other Eckhartian texts maintain that God is the only Being and creature is nothingness: "All things are nothing in themselves: that is why I have said to you, 'Abandon Nothing,' and take on perfect being, in which the will is just. . . . If the spirit were aware of its pure detachment, it would be unable to stoop to anything, but must remain in its bare detachment."[17]

Detachment means a radical movement from the created world to God. It means abandoning oneself as creature to become one with the uncreated Godhead. This dialectical opposition between created and uncreated is incarnated, in Eckhart's preaching, as a paradoxical speech.

---

15. Eckhart, *On Detachment* (McGinn, 2009, 567).
16. Idem, *Sermon 9* (McGinn, 2009, no. 67:342).
17. Idem, *Sermon 10* (McGinn, 2009, no. 66:337–38).

The Nobelman

Only he who knows God is able to realize the detachment. In Eckhart's sermons, he is named the "detached man," or the "nobleman," or the "divine man," or the "just man." The just man is the man who "sets at naught" all created things[18] and he desperately needs justice, because he does not love anything but justice.[19] Created things are nothing for the just man, because he loves justice (i.e., God). In fact, this is the process of detachment: disregarding the nothingness and loving justice. The nobleman is the man who is not satisfied with anything, except with the One.[20] The concept of "nobleman" is so important for Eckhart, that he consecrated a German sermon, titled *The Nobleman*.[21] For Eckhart, the "nobility" is a biblical concept inspired by Luke 19:12 (the parable of the ten minas): "A man of noble birth went to a distant country to have himself appointed king and then to return." In Eckhart's interpretation, the nobleman is the man who abandons himself and all the created realities in exchange for God. In this sermon Eckhart opposes the "outer man" and the "inner man." The outer man knows the created realities as individuals, in their materiality. On the contrary, the inner man knows himself and knows God, and in doing so, he knows everything in himself and in God. Knowing yourself and knowing God are quite the same, for Eckhart, as the little spark of the soul is akin to God. Or, in other words, the ground of the soul and the ground of God are one and the same, and this is the basis of the mystical union. Detaching oneself from the world is not completely ignoring the world, but knowing all created things in their essence, in God.[22] God is also the way one can know his or her real identity: "For the eternal light makes known oneself and God, not oneself apart from God."[23]

METHODOLOGY FOR PREACHING

Symbolic Theology

The theology in Eckhart's sermons is a symbolic theology. Eckhart is aware of the need for images to speak about the unspeakable. His preference for parable, as well as for fictional and symbolic narratives, helps him in his pastoral work with the beguines. Eckhart is aware that, if one is supposed to speak about God, he should use icons and images—the language of the people. He is also aware he

---

18. Idem, *Sermon 16b* (McGinn, 2009, no. 14b:116–17).

19. Idem, *Sermon 41* (McGinn, 2009, no. 43:239).

20. *In agro dominico*, n. 65, LW V, 599:70–71 (McGinn, 2009: 27).

21. It seems that, originally, *The Nobleman* was a sermon integrated in the *Book of Divine Consolation*. Cf. de Libera, *La mystique rhénane*, 40.

22. Meister Eckhart, *The Nobleman* (McGinn, 2009: 557–58).

23. Idem, *Sermon 86* (McGinn, 2009, no. 9:84).

should use the language of his parishioners, the beguines—Middle High German. These two requirements are the point of reference that generated the canon of what we know today as Eckhart's German sermons.

Parables and Timeless Meanings

Eckhart's preaching style is a mystical one, made up of philosophical and theological concepts from Plato, Aristotle, Augustine, Pseudo-Denys the Areopagite, Avicenna, and Moses Maimonides, as well as the apocryphal Neoplatonic *Book of Causes*. Eckhart is a scholastic theologian as well as a mystical preacher. In his sermons, he mentions the University of Paris,[24] as well as various masters and philosophers, to support his mystical preaching. There is no true separation between Eckhart the philosopher and Eckhart the preacher or the mystic. Also, as shown before, Eckhart's German preaching for the layperson and his Latin commentaries for the academic overlap—they both share philosophical concepts. While both embody philosophical concepts, they still exist as mystical contributions of theology.

Eckhart's preaching is certainly not exegetical. Of course, Eckhart bases his preaching on biblical texts, but each verse gives rise to mystical or philosophical reflection. Eckhart shows a clear predilection for particular Scriptures to use as a basis for his sermons. Eckhart often quotes from canonical books (such as Genesis, Exodus, Proverbs, the Gospel of John, the Gospel of Luke) and apocryphal texts (Wisdom of Solomon, Ecclesiasticus), as he does in his commentaries. He often uses other passages found in Scripture, but his predilection for those above is clear by the secondary references he uses in his sermons. There is a definite preference for the wisdom literature in the Old Testament, probably because the biblical sapiential books are the most likely ones to be interpreted in a philosophical sense. For instance, *Sermon 6*[25] is based on the Wisdom of Solomon 5:15 ("The just shall live forever"). This sermon defines "the just" as those who go out of themselves and who look for nothing inside them, beside them, over them, etc., because the just look for God only. This is a demonstration of negative theology, as Eckhart says what a just man does not look for. The just are "so firmly established in justice and so thoroughly self-abandoned" that they take heed at no thing or feeling that could disturb them.[26] The Book of Ecclesiasticus inspired different sermons such as: *Sermon 9*[27] (50:6–7), which is a plea for detachment, defined as abandoning any created being

---

24. Idem, *Sermon 9* (McGinn, 2009, no. 67:342); *Sermon 14* (McGinn, 2009, no. 50:267); *Sermon 16b* (McGinn, 2009, no. 14b: 116).

25. Idem, *Sermon 6* (McGinn, 2009, no. 65:328).

26. Idem, *Sermon 6* (McGinn, 2009, no. 65:329).

27. Idem, *Sermon 9* (McGinn, 2009, no. 67:341–46).

in favor of God beyond (created) being; *Sermon 10* [28] (44:16–17), which speaks of the just who sees God with their inner eye; *Sermon 40* [29] (in this case, Sir 14:21 is a secondary reference only). The theme of the just (righteous man or "nobleman," in Eckhart's terminology) in his relation to justice (God) is also approached in the *Sermon 41*, on Proverbs 15:9 ("He loves those who pursue righteousness").[30] This text is interpreted in the light of the fourth beatitude in Matthew 5:6 ("Blessed are those who hunger and thirst for righteousness, for they will be filled"). Longing for justice is not desiring a moral virtue, but desiring God himself! Another sermon (*Sermon 32*)[31] is inspired by the praise of a woman of noble character (Prov 31:27) who, according to Eckhart, stands for the soul who seeks God.

Eckhart's preference for the nonhistoric narratives is clear from his selections from the Gospel of Luke. Different sermons inspired from Luke are based on parables, rather than on the historical narrative of the life of Jesus. The nobleman, from the Parable of the Ten Minas (Luke 19:12), is the metaphor of he who "has gone out of himself," abandoning everything and giving up the self. He returns richer, because "all things, just as he had fully abandoned them in multiplicity, will be entirely returned to him in simplicity, for he finds himself and all things in the present 'now' of unity."[32] In other words, the mystical union with God requires total abandonment of the self and of the world, but everything is given back at another level, in God. In his abandonment, the mystic learns to know the created through God and in God. In another sermon, Eckhart deals with the Parable of the Great Banquet (Luke14:16) initiated by a "certain man." That man "had no name, for that man is God;" he is the "inexpressible man."[33]

The Gospel of John and John's first epistle are used to approach the theme of love. Here, again, love has a mystical meaning: he who loves God must "give up" himself, "altogether give up self," says Eckhart in *Sermon 28* (based on John 15:16). "If you could naught yourself for an instant, indeed I say less than an instant, you would possess" everything which is in God. [34] Giving up the created being (including the self) means touching the desert of God's plenitude. The new commandment (John 15:12) is interpreted, in *Sermon 27*, as the result of detachment, because "love is quite pure, quite bare, quite detached" and God must be loved "for God's sake," not for any other reason.[35] Commenting on

---

28. Idem, *Sermon 10* (McGinn, 2009, no. 66:334–39).

29. Idem, *Sermon 40* (McGinn, 2009, no. 60:318–21).

30. Idem, *Sermon 41* (McGinn, 2009, no. 43:238–42).

31. Idem, *Sermon 32* (McGinn, 2009, no. 52:275–78).

32. Idem, *Sermon 15* (McGinn, 2009, no. 51:270–74).

33. Idem, *Sermon 20a* (McGinn, 2009, no. 32a:191–95).

34. Idem, *Sermon 28* (McGinn, 2009, no. 17:129–32, especially 130–31).

35. Idem, *Sermon 27* (McGinn, 2009, 12:99–103).

1 John 4:9,[36] Eckhart says "all creatures are mere nothing," because the change and destruction define them. Nevertheless, the created things are not completely abandoned. If they have no being in themselves, their being is recovered in God. Providentially, God knows everything in himself ("God knows nothing outside of Himself. What He sees, He sees entirely within Himself"). By loving God, we can have everything in God and know "All things are equally my own in Him."[37]

This search for a parabolic and timeless meaning in historical biblical texts proves that Eckhart's hermeneutics and preaching are a search for the timeless mystical experience of the Godhead, which explains why Eckhart's sermons include a unique style of preaching.[38]

Stylistic Preaching and the Use of Metaphor

Various figures of speech are present in Eckhart's sermons. Some of them are widely present in other mystical texts. This is the case of the metaphor. The metaphor of the "eye" is one of the most frequent in Eckhart's writings. It is usually a symbolic name for the intellect or for its higher uncreated part—the little spark of the soul. "My eye and God's eye are one eye, one seeing, one knowing and one love."[39] The "morning star" symbolizes the person who desires to be always in God's presence.[40] The "temple" or the "citadel" is the soul Jesus intends to enter.[41]

Paradox is another frequently used figure of speech. Eckhart speaks about a "length without length" and "breadth without breadth,"[42] as well as a "wayless way."[43] Another interesting figure of speech used by Eckhart is the repetition of the names. The model for the repetition is God's name, "I am that I am" (*ego sum qui sum*). This is not a simple imitation of God's name, but a deeper nomination of God.[44] This is also the case with the use of human names. Jesus calls Martha twice ("Martha, Martha!"), because, as Eckhart explains, the first mention of her name shows her perfection in temporal works, while the second call of her name points to her identity in the eternal bliss.[45]

---

36. "This is how God showed his love among us: He sent his one and only Son into the world that we might live through him" (1 John 4:9).

37. Idem, *Sermon 5a* (McGinn, 2009, 13a: 104–07).

38. On the style of Eckhart's preaching, as well as on different interpretative strategies of Eckhart's sermons, see Bruce Milem, "Meister Eckhart's Vernacular Preaching," in *A Companion to Meister Eckhart*, ed. Jeremiah M. Hackett (Leiden: Brill, 2013), 345.

39. Meister Eckhart, *Sermon 12* (McGinn, 2009, no. 57:298). See also: *Sermon 9* (McGinn, 2009, no. 67:343); *Sermon 10* (McGinn, 2009, no. 66:336).

40. Idem, *Sermon 9* (McGinn, 2009, no. 67:345).

41. For the "temple," see *Sermon 1* (McGinn, 2009, no. 6:66–70). For the the "citadel," see *Sermon 2* (McGinn, 2009, no. 8:77–81).

42. Eckhart, *Sermon 19* (McGinn, 2009, no. 35:208).

43. Idem, *Sermon 86* (McGinn, 2009, no. 9:86).

44. Idem, *In Genesim*, n. 179, LW I, 70:71–73.

45. Idem, *Sermon 86* (McGinn, 2009, no. 9:85).

CONTRIBUTIONS TO PREACHING

Meister Eckhart is a mystical preacher who uses philosophy to support a negative theology of the union between the human soul and God. Preaching is the impossible speech for every mystic, including Eckhart. For the mystic, speaking about the unspeakable is not possible, yet it is a duty! The use of images equally serves as an admission of this impossibility. But here is the real paradox of Eckhart's mystical preaching: God can be seen by the pure and naked intellect, separated not only of any materiality, but by any created reality as well. Still, the preacher must use sensible representations to reference a reality completely different than what can be sensed: this is the uncreated intellect.

Eckhart does not represent the mainstream of the Christian theology of his time. While he pretended to be a spiritual descendent of his Dominican fellow Thomas Aquinas, his preaching and theology are less rigorous than those of the angelic doctor. To be sure, Eckhart represents an innovation in late thirteenth-century and early fourteenth-century theology. The interest for the inner life is a subtle criticism of the natural theology of that time. Eckhart does not focus on doctrine or on rational arguments for the existence of God, but on the inner life of the individual.

Eckhart was probably one of the first scholars of his age to use a vernacular language to pass the message of the gospel to his parishioners. The exploration of the theological concept of "justice," as well as the interest for the individual in his encounter with God and his theology of grace could rightfully be interpreted as an anticipation of a theology to come.

Sermon Excerpt

Sermon 9: *Quasi stella matutina*[46]

Everything works in [its] being, nothing can work except in its being. Fire cannot work except in wood. God works beyond being, in breadth, where He can move, and He works in nonbeing: before there was being, God was working: He wrought being where no being was. Masters of little subtlety say God is pure being. He is as high above being as the highest angel is above a midge. I would be as wrong to call God a being as if I were to call the sun pale or black. God is neither this nor that. And

---

46. Meister Eckhart, *Sermon 9* (McGinn, 2009, no. 67:342).

one master says, "Whoever thinks he has known God, if he has known anything, it was not God he knew." But when I have said God is not a being and is above being, I have not thereby denied Him being: rather I have exalted it in Him. If I get copper in gold, it is there and it is there in a nobler mode than it is in itself. St. Augustine says, "God is wise without wisdom, good without goodness, powerful without power." ◆

BIBLIOGRAPHY

Meister Eckhart. *The Complete Mystical Works of Meister Eckhart*. Trans. by Maurice O'C Walshe. Edited by Bernard McGinn. New York: Crossroad, 2009. (McGinn, 2009).

———. *Die deutschen werke*. Stuttgart: Kohnhammer, 1958–. Vol. 1 (DW I) Edited by Josef Quint. 1958; vol. 2 (DW II) Edited by Josef Quint, 1971; vol. 3 (DW III) Edited by Josef Quint, 1976; vol. 4,1 (DW IV,1) Edited by Georg Steer, 1997–2003; vol. 4,2 (DW IV,2) Edited by Georg Steer (ongoing).

———. *Die lateinischen werke*. Stuttgart: Kohnhammer. Vol. 4 (LW IV) Edited by Ernst Benz, Bruno Decker, and Joseph Koch. 1956; Vol. 5 (LW V) Edited by Albert Zimmermann and Loris Sturlese. 2006.

———. *The Essential Sermons, Commentaries, Treatises and Defense*. Trans. by Edmund Colledge, Bernard McGinn, and Houston Smith. Mahwah, NJ: Paulist, 1981.

Beccarisi, Alessandra. "Eckhart's Latin Works." Pages 85–124 in *A Companion to Meister Eckhart*. Edited by Jeremiah M. Hackett. Leiden: Brill, 2013.

Baker, Denise N. "The Structure of the Soul and the 'Godly Wylle' in Julian of Norwich's *Showings*." Pages 37–49 in *The Medieval Mystical Tradition. Exeter Symposium VII*. Edited by E. A. Jones. Cambridge: Brewer, 2004.

Daiber, Hans. *Islamic Thought in the Dialogue of Cultures. A Historical and Bibliographical Survey*. Leiden: Brill, 2012.

Fărcaş, Daniel. *Le transcendantal et le discours théologique: Métaphysique et analogie chez Albert le Grand et Maître Eckhart*. PhD diss., Université de Paris IV—Sorbonne, 2008.

———. *Meister Eckhart: misticul din căuşul ochiului*. Iaşi: Polirom, 2010.

Flasch, Kurt. *Meister Eckhart: Die Geburt der Deutschen 'Mystik' aus dem Geist der arabischen Philosophie*. München: Beck, 2008.

———. *Meister Eckhart: Philosoph des Christentums*. München: Beck, 2010.

Libera, Alain de. *Eckhart, Suso Tauler ou la divinisation de l'homme*. Paris: Seuil, 1996.

———. *La mystique rhénane d'Albert le Grand à Maître Eckhart*. Paris: Seuil, 1994.

Lossky, Vladimir. *Théologie négative et connaissance de Dieu chez Maître Eckhart*: Paris: Vrin, 1960.

Milem, Bruce. "Meister Eckhart's Vernacular Preaching." Pages 337–57 in *A Companion to Meister Eckhart*. Edited by Jeremiah M. Hackett. Leiden: Brill, 2013.

———. *The Unspoken Word: Negative Theology in Meister Eckhart's German Sermons*. Washington, DC: Catholic University of America Press, 2002.

Ozment, Steven E. "Eckhart and Luther: German Mysticism and Protestantism." *The Thomist*, 42 (1)/1978: 259–80.

Schürmann, Reiner. *Wandering Joy: Meister Eckhart's Mystical Philosophy*. Great Barrington, MA: Lindisfarne Books, 2001.

Sturlese, Loris. "Eckhart as Preacher, Administrator and Master of Sentences. From Erfurt to Paris and Back: 1294–1313. The Origins of the *Opus tripartitum*." Pages 125–35 in *A Companion to Meister Eckhart*. Edited by Jeremiah M. Hackett. Leiden: Brill, 2013.

Wendlinder, Anastasia. *Speaking of God in Thomas Aquinas and Meister Eckhart: Beyond Analogy*. Burlington, VT: Ashgate, 2014.

Zum Brunn, Émilie, ed. *Voici Maître Eckhart*. Grenoble: Jérôme Million, 1998.

Johannes Tauler
Preaching Repentance and the Soul's Return to God

BYARD BENNETT

Between the fourteenth and the seventeenth centuries, Johannes Tauler's sermons were very popular because of the simple and vivid guidance they gave on returning to God and knowing God personally and experientially. Tauler's sermons, originally delivered in Middle High German, had a significant impact on later German preaching and movements of spiritual renewal, including the Lutheran Reformation, the Catholic Counter-Reformation, and early German Pietism. Tauler (ca. 1300–1361) emphasized that spiritual renewal was possible only when one came to a searching, thoroughgoing repentance and turned one's attention wholly to God.

HISTORICAL BACKGROUND

Relatively little is known about the life of Johannes Tauler. He was born in Strasbourg around AD 1300 and entered the Dominican order around 1315. Like others entering the Dominican order at that time, Tauler probably spent one year in the novitiate. The novitiate involved living in a monastery or religious house and undergoing spiritual training while the candidate's suitability for entering a religious order was assessed. After completing the novitiate, the candidate would then take vows of chastity, poverty, and obedience to the order. After entering the order, one was required to spend three years studying logic and two years studying the natural sciences and metaphysics. Theology was then studied, using the standard contemporary textbook, the *Sentences* of Peter Lombard (d. 1160).

Tauler was ordained around 1325 and by 1335 was acting as a preacher and spiritual director to Dominican nuns and devout women living in the beguine houses in Strasbourg.[1] Tauler is also known to have been part of a loose network

---

1. On vernacular preaching and spiritual formation in contemporary German Dominican convents, see Marie-Luise Ehrenschwendtner, *Die Bildung der Dominikanerinnen in Süddeutschland vom 13. bis 15. Jahrhundert* (Stuttgart: Franz Steiner, 2004). Tauler's sermons will be cited by the numbers used in the critical edition of the Middle High German text in Ferdinand Vetter, *Die Predigten Taulers* (Berlin: Weidmann, 1910; repr., 2000). All quotations from Tauler's works will be given in the English translation of *Johannes Tauler: Sermons,* ed. Josef Schmidt, trans. Maria Shrady (New York: Paulist, 1985).

of devout laypeople and clergy known as the "Friends of God," who were active in the Rhine River valley and were influenced by the mystical spirituality of the German Dominican Meister Eckhart (ca. 1260–1329).[2] Because of his connection with the "Friends of God," Tauler's influence soon extended well beyond Strasbourg. Tauler is known, for example, to have visited and served as a spiritual adviser to Margareta Ebner (d. 1351), a Dominican nun and visionary mystic who lived in a monastery over 140 miles to the east of Strasbourg.[3]

A conflict between the pope and Emperor Ludwig resulted in Tauler and the other Dominicans withdrawing to Basel in Switzerland from 1338 or 1339 until 1343. Tauler remained in contact with colleagues in Germany, making at least two visits to Cologne between 1339 and 1346. Tauler apparently returned to Strasbourg around 1343 and died there on June 16, 1361.

Tauler's sermons were very popular in the fourteenth to seventeenth centuries.[4] Tauler's program of spiritual renewal provided resources for later reform movements, including the Lutheran Reformation, the Catholic Counter-Reformation, and early German Pietism.[5]

---

2. On the "Friends of God," see Marie-Anne Vannier, "Jean Tauler et les Amis de Dieu," *Revue des sciences religieuses* 75 (2001): 456–64; Regina D. Schiewer, *"Vos amici dei estis*: Die 'Gottesfreunde' des 14. Jahrhunderts bei Seuse, Tauler und in den 'Engelberger Predigten': Religiöse Elite, Verein oder Literaturzirkel?" *Oxford German Studies* 36 (2007): 227–46. On Tauler's indebtedness to Meister Eckhart, see Georg Steer, "Die literarische Abhängigkeit Johannes Taulers von Meister Eckhart und das Problem der Orthodoxie," in *Das Gottesverständnis der deutschen Mystik (Meister Eckhart, Johannes Tauler, Heinrich Seuse) und die Frage nach seiner Orthodoxie*, ed. Markus Enders (Münster: Lit, 2011), 59–78; Christine Büchner, *Die Transformation des Einheitsdenkens Meister Eckharts bei Heinrich Seuse und Johannes Tauler* (Stuttgart: Kohlhammer, 2007).

3. Schmidt, *Johannes Tauler*, 5–6.

4. See Henrik Otto, *Vor- und frühreformatorische Tauler-Rezeption: Annotationen in Drucken des späten 15. und frühen 16. Jahrhunderts* (Gütersloh: Gütersloher Verlagshaus, 2003).

5. The literature on the influence and reception of Tauler's thought is quite extensive. Among the studies that have appeared in the last twenty-five years, one might note especially Maarten J. F. M. Hoenen, "Johannes Tauler († 1361) in den Niederlanden: Grundzüge eines philosophie- und rezeptionsgeschichtlichen Forschungsprogramms," *Freiburger Zeitschrift für Philosophie und Theologie* 41 (1994): 389–444; Marco Vannini, "La postérité de Tauler: La théologie allemande, Luther et les autres," *La vie spirituelle* 738 (2001): 115–32; Gérard Pfister, "La postérité de Jean Tauler," *Revue des sciences religieuses* 75 (2001): 465–78; Marie-Anne Vannier, ed., *Encyclopédie des mystiques rhénans d'Eckhart à Nicolas de Cues et leur réception* (Paris: Cerf, 2011); Hans-Peter Hasse, *Karlstadt und Tauler: Untersuchungen zur Kreuzestheologie* (Gütersloh: Gütersloher Verlagshaus Gerd Mohn, 1993); Hans-Peter Hasse, "Tauler und Augustin als Quelle Karlstadts: am Beispiel von Karlstadts Marginalien zu Taulers Predigt zum Johannistag über Lk 1, 5–23," in *Andreas Bodenstein von Karlstadt (1486–1541), ein Theologe der frühen Reformation: Beiträge eines Arbeitsgesprächs vom 24.-25. November 1995 in Wittenberg*, eds. Sigrid Looß and Markus Matthias (Lutherstadt Wittenberg: Drei Kastanien Verlag, 1998), 247–82; P. J. Stam Jr., *Mystiek geloof: Tauler, Luther, Kohlbrugge* (Kampen: De Groot Goudriaan, 1990); Volker Leppin, *Transformationen: Studien zu den Wandlungsprozessen in Theologie und Frömmigkeit zwischen Spätmittelalter und Reformation* (Tübingen: Mohr Siebeck, 2015); Eric Lund, "Tauler the Mystic's Lutheran Admirers," in *Piety and Family in Early Modern Europe: Essays in Honour of Steven Ozment*, eds. Marc R. Forster and Benjamin J. Kaplan (Burlington, VT: Ashgate, 2005), 9–27; John P. H. Clark, "Father Augustine Baker's Translations from the Works of John Tauler in the Latin Version of Laurentius Surius," in *Analecta Cartusiana 201*, eds. James Hogg, Alain Girard, and Daniel Le Blévec (Salzburg: Institut für Anglistik und Amerikanistik, 2003), 49–90.

THEOLOGY OF PREACHING

Tauler emphasized that the goal of the Christian life is to know God, be united with God, and become as much like God as is possible for a created being.[6] Because human beings were created in the image and likeness of God, our minds reflect the noble image of the Trinity.[7] Following Augustine, Tauler argues that the higher functions of our minds—memory, intellect, and will—reflect the dynamic relationships in the inner life of God.[8] Because of the way we were created, we possess a fundamental connection with God, are able to know and relate to God, and were made to enter into communion with him. Indeed, it is not hard to know God, for his image and activity are already present within us.

Besides the higher functions of the mind, humans also possess other faculties that equip them for life in the created world, including sense perception, simple discursive reasoning, and certain desires and cravings for what we see. When human beings turned their minds away from God and directed their attention and love toward created things without reference to God, disorder, distortion, alienation, and conflicts appeared in the inner life. In place of union with God, the mind's attention was now scattered and dispersed among the many different things that are seen. One's desires always want more of everything that can be seen or experienced and demand gratification. Thus, having detached from God, the fallen person has reattached to created things in such a way that created things take the place of God. As a result of this obsessive and disordered attachment, the fallen person has come to be possessed by created things, rather than being possessed and indwelt by God.

In this fallen state, one is unwilling to give up the satisfactions one derives from created things and stubbornly clings to one's own way of doing things. Such self-absorption and self-will are rooted in sinful pride. Pride produces rash judgments and harsh words that belittle others, but encourages the sinner to defend and excuse such behavior rather than feel sorrow for it.

Self-willed persons may sometimes adopt the outward form of religion, which then becomes a means through which they express their self-assertion and self-indulgence. Imagining themselves to be superior to others, they produce all kinds of conflicts.

---

6. On Tauler's development of this theme, see Alain de Libera, *Eckhart, Suso, Tauler ou la divinisation de l'homme* (Paris: Bayard Éditions, 1996). A helpful summary of Tauler's spiritual teaching can be found in Jörg Gabriel, *Rückkehr zu Gott: Die Predigten Johannes Taulers in ihrem zeit- und geistgeschichtlichen Kontext. Zugleich eine Geschichte hochmittelalterlicher Spiritualität und Theologie* (Würzburg: Echter Verlag, 2013).

7. Gabriel, *Rückkehr zu Gott,* 341–43.

8. Ibid., 344–48.

All their striving is centered upon themselves. Outwardly one can barely tell them from God's friends, for they often spend more time on pious exercises than God's friends: One can always see them reciting prayers, keeping fasts and strict rules . . . They are always sitting in judgment upon others, also upon those who love God: but you never see them judging themselves, whereas the true lovers of God judge no one but themselves. In everything, in God and in His creatures, such people seek nothing but their own gratification. So deeply embedded is this pharisaical tendency in their nature that every corner of the soul is invaded by it. It is impossible to overcome this habit by natural means; one might as well break down mountains of iron. There is only one way, and that is for God to take over and inhabit man. And this He does only for those who love him.[9]

Since self-willed persons are inclined to defend and excuse themselves, God allows them to experience pain, loss, and disappointments. The anguish and desolation they feel when they lose the support of worldly comforts becomes a means by which God invites them to return to him.[10] No longer able to rely on or find pleasure in their outward works, "everything they cleave to crumbles, and they are brought face-to-face with their bare nothingness. Thus they are shown how total is their dependence on God, and they learn to confess Him with a pure and simple faith, with no other support to sustain them."[11]

To accept God's call to conversion and inward renewal requires more than nominal belief; it requires repentance and detachment from all things that are less than God. Like Jesus's disciples in the Gospels, one must be able to say, "We have left everything to follow you!" (Mark 10:28). When, with the help of God, one arrives at detachment and becomes poor in spirit (Matt 5:3), one is able to experience a spiritual breakthrough (*durchbruch*) in which one's soul returns to God and is united to God, as the Son of God takes up his dwelling within the soul.[12]

---

9. *Sermon* 10; Schmidt and Shrady, *Johannes Tauler,* 51. Despite Tauler's opposition to the private devotions performed or imposed by the proud, Tauler continued to see spiritual value in liturgical chant and corporate worship and therefore was not opposed in principle to outward devotional practices; see Joachim Theisen, "Tauler und die Liturgie," in *Deutsche Mystik im abendländischen Zusammenhang,* eds. Walter Haug and Wolfram Schneider-Lastin (Tübingen: Niemeyer, 2000), 409–24; Claire Taylor Jones, "Communal Song and the Theology of Voice in Medieval German Mysticism" (PhD diss., University of Pennsylvania, 2012).

10. Tauler's account of suffering and its relation to spiritual progress is discussed by Christine Pleuser, *Die Benennungen und der Begriff des Leides bei J. Tauler* (Berlin: Erich Schmidt Verlag, 1967).

11. *Sermon* 21; Schmidt and Shrady, *Johannes Tauler,* 76. Compare *Sermon* 35 (Schmidt and Shrady, *Johannes Tauler,* 118), where experiences of loss and desolation show us "how inadequate our nature is, always craving things, always consuming them, and all ending in nothing."

12. Meister Eckhart's account of the birth of the Son of God in the soul is discussed in Marie-Anne Vannier, ed., *La naissance de Dieu dans l'âme chez Eckhart et Nicolas de Cues* (Paris: Cerf, 2006). On Tauler's

Having been united to God, one becomes aware that without God one is nothing and apart from the love of God one can do nothing (John 15:5; 1 Cor 13:2). In this poverty of spirit, one desires only to be moved by God, to do what God loves and wills, and to find one's joy in God. Thinking only of God's glory and honor, "we must intend and seek everything from Him alone."[13]

In those who have surrendered to God, the Holy Spirit produces a burning love that warms the heart and sets it on fire. Burning with ardent desire for God, the soul can no longer find comfort in things that are less than God. This makes it possible for the mind to return to God spontaneously and often, without effort, and to rejoice in God even when one's outward circumstances are painful and difficult. Suffering is the touchstone that reveals whether one's love for God is real or only imaginary.

> Grievous sufferings . . . make us aware whether we possess the true love of God or not. God's true friends take refuge in Him and accept all sorrow freely for His sake, thus suffering with Him and in Him. Or they lose themselves in Him in such a loving union that suffering ceases to be felt as such and turns into joy. For those whose spirit is false, it is quite otherwise: When afflicted with sorrow, they do not know which way to turn; they run this way and that, looking for help and advice and comfort, and when they do not find it, they break down and fall into despair.[14]

The presence and unhindered action of God in the soul leaves the soul rapt with ecstasy as it rests in God.[15] Words, images, concepts, feelings, and all perceptions of form, space, and time prove inadequate to represent the reality of God and are set aside.[16] One's wanting, knowing, loving, and understanding all

---

reception and development of this theme, see Jean Reaidy, "Trinité et naissance mystique chez Eckhart et Tauler," *Revue des sciences religieuses* 75 (2001): 444–55; Caroline F. Mösch, *"Daz disiu geburt geschehe": Meister Eckharts Predigtzyklus Von der êwigen geburt und Johannes Taulers Predigten zum Weihnachtsfestkreis* (Fribourg, Switzerland: Academic Press, 2006).

13. *Sermon 10*; Schmidt and Shrady, *Johannes Tauler,* 52.

14. *Sermon 10*; Schmidt and Shrady, *Johannes Tauler,* 52–53.

15. On Tauler's notion of *Gelassenheit* (resting in God in a calm, serene, composed manner, with complete surrender and resignation to the will of God), see Gabriel, *Rückkehr zu Gott,* 564–73; Imke Früh, "Im Zeichen und im Kontext von *gelossenheit.* Semantisierungsstrategien in den Predigten Johannes Taulers," in *Semantik der Gelassenheit: Generierung, Etablierung, Transformation,* eds. Burkhard Hasebrink, Susanne Bernhardt, and Imke Früh (Göttingen: Vandenhoeck & Ruprecht, 2012), 143–70; Markus Enders, *Gelassenheit und Abgeschiedenheit—Studien zur Deutschen Mystik* (Hamburg: Kovač, 2008), 361–62.

16. On Tauler's conception of *Bildlosigkeit* (imagelessness), see Richard F. Fasching, "Aber so sol man die bilde schiere lossen varn: zum Konzept der 'Bildlosigkeit' bei Johannes Tauler," in *Die Predigt im Mittelalter zwischen Mündlichkeit, Bildlichkeit und Schriftlichkeit,* eds. René Wetzel and Fabrice Flückiger (Zürich: Chronos, 2010), 397–410. On the need to transcend time and temporal concepts, see Niklaus Largier, "Time and Temporality in the 'German Dominican School.' Outlines of a Philosophical Debate between Nicolaus of Strasbourg, Dietrich of Freiberg, Eckhart of Hoheim, and Ioannes Tauler," in *The Medieval Concept of Time:*

go back to God and are lost in God. Setting aside all that one has previously known, the higher faculties of one's mind remain steeped and immersed in God, resting in the depths of God where God knows himself, and understands himself, and delights in his own being.

The complete surrender of the mind's higher faculties to God and the intensity and intimacy of the soul's union with God allow God to move, affect, and transform the soul without any hindrance from created things or self-will: "Here everything that is done in the soul God himself performs: acting, knowing, loving, praising, enjoying. And the soul lets it be."[17] By God's immediate action upon the soul, the soul is not only moved, but also reformed and transformed, so that we become partakers of the divine nature (2 Pet 1:4), becoming as much like God as is possible for a creature: "By this action the soul becomes God-hued, divinized and reformed in the form of God. It possesses everything by grace which God possesses by nature by way of its union with Him and by sinking into Him."[18]

The mind's lower faculties, which deal with discursive reason and judgment, are also affected and transformed by union with God. This leads us to "reflect in the light of reason on our words and thoughts and deeds in an understanding spirit to see if there is perhaps anything that is not oriented toward God as its sole and supreme Good."[19] Reason thus moves quickly and spontaneously to cut off and eradicate any false and hidden motives and any tendency toward self-indulgence.

The healing of reason leads us to see the significance of all created things in light of God's higher purpose for our lives: "[T]here is no work . . . so small and insignificant—be it the ringing of the bells or the lighting of a candle—that it does not serve the perfection of this interior work."[20]

Though one was once moved to envy or pass judgment on the neighbor, now one's reason is "animated by an impulsive love for our neighbor, which increases the more he is loved by Christ our Head."[21] This impulsive love rejoices in every good thing God has given to the neighbor, regardless of whether one has received a similar gift oneself.[22] Because divine love brings us into the most intimate union

---

Studies on The Scholastic Debate and Its Reception in Early Modern Philosophy, ed. Pasquale Porro (Leiden: Brill, 2001), 241.

17. *Sermon* 26; Schmidt and Shrady, *Johannes Tauler*, 97. Compare *Sermon* 40 (Schmidt and Shrady, *Johannes Tauler*, 143) for a similar description of God's action in the soul during ecstatic union: "[E]verything which he is and does, God is and does in him."

18. *Sermon* 37; ibid., 128.

19. *Sermon* 23; ibid., 80.

20. *Sermon* 40; ibid., 140.

21. *Sermon* 40; ibid., 141. On the solidarity of all who are united in the *corpus mysticum* with Christ as their head, see Rémy Valléjo, "Église et unité, 'Corpus mysticum' selon Jean Tauler," in *La prédication et l'Église chez Eckhart et Nicolas de Cues*, ed. Marie-Anne Vannier (Paris: Cerf, 2008), 201–13.

22. On Tauler's account of human love and its transformation by God, see Markus Enders,

with God and the neighbor, if God wills to give something good to our neighbor, we view this good as something we share in and rejoice over.[23]

> [W]hatever good our Lord wishes to give him would be the same as if it were mine... If I love the good in him more than he does himself, then it is more mine than his... That Saint Paul was rapt in ecstasy was granted by God to him, not to me. But if I savor [in this event] God's will, then I had rather that this ecstasy were his than mine, and by my loving it in him, it becomes truly mine. This should be my attitude toward every living person, even if he were on the other side of the ocean, even if he were my enemy... Here it becomes quite clear whether we love God and His will more than we love ourselves and our own will.[24]

Thus, in both our higher and lower faculties, the life of the Son of God is constantly being begotten in us, changing us to make us more like God.[25] Though God's being born in the soul may begin at conversion, it is also an ongoing process that transforms and reshapes every aspect of one's life.[26]

METHODOLOGY FOR PREACHING

About eighty sermons that can reasonably be attributed to Tauler have survived. The text of these sermons appears to be based upon transcriptions (*reportationes*) of Tauler's sermons made by persons who were present at the time, but have wide variations in spelling and represent a variety of Germanic dialects.[27] Some of the

---

"La compréhension mystique de l'amour humain chez Jean Tauler," *Revue des sciences religieuses* 75 (2001): 429–43; Enders, *Gelassenheit*, 320–48.

23. See the discussion in Enders, "Compréhension," 439.

24. *Sermon 33*; Schmidt and Shrady, *Johannes Tauler*, 141.

25. Cf. *Sermon 10* (Schmidt and Shrady, *Johannes Tauler*, 53): God's grace acts upon all parts of the soul so that the Son of God's "suffering should draw us out of ourselves, and that we should extinguish our own dark light in His true, essential light."

26. See Michael Schneider, *Krisis. Zur theologischen Deutung von Glaubens- und Lebenskrisen: ein Beitrag der theologischen Anthropologie*, 2nd ed. (Frankfurt am Main: Knecht, 1995).

27. For a brief summary of recent research, see Peter Dinzelbacher, *Deutsche und niederländische Mystik des Mittelalters: Ein Studienbuch* (Berlin: De Gruyter, 2012), 223; David Blamires, *The Book of the Perfect Life: Theologia Deutsch—Theologia Germanica* (Walnut Creek, CA: AltaMira, 2003), 14–15; Geert Warnar, "Tauler's *Minnenclich Meister*: Charisma and Authority in the Vernacular Mystical Tradition of the Low Countries and the Rhineland," in *Charisma and Religious Authority: Jewish, Christian, and Muslim Preaching, 1200–1500*, eds. Katherine L. Jansen and Miri Rubin (Turnhout: Brepols, 2010), 55. For a more detailed discussion of the manuscript tradition of Tauler's sermons, see G. I. Lieftinck, *De Middelnederlandsche Tauler-handschriften* (Groningen: Wolters, 1936); Johannes G. Mayer, *Die "Vulgata"-Fassung der Predigten Johannes Taulers. Von der handschriftlichen Überlieferung des 14. Jahrhunderts bis zu den ersten Drucken* (Würzburg: Königshausen & Neumann, 1999); Marie-Anne Vannier, "Les œuvres du *corpus* de la mystique rhénane numérisées par la Bibliothèque Nationale et Universitaire de Strasbourg," *Revue des sciences religieuses* 75 (2001): 496–502; Rudolf Kilian Weigand, "Predigen und Sammeln: die Predigtanordnung in frühen Tauler-Handschriften,"

surviving sermons show varying degrees of revision, perhaps by Tauler himself, before being more broadly circulated.

In the manuscript tradition, an introductory heading typically precedes each sermon. This introductory heading indicates the biblical text expounded in the sermon, relates that text back to the current season in the liturgical calendar, and summarizes the spiritual teaching that will be derived from the text. Thus, for example, the heading preceding *Sermon 26* (Pentecost II) indicates the biblical text that will be expounded (Acts 2:4: "All of them were filled with the Holy Spirit") and then summarizes the teaching that the preacher will derive from that text: "The second interpretation of the sublime event of Pentecost teaches us how to bring ourselves to a focus and shut out external matters, so that we may prepare a dwelling-place for the Holy Spirit Who makes us receptive to His divine operation within us."[28]

Tauler's sermons are remarkable because of the way they bring together elements from different types of preaching.[29] His sermons can be regarded as intermediate between the homily and the thematic sermon, drawing on elements of each.

The Homily

The homily involved a short exposition of a Scripture reading set for that Sunday or feast day in the liturgical calendar. A homily might begin with an informal direct address to the audience, use a simple form of verse-by-verse exposition, and appeal to familiar images from everyday life and proverbial sayings in the vernacular language to engage the hearer's attention and create a connection between the preacher and the audience.

Tauler's sermons are commonly structured in ways that reflect the conventions of the popular homily. Thus, for example, Tauler often addresses the audience directly but quite informally at the beginning of the sermon. He may then strategically use a direct address again later in the sermon to revive the hearers' concentration when a matter of central importance to the sermon is about to be discussed.[30] The reuse of informal direct address later in the sermon often has an emotional tone and reveals the preacher's personal knowledge of his audience, the

---

in *Studien zur deutschen Sprache und Literatur: Festschrift für Konrad Kunze zum 65. Geburtstag*, eds. Václav Bok, Ulla Williams, and Werner Williams-Krapp (Hamburg: Kovač, 2004), 114–55; Helga Dierckx, "De overlevering van pseudo-Taulerpreken in het handschrift Hildesheim, Dombibliothek, 724b en de Bazelse Taulerdruk (1521)," *Ons Geestelijk Erf* 84 (2013): 20–40.

28. Schmidt and Shrady, *Johannes Tauler*, 91.

29. On Tauler's preaching, see especially Freimut Löser, "Predigt über Predigt—Meister Eckhart und Johannes Tauler," in *Predigt im Kontext*, eds. Volker Mertens, Hans-Jochen Schiewer, Regina Dorothea Schiewer, and Wolfram Schneider-Lastin (Berlin: De Gruyter, 2013), 155–80.

30. Compare Sabine Volk-Birke, *Chaucer and Medieval Preaching: Rhetoric for Listeners in Sermons and Poetry* (Tübingen: Gunter Narr Verlag, 1991), 74.

mundane routines of their lives, and their present concerns; this helps to create and sustain a connection between the preacher and his audience.

Thus, for example, in *Sermon* 33 (Feast of Corpus Christi IV), Tauler begins by directly addressing the audience and casually alludes to a homily he had delivered on the preceding day: "Yesterday I said I wanted to speak about the glory of the Blessed Sacrament . . . but I did not manage to speak about preparation [to receive it]."[31] He then appeals to his audience's knowledge of local conditions and uses this to enlist them in considering a practical problem that will be addressed in the sermon: "Here in Cologne people are in the habit of receiving the Body of Our Lord frequently, and this is a good thing; but they do not all receive it in the same way." After speaking for about fifteen minutes on the inward attitude that should accompany participation in the sacrament, Tauler reengages the audience with an informal but emotional direct address: "My Beloved! What wonders we could work with God's help if we would turn into our depths and remain there and avail ourselves of the grace that is in us!"[32] Having gained the audience's attention, he then makes a searching personal application, warning against the gossip and conflicts that occur in convent life but are a serious obstacle to union with God: "Unfortunately there are some religious communities where there is altogether too much talk going on; what this or that one has said or done, or what the latest news is. Such nonsense can hinder the soul's union with God . . . I beg you to keep away from such places and such conversations; retire to your room, open your heart to God and His will, and then follow it!"[33]

Tauler's sermons, like the popular homily, also make extensive use of familiar imagery drawn from everyday life to create a connection between the preacher and the audience. This use of familiar imagery gives the sermon a more varied tone, balancing the more abstract words and concepts used by the preacher with concrete pictures that have an immediate personal and emotional resonance for hearers who have had little formal education. In *Sermon* 37, Tauler uses one of the most mundane agricultural tasks to illustrate how God uses trials to bring the unregenerate to conversion:

> And others are so stubbornly attached to their worldly ways that they can be compared to a barn floor which has to be prepared for the threshing: It is so rough and uneven that it needs scrubbing with a strong, stiff broom to even it out. If a threshing floor is already smooth, then it only takes a feather duster to make it shiny. It is the same with people who are crude and

---

31. Schmidt and Shrady, *Johannes Tauler,* 109.
32. Ibid., 114.
33. Ibid., 115.

uneven and unregenerate; they are in need of God's strong and stiff broom, trials and temptations of all kinds, to teach them how to surrender to Him. Those blessed men, however, who are pure of heart and utterly detached, they have no need of this.[34]

Tauler also refers to popular proverbs to build a connection with his hearers, a device commonly used in the homily. Thus, for example, in *Sermon* 1, Tauler uses a well-known German proverb to illustrate the difficulty worldly people have in returning to God: "A proverb says that a child kept too much at home remains uncouth abroad. That holds true of those people who have never left the house of their natural inclinations, who have not gone beyond their nature or beyond all those messages they have received from seeing and hearing, from emotions and excitements. Such people, who have never moved away from sensible things and have never risen above them, will indeed be uncouth when brought face-to-face with divine things."[35]

The Thematic Sermon

Besides certain elements derived from the popular homily, Tauler's preaching also drew upon the conventions and structures of the thematic sermon. The thematic sermon was a systematic and logically ordered form of preaching that was more commonly found in university contexts.[36] At the beginning of the thematic sermon, a biblical quotation was used to identify a theme from Scripture; other biblical passages with similar content might then be cited to show the importance of this theme throughout Scripture. The exposition of the theme was then divided into three or more parts, each of which sought to answer a distinct question;[37] these divisions were sometimes tied back to particular words in the biblical quotation. The preacher might also identify a term essential for understanding the theme and then define that term, often by citing a definition given by a much earlier teacher whose authority was accepted within scholastic education (e.g., Augustine, Proclus, ps.-Dionysius, John of Damascus, or Anselm). In establishing certain points, the preacher would also appeal to stock examples

---

34. Schmidt and Shrady, *Johannes Tauler,* 127. In his sermons Tauler often expresses his appreciation for the work of farmers and craftsmen, even commenting in *Sermon* 47, "Believe me, if I were not a priest and religious, I should be very proud to make shoes, and I should try to make them as best as I can, and I should be glad to earn my living with my own hands" (Schmidt and Shrady, *Johannes Tauler,* 154).

35. Schmidt and Shrady, *Johannes Tauler,* 38–39.

36. On the origin of the thematic sermon in a university context, see the classic study of Marie-Madeleine Davy, *Les Sermons universitaires parisiens de 1230–1231: contribution à l'histoire de la prédication médiévale* (Paris: Vrin, 1931).

37. James R. Ginther, *The Westminster Handbook to Medieval Theology* (Louisville: Westminster John Knox, 2009), 152.

drawn from biblical history or nature in order to elicit a particular reaction from his audience.[38] A thematic sermon would conclude with a brief summary of the discussion and an application of these conclusions to the hearers, stating what was to be believed and done.

Tauler's use of the divisions commonly found in the thematic sermon can be illustrated by examining *Sermon* 40.[39] In that sermon Tauler uses the biblical text set for the day from 1 Pet 3:8, saying, "Beloved, *be you all of one mind* in prayer" to identify and explore the theme of prayer.[40] The theme of prayer is then divided into three parts: (1) the nature of prayer; (2) the method of prayer, including how one should enter into it and how one should be disposed; and (3) in what place one ought to pray. The first section, dealing with the nature of prayer, is quite brief. A definition of prayer by a recognized authority, one familiar from the scholastic curriculum, is offered: Prayer "is an ascent of the mind and heart to God."[41] The second section, which is slightly longer, considers the method of prayer, discussing preparation for prayer and the relation of vocal prayer to contemplative prayer. This prepares for a transition to the third section, namely contemplative prayer as an inward activity, which is Tauler's primary interest and to which he devotes the majority of the sermon. Tauler describes God's activity within the soul and the need to turn one's mind wholly to God, followed by a description of the stages of mystical prayer by which the mind ascends toward God.[42] He concludes by exhorting his hearers to persevere until they have attained the last and highest of these stages of prayer.

---

38. Fritz Kemmler, *"Exempla" in Context: A Historical and Critical Study of Robert Mannyng of Brunne's "Handlyng Synne"* (Tübingen: Gunter Narr Verlag, 1984), 182.

39. Schmidt and Shrady, *Johannes Tauler,* 136–44.

40. On the relation between Tauler's exposition of biblical texts and his systematic exploration of contemplative and mystical themes, see Ludger Schwienhorst-Schönberger, "Johannes Tauler (1300–1361): Mystik und Schriftauslegung" in *Text und Mystik: Zum Verhältnis von Schriftauslegung und kontemplativer Praxis*, eds. Karl Baier, Regina Polak, and Ludger Schwienhorst-Schönberger (Göttingen: Vandenhoeck & Ruprecht, 2013), 83–116.

41. The definition of prayer as "an ascent of the mind to God" first appeared in Evagrius *On Prayer* 36. From there it was cited by John of Damascus *On the Orthodox Faith* 3.24, a work that was known to scholastic theologians through the twelfth-century Latin translation of Burgundio (Eligius M. Buytaert, *Saint John Damascene. De fide orthodoxa. Versions of Burgundio and Cerbanus* [St. Bonaventure, NY: The Franciscan Institute, 1955], 267 [68.1]). One also notes passing references in Tauler's sermons to the Neoplatonist Proclus as an authority and a source of definitions, reflecting the study of Proclus's *Elements of Theology* in the university curriculum during the late thirteenth and fourteenth centuries; see, e.g., *Sermons* 29, 44, and 59 (Schmidt and Shrady, *Johannes Tauler,* 105, 149, 168). On Tauler's reception and use of Proclus, see Loris Sturlese, "Tauler im Kontext: Die philosophischen Voraussetzungen des 'Seelengrundes' in der Lehre des deutschen Neoplatonikers Berthold von Moosburg," *Beiträge zur Geschichte der deutschen Sprache und Literatur (Tübingen)* 109 (1987): 390–426 (reprinted in Loris Sturlese, *Homo divinus: Philosophische Projekte in Deutschland zwischen Meister Eckhart und Heinrich Seuse* [Stuttgart: Kohlhammer, 2007], 169–97); Loris Sturlese, "Tauler e Bertoldo di Moosburg. I presupposti filosofici della dottrina del 'fondo dell'anima,'" in Loris Sturlese, *Eckhart, Tauler, Suso: Filosofi e mistici nella Germania medievale* (Florence: Le Lettere, 2010), 157–94.

42. For Tauler's teaching on the three stages of mystical prayer, see Marcus Straubmüller, *Weltmodell Mystik: Eine raumsemantische Analyse ausgewählter Predigten Meister Eckharts und Johannes Taulers* (Hamburg: Diplomica, 2015), 47–52; Jole D'Anna, *Johannes Tauler, dottore illuminato e sublime* (Rome: Simmetria, 2006), 41–42.

Like contemporary thematic sermons, Tauler's preaching made use of stock examples derived from contemporary *exemplaria* (collections of exemplary moral or spiritual narratives that could serve as sermon illustrations).[43] In *Sermon* 11, for example, the gospel text set for the day (John 7:37) deals with spiritual thirst, and this leads Tauler to cite another text with the same theme, Psalm 42:1 ("As the deer pants for streams of water, so my soul pants for you, my God"). Tauler next wished to discuss how the vices diminish spiritual thirst. In medieval literature the hart pursued by hounds was a common picture of the Christian soul pursued by evil powers.[44] Tauler is therefore able to retain the basic symbol of the hart and use it to make a transition from the theme of spiritual thirst to a reflection on the vices as obstacles to spiritual thirst, using a story drawn from the *exemplaria:*

Just as the hart is hunted by hounds, so men who are beginners in the spiritual life are pursued by temptations as soon as they turn away from the world. They are particularly pursued by their grave and great sins . . . Now it may happen occasionally that one of the hounds will overtake the hart and seize it by the belly with its teeth. When the hart tries to shake itself free of the hound, he will drag it to a tree, dash it against the trunk and crush its head to be freed. This is just the way we should act. If we find that we cannot overcome the hounds, our temptations, we should run with great haste to the Tree of the Cross and Passion of our Lord Jesus Christ, and thus crush the head of the hound which is our temptation. In this way we should overcome the whole lot of them, and be freed of them at once.

However, when the hart has overcome the big hounds, the little ones come running around, snapping at him. He takes hardly any notice of them, yet they maul him badly and do him genuine harm. The same happens to us: When we have conquered and overcome our grave sins, we take no notice of the little hounds, which signify superficial concerns, frivolous occupations, and all such trivialities. These things take little bites out of us, distracting our hearts and stifling true inwardness; they weaken the divine life within the soul to such an extent that in the end grace and love begin to seriously diminish.[45]

---

43. On the Dominican use of *exemplaria*, see M. Michèle Mulchahey, *"First the Bow is Bent in Study . . .":* *Dominican Education before 1350* (Toronto: Pontifical Institute of Mediaeval Studies, 1998), 459–66. On Tauler's use of *exempla* in his preaching, see Michael Egerding, *Die Exempla in der deutschen Mystik: systemtheoretisch beobachtet* (Paderborn: Schöningh, 2010), 156–210.

44. Richard N. Bailey, *Viking Age Sculpture in Northern England* (London: Collins, 1980), 174; Anne Rooney, *Hunting in Middle English Literature* (Rochester: Boydell & Brewer, 1993), 26–27; Kathleen R. Sands, *Demon Possession in Elizabethan England* (Westport, CT: Praeger, 2004), 73.

45. Schmidt and Shrady, *Johannes Tauler,* 56.

Although Tauler made use of elements drawn from both the thematic sermon and the homily, matters of form and convention always remained subordinate to Tauler's broader goal of communicating a distinct spiritual vision and promoting certain practices of contemplative prayer. Thus, for example, Tauler sometimes originally announces a division of the theme into several points, but then spends most of the sermon dealing with only one of these points. In other cases, he changes the order of presentation announced at the beginning of the sermon to emphasize the importance of one particular matter to his hearers. Tauler also often departs from the stated order of presentation by introducing ad hoc illustrations or separate self-contained units within the sermon when he felt this was necessary to address the needs of his hearers.[46] Tauler's sermons, therefore, always exhibit a dynamic, fluid quality, arising from the need to communicate a distinctive spiritual vision to an audience whose needs and responses could not always be predicted in advance.

CONTRIBUTIONS TO PREACHING

Johannes Tauler played an important role in the rise of vernacular preaching in late medieval Europe. Like the mendicant preachers of the preceding century, Tauler was concerned to instruct those who had little or no formal education but had a sincere interest in spiritual growth. Tauler's principal concern was to show the spiritually awakened how they could return to God through repentance and self-denial.

In his sermons, Tauler was able to translate the scholastic learning of the late medieval university and the mystical piety of the religious orders into a vernacular language that devout people with little formal education could understand and embrace. His sermons offered a compelling lived theology, using familiar, mundane images to show what it means to experience the love of God and be formed in Christ.

Tauler's sermons remained popular in Germany for centuries because they provided a detailed road map of the inner life that could guide one's return to God.[47] Tauler's development of the theme of repentance as detachment from all that is less than God had a significant influence on later German and Dutch spirituality. His descriptions of contemplative prayer, religious ecstasy, and union with God also supplied religious language and spiritual ideals that were adopted by later Catholic and Protestant renewal movements.

---

46. Schmidt and Shrady, *Johannes Tauler,* 18–19.

47. Cf. Annette Volfing, "*Du bist den Rin herabe geflossen*: Topographical Metaphors and Interior Geography in the Sermons of Johannes Tauler," in *Schreiben und Lesen in der Stadt: Literaturbetrieb im spätmittelalterlichen Straßburg,* eds. Stephen Mossman, Nigel F. Palmer, and Felix Heinzer (Berlin: De Gruyter, 2012), 17–28.

Sermon Excerpt

Ascension IV[48]

The fourth Sermon for the Ascension [on Acts 1:11: "This same Jesus, who has been taken from you into heaven . . ."] teaches us to seek peace in the midst of trials, joy in tribulation, and comfort in bitterness. We are to be God's witnesses on earth, following Him not only in good times but also in sadness and affliction.

. . . Many people would gladly be God's witnesses when everything goes according to their wishes. They like to be holy, as long as their devotions are not too much of a burden; they would be happy enough to experience great fervor and profess their faith openly, if only there were no distress, no grief, no drudgery involved. Once, however, they know the terrors and temptations of spiritual darkness, as soon as they no longer experience the emotional comfort of God's closeness, and feel forsaken within and without, they turn back and they are no witnesses at all. All men desire peace and they look for it in all kinds of ways and places. Oh, if they only could free themselves of this illusion, and learn to look for it in tribulation. Only there is born abiding peace, lasting peace that will endure; if you look for it elsewhere, you will fail miserably. You ought to seek joy in sadness, detachment in the midst of disaster, and comfort in bitterness; this is the way to become a true witness of God. Before His death, our Lord always promised peace to His disciples; before and after the Resurrection He did so. And yet they never obtained an outward peace. Nonetheless, they found peace in sorrow, and joy in tribulation. In death they found life, and to be judged, sentenced, and condemned was for them a joyous victory. They were God's witnesses. ◆

BIBLIOGRAPHY

Bailey, Richard N. *Viking Age Sculpture in Northern England*. London: Collins, 1980.

Blamires, David. *The Book of the Perfect Life: Theologia Deutsch—Theologia Germanica*. Walnut Creek, CA: AltaMira, 2003.

Büchner, Christine. *Die Transformation des Einheitsdenkens Meister Eckharts bei Heinrich Seuse und Johannes Tauler*. Stuttgart: Kohlhammer, 2007.

Buytaert, Eligius M. *Saint John Damascene. De fide orthodoxa. Versions of Burgundio and Cerbanus*. St. Bonaventure, NY: The Franciscan Institute, 1955.

Clark, John P.H. "Father Augustine Baker's Translations from the Works of John Tauler in the Latin Version of Laurentius Surius." Pages 49–90 in *Analecta Cartusiana 201*. Edited by James Hogg, Alain Girard, and Daniel Le Blévec. Salzburg: Institut für Anglistik und Amerikanistik, 2003.

---

48. *Sermon* 21; Schmidt and Shrady, *Johannes Tauler*, 75.

D'Anna, Jole. *Johannes Tauler, dottore illuminato e sublime*. Rome: Simmetria, 2006.

Davy, Marie-Madeleine. *Les Sermons universitaires parisiens de 1230–1231: contribution à l'histoire de la prédication médiévale*. Paris: Vrin, 1931.

Dierckx, Helga. "De overlevering van pseudo-Taulerpreken in het handschrift Hildesheim, Dombibliothek, 724b en de Bazelse Taulerdruk (1521)." *Ons Geestelijk Erf* 84 (2013): 20–40.

Dinzelbacher, Peter. *Deutsche und niederländische Mystik des Mittelalters: Ein Studienbuch*. Berlin: De Gruyter, 2012.

Egerding, Michael. *Die Exempla in der deutschen Mystik: systemtheoretisch beobachtet*. Paderborn: Schöningh, 2010.

Ehrenschwendtner, Marie-Luise. *Die Bildung der Dominikanerinnen in Süddeutschland vom 13. bis 15. Jahrhundert*. Stuttgart: Franz Steiner, 2004.

Enders, Markus. "La compréhension mystique de l'amour humain chez Jean Tauler." *Revue des sciences religieuses* 75 (2001): 429–43.

_____. *Gelassenheit und Abgeschiedenheit—Studien zur Deutschen Mystik*. Hamburg: Kovač, 2008.

Fasching, Richard F. "Aber so sol man die bilde schiere lossen varn: zum Konzept der 'Bildlosigkeit' bei Johannes Tauler." Pages 397–410 in *Die Predigt im Mittelalter zwischen Mündlichkeit, Bildlichkeit und Schriftlichkeit*. Edited by René Wetzel and Fabrice Flückiger. Zürich: Chronos, 2010.

Früh, Imke. "Im Zeichen und im Kontext von *gelossenheit*. Semantisierungsstrategien in den Predigten Johannes Taulers." Pages 143–70 in *Semantik der Gelassenheit: Generierung, Etablierung, Transformation*. Edited by Burkhard Hasebrink, Susanne Bernhardt and Imke Früh. Göttingen: Vandenhoeck & Ruprecht, 2012.

Gabriel, Jörg. *Rückkehr zu Gott: Die Predigten Johannes Taulers in ihrem zeit- und geistgeschichtlichen Kontext. Zugleich eine Geschichte hochmittelalterlicher Spiritualität und Theologie*. Würzburg: Echter Verlag, 2013.

Ginther, James R. *The Westminster Handbook to Medieval Theology*. Louisville: Westminster John Knox, 2009.

Hasse, Hans-Peter. *Karlstadt und Tauler: Untersuchungen zur Kreuzestheologie*. Gütersloh: Gütersloher Verlagshaus Gerd Mohn, 1993.

Hasse, Hans-Peter. "Tauler und Augustin als Quelle Karlstadts: am Beispiel von Karlstadts Marginalien zu Taulers Predigt zum Johannistag über Lk 1, 5–23." Pages 247–82 in *Andreas Bodenstein von Karlstadt (1486–1541), ein Theologe der frühen Reformation: Beiträge eines Arbeitsgesprächs vom 24.-25. November 1995 in Wittenberg*. Edited by Sigrid Looß and Markus Matthias. Lutherstadt Wittenberg: Drei Kastanien Verlag, 1998.

Hoenen, Maarten J. F. M. "Johannes Tauler († 1361) in den Niederlanden: Grundzüge eines philosophie- und rezeptionsgeschichtlichen Forschungsprogramms." *Freiburger Zeitschrift für Philosophie und Theologie* 41 (1994): 389–444.

Jones, Claire Taylor. "Communal Song and the Theology of Voice in Medieval German Mysticism." PhD diss., University of Pennsylvania, 2012.

Kemmler, Fritz. *"Exempla" in Context: A Historical and Critical Study of Robert Mannyng of Brunne's "Handlyng Synne."* Tübingen: Gunter Narr Verlag, 1984.

Largier, Niklaus. "Time and Temporality in the 'German Dominican School.' Outlines of a Philosophical Debate between Nicolaus of Strasbourg, Dietrich of Freiberg, Eckhart of Hoheim, and Ioannes Tauler." Pages 221–53 in *The Medieval Concept of Time: Studies on The Scholastic Debate and Its Reception in Early Modern Philosophy*. Edited by Pasquale Porro. Leiden: Brill, 2001.

Leppin, Volker. *Transformationen: Studien zu den Wandlungsprozessen in Theologie und Frömmigkeit zwischen Spätmittelalter und Reformation*. Tübingen: Mohr Siebeck, 2015.

Libera, Alain de. *Eckhart, Suso, Tauler ou la divinisation de l'homme*. Paris: Bayard Éditions, 1996.

Lieftinck, G. I. *De Middelnederlandsche Tauler-handschriften*. Groningen: Wolters, 1936.

Löser, Freimut. "Predigt über Predigt—Meister Eckhart und Johannes Tauler." Pages 155–80 in *Predigt im Kontext*. Edited by Volker Mertens, Hans-Jochen Schiewer, Regina Dorothea Schiewer, and Wolfram Schneider-Lastin. Berlin: De Gruyter, 2013.

Lund, Eric. "Tauler the Mystic's Lutheran Admirers." Pages 9–27 in *Piety and Family in Early Modern Europe: Essays in Honour of Steven Ozment*. Edited by Marc R. Forster and Benjamin J. Kaplan. Burlington, VT: Ashgate, 2005.

Mayer, Johannes G. *Die "Vulgata"-Fassung der Predigten Johannes Taulers. Von der handschriftlichen Überlieferung des 14. Jahrhunderts bis zu den ersten Drucken*. Würzburg: Königshausen & Neumann, 1999.

Mösch, Caroline F. *"Daz disiu geburt geschehe": Meister Eckharts Predigtzyklus Von dem êwigen geburt und Johannes Taulers Predigten zum Weihnachtsfestkreis*. Fribourg: Academic Press, 2006.

Mulchahey, M. Michèle. *"First the Bow is Bent in Study . . .": Dominican Education before 1350*. Toronto: Pontifical Institute of Mediaeval Studies, 1998.

Otto, Henrik. *Vor- und frühreformatorische Tauler-Rezeption: Annotationen in Drucken des späten 15. und frühen 16. Jahrhunderts.* Gütersloh: Gütersloher Verlagshaus, 2003.

Pfister, Gérard. "La postérité de Jean Tauler." *Revue des sciences religieuses* 75 (2001): 465–78.

Pleuser, Christine. *Die Benennungen und der Begriff des Leides bei J. Tauler.* Berlin: Erich Schmidt Verlag, 1967.

Reaidy, Jean. "Trinité et naissance mystique chez Eckhart et Tauler." *Revue des sciences religieuses* 75 (2001): 444–55.

Rooney, Anne. *Hunting in Middle English Literature.* Rochester: Boydell & Brewer, 1993.

Sands, Kathleen R. *Demon Possession in Elizabethan England.* Westport, CT: Praeger, 2004.

Schiewer, Regina D. "*Vos amici dei estis*: Die 'Gottesfreunde' des 14. Jahrhunderts bei Seuse, Tauler und in den 'Engelberger Predigten': Religiöse Elite, Verein oder Literaturzirkel?" *Oxford German Studies* 36 (2007): 227–46.

Schmidt, Josef, ed. *Johannes Tauler: Sermons.* Trans. by Maria Shrady. New York: Paulist, 1985.

Schneider, Michael. *Krisis. Zur theologischen Deutung von Glaubens- und Lebenskrisen: ein Beitrag der theologischen Anthropologie.* 2nd ed. Frankfurt am Main: Knecht, 1995.

Schwienhorst-Schönberger, Ludger. "Johannes Tauler (1300–1361): Mystik und Schriftauslegung." Pages 83–116 in *Text und Mystik: Zum Verhältnis von Schriftauslegung und kontemplativer Praxis.* Edited by Karl Baier, Regina Polak and Ludger Schwienhorst-Schönberger. Göttingen: Vandenhoeck & Ruprecht, 2013.

Stam, P. J., Jr. *Mystiek geloof: Tauler, Luther, Kohlbrugge.* Kampen: De Groot Goudriaan, 1990.

Steer, Georg. "Die literarische Abhängigkeit Johannes Taulers von Meister Eckhart und das Problem der Orthodoxie." Pages 59–78 in *Das Gottesverständnis der deutschen Mystik (Meister Eckhart, Johannes Tauler, Heinrich Seuse) und die Frage nach seiner Orthodoxie.* Edited by Markus Enders. Münster: Lit, 2011.

Straubmüller, Marcus. *Weltmodell Mystik: Eine raumsemantische Analyse ausgewählter Predigten Meister Eckharts und Johannes Taulers.* Hamburg: Diplomica, 2015.

Sturlese, Loris. "Tauler im Kontext: Die philosophischen Voraussetzungen des 'Seelengrundes' in der Lehre des deutschen Neoplatonikers Berthold von Moosburg." *Beiträge zur Geschichte der deutschen Sprache und Literatur (Tübingen)* 109 (1987): 390–426. Reprinted on pages 169–97 in Loris Sturlese, *Homo divinus: Philosophische Projekte in Deutschland zwischen Meister Eckhart und Heinrich Seuse.* Stuttgart: Kohlhammer, 2007.

———. "Tauler e Bertoldo di Moosburg. I presupposti filosofici della dottrina del 'fondo dell'anima.'" Pages 157–94 in Loris Sturlese, *Eckhart, Tauler, Suso: Filosofi e mistici nella Germania medievale.* Florence: Le Lettere, 2010.

Theisen, Joachim. "Tauler und die Liturgie." Pages 409–24 in *Deutsche Mystik im abendländischen Zusammenhang.* Edited by Walter Haug and Wolfram Schneider-Lastin. Tübingen: Niemeyer, 2000.

Valléjo, Rémy. "Église et unité, '*Corpus mysticum*' selon Jean Tauler." Pages 201–13 in *La prédication et l'Église chez Eckhart et Nicolas de Cues.* Edited by Marie-Anne Vannier. Paris: Cerf, 2008.

Vannier, Marie-Anne. "Jean Tauler et les Amis de Dieu." *Revue des sciences religieuses* 75 (2001): 456–64.

———. "Les œuvres du *corpus* de la mystique rhénane numérisées par la Bibliothèque Nationale et Universitaire de Strasbourg." *Revue des sciences religieuses* 75 (2001): 496–502.

———, ed. *La naissance de Dieu dans l'âme chez Eckhart et Nicolas de Cues.* Paris: Cerf, 2006.

———, ed. *Encyclopédie des mystiques rhénans d'Eckhart à Nicolas de Cues et leur réception.* Paris: Cerf, 2011.

Vannini, Marco. "La postérité de Tauler: La théologie allemande, Luther et les autres." *La vie spirituelle* 738 (2001): 115–32.

Vetter, Ferdinand. *Die Predigten Taulers.* 1910. Repr., Berlin: Weidmann, 2000.

Volfing, Annette. "*Du bist den Rin herabe geflossen*: Topographical Metaphors and Interior Geography in the Sermons of Johannes Tauler." Pages 17–28 in *Schreiben und Lesen in der Stadt: Literaturbetrieb im spätmittelalterlichen Straßburg.* Edited by Stephen Mossman, Nigel F. Palmer, and Felix Heinzer. Berlin: De Gruyter, 2012.

Volk-Birke, Sabine. *Chaucer and Medieval Preaching: Rhetoric for Listeners in Sermons and Poetry.* Tübingen: Gunter Narr Verlag, 1991.

Warnar, Geert. "Tauler's *Minnenclich Meister*: Charisma and Authority in the Vernacular Mystical Tradition of the Low Countries and the Rhineland." Pages 49–70 in *Charisma and Religious Authority: Jewish, Christian, and Muslim Preaching, 1200–1500.* Edited by Katherine L. Jansen and Miri Rubin. Turnhout: Brepols, 2010.

Weigand, Rudolf Kilian. "Predigen und Sammeln: die Predigtanordnung in frühen Tauler-Handschriften." Pages 114–55 in *Studien zur deutschen Sprache und Literatur: Festschrift für Konrad Kunze zum 65. Geburtstag.* Edited by Václav Bok, Ulla Williams, and Werner Williams-Krapp. Hamburg: Kovač, 2004.

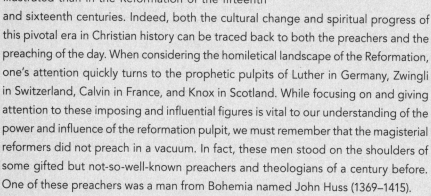

John Huss
Forerunner to the Reformation

MARK A. HOWELL

The connection between pulpit prowess and cultural progress is perhaps nowhere more clearly illustrated than in the Reformation of the fifteenth and sixteenth centuries. Indeed, both the cultural change and spiritual progress of this pivotal era in Christian history can be traced back to both the preachers and the preaching of the day. When considering the homiletical landscape of the Reformation, one's attention quickly turns to the prophetic pulpits of Luther in Germany, Zwingli in Switzerland, Calvin in France, and Knox in Scotland. While focusing on and giving attention to these imposing and influential figures is vital to our understanding of the power and influence of the reformation pulpit, we must remember that the magisterial reformers did not preach in a vacuum. In fact, these men stood on the shoulders of some gifted but not-so-well-known preachers and theologians of a century before. One of these preachers was a man from Bohemia named John Huss (1369–1415).

HISTORICAL BACKGROUND

To grasp the historical significance of John Huss's ministry, one must go no further than the personal testimony of Martin Luther. In describing the early days of the Reformation, Luther draws attention to Huss's indelible mark on the pages of church history when he admits: "Our reform movement was weak at first, but it grew from day to day. John Huss was the seed; he must first die, burned at the stake. Would not that seem to human reason great weakness? But see what, after a hundred years, has come of it!"[1] Luther, of course, was referring to Huss's martyrdom at the Council of Constance nearly a century earlier.[2]

In his book on the history of preaching, David Larsen notes how much Huss influenced Luther. As Larsen puts it, so significant was Huss's influence

---

1. Martin Luther, *Table Talk: Conversations with Martin Luther*, trans. Preserved Smith, eds. Herbert Percival Gallinger and Preserved Smith (New Canaan, CT: Keats Publishing, 1979), 198.
2. See Matthew Spinka, *John Hus at the Council of Constance* (New York: Columbia University Press, 1965), 3–86.

on him that Luther was constantly under "the shadow of the life and death of John Huss."[3] The remainder of this chapter will explore who Huss was, how this obscure Bohemian could leave such an indelible mark on arguably one of the most influential figures in Christian history, and finally, how his theology for preaching should encourage those preaching today.

Forerunner to a Reformation

How Luther discovered Huss is attributable only to the providence of God. One day while rummaging through the library stacks at the University of Erfurt, Luther came across some printed sermons of Huss. Upon reading them, Luther is said to have exclaimed: "I was overwhelmed with astonishment. I could not understand for what cause they had burnt so great a man, who explained the Scriptures with so much gravity and skill."[4] Indeed, Luther's statement reveals two key truths about Huss. First, he was executed in the most heinous way— burned at the stake; and second, he was passionately committed to the proclamation of biblical truth.

Thomas Fudge provides us with a historical look at and an inspirational account of the fateful day when Huss was burned at the stake: "On 6 July, 1415 the Prague university professor, parish priest and condemned heretic Jan Hus was executed by order of the Council of Constance. He died singing. The grotesque comedy of a man wearing a dunce cap standing on a burning pyre chained to a post transmitted enough raw emotion to influence an entire nation. The result was the Bohemian Reformation and the Hussite Revolution. The blood of the martyr produced seed. The ink of the scholar brought forth substance and the 'man' made 'saint' in the hands of others gave birth to a [movement] that whispered in Prague, sang in Constance and shouted across Europe."[5]

As horrifying as his death was, Huss died for a reason. He viewed his world, his church, and his life through a biblical lens. This conviction, of course, is what placed him at odds with the church, and not merely because he believed the Bible, but rather because he boldly declared those beliefs—even when those beliefs both challenged and called into question the authority of a powerful religious system . . . the power of the papacy. This is precisely the reason why Huss's name is forever etched on the pages of Christian history. Huss biographer David Schaff agrees with such a conclusion. In the preface of his biography, Schaff notes the far-reaching influence of Huss:

---

3. David L. Larsen, *The Company of Preachers* (Grand Rapids: Kregel, 1998), 148–49.
4. Martin Luther cited in Herbert B. Workman, *The Age of Huss* (London: Kelly, 1902), 148.
5. Thomas A. Fudge, "The Shouting Hus: Heresy Appropriated as Propaganda in the Sixteenth Century," *Communio Viatorum* 38, no. 3 (1996): 197.

John Huss belongs not to Bohemia alone. He has a place in the religious history of Europe and the West. . . . Some will be attracted to Huss chiefly by the fidelity to conviction which he maintained even in the presence of horrible death; others by those principles which . . . were opposed to the system built up during the Middle Ages and abhorred by the churchmen and theologians of Huss's own age. From whatever standpoint he may be regarded, as a heretic or as an advocate of forgotten Scriptural truth, as a contumacious rebel against constituted church authority or as an advocate of the just rights of conscience, . . . this biography is intended not only to set forth the teachings and activity of John Huss and the circumstances of his death but also to show the perpetuation of his influence upon the centuries that have elapsed since he suffered at the stake, "He being dead yet speaketh."[6]

Given such lofty avowals, to hear Luther refer to Huss as the "seed" of the Reformation is not surprising. In fact, Luther was convinced that despite attempts to mute Huss's message, it continued to reverberate throughout the land. In inimitable Luther fashion, he quips: "How could John Hus ever have reached the point in [his] lifetime where [he] could be in all places? But now that [he is] dead, [he is] made to appear everywhere. In every pulpit one must cope with him. He must be in my mouth and in your mouth, in every book and every ear."[7] What was it about Huss that prompted Luther to offer such a lofty avowal? Was it the man himself or the message he preached? A closer look at his life and his preaching will give some much-needed perspective.

From Obscurity to Prominence to Martyrdom

The remarkable story of Huss's life illustrates how God often works through tragedy to bring about some of history's most significant triumphs. Born to Bohemian peasants in 1373 and raised predominantly by his mother (his father died when he was a child), Huss still managed to attend the University of Prague. While at the university, he supported himself by singing on the streets and in the churches. He made the most of his time at the university by completing both a bachelor's and master's degree. Additionally, his academic prowess coupled with his moral integrity enabled him to gain favor with his colleagues. He was thus made dean of the philosophy faculty in 1401 and then ultimately rector of the university in 1402. While Huss was born to ordinary peasants, it was obvious to

---

6. David S. Schaff, *John Huss: His Life, Teachings and Death, After Five Hundred Years* (Eugene, OR: Wipf & Stock, 2001), vii.

7. Luther, cited in Fudge, "The Shouting Hus," 197.

many that he was anything but ordinary. As Schaff notes: "The qualities of eloquence, moral elevation and personal magnetism ascribed to him at a later period must already have had prominent exercise to explain this gift of the highest university distinction. He was a marked man in the eyes of students and faculties."[8] While serving on the faculty of the university, Huss was ordained to the priesthood. Remarkably, by his own attestation, he opted to pursue the priesthood not because he was called to it, but rather because it offered him a comfortable living.[9]

A key turning point in Huss's life occurred in 1402 when he was appointed to the pulpit of Bethlehem Chapel in Prague. Not yet thirty years of age, Huss's popularity began to rise. Bethlehem Chapel's three thousand seats were regularly filled with those eager to hear him preach. As Jan Ligus notes, his crowds were as diverse as they were large: "Those who listened to Huss's sermons . . . were poor people, students, wealthy Czech citizens and craftsmen; occasionally members of the nobility appeared to hear his sermons as well, courtiers of King Wenceslaus IV, and even queen Sophie (Sofia) herself listened to the words of the local preacher."[10] During his years at Bethlehem Chapel, Huss likely preached more than three thousand sermons.

Although Huss's initial desire for the priesthood was less than noble, he experienced a radical transformation in his early years at Bethlehem Chapel. Influenced and challenged by the writings of John Wycliffe, buoyed by a firm resolve to preach the Scripture, and determined to preach in the language of the people, Huss was no longer an obscure peasant—he became a thundering voice calling for biblical fidelity, moral purity, and ecclesiastical reform. As Schaff insightfully notes: "Huss was a preacher to the age in which he lived, to the congregations which pressed to hear him. His messages burn with zeal for pure religion and with sympathy for men. With his whole heart he was a preacher. Christ's chief command, as he reminded the archbishop of Prague, was to preach the Gospel to every creature, and when he was forbidden by archbishop and pope to no longer occupy his pulpit he solemnly declared, in a letter to the chief civil officials of Bohemia, that he dared not obey the commands, for to do so would be to offend 'against God and his own salvation.'"[11]

Huss's disdain for the corrupt state of the church became more and more evident in his preaching. And although his popularity among the people continued to grow, Huss soon found himself at odds with the archbishop of Prague concerning the controversial teachings of John Wycliffe.

---

8. Schaff, *John Huss*, 22.
9. Ibid.
10. Jan Ligus, "Master Jan Hus—Obedience or Resistance," *European Journal of Theology* 24:1 (2015): 50.
11. Schaff, *John Huss*, 41.

Wycliffe's controversial writings made their way to Bohemia when England's King Richard II married the King of Bohemia's daughter Anne. To say his sermons and writings were creating quite a stir is an understatement. Among his teachings were such themes as: (1) the Bible is the ultimate authority by which life is measured, (2) justification is possible only by the righteousness of Jesus Christ, (3) the papacy is a man-made and corrupt institution, and (4) the true church consists not of an institutionalized hierarchy but rather the invisible church of the elect.[12]

Understandably, the promulgation of such themes throughout Bohemia presented a real threat to the power of the papacy. Not surprisingly, a papal bull (issued at the insistence of the archbishop) declared Wycliffe's writings to be heretical. Hence, any preacher who championed them was to be silenced and punished. The archbishop was entrusted with the task of enforcing the bull and therefore sought to silence Huss. Huss was undeterred. In fact, the threats only served to intensify his passion for the truth and his desire for reform. His response to the papal bull was swift and pointed. Huss referred to the archbishop and pope as "scribes." "Because our scribes desire the same, commanding that there be no preaching in chapels, even such as had been approved by the apostolic authority, therefore I, wishing to obey God rather than men, and to conform to the acts of Christ rather than to theirs, appeal this wrongful command first of all to God, to whom belongs the principal authority to grant the power to preach."[13]

The authorities were not impressed by his recalcitrance. Still, Huss refused to be silent and continued to use his Bethlehem pulpit to affirm the absolute authority of Scripture and to decry the opulence and oppression of the papacy. Huss's courage is admirable. In the face of increasing pressure to acquiesce to the will of the authorities, Huss offered this classic response during one of his Sunday sermons: "Someone will say, 'But you, Hus, do not wish to be subject to your prelates, do not obey the elders, not even the archbishop' . . . I reply that I desire to be as Balaam's ass. Because the prelates sit on me, wishing to force me to go against the command of God . . . I will press the feet of their desire and will not obey them, for the angel of the Lord stands before me in the way."[14]

With mounting pressure from the authorities, Huss's presence in Prague was becoming problematic both for his church and for the city. Huss thus made the

---

12. For a brief overview of the life, ministries, and lasting contributions of Wycliffe, Huss, and others during the tumultuous fourteenth and fifteenth centuries, see John D. Woodbridge, ed., *Great Leaders of the Christian Church* (Chicago: Moody Press, 1988).

13. Huss cited in Ligus, "Master Jan Hus," 52.

14. Ibid.

difficult decision to vacate his pulpit at Bethlehem. He would spend the next two years living in the southern countryside. During this time of exile, he wrote one of his most important contributions to church history, a treatise called *The Church*.[15] He sent his treatise to Prague and insisted that it be read publicly from the Bethlehem pulpit. While his physical voice was no longer reverberating from his pulpit in Prague, Huss's message continued to echo throughout Bohemia.

While his treatise enjoyed a favorable hearing from those who loved him, Will Durant notes how this document ultimately marked the beginning of the end for Huss. Durant called his work both "his *apologia* and his ruin." With Huss's treatise in hand, the authorities had all the evidence necessary to silence him. As Durant succinctly puts it, "from its pages were drawn the heresies for which he was burned."[16]

In both his preaching and writing, Huss was adamant that Christ—not the pope—was the true head of the church. Further, he argued that the Bible—not the church—was the final authority in faith and practice. Convinced of and ready to die for these truths, Huss would affirm: "I hope by God's grace, that I am truly a Christian, not deviating from the faith, and that I would rather suffer the penalty of terrible death than to wish to affirm anything outside of the faith or transgress the commandments of our Lord Jesus Christ."[17] These were not wasted words. Nearly a century later, Martin Luther would speak with the same courage, clarity, and conviction as that of Huss when he avowed: "Unless I am convicted by Scripture and plain reason, I do not accept the authority of popes and councils—for they have contradicted each other—my conscience is captive to the Word of God. I cannot and will not recant anything, for to go against conscience is neither right nor safe. Here I stand, I can do no other, so help me God. Amen."[18]

Faithful to the End

Ultimately, Huss died both for what he believed and for what he preached. History has provided much insight into the events surrounding his martyrdom. One such insight comes from a man named Poggius. He was charged with the dual responsibility of delivering to Huss a summons to appear before the Council of Constance and also with serving as a voting member of the Council. With vivid

---

15. See John Huss, *The Church*, trans. David S. Schaff (New York: Scribner's Sons, 1915).

16. Will Durant, *The Reformation: A History of European Civilization from Wycliffe to Calvin: 1300–1564*, vol. 6 in *The Story of Civilization* (New York: Simon & Schuster, 1957), 164–65.

17. John Huss, *The Letters of John Hus: With Introductions and Explanatory Notes,* comp. Herbert B. Workman and R. Martin Pope (New York: Hodder & Stoughton, 1904), v.

18. Martin Luther, cited in Roland H. Bainton, *Here I Stand: A Life of Martin Luther* (New York: Abingdon-Cokesbury, 1950), 185.

detail, he gives us a firsthand account of how Huss responded to the Council's final attempt to solicit a recantation of his teachings. According to Poggius, Huss responded: "I stand here under the eye of God, and I can never do what you ask me, were I not to blaspheme Him and prostitute my conscience. . . . My trust is in the almighty God and in my Lord Jesus Christ, who has redeemed me and has called me to preach His gospel to the last breath of my life."[19] With those words his fate was sealed, and Huss was ultimately sentenced to be burned at the stake. Another eyewitness recounts the final moments of his life:

> He was handed over to the secular authorities who led him to the place of his execution and death. On the way he shouted that false and twisted testimonies were submitted and that no one should believe that he advocated any heretical article. When he arrived at the place of execution, he knelt down and prayed with a joyful heart and a bright countenance. Then they stripped him down to his shirtsleeves, chained and roped him to a stake and piled wood around him to such a height that his head was barely visible—I omit other details. When the strong flames blazed up, he stopped singing and praying. But his spirit as we devoutly believe, reached with the flames to heaven, to the company of angels, just as Elijah did.[20]

While the final chapter of his earthly journey had come to an end, the story of Huss's life continues. Nowhere is this ongoing story more important than in the legacy of his preaching.

THEOLOGY OF PREACHING

Preaching a sermon is one thing; having something worthwhile to say in that sermon is another. John Huss was not only a preacher; he was a man with a message. As Thomas Fudge notes, Huss's followers celebrated their preacher's commitment to biblical truth by affirming: "If you want to know the Bible, you must go to Bethlehem and learn it on the walls as Master Jan of Husinec preached it."[21] The "walls" were a clear reference to the actual walls of Bethlehem Chapel where Huss had inscribed Scripture texts to remind his people of the centrality of the Bible in all matters of faith. For Huss, the pulpit at Bethlehem did not belong to

19. Poggio Bracciolini, *Hus the Heretic* (Poland, ME: Shiloh Publications, 1997), 70–71.

20. Thomas A. Fudge, *The Trial of John Huss: Medieval Heresy and Criminal Procedure* (Oxford: Oxford University Press, 2013), 347.

21. Thomas A. Fudge, "'Feel this!' Jan Huss and the Preaching of the Reformation," in *The Bohemian Reformation and Religious Practice*, vol. 4 (Czech Republic: Academy of Sciences, 2002), 107. Interestingly, Fudge suggests that these words were actually the lyrics of a song.

him but to God. Thus, he recognized his solemn responsibility to confront his people with God's Word. Even as he faced death, he exhorted his congregation "to obey God, reverence His word, and live according to it."[22]

David Schaff explains how Huss's popularity had as much to do with his message as it did with the man himself. "It's no wonder that Bethlehem Chapel was thronged," writes Schaff, "Its pulpit dealt in no theological abstractions. The sword of the Spirit, which is the Word of God, was in the preacher's hand a sharp weapon, wielded dexterously to lay open the sins and subterfuges of the conscience. It was the Word of Life offering the comforts of saving grace."[23] Huss did not merely talk about the Bible; he preached from the Bible. More than three quarters of his sermons contain direct quotations of the Bible, with majority of the remaining one third containing quotes from the Early Church Fathers who themselves quote the Scriptures.[24] Huss was steadfast in his commitment "to hold, believe, and assert whatever is contained in [the Scriptures]." Hence, he plainly declared: "I rest with the conviction that every word of Christ is true; and what I do not understand, I commit to His grace in the hope, that I shall understand it after my death."[25] Given his high view of Scripture, one may see why Huss was so troubled by the sinful state of the church, the abuses of the papacy, and the carnality of the priests. As Ligus writes, since Huss believed the Bible to be God's Word, the Bible was therefore "the only applicable standard for the life of the Church, its traditions, society, proclamation, liturgy, teaching and pastoral ministry." Huss therefore believed that "individual believers, churches and state authorities [must] be obedient to the Holy Scripture."[26] Knowing what he did about Scripture and seeing what he saw in the life of the church, Huss could not remain silent.

His high view of Scripture was evident not only in what he preached but also in what he wrote. For example, many of Huss's personal letters have been preserved. A majority of his letters read like sermons and provide us with an intimate look into his heart and his convictions. For example, in a letter written from exile and sent to his Bethlehem Chapel congregation, Huss shared the following poignant words: "I . . . would like to see you and preach God's word to you, for it is in this that the other priests also ought to show their greatest earnestness. Woe to the priests who count the word of God as naught! Woe to those who are

22. Huss, cited in E. H. Gillett, *The Life and Times of John Huss*, vol. 2 (Boston: Gould & Lincoln, 1863), 17.

23. Schaff, *John Huss*, 41.

24. Pavel Soukup, "Jan Hus as a Preacher," in *A Companion to Jan Hus*, Vol. 54, eds. Ota Pavlicek and Frantisek Smahel (Czech Republic: Brill), 120.

25. Huss, cited in Spinka, *John Huss at the Council of Constance*, 189–90.

26. Ligus, "Master Jan Hus," 53.

supposed to preach and do not preach! Woe to those who hinder from preaching and hearing! But praise be to those who hear the word and keep it, for it is Christ that gives to them His indulgences, saying: *Blessed are they who hear the word of God and keep it* (italics his)."[27]

In another letter written to the people of Prague, Huss points clearly to the Word of God as the sole avenue by which one could discover the way of eternal life. He writes: "Stand in the ways, constantly asking which are those that lead from eternal death to eternal life, and from misery to eternal joy. And this way is the gospel of the Lord Almighty, the apostolic epistles, the Old Testament, the lives also of the saints which are contained in the sacred letters, saints who shine forth in their lives as the sun, moon, and stars. Therefore, dear brothers and dear sisters in the Lord God, I beg you by the martyrdom of God's Son gladly to attend the preaching, to gather together and hear it diligently; to understand as ye hear, to observe as ye understand; to learn as ye observe."[28]

Huss clearly saw preaching as both central to the worship of the church and as critical for the spiritual growth and development of the Christian. Spinka's observation is insightful when he writes: "The scriptural emphasis [in Huss's preaching] implied the duty of preaching as central to the service of worship, rather than the ceremonialism and outward acts of devotion of which much of the worship then consisted. The preaching of the Word was not only to instruct and confirm the believer in his faith, but to deepen his spiritual life, in which true religion consisted."[29]

METHODOLOGY FOR PREACHING

Above all, John Huss was a preacher. Though he busied himself with other pastoral duties, the main priority of the pastor of Bethlehem Chapel was to preach. The thousands who gathered to hear him expected such. As noted, during his twelve-year preaching span, Huss most likely preached more than three thousand sermons, perhaps even as many as 3,500.[30] To accomplish such a task required him to maintain an arduous preaching schedule. According to one researcher's analysis of Huss's sermons at Bethlehem Chapel, he "preached daily during Lent, in most cases even twice a day, and might have even preached three sermons on major feasts . . . or when a saint's day fell on a Sunday. . . . Outside Advent, Lent,

27. John Huss, *The Letters of John Hus*, 108.

28. Ibid., 137–38.

29. Spinka, *John Huss at the Council of Constance*, 63.

30. In his biography on Huss, Schaff provides an extensive list of primary and secondary resources on his writings, sermons, and letters. Many of these sources are in Latin, Czech, and German. See Schaff, *John Huss*, vi–x.

and major feast periods, Hus usually preached two Sunday sermons (gospel and epistle) and one or two sermons on saints per week."[31]

Even after the Wycliffe controversy forced him to abandon his position at Bethlehem Chapel, Huss continued preaching in exile. Every preacher knows something of the burden Huss must have felt when he forfeited his pulpit. While it's possible to remove a preacher from their pulpit, it is not possible to take the message out of the preacher. Hence, Huss would not be silenced. From the grandeur of castles to the simplicity of fields in the countryside, he would not abdicate his responsibility to preach the Word. As he saw it, he was fulfilling the mandate of Jesus to proclaim the Word in the "highways and hedges" (Luke 14:23, ESV). Applying that biblical passage to his own predicament, he wittingly quipped, "Now I preach between hedges around the castle called Kozi, in highways to towns and villages."[32] Amazingly, even in exile the crowds still gathered to hear him preach.

At the heart of Huss's preaching was the inescapable call of God upon his life. Armed with this calling, Huss faced adversity with a calm assurance. Nowhere is this assurance more on display than in the final days leading up to his martyrdom. Only days before he would be burned at the stake, Huss penned these words:

> I, John Hus, in hope a priest of Jesus Christ, fearing to offend God, and fearing to fall into perjury, do hereby profess my unwillingness to abjure all or any of the articles produced against me by false witnesses. For God is my witness that I neither preached, affirmed, nor defended them, though they say that I did. Moreover, concerning the articles that they have extracted from my books, I say that I detest any false interpretation which any of them bears. But inasmuch as I fear to offend against the truth, or to gainsay the opinion of the doctors of the Church, I cannot abjure any one of them. And if it were possible that my voice could now reach the whole world, as at the Day of Judgment every lie and every sin that I have committed will be made manifest, then would I gladly abjure before all the world every falsehood and error which I either had thought of saying or actually said. I say I write this of my own free will and choice.[33]

Indeed, Huss lived passionately for what he believed and he was willing to die for those beliefs. In the final hours of his life he would exclaim: "But I am anxious now as ever that they will show me scriptures of greater weight and value than

---

31. Soukup, "Jan Hus as a Preacher," 106.
32. Huss, cited in Soukup, "Jan Hus as a Preacher," 110.
33. Huss, *The Letters of John Hus*, 275–76.

those which I have quoted in writing and teaching."[34] Of course, Huss knew no such evidence existed, because his preaching, teaching, and writing were faithful to the Scriptures. As his executioners made their final preparations, Huss spoke these final words of assurance: "I have never thought nor preached save with the one intention of winning men, if possible, from their sins. In the truth of the gospel I have written, taught, and preached, today I will gladly die."[35]

CONTRIBUTIONS TO PREACHING

John Huss was a remarkable man who lived a remarkable life. Although those who opposed his message thought they could silence him by taking his life, his martyrdom only served to influence one of history's most influential theologians, Martin Luther. Whatever else might be said of Huss, he was first and foremost a preacher of the Bible. A survey of his life and ministry confronts us with at least three lessons. First, a call to preach is a call to preach the Bible. To be sure, Huss's biblical convictions put him at odds with the ecclesiastical hierarchy and prevailing religious culture of his day. Still, he never ceased both to believe what the Bible taught and to explain it to his people. For him, the Bible was not a part of the sermon—it *was* the sermon. As such, it was the source and substance of everything he had to say.

Second, a careful look at Huss's life highlights the difficulties and challenges pastors often face in Christian ministry. Huss's biblical convictions collided with the convictions of those in power. As a result, Huss spent the final years of ministry separated from both the church to which he was called and the people he loved. He ultimately paid for his convictions with his life. He was a man who spoke the truth even in the very last words he uttered.

Though the authorities had forbid Huss to preach, he knew he was accountable to a higher authority—a calling from God. As Ligus notes, Huss never lost sight of his calling: "It was the Triune God, Father, Son and Holy Spirit, who had called him to have a ministry in the church. . . . Along with this, Hus had a calling from the church . . . Both of these callings and his knowledge of them helped him to overcome all obstacles, pressures and inner anxieties that he felt when he refused to be subjected to the regulations of the ecclesiastical authorities."[36] A call to ministry is often a call to suffer for the sake of Christ. Yet, with God's call comes God's assurance that he will sustain you even in the most trying days of ministry.

---

34. Ibid., 277.
35. Ibid., 279.
36. Ligus, "Master Jan Hus," 53.

A third and final lesson to be learned from Huss relates to the eternal impact of a biblically grounded, God-saturated ministry. The authorities believed that by burning both a heretic and his books, they could mute the man and eliminate his message. However, as we have seen, history reveals otherwise. In many ways, the message Huss proclaimed is more alive today than it was in the fifteenth century. Huss reminds us how the person who focuses on the depth of their walk with God can trust God to take care of the breadth of their influence for his purposes. This side of heaven you and I may never see the entire picture of what God is doing with us and through us. Yet, with conviction, resolve, and faith, we press on because we know that in the end God will always have the last word. If we are ever in doubt of this truth, we need to look no further than at the remarkable life of John Huss.

Sermon Excerpt

A Letter to the People of Prague (Advent 1412)[37]

Dear friends, although I am now separated from you, because perchance I am unworthy to preach much to you, nevertheless the love which I bear towards you urges me to write at least some brief words to my loved ones.

Lo! dear friends, to-day, as it were, an angel is saying to the shepherds: I bring you good tidings of great joy that shall be to all people. And suddenly a multitude of angels breaks into praise, saying: Glory to God in the highest, and on earth peace to men of goodwill!

As you commemorate these things, dear friends, rejoice that to-day God is born a man, that there may be glory to God in the highest and on earth peace to men of goodwill. Rejoice that to-day the infinitely Mighty is born a child, that there may be glory to God in the highest, etc. Rejoice that to-day a Reconciler is born to reconcile man to God, that there may be glory to God in the highest, etc. Rejoice that today He is born to cleanse sinners from their sin, to deliver them from the devil's power, to save them from eternal perdition, and to bring them to eternal joy, that there may be glory to God in the highest, etc. Rejoice with great joy that today is born unto us a King, to bestow in its fullness upon us the

---

37. This citation is a letter/sermon written to Bethlehem Church while Huss was in exile. The letter is dated December 25, 1412. Huss, *The Letters of John Huss*, 108–10.

heavenly kingdom, a Bishop to grant His eternal benediction, a Father of the ages to come, to keep us as His children by His side forever: yea, there is born a Brother beloved, a wise Master, a sure Leader, a just Judge, to the end that there may be glory to God in the highest, etc. Rejoice, ye wicked, that God is born as a Priest, Who hath granted to every penitent absolution from all sins, that there may be glory, etc. Rejoice that to-day the Bread of Angels—that is, God—is made the Bread of men, to revive the starving with His Body, that there may be peace among them, and on earth, etc. Rejoice that God immortal is born, that mortal man may live forever. Rejoice that the rich Lord of the Universe lies in a manger, like a poor man, that he may make us rich. Rejoice, dearly beloved, that what the prophets prophesied has been fulfilled, that there may be glory to God in the highest, etc. Rejoice that there is born to us a Child all-powerful, and that a Son is given to us, all-wise and gracious, that there may be glory to God in the highest, etc. Oh, dear friends, ought there to be but a moderate rejoicing over these things? Nay, a mighty joy! Indeed, the angel saith: I bring you good tidings of great joy, for that there is born a Redeemer from all misery, a Saviour of sinners, a Governor of His faithful ones; there is born a Comforter of the sorrowful, and there is given to us the Son of God that we may have great joy, and that there may be glory to God in the highest and on earth peace to men of goodwill. May it please God, born this day, to grant to us this goodwill, this peace, and withal this joy! ◆

BIBLIOGRAPHY

Bracciolini, Poggio. *Hus the Heretic*. Poland, ME: Shiloh Publications, 1997.

Durant, Will. *The Reformation: A History of European Civilization from Wycliffe to Calvin: 1300–1564*. Vol 6 of *The Story of Civilization*. New York: Simon & Schuster, 1957.

Fudge, Thomas A. "'Feel This!' Jan Has and the Preaching of Reformation." Pages 107–26 in *The Bohemian Reformation and Religious Practice*. Vol. 4. Czech Republic: Academy of Sciences, 2002.

————. "The Shouting Hus: Heresy Appropriated as Propaganda in the Sixteenth Century." *Communio Viatorum* 38.3 (1996): 197–231.

————. *The Trial of Jan Hus: Medieval Heresy and Criminal Procedure*. Oxford: Oxford University Press, 2013.

Gillett, E. H. *The Life and Times of John Huss: Or, The Bohemian Reformation of the Fifteenth Century*. Vol. 2. Boston: Gould & Lincoln, 1863.

Huss, John. *The Church*. Trans. by David S. Schaff. New York: Scribner's Sons, 1915.

————. *The Letters of John Hus: With Introductions and Explanatory Notes*. Compiled by Herbert B. Workman and R. Martin Pope. New York: Hodder & Stoughton, 1904.

Kaminsky, Howard. *A History of the Hussite Revolution*. Eugene, OR: Wipf & Stock, 1967.

Larsen, David L. *The Company of the Preachers: A History of Biblical Preaching from the Old Testament to the Modern Era*. Grand Rapids: Kregel, 1998.

Ligus, Jan. "Master Jan Hus: Obedience or Resistance." *European Journal of Theology* 24.1 (2015): 49–56.

Loserth, Johann. *Wiclif and Hus*. London: Hodder & Stoughton, 1884.

Luther, Martin. *Table Talk: Conversations with Martin Luther*. Translated by Perserved Smith. Edited by Herbert Percival Gallinger and Perserved Smith. New Caanan, CT: Keats, 1979.

Schaff, David S. *John Huss: His Life, Teachings and Death, After Five Hundred Years*. Eugene, OR: Wipf & Stock, 2001.

Soukup, Pavel. "Jan Hus as a Preacher." Pages 96–129 in *A Companion to Jan Hus*. Edited by Ota Pavlicek and Frantisek Smahel. Vol. 54. Czech Republic: Brill, 2015.

Spinka, Matthew. *John Hus: A Biography*. Westport, CT: Greenwood, 1968.

_____, ed. and trans. *John Hus at the Council of Constance*. New York: Columbia University Press, 1965.

Woodbridge, John D., ed. *Great Leaders of the Christian Church*. Chicago: Moody Press, 1988.

Workman, Herbert B. *The Age of Huss*. London: Kelly, 1902.

HIERONYMI·FERRARIENSIS·ADEO
·MISSI·PROPHETÆ·EFFIGIES·

Girolamo Savonarola

Apocalyptic Preacher and Martyr to Opulence

W. BRIAN SHELTON

Girolamo Savonarola (1452–1498) is among the most irreplaceable of historical preachers. As prior of the monastery of San Marco in Florence, he delivered fiery sermons against opulence and apathy in the birthplace of the humanistic Renaissance. While his ministry shows historic marks of repentance in his congregation and the larger city, his preaching ran afoul of the political and ecclesiastical establishment of central Italy. The result was that the "bonfires of vanity," which burned humanistic works of art and writing, spread to the bonfire of his execution. The result is a preacher who models bold and passionate conviction, while serving as a case study in one preacher's confrontation with culture.

HISTORICAL BACKGROUND

Scandal elicits attention. While provocative religious figures abound in church history, the church must explore and evaluate these figures that inspired and motivated communities to repentance. Girolamo Savonarola is one such figure. Confronted with an unpredictable and unfavorable audience, he preached a simple gospel in a complex cultural milieu that prompted his execution. His unbridled passion, which led to tragedy, can be an instructive warning for preachers today.

The historical setting for the preaching of Girolamo Savonarola is unique. His approach to preaching, his audience, and the context of his sermons are equally complicated. The context for Savonarola's short, Florentine life is crucial to understanding his exegesis and homilies as well as the preacher's execution in May 1498.

Savonarola received his pastoral assignment to the congregation of the Church of San Marco in 1490. The church was located in Florence, the heart of the Italian renaissance, a city that celebrated the cultural shift in art, architecture, literature, music, philosophy, and science. Closely allied with the papacy, the city was wealthy and proud of its contribution to the modern era. Florence would be a center stage for the Italian War of 1494–1498, including the French invasion of the peninsula. Meanwhile, the city accommodated the Holy See, which had plunged itself into opulence and caused moral suspicion for some clergy. There was a substantial contrast between the realm of humanistic art, dense politics, opulent lifestyles, and autocratic power and the private life of a friar who took a vow to poverty, chastity, and self-sacrifice in an order of preachers. For Savonarola, the pulpit was a commission from God to promote the gospel by rebuking the sin that accompanied such wealth, even amid the cultural and political establishment.[1] It was an appointment for divine correction to the church, like that of an Old Testament prophet in corrective service to the people of God. Sermons about simplicity against the backdrop of Florence's luxury, homilies about helping the poor living among the rich, and addresses calling for repentance preached among the comfortable were radically refreshing to many, and yet hostilely received by others. France's invasion was an apocalyptic opportunity for Savonarola to call the Florentine citizens to repentance and to burn humanistic art, lavish jewelry, and pagan writings in bonfires that served as a protest against the affluent establishment.

Personal Life

Girolamo Savonarola was born in 1452 in Ferrara, Italy, in the northeastern sector close to the Adriatic Sea. His most significant influence was his grandfather, a physician who sponsored him toward a master's degree at the University of Ferrara. He seems to have been highly intellectual, a gifted orator, and devoted to study. There are legends of his early attitude toward wealth, but for the purposes of this volume, the timeline begins as he entered the Dominican order at Bologna, the Order of Friars Preachers, in 1475. He preached in various cities throughout Italy for four years before he was assigned as pastor to the Church of San Marco in Florence in 1490. A year later he received his appointment to prior of the monastery, the post in which he served until his death. He is noted for initiating internal reform at the monastery, including strict adherence to the Rule of Saint Augustine, the guidelines adopted by Dominic to govern the order. Like so many monastic reform movements, he sought a restoration toward earthly simplicity and poverty.[2]

---

1. For a summary of the complexities of his life and contribution, see Alison Brown, "Introduction," *Selected Writings of Girolamo Savonarola: Religion and Politics, 1490–1498*, ed. and trans. by Anne Borelli and Maria Pastore Passaro (New Haven: Yale University Press, 2006), xv–xxxi.

2. For a summary of Savonarola's Dominican roots in the making of a preacher, see Donald Weinstein, *Savonarola: The Rise and Fall of a Renaissance Prophet* (New Haven: Yale University Press, 2011), 16–27.

Savonarola's pastoral career would likely have disappeared in history if not for the contrast between his own personality and the immoral, spiritually apathetic environment of Florence. Set against this backdrop, his sermons mesmerized the city, motivating part of the population to repentance while catalyzing another to conflict.[3] Yet in this complex context came a clear message of purity, passion, and dedication to the gospel of Christ and Scripture as the Word of God. This determination is only understood in the context of the era, explaining how a popular orator would become a legendary martyr.

Florentine Milieu

Context informs the sermon methodology and content for Savonarola. The extreme nature of his preaching is inseparable from his mission to champion repentance in Italy's center of humanism.

Savonarola believed two sectors of immoral influence threatened his flock in Florence: humanistic and religious abuses.[4] The cultural threat centered on the humanistic spirit of the Renaissance, stimulating the church to worldliness. This led to two reforming acts inspired by Savonarola. First, so-called bonfires of vanity were initiated in which townspeople brought worldly relics and threw them into a heap. Playing cards, paintings containing nudity, pagan writings, and artifacts of personal ornamentation were set to flames—an act seen as sanctifying the town. These artifacts were particularly important to Florence, as the crafts-manship and art represented the spirit of the Renaissance for which the town was known. It is hard to know the exact association of the bonfires with the priest, but he was likely pleased with them. This heightens the irony that the preacher would eventually fall victim to flames in the same city square.

Additionally, the youth of the city were notably unruly; Savonarola's sermons engendered a spirit of reform among them. His sermons so inspired a change in the demeanor of the youth that, rather than traveling house to house throwing rocks in windows, they would now march peacefully in the church festivals of the town and in support of fundraising for the poor. Multiple sources attribute this transformation to the preaching of Savonarola.

The second threat was religious and stemmed from the immorality of the

---

3. That his pastoral preaching was effective is recognized. In a dialog about prophecy, even his philosophical opponent remarks, "No one can now deny that through the exposition of this teaching the good indeed have been made better, the evil, truly worse." Savonarola, *Selected Writings of Girolamo Savonarola*, 87.

4. Weinstein remarks that these threats corresponded to the people's civic hope: "In both popular and sophisticated expression we find not one but two central themes of civic destiny—the idea of Florence as the daughter of Rome and the idea of Florence as the center of rebirth and Christian renewal." Donald Weinstein, *Savonarola and Florence: Prophecy and Patriotism in the Renaissance* (Princeton, NJ: Princeton University Press, 1970), 35.

Catholic Church leadership, including the papacy. Pope Alexander VI, who would excommunicate Savonarola, was of the Borgia family. He appointed family members to offices and and personally fathered multiple children in the face of his vow of celibacy. The lifestyles of immorality and simony of offices led to Savonaroloa's moral disgust with the church. In general, Savonarola used the neglect of the poor as an example to buttress his sharp rebuke of the opulence of the pope and papal curia. In 1495, Florence defied the papacy by siding with the French King Charles VIII during the invasion. Savonarola had personally appealed to the king on behalf of the city, supporting the ousting of the Medici rule in Florence and creating a popular republic. These political realities seemed to illustrate and confirm the apocalyptic preaching of Savonarola, terrifying the townspeople and convicting them for not following the preached Word of the Lord, much like the medieval firebrand Joachim of Fiore had done. One medieval scholar writes: "The Joachimist marriage of woe and exaltation exactly fitted the mood of late fifteenth century Italy, where the concept of the humanist Age of God had to be brought into relation with the ingrained expectation of Antichrist."[5]

Excommunication and Execution

By May 1497, Savonarola was excommunicated and banned from preaching. The pope threatened to place Florence under an interdict, which prohibited priests from dispensing the sacraments except in emergencies. Savonarola and two other Dominican friars were imprisoned. Torture would lead to his confession that he had feigned the visions and prophecies from God, revelations that were the basis for many of his sermons.[6] Today, scholars speculate his confession was either coerced or fabricated by the church. Johann Burchard reported in 1498 that Savonarola was "tortured seven times before he pleaded mercy and offered to say and to commit to writing all the matters in which he had erred. And taken away from the torture chamber back to his cell, he was given paper and ink, and he wrote down all his crimes and faults . . . filling it was said, eighty scrolls or more."[7] May 23, 1498, saw the church join with Florentine civil authorities to hang and then burn three friars in the Piazza della Signoria.

---

5. Marjorie Reeves, *The Influence of Prophecy in the Later Middle Ages: A Study in Joachimism* (New York: Oxford, 1969), 431.

6. Savonarola adopted apocalyptic themes in his sermons, including claiming visions of divine judgment against the consequences of Florence's spiritual apathy. The most notable example of temporal judgment was the impending invasion by France, where God's supposed revelation to the friar was the basis of his command to repent, explained below.

7. Andrew McCall, *The Medieval Underworld* (New York: Barnes & Noble, 1979), 67. McCall states, "Among his cited faults were making no confession since the age of twenty, giving communion with an unconsecrated host and using various tricks, including getting details of people's confessions from other friars, so as to pretend to have been granted divine revelations." Ibid., 67.

Such was the personal fate of this Dominican friar who chose to prophetically confront and make appeals to a city whose culture allowed more accommodating preachers to survive. The theology and shape of Savonarola's preaching helps to elucidate the conviction that motivated the pious faithful of the church to repentance, while perturbing the wealthy of the church to enmity and violence.

THEOLOGY OF PREACHING

Spiritual rebuke and apocalyptic overtones stand out as unique features of Savonarola's preaching. But these elements should not detract from his emphasis on prayer, charity, and personal holiness, which remained at the core of his preaching. In the spirit of 2 Timothy 3:16, Savonarola drew richly from the Old and New Testaments to teach, reprove, correct, and train in righteousness. His sermons never failed to center on the gospel call to godliness, while his conviction echoed the Old Testament prophets with rebuke and invitation to repent.

Rebuke to a Collective City

Savonarola has long been viewed as a fundamentalist preacher placed in the middle of free-thinking cultural elitism, rejecting progressive values for spiritual ones. This stereotypical view of him as a fire and brimstone missionary is not misdirected, but such a view constitutes only a partial understanding of his motivation that was also equally intellectual, passionate, biblical, and reactionary. While the Renaissance flourished with its Greco-Roman revival of humanistic values in art and literature, Savonarola despised the paganism that characterized the culture. While this analysis of his rejection of Renaissance art seems true, rarely does Savonarola name art as an object of condemnation. On the other hand, the social milieu that allowed for the artisan to thrive also meant that society had fluid wealth to afford the rise of this special class. It was the opulence, comfort, and apathy of Florence that prompted the friar to preach against the surge in humanistic art. When he did, the whole city often became the personification of his sermon audience.

In his sermon "The Art of Dying Well," he preached about congregational desires without mentioning specific sins: "Appetite for existence draws man so forcefully that it makes him remain fixed on this thought to such an extent that all his mental concentration and virtually all his actions are ordered toward this will, and he does everything to sustain it."[8] In this sermon on the importance of

---

8. Savonarola, "The Art of Dying Well," in *Selected Writings of Girolamo Savonarola: Religion and Politics, 1490–1498*, ed. and trans. by Anne Borelli and Maria Pastore Passaro (New Haven: Yale University Press, 2006), 34.

reflecting on death, he says: "All man's concern seems to be thinking about how to stay here and build beautiful palaces and amass possessions and so to become rich."[9] On the other hand, "If you were to think continually of death; you would abstain by and large from sin because there are two things which lead one to perform any good deed, love and fear, and these two spurs are the teachers of the arts."[10]

In a sermon from Exodus, he remarked that the spiritual condition of Italy was easily evidenced because "in this country more sins and greater were committed, and more frequently, than had ever been done before in times past since this mode of living commenced among the people. Therefore, I tell you that God is greatly enraged against you. I speak, I say, about the wicked."[11] A typical exhortation to the collective city can be illustrated: "Florence ... do, then, what I have told you; entrust yourselves to God, live in charity, do away with all hatred."[12] His Exodus sermon challenges the comfortable citizens of the city: "You lukewarm, I remind you of one thing: take care that you do not become martyrs for the devil.... I tell you, you lukewarm, that although you may be able to perform good exterior works, if you do not have charity and this law of Christ in your heart, you accomplish nothing, and you will end up in the house of the devil.... Come along this way, you lukewarm, for I have taken you by the arm this morning."[13]

These indifferent citizens of Florence are described using biblical imagery for apathy: "They have eyes, and they will not see," "they have ears, and they will not hear," while "they have noses, and they will not smell."[14] His appeal to spiritual health and countercultural initiatives often mark him among the "pre-Reformers" of the Protestant Reformation. His passionate appeal to righteousness against a Catholic establishment is illustrated by his Exodus sermon: "O you religious, O Rome, O Italy, I call on the whole world: come forward ... O Rome, it is hard for you to kicks [*sic*] against the goad."[15] While appealing to individual holiness, Savonarola also appealed to collective Florence, the country of Italy, and the Holy See itself. His boldness is convicting: "Consider if any prelates who are the leaders of the priests today believe in Him."[16]

---

9. Ibid., 35.
10. Ibid.
11. Ibid., 316.
12. Ibid., 30.
13. Girolamo Savonarola, "Exodus, Sermon III," in *Selected Writings of Girolamo Savonarola: Religion and Politics, 1490–1498,* ed. and trans. by Anne Borelli and Maria Pastore Passaro (New Haven: Yale University Press), 324. Donald Weinstein comments, "He exploited the lukewarmness theme in new ways and to an unprecedented degree," Weinstein, "Explaining God's Acts to his People: Savonarola's Spiritual Legacy to the Sixteenth Century," in *Humanity and Divinity in Renaissance and Reformation: Essays in Honor of Charles Trinkaus,* eds. John W. O'Malley, Thomas M. Izbicki, and Gerald Christenson (Leiden: Brill, 1993), 218.
14. Ibid., 328. Cf. Jer 5:21, Ezek 12:2, Matt 13:15, and Rom 11:8.
15. Ibid., 332. Cf. Acts 9:5.
16. Ibid., 320.

Apocalyptic Overtones

The recorded preaching of Savonarola centers on an apocalyptic threat that is indelibly contextualized in the perceived vices of Florence, the larger Roman Catholic Church, and the geography of Italy. In the face of the invading armies of Charles VIII of France, he reminded his congregants of the analogy of the ark: the righteous are delivered and the wicked are punished.[17] Such dramatic illustrations characterized many of his recorded sermons, adding a heightened sense of doom and apocalyptic threat in order to foster repentance. This is best illustrated in his "Renovation Sermon" for Florence. Here, the phrase *Ecce gladius Domini super terram cito et velociter* governs the sermon, "Behold, the sword of the Lord [will be] over the earth soon and swiftly,"[18] while the phrase, "The scourge is near," figures multiple times in the sermon.[19] Meanwhile, the work contains ten reasons that demonstrate and herald the coming renewal of the church through this work of God.[20]

Bernard McGinn summarizes how Savonarola "expected a confrontation between the revitalized church and the Final Enemy of the Fifth Age and a millennial period that would succeed this struggle."[21] Other friars and humanists called Savonarola the antichrist, while his followers continued to announce the apocalyptic message.[22] Weinstein describes the friar who can be perceived as prophet: "Savonarola the preacher catches the attention of sinners by means of threats of hellfire and such vivid imagery as the Devil's chessgame, and gives them a simple formula for avoiding sin, and from there Savonarola the writer takes over to pursue a more subtle and demanding, but ultimately more fulfilling, message of love and faith."[23]

Apocalyptic material applied to Florence is an abundant element in Savonarola's sermons. His sermon on Amos and Zechariah illustrates his use of visions and the extent to which he would dramatize his appeal: "I saw the whole world before my eyes, bit by bit, on a very great plain all full of many men and women of every condition in the world . . . Lo and behold! Lances, swords, bombs,

---

17. Savonarola, "On Social Order," in *Selected Writings of Girolamo Savonarola*, 139. Weinstein comments that the destiny of Florence was linked to the popular expectation that a French Charles could restore prominence for Florence as Charlemagne had done after the sixth-century Ostrogoth destruction. Weinstein, *Savonarola and Florence*, 38–40.

18. Savonarola, "Renovation Sermon," in *Selected Writings of Girolamo Savonarola*, 59 n.1.

19. Ibid., 62–74.

20. Ibid., 62–64.

21. Bernard McGinn, *Antichrist: Two Thousand Years of the Human Fascination with Evil* (San Francisco: HarperSanFrancisco, 1994), 188.

22. Ibid., 188, including specific names and accusation of friars.

23. Donald Weinstein, "The Art of Dying Well and Popular Piety in the Preaching and Thought of Girolamo Savonarola" in *Life and Death in Fifteenth-Century Florence*, eds. M. Tetel, R. G. Witt, and R. Goffin (Durham, NC: Duke University Press, 1989), 102.

and pestilence were coming . . . thus says the Lord God."[24] When the king of France prompted the expulsion of the Medici with the cooperation of Florence, the preacher remarked: "God has loved you, Florence, for He has shown you mercy, not for the sake of any advantage to Him, but solely on account of love from true friendship, and in order to do you good, although He has no need of you . . . Acknowledge, then, Florence, the grace that you have received."[25]

This use of the apocalyptic can be biblical, but it can also be dangerous. Savonarola employed the sacred text in an effort to motivate his congregation toward repentance, even in the face of Florence's critics.[26] The attacks came from all camps, as his radical rhetoric made him an easy target for criticism. Yet, the pastor defended his visions and his message. In part, his defense was due to a passion for the purpose of apocalyptic literature: the repentance of God's people in preparation for the tribulation to come. Furthermore, he observed how fear was able to lead the people to holiness. "If, therefore, to think this [Florence's sin] is sacrilege, let us concede that this which I prophesy is truth, and moreover, let no one presume either that I am deceived or that I deceive others."[27]

Call to Righteousness and Charity

The ongoing themes of rebuke and apocalyptic threat were part of the uniqueness of Savonarola's homiletics. But these threats are inseparable from the call to personal and civic obedience and righteousness. For example, "O citizens, devote yourselves to living uprightly and to doing good deeds,"[28] is delivered in a context of a need to put aside wealth, and instead sacrifice in giving. For this passion, the church today can find an appreciation of the driving force of preaching: a call to repentance. The central focus of Savonarola's sermons was the gospel message. "I set the Crucifix in the middle of the world, and I want to show you that this is the intended end of man, which moves everyone as the thing he loves and desires."[29] This is a call to personal righteousness and charity, both of which

---

24. Savonarola, "The Art of Living Well," in *Selected Writings of Girolamo Savonarola*, 9–10.

25. Savonarola, "On Social Order," in *Selected Writings of Girolamo Savonarola,* 143.

26. One noteworthy critic was Niccolò Machiavelli in the great Renaissance work *The Prince*, which sees Savonarola as inept, particularly because of his ideal for the state: "Moses, Cyrus, Theseus, and Romulus could never have made their ordinances be observed for any length of time had they been unarmed, as was the case in our own days, with the Friar Girolamo Savonarola, whose new institutions came to nothing so soon as the multitude began to waver in their faith . . ." Niccolò Machiavelli, *The Prince* (New York: Dover, 1992), 14. Martines remarks, "The figure of the great preacher is always present in Machiavelli's imagination." Lauro Martines, *Fire in the City: Savonarola and the Struggle for the Soul of Renaissance Florence* (Oxford: Oxford University Press, 2006), 312.

27. Savonarola, "A Dialog Concerning Prophetic Truth," in *Selected Writings of Girolamo Savonarola,* 5, 91.

28. Savonarola, "On Social Order," 147.

29. Savonarola, "The Art of Living Well," 6.

are sacrificial. His sermon on Exodus is typical of his appeal to Christian living: "I will exult this morning that you are the epistle of Christ, wherein through our ministry His law is written; you do not have it written in a book, but in your hearts. There a very great difference between having it written in the heart and having it written in books, as great as that between grace and ink, between the pen and the Holy Spirit, between man and God, between paper and the heart. Oh, a great difference, indeed!"[30]

In his sermon on Haggai, he called for two collections on the upcoming Sunday: "One will be for the poor who are in the city, the other for those who are outside . . . I exhort the citizens and anyone who is concerned at this time and for this charity for the poor, the money which you spend for the University be converted to relief for the poor, because this for now is more necessary and charitable than the other. . . . The other good provision is that the shops be opened and that everyone, and especially the poor, be able to work and support himself in this labor."[31]

The examples of his call for righteousness seem unending. "Florence . . . do, then, what I have told you; entrust yourselves to God, live in charity, do away with all hatred."[32]

METHODOLOGY FOR PREACHING

Savonarola approached the task of communicating his message with sobriety, conviction, and rhetorical skill. Compelling oratory and paraenetic appeal particularly characterize Savonarola's practice.

Compelling Oratory

The church has always valued excellent preaching with compelling oratory. Martines remarks of the Renaissance era: "Eloquence was part of the city's innermost self. With Dante, Petrarch, and Boccacio at the head of its outstanding constellation of writers, Florence was the literary city *par excellence*."[33] Likewise, "Florentines had a peninsula-wide reputation for wit and words."[34] Martines describes the posture of Savonarola's congregants: "They were therefore bound to study and weigh the words of a phenomenal preacher, while drawing on standards of eloquence that were exacting. In this test, Savonarola's sermons and delivery

---

30. Savonarola, "Exodus, Sermon III," in *Selected Writings of Girolamo Savonarola*, 319.
31. Savonarola, "On Social Order," 149–50.
32. Savonarola, "The Art of Living Well," 30.
33. Martines, *Fire in the City*, 288.
34. Ibid., 288.

conquered the city even more, much more [than his predecessor]. His flow of galvanizing words, in sermons that often lasted for more than two hours, touched something deeply receptive in Florentine people."[35]

In a context that valued excellent sermon delivery, Savonarola performed exceptionally. Donald Weinstein has called him "a spectacularly effective preacher."[36] Likewise, "The content of Savonarola's religious message was as carefully tuned to his sermon audience as were his rhetoric and language."[37] His popular preaching often included clever apologetics: "But I want to say a word about this Crucifix to the Jews and to the pagans," he remarked in one sermon. "Jew come forward. Either this is the Messias or He is not: if you affirm that He is, then convert; if you say that He is not, I ask you what it means that all the prophecies are verified in Him and that all fit Him, not by distorting them, but easily."[38] His preaching was equally epic: "O man, behold your Lord nailed and dying for you on this wood. Acknowledge this favor, leave your wicked life, return to Him Who waits for you with arms wide open, call for mercy from Him, for he wants to grant it to you. Mercy!"[39]

Paraenetic Appeal

At the heart of this preaching was a gentle, convincing appeal to godly living. Paraenesis is defined as an "exhortation, advice, counsel," or is a "hortatory composition."[40] The method of Savonarola was direct, bold, and critical, but concurrently, it was sometimes bridled in a tension/release fashion. His methodology can be restrained and hortatory, appealing and convincing. He strategically centers his sermon on a thematic point—always related to godliness—to which he wisely returns throughout the sermon as an appeal to action. "Praise Him with your whole heart and mind, an interior conjunction which cannot take place without knowing God and His grace."[41] Likewise, he preaches: "Above all, let everyone pray, for by this means all good works are always done. And if you will do this, you will be able to say along with the last verse of our Psalm 114:9 [Latin Vulgate]: 'I will please the Lord in the land of the living'"[42] In his sermon "The Art of Dying Well," which focuses parishioners on a view of death that motivates one to right perspective, he appeals to various groups of individuals

---

35. Ibid., 288–89.
36. Weinstein, "The Art of Dying Well," 91.
37. Ibid., 98.
38. Savonarola, "The Art of Living Well," 7.
39. Ibid., 31–32.
40. *The Oxford English Dictionary*, 2nd ed. (Oxford: Clarendon, 1989), 186.
41. Savonarola, "On Social Order," 144–45.
42. Ibid., 145.

then returns to the formula, "Put on these spectacles of death" for perspective on life.[43] Weinstein describes how Savonarola's sermons are written from "moral formal theological works and devotional treatises for clerics and Latin-reading laypeople." This effort comes "notwithstanding the heavy demands of almost daily sermons and religious and political mentoring."[44] Such a commitment to paraenesis comes from his deep commitment to the Lord and the pastor's task. Weinstein remarks: "Laypeople of every condition were redeemable; that was the premise of the friar's whole career as preacher, prophet, and reformer."[45] One final example suffices: with a vision of a ladder ascending heaven, he remarks, "Set your foot up here and listen to what the Lord says: 'Come to me all who labor.' . . . He is your Lord, your Physician, and that He acts in this way because he loves you, and then you would think that in any case you must die, and love will bear the burden of it."[46]

CONTRIBUTIONS TO PREACHING

As with all preachers of history, there are aspects of their ministry which were tied to their context. Other aspects transcended their time and space, giving insight to our place and ministry. Several unique contributions from the preaching of Savonarola can still provide instruction to the church today.

Passionate Conviction with Personal Endurance

A lesson for the contemporary church from Savonarola's legacy is the balance between zealous conviction in preaching and the risk of audience acceptance of the message. Overzealous preaching can be questionable, but zealous preaching has its place, while mitigated renunciation of sin can be compromising. The preacher must weigh the times, the audience, and his own personal conviction to know the application force of a sermon. Desperate times call for desperate measures, but wisdom to know the degree of pastoral desperation must be calculated. For Savonarola, the calculation seemed to require fiery sermons.

His conflicted personal soul was an appealing motivator to some of Florence, yet vulnerability and authenticity is always a risk for a preacher. Yet, at times the compulsion to preach a sense of truth overcomes the possibility of rejection, misunderstanding, and annoyance by the audience. Savonarola models personal endurance in the face of personal rejection: "If, therefore, I were bruised solely

---

43. Savonarola, "The Art of Dying Well," 44–45.
44. Weinstein, "The Art of Dying Well," 91.
45. Ibid., 101.
46. Savonarola, "The Art of Living Well," 12–13.

with the hope of this world, and if, for the sake of obtaining what I desire, I were to deceive people, and by deceiving them I were to stir up against myself the wealthy and the powerful and nearly the whole world besides, truly I would not be cunning, but mindless and insane, nor indeed would I be deceiving, but I myself would be utterly deceived."[47]

Meanwhile, for others in his audience, politics and the popular opinion would overshadow this powerful conviction in preaching. The divide between a dedicated cleric and an apathetic layperson was a source of anxiety for Savonarola that he regularly had to overcome. His endurance can be perceived even more powerfully when one considers his personal success at dedicated prayer and obedience in contrast to a culture of apathy. Regarding the sermon on "The Art of Dying Well," Weinstein remarks, "There is in these passages more than a little of the clerical ascetic's traditional misgivings, if not contempt, toward the lay condition . . . indeed, these, being the disabilities of the simple and humble, could even be turned into assets, since they were protections against ambition for power, riches, and knowledge."[48] What follows is a deep, personal struggle to maintain the sanity of one's efforts against a tide of indifference. The tracking of Savonarola's endurance is a lesson for spiritual leaders.

His passionate conviction translated into personal endurance when he received news of his excommunication from the Holy See. He insists in one 1498 sermon: "I have not sinned in this, in not observing the excommunication."[49] Likewise, "These excommuncations today are cheap commodities; for four lire anyone can have anyone he likes excommunicated. They can be given to anybody who wants them, these excommunications. I tell the truth: I do not believe such excommunciations carry weight with God, because of the liberality and abundance with which they are handed out."[50]

Meanwhile, Mazotta observes about Savonarola's inevitable demise: "He recognized that his destiny was to lose himself."[51] He preaches about himself and seems to promote his own endurance to his congregation: "'O, friar, a great war will be waged against you.' Was not a great war waged against our Lord until they finally crucified him? I fear nothing; make war as much as you want; it is enough for me that the Lord is with me. But you do not believe that the Lord is with us;

47. Savonarola, "A Dialog Concerning Prophetic Truth" in *Selected Writings of Girolamo Savonarola*, 1, 79–80.

48. Weinstein, "The Art of Dying Well," 101.

49. Savonarola, "Exodus, Sermon III," 331.

50. Ibid., 332.

51. Giuseppe Mazotta, "Foreword" in *Selected Writings of Girolamo Savonarola: Religion and Politics, 1490–1498*, ed. and trans. by Anne Borelli and Maria Pastore Passaro (New Haven: Yale University Press, 2006), xii.

believe that I am not crazy, that I know where I am, and that I would know how to get out of here, if I wanted by human means . . . Because I know that the Lord is with me, I fear nothing."[52]

The personal depth of this monk should not be overlooked. Mazotta recognizes Savonarola's angst, "Above all, he was a revolutionary because he struggled to overcome himself. His perpetual lamentations adumbrate the phantasms of this inner struggle, the tragic knowledge of a man who lived before his time and, like the true prophets, outside of his own time, and who recognized that his destiny was to lose himself."[53]

Cultural Confrontation

Another lesson for the contemporary church is the relationship between the preacher and culture. Savonarola was offended by the humanistic spirit of the Renaissance that he believed led to the moral laxity of Florence. By learning from his confrontation with culture, a preacher can see that wisdom must characterize the balance between rebuke and appeal. Without here weighing in on the judgment of the Renaissance spirit, Savonarola unintentionally might instruct us to beware the use of polemics. In the case of the preaching of the gospel, the principle of "stumbling block" must be balanced with cultural sensitivity to the audience receiving the message.

Savonarola's style of cultural confrontation could be recognized by Richard Niebuhr as a "Christ against culture" theory of relationship. In his classic work, *Christ and Culture*, Niebuhr remarks that "culture is the 'artificial, secondary environment' which man superimposes on the natural. It comprises language, habits, ideas, beliefs, customs, social organization, inherited artifacts, technical processes, and values."[54] Niebuhr has shown that anticulture, apocalyptic responses are dissociative reactions to a preacher's frustrating situation: "To know one's theological enemies and to know how to respond to their positions was key to their legal responses and is key for the *contra* approach. The church [in the past] directly engaged and rejected certain alternative theologies that were spiritually harmful."[55] Savonarola's aim particularly targeted the corrupt clergy of his day: "O clergy, clergy, 'On account of you this tempest has arisen.' Know that it was for the purpose of avoiding these tribulations, which today are seen coursing throughout Italy, that these prayers were made to which I have exhorted you for

---

52. Savonarola, "Exodus, Sermon III," 327.

53. Mazotta, "Foreword," xii.

54. H. Richard Niebuhr, *Christ and Culture* (New York: Harper & Row, 1951), 32.

55. W. Brian Shelton, "Learning from Patristic Responses to Culture," in *The Contemporary Church and the Early Church: Case Studies in Ressourcement*, ed. Paul A. Hartog (Eugene, OR: Wipf & Stock, 2010), 126.

so long, and let us pray to God that they turn into plague rather than war. But I hope to God that the Lord may free us of them, if not completely, at least in part, if you will do this which is the will of God."[56]

His cultural confrontation has led historians such as Giuseppe Mazotta to declare him a radical innovator: "More than a moral reformer, Savonarola can be called a moral revolutionary."[57] For these reasons, as well as his call to biblical obedience, his defiance against clerical abuses, and the promotion of a government outside the Holy Roman Empire, he is often depicted as a "forerunner of the Reformation," along with John Huss and John Wycliffe. Certainly Germany recognized his influence, placing him at the foot of Luther's monument at Worms.

CONCLUSION

Girolamo Savonarola was a fiery preacher whose sermons ignited a bonfire of political resistance in a city in desperate need of repentance. His homiletics perpetually refocused his congregation on self-examination and action in perpetuation of the gospel. Unfortunately, the combination of his passionate, confrontational style and the opposition to his sermons saw his own legacy suffer on a pyre in the center square of Florence. The present plaque commemorating the event in the Piazza della Signoria seeks his redemption, "Here . . . on March 23, 1498, by unfair judgment was hanged and burned Giroloamo Savonarola."

This combination preacher and prophet rebuked a papacy and beckoned a city to repentance in an imaginative style. Giuseppe Mazotta remarks, "He was well aware of the creative, deeply subversive powers of the imagination, and, specifically, of the religious and prophetic imagination. He thought of himself as, and was, a preacher-prophet."[58] Perhaps the line that best embodies his appeal to the local church and captures his intention to godliness is seen in his "Art of Living Well" sermon, repeated here: "Florence . . . do, then, what I have told you; entrust yourselves to God, live in charity, do away with all hatred."[59]

---

56. Savonarola, "On Social Order," 147.
57. Mazotta, "Foreword," xi.
58. Ibid.
59. Savonarola, "The Art of Living Well," 30.

Sermon Excerpt:
Haggai Sermon VII "On Social Order"[60]

O citizens, devote yourselves to living uprightly and to doing good deeds. Devote yourselves to simplicity; otherwise, God will be angry with you, should you be ungrateful and not acknowledge the favor which God has done for you. And you, women, I declare to you that, if you do not forgo your pomp and your superfluities and vanities and do not devote yourselves to simplicity, then if the plague comes, you will die like dogs. Devote yourselves, I say, to simplicity, and do not be ashamed to go dressed more simply than you do, for this is not shame whatsoever to you, if you consider it well, but rather honor and usefulness. And you well-to-do women, who are among the first rank, start giving this good example to the others, and you will cause many others to follow you and do good, and you will have merit with God for this. Look, our psalm says, "The Lord watches over little ones." The little ones are those who humble themselves and abase themselves and go about simply. ♦

BIBLIOGRAPHY
Primary Sources

Machiavelli, Niccolò. *The Prince*. New York: Dover, 1992.

Savonarola, Girolamo. *Selected Writings of Girolamo Savonarola: Religion and Politics, 1490–1498*. Trans. and edited by Anne Borelli and Maria Pastore Passaro. New Haven: Yale University Press, 2006.

Secondary Sources

Brown, Allison. "Introduction." *Selected Writings of Girolamo Savonarola: Religion and Politics, 1490–1498*. Trans. and edited by Anne Borelli and Maria Pastore Passaro. New Haven: Yale University Press, 2006.

Martines, Lauro. *Fire in the City: Savonarola and the Struggle for the Soul of Renaissance Florence*. Oxford: Oxford University Press, 2006.

Mazotta, Giuseppe. "Foreword." *Selected Writings of Girolamo Savonarola: Religion and Politics, 1490–1498*. New Haven: Yale University Press, 2006.

McCall, Andrew. *The Medieval Underworld*. New York: Barnes & Noble, 1979.

McGinn, Bernard. *Antichrist: Two Thousand Years of the Human Fascination with Evil*. San Francisco: HarperSanFrancisco, 1994.

Niebuhr, H. Richard. *Christ and Culture*. New York: Harper & Row, 1951.

The Oxford English Dictionary, 2nd ed. Oxford: Clarendon, 1989.

Reeves, Majorie. *The Influence of Prophecy in the Later Middle Ages: A Study in Joachimism*. New York: Oxford University Press, 1969.

Shelton, W. Brian. "Learning from Patristic Responses to Culture." *The Contemporary Church and the Early Church: Case Studies in Ressourcement*. Edited by Paul A. Hartog. Eugene, OR: Wipf & Stock, 2010.

---

60. Savonarola, "On Social Order," 147–48.

Weinstein, Donald. "The Art of Dying Well and Popular Piety in the Preaching and Thought of Girolamo Savonarola." Pages 88–104 in *Life and Death in Fifteenth-Century Florence*. Edited by M. Tetel, R. G. Witt, and R. Goffin. Durham, NC: Duke University Press, 1989.

_____. "Explaining God's Acts to his People: Savonarola's Spiritual Legacy to the Sixteenth Century." Pages 205–25 in *Humanity and Divinity in Renaissance and Reformation: Essays in Honor of Charles Trinkaus*. Edited by John W. O'Malley, Thomas M. Izbicki, and Gerald Christenson. Leiden: Brill, 1993.

_____. *Savonarola: The Rise and Fall of a Renaissance Prophet*. New Haven: Yale University Press, 2011.

_____. *Savonarola and Florence: Prophecy and Patriotism in the Renaissance*. Princeton, NJ: Princeton University Press, 1970.

PART Three

Preaching among the Reformers

Hughes Oliphant Old characterizes the Reformation in the following way, "At its core, the Reformation was as much a reform of preaching as it was preaching of reform."[1] In Part III, *Preaching among the Reformers,* we will begin to see this trajectory taken because of the Protestant Reformation. Here, the preaching of **Martin Luther** (1483–1546), **Ulrich Zwingli** (1484–1531), **Balthasar Hubmaier** (1480–1528), **William Tyndale** (1494–1536) and **John Calvin** (1509–1564) will be examined. A common bond in their approach to preaching is their commitment to the Word of God, and there are four areas of agreement in their application of the Word of God.

The first startling difference between the preaching of the Reformation and the preaching of the medieval era is a return to the emphasis on the *lectio continua.* The reform in preaching eventually leads to liturgical reform. The Mass will be eliminated. The Eucharist will no longer be preeminent. Preeminence will be given to the sermon, the preaching of the Word of God. Each of the preachers examined in this section had been educated by and served in the Roman Catholic Church. They stood as inheritors of the preaching tradition of the medieval church, but each, in his own search for truth, would eventually leave the Roman Catholic Church and launch a profound ministry of preaching that changed the sermonic landscape.

The second area of agreement can be found in the form of the sermon. The expository sermon was given the place of prominence. The preaching exemplars of this section all had obtained excellent exegetical skills, had benefited from some of the best education of their day, and possessed language skills that rival

---

1. Hughes Oliphant Old, *The Reading and Preaching of the Scriptures in the Worship of the Christian Church, Volume 4: The Age of Reformation* (Grand Rapids: Eerdmans), 1.

most in the academy today. In fact, their examples serve as a challenge to contemporary homileticians to strive for excellence and mastery of the biblical languages. Their confidence in the Word of God led them to the historical grammatical hermeneutic—which prioritizes the authorial intent of a passage. This was no wooden biblical literalism, but rather an approach that rejected the twisting in the wind of allegorical approaches to the Scriptures that had characterized the preaching of the medieval church.

A third area of agreement was on the preeminence of Christ. It was Christ alone that could save. No amount of good works, penance, or any other machination of the Roman Catholic Church could secure a person's relationship with God and ensure one's home in eternity. These preachers pointed their congregations toward Jesus as the sole mediator between humanity and God. Here the influence of Erasmus is evident. For some the influence is explicit and direct, and for others the influence was more tacit, but nonetheless, Erasmus deserves mention for reestablishing the central role of the Evangel.

A fourth area of agreement can be found in the praxis of the faith for the laity. Since the Bible was the Word of God and intended for all to hear and obey, these preachers were very intentional in preaching sermons in the language of the common people. What benefit could there be in a sermon that was preached if no one understood its meaning? The Reformation displays on a grand stage the impact the Word of God has when people hear and understand the Word in their own language.

Martin Luther
Preaching a Theology of the Cross

ROBERT KOLB

By the time Martin Luther (1483–1546) achieved European-wide attention through the medium of print, he had mastered the oral delivery of the Bible's message as a popular monastic preacher. The swift and widespread distribution of the "Ninety-Five Theses" on indulgences created a media revolution. Printers had sensed a market; Luther quickly capitalized on their enterprise and their craft, and within weeks of the "success" of the Theses, spread his still-forming ideas of the reform of the church's public teaching through the medium of print. But he remained first and foremost a university lecturer and monastic preacher focused on addressing the theological deficiencies he saw in the Catholic Church. Within the framework of his "theology of the cross," and using the proper distinction of law and gospel, Luther sought to bring hearers and readers of his sermons into the text, where God addresses them, and to bring the text into his own world so that it could make an impact on the lives of those hearers and readers. Many of those who heard his preaching were students at the University of Wittenberg, and thus, they took his message and method of preaching to countless places. In addition, he shaped preaching across the German lands and beyond through his model sermons, individually printed or in his postils, the collections designed for the traditional pericopal system of lessons assigned for Sundays and festivals.

HISTORICAL BACKGROUND

As a member of the order of Augustinian Eremites, Luther probably counted his celebration of the Mass as more important than his preaching, but the Augustinians did dedicate themselves to preaching in villages and towns. David Steinmetz accurately observes that, even with its increasing popularity in the fifteenth century, the sermon remained a preface to the heart of medieval piety, the Mass.[1] Nonetheless, Luther's sermons in the monastery and in the pulpits of the town

---

1. David Steinmetz, "Luther, the Reformers, and the Bible," in *Living Traditions of the Bible*, ed. James E. Bowley (Saint Louis: Chalice. 1999), 164–66.

and castle churches in Wittenberg had won him the admiration and affection of the local populace before he had come to his evangelical convictions. At that time he was preaching largely in the moralistic style of his teachers, with ever more mystical elements that sought to foster increasing devotion to Jesus.[2]

His monastic life drilled the psalms into his head. As an Augustinian friar, he prayed psalms seven times a day, and he heard daily Bible readings along with readings from the stories of the saints at mealtime. His curiosity about Scripture deepened into a love for its narrative and message as he read it as often as possible in the library of the monastery. But his childhood had mixed the Bible stories with the legends of the saints, and for a long time he probably could not distinguish sharply between Daniel with the lions and George, the patron of the local church in Mansfeld where he grew up, with his dragon. Furthermore, he learned that the bishop of Rome had final interpretive power in the reading of Scripture and the final say in the life of the church. The medieval tradition framed his appreciation of Scripture.[3]

Luther's superiors recognized his innate gifts and ended his dream of earning God's favor by being the lowest of the lay brothers among the Augustinians. His talent for leadership and his keen mind and command of Scripture won their attention. His ultimate German superior, the general-vicar of the Observant wing of the Augustinian Eremites, Johann von Staupitz, had aided Elector Frederick the Wise in founding the University of Wittenberg in 1502, three years before Luther entered the Augustinian cloister in Erfurt. Staupitz became dean of the theological faculty there, but his many other duties made it imperative to find a replacement. Brother Martin was his man. Reluctantly, under protest, Luther pursued the course to the height of the discipline of theology, the queen of the university disciplines, and on October 12, 1512, received the title of *Doctor in Biblia*. With it, he assumed under oath the obligation to teach God's truth to the church. He plunged into his work with trepidation and vigor, marshalling the most recently developed tools for thorough study of the texts in their linguistic and historical contexts. Scholars debate whether he was a part of the "humanist movement" that called for a return to the sources and for increased attention to effective communication (emphasizing rhetoric over or alongside the logic that formed the centerpiece of medieval education); he was certainly influenced by humanist development of these tools for interpreting the biblical text, and he

---

2. Elmer Kiessling, *The Early Sermons of Luther and their Relation to the Pre-Reformation Sermon* (Grand Rapids: Zondervan, 1935), 68–108.

3. On the medieval experience of Scripture which Luther had, see Robert Kolb, *Martin Luther and the Enduring Word of God: The Wittenberg School and Its Scripture-Centered Proclamation* (Grand Rapids: Baker Academic, 2016), chapter 1.

attracted many of its followers to his own movement.[4] He used the Hebrew grammar and dictionary of Johannes Reuchlin, absorbed Desiderius Erasmus's *Paraphrases,* put his edition of the Greek New Testament immediately to work, and engaged the interpretation of Jacques Lefévre d'Etaples.[5]

As Luther mounted the pulpit in Wittenberg's town church, he knew the lives of his hearers were filled with fears of many kinds, though probably relatively few had his conscience's scruples and his terror before the wrath of God. They instead feared disorder, for theirs was a world in which peasants were frequently threatening revolts that brought destruction and death in their wake; pestilence and plague along with accident and injury shortened lives, leaving widows, widowers, and orphans behind; and irritable neighbors and family members jeopardized the harmony necessary for a contented life. Luther recognized that problems of multiple kinds disrupted the lives of his hearers, along with their acute sense of their own inability to please God.

The unsettledness which beset Luther and his Wittenberg hearers typified a widespread crisis of piety and pastoral care in late medieval German lands. This crisis had launched many efforts to make the system for establishing and maintaining the relationship between God and his human creatures work more effectively. The predominant teaching and belief for fifteenth-century Germans focused on human efforts to please God through godly deeds, which were deeds chiefly done in the sacred or religious sphere of life. In popular piety and formal public teaching, grace was made easier to earn. For God's grace was necessary to complete—and for some theologians to initiate—the life of good works which God demanded for entering and remaining in his kingdom.[6] Luther learned from his instructors, who had been trained by Gabriel Biel at the University of Tübingen, that he had to do all he could, his best (*facere in se est*), in order to merit the grace that would enable him to do the good works that merited life with God forever.[7] Luther's education in the faith, at home and in the monastery, taught him

---

4. Lewis W. Spitz, *The Religious Renaissance of the German Humanists* (Cambridge: Harvard University Press, 1963) argues for Luther's proximity to the humanists without placing him among them; Leif Gran, *Martinus Noster: Luther in the German Reform Movement 1518–1521* (Mainz: Zabern, 1994); and Helmar Junghans, *Der junge Luther und die Humanisten* (Göttingen: Vandenhoeck/Ruprecht, 1985), place him among them. On his influence on younger humanists, see Lewis W. Spitz, "The Third Generation of German Renaissance Humanists," in *Aspects of the Renaissance: A Symposium,* ed. Archibald R. Lewis (Austin: University of Texas Press, 1967), 105–21.

5. Robert Rosin, "Humanism, Luther, and the Wittenberg Reformation," in *The Oxford Handbook of Martin Luther's Theology,* eds. Robert Kolb, Irene Dingel, and L'ubomír Batka (Oxford: Oxford University Press, 2014), 91–104.

6. Bernd Hamm, *Religiosität im späten Mittelalter: Spannungspole, Neuaufbrüche, Normierungen* (Tübingen: Mohr/Siebeck, 2011).

7. Heiko Augustinus Oberman, *The Harvest of Medieval Theology: Gabriel Biel and Late Medieval Nominalism* (Durham: Labyrinth, 1983), 132–134.

that the righteousness of human performance was the only righteousness that counted in God's sight. And such righteousness consisted first and foremost of sacred or religious works.

As the psalms gave voice to Luther's cries of despair in the face of God's holiness, they also provided him the foundations for exploring a totally different paradigm for understanding what it means to be Christian. As he wrestled through his lectures on Psalms (1513–1515) and then through Romans (1515–1516), Galatians (1516), and Hebrews (1517–1518), the biblical writers addressed his own, scrupulous, sensitive personality on the basis of certain aspects of the Ockhamist philosophy he had learned at the University of Erfurt. Luther found in Scripture that God initiates the relationship with his human creatures, and that he does so not on the basis of works, either in ritual performance or ethical action, but purely, unconditionally, on the basis of love for his creatures and his love for making all things new. Ockham had emphasized God's almighty power, and this sovereign character of the Creator helped Luther become convinced that God is always in charge and in control. Only in this feeling of total dependence on a totally reliable God could human beings be free to be human, that is, to praise God for his sake and not to earn his favor, and to love and serve neighbors without instrumentalizing them as tools for making the performer look good in God's sight. As he read the entire Scripture, from Genesis through Revelation, Luther recognized that this person, the God who has revealed himself in and as Jesus Christ, is a speaking God, and his speaking creates—and in forgiving sins, recreates—children out of sinners.[8]

Twentieth-century scholars wasted much time and ink trying to identify a specific point at which Luther made his "evangelical breakthrough." Luther's ideas, like most people's, ripened slowly, and so it is better to speak of an "evangelical maturation" that took place as he was lecturing on Psalms, Romans, Galatians, and Hebrews in the 1510s. He spoke of a "tower experience," and for some time scholars associated this tower with the location of the cloister's privy. And recent archeological probes on the north side of the building have uncovered the tower in which Luther's study was located. The maturation took place as he devoured and digested the words of the biblical writers. Erik Herrmann has identified the key element in this evangelical maturation: Luther's abandonment of the predominant medieval hermeneutical framework that identified the Old Testament as the time in which the law of Moses taught God's people how to

---

8. For further development of this description, see Robert Kolb and Charles P. Arand, *The Genius of Luther's Theology: A Wittenberg Way of Thinking for the Contemporary Church* (Grand Rapids: Baker, 2008), 129–220; and Robert Kolb, *Martin Luther: Confessor of the Faith,* in Christian Theology in Context (Oxford: Oxford University Press, 2009), 26–71.

please him and the New Testament as the time in which God revealed in Jesus Christ how grace and mercy aid people in performing works that please him. Instead, Luther came to define the law as God's plan or design for human performance and the gospel as the expression of his recreative actions in Jesus Christ. The gospel delivers people from their rebellion against him and restores them to being—and living as—his children.[9]

THEOLOGY OF PREACHING

In the midst of Luther's theological maturation, his theses on the Catholic practice of selling indulgences catapulted him into the limelight in unpleasant ways. The theses challenged the authority and practice of papal power, and his Augustinian order was told to rein him in. In April 1518, the German chapter of the order met in Heidelberg, and Luther was supposed to justify himself before his brothers. Instead of addressing the issues of papal power or of indulgences for those in purgatory, he chose, in his "Heidelberg Theses," to outline his underlying hermeneutic as he formulated it at the time. He called his way of practicing biblical interpretation the "theology of the cross."

Theology of the Cross

This *theologia crucis*, as presented at Heidelberg, posited two major premises: God is larger than the imagination of the sinner or even of the human creature as creature; human beings are totally dependent on God's revelation of himself. God-Revealed, or God-Preached, Luther asserted, is the God who has come to us on the cross. Under the appearance of weakness and foolishness he died, but in his resurrection he has conquered all the evils that threaten his human creatures, including their own sinfulness (1 Cor 1:17–2:16). God-Hidden remains beyond human grasp; it is folly to pursue his hidden ways and counsel. Luther used the term *Deus Absconditus* both for God, as he really is beyond human ken, and for the false gods that sinners invent to substitute for their Creator. He also spoke of the Revealed God hiding himself in the crib and the cross. Also, Luther crucified human efforts of all kinds, including the effort to merit God's favor through works of any kind and the effort to master what God says to his people in Scripture through human reason (again relying on 1 Corinthians 1 and 2).

Luther's entire approach to theology includes three other points for which the cross of Christ is key. Reconciliation with God is accomplished only through

---

9. Erik Herrmann, "Luther's Absorption of Medieval Biblical Interpretation and His Use of the Church Fathers," in *Oxford Handbook,* 71–90; and Herrmann, "'Why then the Law?' Salvation History and the Law in Martin Luther's Interpretation of Galatians 1513–1522" (PhD diss., Concordia Seminary, 2005), esp. 236–47.

the death and resurrection of Jesus, who died for our sins and was raised for our justification (Rom 4:25).[10] First, the daily life of the Christian involves struggles against Satan, the world's alternative plans for life, and his or her own desires to master life without God. Therefore and secondly, the daily crucifixion of these sinful desires and the daily assaults from the devil and all his agencies belong to the routine and rhythm of Christian living on this earth (Rom 6:6, Gal 5:24). And finally, Christians are liberated from sin so they may bear the crosses of others (Matt 10:38, Luke 14:27). Some scholars believe that the *theologia crucis* disappeared from Luther's thinking, but he consistently used elements of it throughout his life.[11]

Luther also made clear throughout his life that his preaching and teaching depended on the proper distinction between God's plan for proper human action (law) and the gospel of the free, unconditional, unmerited forgiveness of sins. His evangelical maturation depended on his transformation of the sacrament of penance, which, along with attendance at mass, formed the centerpiece of medieval pious practice. He rejected the meritorious nature of contrition (though he also regarded it as necessary), and he rejected the necessity of following up absolution with works of satisfaction to allay temporal punishment associated with the forgiven eternal guilt. He rejected the necessity of enumerating sins to the priest to have them forgiven. He made absolution the center of the life of repentance.

In absolution, he believed, any Christian may speak for God and deliver the gospel of the forgiveness of sins. For the power of absolution lies in the Word of God, God's active tool for reconciling sinners to himself (Rom 1:16). The words of the first of the Ninety-Five Theses, "the whole life of the Christian is a life of repentance," should probably be understood in a medieval context.[12] But Luther transformed its sense by 1529, when in his *Small Catechism* he described the daily life of believers as a repetition of what Paul says (in Romans 6:3–4) happens definitively in baptism: "the old creature in us with all sins and evil desires is to be drowned and die through daily contrition and repentance, and on the other hand that daily a new person is to come forth and rise up to live before God in righteousness and purity forever."[13] Luther's sermons often directed this absolution to

10. Robert Kolb, "Resurrection and Justification. Luther's Use of Romans 4,25," *Lutherjahrbuch* 78 (2011): 39–60.

11. Gerhard O. Forde, *On Being a Theologian of the Cross, Reflections on Luther's Heidelberg Disputation, 1518* (Grand Rapids: Eerdmans, 1997); Vitor Westhelle, "Luther's Theologia crucis," in *Oxford Handbook*, 156–67; Robert Kolb, "Luther's Theology of the Cross Fifteen Years after Heidelberg: Luther's Lectures on the Psalms of Ascent, *Journal of Ecclesiastical History* 61 (2010): 69–85.

12. *Martin Luthers Werke* (WA), (Weimar: Böhlau, 1883–1993), WA 1:233,10–11; *Luther's Works* (LW), (Saint Louis/Philadelphia: Concordia/Fortress, 1958–1986), LW 31:25, cf. Volker Leppin, "'Omnem vitam fidelium penitentiam esse voluit,' Zur Aufnahme mystischer Tradition in Luthers erster Ablaßthese," *Archiv für Reformationsgeschichte* 93 (2003): 7–25.

13. Kolb and Arand, The Genius of Luther's Theology, 98. See also, Irene Dingel, ed., *Die Bekenntnis-chrfiten der Evangelische-Lutherischen Kirche* (*BSELK*) (Göttingen: Vandenhoeck & Ruprecht, 2014), 885.

his hearers with the words "for you" and "for us" (*pro te, pro nobis*). He strove to make Christ's saving work personal, specifically applicable to his listeners.

Therefore, all of Luther's teaching and preaching was guided by the distinction between the message delivered by God's plan for human life and the message of what God gives freely in sending Jesus Christ to die and rise to restore sinners to being children of God. He emphasized the crushing power of the law because of sinners' daily rejection of God's plan for their lives, but he also spent much time showing how, by the power of the Holy Spirit, believers can live lives of love and service in accordance with God's plan. Luther's explanation of the law in his *Small Catechism* focuses on the Ten Commandments. His explanations don't point only to what sinners do and fail to do. They explain why, for instance, in the case of the command not to murder, we continue to "endanger [and] harm the lives of our neighbors" and fail to "help and support them in all of life's needs," or why we "tell lies about our neighbors, betray and slander them, and destroy their reputations" and fail to "come to their defense, speak well of them, and interpret everything they do in the best possible light." It's because we fail to "fear and love God." Each of the commandments two through ten is tied back to the first commandment. And for Luther, the phrase, "we should fear, love, and trust God above all things" is what the first commandment means and what the heart and core of human life is designed to be.[14]

Law and Gospel

Twice, Luther published sermons he had preached to the Wittenberg congregation on the proper distinction of law and gospel. One was from 1532, when the defense of the conditional gospel of forgiveness, life, and salvation in Christ was at stake in disputes with Roman Catholics. The other was in 1537, when, in Wittenberg, one of his disciples, Johann Agricola was challenging the proper distinction of law and gospel by teaching that the gospel does the work of the law, calling to repentance and informing the shape of the Christian life.[15] In fact, his distinction of law and gospel is made of the stuff that all human drama is made of: problem and solution. His definition of the problem takes very seriously the sinful doubt of God's Word and the denial of God's lordship that it exhibits. Luther labeled this doubt "the original sin," transforming the medieval concept of the term from something every person inherits from Adam and Eve, into something

---

Robert Kolb and Timothy J. Wengert, eds., *The Book of Concord, the Confessions of the Evangelical Lutheran Church* [henceforth BC] (Minneapolis: Fortress, 2000), 360.

14. *BSELK* 862–69, BC 351–53.

15. Robert Kolb, "'The Noblest Skill in the Christian Church': Luther's Sermons on the Proper Distinction of Law and Gospel," *Concordia Theological Quarterly* 71 (2007): 301–18. On Luther's entire hermeneutic, see Robert Kolb, "Luther's Hermeneutics of Distinctions: Law and Gospel, Two Kinds of Righteousness, Two Realms, Freedom and Bondage," in *Oxford Handbook,* 168–84; and Kolb, *Enduring Word of God,* chapter 4.

far more: the original sin of doubt haunts every day of human life and permeates human thinking so that sinners are "turned in upon themselves." Even their pious deeds reflect that they feel they need to secure their lives in God's sight. That this doubt still lurks in the hearts of believers remained a mystery for Luther, which he did not try to solve. He simply addressed it with the law's call to repentance and the gospel's liberating pronouncement of forgiveness.[16] Such a life was freed from the need for self-justification and could concentrate on the neighbor's needs.

Correlative with (though distinct from) the distinction of law and gospel were Luther's anthropological distinctions between the passive and active righteousness of believers. Medieval theology had universally viewed that which establishes the human being's identity before God in terms of his or her good works. That identity was labeled "righteousness." In 1518 and 1519, Luther formulated his anthropology in terms of the distinction between human identity in God's sight, like our identity inherited from and bestowed by our parents—an unrequested, unearned gift—from human identity within creation, especially among human creatures, akin to the relationships among siblings. He originally labeled these two kinds of righteousness "*aliena*"—a righteousness given from outside oneself—and "*propria*"—righteousness performed by oneself. He later designated them as "*passiva*"—the identity the person receives from God in his grace—and "*activa*"—the identity that takes shape in human interactions. Although Luther did not compare this distinction to the relationship between parent and child and children among their siblings, he did increasingly (after the birth of his first child) use the language of father and child to speak of God and his chosen people.[17] Luther presumed that through trust in Christ, the passive righteousness of believers would produce active righteousness, even if Christians constantly combat temptation and sometimes fall back into sinful actions. That made the whole life of the Christian a life of repentance.

METHODOLOGY FOR PREACHING

In his proposal for the German liturgy, composed in 1526, Luther wrote, "preaching and teaching of God's Word are 'the most important part of the divine service'"[18] and the public absolution of the sins of the worshipers 'the true voice of the gospel announcing remission of sins.'"[19] Elsewhere he said, "The highest

---

16. L'ubomír Batka, "Luther's Teaching on Sin and Evil," in *Oxford Handbook*, 233–53. See also Robert Kolb, "The Lutheran Doctrine of Original Sin," in *Adam, the Fall, and Original Sin,* Hans Madueme and Michael Reeves, eds. (Grand Rapids: Baker Academic, 2014), 109–27.

17. Birgit Stolt, "Martin Luther on God as Father," *Lutheran Quarterly* 8 (1994): 385–95.

18. *The German Mass*, 1526, WA19:78,26–27, LW53:68.

19. *An Order of Mass and Communion*, 1523, WA 12:213,9–11, LW53:28.

worship of God takes place in preaching the Word, since God is worshiped when the gospel is preached, thanks is given, and all the sacrifices and worship of the Old Testament are fulfilled. In this form of worship the neighbor is served and the image of God is formed in people, so that they die and come alive in order to be God-like."[20] That appraisal of public preaching rested on his understanding of God as a being who is in conversation with his human creatures, a conversation that creates the community that links them to him and to each other. Luther regarded God's Word as the instrument or agent of his creative and sustaining will. As God had spoken the worlds into existence in Genesis 1, so also his Word of gospel in Jesus Christ created sinners anew, refashioning them into his children.[21] He also believed that God's Word, and thus his saving activity, takes place through oral, written, and sacramental forms of the Word.[22] God was truly present as coauthor when the prophets and apostles wrote the Scriptures, and he is present in its use as the Holy Spirit guides its proclamation throughout the history of the church.[23] For Luther, the sermon was one of the most vital instruments of the Holy Spirit's fostering of repentance, bestowing forgiveness of sins, and empowering the godly life of the reborn child of God. His lectures reflected his concern that his students preach well. His sermons made clear that God was at work in his hearers' minds and hearts as the Word came from the pulpit. His devotional writings sought to cultivate trust in Christ through the promise of the gospel.

Luther never held a pastorate, but his colleague and pastor of the town church in Wittenberg, Johannes Bugenhagen, frequently left Wittenberg to help municipal and princely governments reorganize their churches along Wittenberg lines. Luther often took his place in the pulpit. On Sundays he followed the lessons traditionally appointed for the day, since he believed that the wisdom of the church had so organized these lessons that the vital topics of God's biblical revelation would be covered each year. However, he occasionally preached thematic sermons, and in the regular weekday services in Wittenberg he treated several books which were then edited for publication: Genesis (1523–1524),[24] Exodus

---

20. WA26:110,15, LW28:369.

21. Kolb/Arand, *Genius*, 131–59; Johann Haar, *Initium creaturae Dei. Eine Untersuchung über Luthers Begriff der "neuen Creatur" im Zusammenhang mit seine Verständnis von Jakobus 1,18 und mit seinem "Zeit"-Denken* (Gütersloh: Bertelsmann, 1939).

22. Kolb/Arand, *Genius*, 161–203; Kolb, *Enduring Word of God*, chapter 2.

23. Luther did not address the theodical problem raised by this conviction: why does the Holy Spirit permit differing, contradictory interpretations of the text; he simply proclaimed its content as he found it. See Kolb, *Enduring Word of God*, chapter 3.

24. On these sermons, see Sabine Hiebsch, *Figura ecclesiae: Lea und Rachel in Martin Luthers Genesispredigten* (Münster: LIT, 2002); Robert Kolb, "Models of the Christian Life in Luther's Genesis Sermons and Lectures," *Lutherjahrbuch* 76 (2009): 293–320; and idem, "God and His Human Creatures in Luther's

(1524–1527), Leviticus (1527–1528), Numbers (1528–1529), Matthew (1528–1529, 1530, 1532, 1537–1540),[25] John (1528–1529, 1530–1532, 1537–1540),[26] 1 and 2 Peter, and Jude (1523).

Luther urged readers of his collected works to come to the Scriptures in all humility, ready to learn what God has done for his people and what he expects from the words which the Holy Spirit had coauthored with the prophets and the apostles. Thus, sermon preparation should involve prayer and meditation on the text within the context of the Satanic assaults and other challenges to faith that the preacher is always facing. As a friar in the cloister, he had learned that the reading of Scripture (*lectio*) led to prayer (*oratio*) and meditation (*meditatio*) on its meaning. Presuming the reading of the text, Luther saw that engagement with the Scripture involved simultaneously praying, meditating—turning the text's words over and over, even reciting them aloud to oneself, and exploring their significance—and placing the text in the midst of the eschatological struggle of everyday life. He recognized the assaults of the devil, the world, and his own sinful desires, and he also recognized that the text provides defense against these assaults as well as the basis for counterattack with the sword of the Spirit (Eph 6:17).[27]

Luther's sermons used several basic homiletical devices. First, he insisted on the historical nature of God's interaction with his human creatures and the historical accuracy of the biblical accounts of the activities of patriarchs, prophets, and apostles, as well as of their words. He presumed that the path linking his Saxony and Isaiah's or Jesus's Judaea was a two-way street on which the experiences of God's ancient people came to his hearers as encouragement—a model of interaction with their gracious God. He believed his hearers could understand the biblical text because, despite the historical and cultural differences between the ancient world and his own, they shared common experiences of evil and of God's goodness. Therefore, he took pains to explain, not only in his exegetical lectures to students, but also to the people who came to the town church to hear him preach, the linguistic and historical intricacies of the texts of Scripture.

However, most of his sermons focused on teaching the fundamentals of

Sermons on Genesis: The Reformer's Early Use of His Distinction of Two Kinds of Righteousness," *Concordia Journal* 33 (2007): 166–84.

25. Matt 5–7, 1530/1532, WA32:299–544, LW22:3–294.

26. John 1–4, 1537–1539, WA46:568–789, 47:1–231, LW225–530; John 16, 1538/1539, WA46:1–111, LW24:299–422.

27. WA50:659, 5–660,30, LW34:285–286. Cf. John Kleinig, *Grace Upon Grace: Spirituality for Today* (Saint Louis: Concordia, 2008); and Oswald Bayer, "Oratio, Meditatio, Tentatio. Eine Besinnung auf Luthers Theologieverständnis," *Lutherjahrbuch* 55 (1988): 7–59; idem, *Martin Luther's Theology: A Contemporary Interpretation*, trans. Thomas Trapp (Grand Rapids: Eerdmans, 2008), 29–37, and idem, *Theology the Lutheran Way*, trans. Jeffrey G. Silcock and Mark C. Mattes (Grand Rapids: Eerdmans, 2007), 33–82.

God's law and his gospel: calling for repentance; bestowing forgiveness, life, and salvation; and giving both positive and negative observations about how to live the Christian life. In his world, in which 85–93% of the population could not read nor write, the Bible most of his hearers and readers carried with them was contained in "the catechism," not understood in the Middle Ages as a textbook, but as a program of instruction. This program centered in the Creed, which, Augustine had taught, created faith. According to Augustine, the Lord's Prayer was the expression of hope, and the Ten Commandments or, earlier, lists of virtues and vices—Augustine designated as love.

With a largely illiterate population, medieval "catechism" was practiced through preaching, not through classes that worked with textbooks. The *Enchiridion* or *Handbook* for this instructional program Luther composed in 1529 fairly quickly changed the usage of the word "catechism" to refer to such handbooks.[28] Luther changed the order of these three core elements of medieval instruction in 1520, in his *Personal Prayer Book*, writing that "three things are necessary to know to be saved: first, what one should do and not do; second, when one sees that he cannot do or not do these things by his own strength, that he know where to seek and find it, so that he may do and not do these things; third, that he know how to see and gain it." Sick people must diagnose their illness, then seek the remedy, and consequently desire and strive for healing.[29] His catechisms placed the Ten Commandments (law) first, followed by the Creed (gospel), and the resulting daily life of the Christian, initiated by and centered in prayer (the Lord's Prayer).[30] Luther usually let the appointed reading for the day dictate the starting point for his preaching, and he sometimes worked through the text, expositing on the writer's account or argument. Other times he took one or two ideas and expanded on them. But in every case, he marshalled parallel passages from the whole of Scripture, for he believed the Holy Spirit had spoken and was speaking the same law and gospel throughout the Bible.

He occasionally reinforced the gospel of Christ with typological interpretations of Old Testament passages, for he believed that the Old Testament had foreshadowed the coming of the Messiah and the life of the New Testament church in a variety of ways.[31] He also occasionally employed the allegorical

28. Charles P. Arand, *That I May Be His Own: An Overview of Luther's Catechisms* (Saint Louis: Concordia, 2000).

29. WA7:204,13–27. Cf. Luther's *Prayerbook*, 1522, WA10,2:376,12–377,14. Cf. Joachim Ringleben, *Gott im Wort: Luthers Theologie von der Sprache her* (Tübingen: Mohr/Siebeck, 2010), 250–51; Mark Thompson, *A Sure Ground on Which to Stand: The Relation of Authority and Interpretive Method in Luther's Approach to Scripture* (Carlisle, PA: Paternoster, 2014), 171–77.

30. *BSELK*, 884/885, BC, 360.

31. Heinrich Bornkamm, *Luther and the Old Testament*, trans. Eric W. and Ruth C. Gritsch (Philadelphia: Fortress, 1969), 11–44.

method, through which much of formal exegetical training had come (though not for all among the monastics, including the Augustinians, since a tradition of historical interpretation had existed for several centuries by his time).[32] However, he also criticized allegory strongly, even though he, like all preachers, could not resist using it in sermons from time to time. Instructing his students on how to preach as he lectured on Genesis, he said, "I do not try to find [allegories] unless they in some way enhance the historical meaning which is comprehended from the simple story itself. . . . they prove nothing."[33] Luther admitted "it was very difficult for me to break away from my habitual zeal for allegory, and yet I was aware that allegories were empty speculations and the froth, so to say, of the Holy Scriptures. It is the historical sense alone which supplies the true and sound doctrine."[34]

Finally, to reinforce his catechetical proclamation, Luther employed his linguistic and literary gifts to dramatize the accounts of events and people in both Testaments, because he believed that, despite all the specific cultural differences, Abraham's and Mary's encounters with God reflected the same humanity as that of his hearers and revealed the same God who loved them and sought their welfare. He created monologues in which God addressed the Wittenberg congregation or dialogues between God and Satan, or God and the believer. He retold the stories, sometimes sticking quite closely to the text, sometimes elaborating with imaginative expansions, like the mind-reading of Abraham indulged in by the writer to the Hebrews (11:17–19). He also told of Abraham's struggle of faith, Joseph's confrontation with his brothers, Mary's faithfulness, and Herod's perfidiousness, enlivening their personalities and some of their expressions of trust in the midst of evil's assaults.[35]

His belief in the concrete nature of the experiences of biblical figures matched his appreciation for the concrete problems and challenges to the faith and obedience of his hearers and readers. Luther's sermons breathed real life, as experienced in his day and, *mutatis mutandis*, in every age, he believed.

CONTRIBUTIONS TO PREACHING

Precisely in this concreteness lies Luther's genius as a model for preaching today. His sermons are time-bound because they addressed his sixteenth-century Germans,

---

32. Cf. Christopher Ocker, *Biblical Poetics before Humanism and Reformation* (Cambridge: Cambridge University Press, 2002).

33. WA43:490,15–17, LW5:88.

34. WA42:173,30–174,2, LW1:233.

35. Robert Kolb, *Luther and the Stories of God: Biblical Narratives as a Foundation for Christian Living* (Grand Rapids: Baker, 2012).

who encountered Satanic assaults, worldly allurements, and their own perverted desires in culturally determined and specific ways. But because God remains God, Christ's work through the cross and empty tomb stands forever, and the Holy Spirit continues to work through the Word he gave to the prophets and apostles, reading Luther's sermons can indeed inspire and stimulate the twenty-first century preacher. For biblical preaching always confronts the messy predicaments into which sinful humans entrap themselves. Luther understood that, at its core, God's law posits trust in God as the center and foundation of life. He identified doubt of the Word as the root and heart of all human problems; such doubt is the foolish consignment of the self to misery and tribulation. In the twenty-first century too, the law still helps us diagnose why our contemporaries feel so dissatisfied and discombobulated.

To human tribulations and terrors, Luther brought the presence of God and the promise of life. Luther's command of Scripture and his ability to bring God's voice from even remote corners of the biblical narrative to bear on the real fears and foibles of daily life provide a model for the preacher's preparation today. This model invites intensive study, the devouring and digesting of one biblical book after another, and the imaginative meditation on what the events of God's interaction with his ancient people of Israel and his apostolic church mean for twenty-first century living.

Sermon Excerpt
Luke 7:11–17[36]

Whoever wants to be a Christian should set his heart on this: that he has a God, who deals with that which is nothing. For that is what faith is: that it gives thought to something that is not the case, just as this widow did. She was alone. Her son was dead. Had she thought, "my son is live and is not dead," her mind would have been thinking of something that was not the case. For he was dead. That was clear to see. The life on which she would have been believing did not exist. Despite that, it had to be. In this manner the thoughts and faith of every Christian must be similar in all things, and especially in those that pertain to that life. . . . Therefore our life is simply comprehended in the naked word. For we have Christ.

---

36. This sermon was first preached on October 2, 1530, the sixteenth Sunday after Trinity. See WA 32: 123,8–17, 25–35, 126, 9–33.

We have eternal life, eternal righteousness, God's aid and comfort. But where is it? We do not see it. We do not have it in a box or in our hands, but only in the naked word. God just has placed what he is doing in just nothing tangible. That is the reason why Christians are not distinguishable by their outward appearance. You have to hear them speak to know that they are Christian. For Christ himself said that a Christian is like the wind. You hear the sound of the wind, but you do not know where it is or where it is going (John 3:5), over you or under you. You grab for it but you cannot take hold of it. So it is with a Christian. I cannot guarantee that he will be learned, handsome, rich, wise, etc. I recognize him from the sound of his words. . . . I have said all this, dear friends, so that you pray diligently, that our dear God continue to work miracles and wonders, as he began to do, and preserves us in his Word and in faith, so that there is no reason to fear the devil. We have the guarantee, his dear Word. We will not look for another but press forward, and pray for wisdom as Solomon did (1 Kings 3:7–14). . . . Thus, we have his Word, which is certain, and because of this peace will follow. Therefore, pray diligently and be thankful and do not forget that our faith God and Father has undertaken and done so much with us. He has given us more than the entire world is able to give. He will continue to the best for us and will not abandon us as his children, who desire to remain with his Word. Instead, he intends to save, protect, and shield us against the devil and his minions. God grant us that through Christ our Lord. Amen. ◆

BIBLIOGRAPHY

Arand, Charles P. *That I May Be His Own: An Overview of Luther's Catechisms*. Saint Louis: Concordia, 2000.

Bayer, Oswald. "Oratio, Meditatio, Tentatio. Eine Besinnung auf Luthers Theologieverständnis," *Luther-jahrbuch* 55 (1988): 7–59.

———. *Martin Luther's Theology: A Contemporary Interpretation*. Trans. by Thomas Trapp. Grand Rapids: Eerdmans, 2008.

———. *Theology the Lutheran Way*. Trans. by Jeffrey G. Silcock and Mark C. Mattes. Grand Rapids: Eerdmans, 2007.

Bornkamm, Heinrich. *Luther and the Old Testament*. Trans. by Eric W. and Ruth C. Gritsch. Philadelphia: Fortress, 1969.

Dingel, Irene, ed. *Die Bekenntnisschriften der Evangelische-Lutherischen Kirche*. Göttingen: Vandenhoeck & Ruprecht, 2014.

Forde, Gerhard O. *On Being a Theologian of the Cross: Reflections on Luther's Heidelberg Disputation, 1518*. Grand Rapids: Eerdmans, 1997.

Grane, Leif. *Martinus Noster: Luther in the German Reform Movement 1518–1521*. Mainz: Zabern, 1994.

Grimm, Harold J. *Martin Luther as a Preacher*. Columbus: Lutheran Book Concern, 1929.

Hamm, Bernd. *Religiosität im späten Mittelalter. Spannungspole, Neuaufbrüche, Normierungen*. Tübingen: Mohr/Siebeck, 2011.

Haar, Johann. *Initium creaturae Dei. Eine Untersuchung über Luthers Begriff der "neuen Creatur" im Zusammenhang mit seinem Verständnis von Jakobus 1,18 und mit seinem "Zeit"-Denken.* Gütersloh: Bertelsmann, 1939.

Herrmann, Erik. "'Why then the Law?' Salvation History and the Law in Martin Luther's Interpretation of Galatians 1513–1522," PhD diss., Concordia Seminary, Saint Louis, 2005.

Hiebsch, Sabine. *Figura ecclesiae: Lea und Rachel in Martin Luthers Genesispredigten.* Münster: LIT, 2002.

Junghans, Helmar. *Der junge Luther und die Humanisten.* Göttingen: Vandenhoeck/Ruprecht, 1985.

Kiessling, Elmer. *The Early Sermons of Luther and their Relation to the Pre-Reformation Sermon.* Grand Rapids: Zondervan, 1935.

Kleinig, John. *Grace Upon Grace: Spirituality for Today.* Saint Louis: Concordia, 2008.

Kolb, Robert. "God and His Human Creatures in Luther's Sermons on Genesis: The Reformer's Early Use of His Distinction of Two Kinds of Righteousness," *Concordia Journal* 33 (2007): 166–84.

_____. *Luther and the Stories of God: Biblical Narratives as a Foundation for Christian Living.* Grand Rapids: Baker, 2012.

_____. "Luther's Theology of the Cross Fifteen Years after Heidelberg: Luther's Lectures on the Psalms of Ascent." *Journal of Ecclesiastical History* 61 (2010): 69–85.

_____. *Martin Luther: Confessor of the Faith.* Christian Theology in Context series. Oxford: Oxford University Press, 2009.

_____. *Martin Luther and the Enduring Word of God: The Wittenberg School and Its Scripture-Centered Proclamation.* Grand Rapids: Baker Academic, 2016.

_____. "Models of the Christian Life in Luther's Genesis Sermons and Lectures," *Lutherjahrbuch* 76 (2009): 293–320.

_____. "The Lutheran Doctrine of Original Sin." Pages 109–28 in *Adam, the Fall, and Original Sin.* Edited by Hans Madueme and Michael Reeves. Grand Rapids: Baker Academic, 2014.

_____. "'The Noblest Skill in the Christian Church': Luther's Sermons on the Proper Distinction of Law and Gospel," *Concordia Theological Quarterly* 71 (2007): 301–18.

_____. "Resurrection and Justification. Luther's Use of Romans 4,25," *Lutherjahrbuch* 78 (2011), 39–60.

Kolb, Robert, and Charles P. Arand, *The Genius of Luther's Theology: A Wittenberg Way of Thinking for the Contemporary Church.* Grand Rapids: Baker, 2008.

Kolb, Robert, Irene Dingel, and L'ubomír Batka, eds. *The Oxford Handbook of Martin Luther's Theology.* Oxford: Oxford University Press, 2014.

Kolb, Robert, and Timothy J. Wengert, eds. *The Book of Concord.* Minneapolis: Fortress, 2000.

Luther, Martin. D. *Martin Luthers Werke.* Weimar: Böhlau, 1883–1993.

_____. *Luther's Works.* Saint Louis/Philadelphia: Concordia/Fortress, 1958–1986.

Leppin, Volker. "'Omnem vitam fidelium penitentiam esse voluit,' Zur Aufnahme mystischer Tradition in Luthers erster Ablaßthese," *Archiv für Reformationsgeschichte* 93 (2003): 7–25.

Meuser, Fred W. *Luther the Preacher.* Minneapolis: Augsburg, 1983.

Nembach, Ulrich. *Predigt des Evangeliums: Luther als Prediger Pädagoge und Rhetor.* Neukirchen: Neukirchener Verlag, 1972.

Oberman, Heiko Augustinus. *The Harvest of Medieval Theology: Gabriel Biel and Late Medieval Nominalism.* Durham: Labyrinth, 1983.

Ocker, Christopher. *Biblical Poetics before Humanism and Reformation.* Cambridge: Cambridge University Press, 2002.

Ringleben, Joachim. *Gott im Wort: Luthers Theologie von der Sprache her.* Tübingen: Mohr/Siebeck, 2010.

Spitz, Lewis W. *The Religious Renaissance of the German Humanists.* Cambridge: Harvard University Press, 1963.

_____. "The Third Generation of German Renaissance Humanists." Pages 105–21 in *Aspects of the Renaissance: A Symposium.* Edited by Archibald R. Lewis. Austin: University of Texas Press, 1967.

Steinmetz, David. "Luther, the Reformers, and the Bible." Pages 163–76 in *Living Traditions of the Bible.* Edited by James E. Bowley. Saint Louis: Chalice, 1999.

Stolt, Birgit. "Martin Luther on God as Father," *Lutheran Quarterly* 8 (1994): 385–95.

Thompson, Mark. *A Sure Ground on Which to Stand: The Relation of Authority and Interpretive Method in Luther's Approach to Scripture.* Carlisle: Paternoster, 2004.

Ulrich Zwingli

Pastor, Patriot, Prophet, and Protestant

KEVIN L. KING

Ulrich Zwingli (1484–1531) stands with Martin Luther as one of two giants among the first generation of Reformers. In what proved to be a relatively short time in ministry, Zwingli's influence was substantial. His expositional preaching was instrumental in the Reformation in Zurich. His position on Swiss mercenary service led to Swiss neutrality, which is embraced to this day. He was the first writer of Reformed theology, established a school for training clergy, and after debating Luther, formulated what would become the memorial view on the presence of Christ in the Eucharist.

HISTORICAL BACKGROUND

Born in the mountainous farming village of Wildhaus, Switzerland, Zwingli was born to parents who were able to give him an education, planting knowledge in the fertile soil of his intellect and zeal that he would later display. Zwingli's early years had a profound effect on him. He proudly referred to himself as a peasant and allowed himself to be called a Toggenburger.[1] Zwingli developed a strong sense of Swiss patriotism, as children of his time were often told of the heroics of Swiss heroes such as William Tell. The clear message was that to be a good Swiss, one must emulate those qualities and heroics.[2]

Zwingli progressed rapidly in his early studies by demonstrating proficiency in Latin, dialectic, and music. He studied with his uncle who was a parish priest in Wesen. Following this tutelage from his uncle, he traveled to Basel and then to Bern for advanced education. In Bern, his lifelong enthusiasm for humanistic

---

1. Oskar Farner, *Zwingli The Reformer: His Life and Work*, trans. D. G. Sear (Hamden, CT: Archon Books, 1968), 7. "I am a peasant through and through." Toggenburg is the name of the region that Zwingli was born in. To be called a Toggenburger would be akin to being called a Southerner if one was born in the southeastern portion of the United States.
2. Ibid., 12.

studies was birthed.[3] He received his first degree in 1504 and his second two years later. He was introduced to Thomas Wyttenbach at the University of Basel, an association that would eventually play a formative role in his disagreement with Luther at Marburg in 1529.

Up to this point, there are two major factors that shaped Zwingli's thought: Swiss patriotism and humanism.[4] Eventually, a strong theological conviction would be added as a shaping element.[5] As one writer has put it, if Martin Luther was a monk concerned for his own salvation, Ulrich Zwingli was a "parish priest and Swiss patriot who was concerned for the salvation of his own people."[6]

Zwingli's ministry is framed around his two pastoral roles. The first phase of his ministry is as the parish priest in Glarus and Einsiendeln (1506–1518), while he was still a part of the Catholic Church. During this season, he continued growing as a humanist, which eventually led to his departure from the church. The second phase of ministry started when he became the people's priest at the Grossmunster in Zurich (1519–1531).

Parish Priest (1506–1518)

The next ten years of Zwingli's life (1506–1516) would be spent as the parish priest of Glarus, a small market town of less than two thousand inhabitants. The position was probably secured with the assistance of his uncle in Wesen and would prove to be a mutually-beneficial place of service. Zwingli was twenty-two when he started, and he had no experience. He was fortunate to secure this position for two reasons. First, many of his contemporaries had to wait much longer to secure this kind of position. Second, he was able to continue his development as a humanist, which led to him, in a remarkable way, becoming the Reformer of Zurich.[7] Potter called this season as parish priest Zwingli's "time of preparation."[8]

The young pastor immersed himself in his priestly duties with characteristic energy and zeal. He oversaw a building expansion at the church, founded a school where he taught Latin to the local young men (some of whom would go on to university studies), gave himself to humanist studies, and served as a military chaplain.[9]

---

3. Rupert E. Davies, *The Problem of Authority in the Continental Reformers* (Westport, CT: Greenwood, 1946), 63.

4. Timothy George, *Theology of the Reformers*, rev. ed. (Nashville: B & H Academic, 2013), Kindle edition.

5. H. Wayne Pipkin, "The Making of a Pastor: Huldrych Zwingli's Path from Humanism to Reformation." *Reformed Review* 37, no. 2. (1984): 54, 64–65.

6. John B. Payne, "Zwingli and Luther: The Giant vs. Hercules," *Christian History* 3, no. 4 (1984): 6, http://www.christianitytoday.com/history/issues/issue-4/zwingli-and-luther-giant-vs-hercules.html.

7. G. R. Potter, *Zwingli* (Cambridge: Cambridge University Press, 1976), 22.

8. Farner, *Zwingli the Reformer*, 17.

9. G. R. Potter, *Huldrych Zwingli: Documents of Modern History* (New York: St. Martin's Press, 1977), 4.

The long winters provided Zwingli with ample time to read widely. He later wrote, "from my youth up God granted me grace that I industriously and willingly studied things divine and human . . . I was always determined that what I wrote should be my own, not someone else's."[10]

Without aid of an instructor, Zwingli taught himself Greek and Hebrew. He read extensively among the Early Church Fathers and built an impressive library containing the works of Ambrose, John Chrysostom, Gregory of Nazianzus, and Augustine. When the nine folio volumes of the works of Jerome were published by Erasmus, Zwingli was one of the first to study it.[11] One of the most remarkable accomplishments of Zwingli during this period was that he copied most of the epistles of Paul in Greek and memorized them.[12] Zwingli gave himself to study to enable himself to better preach and teach the Scriptures.

This period of preparation is marked by two other events that would profoundly impact the young priest: the military campaigns of 1512–1515, and his meeting and subsequent friendship with Erasmus.[13] Swiss mercenary service was both a curse and blessing. It provided a source of income, but came at a great price in terms of the lives of the young men of Switzerland. In 1510, Zwingli wrote a fable entitled *The Ox*. It examines Swiss patriotism in light of the competing international influences that robbed Switzerland of its most prized natural resource, its young men. The dangers outlined in Zwingli's cautionary tale would come home to roost in the disastrous battle of Marginano of 1515. On that field would lay ten thousand of Switzerland's finest. Zwingli realized the damage caused by mercenary service was staggering in the cost of lives and morals. The cost to Swiss unity was also staggering.

When Zwingli returned home from the battlefield, he was a changed man. His opposition to mercenary service was more pronounced and public. Consequently, he found himself at odds politically in Glarus, and it soon became necessary that he move on to another ministry assignment. Einsiedeln would provide the next step on the road to Reformation.[14] The two years spent in Einsiedeln were, in many ways, a dress rehearsal for the Swiss Reformation in Zurich. It is only in retrospect that one can see this aspect of his preparation. When Zwingli moved to Einsiedeln, he found the sale of indulgences on full display in the abbey of this small town. Faithful Catholics were asked to purchase grace as they

---

    10. Ibid., 5.

    11. Hughes Oliphant Old, *The Reading Preaching of the Scriptures in the Worship of the Christian Church* (Grand Rapids: Eerdmans, 2002), 45.

    12. Potter, *Huldrych Zwingli*, 39.

    13. Pipkin, "The Making of a Pastor," 56.

    14. Ibid.

venerated the statue of the Virgin Mother. Over the gate of the abbey were these words: *"Hic est plena remissio omnium peccatorum a culpa et poena."*[15]

Zwingli, as he was still developing his theology, took a moderate course in response to this practice: he quietly had the sign removed. While at the abbey, his sermons developed a strong christocentric and evangelical emphasis, in spite of his continued role as a Catholic priest.[16] There are two pieces of evidence of this developing trend during his time at Einsiedeln: (1) Zwingli's exposition of the gospel of the day, in lieu of the usual practice of the discussion of some theological or topical discussion, and (2) his opposition to the Franciscan preacher Samson. Zwingli's opposition to Samson, although not as celebrated as Luther's opposition to Tetzel's selling of indulgences,[17] was nonetheless as principled, especially as it was part of the developing evangelical core of Zwingli's thought and preaching.[18] Zwingli later identified the years 1515–1516 as being foundational for his development as a Reformer. The convergence of events, people, patriotism, and his personal development through a study of the Scriptures led toward new convictions. All that needed to happen next was for Zwingli to be put in the right position for these seeds of Reformation to burst forth into a full flowering.

The second significant event for Zwingli during this period was his meeting and subsequent friendship with Erasmus of Rotterdam.[19] The influence of Erasmus on Zwingli was profound. Under the influence of Erasmus, Zwingli would eventually conclude that in the Scriptures there is nothing to be found regarding the necessity of intercession by the saints. No one but Christ could serve as a mediator between God and humanity. This led to Zwingli's immersion into the writings of Erasmus, which in turn, led to a meeting in Basel in 1516, the same

---

15. "This is a full remission of sins of both guilt and punishment," is the English translation of this phrase. Samuel Simpson, *The Life of Ulrich Zwingli: The Swiss Patriot and Reformer* (New York: Baker & Taylor Co., 1902), 62. This belief was due in part to the Angelic Dedication of an alleged papal bull of Leo XIII, which promised plenary indulgences to those that visited the chapel. Samuel Macauley Jackson, *Huldreich Zwingli: The Reformer of German Switzerland (1484–1531)*, Heroes of the Reformation (New York: G. P. Putnam's Sons, 1901), 101.

16. Simpson, *The Life of Ulrich Zwingli*, 104.

17. Justo Gonzalez, *The Story of Christianity*, vol. 2 of *The Reformation to the Present Day* (New York: HarperOne, 2010), 27.

18. G. W. Bromiley, *Zwingli and Bullinger* (Louisville: Westminster John Knox, 2006), 17–18.

19. Pipkin, "The Making of a Pastor," 57. Pipkin makes the comment that Gottfried Locher provides an excellent analysis of the influence and relationship of and between Erasmus and Zwingli in *Zwingli's Thought* (Leiden: Brill, 1981). Their relationship would become strained as Zwingli developed his program of Reform in Zurich and, unfortunately, suffer an irreparable breach in 1523, when Zwingli provided shelter for Ulrich von Hutten. Hutten was an erstwhile Reformer who embraced military action in the cause of reformation. He took the losing side of what is known as the Knight's Revolt in 1522. This lead to Hutten's attempt to enlist Erasmus to the Reformation. When Erasmus refused him, it resulted in an exchange of letters that sealed their estrangement. The more significant break for our story is that between Zwingli and Erasmus when Zwingli provided him refuge.

year Erasmus released his critical edition of the Greek New Testament.[20] Years later, Zwingli would mark 1516 as the year he began his evangelical preaching.[21] Now Zwingli had a model for engaging to serve the church through a humanistic study of the Word.[22] Zwingli wrote *The Labyrinth* in 1516. It was a fable that paralleled *The Ox* (1510), but with the addition of a religious element. The fruit born from this was a theology that centered the Reformation in Zurich and was "both biblical and centered in Christ."[23]

The Reformer of Zurich (1518–1531)

There are moments when certain circumstances and certain people converge at just the right time. This was certainly the case for Luther and Wittenberg, as well as for Zwingli and Zurich. In October of 1518, the position of the people's priest at the Grossmunster in Zurich became open. Zwingli's reputation as a preacher had garnered the attention of the city council of Zurich. He accepted the position in late 1518. By birth, training, and calling, Zwingli stepped into the most influential pulpit of the canton of Zurich and captivated its people with his powerful preaching that contained an unmistakable christocentric core.

Zwingli began his ministry in Zurich on Saturday, January 1, 1519. It was his thirty-fifth birthday. He announced that he would begin preaching the following day from Matthew's gospel, abandoning the standard practice of "canned messages" and following the *lectio continua* practiced by Chrysostom centuries before. Zwingli had been given a copy of Chrysostom's sermons from Matthew by a leading publisher from Basel. And following the example of Chrysostom, Zwingli made the first liturgical reform of Protestantism[24] Throughout his ministry in Zurich, Zwingli would preach expositionally following the *lectio continua*, while preaching the "occasional" sermon as the circumstances dictated.

---

20. James M. Stayer, "Zwingli and the 'Vir Multi Et Excellentes:' The Christian Renaissance's Repudiation of Neoterci and the Beginnings of Reformed Protestantism," in *Prophet, Pastor, Protestant: The Work of Huldrych Zwingli after Five Hundred,* eds. E. J. Furcha and H. Wayne Pipkin (Allison Park, PA: Pickwick, 1984), 142.

21. Davies, *The Problem of Authority,* 66.

22. W. P. Stephens, *Zwingli: An Introduction to His Thought* (Oxford: Clarendon, 1992), 15. The relationship between Zwingli and Erasmus while significant for Zwingli, would eventually suffer an irreparable breach. The break came when Zwingli entered the debate between Luther and Erasmus over free will. When in 1525, Zwingli sides with Luther in his Commentary on True and False Religion, there was no mending the relationship. The final nail in the coffin came when Zwingli offered refuge for Ulrich von Hutten, a repudiated disciple of Erasmus (cf. Bruce Gordon, "Huldrych Zwingli," *Expository Times* 126, no. 4 [2015]: 161).

23. Ibid. For additional insight on the impact of Erasmus on Zwingli, who owned many of Erasmus's books, read *Handbook of the Christian Soldier* and *Account of True Theology.* Pipkin concludes at this point that Erasmus was intent on ridding the church of the distraction of all the excesses of the day by a return to a more pristine practice as found in the early church. This goal becomes a key element in the Zwinglian reform in Zurich. Pipkin, "The Making of a Pastor," 59.

24. Old, *The Reading and Preaching of the Scriptures,* 46.

Zwingli's first year in Zurich was an eventful one. In June of 1519, Luther would debate Johann Eck in Leipzig. Zwingli was so impressed with Luther's boldness that he referred to him as "Elijah" and allowed the sale of Luther's works in Zurich.

In August of 1519, the plague hit Zurich. Two thousand of the seven thousand inhabitants of the city died. Zwingli was away at a nearby mineral spring when the plague broke out, but he hurried back to tend to his flock. In September, he contracted the plague and nearly died. He eventually recovered and wrote *The Plague Song*, which displays his understanding of "God's sovereignty and his submission to God's will."[25] Zwingli was a changed man after this experience. His preaching, according to Farner, "reached the heights of absolute clarity and determination."[26] The impact of his preaching was such that the city council gave Zwingli's expositional preaching a vote of confidence and required that all "priests were to preach the Gospels and the Epistles in accordance with pure texts of the two testaments, avoiding human additions and explanations."[27]

In 1521, Zwingli was elected as a canon in the Grossmunster and became a full citizen of Zurich. Just as his influence was on the rise, he was tested. Francis I was at war with Charles V. Because Francis I was an ally of the pope, he requested that Zurich send him troops as part of their fidelity to the pope. Zwingli opposed this and the council followed their young priest. On January 11, 1522, they issued the following decree: "No one shall enter the service of, or go on foot or horseback to the armed forces of the pope, Holy Roman Emperor, or king of France."[28] The break with Rome officially started. In April, the famous "Sausage Affair" prompted Zwingli to assert that unless Scripture explicitly demands a practice that a person is not bound to adhere to it.[29] Zwingli's sermon "Concerning Choice and Liberty Respecting Food," occasioned the first clearly delineated Reformation writing by Zwingli.[30] Zwingli followed this with an appeal to the Bishop of Constance to allow priests to marry. The Bishop refused. While this decision was anticipated, Zwingli established the principle of conformity to Scripture.

---

25. Stephens, *Zwingli: An Introduction to His Thought*, 17.

26. Farner, *Zwingli the Reformer*, 34–37.

27. Potter, *Huldrych Zwingli: Documents of Modern History*, 73. In 1522, Zwingli resigned as the "people's priest" and was retained in Zurich as a preacher to the entire city of Zurich (George, *Theology of the Reformers*, Kindle edition).

28. Potter, *Huldrych Zwingli: Documents of Modern History*, 7.

29. Gonzalez, *The Story of Christianity*, 60–61. Zwingli had preached against laws on fasting and abstinence and several parishioners defied the Lenten fast and were arrested. After Zwingli's sermon in the Grossmunster, the parishioners were released. Cf. John D. Woodbridge and Frank A. James III, *Church History*, vol. 2 in *From the Pre-Reformation to the Present Day*. (Grand Rapids: Zondervan, 2013).

30. Pipkin, "The Making of a Pastor," 60. "If Luther's protest against the indulgence traffic was a legitimate protest against an abuse of Catholic practice, then the event in Zurich represents a more radical attack on the whole of Catholic spirituality."

He also understood for reform to happen, the city council of Zurich would have to buy into it as well. Zwingli attacked the unbiblical requirement of fasts and abstinence, appealing to the authority of Scripture. The city council had previously passed a requirement that all priests in Zurich follow *the lectio continua* and preach expositionally. When the representative of the Bishop of Constance accused Zwingli before the city council, the council called for a disputation to settle the matter.

The first Zurich disputation took place in January 1523, and it was then that the pace of the Reformation picked up. Here Zwingli presented the *Sixty-Seven Articles,* the first written document that articulated the principles of the reform. These articles were to serve as the basis for the disputation. In them, Zwingli asserted the supremacy of the Word of God and sufficiency of the atoning work of Jesus Christ. In light of his understanding of the sufficiency of Christ alone in salvation, he also rejected "the papacy, priestly mediation, the mass, and good works as contrary to Holy Scripture."[31] Six hundred people attended the disputation and at its conclusion, Zwingli was declared the winner by the vote of the council.[32] Zwingli followed this up by publishing an *Exposition of the Articles* so the people of Zurich would understand the direction they were heading.

There are two great principles that Zwingli held to that governed the remainder of his ministry. First, all doctrinal and ecclesiastical questions have to be settled in accordance with the teaching of Scripture. Second, a Christian government has both the right and the duty to see that the teachings of Scripture are obeyed.[33] It is the second principle that undergirds the cautious pace of reform which Zwingli used in Zurich. He was by nature a cautious man. He did not want to jeopardize his cause by ill-timed actions. This proved costly in his disagreement with the Swiss Brethren.[34]

The second Zurich disputation took place in October of 1523. The focus of

---

31. Simpson, *The Life of Ulrich Zwingli,* 119. From the preface to the Sixty-Seven Articles:
The articles and opinions below, I, Ulrich Zwingli, confess to have preached in the worthy city of Zurich as based upon the Scriptures which are called inspired by God, and I offer to protect and conquer with the said articles, and where I have not now correctly understood said Scriptures I shall allow myself to be taught better, but only from said Scriptures. "Zwingli's Sixty Seven Articles," Christian History Institute, https://christianhistoryinstitute.org/study/module/zwinglis-sixty-seven-articles/.

32. Ibid., 123–24. When the Council convened again, a paper was read embodying their decision, i.e., "that Master Ulrich Zwingli continue to proclaim the Holy Gospel as long and as often as he will until something better is made known to him. Furthermore, all priests, curates, and preachers in cities, cantons and dependencies, shall undertake and preach nothing but what can be proved by the Holy Gospel and the Scriptures; furthermore, they shall not in future slander, insult, or call each other heretics."

33. James Atkinson, "Huldreich Zwingli: Swiss Reformer," *Churchman* 75, no. 1 (1961): 3, http://churchsociety.org/docs/churchman/075/Cman_075_1_Atkinson.pdf.

34. Woodbridge and James, *Church History,* Kindle edition, chapter 4.2, The Swiss Reformations: The Maturation of International Calvinism (16th Century).

the debate was on "image and the mass."[35] The issue was settled rather easily. As images and the Mass were found without benefit or Scriptural warrant.

An underlying issue was the pace of the reform. There were those aligned with Zwingli, later identified as the Swiss Brethren,[36] who were unhappy with the slowness in which the reform was being carried out. While the second disputation resulted in the decision that the images and Mass were unscriptural, they were not immediately discontinued. Zwingli was not willing to move faster than the people of Zurich, and this caused tension between himself and his young followers.

Conrad Grebel and Feliz Manz, who would emerge as two of the leaders of the Swiss Brethren, increasingly became frustrated at the slow pace of reform in Zurich. They continued the practice of studying the Bible as they had learned from Zwingli, and became convinced more radical reformation was necessary. As 1524 neared its end, the Swiss Brethren began to question the legitimacy of infant baptism. Manz made his views public and the council called for a disputation in 1525. The views of Manz, Grebel, and other like-minded Swiss Brethren were rejected at the council. The council mandated that any unbaptized infants were to be baptized within eight days of the council's ruling.[37] At this time in Zurich, infant baptism signified not only church membership but also citizenship. In rejecting infant baptism, Manz, Greble, et al. were, in the eyes of Zwingli and the council, a threat religiously and politically.[38] Believing that infant baptism was not supported by Scripture, the Swiss Brethren took a radical step in baptizing each other as a profession of their faith in Jesus Christ.[39] The council was swift in taking action: these leaders were arrested and banished from Zurich. Grebel, Manz, and George Blaurock were rearrested at a nearby town of Zurich later that summer. Another disputation was held in addition to two trials, and all three men were given life sentences. Grebel died of the plague while in exile. Blaurock was captured and burned at the stake. Manz was eventually arrested and drowned in the Limant River in Zurich, an explicit castigation of his views on believer's baptism.[40]

35. Gordon, "Huldrych Zwingli," 162.

36. Woodbridge and James, *Church History,* Kindle edition, chapter 4.2, The Swiss Reformations: The Maturation of International Calvinism (16th Century).

37. H. Wayne Pipkin, "Impatient Radicals: The Anabaptists," *Christian History* 3, no. 4 (1984), https://christianhistoryinstitute.org/magazine/article/impatient-radicals-the-anabaptists/.

38. Woodbridge and James, *Church History,* chapter 4, The Swiss Reformations: The Maturation of International Calvinism (16th Century).

39. Gozalez, *The Story of Christianity,* 69.

40. Ibid., 3, "George Blaurock asked Conrad Grebel to baptize him. He in turn baptized those who were present. This event is considered today to be the beginning of the Anabaptist movement." William R. Estep has a particularly moving description of the martyrdom of Felix Manz in *The Anabaptist Story,* 3rd ed. (Grand Rapids: Eerdmans, 1995).

Zwingli had always faced opposition in implementing his vision of reform in Zurich. Now a new problem had arisen. Johann Eck, the Catholic theologian, noted for his confrontation with Luther, had made the observation that Luther and Zwingli were saying different things when it came to the presence of Christ in the Lord's Supper. Indeed, they were. Painfully and regrettably, the meeting at Marburg of 1529 ended with the leaders of the Reformation parting ways and the hope of a united Protestant front was lost.[41]

Zwingli had hoped to be able to build an alliance that would protect Zurich and like-minded cantons from hostile advances from the Catholic forces. This was a factor in his going to Marburg to meet with Luther. He wanted to build an alliance between Protestant territorial states and Protestant Swiss Cantons.[42]

Zwingli not only miscalculated what it would take to build an alliance with Protestant princes in Germany, but he also misjudged the leverage he had in Switzerland. Having brought reform to Zurich, he had hoped it would serve as a model for a Swiss National Protestant Church. He then wanted to expand this model across Europe. Within the old Swiss Confederacy, some cantons sided with Zwingli and became Protestant, while others did not. As tensions mounted, each side began to prepare for war. With both sides on the field of battle, a compromise was reached at the First Battle of Kappel. It ended without any bloodshed, though peace was short-lived, as the terms allowed for individual congregations to determine if they would or would not accept the Reformation. This "freedom" was extended to the Forest (Mountain) Cantons where Catholic sentiment was stronger. Also unacceptable to the Forest Cantons was the prohibition of mercenary service. Without this source of income, they were fearful they would not be able to buy grain. To aggravate their fears, the Protestant Cantons began a blockade of grain being shipped to the Forest Cantons. Zwingli opposed the move, opting for outright war rather than the slow process of starvation.[43]

On October 11, 1531, the Forest Cantons launched a surprise attack against Zurich. The people of Zurich did not know they were under attack until they saw the banners of the enemy. Zwingli marched out with his undersized "rapid response force," hoping to last long enough for reinforcements to arrive. Zwingli was wounded in the battle and the defensive force of Zurich was routed. As the victors went over the field looking for wounded, Zwingli was discovered and

41. Gordon, "Huldrych Zwingli," 163.

42. Robert C. Walton, "The Spread of the Zwingli Reformation," *Church History* 3, no. 4 (1984), https://christianhistoryinstitute.org/magazine/article/spread-of-zwingli-reformation/.

43. Ibid., 6.

killed. His body was quartered and burned.[44] It was a sudden and tragic ending for the reformer of Zurich. Zwingli is memorialized at Wasserkirche with a Bible in one hand and a sword in the other. While the meaning of his legacy has prompted various interpretations, two facts seem beyond debate: love for the Word of God and the love for God's people. He gave his life in defense of both.

THEOLOGY OF PREACHING

"The Bible was at the heart of Zwingli's reformation."[45] For the twelve years of Zwingli's ministry in Zurich, the central element of his ministry was the preaching of the Word. He preached regularly in the Grossmunster, and would eventually preach most of the Bible, both Old and New Testaments. His sermons were practical, addressing religious, social, and political issues.[46] It is beyond debate that preaching the Word of God was at the heart of the reform in Zurich, but the theological focus of Zwingli's preaching can be summarized using the following four themes: (1) *sola scriptura*, (2) the sovereignty of God, (3) a christocentric view of the goal and purpose of Scripture, and (4) the role of the Holy Spirit.

Sola Scriptura

Zwingli's theology of preaching is rooted in a high view of Scripture. One can see this by Zwingli's action from the very first day he set foot in the Grossmunster, when he announced that on the next day he would preach from Matthew's gospel. He began with the "genealogy of Christ and expound the whole text."[47] In the *Archeteles* (1522), Zwingli asserts: "For three years ago now (to give you an account of the preaching I have done at Zurich), I preached the entire Gospel according to Matthew, and at that time I had not even heard the name of those persons to whose faction you accuse me of belonging. I added the Acts of the Apostles to the Gospel immediately, that the Church of Zurich might see in what way and with what sponsors the Gospel was carried forth and spread abroad. Presently came the First Epistle of Paul to Timothy, which seemed to be admirably adapted to my excellent flock."[48]

Zwingli believed that all authority was vested in the Scriptures. This position set the ground work for his and Zurich's eventual break with Rome. In the

---

44. Gonzalez, *The Story of Christianity*, 61.

45. Stephens, *Zwingli: An Introduction to His Thought*, 30.

46. Ibid.

47. Potter, *Huldrych Zwingli: Documents of Modern History* 13.

48. Huldreich Zwingli, *The Latin Works and The Correspondence of Huldreich Zwingli: Together with Selections from His German Works,* vol. 1, ed. Samuel Macauley Jackson, trans. Henry Preble, Walter Lichtenstein, and Lawrence A. McLouth (London; New York: G. P. Putnam's Sons; Knickerbocker, 1912), 238.

first two disputations, Zwingli set the Bible as the final authority in all matters. In the preface to the *Sixty-Seven Articles*, Zwingli asserted the principle of *sola scriptura*: "I, Ulrich Zwingli, confess that I have preached in the worthy city of Zurich these sixty-seven articles or opinions on the basis of Scripture, which is called *theopnuestos* (that is inspired by God). I offer to defend and vindicate these articles with Scripture. But if I have not understood Scripture correctly, *I am ready to be corrected, but only from Scripture.*"[49]

The Word of God has authority because it is the Word of God. Its authority is not established rationally nor ecclesiastically. It has a self-authenticating authority. A common objection at this point is that Zwingli is holding to a naïve Biblicism. However, in Zwingli's case, that objection does not stand. As Hughes Oliphant Old writes, "When one realizes the high level of Zwingli's biblical scholarship, one can hardly look at it this way. Zwingli was an accomplished scholar who knew the Scriptures in the original languages and had studied deeply in the Fathers. When such a man tells us that the Scriptures have a self-authenticating authority which outstrips the recommendation of the Fathers, the councils, or any other human authority simply because it is the Word of God, that cannot be tossed off as naive enthusiasm."[50]

Zwingli makes this argument in his sermon entitled "Of the Clarity and the Certainty of the Word of God." The present version is revised and edited for publication. Originally, it was preached in summer of 1522 to the nuns of the Oetenbach convent. Another aspect of Zwingli's view of *sola scriptura* is that the Word of God is common property of the people of God. It nourishes and refreshes our faith.[51] "There is nothing which can give great assurance or comfort to the soul than the Word of its creator and maker."[52] This nourishing effect is a result of the *imago Dei* in humanity. In humanity there is a desire for and an affinity for the Word of God. According to Zwingli, this is a constituent element of the image of God in all people, saved and unsaved. It is the spiritual air we breathe in which life itself is based.[53]

Sovereignty of God

The second element of Zwingli's theology of preaching is his confidence in the sovereignty of God. As important as the other *solas* are in Reformation

---

49. Ulrich Zwingli, "The Sixty-Seven Articles," ed. Mark Knoll, *Confessions and Catechisms of the Reformation* (Grand Rapids: Baker, 1991), 39, emphasis added.
50. Old, *The Reading and Preaching of the Scriptures*, 48.
51. Ibid.
52. Bromiley, *Zwingli and Bullinger*, 68.
53. Carl M. Leth, "Signs and Providence: A Study of Ulrich Zwingli's Sacramental Theology" (unpublished diss., Duke University, 1992).

constellation, none would outshine *soli Deo gloria*. A characteristic phrase of Zwingli would be never to substitute the creature for the Creator.[54]

If the center of the reformation in Zurich was the Word of God, at the center of the Word of God was God. Zwingli believed the church and its teaching had lost its center; God was not the core of the church and its teaching. Zwingli not only knew the revealed Word of God and its teaching of God's sovereignty, but he was willing to embrace the implications of God's sovereignty, regardless of the cost.[55]

He states his view in A Commentary on True and False Religion in 1525:

> It is false religion or piety when trust is put in any other than God. They, then, who trust in any created thing whatsoever are not truly pious. They are impious who embrace the word of man as God's. It is, therefore, madness and utter impiety to put the enactments and decrees of certain men or certain councils upon an equality with the word of God. For if their dicta are like God's word, it is the word that must be embraced, not the authority of men; if they are unlike it, they are to be rejected and shunned, as the Children of Israel avoided marriage with the women of the Moabites and other Gentiles [cf. Ezra 10:2–4].[56]

Combating the tendency to substitute the creature for the Creator was a reoccurring theme and one that Zwingli steadfastly held to throughout his ministry in Zurich. God's sovereignty is prominent in his view of providence and predestination.[57] In the closing section of "God and His Worship" in *A Short and Clear Exposition of the Christian Faith* 1531, Zwingli succinctly sums up his view of the *soli Deo gloria*: "To sum up: This is the fountainhead

---

54. Zwingli, *The Latin Works of Huldreich Zwingli*, vol. 2, ed. William John Hinke (Philadelphia: Heidelberg), 238–39. The following is an excerpt from Zwingli's sermon entitled *A Short and Clear Exposition of The Christian Faith*. The sermon was written in July 1531 but was not published until 1536:

All the things that are either created or uncreated. The one and only uncreated thing is God, for there can be but one uncreated thing . . . On this depends also the origin, source and foundation of the first article of our faith, that is, when we say, "I believe in one God, the Father Almighty, Creator of heaven and earth," we confess and declare that we have an infallible faith, since it is one resting securely upon one only Creator . . . it is certain that the one and only uncreated thing is God . . . For that in which one should trust with absolute assurance must be God. But if one should trust in a created thing, then the created thing would have to be the Creator, and if in sacraments, then the sacraments would have to be God, so that not only the sacrament of the Eucharist, but baptism and the laying on of hands also would be God. How absurd that is to learned, to say nothing of pious men.

55. In the *Plague Song*, a poem of Zwingli, he says, "To Thee I call, Be it Thy will, Pluck out the dart, That wounds my heart . . . And if Thou yet, Wouldst have me dead, Amidst my earthly days, Yet may I still Thee praise, Thy will be done!" Farner, *Zwingli The Reformer*, 35.

56. Huldreich Zwingli, *The Latin Works of Huldreich Zwingli*, vol. 3, ed. Clarence Nevin Heller (Philadelphia: Heidelberg Press, 1929), 97–98.

57. Stephens, *Zwingli: An Introduction to His Thought*, 43.

of my religion, to recognize God as the uncreated Creator of all things, who solely and alone has all things in His power and freely giveth us all things. They, therefore, overthrow this first foundation of faith, who attribute to the creature what is the Creator's alone. For we confess in the creed that it is the Creator in whom we believe. It cannot, therefore, be the creature in whom we should put our trust."[58]

Christocentric Preaching

The third element of Zwingli's theology of preaching is the sufficiency of Christ. This represents a radical departure from the medieval church. When Zwingli read Erasmus's poem the *Expostulation of Jesus with a Man Perishing Through His Very Own Fault*, the impact was profound. "I shall not conceal from you, dearly beloved brethren, the manner in which I arrived at this opinion, the utterly sure conviction that we have no need of any mediator apart from Christ... I read a poem of that most learned man, Erasmus of Rotterdam, in which Christ pleads with men as to the reason why men are so stupid as not to seek all things in Him."[59]

One can see the prominent place that Jesus Christ plays in Zwingli's thought from the *Sixty-Seven Articles* and in the *Exposition of the Articles*. Jesus Christ is the unifying theme of Scripture and the center of the Christian faith. This focus on Christ as the center of the Christian faith is directly attributable to the influence of Erasmus.[60] One can see the christocentricism of Zwingli from the first four articles of the *Sixty-Seven Articles* that Zwingli composed in preparation of the first Zurich disputation in 1523:

1. All who say that the gospel is nothing without the confirmation of the church make a mistake and blaspheme God.
2. The sum of the gospel is that our Lord Jesus Christ, true Son of God, has made known to us the will of his heavenly Father, redeemed us from death by his innocence, and reconciled us to God.
3. Therefore, Christ is the only way to salvation for all who have been, who are and who will be.
4. Whoever seeks or points out any other way to God is a murderer of souls and a thief.[61]

58. Zwingli, *The Latin Works of Huldreich Zwingli*, vol. 2, 241.

59. Ford Lewis Battles, "Jesus Christ the sole mediator between God and man." *Hartford Quarterly* 5, no. 4 (1965): 67. *ATLASerials, Religion Collection*, EBSCO.com.

60. Stephens, *Zwingli: An Introduction to His Thought*, 54.

61. Knoll, *Confessions and Catechisms of the Reformation*, 40. Articles 1–4 of the *Sixty-Seven Articles*.

Role of the Holy Spirit for Preaching

The fourth element of Zwingli's theology of preaching is the role of the Holy Spirit, and it is likely the most controversial of the area of Zwingli's theology of preaching. He does not use the word Spirit as a synonym for God, but for the third person of the Trinity, the Holy Spirit. The Holy Spirit is the author of the Bible in a way that does not do violence to the individuality of the human authors. The Holy Spirit is related to the Word, the written Word, and the incarnate Word. And yet, Zwingli does not limit the Holy Spirit to the Bible. He dissociates the Spirit from the Word and or sacrament.[62] At first glance, this seems problematic, because Zwingli appears to be in the precarious position of embracing a more spiritualist position, as some Anabaptists are known to have embraced.[63]

Zwingli, however, noted that the Word and sacrament were ineffective without the Spirit, but the Spirit is not ineffective without them. "Moreover, a channel or vehicle is not necessary to the Spirit, for He Himself is the virtue and energy whereby all things are borne, and has no need of being borne; neither do we read in the Holy Scriptures that visible things, as are the sacraments, carry certainly with them the Spirit, but if visible things have ever been borne with the Spirit, it has been the Spirit, not the visible things that have done the bearing."[64]

His emphasis on the Spirit can also be seen in how the Spirit teaches through the Word. "Even if you hear the gospel of Jesus Christ from an apostle you will not follow it unless the heavenly Father teaches and draws you by his Spirit."[65] Zwingli attempted to frame his theology of preaching in such a way as to incorporate both rational and pneumatological aspects of Scripture in a robust and practical manner.

METHODOLOGY FOR PREACHING

Zwingli's method of preaching can be described as expositional and prophetic.[66] While there are not many extant sermons available for the English reader, what can be gleaned is that Zwingli preached expositionally, following the *lectio continua*. Bullinger made the following comments regarding Zwingli's sermon

---

62. Stephens, *Zwingli: An Introduction to His Thought,* 64.

63. Huldreich Zwingli, *Selected Works of Huldrich Zwingli (1484–1531): The Reformer Of German Switzerland,* trans. Lawrence A. McLouth, Henry Preble, and George W. Gilmore (New York: Evergreen Review Inc., 2011). Zwingli took special pains to differentiate himself from the Anabaptists, which can be seen in his treatise entitled *Refutation of the Tricks of the Baptists* by Huldreich Zwingli, in which he says, "This inauspicious race of men has so increased within a few years that they cause anxiety to certain cities . . . yet men of this kind are so thoroughly ignorant of that which they boast . . . they talk about 'the spirit' and deny Scripture. As if indeed the heavenly spirit were ignorant of the sense of Scripture which is written under its guidance or were anywhere inconsistent with itself" (p. 126).

64. Zwingli, *The Latin Works of Huldreich Zwingli,* vol. 2, 46.

65. Potter, *Huldrych Zwingli,* 30.

66. Old, *The Reading and Preaching of the Scriptures,* 47.

approach: "After the usual words of thanks and good wishes well . . . he resolved with God's help to preach the gospel according to St. Matthew in full and in consecutive order and not divided into the prescribed extracts. He would expound it from the Bible and not according to other men's commentaries and all this to the honor of God, and his only son Jesus Christ, for the true salvation men's souls and for the instruction of simple pious people."[67]

Lectio Continua

In a letter to the Bishop of Constance in August of 1522, Zwingli outlines what has been his expositional practice from the pulpit of Zurich. He started by preaching through the Gospel of Matthew, which took three years. Following Matthew, he preached works of Luke, Paul, and Peter.[68]

Zwingli continued preaching expositionally and by 1525 had worked his way through the New Testament (except for Revelation) and then turned to the Old Testament.[69] He took particular pains to keep his language in common with the common people. There was no need for scholastic speculation, but instead he used words his listeners could comprehend and apprehend. Zwingli was an exegete of his audience as well as of the text.

Zwingli followed the *lectio continua* for seven years before turning to the Old Testament. That is not to say he did not, as the occasion demanded, preach occasional sermons. *The Shepherd* was preached at the second Zurich disputation. In this sermon, Zwingli contrasts the true shepherd with the false shepherd. H. Wayne Pipkin suggests that if this sermon was read in conjunction with a "Short Christian Instruction," one would get a concise sense of the essence of the Reformation in Zurich.[70] "The Clarity and Certainty of the Word of God" was preached to the Dominican Sisters at Oetenbach and it sets forth Zwingli's view of *sola scriptura*. It can be said without qualification, per Hughes Oliphant Old, that the foundation to Zwingli's preaching ministry was expositional.[71]

The Voice of the Prophet

If expositional preaching was the foundation of Zwingli's preaching ministry, the support for his preaching ministry was a prophetic voice. Zwingli increasingly began to see his role more in the mode of the Old Testament prophet. He preferred the titles "shepherd" and "watchman" over "pastor." He believed the

67. Potter, *Huldrych Zwingli*, 15.

68. Zwingli, *The Latin Works and The Correspondence of Huldreich Zwingli*, vol. 1, 238.

69. George, *Theology of the Reformers*, Kindle edition. George comments that Zwingli did not preach through the book of Revelation because he doubted that it belonged in the canon.

70. H. Wayne Pipkin, trans., *Huldrych Zwingli Writings*, vol. 2 (Eugene, OR: Pickwick, 1984), 79.

71. Old, *The Reading and Preaching of the Scriptures*, 47.

shepherd would battle for his flock against the Evil One and anything that would substitute the creature for the Creator.[72] Zwingli instituted the *Prophezi,* which functioned as a "school of the prophets."[73] He believed if the reform in Zurich was to continue, it would require an educated clergy. As a humanist, Zwingli insisted that his students excel in Hebrew, Greek, and Latin. The school was rigorous, consisting of three hours of daily Bible study, which included etymological, semantic, and translation studies. The *Prophezi* in Zurich served as model in Geneva and was imitated in Strasbourg. By-products of this school was the Zurich Bible and the production of Zwingli's commentaries on the Bible.[74]

A telling example of Zwingli's view of the pastor as prophet occurred at the beginning of his ministry in Zurich when the Swiss "Tetzel," Samson, arrived in Zurich selling indulgences. Zwingli, from the pulpit, denounced Samson with such effectiveness that the monk was not granted permission to sell indulgences by the bishop of the area. Zwingli, in preaching against Samson said, "There were also false prophets among the people of Israel even as there will be false teachers among you . . . In their greed for money they will trade on your credulity with sheer fabrications."[75] In the role of the shepherd/prophet, Zwingli sees himself as looking out not only to protect his flock but to feed his flock. Concerning whether to observe the fast or not, Zwingli preached, "If you want to fast, do so; if you do not want to eat meat, don't eat it; but allow Christians a free choice . . . If you would be a Christian at heart, act in this way. If the spirit belief teaches you thus, then fast, but grant also your neighbor the privilege of Christian liberty."[76]

Just as the Old Testament prophets thundered against idolatry, so did Zwingli. While not an iconoclast, nor an enemy of art, he prevented any substitution of the creature for the Creator. Later, the council authorized the removal of the trappings of idolatry in the churches of Zurich.[77] His prophetic voice eventually abolished the Mass in April of 1525.[78] Also, as a prophetic preacher, he opposed the mercenary system. When Cardinal Schinner came to Zurich to arrange for the recruitment of soldiers, and while the Cardinal was in attendance

---

72. George, *Theology of the Reformers,* Kindle edition.
73. Ibid.
74. Potter, *Huldrych Zwingli,* 62.
75. Ibid., 15.
76. Ibid., 17.
77. Old, *The Reading and Preaching of the Scriptures,* 52. The principle that Zwingli tried to apply was the restoration of biblical faith and practice. It is surprising, considering his considerable scholarly achievement, he would retreat to a wooden Biblicism on this issue. If the Bible did not expressly commend a practice, it was to be excluded in the worship service of the church. He excluded the playing of organs, the violin (which he played with expertise), and other uses of music as well. Even the Lord's Supper was not to be taken too frequently (he preferred four times a year) as anything that might take away from the hearing of the preached Word of God should be prohibited. Cf. Gonzalez, *The Story of Christianity,* 61.
78. George, *Theology of the Reformers,* Kindle edition.

in full vestments sitting just below the pulpit, Zwingli said, "And I could wish that one would declare the alliance with the Pope null and void and would send the treaty back with the messenger . . . Against a wolf one raised the hue and cry, but no one really opposed the wolves who destroyed most people."[79] It's easy to see that even with the limited examples we have, Zwingli's prophetic ministry was as essential to his preaching as was expositional preaching.

CONTRIBUTIONS TO PREACHING

Zwingli's preaching had a vibrant element of expectancy. He expected people would respond to the Word of God and change accordingly. His life had been changed dramatically and significantly. He had a strong love for country and his countrymen, hoping all the Swiss people might know Jesus Christ as Savior. Zwingli was committed to expositional preaching and faithfully modeled this throughout his twelve-year ministry in Zurich. His commitment to the method of expositional preaching was based on his absolute conviction that the Bible was the Word of God. The pastor is to feed the flock the Word of God through faithful expositional preaching, but also is to protect the flock. At times the protecting role will mean the pastor, based on the teaching of the Word of God, will address those thoughts and actions that distract people when their focus begins to drift to the creature rather than the Creator. Zwingli is a model for the modern preacher to have the same indefatigable commitment to pointing the way to Christ as the only way to salvation.

Sermon Excerpt

Concerning Choice and Liberty Respecting Food—Concerning Offence and Vexation—Whether Anyone Has Power to Forbid Foods at Certain Times[80]

What should I do, as one to whom the care of souls and the Gospel have been entrusted, except search the Scriptures, particularly again, and bring them as a light into this darkness of error, so that no one, from

---

79. Zwingli, *The Latin Works and The Correspondence of Huldreich Zwingli*, vol. 1, 69.

80. Zwingli, *The Latin Works and The Correspondence of Huldreich Zwingli*, vol. 1, 70. This is the sermon that Zwingli preached on April 16, 1522, where he demonstrates the principle of Christian liberty in light of the Lenten fast, or the "Sausage Affair." This is the expansion of a sermon Zwingli preached on March 23rd, 1522, together with an appendix addressed to the chapter of the Great Minster, Zwingli's church, on the question whether anyone had authority to forbid flesh at any particular time. It was the first of Zwingli's publications in the interest of the Reformation. It shows the practical order of his mind.

ignorance or lack of recognition, injuring or attacking another come into great regret, especially since those who eat are not triflers or clowns, but honest folk and of good conscience? Wherefore, it would stand very evil with me, that I, as a careless shepherd and one only for the sake of selfish gain, should treat the sheep entrusted to my care, so that I did not strengthen the weak and protect the strong. I have therefore made a sermon about the choice or difference of food, in which sermon nothing but the Holy Gospels and the teachings of the Apostles have been used, which greatly delighted the majority and emancipated them. But those, whose mind and conscience is defiled, as Paul says [Titus, 1:15], it only made mad. But since I have used only the above-mentioned Scriptures, and since those people cry out none the less unfairly, so loud that their cries are heard elsewhere, and since they that hear are vexed on account of their simplicity and ignorance of the matter, it seems to me to be necessary to explain the thing from the Scriptures, so that everyone depending on the Divine Scriptures may maintain himself against the enemies of the Scriptures. Wherefore, read and understand; open the eyes and the ears of the heart, and hear and see what the Spirit of God says to us. ✦

BIBLIOGRAPHY

Atkinson, James. "Huldreich Zwingli, Swiss Reformer." *Churchman* 75, no. 1 (March 1961). http://church-society.org/docs/churchman/075/Cman _075_1_Atkinson.pdf.

Battles, Ford Lewis, "Jesus Christ the Sole Mediator between God and Man." *Hartford Quarterly* 5, no. 4 (Summer 1965): 63–74. EBSCO.com.

Bromiley, G. W., ed. *Zwingli and Bullinger*. Louisville: Westminster John Knox, 2006.

Davies, Rupert E. *The Problem of Authority in the Continental Reformers*. Westport, CT: Greenwood, 1946.

Estep, William R. *The Anabaptist Story*. 3rd ed. Grand Rapids: Eerdmans, 1995.

Farner, Oskar. *Zwingli The Reformer: His Life and Work*. Trans. by D. G. Sear. Hamden, CT: Archon Books, 1968.

Furcha, E. J., and H. Wayne Pipkin, eds. *Prophet, Pastor, Protestant: The Work of Huldrych Zwingli After Five Hundred Years*. Allsion Park, PA: Pickwick, 1984.

George, Timothy. *Theology of the Reformers*. Rev. ed. Nashville: B & H Academic, 2013. Kindle edition.

Gonzalez, Justo L. *The Story of Christianity*. Vol. 2 in *The Reformation to the Present Day*. New York: HarperOne, 2010.

Gordon, Bruce. "Huldrych Zwingli." *Expository Times* 126, no. 4 (2015): 157–68.

Jackson, Samuel Macauley. *Huldreich Zwingli: The Reformer of German Switzerland (1484–1531)*. Heroes of the Reformation. New York: G. P. Putnam's Sons, 1901.

Leth, Carl M. "Signs and Providence: A Study of Ulrich Zwingli's Sacramental Theology." PhD diss., Duke University, 1992.

Locher, Gottfried. *Zwingli's Thought*. Leiden: Brill, 1981.

Noll, Mark A., ed. *Confessions and Catechisms of the Reformation*. Grand Rapids: Baker Book House, 1991.

Old, Hughes Oliphant. *The Age of the Reformation* Vol. 4 in *The Reading and Preaching of the Scriptures in the Worship of the Christian Church*. Grand Rapids: Eerdmans, 2002.

Payne, John B. "Zwingli and Luther: The Giant vs. Hercules," *Christian History* 3, no. 4 (1984). http://christianitytoday.com/history/issues/issue-4/zwingli-and-luther-giant-vs-hercules.html.

Pipkin, H. Wayne. "The Making of a Pastor: Huldrych Zwingli's Path from Humanism to Reformation." *Reformed Review* 37, no. 2. (1984): 54–68.

_____. "Impatient Radicals: The Anabaptists," *Christian History* 3, no. 4 (1984). https://christian historyinstitute.org/magazine/article/impatient-radicals-the-anabaptists/.

_____, trans. *Huldrych Zwingli Writings*. Vol. 2. Eugene, OR: Pickwick, 1984.

Potter, G. R. *Huldrych Zwingli: Documents of Modern History*. New York: St. Martin's Press, 1977.

_____. *Zwingli*. Cambridge: Cambridge University Press, 1976.

Simpson, Samuel. *The Life of Ulrich Zwingli*. New York: Baker & Taylor Co., 1902.

Stayer, James M. "Zwingli and the 'Vir Multi Et Excellentes:' The Christian Renaissance's Repudiation of Neoterci and the Beginnings of Reformed Protestantism." Pages 137–54 in *Prophet, Pastor, Protestant: The Work of Huldrych Zwingli after Five Hundred Years*. Edited by E. J. Furcha and H. Wayne Pipkin. Allison Park, PA: Pickwick, 1984.

Stephens, W. P. *The Theology of Huldrych Zwingli*. Oxford: Clarendon, 1986.

_____. *Zwingli: An Introduction to His Thought*. Oxford: Clarendon, 1992.

Walton, Robert C. "The Spread of the Zwingli Reformation," *Church History* 3, no. 4 (1984). https:// christianhistoryinstitute.org/magazine/article/spread-of-zwingli-reformation/.

Woodbridge, John D., and Frank A. James III. *Church History*. Vol. 2 in *From the Pre-Reformation to the Present Day*. Grand Rapids: Zondervan, 2013. Kindle edition.

Zwingli, Huldreich. *The Latin Works and The Correspondence of Huldreich Zwingli: Together with Selections from His German Works*. Vol. 1. Edited by Samuel Macauley Jackson. Trans. by Henry Preble, Walter Lichtenstein, and Lawrence A. McLouth. London; New York: G. P. Putnam's Sons; Knickerbocker, 1912.

_____. *The Latin Works of Huldreich Zwingli*. Vol. 2. Edited by William John Hinke. Philadelphia: Heidelberg Press, 1922.

_____. *The Latin Works of Huldreich Zwingli*. Vol. 3. Edited by Clarence Nevin Heller. Philadelphia: Heidelberg Press, 1929.

_____. *Selected Works of Huldrich Zwingli (1484–1531): The Reformer of German Switzerland*. Trans. by Lawrence A. McLouth, Henry Preble, and George W. Gilmore. New York: Evergreen Review, Inc., 2011. Kindle edition.

_____. *Writings*. Vol. 2 of *In Search of True Religion: Reformation, Pastoral and Eucharistic Writings*. Trans. by H. Wayne Pipkin. Eugene, OR: Pickwick, 1984.

Balthasar Hubmaier

Catholic, Evangelical, and Anabaptist Preacher

CORNELIU C. SIMUŢ

Looking back in history, Balthasar Hubmaier's rather short but very intense preaching ministry has had a global impact. During his life Hubmaier (1480–1528) went through all the confessional parties of sixteenth-century Western Christianity, having preached as a Catholic, Evangelical, and Anabaptist theologian. But after his death his theological legacy extended toward Eastern Europe, when in the eighteenth-century Anabaptists were invited by Tsarina Catherine II to settle in Eastern Orthodox Russia. Putting things into perspective, it is only fair to say that Hubmaier's preaching ministry positively influenced not only Catholicism, mainline Protestantism, and Anabaptism in Western Europe, but also the unreformable Eastern Orthodoxy of the lands stretching from Russia to the Balkans.

HISTORICAL BACKGROUND

Balthasar Hubmaier is well-known among the Anabaptists, not only for being the movement's only theologian with a doctoral degree, but also as one of their earliest martyrs. A Catholic for most of his life, Hubmaier studied and worked under the famous Johann Eck, who engaged in theological debates with Martin Luther in the first years of the German Reformation. Although Hubmaier moved up the academic ladder to the position of vice-rector of the University of Ingolstadt in 1515,[1] he was much more attracted by the practical side of theology, which prompted him to accept a pastoral invitation as preacher for Regensburg's Catholic Catedral in 1516.[2] It became evident rather swiftly that Hubmaier had a passion for preaching, not only because he spoke fervently from the pulpit, but also because his ministry became extremely

---

1. Graeme R. Chatfield, *Balthasar Hubmaier and the Clarity of Scripture: A Critical Reformation Issue* (Cambridge: Clarke, 2013), 11.

2. Martin H. Jung, *Die Reformation: Theologen, Politiker, Künstler* (Göttingen: Vandenhoek & Ruprecht, 2008), 56.

successful in a very short period of time.[3] Forced to leave Regensburg in 1520 because of his unexpected success, Hubmaier went to a smaller parish in Waldshut, where he moved from Catholicism to evangelicalism[4]—or early magisterial Lutheran and Zwinglian Protestantism—as he became acquainted with Joachim von Watt, also known as Vadian, the reformer of St. Gallen.[5] Hubmaier's time in Waldshut during 1521–1525 was by no means an easy one; he was forced to leave the town several times, going back to either Regensburg or Schaffhausen or to Nikolsburg (now Mikulov)[6] in Moravia,[7] while also moving from a promising friendship with Zwingli to an unfortunate detachment from the Zurich reformer.[8] During his last year in Waldshut, the Protestant Hubmaier confirmed his evangelical convictions by getting married.[9] Shortly thereafter, he was baptized as an adult, thus formally joining the Anabaptist movement which he served in Nikolsburg from 1526 until his trial and execution in 1528 by burning at the stake in Vienna.[10] Three days after his execution, the foremost Anabaptist preacher was joined in death by his wife who was drowned in the Danube with a stone tied to her neck.[11] Beyond his personal tragedy, however, Hubmaier is survived by his ministry and especially by his passionate preaching, which was always fervent and effective irrespective of his Christian confession, so that not only Anabaptism benefitted from it, but also Catholicism and mainstream Protestantism.

THEOLOGY OF PREACHING

Hubmaier's Catholic Preaching

While in Regensburg, as preacher of the city's Catholic cathedral, Hubmaier established himself not only as an exceptional orator, but also as an equally

3. William R. Estep, *Renaissance and Reformation* (Grand Rapids: Eerdmans, 1995), 206.

4. For the use of the term Evangelicalism as opposed to Catholicism in order to designate the earliest efforts to promote the reformation of the church in the first decades of the sixteenth century under Luther and Zwingli, see John A. Maxfield, *Luther's Lectures on Genesis and the Formation of Evangelical Identity* (Kirksville, MO: Truman State University Press, 2008), 3; and Joachim Whaley, *Germany and the Holy Roman Empire, Volume 1: Maximilian I to the Peace of Westphalia, 1493–1648* (Oxford: Oxford University Press, 2012), 241.

5. C. Arnold Snyder, "Swiss Anabaptism: The Beginnings, 1523–1525," in *A Companion to Anabaptism and Spiritualism, 1521–1700,* eds. John D. Roth and James M. Stayer (Leiden: Brill, 2007), 56.

6. In the first decades of the Reformation, Nikolsburg was famous for its association with the Anabaptist movement. See Paul Brand, "Standing Still or Running On? Reconsidering Rhetoric in the Strasbourg Anabaptist-Spiritualist Debates, 1530–1531," in *Journal of Ecclesiastical History* 62.1 (2011): 23.

7. J. Travis Moger, "Hubmaier, Balthasar," in *The New Westminster Dictionary of Church History. Volume 1: The Early, Medieval, and Reformation Eras,* eds. Robert Benedetto, James O. Duke, Carter Lindberg, Christopher Ocker, and Rebecca H. Weaver (Louisville: Westminster John Knox, 2008), 321.

8. Eddie L. Mabry, *Balthasar Hubmaier's Understanding of Faith* (Lanham, MD: University Press of America, 1998), 21.

9. Michael I. Bochenski, *Transforming Faith Communities: A Comparative Study of Radical Christianity in Sixteenth-Century Anabaptism and Late Twentieth-Century Latin America* (Eugene, OR: Pickwick; Eugene, OR: Wipf & Stock, 2013), 45.

10. See also Bryan D. Spinks, *Reformation and Modern Rituals and Theologies of Baptism: From Luther to Contemporary Practices* (Aldershot, UK: Ashgate, 2006), 84.

11. Rudolph W. Heinze, *Reform and Conflict: From the Medieval World to the Wars of Religion, AD 1350–1648* (Oxford: Monarch Books; Oxford: Lion Hudson, 2006), 159.

thriving pastor, a fact demonstrated by the support he received from the citizens of Regensburg. During his time there, Hubmaier developed a Catholic theology of preaching[12] which was deeply rooted in two main aspects: first, a stern criticism of the Jews,[13] and second, an undeterred devotion to Virgin Mary.[14]

Anti-Semitism

Hubmaier became involved in a fierce fight against the Jews' use of money,[15] although the reason behind his actions had to do with the general desire of the citizens to rid themselves of the city's Jewish population.[16] Although it seems Hubmaier was not personally against the Jews in the sense that he nurtured hatred or similar antagonistic feelings toward them, he nonetheless decided to act on all his preaching responsibilities as minister of the Word at the Regensburg Catholic cathedral.[17] One of his main duties as cathedral preacher was to make sure the Jewish population was carefully controlled, to the point of civil restraint, in a time when Jews had already been expelled from most German burgs. Thus, even if he had nothing against individual Jews,[18] Hubmaier resented Jewish fiscal philosophy and especially the very high interest rates they used to charge for loans.[19] Thus, Hubmaier's disapproval of Jewish financial dealings turned into a rather fierce antagonistic position—considering these high interest rates as nothing less than sins—which resulted in his passionate preaching against them. Hubmaier was so extremely successful in his preaching against the Jews that they were eventually forced to leave Regensburg.[20] The fact that the Jews were expelled from the city appears not to have been enough; Hubmaier's fiery preaching against the Jews also led to the burning and demolition of the city's

---

12. Regarding the theology Hubmaier professed as a Catholic, he is considered a "systematic theologian in the Roman Catholic Church at the inception of the Reformation" most probably because of his previous connections with Johann Eck. See Todd E. Johnson, "Hoping to Death: Baptism, Eschatology, and Ethics," *Liturgy* 22.1 (2007): 59.

13. Bernhard Lohse, *Luthers Theologie in ihrer historischen Entwicklung und in ihrem systematischen Zusammenhang* (Göttingen: Vandenhoek & Ruprecht, 1995), 358.

14. See also Peter Matheson, *Argula von Grumbach: Eine Biographie* (Göttingen: Vandenhoek & Ruprecht, 2014), 48.

15. James I. Lichti, *Houses on the Sand?: Pacifist Denominations in Nazi Germany* (New York: Lang, 2008), 156.

16. Allison P. Coudert, "Judaizing in the Seventeenth Century: Francis Mercury van Helmon and Johan Peter Späth (Moses Germanus)," in *Secret Conversion to Judaism in Early Modern Europe*, eds. Martin Mulsow and Richard H. Popkin (Leiden: Brill, 2004), 85.

17. For the general context, see Dean P. Bell, *Secret Communities: Jewish and Christian Identities in Fifteenth-Century Germany* (Leiden: Brill, 2001), 119.

18. The theory that Hubmaier had nothing against Jews during his Catholic service is still disputed, but what appears to be clear is that he displayed a favorable attitude towards Jews after he joined the Anabaptist movement. See Lichti, *Houses on the Sand?*, 156.

19. Estep, *Renaissance and Reformation*, 206.

20. Eric W. Gritsch, *Martin Luther's Anti-Semitism: Against His Better Judgment* (Grand Rapids: Eerdmans, 2012), 25.

famous synagogue.[21] Hubmaier's theology of preaching during his Catholic phase in Regensburg emphasized not only the sinful nature of Jewish use of money, but also some of their reportedly wicked features of character, which amounted to the point that Hubmaier described the Jews as "idle," "lecherous," and "greedy."[22] By Hubmaier's out-of-the-pulpit actions, he seems to have favored individual Jews,[23] but he nonetheless rapidly became infamous as an anti-Jewish preacher because his sermons appear to have been filled with these adjectives directed against the Jewish population in general. Moreover, he did not forget to mention in his sermons that Christians suffer constantly from the mere presence of Jews in the city, mainly because their loan policy was utterly unbearable and deceitfully exploiting.[24] One can only imagine Hubmaier's preaching passion when he fraternally rallied in support of a Franciscan monk who reported that a baker from the city was coerced into giving his Jewish lender bread for a whole year as a result of borrowing only six gulden. Such a story, vigorously told and retold in passionate sermons, most certainly turned Hubmaier not only into a person who was highly respected by Regensburg's Catholic Christians, but also into the *éminence grise* who orchestrated the expulsion of Jews from the city.[25]

The Doctrine of Mary

The second aspect of Hubmaier's Catholic theology of preaching, namely his devotion to the Virgin Mary, followed quite naturally from his critical position on Jewish finances. Following his extremely successful sermons against the sins of the Jews, which resulted in their expulsion from Regensburg, Hubmaier was left with an empty synagogue at his disposal. He swiftly preached in favor of burning it down and demolishing it,[26] under the pretenses of the need to erect a shrine to honor the Virgin Mary. It was the demolition itself that provided Hubmaier with the perfect excuse to develop his Mariology from mere personal and communitarian devotion to an extremely famous and financially lucrative endeavor. Thus, when, during the demolition of the synagogue, a certain stone worker called Jakob

---

21. Mabry, *Balthasar Hubmaier's Understanding of Faith*, ix.

22. Gritsch, *Martin Luther's Anti-Semitism*, 25; and Michael T. Walton, *Anthonius Margaritha and the Jewish Faith: Jewish Life and Conversion in Sixteenth-Century Germany* (Detroit: Wayne State University Press, 2012), 11.

23. One story references that in spite of his anti-Semitism in general, he appears to still care for individuals which was evidenced by his attempt to help an older Jewish person as he was about to be defrauded by family members. See Estep, *Renaissance and Reformation*, 206.

24. See also R. Po-chia Hsia, "Jews as Magicians in Reformation Germany," in *Anti-Semitism in Times of Crisis*, eds. Sander L. Gilman and Steven T. Katz (New York: New York University Press, 1991), 128.

25. For details, see Walton, *Anthonius Margaritha and the Jewish Faith*, 11.

26. See Francis Rapp, *Christentum IV: Zwischen Mittelalter und Neuzeit, 1378–1552* (Stuttgart: Kohlhammer, 2006), 235.

Kern was seriously injured,[27] but then had his health restored in a rather uncanny way following a special prayer to the Virgin Mary. Hubmaier seized the opportunity to boisterously preach about the healing.[28] Immediately after the demolition of the Jewish synagogue, a wooden shrine was built for Mary. Given Hubmaier's passionate advocacy of Mary's healing powers, the venue became a pilgrimage site with over fifty thousand people travelling to Regensburg within weeks of Kern's reportedly miraculous healing. Regensburg's economy began to flourish almost overnight, which sparkled the envy of the local Dominican monks who rather abruptly no longer benefited from either the people's attention or their money.[29] The conversion of the Jewish synagogue into a place of Christian devotion was aptly supported by Hubmaier's exceptional sermons which seem to have constantly praised the rather wide range of spiritual results associated with the shrine. Most of the results of the shrine were miraculous recoveries from various illnesses and physical handicaps as described in Hubmaier's *Booklet Containing Proof of the Wonderful Signs [which] Happened in Regensburg [at the Chapel to] the Beautiful Mary, the Mother of God*, published in 1520.[30]

The Regensburg marvel, however, did not last long. Pilgrims flooded into the city by hundreds of thousands, bringing with them not only economic prosperity, but also ecstatic manifestations which did not appeal to Hubmaier. The famous city preacher was forced to take an official stand against such events, so he began to use his exceptional rhetorical skills to speak against the pilgrims who were dancing around the shrine or were "bellowing like cattle," enough to convince Hubmaier that they were literally mad.[31] This particular situation, coupled with the increasingly evident discontent of the Dominican monks in Regensburg, whose monastery was left without financial contributions since Hubmaier's Chapel had been erected, caused Hubmaier to fall into disrepute both with the city council and with the local bishop. Thus, despite his preaching effectiveness which brought significant popularity as well as prosperity not only to the city of Regensburg, but also to Catholic faith and practice, Hubmaier was obligated to reconsider his position in the city. The vivacious Catholic preacher eventually decided to leave the city given the new perception about him in the leading political and ecclesiastical quarters of Regensburg, although he is said to have claimed that his intention to

---

27. Alexander Smoltczyk, "Regensburg," in *Erinnerungsorte des Christentums*, eds. Christoph Markschies and Hubert Wolf (München: Beck, 2010), 349.

28. Carter Lindberg, *The European Reformations* (Oxford: Blackwell, 2002), 28.

29. Changkyu Kim, *Balthasar Hubmaier's Doctrine of Salvation in Dynamic and Relational Perspective* (Eugene, OR: Pickwick; Eugene, OR: Wipf & Stock, 2013), 3.

30. Balthasar Hüebmör, *In disem Buchlein seind begriffen die wunderbarlichen Zaychen beschehen zu Regensburg zu der schönen Maria der Mutter Gottes* (Nürberg: Höltzel, 1520).

31. Erik Midelfort, *A History of Madness in Sixteenth-Century Germany* (Stanford, CA: Stanford University Press, 1999), 306.

look for another place of ministry was the result of totally different circumstances, such as the outbreak of the plague, which struck the city late in 1520.[32]

Hubmaier's Evangelical Preaching

Having left Regensburg, Hubmaier accepted a preaching position in Waldshut, where he gradually became interested in the Reformation.[33] A fervent Catholic in his first year in Waldshut, Hubmaier came into contact with the Swiss reformers; it was in this new theological context that he visited Basel and Zurich to meet Erasmus and Zwingli.[34] It appears that after a short return to Regensburg—in a Catholic capacity—Hubmaier eventually embraced the theology of the magisterial Reformation, first in its evangelical Lutheran form, and then in its Reformed Zwinglian version, which—for the sake of simplicity—are going to be referred to by the term "evangelical."[35] By 1523, Hubmaier was decisively associated with the Zwinglian Reformation when he participated at the second Zurich disputation alongside Zwingli.[36]

The Centrality of Christ

In April 1524, Hubmaier wrote *Eighteen Articles*, his first Protestant booklet, in which he teaches that each Christian believes for themselves that Christ died for our sins and is therefore our only Savior.[37] This work also presents some key themes which must have been constantly present in Hubmaier's preaching ministry. Thus, according to his evangelical theology of preaching, the model for our lives is Christ, not church tradition, and what should guide Christians is not violence and killing but rather the "bond of brotherly love." This special connection between Christians cannot exist or manifest itself apart from Christ, so Hubmaier insisted that whatever happens among Christians must be done "through the peace of Christ and in the name of our Lord Jesus Christ." Such a blessed state is possible because of faith, which makes us godly before God, Hubmaier writes, but this faith is really capable of working wonders among Christians because it

---

32. David C. Steinmetz, *Reformers in the Wings: From Geiler von Kaysersberg to Theodore Beza,* 2nd ed. (Oxford: Oxford University Press, 2001), 140.

33. Chatfield, *Balthasar Hubmaier and the Clarity of Scripture,* 13.

34. George Huntston Williams, *The Radical Reformation,* 3rd ed. (Kirksville, MO: Truman State University Press), 149.

35. "Evangelical" is used as a generic term here to designate the first Reformation attempts under Luther and Zwingli. In this sense, the word "Evangelical" is opposed to "Catholic" and different from "Anabaptist." For details about this differentiation, see Sigrun Haude, "Anabaptism," in *The Reformation World,* ed. Andrew Pettegree, (London: Routledge, 2000), 240.

36. Simon V. Goncharenko, *Wounds that Heal: The Importance of Church Discipline within Balthasar Hubmaier's Theology* (Eugene, OR: Pickwick; Eugene, OR: Wipf & Stock, 2012), 8.

37. More on Hubmaier's Eighteen Articles in William R. Estep, *The Anabaptist Story: An Introduction to Sixteenth-Century Anabaptism,* 3rd ed. (Grand Rapids: Eerdmans, 1996), 197.

is a kind of knowledge. Thus, Hubmaier preaches the need for Christians to be aware of their faith as "knowledge of God's mercy," the only spiritual reality that can provide the church with "brotherly love."[38]

Responding to Heresy

It was anything but brotherly love that was extended to him by Catholic authorities. So in August 1524, Hubmaier had to flee from Waldshut to Schaffhausen,[39] where he wrote *Concerning Heretics and Those Who Burn Them*, a work which sheds significant light on the kind of issues he preached about—from a mainline Protestant perspective—during his ministry in Waldshut. The book establishes Hubmaier as a Protestant moving between evangelical Lutheranism and Reformed Zwinglianism, but not yet as an Anabaptist because of the then Catholic tendency to treat harshly all those who disagreed, to the point of torture and execution. Though he would later find out that evangelicals were capable of the same horrors. Even if Hubmaier wrote down his arguments on religious liberty for the sake of the state-church, it is very likely that he preached the same ideas. And one can easily imagine the pathos he must have poured over his sermons in defending those who err in matters related to faith and practice from those who are ready to burn them alive for those supposedly heretical beliefs.[40]

At this point of his career, Hubmaier was not preaching against the separation between church and state, so it was in this mainline Protestant vein that he instructed religious and civil authorities to treat those whom they consider heretics in a spiritual way, not through the employment of physical abuse like torture or execution.[41] Thus, Hubmaier passionately advocates the use of doctrinal apologetics in dealing with heretics, because the ultimate aim in such cases is not the destruction of those who hold different beliefs but, quite *au contraire*, winning them back for the church, which, in this case, is still the state church. Dissenting from the teachings of the state church is a very serious situation in Hubmaier's mind; this is why he defends those who err in issues concerning theology by urging true believers to understand that heresy is nothing less than misery. Since heretics are people who suffer spiritually, Hubmaier preaches tolerance, understanding, and meekness toward them, but also concrete action (like attempting to

---

38. Balthasar Hüebmör, *Acht und dreyssig Schlussrede* (1524), 4–7.

39. More details about the political context which caused Hubmaier's departure from Waldshut to Schaffhausen can be found in Bruce Gordon, *The Swiss Reformation* (Manchester: Manchester University Press, 2002), 199–200.

40. Kirk R. McGregor, *A Central European Synthesis of Radical and Magisterial Reform: The Sacramental Theology of Balthasar Hubmaier* (Lanham, MD: University Press of America, 2006), 146.

41. Thomas White, "The Anabaptists and Religious Liberty," in *The Anabaptists and Contemporary Baptists. Restoring New Testament Christianity,* ed. Malcolm B. Yarnell III (Nashville: Broadman & Holman, 2013), 76.

convince heretics of their faulty doctrines), which must always follow the example of Christ.[42] Heretics, he underlines, are miserable even without being aware of their wretched state, because being a heretic means being against Christ himself and his example.[43] Since those who go against Christ's example are considered heretics, true believers are those who follow Christ's example. In this respect, however, Hubmaier emphatically points out that Christ did not come to kill people but to bring life to them.[44] This is the example of Christ, namely the way to life and instruction, not the path to death and destruction. Consequently, Hubmaier is convinced that certain measures must be taken against heretics, but with prayer, hope, and repentance rather than violence, torture, and killing. Hubmaier's preaching focuses on the need of true believers to pray for those who depart from the orthodoxy of faith and church, as well as to hope for their return and to act in such a way that repentance is being shown in all deeds.[45]

At this stage of his ministry, Hubmaier's preaching is directed against self-righteousness or the kind of attitude which always sees faults in others, not in oneself. This is pure deception, he points out, because in wholeheartedly wishing to wipe out heretics from the face of the earth, some people may ignore the fact that they can be heretics as well—if not in the sense of getting doctrines wrong then at least in failing to appreciate God's sovereignty, Christ's example, and Scripture's guidance. This particular zeal for God is anything but godly because it is not rooted in Scripture; it is deeply embedded in humanity's natural, and hence sinful, constitution. In Hubmaier's reasoning, the light of nature can never overcome the light of Scripture;[46] this is why torturing and killing heretics must never be mistaken for the salvation of souls. Thus, Hubmaier preaches against a false understanding not only of salvation, but also the church, truth, traditions, and even human reason. Thinking that all these aspects can be followed and practically implemented without Scripture is a deadly error which leads away from true prayer, earnest hope, and genuine repentance.[47] Hubmaier sought to apply all these Christian virtues in his practical theology as well as in his personal life as he returned to Waldshut in October 1524 to preach the "holy gospel" not only to his church but also to the people of the city.[48]

42. See Thomas White, "The Defense of Religious Liberty by the Anabaptists and the English Baptists," in *First Freedom: The Baptist Perspective on Religious Liberty*, eds. Thomas White, Jason G. Duesing, Malcolm B. Yarnell III (Nashville: Broadman & Holman, 2007), 52.

43. For more details about the relationship between the so-called heretics and Christ in Hubmaier, see Andrew A. Chibi, *The Wheat and the Tares: Doctrines of the Church in the Reformation, 1500–1590* (Eugene, OR: Pickwick; Eugene, OR: Wipf & Stock, 2015), 137–38.

44. Edward Peters, *Inquisition* (Berkeley: University of California Press, 1989), 158–59.

45. Balthasar Hüebmör, *Von ketzern und iren verbrennern* (1524), 6.

46. Chatfield, *Balthasar Hubmaier and the Clarity of Scripture*, 87.

47. Hüebmör, *Von ketzern und iren verbrennern*, 5–6.

48. Estep, *Renaissance and Reformation*, 209.

Hubmaier's Anabaptist Preaching

The return to Waldshut late in 1524 marks Hubmaier's transition from evangelicalism to Anabaptism. In January 1525, he married Elsbeth Hugline, having been convinced that marriage was ordained by God for ministers of the gospel,[49] and then he began to be increasingly critical of infant baptism[50] because he considered children unsuitable candidates for baptism.[51] Reaching the conclusion that each believer must accept baptism as a command of the Lord Jesus Christ, he allowed Wilhelm Reublin to baptize him in April 1525, and then, in early June, he wrote *The Christian Baptism of Believers* not only to respond to Zwingli's criticism of adult baptism and defense of infant baptism, but also to explain, from a distinctively Anabaptist perspective, what he meant by true biblical baptism.[52] This work on baptism also contains an exceptional presentation of Hubmaier's view of preaching, which he masterfully weaves around his defense of adult baptism.

Hubmaier builds his Anabaptist theology of preaching on the ministry of John the Baptist,[53] which can be summarized in three distinct aspects: (1) John the Baptist preached, (2) he baptized, and (3) he pointed to Christ. These three issues are extremely important for Hubmaier because they disclose his understanding of the mechanism and results of preaching. Preaching leads to baptism, so baptism must never be done before or without preaching, but only as a result of preaching.[54] Also, preaching must always point to Christ, who is not only the content of preaching but also its most important and most celebrated aim. Again pointing to John the Baptist's ministry, Hubmaier indicates that preaching also leads to some concrete effects in those who listen: (1) they can become better people, (2) they are able to change their lives, and (3) they have the power to recognize their sins.

The Methodology of John the Baptist as an Archetype

Although, for Hubmaier, John the Baptist stands between the prophets of the Old Testament[55] and Christ and the apostles of the New Testament, his preaching ministry can serve as an exceptional model for any preacher. Consequently, despite that John did not preach like Christ and the apostles, as Hubmaier points

---

49. See also Robert D. Linder, *The Reformation Era* (Westport, CT: Greenwood Press, 2008), 90.

50. Compare with Jonathan H. Rainbow, "Confessor Baptism: The Baptismal Doctrine of the Early Anabaptists," in *Believer's Baptism: Sign of the New Covenant in Christ,* eds. Thomas R. Schreiner and Shawn D. Wright (Nashville: Broadman & Holman, 2006), 201.

51. Brian C. Brewer, "To Defer and Not to Hasten: the Anabaptist and Baptist Appropriations of Tertullian's Baptismal Theology," *Harvard Theological Review* 106.3 (2013): 295.

52. Estep, *Renaissance and Reformation,* 210–11.

53. For details about Hubmaier's view of John the Baptist, see Chatfield, *Balthasar Hubmaier and the Clarity of Scripture,* 118–99.

54. See also Goncharenko, *Wounds that Heal,* 47–48.

55. Kim, *Balthasar Hubmaier's Doctrine of Salvation,* 101.

out, he nonetheless always pointed to Christ, because it is through Christ that people can find the gospel and the forgiveness of sins. According to Hubmaier, John the Baptist preached based on the law and even taught the law,[56] but his constant emphasis on Christ and his gospel turns his preaching into a model which can and should be followed because of his deep conviction that Christ alone is capable of moving and making all things alive.[57] Hubmaier's theology of preaching establishes the priority of preaching over baptism, which not only indicates that salvation from sin is dependent on preaching but also reveals that preaching is the only way through which people have the chance to hear about their sins and God's salvation.[58]

Christ, the Forgiver of Sins

Regarding salvation, Hubmaier is very careful to establish what one can and cannot do in this respect, and it is preaching which discloses these crucial aspects of one's life. For instance, preaching shows that one can never become good solely by one's own efforts.[59] Preaching must always insist on the necessity that one's life should become better, but the mere acknowledgment of this need will never change anyone. Preaching must therefore always lead people to Christ, the only one who is capable of improving people's lives, so people must make a decision regarding Christ.[60] People, however, will never be able to do so unless this news is preached to them. Hence, Hubmaier's insistence on the necessity that those who preach the gospel should be voices like John the Baptist. It does not matter whether one is a voice in the desert or not; what matters is that Christians become voices or preachers who draw people's attention to Christ, the only One capable of lifting up or forgiving their sins.[61]

This is the very essence of Hubmaier's Anabaptist theology of preaching: Christ as forgiver of sins, an image confirmed by adult baptism.[62] Preaching Christ is compulsory for faith, because preaching Christ can provide people with faith without doubt. For Hubmaier, whenever Christ is preached to people, they are enabled to receive him and trust him fully. Preaching, therefore, leads to faith,

---

56. See also Susan E. Schreiner, *Are You Alone Wise?: The Search for Certainty in the Early Modern Era* (Oxford: Oxford University Press, 2011), 247.

57. See David C. Steinmetz, "The Baptism of John and the Baptism of Jesus in Huldrych Zwingli, Balthasar Hubmair, and Late Medieval Theology," in *Continuity and Discontinuity in Church History: Essays Presented to George Huntston Williams*, eds. F. Forrester Church and Timothy George (Leiden: Brill, 1979), 180.

58. Balthasar Hüebmör, *Von dem christlichen Tauff der glaübigen* (Straßburg: Matthias Schürer, 1525), 15–17. Compare with Kim, *Balthasar Hubmaier's Doctrine of Salvation*, 189.

59. Compare with Kim, *Balthasar Hubmaier's Doctrine of Salvation*, 189.

60. Hughes Oliphant Old, *The Shaping of the Reformed Baptismal Rite in the Sixteenth Century* (Grand Rapids: Eerdmans, 1992), 99–100.

61. Hüebmör, *Von dem christlichen Tauff der glaübigen*, 25–26.

62. Kim, *Balthasar Hubmaier's Doctrine of Salvation*, 101.

and faith leads to baptism.[63] All those who put their trust in Christ allow them-selves to be baptized, and since baptism is performed in the name of Christ, they build their entire faith—as well as their lives—on the grace and power of "our Lord Jesus Christ." They then publicly demonstrate their belief in the remission of sins by accepting baptism. In this context, however, preaching is based on a threefold reality, which must also become a firm conviction for all believers: (1) God forgives sins, (2) God sent his Word in the world, and (3) God's Word became man in Jesus Christ, who is described by Hubmaier as "our Savior."[64]

Once Hubmaier reaches the conclusion that Christ is "our Savior"—a cru-cial realization in Anabaptist circles where Christ was often seen in lesser terms, having been considered merely a great prophet rather than humanity's Savior and God's Son[65]—the connection between Christ, faith, and the gospel becomes the prominent theme of Hubmaier's theology of preaching.[66] He establishes a clear *ordo actionis*—if not a genuine *ordo salutis*—which lists what Christians must do: first, they must go everywhere in the world; second, they must preach; third, they must see who has faith as trust in God; fourth, they must baptize those who have faith; and finally, they must understand that those who have faith and were baptized are saved from sin. All these five steps (of the *ordo salutis*), however, are possible because of Christ, the "healer and pardoner of sins."[67] This is, according to Hubmaier, how the connection between preaching and the gospel must be applied by Christians, namely they must preach the gospel of Christ.[68] This must be done at all costs, even if it leads to torture and death, as the personal example of Hubmaier plainly demonstrates. He was first tortured on the rack following the decision of the Reformed city council in Zurich, and then, some years later, as he was executed by burning at the stake by Catholic authorities in Vienna.[69]

METHODOLOGY FOR PREACHING

Hubmaier's most important theological contribution to preaching is perhaps his capacity to adapt his sermon delivery not only to his evolving religious con-victions as he moved from Catholicism to mainline Protestantism and then to

---

63. Goncharenko, *Wounds that Heal*, 48.
64. Hüebmör, *Von dem christlichen Tauff der glaübigen*, 28, 31.
65. McGregor, *A Central European Synthesis of Radical and Magisterial Reform*, 2006), 249. See also Chatfield, *Balthasar Hubmaier and the Clarity of Scripture*, 315, n. 475.
66. See C. Douglas Weaver, ed., *From Our Christian Heritage: Hundreds of Ways to Add Christian History to Teaching, Preaching, and Writing* (Macon, GA: Smyth & Helwys, 1997), 124.
67. Hans-Jürgen Goertz, *The Anabaptists* (London: Routledge, 1996), 75.
68. Hüebmör, *Von dem christlichen Tauff der glaübigen*, 37, 40–41, 49–50, 56.
69. Roger E. Olson, *The Story of Christian Theology: Twenty Centuries of Tradition and Reform.* (Downers Grove, IL: InterVarsity Press, 1999), 237.

Anabaptism, but also to new audiences. His impact on people remained as powerful as ever, regardless of whether he preached to the same audience or to new ones. If as a Catholic, Hubmaier directed his attention at anti-Jewish discourses and praises to the Virgin Mary, when he turned toward Protestant beliefs, his sermons underwent a dramatic theological shift from such anthropological preoccupations to clear christological interests, as he began to focus on the centrality of Christ and his redemptive work. It takes strong theological convictions to go through so evident a change and remain at least equally effective in preaching if not even more so over the years since Hubmaier's preaching ministry led to the widespread of Anabaptism in Europe.

Given that he was one of the earliest Protestant theologians and preachers, Hubmaier also contributed to the development of a specifically Protestant homiletical methodology in the sense that he switched from nonbiblical aspects to issues found exclusively in Scripture. Thus, his former Catholic sermons revolving around the criticism of Jewish financial practices and the Virgin Mary's miraculous powers of physical healing turned into completely different homiletical enterprises when he started to concentrate on the person and work of Christ as depicted in Scripture. In other words, as far as his preaching methodology is concerned, Hubmaier moved from a politically motivated preaching with little, if any, biblical support to a new homiletical model deeply rooted in the Bible and decisively focused on Christology, soteriology, and ecclesiology. His methodological shift resulted in an equally determined move from a Catholic understanding of human healing by banishing the Jews and idolizing the Virgin Mary to a subsequently Protestant understanding of healing, which is not only essentially spiritual but also exclusively christological.

CONTRIBUTIONS TO PREACHING

Hubmaier was an exceptionally gifted public speaker, distinguished by rhetoric skill and preaching power whenever he delivered sermons. Regardless of whether he spoke to the public as a Catholic theologian, an evangelical pastor, or an Anabaptist leader, Hubmaier preached with passion and simplicity. As a Catholic he effectively spoke against Jews and in favor of Virgin Mary, which immediately resulted in endless pilgrimages to the site of the Chapel for Beautiful Mary, a building which was erected on the site of the former Jewish synagogue in Regensburg. As an evangelical, he strongly defended everybody's freedom of conscience, especially in matters of religious belief, and sternly criticized the criminal attitude of both Protestants and Catholics to torture and burn anyone who dissented and disagreed with what was considered dogmatically orthodox in either circle. As an Anabaptist, he relentlessly insisted on the necessity of preaching the gospel of Jesus Christ, faith as trust in him, and adult baptism as external demonstration of one's inner convictions, a teaching which caused him much personal distress and physical suffering. He suffered both by the hands of his fellow Protestants, who tortured him in Zurich, and by the Catholic authorities in Vienna, who infamously decided to execute not only him, by burning at the stake, but also his wife, by drowning her in the Danube. From a historical perspective, however, it appears that Hubmaier's troubled life was the very aspect which cemented his priceless legacy of faithfulness to God in the face of adversity, by unflinchingly preaching God's salvation, the necessity of faith, and the command to accept baptism as a public display of the believer's trust in the Lord Jesus Christ, the only Savior. Viewed from the same historical perspective, Hubmaier's legacy goes beyond the traditional dogmatic borders of confessional Christianity to the point of realization that not only Protestantism, magisterial and radical, but also Catholicism have been enriched by Hubmaier's exceptional contribution to the dissemination of the gospel and the expansion of God's kingdom.

Sermon Excerpt
On the Lord's Prayer[70]

Gracious Father, I am not worthy to be called a child of yours or that I should be able to call you my Father. I have not always done your will. I have often done the will of the Father of Lies. . . . Father of goodness, look upon us, we who live in this miserable state of woe. We know that children cannot find a better condition than to be with their loving father, who feeds them, gives them drink, clothes them, protects them, and shields them from all needs. . . . Merciful Father, we know that we are guilty of continually dishonoring your name with our words and actions. The suffering of Christ, which for us is medicament for eternal life, we make into an eternal reproach by our cursing and rebuking. . . . Gracious Father, we know that we are captives to sin, the devil, hell, and eternal death. But Father, we cry out and call to you as our loving Father to come quickly with your kingdom of grace, peace, joy, and eternal salvation. . . . Good Father, we confess publicly that your fatherly will does not suit us

70. Balthasar Hubmaier, "A Short Meditation on the Lord's Prayer (1526)," in *Early Anabaptist Spirituality: Selected Writings,* ed. Daniel Liechty (Mahwah, NJ: Paulist, 1994), 39–40.

earthly people. Our will is completely and totally hostile to your divine will. . . . Compassionate Father, we live not by bread alone, but by every word that comes from your holy mouth. Therefore, we humbly pray that you will feed us with the bread of your holy word. This is the bread of heaven, and whoever eats it will be eternally filled. . . . Kind Father, we know that we are guilty of having sinned in words, deeds, and evil thoughts. We do not even know the number, portion, and extent of our sins. Father, forgive us and give us power to better our way of living, even as we forgive those who have caused our suffering. . . . Enlighten all those who misunderstand your holy word, who abuse and persecute us, so that they might come to the true way that leads to eternal life. . . . Heavenly Father! Look on the fear, bareness, misery, persecution, and hardship which we must endure here on earth, and ponder also our human weakness. . . . Do not allow us to be tempted beyond that which we can endure. We are weak and frail, while our enemies are strong, powerful, and heartless. You know these things, merciful Father. . . . Deliver us from evil, from sin, from the devil, from our own lust, which is our greatest enemy. Deliver us from all that keeps us far from you. Moreover, give us all that brings us closer to you. Eternal Father, as we have prayed to you here, bring it to fulfillment according to your Fatherly good will. . . . But we pray this especially, pleading with you, through your most beloved son, our Lord Jesus Christ. He has surely promised us, and proved it through his bitter death, that whatever we pray for in your name you will give us. ◆

BIBLIOGRAPHY

Primary Sources

Hüebmör, Balthasar. *In disem Buchlein seind begriffen die wunderbarlichen Zaychen beschehen zu Regensburg zu der schönen Maria der Mutter Gottes.* Nürberg: Höltzel, 1520.
_____. *Acht und dreyssig Schlussrede.* 1524.
_____. *Von ketzern und iren verbrennern.* 1524.
_____. *Von dem christlichen Tauff der glaübigen.* Straßburg: Matthias Schürer, 1525.

Books

Bell, Dean P. *Secret Communities: Jewish and Christian Identities in Fifteenth-Century Germany.* Leiden: Brill, 2001.
Bochenski, Michael I. *Transforming Faith Communities: A Comparative Study of Radical Christianity in Sixteenth-Century Anabaptism and Late Twentieth-Century Latin America.* Eugene, OR: Pickwick; Eugene, OR: Wipf & Stock, 2013.
Chatfield, Graeme R. *Balthasar Hubmaier and the Clarity of Scripture: A Critical Reformation Issue.* Cambridge: Clarke, 2013.

Chibi, Andrew A. *The Wheat and the Tares: Doctrines of the Church in the Reformation, 1500–1590*. Eugene, OR: Pickwick; Eugene, OR: Wipf & Stock, 2015.

Estep, William R. *Renaissance and Reformation*. Grand Rapids: Eerdmans, 1995.

————. *The Anabaptist Story: An Introduction to Sixteenth-Century Anabaptism*. 3rd ed. Grand Rapids: Eerdmans, 1996.

Finger, Thomas N. *A Contemporary Anabaptist Theology: Biblical, Historical, Constructive*. Downers Grove, IL: InterVarsity Press, 2004.

Goertz, Hans-Jürgen. *The Anabaptists*. London: Routledge, 1996.

Goncharenko, Simon V. *Wounds that Heal: The Importance of Church Discipline within Balthasar Hubmaier's Theology*. Eugene, OR: Pickwick; Eugene, OR: Wipf & Stock, 2012.

Gordon, Bruce. *The Swiss Reformation*. Manchester: Manchester University Press, 2002.

Gritsch, Eric W. *Martin Luther's Anti-Semitism: Against His Better Judgment*. Grand Rapids: Eerdmans, 2012.

Heal, Bridget. *The Cult of the Virgin Mary in Early Modern Germany. Protestant and Catholic Piety, 1500–1648*. Cambridge: Cambridge University Press, 2007.

Heinze, Rudolph W. *Reform and Conflict: From the Medieval World to the Wars of Religion, AD 1350–1648*. Oxford: Monarch Books; Oxford: Lion Hudson, 2006.

Jung, Martin H. *Die Reformation: Theologen, Politiker, Künstler*. Göttingen: Vandenhoek & Ruprecht, 2008.

Kim, Changkyu. *Balthasar Hubmaier's Doctrine of Salvation in Dynamic and Relational Perspective*. Eugene, OR: Pickwick; Eugene, OR: Wipf & Stock, 2013.

Lichti, James I. *Houses on the Sand?: Pacifist Denominations in Nazi Germany*. New York: Lang, 2008.

Lindberg, Carter. *The European Reformations*. Oxford: Blackwell, 2002.

Linder, Robert D. *The Reformation Era*. Westport, CT: Greenwood, 2008.

Lohse, Bernhard. *Luthers Theologie in ihrer historischen Entwicklung und in ihrem systematischen Zusammenhang*. Göttingen: Vandenhoek & Ruprecht, 1995.

Mabry, Eddie L. *Balthasar Hubmaier's Understanding of Faith*. Lanham, MD: University Press of America, 1998.

Matheson, Peter. *Argula von Grumbach. Eine Biographie*. Göttingen: Vandenhoek & Ruprecht, 2014.

Maxfield, John A. *Luther's Lectures on Genesis and the Formation of Evangelical Identity*. Kirksville, MO: Truman State University Press, 2008.

McGregor, Kirk R. *A Central European Synthesis of Radical and Magisterial Reform: The Sacramental Theology of Balthasar Hubmaier*. Lanham, MD: University Press of America, 2006.

Midelfort, Erik. *A History of Madness in Sixteenth-Century Germany*. Stanford, CA: Stanford University Press, 1999.

Muers, Rachel. *Testimony: Quakerism and Theological Ethics*. London: SCM, 2015.

Old, Hughes Oliphant. *The Shaping of the Reformed Baptismal Rite in the Sixteenth Century*. Grand Rapids: Eerdmans, 1992.

Olson, Roger E. *The Story of Christian Theology: Twenty Centuries of Tradition and Reform*. Downers Grove, IL: InterVarsity Press, 1999.

Peters, Edward. *Inquisition*. Berkeley: University of California Press, 1989.

Rapp, Francis. *Christentum IV. Zwischen Mittelalter und Neuzeit, 1378–1552*. Stuttgart: Kohlhammer, 2006.

Schreiner, Susan E. *Are You Alone Wise? The Search for Certainty in the Early Modern Era*. Oxford: Oxford University Press, 2011.

Spinks, Bryan D. *Reformation and Modern Rituals and Theologies of Baptism: From Luther to Contemporary Practices*. Aldershot, UK: Ashgate, 2006.

Steinmetz, David C. *Reformers in the Wings. From Geiler von Kaysersberg to Theodore Beza*. 2nd ed. Oxford: Oxford University Press, 2001.

Stout, Tracey M. *A Fellowship of Baptism: Karl Barth's Ecclesiology in Light of His Understanding of Baptism*. Eugene, OR: Pickwick; Eugene, OR: Wipf & Stock, 2010.

Walton, Michael T. *Anthonius Margaritha and the Jewish Faith: Jewish Life and Conversion in Sixteenth-Century Germany*. Detroit: Wayne State University Press, 2012.

Weaver, C. Douglas, ed. *From Our Christian Heritage: Hundreds of Ways to Add Christian History to Teaching, Preaching, and Writing*. Macon, GA: Smyth & Helwys, 1997.

Whaley, Joachim. *Germany and the Holy Roman Empire: Volume 1: Maximilian I to the Peace of Westphalia, 1493–1648*. Oxford: Oxford University Press, 2012.

Williams, George H. *The Radical Reformation*. 3rd ed. Kirksville, MO: Truman State University Press, 2000.

Windhorst, Christof. *Täuferisches Taufverständnis: Balthasar Hubmaiers Lehre zwischen traditioneller und reformatorischer Theologie*. Leiden: Brill, 1976.

Book Chapters

Coudert, Allison P. "Judaizing in the Seventeenth Century: Francis Mercury van Helmon and Johan Peter Späth (Moses Germanus)." Pages 71–122 in *Secret Conversion to Judaism in Early Modern Europe*. Edited by Martin Mulsow and Richard H. Popkin. Leiden: Brill, 2004.

Haude, Sigrun. "Anabaptism." Pages 237–56 in *The Reformation World*. Edited by Andrew Pettegree. London: Routledge, 2000.

Hsia, R. Po-chia. "Jews as Magicians in Reformation Germany." Pages 115–39 in *Anti-Semitism in Times of Crisis*. Edited by Sander L. Gilman and Steven T. Katz. New York: New York University Press, 1991.

Moger, J. Travis. "Hubmaier, Balthasar." Pages 321–22 in *The New Westminster Dictionary of Church History: Volume 1: The Early, Medieval, and Reformation Eras*. Edited by Robert Benedetto, James O. Duke, Carter Lindberg, Christopher Ocker, and Rebecca H. Weaver. Louisville: Westminster John Knox, 2008.

Patterson, Paige. "Mutually Exclusive or Biblically Harmonious? Religious Liberty and Exclusivity of Salvation in Jesus Christ." Pages 31–48 in *First Freedom: The Baptist Perspective on Religious Liberty*. Edited by Thomas White, Jason G. Duesing, Malcom B. Yarnell III. Nashville: Broadman & Holman, 2007.

Rainbow, Jonathan H. "Confessor Baptism: The Baptismal Doctrine of the Early Anabaptists." Pages 189–206 in *Believer's Baptism: Sign of the New Covenant in Christ*. Edited by Thomas R. Schreiner and Shawn D. Wright. Nashville: Broadman & Holman, 2006.

Smoltczyk, Alexander. "Regensburg." Pages 345–58 in *Erinnerungsorte des Christentums*. Edited by Christoph Markschies and Hubert Wolf. München: Beck, 2010.

Snyder, C. Arnold. "Swiss Anabaptism: The Beginnings, 1523–1525." Pages 45–82 in *A Companion to Anabaptism and Spiritualism, 1521–1700*. Edited by John D. Roth and James M. Stayer. Leiden: Brill, 2007.

Steinmetz, David C. "The Baptism of John and the Baptism of Jesus in Huldrych Zwingli, Balthasar Hubmair, and Late Medieval Theology." Pages 159–81 in *Continuity and Discontinuity in Church History: Essays Presented to George Huntston Williams*. Edited by F. Forrester Church and Timothy George. Leiden: Brill, 1979.

White, Thomas. "The Anabaptists and Religious Liberty." Pages 65–82 in *The Anabaptists and Contemporary Baptists: Restoring New Testament Christianity*. Edited by Malcolm B. Yarnell III. Nashville: Broadman & Holman, 2013.

White, Thomas. "The Defense of Religious Liberty by the Anabaptists and the English Baptists." Pages 49–66 in *First Freedom: The Baptist Perspective on Religious Liberty*. Edited by Thomas White, Jason G. Duesing, and Malcolm B. Yarnell III. Nashville: Broadman & Holman, 2007.

Williamson, Darren T. "The Reformation and Believer's Baptism. Erasmus and the Anabaptists on the Great Commission." Pages 267–82 in *Renewing Tradition: Studies in Texts and Contexts in Honor of James W. Thompson*. Edited by Mark W. Hamilton, Thomas H. Olbricht, and Jeffrey Peterson. Eugene, OR: Pickwick; Eugene, OR: Wipf & Stock, 2007.

Journal Articles

Brand, Paul. "Standing Still or Running On? Reconsidering Rhetoric in the Strasbourg Anabaptist-Spiritualist Debates, 1530–1531." *Journal of Ecclesiastical History* 62, no. 1 (2011): 20–37.

Brewer, Brian C. "To Defer and Not to Hasten: The Anabaptist and Baptist Appropriations of Tertullian's Baptismal Theology." *Harvard Theological Review* 106, no. 3 (2013): 287–308.

Johnson, Todd E. "Hoping to Death: Baptism, Eschatology, and Ethics." *Liturgy* 22, no. 1 (2007): 55–62.

MacGregor, Kirk R. "The Eucharistic Theology and Ethics of Balthasar Hubmaier." *Harvard Theological Review* 105, no. 2 (2012): 223–45.

Suderman, Henry. "Place and Power in Radical Baptism." *Studies in Religion/Sciences Religieuses* 39, no. 2 (2010): 219–39.

William Tyndale
Translation for the Task of Proclamation

SCOTT A. WENIG

William Tyndale (1494–1536) was a preacher, biblical theologian, and linguist who greatly influenced the advance of the Reformation in England via his translation of much of the Bible into English. Moreover, his long-term impact on the preaching in the Protestant Church in particular and on Western Civilization in general has been immense, because the King James Version of 1611 was based on his original work of Bible translation.

HISTORICAL BACKGROUND

One of the most famous movie introductions of the past fifty years begins with the arresting phrase "A long time ago in a galaxy far, far away. . . ."[1] Perhaps more than we realize, that is how many people today view the era traditionally labeled as the Middle Ages. Without question it was a world very different from our own, not least in the nature and function of the Christian faith. From the late eleventh century through the early decades of the sixteenth, the Roman Catholic Church essentially dominated the society known as Western Christendom. As the largest landowner in what eventually became known as Europe, the Church had constructed thousands of parish churches, hundreds of abbeys and monasteries, as well as numerous cathedrals with their massive spires reaching to the heavens. It also had its own legal system, known as canon law, and was served by a massive bureaucracy of clergy from the pope downward to cardinals, archbishops, bishops, deans, monks, friars, and parish priests. From what is now Poland in the east to Spain in the west, from Italy in the south to Scotland in the north, the Church was omnipresent in the lives of all those who inhabited the cities, towns, and villages under its purview. Moreover, the Church defined and controlled the worship of God by centering it in the Eucharistic Mass, which was performed in Latin, the official ecclesiastical language of the West. And while the Church possessed Jerome's Latin translation of the Bible known as the Vulgate, Scripture was

---

1. George Lucas, *Star Wars, Episode IV: A New Hope*, 20th Century Fox, 1977.

functionally unknown to the vast majority of people who composed the *corpus christianum*.[2]

In the latter part of the fourteenth century, however, a biblical and theological explosion rocked the environs of Oxford, England, when a fierce and unrelenting professor of theology began to press for church reform. His name was John Wycliffe (1324–1384), and after attaining his post at the university, he also became the rector of the parish in Ludgershall in Buckinghamshire, not far from Oxford. Following an intense and systematic study of the Scripture, Wycliffe rejected his "years as a logician" (meaning scholasticism) and gave a series of lectures where he taught that the Church had been severely corrupted by its massive wealth. In Wycliffe's view, its only hope for reform was to eliminate a number of unbiblical religious rituals that had accrued over the centuries, such as auricular confession, and a return to the poverty exemplified by Christ and the apostles.[3] This embroiled him in an intense conflict between various ecclesiastical authorities and the English crown over exactly who was in charge of the Church and her revenues. Articulating a view later known as Erastianism, Wycliffe argued on behalf of the Crown, citing numerous biblical examples to make his case.[4] As he clearly saw, the heart of the battle was over the issue of spiritual authority much more than money. It was his firm belief that Scripture should be the guide and authority of the church and not the canonized law that ruled through the papacy.

Wycliffe's foray into this political maelstrom was merely the first step toward promoting further ecclesiastical reform. To reignite spiritual devotion throughout the realm, he called on the clergy to give up their property and become preachers and pastors in line with the original call of Christ to his disciples. To accomplish this he sent out barefoot, itinerant preachers two by two, cloaked in red robes and carrying a staff as they taught God's Word. The staff symbolized their pastoral function, and their preaching was to stress God's sovereignty and the sheer grace of his salvation apart from church ritual or good works. In a radically dangerous move, Wycliffe went on to attack the doctrine of transubstantiation as both illogical and unbiblical, making him a fanatical heretic in the eyes of the authorities.[5]

Underlying all Wycliffe's efforts was his fundamental conviction that Scripture was the law of the church, not canon law or papal pronouncements. It was "the highest authority for every Christian, and the standard of faith and

---

2. *Corpus christianum* means "the body of Christians"; it is a term used to describe Latin Western Christendom in the medieval era.

3. Brian Moynahan, *William Tyndale: If God Spare My Life* (Boston: Little, Brown, 2002), xiii–xiv.

4. Erastianism is the belief that civil magistrates should have ultimate say over church affairs. The term was derived from the view of Thomas Erastus (1524–83), a pupil of Henry Bullinger at Zurich. Owen Chadwick, *The Reformation* (Middlesex, England: Penguin, 1972), 150.

5. Ibid., xvii.

all human perfection."[6] For him, the individual rank or power of the clergy was irrelevant; a priest, friar, monk, or cardinal should only be given heed if their life and teaching agreed with Scripture. But given the inaccessibility of the Vulgate to the laity, and even many of the clergy, Wycliffe set himself to the task of translating the Bible into English for the good of all the people of England. He was joined in this by some other scholars and, while it is impossible from this distance to determine Wycliffe's exact part in the process, there is no doubt that he led it. By 1388, there were completed English versions of both the Old and New Testaments, leading Wycliffe's increasingly venomous opponents to label him and his followers "'Bible men,'" a term of derision which came to be supplanted by the name Lollard.[7]

Wycliffe died of a stroke on the last day of 1384 and was buried in the chancel of St. Mary's church in Lutterworth. In May 1415, he was declared an unrepentant heretic by the Council of Constance, and his remains were exhumed and burned by the English authorities in 1428. The Lollards remained visible in the late fourteenth and early fifteenth centuries but apparently went underground around 1450 only to reemerge in the early sixteenth century just as Lutheranism began to creep into England.[8] They had maintained copies of the Scripture in English and promoted Wycliffe's reformist doctrines for over a century. Without question, Wycliffe's vernacular translation and its preservation by the Lollards laid the biblical and theological groundwork for England's greatest Bible translator and one of its earliest Protestant preachers, William Tyndale.[9]

EARLY LIFE AND PREACHING

Sometime between 1491 and 1495, just on the eve of the Reformation, William Tyndale was born. One Tudor chronicler stated that he was from the borders of Wales, but his most recent biographers argue that he and his family were residents of Gloucestershire in the diocese of Hereford.[10] It appears that around the age of seventeen Tyndale enrolled as a student at Magdalen College in Oxford, which at that point, functioned like a prep school attached to the university. He was

---

6. Ibid., xiii.

7. Lollard was a derivation from the Dutch *lollen,* meaning "to mumble" and was used to describe religious eccentrics and vagabonds. Ibid., xx.

8. A. G. Dickens, *The English Reformation*, 2nd ed. (London: Batsford, 1989), 26–37.

9. For the connections between Wycliffe, the Lollards, and Tyndale, see Anne Hudson, *The Premature Reformation* (Oxford: Clarendon, 1988); Donald Dean Smeeton, *Lollard Themes in the Reformation Theology of William Tyndale* (Kirksville, MO: Truman State University Press, 1986); Ralph S. Werrell, *The Roots of William Tyndale's Theology* (Cambridge: Clarke, 2013).

10. Moynahan, *If God Spare My Life*, 2–5; David Daniell, *William Tyndale: A Biography* (New Haven: Yale University Press, 1994), 11–13.

awarded his MA in 1515 and not long thereafter was ordained as a priest.[11] He moved on to Cambridge in 1519 for further study but left in 1521 due to his growing frustration with the nature of classical medieval education. Years later he wrote that "In the universities they have ordained that no man shall look on the Scriptures until he be nozzled in heathen learning eight or nine years, and armed with false principles with which he is clean shut out of the understanding of the Scripture."[12] By this point, Lutheran ideas were widely known in England, prompting Cardinal Wolsey to publicly burn some of Luther's writing at Paul's Cross in London in 1521. That same year, Henry VIII was awarded the title "Defender of the Faith" by the papacy for an anti-Lutheran treatise he had composed. Soon thereafter, Cambridge became a hotbed of Lutheran doctrine, making it almost certain that Tyndale encountered the broad outline of Luther's doctrine before his departure.[13] A much later comment, surprisingly made by Tyndale's greatest adversary Sir Thomas More, indicates that Tyndale was known in town as a good man and preacher, well versed in the Scripture.[14] Given his exposure to Luther's ideas, some ongoing influence of Wycliffe via the Lollards, and his knowledge of the great humanist scholar Erasmus's Greek New Testament, Tyndale almost certainly would have expounded Protestant doctrines such as *sola fide* and *sola scriptura* in his Cambridge sermons.

His next stop was the household of Sir John Walsh in Little Sodbury Manor, north of the city of Bath. The records are unclear as to his exact role, but it appears he served as a tutor to Walsh's children and may have supplemented that by working as a secretary for Sir John. Walsh seems to have been prominent in the larger community, not the least of which with the local clergy. He welcomed a number of them to his home on a regular basis for dinner and theological discussions. Tyndale participated in these and grew increasingly ill at ease with the apparent lack of biblical knowledge and theological acumen on the part of the priests. Moreover, we know that he was now preaching in public on a regular basis, causing a stir for basing his sermons on Scripture.[15] Unfortunately, any records of these sermons have long since been destroyed or lost, making it difficult to nail down his content. The great martyrologist John Foxe reported that

---

11. William E. Campbell, *Erasmus, Tyndale and More* (London: Eyre and Spottiswoode, 1949), 101–2.

12. Quoted by Tony Lane, "A Man for All People: Introducing William Tyndale," *Christian History*, no. 16 (1987): 2.

13. During the early 1520s, a group of scholars known as "Little Germany" met at the White Horse Inn in Cambridge to discuss Protestant ideas. Tyndale was almost certainly a part of this group. Lewis W. Spitz, *The Protestant Reformation 1517–1559* (New York: Harper & Row, 1985), 246.

14. Quoted by Moynahan, *If God Spare My Life*, 21.

15. John Foxe, *Acts and Monuments*, V, 117 cited by David Daniell, *William Tyndale: A Biography*, 56; Brian Moynahan, *God's Bestseller: William Tyndale, Thomas More and the Writing of the English Bible—A Story of Martyrdom and Betrayal* (New York: St. Martin's Press, 2002), 24–26.

when criticized by one priest for the biblical basis of his preaching as opposed to asserting papal authority, Tyndale replied that "I defy the pope and all his laws and . . . if God spare my life, ere many years pass, I will cause a boy that driveth the plow shall know more of the Scripture than thou dost."[16] This sharp rejoinder echoes a portion of the preface of Erasmus's Greek New Testament which Tyndale obviously knew well: "I would to God that the plowman would sing a text of the Scripture at his plow and that the weaver would hum them to the tune of his shuttle."[17] His course was now set, and he actively began to pursue what he believed to be God's call on his life.

Unfortunately for Tyndale, the English authorities saw Wycliffe's Bible as a pernicious evil that fomented heresy and rebellion. Thus, under the direction of Archbishop Arundel in 1408, any translation of the Bible into English was banned as unlawful.[18] Recognizing this as a formidable obstacle, Tyndale left Little Sodbury in 1524, seeking ecclesiastical approval for his projected work. In what at the time seemed a shrewd move, he sought an audience with Cuthbert Tunstall, the bishop of London. Tunstall was noted to be a humanist scholar, a friend of Erasmus, and gentle in both spirit and tone. He was deeply committed to traditional doctrine and practice and clearly opposed to Lutheran ideas, yet recognized the growing need for ecclesiastical reform within the realm. It is unclear whether Tyndale ever had a face-to-face meeting with the bishop, but eventually Tunstall made it clear that his own house was full and encouraged the young priest to look for work elsewhere.[19] Prior to hearing from the bishop, however, Tyndale began to preach in the parish of St. Dunstan-in-the-West in Fleet Street. Once again no records of these sermons survive, but his preaching did attract the attention of a reform-minded merchant, Humphrey Monmouth. Years later, Monmouth was interrogated about his relationship with Tyndale by Sir Thomas More, then England's chancellor and Tyndale's implacable foe. Monmouth testified that he took in Tyndale for a little over six months, believing him to be a good priest. From Monmouth's description it appears that Tyndale lived like a Protestant monk, eating and drinking little, giving scant attention to his clothes and devoting himself "most of the day and of the night at his book."[20]

The time at Monmouth's house in late 1523 served Tyndale in at least two ways. First, as noted by his host's testimony, he was able to give himself to

---

16. John Foxe, *The Acts and Monuments of John Foxe* (London: The Religious Tract Society, 1563), 514.

17. Quoted by Lane, "A Man for All People," 3.

18. Gordon Rupp, *Six Makers of English Religion, 1500—1700* (New York: Harper & Brothers, 1957), 13.

19. Daniell, *William Tyndale: A Biography*, 85.

20. Quoted by Moynahan, *If God Spare My Life*, 47.

the initial phases of his project of translation. Second, and more ominously, it became clear that neither he nor his work had any future in England. The church authorities, most notably Cardinal Thomas Wolsey, were ramping up their efforts to stamp out Protestant ideas, particularly those of Luther which had now infiltrated much of the country. In addition, Wolsey, along with Archbishop Warham, Bishop John Fisher, and Bishop Tunstall, composed a newly created board of censors which had complete control over what was—and was not—to be published in England. It finally dawned on Tyndale that he would never be able to fulfill his mission in his homeland. In early 1524, he set his sights on Germany, noting that "not only . . . was there no room in my Lord of London's [Tunstall] palace to translate the New Testament, but also there was no place to do it in all England, as experience doth now openly declare."[21] A month or so later, in April 1524, he set sail for Hamburg, never to see his homeland again.

TRANSLATIONS, OTHER WRITINGS, AND SUBSEQUENT MARTYRDOM

Shortly thereafter Tyndale arrived in the German city of Cologne and settled in to begin his work of translating the New Testament into English. Cologne was under Roman Catholic jurisdiction, necessitating that Tyndale keep his whereabouts quiet. He had with him Erasmus's Greek New Testament in its third edition, the Latin Vulgate, and Luther's September Testament of 1521. He later noted that he did not possess a Lollard Bible, meaning Wycliffe's translation, or any other help with the English language as it directly pertained to Scripture.[22] A little over ten months later, in the summer of 1525, he had completed his initial translation and found a printer willing to produce the work. Unfortunately, he was discovered by a Catholic scholar-writer, John Dobneck, who also went by the Latin name Cochlaeus and who had arranged for a raid on the press. Warned at the last moment, Tyndale narrowly escaped to the city of Worms with just the pages that had first been printed. Worms was a more reform-minded city and within months the complete New Testament was printed in over six thousand copies. By February 1526, these were circulating back in England, forcing the bishops to spend valuable resources of time, energy, and money gathering them up for destruction. In an ironic turn of events, none other than Bishop Tunstall preached against the translation and had numerous copies which he had purchased, publically burned at St. Paul's Cathedral in London.

---

21. Ibid., 52.
22. Ibid., 56.

Sometime between 1526 and 1528, Tyndale moved from Worms to the commercial city of Antwerp. Antwerp was a large and thriving cosmopolitan center with an expanding printing industry. It was a smart move on Tyndale's part, because his new residence gave him both a greater degree of anonymity and more options by which to see his New Testament printed and then shipped back to England. He now began to revise his original translation in view of some suggestions he had received from his English readers, as well as drawing on refinements in his own thinking. He also began translating the Pentateuch with the goal of completing the entire Old Testament over the next few years. Moving directly from either the Greek or Hebrew with only occasional references to the Vulgate or Luther's German edition, Tyndale's work was nothing short of brilliant. In keeping with his original intent to make the Bible as accessible to as many English readers as possible, his genius in communicating in the vernacular shines forth time and again. Phrases from the New Testament such as "Eat, drink and be merry," "the salt of the earth," "greater love than this hath no man, than he lay down his life for his friends," all entered the bloodstream of the English language. Tyndale found that English lent itself to the original biblical text far better than Latin, and he leveraged his skill with short words and short sentences to make it clear. It was the sheer plainness of his prose which made the Scriptures come alive and draw in a growing number of new readers. No wonder that in 1527 Archbishop Warham ordered that every copy of Tyndale's New Testament be bought off the streets so they might all be burned! He rightly feared it would not serve the late medieval English Church well to have such a powerful document in the language of the laity.

By 1530 Tyndale had finished his translation of the Pentateuch and the printed copies soon made their appearance in England. In addition, he also produced some other works of theology, Christian living, political theory, and polemics. His most famous, *The Parable of the Wicked Mammon*, focused on the doctrine of justification by faith alone. Although dependent on Luther, Tyndale was biblically and theologically original enough to move beyond Luther's dictums to develop out his own perspective on *sola fide*. This is perhaps most clearly seen in his controversial diatribe against Sir Thomas More. More saw himself as the protector of traditional doctrine and papal supremacy and thought it his divine mission to hunt down and destroy every heretic in England. Tyndale became the focus of his wrath and the two men engaged in a literary battle as notorious for its abusive language as for its competing theologies.[23] Yet it is here that Tyndale's

---

23. See More's *Dialogue Concerning Heresies* (1529), Tyndale's *An Answer to Sir Thomas More's Dialogue* (1531), and More's *Confutation*, (1532–1533).

Protestantism burst forth with a resounding declaration of justification by faith. For Tyndale, the law is good but cannot be kept by frail and fallen human beings. In his mercy, God provides the cure for sin in the passion and death of his Son, Jesus. God's Spirit provides the light which allows for individual repentance, which then produces the trust and confidence necessary to appropriate his mercy as given in the gospel. Thus, in Tyndale's paradigm, it is one's belief in the good news of God's forgiveness in Christ that saves—quite apart from religious ritual, good works, or participation in the Mass.[24]

Another of Tyndale's major publications was *The Obedience of a Christian Man*. In it, he argued forcefully that believers have a duty to obey both family and civil authorities, except where loyalty to God is concerned. He went on to show how the papacy had undermined the essential nature of God's authoritative role in human life and led people away from their proper duties, specifically through the imposition of the sacramental system. In one of the innumerable paradoxes of the English Reformation, Henry VIII was given a copy of this treatise by his then queen, Anne Boleyn, and liked it so much that he sought to bring Tyndale back from exile to serve as his court propagandist. This, of course, did not happen as Anne was unable to produce a male heir and was eventually accused of adultery by her Catholic enemies at court and promptly executed by the king. Yet, like Tyndale's translations of the Scriptures, *The Obedience of a Christian Man* found a receptive audience in England and further solidified his place in the cause of reform.

By 1534, Tyndale had found a position of apparent stability with some English merchants in Antwerp under the patronage of Thomas Poyntz, a friend of Lady Walsh of Little Sodbury. Paid a regular stipend and seemingly secure in his new surroundings, he focused his efforts on translating the remainder of the Old Testament. But his Catholic enemies in England were undeterred in their hunt to capture the great translator. Sometime in the late spring of 1535, a certain Henry Phillips arrived in Antwerp, portraying himself as a friend of reform and ingratiating himself with the English merchants who lived and worked there. It is still unknown whether Phillips was working for Sir Thomas More or John Stokesley, newly consecrated bishop of London and a notorious burner of Protestants, but Phillips was clearly well-financed in his task. Over a series of weeks, he found himself at dinner with Tyndale, who was attracted to Phillips by his manners, speech, and knowledge of events in England. Projecting friendship, Phillips coyly began testing the merchants around Tyndale to see if any might betray him. When these efforts proved fruitless, he set the trap himself. He recruited

---

24. *Answer to More* quoted by Daniell, *William Tyndale: A Biography*, 271.

some Catholic officers from Brussels, about twenty-five miles from Antwerp, and then returned and invited Tyndale to lunch at an open place in town. Suspecting nothing but goodwill, Tyndale accepted, journeyed into the streets, was arrested and brought to the grim castle of Vilvoorde, six miles north of Brussels. There he was held in a gruesome prison for over a year awaiting execution. He was tried in August of 1536, convicted on numerous counts of heresy and strangled to death in early October. By all counts Tyndale stood immovable and at the last moment prayed in a loud, passionate voice, "Lord, open the king of England's eyes."[25]

THEOLOGY OF PREACHING

What we know of Tyndale's preaching must be carefully construed from a study of his hermeneutical approach and the subsequent development of his theology. Reflecting the influence of Christian humanism and its emphasis on textual analysis, Tyndale's interpretative methodology was always centered in the literal meaning of Scripture. As he noted, "The Scripture hath but one sense, which is the literal sense. And that literal sense is the root and ground of all, and the anchor that never faileth, whereunto if thou cleave, thou canst never err or go out of the way. The Scripture indeed useth proverbs, similitudes, riddles, or allegories, as all other speeches do; but that which the proverb, similitude, riddle or allegory signifieth is ever the literal sense, which thou must seek out diligently."[26]

In the contemporary era, we often define this as the historical-grammatical approach. Tyndale stressed this technique as he worked on his translation of the New Testament. "Except of the parables, all the rest has the sense that appears on the surface, nor is one thing said and another meant, but the very thing is meant which is said and the sense is literal."[27] As he wryly noted, "God is a spirit and all of his words are spiritual. His literal sense is spiritual and all his words are spiritual."[28]

This perspective stood in stark opposition to the traditional fourfold meaning of medieval hermeneutics, which consisted of the literal, allegorical, tropological, and anagogical.[29] The classic illustration of this was how the Scripture's use of Jerusalem was interpreted. Literally, it would be understood as the city of the Jews, allegorically as the church, tropologically as the human soul, and anagogically as the heavenly city. Tyndale saw this hermeneutic as a major reason why the

---

25. Foxe, *Acts and Monuments*, V, 127.

26. William Tyndale, *Doctrinal Treatises*, vol. I, (London: Cambridge University Press, 1848), 303, quoted in Philip Hughes, *The Theology of the English Reformers* (Grand Rapids: Eerdmans, 1966), 43.

27. Quoted in David Daniell, *Tyndale's New Testament*, trans. William Tyndale (New Haven: Yale University Press, 1989), vii.

28. William Tyndale, *The Obedience of a Christian Man* (Cambridge: Parker Society, 1849), 309.

29. Tropological refers to a moral element of the text and anagogical refers to a heavenly aspect.

church of his day had lost the truth of the gospel and the vibrancy of saving faith. Dialing back to the era of the early church, he focused his attack on Origen and some of the other church fathers.

> The greatest cause of which captivity and the decay of the faith, and this blindness wherein we now are, spring first of allegories. For Origen and the doctors of his time drew all the Scripture unto allegories; whose example that came after followed so long, till they at last forgot the order and process of the text, supposing that the Scripture served but to feign allegories upon; make descant upon song. Then came our sophisters with their anagogical and "chopological" sense and with an antitheme of half an inch, out of which some of them drew a thread nine days long.[30]

For Tyndale, however, Scripture was a light that simply needed to be uncovered. It alone "showeth us the true way, both what to do and what to hope for, and a defense from all error, and a comfort in adversity that we despair not, and feareth us in prosperity that we sin not."[31]

Given Tyndale's approach to Scripture and the fact that he never composed a formal systematic theology, a la John Calvin's *Institutes of Christian Religion*, he might best be described as a biblical theologian. From his various treatises and collective works, we can discern some of the major themes of his theological framework, which almost certainly composed the content of his preaching. First, the foundation of Tyndale's theological paradigm was his understanding of God's immoveable covenant with his people.[32] In his view, God knew from eternity past that humanity would fall into sin, thus bringing evil and disaster to itself and God's creation. Yet before the foundation of the world and the entrance of original sin, the triune God covenanted to redeem both his elect and his creation from the disastrous effects of evil. The Father chose his own, the Son shed his blood to make their redemption possible, and the Spirit applied the effects of the Father's choice and the Son's redemption to them so they would be God's children rather than the offspring of the devil. Christ's blood satisfied God's justice and broke the barrier between sinful humanity and the holy God, thus fulfilling the legal aspect of the covenant. Yet there is more going on in Christ's death than a forensic transaction. Humanity is tragically dead in sin and completely incapable of responding to God. As Tyndale noted, "We can do no good works unto God,

---

30. Quoted in Daniell, *Tyndale's New Testament*, xvi.
31. Tyndale, *Doctrinal Treatises*, vol. I, 399 ff, quoted in Hughes, *English Reformers*, 40.
32. Michael McGiffert, "William Tyndale's Conception of Covenant," *Journal of Ecclesiastical History* vol. 32, no. 2 (1981): 167–84.

but receive only of His mercy with our repenting faith."[33] Thus, it is only by the Spirit's sprinkling of Christ's blood on the hearts of people that they can be made regenerate and be part of God's family.

A second and closely related element of Tyndale's theology of salvation is his emphasis on good works. As noted, in Tyndale's theological framework good works cannot save a person; only those born again by God's Spirit and who trust in Christ alone are deemed the children of God.[34] But in time, these will live out their salvation by obeying God and doing good works. Tyndale consistently reiterated this intimate connection between saving faith and the law of love. He argued, "When the gospel is preached unto us we believe the mercy of God, and in believing we receive the Spirit of God, which is the earnest of eternal life, and we are in eternal life already, and feel already in our hearts the sweetness thereof, and are overcome with the kindness of God and Christ and therefore love the will of God, and of love are ready to work freely, and not to obtain that which is given us freely and whereof we are heirs already."[35]

This "readiness to work freely" invoked a third major aspect of Tyndale's theology. In his view, all humanity, including those who are part of God's saving covenant, are fundamentally indebted to God. While that debt was paid by Christ and applied to the elect, the concept of indebtedness to the Savior remained central to his thought. Specifically, this played out in Tyndale's understanding of stewardship. What we possess, be it the grace of God, spiritual gifts, or material possessions, is not ours; it has been given to us by our Father, through the Son, and by the Spirit. Any prosperity or good welfare we might possess is always the result of divine action. Therefore, the idea of grasping these things or leveraging them in a selfish manner fundamentally works against the divine love inherent in God's covenant. Instead, the Christian should be willing to share what he or she possesses with those in need, be it a friend, a neighbor, or even those far away who do not share the same faith.[36] In Tyndale's words, "Deeds are the fruit of love and love is the fruit of faith."[37]

CONTRIBUTIONS TO PREACHING

As noted, Tyndale was not a systematic theologian but a Bible-focused linguistic genius who vigorously stressed and practiced the clear exposition of God's Word.

---

33. Tyndale, *Doctrinal Treatises*, vol. I, 466, quoted in Hughes, *English Reformers*, 84.

34. Tyndale, *Doctrinal Treatises*, vol. I, 349, quoted by McGiffert, "William Tyndale's Conception of Covenant," 169.

35. Tyndale, *The Parable of the Wicked Mammon*, quoted by Daniell, *William Tyndale: A Biography*, 164.

36. *Parable of the Wicked Mammon*, 93–99 as cited by Rowan Williams, *Why Study the Past? The Quest for the Historical Church* (Grand Rapids: Eerdmans, 2005), 76.

37. Tyndale, *Doctrinal Treatises*, vol. I, 57, quoted by Hughes, *English Reformers*, 103.

Given the enormous emphasis in late medieval piety on good works as a means of securing one's salvation or reducing time in purgatory, it is not surprising that Tyndale's preaching rankled many. While still residing in Gloucester at the home of Sir John Walsh, Tyndale preached regularly in and around the alehouse which served as a place for public discussion and the exchange of ideas. Given his theological orientation his sermons were rooted in the text of Scripture and clearly expounded the doctrines of being dead in our trespasses and sins (Eph 2:1) and the need of *sola fide*. Having laid a foundation that undercut any sense of works righteousness, it would not be too far-fetched to imagine that he then stressed the need for repentance from many of the religious practices of the day. That would have been followed with a call to receive Christ as Savior and Lord in a manner in which the majority of his hearers were unaccustomed. Given that Tyndale would have stressed an expansive social ethic which required believers to live out the law in love of Christ, it is a small wonder he created a high degree of anxiety whenever he spoke. John Foxe relates that Tyndale's preaching so upset the local clergy of Gloucester that they recruited the chancellor of the diocese, a certain Dr. Parker, to interrogate him into silence. It went badly. Tyndale later recounted that "he threatened me grievously, and reviled me, and rated me as though I had been a dog."[38]

Tyndale would also have taught publicly on the doctrines of election and covenant, because of their theological importance. He saw these as fundamental elements of God's relationship with humanity and his church, concepts which every Christian needed to know. Moreover, Tyndale deeply believed that the papacy had undermined Christendom in general and English society in particular with intentional falsehoods, moral corruption, and evil doctrine. The only correction to this chaotic and destructive mess, as well as the only hope of personal and social redemption, was the principle of perfect fidelity revealed in God's covenant with humanity.[39] Certainly it would have taken some diligence on his part to make these concepts clear to audiences wholly unaccustomed to explicit biblical teaching. But above all else, Tyndale desired to communicate the whole counsel of God in a way that was intelligible and attractive. The clarity, power, and beauty of his biblical translations vividly demonstrates his passion as well as his skill in this regard.

From the late fourteenth century on, the men and women who committed themselves to the cause of reform relied on the unremitting power of God's Word to shape the direction of the Christian faith. William Tyndale may have been the

---

38. Foxe, *Acts and Monuments*, vol. III, 514.
39. McGiffert, "William Tyndale's Conception of Covenant," 169.

preeminent example of this. He serves as a historical, biblical, and homiletical bridge between Wycliffe and the Lollards to the English divines who constructed the Authorized Version of 1611.[40] Yet his greatest contribution to the task of preaching was to give us the Bible in English, the one indispensable element in the expansion of Protestantism in the Western World from the sixteenth century to the present.

Following his martyrdom in 1536, Tyndale's work of translation was taken up by Miles Coverdale, another Protestant who had fled from the persecution of Henrician England. Coverdale's work was eventually labeled Matthew's Bible because its editor, John Rogers, a friend of Tyndale's, published it under the assumed name Thomas Matthew. This was the version which Archbishop Thomas Cranmer persuaded Henry VIII to publish in 1537. It was licensed to be produced in 1,500 copies and contained the initials W.T. between the two testaments to reflect that it was, in essence, Tyndale's translation.[41]

Other Bibles in English followed, most notably the Great Bible, printed under the patronage of Thomas Cromwell in 1539, the Geneva Bible of 1560, and the Bishops Bible of 1568. Yet Tyndale's genius was enshrined in the Authorized, or "King James," Version of 1611. Commissioned by James I in 1604, it was composed over a period of seven years by fifty-four clergymen at Westminster, Oxford, and Cambridge. It became the standard translation for the English-speaking world until the latter part of the twentieth century and undoubtedly helped to shape the culture of Western Civilization over the past four centuries. A textual analysis of the King James Version has revealed that Tyndale's words make up 84 percent of the New Testament and 76 percent of the Old Testament. This makes it, by any reasonable standard, Tyndale's Bible. Produced at enormous cost in both labor and life, it has served for decades as the foundation for preaching in Protestant churches and remains an incalculable treasure of the church in the English-speaking world.[42]

It has been noted in this survey of Tyndale's works and preaching that no specific extant sermons of his have survived. Yet his writings convey not only heart-felt conviction but also such vast biblical and theological knowledge that it seems not far-fetched to imagine that Tyndale preached in much the same manner. And while he was never fearful of controversy, Tyndale's concern for God's truth and the good of his people regularly shines forth in his writings. Thus, for

40. Jens G. Møller, "The Beginnings of Puritan Covenant Theology," *Journal of Ecclesiastical History* no. 14 (1963): 46–67.

41. Moynahan, *If God Spare My Life*, 388.

42. Hugh Oliphant Old, *The Age of the Reformation*, vol. 4 of *The Reading and Preaching of the Scriptures in the Worship of the Christian Church* (Grand Rapids: Eerdmans, 2003), 138.

the purpose of illustration, the following paragraph from his *A Brief Declaration of the Sacraments* is provided in the hope that it illuminates the content of what his preaching may have been like, as well as the pastoral tone in which it was generally delivered.

Sermon Excerpt

A Brief Declaration of the Sacraments[43]

Wherefore, to avoid this endless brawling, which the devil hath no doubt stirred up, to turn the eyes of our souls from the everlasting covenant made us in Christ's blood and body, and to nosel us in idolatry, which is trust and confidence in false worshipping of God; and to quench first the faith to Christ-ward, and then the love due to our neighbor; therefore methinketh that the party that hath professed the faith of Christ, and the love of his neighbor, ought of duty to bear each other, as long as the other opinion is not plain wicked through false idolatry, nor contrary to the salvation that is in Christ, nor against the open and manifest doctrine of Christ and his apostles, nor contrary to the general articles of the faith of the general church of Christ, which are confirmed with open scripture; in which articles never a true church in any land dissenteth. ♦

BIBLIOGRAPHY

Primary Sources

Foxe, John. *The Acts and Monuments of John Foxe*, 8 vols. 4th ed. Edited and corrected by J. Pratt; introduction by J. Stoughton. London: The Religious Tract Society, 1877.

Tyndale, William. *The Obedience of a Christian Man*. Cambridge: Parker Society, 1849.

_____. *The Parable of the Wicked Mammon* in *Doctrinal Treatises and Introductions to Different Portions of the Holy Scriptures*. Edited by Henry Walter and The Parker Society. Cambridge: Cambridge University Press, 1848.

_____. *Preface That He Made Before the Five Books of Moses* in *Doctrinal Treatises and Introductions to Different Portions of the Holy Scriptures*. Edited by Henry Walter and The Parker Society. Cambridge: Cambridge University Press, 1848.

_____. *Prologue Upon the Gospel of St. Matthew* in *Doctrinal Treatises and Introductions to Different Portions of the Holy Scriptures*. Edited by Henry Walter and The Parker Society. Cambridge: Cambridge University Press, 1848.

_____. *An Answer to Sir Thomas More's Dialogue*. Edited by Henry Walter and The Parker Society. Cambridge: Cambridge University Press, 1850.

Tyndale's New Testament. Intro. by David Daniell. New Haven: Yale University Press, 1989.

---

43. William Tyndale, *Doctrinal Treatises and Introductions to Different Portions of the Holy Scriptures*, ed. Henry Walter (Cambridge: Cambridge University Press, 1848), 384.

Secondary Sources

Campbell, William Edward. *Erasmus, Tyndale and More*. London: Eyre & Spottiswoode, 1949.

Chadwick, Owen. *The Reformation*. Middlesex, England: Penguin, 1972.

Clebsch, William A. *England's Earliest Protestants 1520–1535*. New Haven: Yale University Press, 1964.

Daniell, David. *William Tyndale: A Biography*. New Haven: Yale University Press, 1994.

Demaus, Robert. *William Tindale, a Biography: A Contribution to the Early History of the English Bible*. Nashville: Cokesbury, 1927.

Dickens, A. G. *The English Reformation*, 2nd ed. London: Batsford, 1989.

Hudson, Anne. *The Premature Reformation*. Oxford: Clarendon, 1988.

Hughes, Philip Edgcumbe. *Theology of the English Reformers*. Grand Rapids: Eerdmans, 1966.

Lane, Tony. "A Man for All People: Introducing William Tyndale." *Christian History* 16 (1987): 2–3.

McGiffert, Michael, "William Tyndale's Conception of Covenant." *Journal of Ecclesiastical History* 32 (1981): 167–84.

McGoldrick, James Edward. *Luther's English Connection: The Reformation Thought of Robert Barnes and William Tyndale*. Milwaukee: Northwestern, 1979.

Møller, Jens G. "The Beginnings of Puritan Covenant Theology." *Journal of Ecclesiastical History* 14 (1963): 46–67.

Moynahan, Brian. *God's Bestseller: William Tyndale, Thomas More and the Writing of the English Bible—A Story of Martyrdom and Betrayal*. New York: St. Martin's Press, 2002.

_____. *William Tyndale: If God Spare My Life*. London: Little, Brown, 2002.

Mozley, J. F. *William Tyndale*. Reprint, Westport, CT: Greenwood, 1971.

Olds, Hugh Oliphant. *The Age of the Reformation*. Vol. 4 of *The Reading and Preaching of the Scriptures in the Christian Church*. Grand Rapids: Eerdmans, 2003.

Pilgrim, A. Christian. *The Forbidden Book: William Tyndale and the First English Bible*. Shippensburg, PA: Lollard House, 1992.

Rex, Richard. "New Light on Tyndale and Lollardy." *Reformation* 8 (2003): 143–71.

Rupp, E. Gordon. *Six Makers of English Religion, 1500–1700*. New York: Harper & Brothers, 1957.

Smeeton, D. D. *Lollard Themes in the Reformation Theology of William Tyndale*. Vol. 6 of *Sixteenth Century Essays and Studies*. Edited by C. G. Nauert. Kirksville, MO: Truman State University Press, 1984.

Spitz, Lewis W. *The Protestant Reformation 1517–1559*. New York: Harper & Row, 1985.

Werrell, Ralph S. *The Roots of William Tyndale's Theology*. Cambridge: Clarke, 2013.

Williams, Charles Harold. *William Tyndale*. London: Nelson, 1969.

Williams, Rowan. *Anglican Identities*. Cambridge, MA: Cowley, 2003.

_____. *Why Study the Past? The Quest for the Historical Church*. Grand Rapids: Eerdmans, 2005.

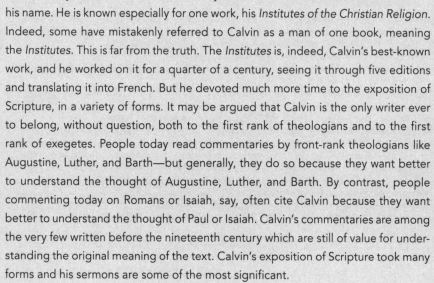

John Calvin
Preaching the Glorious Christ

ANTHONY N. S. LANE

Calvin (1509–1564) is best known as a theologian. Any list of the most significant theologians
in the history of the church would be likely to include
his name. He is known especially for one work, his *Institutes of the Christian Religion*.
Indeed, some have mistakenly referred to Calvin as a man of one book, meaning
the *Institutes*. This is far from the truth. The *Institutes* is, indeed, Calvin's best-known
work, and he worked on it for a quarter of a century, seeing it through five editions
and translating it into French. But he devoted much more time to the exposition of
Scripture, in a variety of forms. It may be argued that Calvin is the only writer ever
to belong, without question, both to the first rank of theologians and to the first
rank of exegetes. People today read commentaries by front-rank theologians like
Augustine, Luther, and Barth—but generally, they do so because they want better
to understand the thought of Augustine, Luther, and Barth. By contrast, people
commenting today on Romans or Isaiah, say, often cite Calvin because they want
better to understand the thought of Paul or Isaiah. Calvin's commentaries are among
the very few written before the nineteenth century which are still of value for understanding the original meaning of the text. Calvin's exposition of Scripture took many
forms and his sermons are some of the most significant.

HISTORICAL BACKGROUND[1]

John Calvin was born in 1509 at Noyon, in northern France. He studied at
Paris, Orleans, and Bourges universities and became an admirer of Erasmus and
humanism. He himself produced a work of humanist scholarship in 1532, a commentary on the Roman philosopher Seneca's *De clementia*, which failed to make
the impact he had hoped for. At about this time Calvin was converted to the
Protestant cause and immediately devoted himself to theological study.[2]

---

1. This chapter is dedicated to my former doctoral supervisor, T. H. L. Parker, who died on April 25, 2016, just short of his 100th birthday. He was one of the leading students of Calvin's commentaries and sermons.
2. The best biography of Calvin is Bruce Gordon, *Calvin* (New Haven: Yale University Press, 2009).

In 1533, Calvin was associated with a mildly Protestant speech given by the new rector of Paris University, Nicholas Cop, and had to leave town in a hurry. The following year, he left France and settled in Basel to study and write. By the summer of 1535 he had finished the first edition of his *Institutes*. His season of peaceful scholarship, however, was to be short-lived. In 1536, he was forced by a local war to make a detour through Geneva, which had just accepted the Reformation. Calvin planned to stop for one night only, but Farel, the leader of the Genevan Reformers, prevailed upon him to stay.

Calvin's ministry in Geneva lasted until his death in 1564, though not without interruption. In 1538, a dispute over the issue of church government led to his exile and he withdrew to Basel, hoping to resume his studies. Again, this was not to be. Martin Bucer persuaded him to come to Strassburg to minister to the small congregation of French refugees there.[3] He stayed until 1541, profiting from contact with other Reformers, especially Bucer. But while Calvin was at Strassburg, the church at Geneva was going from bad to worse and eventually Calvin was prevailed upon to return. There followed a long and bitter struggle in which Calvin fought for the spiritual independence of the Genevan church and for the imposition of rigorous discipline. For many years Calvin had to face intense opposition from the magistrates, but eventually his opponents were discredited and there was a pro-Calvin city council. In the final years of his life, he was highly respected, though his wishes were not always obeyed. He died in 1564.

CALVIN AND SCRIPTURE

Calvin's exposition of Scripture comes in four forms. Best known are his commentaries, which are still widely used and which have been translated into many languages. First to appear was the commentary on Romans (1540), Calvin seeing Romans as crucial for the understanding of the gospel. After a slow start, Calvin completed the New Testament letters by 1551. Over the next four years he completed the Gospels and Acts, thus covering the whole New Testament apart from 2 & 3 John and Revelation. In the 1550s, Calvin turned his attention to the Old Testament. He produced commentaries on Isaiah, Genesis, Psalms, a Harmony of Exodus to Deuteronomy, and eventually a brief commentary on Joshua near the end of his life.

As well as writing commentaries, Calvin also *lectured* on the Bible—on the New Testament in his first stay at Geneva and at Strassburg and on the Old

---

3. I use the German name for Strasbourg as a reminder that in the sixteenth century this was still a German city.

Testament after his return to Geneva. In 1556, he was lecturing on Hosea and from that point on, all of his lectures were published based on transcripts taken by his students. The books covered are Jeremiah, Lamentations, Daniel, and the Minor Prophets. At the time of his death, he was lecturing on Ezekiel, but got no further than 20:44. Earlier lectures on Isaiah, Genesis, and Psalms had paved the way for his commentaries on these books.[4]

Starting in 1536, the Genevan ministers had a weekly meeting (called a *con-grégation*) in which a passage of Scripture was expounded by one minister and then discussed by all. From 1549, a transcript was taken of each of these exposi-tions, only a small number of which survive.[5] This is partly because Calvin used the *congrégations* as a stage in his preparation of commentaries and there was no need to keep them once the latter had appeared. In 1542, Calvin published a brief exposition of Jude in French. Erik de Boer argues persuasively that this probably originated as a presentation at a *congrégation*.[6]

In addition to Calvin's commentaries, lectures, and *congrégations* there is a fourth group of expositions, his *sermons,* and it is these that concern us here.

PREACHING

Calvin preached regularly from 1536 on, both in Geneva and in Strassburg. Our knowledge of how often he preached prior to 1549 and on which books is limited. His method was to preach consecutively through whole books of the Bible, seeing this as the practice of the early church.[7] So there are, for example, two hundred sermons on Deuteronomy, 159 sermons on Job, and forty-three on Galatians. Normally the Sunday sermons were on the New Testament (though at times the afternoon sermons were on the Psalms) and the weekday sermons on the Old Testament. He would interrupt the series to preach specific sermons for the church festivals of Christmas, Easter, and Pentecost. In 1550, the city council abolished all holidays apart from Sunday, and Christmas was celebrated on the first Sunday after the 25th of December.[8]

In 1549, the French refugee Denis Raguenier was hired to take down Cal-vin's sermons in shorthand and to oversee their transcription, which he continued to do until his death sometime between December 1560 and February 1561.[9]

---

4. The first edition of the Isaiah commentary (1551) was written up from Calvin's lectures by a student, Nicolas Des Gallars, and revised by Calvin. Calvin himself wrote a much fuller second edition (1559).

5. All that survives, including Calvin's comments on the presentations of others, is to be found in COR 7/1. For more on the *Congrégations*, see E. A. de Boer, *The Genevan School of the Prophets: The Congrégations of the Company of Pastors and Their Influence in 16th century Europe* (Geneva: Droz, 2012).

6. COR 7/1:3–4.

7. Second Defence of the Sacraments (CTS 2:323; CO 9:104).

8. COR 5/8:XIX-XX.

9. COR 7/1:XX-XXI.

Raguenier also compiled a catalog of Calvin's sermons.[10] Given the number transcribed from 1549 to 1560, and allowing for those which Raguenier missed due to ill health, we see that Calvin preached on average nearly two hundred times per year. The default setting was for Calvin to preach twice on Sundays and daily during alternate weeks.[11] This would amount to over 230 times a year, but sometimes Calvin did not preach because he was ill or was away from Geneva.

After Raguenier's death, someone else took on the task of recording Calvin's weekday (but not Sunday) sermons, covering 1 and 2 Samuel and as far into 1 Kings as Calvin reached. Maybe the decision to focus on the weekday sermons was because these, unlike the Sunday sermons, were on Old Testament books on which Calvin had written no commentary. There seems to have been a gap, as there is no mention of a transcript of Judges, on which Calvin preached between his sermons on Genesis and 1 Samuel.

The transcribed sermons give the date of delivery but unfortunately, apart from the Deuteronomy sermons, the sixteenth-century publishers omitted this in their printed editions. In many instances, the dates can be reconstructed using indications in the sermons themselves and external evidence.[12]

THE FATE OF CALVIN'S SERMONS

At Calvin's death, there were many volumes of transcribed copies of his sermons. Some were published in the sixteenth century; most were left in manuscript form in the Genevan library. In 1805, the librarian sold these off to booksellers by weight! His justification was that they were not in Calvin's hand and that they were hard to read. A few were recovered by some theological students and some others have subsequently been recovered, but the great majority of the transcribed volumes have been lost.[13]

The transcribed sermons of Calvin fall into four groups:

1. Some were published in the sixteenth century:[14] Calvin himself oversaw the publication of a single volume of five sermons (1552).[15] Many others

---

10. SC 1:XXXIV-XXXVI; SC 2:XV-XVII; ET: T. H. L. Parker, *Calvin's Preaching* (Edinburgh: T&T Clark, 1992), 153–56.

11. Sometimes he also preached on the Wednesday of his "week off."

12. Parker, *Calvin's Preaching*, 163–71 does this for 1 & 2 Timothy and Job; COR 5/8:XXVIII-XXXV for some others.

13. For this saga, see SC 2:XX-XXVIII; Parker, *Calvin's Preaching*, 68–70.

14. For the list, see Parker, *Calvin's Preaching*, 180–90 and, more fully and more accurately, R. Peter & J.-F. Gilmont, *Bibliotheca Calviniana. Les oeuvres de Jean Calvin publiées au XVI siècle*, 3 vols. (Geneva: Droz, 1991–2000).

15. On Psalms 16:4, 27:4, 27:8; Hebrews 13:13, together with an exposition of Psalm 87.

were published based on transcripts without further collaboration from him. (Indeed, he had strong reservations about their publication.)[16] These covered a range of biblical books: Deuteronomy (1562),[17] Job (1563), Daniel 5–12 (1565),[18] the Synoptic Gospels (1562),[19] 1 Corinthians 10–11 (1558),[20] Galatians (1563), Ephesians (1562), the Pastoral Epistles (1561), as well as a few Psalms [115, 124 (1546) and 119 (1554)]. There were also thematic extracts from the Genesis and Isaiah sermons: on Melchizedek and Abraham (1560),[21] on Jacob and Esau (1560),[22] and on Hezekiah's canticle (1562).[23] A volume of sermons from church festivals was published: on Christ's Deity, Nativity, Passion, Resurrection, and Ascension, as well as Pentecost and Last Advent, together with Isaiah 52:12–53:12 (1558).[24] In 1604, Calvin's sermons on 1 Samuel were published in Latin. All of these are found in the nineteenth-century *Calvini Opera*.[25] In addition, three sermons on Psalms 46 and 48 were published in English only (1562), having been translated from Raguenier's transcription.[26]

Some of the series published in the sixteenth century were translated into other languages. A few were translated into German, Dutch, or Italian, but a far greater number into English, including all the complete sets on whole books.[27]

---

16. For these reservations, see E. A. McKee, "Calvin's Sermons: Suspected, Unique and Prized" in *Calvin Studies XII*, ed. Michael D. Bush (Due West, SC: Erskine Seminary, 2006), 99–103.

17. The Ten Commandments appeared on their own in 1557.

18. The sermons on Chapters 1–4 are not included because Raguenier was unwell and so unable to transcribe them.

19. The sixty-five sermons that Raguenier transcribed before his death. Calvin continued to preach on the Synoptic Gospels until his death, but those sermons were not transcribed.

20. These sermons are excerpted from Calvin's series on 1 Corinthians.

21. On Genesis 14:13–15:7, 21:33–22:14. There were two similar Genevan editions in 1560. The first contains the sermons on Genesis 14–15, together with eleven sermons on Luke 1–2, excerpted from the sixty-five sermons on the Synoptic Gospels which were to be published in 1562. The other edition erroneously has a similar title page to the first but in fact contains simply the sermons on Genesis 14–15, 21–22. See Peter & Gilmont, *Bibliotheca Calviniana*, 2:745–52.

22. Covering all of Genesis 25:12–27:38, initially published as an appendix to the French translation of Calvin's *Eternal Predestination*. They were later published in a separate edition on their own (1562).

23. On Isaiah 38.

24. These sermons are drawn from a range of sources. The first sermon, on John 1:1–5, is the publication of a *congrégation*. The next ten, on the Nativity Passion and Resurrection, were preached for Christmas and Easter. One sermon on Pentecost was preached for that feast but the remaining seven sermons on the Ascension and Pentecost are excerpted from Calvin's series on Acts. The sermon on the Last Advent is excerpted from Calvin's otherwise missing series on 1 & 2 Thessalonians. Finally, the sermons on Isaiah 52:12–53:12 are excerpted from Calvin's series on Isaiah.

25. All will also appear in COR 5/1–12, apart from those on Isaiah, which have already appeared in SC 3 & 4/1.

26. For two of these Raguenier's transcription survives. These, together with the English version of the third, are found in SC 7.

27. Parker, *Calvin's Preaching*, 71–73, 188–94.

2. A number of the series which survive in manuscript have been published since 1936 in the *Supplementa Calviniana* series: Genesis 1:1–20:7, 2 Samuel, selected Psalms,[28] Isaiah 13–41 and 52–66, Jeremiah 14:19–18:23, Lamentations 1:1–5, Ezekiel 36–48, Micah, and Acts 1–7, together with some sermons on Easter and Pentecost.[29]

3. Some manuscripts still await publication: Isaiah 42–51, Ezekiel 1–15 and 23–35, and 1 Corinthians 1–9.

4. This leaves a number of volumes and part-volumes of transcribed sermons still missing: Genesis 20:8–21:32 and 22:14–25:11, 1 Kings 1-c. 18,[30] further Psalms, Isaiah 1–12, Jeremiah 1:1–14:18 and 19–52, Lamentations 1:6–5:22, Ezekiel 16–22, Hosea, Joel, Amos, Zephaniah, Obadiah, Jonah,[31] Acts 8–28, 1 Corinthians 12–16, 2 Corinthians, and 1 and 2 Thessalonians. There is also evidence that further sermons on the church festivals were transcribed but have since been lost.[32]

In 1561, after Raguenier's death, Calvin preached on Judges before moving on to 1 and 2 Samuel.[33] There is no evidence that the sermons on the Judges were transcribed. It is most likely that Raguenier's replacement was not in place until the sermons on 1 Samuel.

The varied fate of the Genesis sermons illustrates the complexity of the situation. Raguenier's catalog mentions two complete volumes on Genesis, comprising 123 sermons. These volumes have been lost, but partial copies survive elsewhere, containing the ninety-seven sermons on 1:1–20:7. In addition, selected sermons on chapters 14:13–15:7, 21:33–22:14, and 25:12–27:38 were published in the sixteenth century, yielding another sixteen sermons. We thus have today 113 sermons, while Raguenier's two volumes contained 123. We lack sermons on 20:8–21:32 and 22:14–25:11 and these four and a half chapters could not possibly have been covered by ten sermons. So in addition to the two completed volumes, Raguenier must have prepared a number of further sermons prior to his death or incapacity; but how many? Subsequent catalogs of the sermons mention only the

---

28. Passages from Psalms 46, 48, 65, 80, 89, 147–49.

29. Sermons on passages from Matthew 26–28 and Acts 2.

30. CO 21:48 has Beza's catalogue of unpublished OT sermons (taken from his 1564 first Life of Calvin), which includes sermons "Sur le premier livre des Rois." Note 6 adds "In prioris regum 18 capita circiter," this addition coming from Beza's 1575 Latin *Iohannis Calvini Vita* found at the beginning of his edition of Calvin's letters (4a). CO 21 omits this catalogue from Beza's 1575 *Vita*, hence the footnote on CO 21:48. Beza would have had access to the transcript in the library but his note suggests that he did not take the time to check.

31. Only six sermons on Jonah were transcribed, Raguenier missing the rest because of ill health. The sermons on Nahum were were not transcribed for the same reason.

32. Parker, *Calvin's Preaching*, 160–62.

33. According to Colladon (CO 21:91). He makes no mention of Ruth, but maybe we are meant to understand "Judges and Ruth."

two volumes of Genesis sermons,[34] so maybe the extra sermons covered 25:12–27:38 and these manuscripts were destroyed once they had been printed. That would mean that 20:8–25:11 must have been contained in Raguenier's second volume, which means Calvin would have covered these five chapters in twenty-six sermons.[35] That is a very reasonable average number of sermons per chapter.[36]

Raguenier transcribed 2,042 sermons and a further 262 were transcribed after his death, yielding a total of 2,304.[37] Of these 1,547 survive as transcripts or were published by 1604.[38] This yields a total of 757 transcribed sermons still missing. These figures may not be 100 percent correct, but they give a reliable idea of the proportion of sermons that have been lost, i.e. about a third. Two observations may be made about the missing sermons. First, some may be sitting in a library awaiting discovery. In 1995, Max Engammare discovered 243 sermons covering Isaiah 23:15–66:24 in the library of the French Protestant Church in London. Most of these were already known, but eighty-seven were previously missing.[39] Second, with the exception of 1 Kings 1-c. 18 and Ezekiel 21–22, all of the missing material relates to passages for which we have Calvin's commentaries or lectures. There are no profound insights into Calvin's exegesis awaiting in the missing material. It would be a different matter if there were missing sermons from, say, Proverbs, Ecclesiastes, Song of Solomon, or Revelation. Sermons on Judges, Ruth, and 1 Kings to Esther would also fill gaps but would be less informative.

There are three surprising omissions in the list of books on which Calvin preached: John, Romans, and Hebrews, books Calvin regarded as of prime importance. It is inconceivable that he did not preach on these and the likelihood is that because of their importance, he preached on them first, thus before his sermons began to be transcribed.[40] We do, of course, have his commentaries on these books.

PREPARATION AND DELIVERY OF SERMONS

Calvin preached extempore and did not write his sermons down before or after preaching them. This does not mean that he did not prepare them. "God has

---

34. Parker, *Calvin's Preaching*, 157, 159.

35. Raguenier's 123 sermons minus the ninety-seven sermons on 1:1–20:7.

36. Max Engammare notes in SC 11/1:XXI that Calvin averages five sermons per chapter of Genesis.

37. W. Moehn, "Sermons" in *The Calvin Handbook,* ed. Herman J. Selderhuis (Grand Rapids: Eerdmans, 2009), 175.

38. J. Leith, "Calvin's Doctrine of the Proclamation of the Word and Its Significance for Today" in *John Calvin and the Church*, ed. T. George (Louisville: Westminster John Knox, 1990), 207, gives the figure of 1,460, to which must be added the eighty-seven discovered by Max Engammare, as described below.

39. Max Engammare, "Calvin Incognito in London: The Rediscovery in London of Sermons on Isaiah," *Proceedings of the Huguenot Society* 26 (1996): 453–62.

40. McKee, "Calvin's Sermons: Suspected, Unique and Prized," 89–92.

promised that his blessing shall be upon the hands of those who work. . . . If I should climb into the pulpit without deigning to glance at a book, and frivolously imagine to myself, 'Oh well, when I preach God will give me enough to say,' and come here without troubling to read, or thinking what I ought to declare, and do not carefully consider how I must apply Holy Scripture to the edification of the people, then I should be an arrogant upstart and God would put me to shame for my audacity!"[41]

Calvin sees this attitude as analogous to the way in which the people of Israel tested God at Massah (Deut 6:16) and the way in which Satan tempted Jesus to test God (Matt 4:7). His preparation consisted primarily in his wide reading and learning. It is unlikely he would have been able to devote more than an hour to preparing for a specific sermon.[42] He generally took into the pulpit a Hebrew Old Testament (the 1534–35 edition of Sebastian Münster's *Biblia Hebraica*) or a Greek New Testament and gave his own translation on the spot.[43] Max Engammare has shown how Calvin would make a mistake in his translation one day, not having prepared adequately. For the next few days he prepared rigorously and then with time he prepared less until eventually he made another mistake. And the cycle started all over again.[44] It is reassuring to learn that Calvin was human like the rest of us!

Calvin stressed that the preacher's life should accord with their sermons: "If we were like angels in the pulpit, but then led a licentious life and people detected in our life nothing but contempt for God, that we were mockers and prophane people, what would that communicate? Would this not cause God's name to be despised?"[45]

In his "last will and testament" Calvin declared concerning his sermons that "I have endeavoured, according to the measure of grace that [God] has given me, both in my sermons and in my writings, to teach his word purely and faithfully interpret Holy Scripture."[46]

---

41. Sermon 49 on Deuteronomy 6:15–19. CO 26:473–74. ET 292. (For details of the ET of sermons and *Institutes*, see the bibliography. With older translations I have sometimes modernised the translation.) This is cited, with two different translations, by T. H. L. Parker, *The Oracles of God: An Introduction to the Preaching of John Calvin* (London: Lutterworth, 1947), 69; and Parker, *Calvin's Preaching*, 81.

42. This was true of his lectures on the Old Testament, as Colladon notes in his *Vie de Calvin* (CO 21:109). For more evidence, see M. Engammare, "Calvin connaissait-il la Bible?," *Bulletin de la Société de l'Histoire du Protestantisme Français* 141, no. 8 (1995): 165. It is said of C. H. Spurgeon, one of the greatest of preachers, that he prepared his Sunday evening sermon on Sunday afternoon (L. A. Drummond, "The Secrets of Spurgeon's Preaching," *Christian History* 29 [1991]: 16), but that was on top of many hours of study each week.

43. Parker, *Calvin's Preaching*, 172–78; SC 11/1:XLIV-XLV.

44. M. Engammare, "Joannes Calvinus trium linguarum peritus? La question de l'hébreu," *Bibliothèque d'Humanisme et Renaissance* 58 (1996): 58.

45. Sermon 51 on 1 Tim 6:4 (CO 53:614; ET 615; cited by Moehn, "Sermons," 178).

46. CO 20:299. CTS 1:lxxxvi.

Beza, in his first *Life of Calvin* compared Calvin's preaching with that of Farel and Viret: "Farel excelled in a certain sublimity of mind, so that nobody could either hear his thunders without trembling, or listen to his most fervent prayers without feeling almost as it were carried up into heaven. Viret possessed such winning eloquence, that his entranced audience hung upon his lips. Calvin never spoke without filling the mind of the hearer with most weighty sentiments. I have often thought that a preacher compounded of the three would have been absolutely perfect."[47]

THEOLOGY OF PREACHING

It will come as no surprise to learn that Calvin regarded the Bible as the Word of God and that all preaching is to be based on this norm: "No other word is to be held as the Word of God, and given place as such in the church, than what is contained first in the Law and the Prophets, then in the writings of the apostles; and the only authorized way of teaching in the church is by the prescription and standard of his Word."[48]

The *Second Helvetic Confession*, written by Bullinger (1566), famously states that "the preaching of the Word of God *is* the Word of God."[49] Calvin never states this so succinctly, but he would not have disagreed with Bullinger. In his commentary on Exodus 14:31, he states that we must not reject the outward preaching of Word but those who faithfully deliver God's commands should be heeded as if God openly descended from heaven to speak to us, citing Matthew 10:40. This assumes that the preacher is preaching God's Word and does not mean that we should heed the pope.[50] In the Genevan Catechism (Q. 307), children are taught that they should hear pastors when they preach and to listen with fear and reverence to the doctrine of Christ that they preach.[51]

There is a parallel here between preaching and the sacraments.[52] The sacrament is a "visible Word," just as preaching is the preached Word. In both, Christ is set before us and offered to us in the gospel. With both, faith is required to lay hold of what is offered. There is not parity between the two, however, as it

47. CO 21:132; CTS 1:xxxix.

48. J. T. McNeill and F. L. Battles, eds., *Calvin: Institutes of the Christian Religion*. (Hereafter as *Inst.*) *Library of Christian Classics* (London: SCM; Philadelphia: Westminster), 4:8:8.

49. Chapter 1 (A. C. Cochrane, ed., *Reformed Confessions of the Sixteenth Century* [Louisville: Westminster John Knox, 2003], 225), my emphasis.

50. CO 24:156.

51. OS 2:130; CTS 2:83.

52. Rightly noted by Dawn DeVries, "Calvin's Preaching" in *The Cambridge Companion to John Calvin*, ed. Donald K. McKim (Cambridge: CUP, 2004), 108–10.

is wrong to celebrate the sacraments without explanatory preaching, but it is all right to preach without celebrating a sacrament.[53]

Calvin did not devote a chapter of the *Institutes* to preaching but mentions it a number of times in that work. Its importance is made clear by his criteria for where a church of God is to be found: "wherever we see the Word of God purely preached *and heard*, and the sacraments administered according to Christ's institution."[54] God chooses to speak to us not directly, not through angels, but through human beings. This "is a singular privilege that he deigns to consecrate to himself the mouths and tongues of men in order that his voice may resound in them."[55]

Why does he do this? First, it is a test of our obedience, that we are willing to submit ourselves to the teaching of others. We show our piety and obedience by being teachable "when a puny man, risen from the dust, speaks in God's name." Those who consider preaching superfluous "are led either by pride, dislike, or rivalry to the conviction that they can profit enough from private reading and meditation." Second, this is a concession to our weakness, in that God addresses us in a human way, rather than thunder at us from heaven and scare us away.[56] Third, God's use of human ministers to bestow his gifts on the church fosters mutual love and binds the church together in one body.[57] Calvin cites two examples from Acts to illustrate the necessity for this human ministry. When God wanted to lead Cornelius to an understanding of the gospel, he did not do so by an angel but rather used the angel to tell him to send for Peter (Acts 10:1–33). Paul likewise was blessed with an appearance of the risen Christ, but had to wait for Ananias to come to him to teach him and baptize him (Acts 9:1–19). If even the apostle Paul had to learn from such human ministry, how can we despise it or regard it as superfluous?[58]

The "Cathedral" at Ulm in southern Germany has a distinctive baroque canopy above the pulpit. In this canopy there is a miniature pulpit, indicating the role of the invisible preacher, the Holy Spirit. The symbolism is clear: unless the divine Preacher is at work in the hearts of the congregation, the words of the human preacher will be ineffective. Calvin believed this very strongly. By nature, we are all blind and the Word of God "cannot penetrate into our minds unless the Spirit, as the inner teacher, through his illumination makes entry for it."[59]

---

53. For the foregoing, see *Inst.* 4:14:1–6.
54. *Inst.* 4:1:9 (my emphasis), repeated more briefly in 4:1:10.
55. *Inst.* 4:1:5.
56. *Inst.* 4:1:5; 4:3:1.
57. *Inst.* 4:3:1–2.
58. *Inst.* 4:3:3.
59. *Inst.* 3:2:34. Similarly, *Inst.* 2:2:20; 3:24:8.

Indeed, external preaching is ineffective and pointless without the teaching office of the Spirit. God teaches us outwardly through preaching and inwardly by the Spirit.[60] There is a twofold hearing: outwardly of the voice of the preacher, which is "nothing but a sound that vanishes in the air;" inwardly of the voice of the Spirit, who makes the Word bear fruit.[61]

METHODOLOGY OF PREACHING

Calvin's principles for preaching can be considered under four headings: biblical, theological, applied, and pastoral.[62]

Biblical Principles

The most obvious feature of Calvin's preaching is that it is biblical. He preached continuously through whole books of the Bible and his preaching is closely tied to the text. As with his other teaching, he follows the principle of interpreting Scripture in the light of Scripture. Article 20 of the 39 Articles of the Church of England states that the Church may not "so expound one place of Scripture, that it be repugnant to another." In his preaching, Calvin always aimed to avoid this error.

In the Dedicatory Epistle of his first commentary, on Romans, Calvin set out the principles of interpretation that he shared with Simon Grynaeus.[63] The first was lucid brevity, and it was to this end that he dealt with theological issues in his *Institutes*, obviating the need for long discussions in his commentaries.[64] The goal of lucidity remains in the sermons, but preaching calls for a more discursive style, for lengthier discussion of points so as to communicate them to a congregation. The second principle was that it is almost the interpreter's only task to unfold the mind of the author.

This principle applies as well to the sermons. In his Ephesians sermons, for example, Calvin refers repeatedly to Paul's intentions, to the reason *why* he expresses himself in a certain way, given the circumstances that he faced.[65]

---

60. Comm. John 14:26. Similarly, Comm. Ezek 2:2; *Summa Doctrinae de Ministerio Verbi et Sacramentorum* art. 5 (CO 9:774–75).

61. *Sermons on Election and Reprobation,* 63–64; cited by Leith, "Calvin's Doctrine of the Proclamation of the Word and Its Significance for Today," 227.

62. P. Adam, "'Preaching of a Lively Kind'—Calvin's Engaged Expository Preaching" in *Engaging with Calvin: Aspects of the Reformer's Legacy for Today,* ed. M. D. Thompson (Nottingham: Apollos, 2009), 13–41, describes Calvin's preaching as engaged with the congregation, with God, with the Bible, with theology and with training. All but the last of these are covered here.

63. CO 10b:402–403; COR 2/13:3.

64. See below.

65. R. C. Zachman, "Expounding Scripture and Applying It to Our Use: Calvin's Sermons on Ephesians"

So, for example, in seeking to explain Paul's wording in Ephesians 6:12, Calvin notes that "if we pay attention to St Paul's intention this question will be easily resolved."[66] This "psychological" interpretation, focusing not just on what was said but why it was said, is a mark of Calvin's exegesis, in his commentaries as well as his sermons.[67] This concern extended not just to Paul's intention, but also to God's. "If we consider well the doctrine contained in [Paul's letters] we can easily judge that God wanted to be heard in what is said here, until the end of the world."[68]

Calvin's emphasis on the author's intention meant that Calvin was no lover of allegory.[69] Paul used the word in Galatians 4:24, but Calvin tells the Genevans that "Paul did not wish to deny the literal meaning of Scripture."[70]

Theological Principles

Calvin's interpretation of Scripture was always in the context of his theology as a whole. In his *Letter to the Reader* at the beginning of the 1539 edition of his *Institutes*, Calvin explains how it should be used. It is intended as an introduction and guide to the study of Scripture and to complement his commentaries. Because of the *Institutes*, Calvin need not digress at length on doctrinal matters in his commentaries.[71] The *Institutes* and the commentaries are designed to be used together—the *Institutes* to provide a theological undergirding for the commentaries, and the latter to provide a more solid exegesis of the passages cited in the former. Likewise, the sermons should always be read in the light of the *Institutes*. "The sermons clarify and apply the theology of the *Institutes* to human experience as understood apart from the *Institutes*, and the *Institutes* are illuminated by the sermons."[72]

Applied Principles

The story is told of the novice assistant minister who, having preached his first sermon, tentatively asked the minister, "What about my sermon? Will it do?" "Do what?" was the withering response. Calvin was not vulnerable to that

---

in his *John Calvin as Teacher, Pastor, and Theologian* (Grand Rapids: Baker, 2006), 164–66. In his Ephesians commentary Calvin refers to Paul's mind and his intention, in the sermons only to his intention.

66. Sermon 46 on Eph 6:12 (CO 51:823; ET 663); cited by Zachman, "Expounding Scripture and Applying It to Our Use," 164.

67. This was a point made strongly by the late David Wright in his discussion of Calvin's commentaries on the Old Testament prophets.

68. Sermon 1 on Eph 1:1–3 (CO 51:245; ET 7).

69. *Inst.* 1:5:19: "Allegories ought not to go beyond the limits set by the rule of Scripture, let alone suffice as the foundation for any doctrines."

70. Sermon 29 on Gal 4:22 (CO 50:636; ET 433). See also his nuanced discussion in Comm. Gal 4:22.

71. OS 3:6; ET 4–5.

72. Leith, "Calvin's Doctrine of the Proclamation of the Word and Its Significance for Today," 218–19.

criticism. His sermons were always relevant and applied to his congregation. In preaching, Scripture should be "truly expounded and applied rightly to our use."[73] This involves applying the message, not just in general terms, but to the specific context as Calvin spells out in a sermon on Acts:

> Let us respect this application of the teaching and use it correctly so that this word may have its full and complete effect and so that we may present it seriously, mindful of how we do so. Many people would like me to preach with my eyes closed, not considering where I live, or in what locale, or in what time. As if those whose responsibility it is to proclaim God's message did not proceed the way it was done in the time of the apostles—as if the prophets did not apply the law of Moses to their day and time, and as if the apostles did not follow the same practice! And as if we were not to honour God's command through Paul to apply that teaching as we observe the offences, the dissolution, the vice, and the disruption among us![74]

In his sermons Calvin does not merely teach but exhorts, warns, stimulates, and rebukes, not just in general terms but specifically.[75] He appeals to the mind, the emotions, the memory, the will, and the actions of the people.[76] Paul in 1 Timothy 6:13 refers to both teaching and exhortation. To preach faithfully is not just to present doctrine on a take-it-or-leave-it basis. A sound understanding is needed, but the preacher also needs passion and vehemence so that the teaching may touch people's hearts and move them action. Rhetoric can move hearts to some extent, but zeal is needed alongside it to make preaching effective.[77]

Pastoral Principles

Calvin firmly believed that the Bible was the Word of God, but he also held that in the Bible, God's communication with his people is accommodated to such factors as human frailty, human sinfulness, and the barbarity of primitive ages.[78] Calvin's preaching was likewise accommodated to his audience. Conrad

---

73. Sermon 25 on Eph 4:11–12 (CO 51:555; ET 363); cited by Zachman, "Expounding Scripture and Applying It to Our Use," 161, 163.

74. Sermon 24 on Acts 6:1–6 (SC 8:212; ET 327); cited by Moehn, "Sermons," 179.

75. Zachman, "Expounding Scripture and Applying It to Our Use," 162.

76. Adam, "Preaching of a Lively Kind," 19–20.

77. Sermon 34 on 1 Tim 4:12–13 (CO 53:416; ET 418–19).

78. See, e.g., J. Balserak, *Divinity Compromised: A Study of Divine Accommodation in the Thought of John Calvin* (Dordrecht: Springer, 2006); A. Huijgen, *Divine Accommodation in John Calvin's Theology: Analysis and Assessment* (Göttingen: Vandenhoeck & Ruprecht, 2011). D. Wright, "Accommodation and Barbarity in John Calvin's Old Testament Commentaries," in *Understanding Poets and Prophets*, ed. A. G. Auld (Sheffield: Sheffield Academic, 1993), 416–24, shows how Calvin takes this to the point of describing some Old Testament laws, given by God, as "barbaric."

Badius, who published Calvin's sermons on the Ten Commandments, noted Calvin's hesitation about the wider dissemination of simple and unadorned sermons that he had preached as an accommodation to the roughness of the people, without pomp or polished layout.[79] His style was simple and clear, didactic, lively, polemical, serious, and solid.[80] Rightly handling the Word of Truth (2 Tim 2:15) means "giving such lessons as the hearers are able to bear."[81] Although Calvin was immensely learned, he "never intrudes his learning into his sermons. . . . His learning is so well hidden that one might hear him preach for a month without suspecting that he had read any book other than the Bible . . . The learning is present in his exegesis and interpretation, but he keeps the skeleton well clothed."[82] He assumes of his hearers no more than a knowledge of the French language, the Apostles' Creed, and the Bible.[83]

CONTRIBUTIONS TO PREACHING

Geneva attracted Reformed refugees and pilgrims from all over Western Europe. Many of these were to return to their native lands, where they sought to reform the church in line with what they had seen in Geneva. Doubtless, Calvin's model of preaching would have made its mark on such people. The published volumes of the reformer's preaching would also have influenced many.[84]

Sermon Excerpt

Sermon 32 on Galatians 5:4–6[85]

Now, to conclude, we must seek to live as God has commanded in his Word, and not occupy ourselves with the pomp, splendour and ceremonies that hypocrites love. We are to walk honestly in purity of life, with all equity and straightforwardness, as I have said. But we are to recognise that when we have done all this, it cannot justify us or obtain God's grace for us. Whilst it is true that he is pleased to accept the desire that we have to honour him, he still only accepts us through the Lord Jesus Christ,

---

79. CO 25:597–98.
80. Leith, "Calvin's Doctrine of the Proclamation of the Word and Its Significance for Today," 220–22.
81. Sermon 12 on 2 Tim 2:14–15 (ET 805); cited by Adam, "Preaching of a Lively Kind," 17.
82. Parker, *The Oracles of God*, 75.
83. Zachman, "Expounding Scripture and Applying It to Our Use," 153–56.
84. For Calvin's influence on English preaching, see Parker, *The Oracles of God*, 108–27.
85. ET 488.

as we have explained before. It is here that we are to place our trust for salvation. Thus, even when we have walked in love, and sought to carry out our duty, we must realise that because of our weakness, we cannot approach the standard that God has shown us. We aim to do so, but we need God to look upon us mercifully. Thus, we need not doubt that he is pleased with our works, if they are dedicated to him through the blood of the Lord Jesus Christ, who is the true priest who presents our offerings and makes them acceptable to God. We need our Lord Jesus to intercede, to make our works pleasing to God the Father. Even when we pray or sing praise to him, it would all be dung to him if not purified by the Lord Jesus Christ. Indeed, the apostle says that it is by him that we offer to God the sacrifice of our lips, that is the sacrifice of praise by which he is glorified.

Now let us fall down before the majesty of our great God, acknowledging our sins, and praying that he would help us to be more conscious of them. May we truly be convicted by them so that we are brought to a true repentance and seek in the Lord Jesus Christ all that we need. May we be so humbled that we are totally cast down and get rid of all false presumption which we may wrongly have. May our only desire be to be received by the mercy of our God and reach the eternal inheritance. May we so strive to walk according to his commandments, that he will be pleased to support us in our weakness until the day that we are altogether free of it. Thus, we all say, Almighty God and our heavenly Father. ◆

BIBLIOGRAPHY

Primary Sources

Barth, P., Wilhelm Niesel, and Dora Scheuner, eds. *Johannis Calvini Opera Selecta.* [OS] 1st–3rd ed. Munich: Kaiser, 1926–68.

Baum, G., E. Cunitz, and E. Reuss, eds. *Ioannis Calvini Opera Quae Supersunt Omnia.* [CO] Braunschweig: Schwetschke, 1863–1900.

Calvin, Jean. *Ioannis Calvini Opera Omnia: denuo recognita et adnotatione, critica instructa, notisque illustrata.* [COR] Edited by Helmut Feld, T. H. L. Parker, A. N. S. Lane, Erik Alexander de Boer, F. P. van Stam, and Brian G. Armstrong. Geneva: Droz, 1992 on.

_____. *Supplementa Calviniana: Sermons inédits.* [SC] Neukirchen-Vluyn: Neukirchener Verlag, 1936 on.

English Translations

Calvin, John. *Selected Works of John Calvin: Tracts and Letters.* [CTS] Edited by Henry Beveridge and Jules Bonet. Calvin Translation Society edition. Reprint. Grand Rapids: Baker, 1983.

_____. *Sermons on Deuteronomy.* 1583. Repr., Edinburgh: Banner of Truth, 1987

_____. *Sermons on Election & Reprobation.* Rev. ed. Willowstreet, PA: Old Paths, 1996.

_____. *Sermons on the Acts of the Apostles, Chapters 1–7*. Trans. by Rob Roy McGregor. Edinburgh: Banner of Truth, 2008.

_____. *Sermons on the Epistle to the Ephesians*. Rev. ed. Edinburgh: Banner of Truth, 1973.

_____. *Sermons on the Epistles to Timothy & Titus*. Repr., Edinburgh: Banner of Truth, 1983.

_____. *Sermons on Galatians*. Trans. by Kathy Childress. Edinburgh: Banner of Truth, 1997.

McNeill, J. T., and F. L. Battles, eds. *Calvin: Institutes of the Christian Religion*. Vols 20–21 of *Library of Christian Classics*. London: SCM; Philadelphia: Westminster, 1960.

Secondary Sources

Adam, Peter. "'Preaching of a Lively Kind'—Calvin's Engaged Expository Preaching." Pages 13–41 in *Engaging with Calvin: Aspects of the Reformer's Legacy for Today*. Edited by Mark D. Thompson. Nottingham: Apollos, 2009.

Balserak, Jon. *Divinity Compromised: A Study of Divine Accommodation in the Thought of John Calvin*. Dordrecht: Springer, 2006.

Boer, Erik A. de. *The Genevan School of the Prophets: The Congrégations of the Company of Pastors and Their Influence in 16th Century Europe*. Geneva: Droz, 2012.

Cochrane, Arthur C., ed. *Reformed Confessions of the Sixteenth Century*. Louisville: Westminster John Knox, 2003.

DeVries, Dawn. "Calvin's Preaching." Pages 106–24 in *The Cambridge Companion to John Calvin*. Edited by Donald K. McKim. Cambridge: CUP, 2004.

Drummond, Lewis A. "The Secrets of Spurgeon's Preaching," *Christian History* 29 (1991): 14–16.

Engammare, Max. "Calvin connaissait-il la Bible?" *Bulletin de la Société de l'Histoire du Protestantisme Français* 141 (1995): 163–84.

_____. "Calvin Incognito in London: The Rediscovery in London of Sermons on Isaiah." *Proceedings of the Huguenot Society* 26 (1996): 453–62.

_____. "Joannes Calvinus trium linguarum peritus? La question de l'hébreu." *Bibliothèque d'Humanisme et Renaissance* 58 (1996): 35–60.

Gordon, Bruce. *Calvin*. New Haven: Yale University Press, 2009.

Huijgen, Arnold. *Divine Accommodation in John Calvin's Theology: Analysis and Assessment*. Göttingen: Vandenhoeck & Ruprecht, 2011.

Leith, John. "Calvin's Doctrine of the Proclamation of the Word and Its Significance for Today." Pages 206–29 in *John Calvin and the Church*. Edited by Timothy George. Louisville: Westminster John Knox, 1990.

McKee, Elsie A. "Calvin's Sermons: Suspected, Unique and Prized." Pages 85–110 in *Calvin Studies XII*. Edited by Michael D. Bush. Due West, SC: Erskine Seminary, 2006.

Moehn, Wim. "Sermons." Pages 173–81 in *The Calvin Handbook*. Edited by Herman J. Selderhuis. Grand Rapids: Eerdmans, 2009.

Parker, T. H. L. *The Oracles of God: An Introduction to the Preaching of John Calvin*. London: Lutterworth, 1947.

_____. *Calvin's Preaching*. Rev. ed. Edinburgh: T&T Clark, 1992.

Peter, R., and J.-F. Gilmont. *Bibliotheca Calviniana. Les oeuvres de Jean Calvin publiées au XVI siècle*. 3 vols. Geneva: Droz, 1991–2000.

Wright, David. "Accommodation and Barbarity in John Calvin's Old Testament Commentaries." Pages 413–27 in *Understanding Poets and Prophets*. Edited by A. G. Auld. Sheffield: Sheffield Academic, 1993.

Zachman, Randall C. "Expounding Scripture and Applying It to Our Use: Calvin's Sermons on Ephesians." Pages 147–72 in his *John Calvin as Teacher, Pastor, and Theologian*. Grand Rapids: Baker, 2006.

PART Four

Preaching among the Puritans

The Reformation gave birth to a unique period of preaching in England from 1550 to 1700. The Elizabethan Settlement (1559) brought back Protestantism to England and there was a growing desire to reform the Church of England from some of its ecclesiastical baggage. So a group of English preachers refused to conform to the structure, liturgy, and hierarchy of the Anglican Church.

Committed to *sola scriptura* as the church's rule of faith and Reformed doctrine to inform all matters of life, a new era of preaching history began. Many of these English Reformers came out of Cambridge University and promoted a plain style of preaching to proclaim the truths of Scripture both to the educated and uneducated alike.

English royalty and the leaders of the Anglican Church opposed these nonconformist preachers, giving them the pejorative label "puritans." Eventually, tensions between the Puritans and English authorities led to a civil war and the brief establishment of the Puritan Commonwealth under the military leadership of Oliver Cromwell (in 1649). Yet most Puritans did not want to be revolutionaries, and the English throne was soon restored. The Puritans failed to reform the Church of England, and after the Act of Uniformity (1662), around two thousand clergymen were expelled from the state Church. Some separatist Puritan leaders, like John Cotton, fled to New England to establish a "New Jerusalem" where the Bible dictated every norm of culture. Puritanism become a way of life. They believed the Bible gave the proper ethic for family, work, culture, and church. For the Puritans, there was no sacred/secular divide.

Puritan preachers were principled men of God. They were concerned that the elect of God live holy lives. Their sermons emphasized doctrine to inform the conscience so the believer would have an informed spirituality. Biblical preaching was as strong as in any other era of church history, and the sermon became central in corporate worship. Pulpits were placed front and center in sanctuaries, and Puritan pastors removed any remaining vestiges of sacerdotalism and sacramentalism from their churches.

Puritan preaching was marked by a simple style over rhetorical eloquence. Certain doctrines dominated their sermons: predestination, Divine Providence, God's covenant, sanctification, and the person and work of Jesus Christ. Most Puritan preaching was heavy on doctrinal instruction and application, maintaining an important balance between the propositional and the personal. The Puritan preacher was to be God's prophet to his people, an under-shepherd of Christ to his church, and a physician of souls.

Although the Puritans were similar in doctrine and shared a nonconformist view of the church, their personalities and ministries were vastly different. **William Perkins** (1558–1602) is considered the father of Puritanism. He promoted an expositional method of preaching and communicated this model via his book *The Art of Prophesying,* which became a significant influence in the preaching of many. **Richard Baxter** (1615–1691) was a model for pastoral ministry who committed to personally discipling his entire congregation on a yearly basis. **John Owen** (1616–1683) became the chief theologian of the Puritans and was eventually Vice-Chancellor of the University of Oxford. **John Bunyan** (1628–1688), perhaps best known as the author of *Pilgrim's Progress,* wrote this book and preached faithfully—even while in prison. He ended up in prison for preaching without license, but continued to preach from the window of his prison cell. **Matthew Henry** (1662–1714) is best known for his expositional commentary on the Bible, and yet he was a committed textual preacher whose exposition encouraged and influenced generations of preachers to come. This brief yet important subculture of biblical proclamation has made the Puritan era one of the most significant in preaching history.

William Perkins
Prince of Puritan Preaching

DWAYNE MILIONI

William Perkins (1558–1602) has been titled the Prince of Puritan Theologians and the Principle Architect of Elizabethan Puritanism. His primary motivation in ministry was to instruct God's people with God's Word. Rather than opposing church authorities, he found a balance in relating to the established Church of England while promoting English Puritanism. This Reformer was devoted to the inerrant Scriptures and combined this with a deep, Calvinistic piety that urged Christians to pursue a vital religion. Perkins was a voluminous writer and gifted lecturer at Cambridge. As pastor of Great St. Andrews Church, his pious temperament allowed him to preach to both the great and small. His method of "plain preaching" allowed him to proclaim the life-transforming Scriptures to the common person. His book on preaching, *The Art of Prophesying*, became *sine qua non* for English pastors with lasting influence to the present day.

HISTORICAL BACKGROUND

In 1558, William Perkins was born of Thomas and Anna Perkins in rural Warwickshire England. His parents were of humble means, but put together enough money to send William to Christ's College, Cambridge. He entered as a pensioner, a middle socioeconomic rank.[1] Perkins was a wild youth given to drunkenness and astrology.[2] He would eventually experience shame for his sordid reputation, and under the conviction of the Holy Spirit, he repented from his sinful lifestyle and committed himself to Christianity.[3]

While Perkins attended Christ's College, the study of rhetoric was primary, having surpassed dialectic and natural philosophy, only later to be replaced with

---

1. W. B. Patterson, *William Perkins and the Making of a Protestant England* (Oxford: Oxford University Press, 2014), 3, 41. I am indebted to Patterson's biography on Perkins and to one of my students, Jeremy Roden, for his research on Perkins compiled for his MA thesis paper.

2. David Larsen, *The Company of Preachers: A History of Biblical Preaching from the Old Testament to the Modern Era* (Grand Rapids: Kregel, 1998), 206.

3. Thomas Fuller, *The Holy State* (Cambridge: Williams, 1642), 89.

the natural sciences. Perkins received a classical education aimed at formulating logical, coherent, and persuasive arguments.[4] He was invited to be a teaching fellow after graduating with a BA in 1581 and a MA in 1584. As a fellow, he would inspire men such as Richard Sibbes, a colleague at Cambridge and fellow puritan.[5]

Perkins had to resign his teaching post in 1595 because of his marriage to Timothye Cradocke.[6] He would continue to lecture and write, eventually leading him to become the most widely known English theologian of the late sixteenth and early seventeenth centuries.[7] While some of his thoughts varied from the teaching of the Church of England, much of his work supported the English crown and Church. His works greatly influenced the Elizabethan Puritan movement and its offshoot in North America's New England.[8]

The influences on William Perkins are numerous, but most are within the Reformed tradition. He was significantly helped by the theology and writings of John Calvin and his successors in the Swiss Reformed tradition.[9] The Reformed influence on Perkins also came from his tutors at Cambridge—Laurence Chaderton, Edward Dering, and Thomas Cartwright.[10] Under the instruction of these tutors, Perkins studied the works of Augustine and Erasmus. He was also influenced by the writings of Matthias Flacius Illyricus, Niels Hemmingsen, Johan Wigandus, and Andreas Gerardus of Yypres. Peter Ramus, a leading rhetorician of the day, would also play a significant role in the development of Perkins's preaching ministry.[11]

While a fellow at Cambridge, Perkins served as pastor of Great St. Andrew's Church, which is directly across the street from the college. He also served in a prison ministry at Cambridge Castle.[12] He actively taught and preached at Great St. Andrews until his death.[13]

William Perkins was a prolific writer. Patterson considers him a "many-sided theologian," some books having heavy theological content, while others were pastoral in nature.[14] Perkins is considered the "father of Puritanism," mainly due to

---

4. Patterson, *William Perkins*, 120.
5. Hughes Oliphant Old, *The Reading and Preaching of the Scriptures in the Worship of the Christian Church, Vol. 4: The Age of the Reformation* (Grand Rapids: Eerdmans, 2002), 270.
6. Patterson, *William Perkins*, 41.
7. Ibid.
8. Patterson, *William Perkins*, 40.
9. Ibid., 4.
10. Ibid.
11. As a reminder, Ramist philosophy sought to reorganize logic and rhetoric. Ramus wanted to liberate logic from the formal confines that bound it through the Middle Ages.
12. Patterson, *William Perkins*, 4.
13. Ibid., 41.
14. Ibid., 46.

his writings promoting the Reformed faith in England.[15] Though his writings are often associated with the Elizabethan Puritan movement, he was as much of an apologist for the Church of England as he was a defender of Puritanism.[16]

Perkins wrote over forty books, about half published after his death. One of the most important theological works was also his first—*A Golden Chain*, first printed in 1591.[17] This text deals with the theological implications of predestination and the covenant grace of salvation. Perkins tried to maintain a balance within Reformed experiential theology, keeping himself from falling into fatalism on one side and works-oriented salvation on the other.[18] For Perkins, salvation was not merely a formal decree of God that predestines a person to faith, but Divine election is always "in Christ," making Christ the heart and center of predestination.[19] In this book, Perkins also gave instruction for the Christian on the moral law found in the Ten Commandments to show what godliness and holiness should look like.[20] This work set a standard for English Calvinism and became a practical guide for English doctrine and preaching, allowing Perkins to promote gospel-centered sermons so congregations would know Christ and be conformed to his righteousness.[21]

Perkins wrote *A Discourse of Conscience* in 1596. This text provides the nature, properties, and differences of conscience to show how a person can keep a good conscience.[22] He argued if a person wants a good conscience, then one should seek "above all things to labor and obtain it: for it is not given by nature to any man, but comes by grace."[23] He came to understand the soul contained both the faculties of understanding and will. Understanding serves to rule and order a person's life. The will determines a person's choices and is associated with emotions. Discerning whether an action is good or evil involves both understanding and will.[24] The law revealed in the Scriptures helps to inform the conscience so the Christian can pursue righteousness. For the one whose conscience

---

15. See Joel Beeke and Mark Jones, *A Puritan Theology: Doctrine for Life* (Grand Rapids: Reformation Heritage, 2012), 117.

16. See Patterson, *William Perkins*, 46. See also page 51 where Patterson notes Perkins would only consider separating from the Church of England if either its worship or doctrine became corrupt in substance.

17. See Patterson, *William Perkins*, 69. This was originally published in Latin as *Armilla aurea* by the University Press in Cambridge, 1590. The English version was translated by Perkin's student, Robert Hill. The full title is *A Golden Chaine: or The Description of Theologie, Containing the Order of the Causes of Saluation and Damnation, According to God's Word.*

18. Beeke and Jones, *A Puritan Theology*, 119.

19. Ibid., 122.

20. Patterson, *William Perkins*, 74.

21. Ibid., 69

22. William Perkins, *A Discourse of Conscience: Wherein Is Set Down the Nature, Properties, and Differences Thereof* (Cambridge: John Legate Printer, 1596), 1.

23. Ibid., 157.

24. Ibid.

is burdened down with sin, Perkins advocates seeking prayer and counsel from a pastor, who serves as a Protestant form of private confessionary.[25] Eventually Perkins's teaching on the conscience and the moral demands of the Scriptures became unpopular in the established church of England, though popular among his readers.[26] His theology of the conscience would influence his sermonic form, since he believed the application of proper doctrine in a sermon would be used by the Holy Spirit to mold and build the conscience of his listeners.

Perkins wrote *A Reformed Catholike* in 1597, comparing the doctrines of the Church of Rome to the Church of England.[27] He argued for the Reformed faith by challenging Catholic dogma. For example, he shows how the Roman Catholic view of justification has two parts, not one. The first is an action by God pardoning the sinner. The second is the work of people to do good deeds and become more righteous.[28] Perkins promotes the teaching of Calvin, that every saint has the capacity to express faith through an understanding of the Scriptures.[29]

Perkins wrote numerous Bible studies. Two of his most famous are a textual-thematic analysis on the Lord's Prayer and the Apostles' Creed. In sum, Perkins became the most prolific and influential theologian of his day. His aim was to "win the ignorant, the superstitious, the uninformed, and those whose faith was still half-Roman Catholic to a religious faith that would transform and renew them from within."[30]

Perkins died of a kidney stone in 1602 at the age of 44. His service as a lecturer, pastor, and author was brief. He left behind his wife, three children, and a fourth who was born after his passing. Perkins's works would be gathered into a single, large collection called *Opera Theologica.*

THEOLOGY OF PREACHING

The Reformation in Great Britain was sporadic due to the changes between Catholic and Protestant monarchs. Henry VIII broke England away from the Roman Catholic Church in 1534. Edward VI briefly continued England's reforms, but Mary I (r. 1553–1558) would convert the country back to Catholicism, though only for five years. Elizabeth I (reigning 1558–1603) would forever entrench Protestantism in England. While much of her early reign was marked by Catholic activists, England would fully align itself under Elizabeth's reign after several

---

25. Patterson, *William Perkins,* 100.
26. Ibid., 114.
27. Ibid., 52.
28. William Perkins, *A Reformed Catholike* (Cambridge: John Legate Printer, 1597), 62–66.
29. Ibid., 271.
30. Patterson, *William Perkins,* 62.

political victories and the failure of the Spanish Armada to defeat the English navy in 1588.[31]

Elizabethan England experienced massive population growth and along with it came low wages due to the increase of the work force. Around one in four households suffered from poverty while Perkins served as pastor.[32] As the gap between the rich and poor widened, Perkins confronted the problem by preaching on social justice. Believing the sanctified life required dealing with difficult moral and cultural issues, he would end up writing more extensively on social issues than any of his English contemporaries.[33] Like Martin Luther, Perkins exalted vocation as a means for the common worker to express the *imago dei* and experience the grace of God through employment. Perkins believed caring for the needs of the poor was a primary responsibility of the church.[34]

Polemical theology was prevalent between hostile Protestants and Catholics when Elizabeth began her monarchy up through Perkin's preaching ministry.[35] The polemical term "Puritan" became used to connote those who wished to rid the Church of England from all the relics and vestiges of Roman Catholicism.[36] Eventually, a growing group of English Protestants would separate from the established Church and pursue an unadulterated Reformed model for church life and practice. The hostile theological environment between Roman Catholics, Anglicans, and Puritans in Britain and Ireland would result in half a century of civil war.[37]

Near the beginning of Elizabeth's reign, there was a shortage of educated clergy. Trained pastors used the *Elizabethan Prayer Book of 1559* to help with sermon preparation. For those not properly educated, the *Book of Homilies* was used to cover basic Christian doctrines in their preaching. The shortage of educated preachers in the mid to late 1500s resulted in preaching or "prophesying" events to provide a means of equipping clergy to preach. Preachers would gather to discuss sermon form, content, and relevance. The clergy would take turns delivering sermons and would receive critique on form and content.[38] These meetings helped sharpen the homiletical skills of ministers, though Queen Elizabeth eventually would see these meetings as potentially subversive and in 1576, ordered them to stop.

---

31. Ibid., 1–2.
32. Ibid., 136.
33. Ibid, 156.
34. Ibid., 149. See also Christopher Hill's chapter, "William Perkins and the Poor" in *Puritanism and Revolution: Studies in Interpretation of the English Revolution of the 17th Century* (London: Secker & Warburg, 1958), 215–38.
35. Ibid., 7.
36. Ibid., 16.
37. Ibid., 30.
38. Ibid., 118.

William Perkins, playing off the name of these meetings, wrote *The Art of Prophesying* to offer a homiletical education similar to the one that the clergy were receiving in these meetings. This influential book was first published in Latin in 1592 and translated into English after Perkins's death.[39] This was the first significant homiletical manual to be written in England by an Englishman. This hermeneutics and homiletics manual filled a void in the education of pastors at Cambridge as well. The classic educational system at Cambridge was concerned more about rhetoric and structuring arguments than about making scriptural arguments and applying biblical truth. Perkins's goal in *The Art of Prophesying* was to argue the substance of preaching must be found in the substance of the Scriptures. The truths of God's Word must be applied to the audience in a way that fits the needs of the congregation, using language accessible to ordinary people and delivering complicated doctrines in plain speech. Perkins saw the modern preacher standing in succession with the prophets and apostles who were committed to expounding God's Word and prayerfully ministering to God's people.[40]

Perkins carried his Reformed doctrine into the pulpit. The sole authority of Scripture was paramount in his preaching, believing the sermon is simply "to set forth the Word of God."[41] Beeke notes, "Perkins' goal was to help preachers realize their responsibility as God's instruments to reveal and realize election and the covenant. Biblically balanced preaching was paramount, for the Word preached is the power of God unto salvation."[42] For Perkins, preaching was the instrument God used to draw the elect to salvation and allure the soul to Christ (Rom 10:14).

Perkins did not dismiss his rhetorical training as a preacher; he simply built upon it. He adapted rhetoric for the purposes of textual preaching. The "plain style" that represents Perkins's preaching relies heavily on Ramist logic. Donald McKim, a noted Ramus and Perkins scholar states, "When put to use for preaching, the Ramist framework became for Perkins a springboard for exhortation and action. Perkins the preacher could appeal to the minds, wills, and emotions of a congregation. He provided the theoretical framework by which the preacher could impart information as well as instruct and correct the lives of the hearers."[43]

The use of "plain speech" in preaching became germane in England. Patterson notes, "In place of the rich, complex, Latinate, and metaphorical prose of many Elizabethan and early Stuart writers, English prose came to be marked by

---

39. William Perkins, *The Art of Prophesying*, 1606, repr. (Edinburgh: The Banner of Truth Trust, 2011), xi.
40. Ibid.
41. Old, *The Reading and Preaching of the Scriptures*, 263.
42. Beeke and Jones, *A Puritan Theology*, 129.
43. Donald K. McKim, "The Functions of Ramism in William Perkins' Theology," *Sixteenth Century Journal* 16, no. 1 (March 1, 1985): 511–12.

other qualities. Brevity, clarity, and concreteness came to be highly regarded."[44] The plain style of Puritan preaching did not mean sermons should be without wit, imagination, or eloquence, but should not be designed to impress the audience with rhetorical grandeur. The purpose of the sermon was to expose scriptural truth to a congregation to effect change in conscience and volition. Perkins's preaching would emphasize a concern for the common person who struggles to understand and practice the Christian faith.[45] The sermon should show an audience how to use theological and moral principles to overcome human problems and experiences. The use of plain style helped William Perkins hold a fruitful, pastoral tenure at Great St. Andrew's Church. He provided the congregation with a purposeful diet of topical and textual thematic sermons that moved through many books of the Bible.

METHODOLOGY FOR PREACHING

Perkins places preaching within rightly-ordered worship, which contains four components: preaching the Word of God, giving alms to the poor, properly administering the sacraments, and conducting public prayers.[46] He modeled his preaching style after the prophets in the Bible, including Moses, Isaiah, John the Baptist, and Paul. He believed unfolding and applying the text of Scripture in a straightforward and simple, yet vigorous and direct style of speech and manner was at the center of biblical preaching.[47] This led Perkins to model a "plain style" of biblical preaching by taking Bible doctrine and making it accessible to his congregation. At times, his preaching style would put him at odds with the traditional style of preaching found in the Church of England, but it quickly became a model for nonconformists.[48]

The gravity and responsibility of reliable preaching is clear in Perkins's preface to *The Art of Prophesying*. He wrote, "The preparation of sermons is an everyday task in the church, but it is still a tremendous responsibility and by no means easy. In fact it is doubtful if there is a more difficult challenge in the theological disciplines than that of homiletics. Its subject matter is prophecy, which is the 'higher gift,' indeed, whether we think about its dignity or its usefulness."[49] Perkins believed preaching had twofold value: gathering the elect for instruction and driving away wolves from the fold. He saw preaching (prophesying) as

---

44. Patterson, *William Perkins,* 132.
45. Ibid., 5.
46. Ibid., 57.
47. Ibid.
48. Ibid., 114.
49. Perkins, *The Art of Prophesying,* 3.

"a solemn public utterance by the prophet, related to the worship of God and the salvation of our neighbours."[50]

In *The Art of Prophesying*, Perkins provides one of the clearest models of expositional preaching in all Christian history. He summarizes his simple method as follows:

1. Reading the text clearly from the canonical Scriptures.

2. Explaining the meaning of it, once it has been read, in the light of the Scriptures themselves.

3. Gathering a few profitable points of doctrine from the natural sense of the passage.

4. If the preacher is suitably gifted, applying the doctrines thus explained to the life and practice of the congregation in straightforward, plain speech.

The heart of the matter is this: Preach one Christ, by Christ, to the praise of Christ. Soli Deo Gloria.[51]

These four steps of sermon development and delivery will be briefly discussed.

Read the Text Directly from the Canon

Perkins believed the canonical Bible to be the Word of God and it should read to the people of God whenever they gather for worship. The scriptures alone are worthy to be proclaimed because they are perfect, pure and eternal (Psa 19).[52] The perfection of Scripture consists of its sufficiency and completeness. Nothing is be added or taken away from its perfection. The purity of Scripture entails its inerrancy and truthfulness.[53] The eternality of Scripture consists in the promise of Jesus that nothing will pass away from it until all its commands have been accomplished. (Matt 5:18)[54] The Bible has also been given to reveal God's wisdom.[55] This wisdom can penetrate the spirit of a person and bind the conscience. Therefore, the preacher should read the entire text the sermon is based upon from the canonical Bible. The rest of the sermon should then reflect upon the text and have its points stem directly from it.

Give the Sense and Understanding of the Text by Scripture Itself

For Perkins, "faith does not exist apart from the Word. It alone is the rule or object of faith; not the judgment of mere men, even the holiest men."[56] So the

---

50. Ibid., 5.
51. Ibid., 75.
52. Ibid., 9.
53. Ibid., 10. Perkins uses the phrase "without either deceit of error."
54. Ibid.
55. Perkins, *The Art of Prophesying*, 9.
56. Ibid., 19.

preacher must understand and interpret the Bible correctly. Perkins writes, "Interpretation is the opening up of the words and statements of Scripture in order to bring out its single, full and natural sense."[57] By contrast, the allegorical method used by Roman Catholics should be avoided.[58] He believed the Holy Spirit to be the principal interpreter of Scripture and there to be "three subordinate means to help when interpreting a passage: the analogy of faith, the circumstances of the particular passage, and comparisons with other passages."[59]

Sermon preparation begins with careful, private study. Perkins advises the preacher to, "fix clearly in your mind and memory the sum and substance of biblical doctrine, with its definitions, divisions and explanations."[60] The preacher should analyze the text using "grammatical, rhetorical, and logical analysis, and the relevant ancillary studies."[61] To understand the literal sense, Perkins urges the preacher to summarize the Scripture, understand the circumstances of the passage, and compare these passages with similar passages. Help when interpreting can be found among orthodox Christian writers of old and contemporary commentators so the preacher will have "both old and new material at hand."[62] Most importantly, Perkins advises preachers to "earnestly seek God in prayer to open blind eyes to the meaning of Scriptures" (Psa 119:18).[63]

Collect a Few Profitable Points of Doctrine from the Natural Sense

Preaching should build up the body of Christ. Once the text has been properly interpreted and explained, "Now we come to consider the right 'cutting' or 'dividing' of it. Right cutting is the way in which the Word is enabled to edify the people of God." (2 Tim 2:15).[64] For Perkins, the skill of pulling out the doctrine contained in the text involves resolution and application. He states, "Resolution is the unfolding of the passage into its various doctrines, like the untwisting and loosening of a weaver's web."[65]

Biblical doctrines found in the text are either overtly stated or must be drawn from the text by way of implication.[66] Perkins encourages that all doctrine taken from the text through proper interpretation should be believed based on

---

57. Ibid., 25.
58. Ibid. Perkins states, "This pattern of the fourfold meaning of Scripture must be rejected and destroyed. Scripture has only sense, the literal one."
59. Ibid.
60. Perkins, *The Art of Prophesying*, 22.
61. Ibid.
62. Ibid., 23.
63. Ibid., 24.
64. Perkins, *The Art of Prophesying*, 46.
65. Ibid.
66. Ibid., 47.

Scripture's own authority and should be declared in the sermon.[67] If a doctrine is clearly found in other Scriptures, these should be mentioned in the sermon too. However, the use of scriptural cross-references should be limited. As for quoting other sources when preaching, Perkins advises, "We should not rest our faith on human testimonies, either from the philosophers, or the Fathers."[68] Quoting secular authors should be done sparingly.

Perkins distinguishes doctrinal preaching from the prevailing allegorical method of his day. He warns the preacher against developing doctrine using allegories, but allows for analogies and some allegories to be utilized based on four caveats:

1. They should be used sparingly and soberly.
2. They must not be far-fetched, but appropriate to the matter at hand.
3. They must be mentioned briefly.
4. They should be used for practical instruction and not to prove a point of doctrine.[69]

Once the resolution of doctrine has been achieved, the dogma of text is to be applied to hearts of the hearers.

Apply the Doctrine Rightly Collected to the Life and Manners of People in Plain Speech

Perkins's homiletical method progressively builds upon itself as the sermon is developed and delivered. First the text is read. Then it is explained in its natural sense. Then its universal truths (doctrine) are revealed. Finally, these truths are to be applied to the lives and lifestyles of the hearers. Perkins defines application as, "the skill by which the doctrine which has been properly drawn from Scripture is handled in ways which are appropriate to the circumstances of the place and time and to the people in the congregation."[70]

Like many reformers, Perkins emphasized a distinction between the law and the gospel. The Law points to the "disease of sin, and as a side-effect stimulates and stirs it up."[71] The gospel teaches the actions that should be taken in light of the disease through the power of the Holy Spirit.[72] Perkins recommends the preacher begin with the law and move to the gospel.

---

67. Ibid., 50.
68. Ibid., 51.
69. Perkins, *The Art of Prophesying*, 50.
70. Ibid., 52.
71. Ibid.
72. Ibid.

Sermon application is driven by the audience. Perkins encourages audience analysis and identifies six types of audience members when considering application. First are the unbelievers who are ignorant and cannot be taught. Their hearts must be prepared to receive God's Word. Second are unbelievers who are ignorant but teachable. Perkins recommends instruction via catechism for these.[73] Third are unbelievers who have some knowledge of Scripture, but have never been humbled. They need to seek repentance and godly sorrow.[74] Fourth are unbelievers who have some knowledge and have been humbled. The extent of their humility should be examined to determine their level of repentance.[75] Fifth are committed believers. They need proper teaching of both law and gospel.[76] Sixth are believers who have fallen back and have partly departed from the state of grace either in faith or lifestyle. They need to be taught specific doctrines that will bring them to confession and repentance. Perkins writes, "Do they hate sin as sin? That is the foundation of the repentance which brings salvation. Then, secondly we must ask whether they have or feel in their heart a desire to be reconciled with God."[77] Finally, Perkins warns the preacher to expect the congregation to be composed of a mixture of all these types.[78]

Perkins believes there are two types of application to be sought after when preaching. First is mental application, which is concerned with the mind and involves doctrinal teaching and reproof. He says, "When [application] involved doctrine, biblical teaching is used to inform the mind to enable it to come to a right judgment about what is to be believed. Reproof is using biblical teaching in order to recover the mind from error."[79] He recommends the preacher only reprove the errors which are currently troubling the church.

The second is practical application, which concerns lifestyle and behavior. For this Perkins recommends instruction and correction, "Instruction is the application of doctrine to enable us to live well in the context of the family, the state and the church. It involves both encouragement and exhortation."[80] He then adds, "Correction is the application of doctrine in a way that transforms lives marked by ungodliness and unrighteousness. This involves admonition."[81] With these in mind, the preacher can apply the doctrines gleaned from the text to the life and manners of the audience.

---

73. Perkins, *The Art of Prophesying*, 54.
74. Ibid., 55.
75. Ibid., 56.
76. Ibid., 57.
77. Ibid., 58.
78. Perkins, *The Art of Prophesying*, 60.
79. Ibid., 61.
80. Ibid., 62.
81. Ibid.

Perkins concludes his instruction on preaching with several, practical guidelines. The first is the use of memory. He discourages the use of pneumonic devices to aid in memory. He also discourages memorizing the sermon word for word. Instead, he commends an extemporaneous approach, "It is more helpful if, when preparing for preaching, we carefully imprint on our mind—with the help of an axiomatical, syllogistical, or methodical way of thinking—the various proofs and application of the doctrines, the illustrations of the applications, and the order in which we plan to expound them."[82] Second, Perkins recommends the preacher to try to hide human wisdom and rhetorical skills. Rather, he should seek a demonstration or manifestation of the Holy Spirit when preaching. He says, "The 'demonstration of the Spirit' (1 Cor 2:4) becomes a reality when, in preaching, the minister of the Word conducts himself in such a way that everyone—even those who are ignorant of the gospel and are unbelievers—recognise that it is not so much the preacher who is speaking but the Spirit of God in him and by him."[83] He encourages both grace and holiness to be manifested in the verbal and nonverbal aspects of sermon delivery. Finally, preaching (prophesying) coincides with public prayers during worship. Perkins believed only the preacher should offer a public prayer and the congregation should indicate their agreement at the end of the prayer by saying, "Amen."[84] Perkins offers three elements of public prayer:

1. Carefully thinking about the appropriate content for prayer.

2. Setting the themes in an appropriate order.

3. Expressing the prayer so that it is made in public in a way that is edifying for the congregation.

He concludes his instruction on preaching with a reverent benediction, "To the Triune God be the glory!"[85]

CONTRIBUTIONS TO PREACHING

William Perkins was the most influential author of his day, publishing more works in the late sixteenth and early seventeenth centuries than any other English theologian.[86] His works were translated into French, Dutch, German, Welsh, Czech, Spanish, and Hungarian. In all, Perkins wrote forty-eight texts

---

82. Ibid., 66–67.

83. Ibid., 68. Perkins adds that the Holy Spirit's presence will express itself in both the preacher's speech and gestures. Also see page 72, although Perkins allows for gestures while preaching, he cautions their use to maintain a sense of "gravity" as a messenger of God.

84. Ibid., 73.

85. Ibid., 74.

86. Patterson, *William Perkins*, 63.

with twenty-one published during his lifetime. The remainder were published posthumously by friends and colleagues.

Both his significant book on preaching, *The Art of Prophesying* and the compiled *Works of William Perkins* helped shape the style of preaching in England after his death. As a rhetorician, expositor, theologian, and pastor, he became a principal architect of the Puritan movement. Beeke notes that by the time of William Perkins's death, his writings in England were outselling those of Calvin, Beza, and Bullinger combined.[87] Some have even classified him alongside Calvin and Beza as the third person in the trinity of the Reformed orthodox.[88] Both Perkin's theology and preaching methodology in *The Art of Prophesying* became a standard for textual preaching in the seventeenth and eighteenth centuries in Britain. This book may be the most significant work on preaching since Augustine's *On Christian Doctrine*. It continues to be read and utilized in homiletics courses in the present day.

Perkins did not lead a movement, but engaged the complex doctrinal and social issues of his era through writing and preaching, resulting in the continuing reform of the Protestant church. His lectures, sermons, and writings gave Cambridge international prominence.[89] His preaching ministry at Great St. Andrews Church became a model for renowned Puritan preachers like John Cotton, Thomas Goodwin, John Preston, and Richard Sibbes.[90] He was seen as a mentor to theologians and pastors, but his writings were primarily directed to the common people of England.

Sermon Excerpt
Commentary on Galatians 1:6[91]

The second point is the fault reproved, and that is, the revolt of the Galatians which was a departure from the calling whereby they were called to the grace of Christ. If it be demanded, what kind of revolt this was? I answer, there be two kinds of revolt, particular and general. Particular, when men profess the name of Christ, and yet depart from the

---

87. Joel Beeke, *Meet the Puritans: With a Guide to Modern Reprints* (Grand Rapids: Reformation Heritage, 2006), 473–74.

88. Beeke and Jones, *A Puritan Theology*, 130.

89. Ibid., 62.

90. Perkins, *The Art of Prophesying*, x.

91. This is taken from Perkin's Commentary on Galatians 1:6, "I marvel that you are so soon removed away to another gospel, from him that hath called you in the grace of Christ." Joel R. Beeke and Derek W. H. Thomas, *The Works of William Perkins*, vol. 2, ed. Paul M. Smalley (Grand Rapids: Reformation Heritage, 2015), 27–28.

faith, in some principal points thereof. Of this kind was the apostasy of the ten tribes, and such is the apostasy of the Roman Church. A general revolt is when men wholly forsake the faith and name of Christ. Thus do the Jews and Turks at this day. Again, a revolt is sometimes of weakness, and human frailty, and sometimes of obstinacy. Now the revolt of the Galatians was only particular in the point of justification, and of weakness, and not of obstinacy; and this Paul signifies when he says they were carried by others. ◆

BIBLIOGRAPHY

Alain, J. C. "William Perkins: Plain Preaching." *Preaching* 11, no. 5 (March 1, 1996): 42–45.

Beeke, Joel. *Meet the Puritans: With a Guide to Modern Reprints*. Grand Rapids: Reformation Heritage, 2006.

Beeke, Joel, and Mark Jones. *A Puritan Theology: Doctrine for Life*. Grand Rapids, Reformation Heritage, 2012.

Beeke, Joel, and Derek W. H. Thomas, *The Works of William Perkins*. Vol. 1. Grand Rapids: Reformation Heritage, 2014.

_____. *The Works of William Perkins*. Vol. 2. Edited by Paul M. Smalley. Grand Rapids: Reformation Heritage, 2015.

Blench, J. *Preaching in England in the Late 15th and 16th Centuries: A Study of English Sermons, 1450–c1600*. Oxford: Blackwell, 1964.

Breward, Ian. "Significance of William Perkins." *Journal of Religious History* 4, no. 2 (December 1, 1966): 113–28.

Broadus, John A. *Lectures on the History of Preaching*. Repr. Miami: HardPress, 2010.

Brown, John. *Puritan Preaching in England: A Study of Past and Present*. New York: Scribner's Sons, 1900.

Bruhn, Karen. "Pastoral Polemic: William Perkins, the Godly Evangelicals, and the Shaping of a Protestant Community in Early Modern England." *Anglican and Episcopal History* 72, no. 1 (March 1, 2003): 102–27.

Chandos, John. *In God's Name: Examples of Preaching in England from the Act of Supremacy to the Act of Uniformity, 1534–1662*. London: Hutchinson, 1971.

Clarke, M. L. *Classical Education in Britain, 1500–1900*. Cambridge: Cambridge University Press, 1959.

Dahlman, Jason E. "Opening a Box of Sweet Ointment: Homiletics within the Church of England, 1592–1678." PhD diss., Trinity International University, 2012.

Dargan, Edwin Charles. *A History of Preaching*. Vol. 2 of *From the Close of the Reformation Period to the End of the Nineteenth Century, 1572–1900*. 1905. Repr. Lexington: Forgotten Books, 2012.

Edwards Jr., O. C. *A History of Preaching*. Nashville: Abingdon Press, 2004.

Erasmus, Desiderius. "Copia: Foundations of the Abundant Style (De duplici copia verborum ac rerum commentarii duo)." *Collected Works of Erasmus*. Vol. 24. Edited by Craig R. Thompson. Toronto: University of Toronto Press, 1978.

Evans, G. R. *The University of Oxford: A New History*. London: Tauris, 2013.

Fuller, Thomas. *The Holy State*. Cambridge: Williams, 1642.

Gane, Erwin R. "The Exegetical Methods of Some Sixteenth-Century Puritan Preachers: Hooper, Cartwright, and Perkins, pt 1." *Andrews University Seminary Studies* 19, no. 1 (March 1, 1981): 21–36.

Hill, Christopher. *Puritanism and Revolution: Studies in the Interpretation of the English Revolution of the 17th Century*. London: Secker & Warburg, 1958.

Howard, Leon. *Essays on Puritans and Puritanism*. Edited by James Barbour and Thomas Quirk. Albuquerque: University of New Mexico Press, 1986.

Kendall, R. T. "Living the Christian Life: In the Teaching of William Perkins and His Followers." Paper presented at the annual meeting of the Westminster Conference, Huntingdon, England, 1974.

Larsen, David. *The Company of Preachers: A History of Biblical Preaching from the Old Testament to the Modern Era*. Grand Rapids: Kregel, 1998.

Mack, Peter. *A History of Renaissance Rhetoric 1380–1620*. New York: Oxford University Press, 2011.

Mahoney, John L. "The Classical Tradition in Eighteenth Century English Rhetorical Education." *History of Education Journal* 9, no. 4 (Summer 1958): 93–97.

McKim, Donald K. "The Functions of Ramism in William Perkins' Theology." *Sixteenth Century Journal* 16, no. 1 (March 1, 1985): 503–17.

————. "Ramism as an Exegetical Tool for English Puritanism as Used by William Perkins." *Society of Biblical Literature*, no. 23 (1984): 11–21.

Morgan, John. *Godly Learning: Puritan Attitudes towards Reason, Learning, and Education, 1560–1640*. Cambridge: Cambridge University Press, 1986.

Old, Hughes Oliphant. *The Age of the Reformation*. Vol. 4 of *The Reading and Preaching of the Scriptures in the Worship of the Christian Church*. Grand Rapids: Eerdmans, 2002.

Overton, John H., and Frederic Relton. *The English Church from the Accession of George I to the End of the Eighteenth Century*. London: Macmillan, 1906.

Packer, J. I. *Among God's Giants: The Puritan Vision of the Christian Life*. Eastbourne: Kingsway, 1991. (Published in USA under the title *A Quest for Godliness*. Wheaton, IL: Crossway, 1990).

Patterson, W. B. *William Perkins and the Making of a Protestant England*. Oxford: Oxford University Press, 2014.

Perkins, William. *A Discourse of Conscience: Wherein Is Set Down the Nature, Properties, and Differences Thereof*. Cambridge: John Legate Printer, 1596.

————. *A Reformed Catholike*. Cambridge: John Legate Printer, 1597.

————. *The Art of Prophesying*. 1606. Repr. Edinburgh: The Banner of Truth Trust, 2011.

Perkins, William, Thomas Pickering, Thomas Pierson, John Legate, and T. T. Waterman. *The Workes of that Famous and Worthy Minister of Christ in the Universittie of Cambridge, Mr. William Perkins*. Cambridge: Library of Congress, 1608–1609.

Pointer, Steven R. "Puritan Identity in the Late Elizabethan Church: William Perkins and a Powerful Exhortation to Repentance." *Fides Et Historia* 33, no. 2 (June 1, 2001): 65–71.

Porter, Stephen. *The London Charterhouse*. Stroud: Amberly, 2012.

Webber, F. R. *A History of Preaching*. Vols. 1–3. Milwaukee: Northwestern, 1952.

Wellcome Images/Wikimedia Commons

Richard Baxter
Preaching as a Dying Man to Dying People

SIMON VIBERT

Richard Baxter

At the heart of Richard Baxter's preaching was a desire to disciple his congregation unto spiritual maturity. It was this focus that pushed him to personally attend to the spiritual nourishment of each member of his flock. Baxter (1615–1691) was a godly Puritan pastor who prized the careful attention to the study, preaching, and application of Scripture, first to his own heart, and then to the people under his care.

HISTORICAL BACKGROUND

Richard Baxter is one of the best-known pastors among the Puritan divines, serving as the vicar of St. Mary's Kidderminster for two decades. He ministered from 1641 to 1660 with a five-year break during the English Civil War. He had several short spells away from the town of Kidderminster after disputes about his perceived hard and disciplinary pastoral style. In 1642, he went to stay with the Curate of Holy Trinity Coventry. He thought this would be brief, but ended up away from Kidderminster till after the war ended, only returning in 1647. During this time, he acted as chaplain to Oliver Cromwell's troops and spoke in support—although not uncritically—of the Parliamentarian cause.

Some of the literature points to him being a complex man with something to say about most subjects, and as noted, one of the more controversial aspects of his ministry was an expectation of church discipline, particularly around the Lord's Table. Certainly he was voluminous, with the four-volume *Practical Works of Richard Baxter* running to over four thousand pages of tightly packed prose. One illustration may be found in Volume 3, *The Special Duties of Husbands to their Wives and Wives Towards Their Husbands*, which includes such wisdom as choosing a good spouse, not marrying too hastily, remembering the commandments to mutual love, living with mutual affections, and overcoming weaknesses with love.[1] A thorough examination of all that Baxter has written would be an

---

1. See Richard Baxter, *The Practical Works of Richard Baxter, Vol. 3: A Christian Directory. Part II Christian Economics* (London: Virtue, 1838).

enormous task, but there is warmth and sincerity to be found through his doctrinal instructions.

Baxter was initially hesitant about making a living in Kidderminster, perhaps in part due to his ongoing poor health, but maybe more so because of his perception of the spiritual challenge which Kidderminster presented. About the people of Kidderminster he said, "[They were] an ignorant, rude and revelling people, for the most part . . . they had hardly ever had any lively serious preaching among them."[2] But, as we shall see, his investment in this town was to bear lasting fruit.

THE PASTOR

Baxter's pastoral practice was written up in his well-known book, *The Reformed Pastor*, published in 1656, which he based on Acts 20:28: "Keep watch over yourselves and all the flock of which the Holy Spirit has made you overseers. Be shepherds of the church of God, which he bought with his own blood." In this text, Baxter sought to model his own ministry on that of the apostle Paul.[3] Paul describes his ministry among the Ephesians in Acts 20:20: "You know that I have not hesitated to preach anything that would be helpful to you but have taught you publicly and from house to house." Thus, following the practice outlined by Paul, Baxter spent two days a week seeing families in their homes at a rate of seven or eight families per day. This allowed him to see his whole parish of about eight hundred families, one hour per household every year.

Baxter prized preaching very highly, but nevertheless expressed concern that too many pastors spent too much time in the study. In this vein, Baxter has much to teach the modern pastor. There is a danger that meaningful pastoral time with people is squeezed out of today's ministry, somewhere between the office, meetings, and administration. Baxter's house-to-house ministry presents quite a challenge to the modern pastor. However, it is also worth noting that these were not just social calls to drink tea and chat about the family. Rather, Baxter had a specific intention to get the families to recite the Westminster Shorter Catechism and then to answer questions he asked of them related to their understanding of Scripture and theology. He also looked for real signs of "affection" and encouraged them to pray out loud together.[4]

---

2. J. I. Packer, *Among God's Giants* (Eastbourne: Kingsway, 1991), 53. Published in USA under the title *A Quest for Godliness* (Wheaton, IL: Crossway, 1990).

3. As did other Puritan contemporaries and forbears. For example, Martin Bucer, *Concerning the True Care of Souls* (1538; repr., Carlisle, PA: Banner of Truth, 2009) speaks of the fivefold pastoral task of leading, restoring, assisting, reestablishing, and protecting God's flock.

4. Wallace Benn has spelled out how he put this into practice in the commuter town of Harold Wood. Aware of the difficulty of finding people in their homes and their reluctance to have unannounced visits,

As a Puritan, Baxter was faithful in his proclamation of the Word—focusing on the meaning and use in the original text. In addition to his preaching, he was actively engaged in personal catechesis of his congregation as he went house-to-house speaking to families.[5] He believed preaching to be "the most excellent means, because we speak to many at once," but preaching alone is insufficient to ensure that the Word has penetrated deeply into a person's heart and life.

> The first and greatest work of ministers of Christ is acquainting men with the God who made them; He is the source of their blessing. We should open up the treasures of His goodness for them and tell them of the glory that is in His presence, a glory that his chosen people shall enjoy. By showing men the certainty and excellence of the promised joy, and by making them aware of the perfect blessedness in the life to come in comparison with the vanities of the present life, we may direct their understanding and affections toward heaven. We shall bring them to the point of due contempt of this world and fasten their hearts on a more durable treasure. This is the work we should be busy with both night and day. For when we have affixed our hearts unfeigned on God and heaven, the major part of this ministry is accomplished. All the rest will follow naturally.[6]

The results of his extended ministry resulted in nearly the whole town of about two thousand people professing conversion. Baxter claimed when he arrived in the town he found the people to be "an ignorant, rude and revelling people." But toward the end of his ministry, he commented:

> The congregation was usually full, so that we were fain to build five galleries after my coming thither. (The Church would have held about a 1000 without galleries). Our private meetings were also full. On the Lord's Days there was no disorder to be seen in the streets, but you might hear a hundred families singing Psalms, and repeating Sermons, as you passed through the streets. In a word, when I came thither first, there was about one family in a street that worshipped God and called on his Name, and when I came away

---

Wallace Benn set up a series of Saturday "surgeries" and one evening per week, with the aim of seeing all members on the electoral role with the purpose of asking searching/catechical questions about congregation members' spiritual health. See *The Baxter Model: Guidelines for Pastoring Today* (Orthos 13, Blackpool, England: Fellowship of Word and Spirit, 2007). See also Leland Ryken and Todd Wilson, "Preaching with a Pastor's Heart: Richard Baxter, The Reformed Pastor," in *Preach the Word: Essays on Expository Preaching in Honor of R. Kent Hughes* (Wheaton, IL: Crossway, 2007).

5. This was not until the last four years of his time in Kidderminster, and he lamented not having done this earlier in his ministry.

6. Ryken and Wilson, *Preaching with a Pastor's Heart*, 108.

there were some streets where there was not past one family in the side of a street that did not so; and that did not by professing serious godliness, give us hopes of their sincerity. And those families that were the worst, being in inns and alehouses usually some persons in each house did seem to be religious … when I set upon personal conference and catechising them, there were very few families in all the town that refused to come … And few families went from there without some tears, or seemingly serious promises of a godly life.[7]

THEOLOGY OF PREACHING

Baxter had several periods of enforced absence from the congregation in Kidderminster. The longest was during the Civil War (1642–1647).[8] J. William Black argues that three convictions shaped the way he went about his ministry when he returned to the church in 1647:

1. the inability of the pulpit alone to bring about the conversion of the ungodly in post-civil war, rural England;
2. the lack of any real sense of discipline of the clergy and discipline for the church, bemoaning Parliament's lack of desire to implement the outcome of the Westminster Assembly; and
3. the proliferation of separatists and sectarians.[9]

The way in which Baxter sought to address those problems was through a combination of faithful pastoral ministry, which was carried out house-to-house and in applied biblical preaching. The teaching and application of the Word of God was, in his mind, powerful to amend lives and give substantial hope; however, he believed the way the land would be changed was through parish-level pastoral duties. Clearly, the substantial number of conversions and numerical growth were brought about by the sovereign work of the Holy Spirit bringing revival to the town of Kidderminster. But at the level of human observation, we see in Baxter a man committed to the rigorous preaching of God's Word, the catechising of his congregation, and an outworking of biblical principles for church order and family life. While there is no guarantee of such an immense response to such biblical faithfulness, modern pastors have much to learn from the diligent attention Baxter paid to his parochial duties.

---

7. Packer, *Among God's Giants*, 53f. Quoting Baxter, *Reliquiae Baxterianae*, 84ff.
8. His political allegiance to Cromwell caused no less controversy than his disciplinary approach to ecclesial life!
9. J. William Black, *Reformation Pastors* (Milton Keynes: Paternoster, 2004), 255.

J. I. Packer underlines this point in *The Redemption and Restoration of Man in the Thought of Richard Baxter,* arguing that Baxter identified himself as a Puritan in two key respects: through his general association with Calvinistic piety, manifesting itself in "strong pastoral concerns," and "with a conscientious nonconformity and, after 1662, non-subscription and with a programme whose permanent element was a demand for competent preaching and discipline in every parish."[10]

THE PREACHER

Baxter believed preaching to be a solemn duty, saying, "It is no small matter to stand up in the face of a congregation, and deliver a message of salvation or damnation, as from the living God, in the name of our Redeemer."[11] Baxter preached the glories of heaven and the terror of hell. The twin Puritan aims of preaching were to bring "light" and "heat." By this they mean illumination of the truth of the Bible alongside the warmth of gospel conviction. But light comes first and then heat. Without doctrinal truth the heart will never be warmed and changed.

Along with other Puritans, Baxter rejected rhetorical eloquence and appealed for plainness in preaching. If the sermon is hard to remember or difficult to follow, then, in Baxter's mind, the preacher was culpable. Aiming for retention and clarity is the key goal for the sermon. Ryrie makes the point that there was considerable concern among sixteenth-century preachers that sermons were to be constructed in such a way as to aid memorization, that they encouraged active listening from the congregation, and that they worked beyond the ear to affect the heart.[12] It should not be inferred from this that preaching is to be a dispassionate monologue. In a section on the need for vigor (sic) and fervency in preaching, Baxter says, "O sirs, how plainly, how closely, how earnestly should we deliver a message."[13] Like other Puritans of his time, Baxter believed the aim of the sermon was to move the affections through the plain preaching of God's Word, "May I speak pertinently, plainly, piercingly and somewhat properly, I have enough."[14] This efficacy of communication is the job of the preacher.

---

10. This is Packer's DPhil thesis, submitted to the University of Oxford in 1954, first published then, but this edition published as J. I. Packer, *The Redemption and Restoration of Man in the Thought of Richard Baxter,* rev. ed. (Carlisle, PA: Paternoster, 2003), 28.

11. See "Christian Economics" in Joel Beeke and M. Jones, *A Puritan Theology: Doctrine for Life* (Grand Rapids: Reformation Heritage, 2012), 684.

12. Alec Ryrie, *Being Protestant in Reformation England* (Oxford: Oxford University Press, 2013), 352–62.

13. Richard Baxter, *The Reformed Pastor* (Edinburgh: Banner of Truth, 1656, 1989), 147f.

14. Quoted in Packer, *Redemption and Restoration,* 163.

It is necessary for the congregation to ponder and digest what is preached, but alongside the preaching of the Word is the absolute necessity for the Spirit of God to drive the Word deep into the hearer's heart. Thus, the role of the Holy Spirit was an important aspect of Baxter's theological commitment to preaching. He wrote about the need to recognize "the Witness of the Indwelling Spirit."[15] The Spirit attests to the truth and evidences the authenticity of the Bible. Without the work of the Spirit, the plainness of the preaching will be to no avail: "Conscience and passion must be roused, for only rational passion will avail to unseat and dethrone irrational passion."[16] Elsewhere he said,

> I seldom come out of the pulpit, but my conscience smiteth me that I have been no more serious and fervent . . . it accuseth me not so much for want of human ornaments or elegance, nor for letting fall an unhandsome word but it asketh me, How . . . woulds't thou preach of heaven and hell, in such a careless, sleepy manner? Dost thou not weep over such a people, and should not thy tears interrupt thy words? . . . Truly, this is the peal that conscience doth ring in my ears, and yet my drowsy soul will not be awakened. Oh what a thing is a senseless, hardened heart! . . . I am even confounded to think what difference there is between my sickness-apprehensions, and my pulpit and discoursing apprehensions, of the life to come.[17]

The Self-Watch of the Preacher

Baxter appealed to the preacher first to take heed to himself or herself. How can one exercise oversight of others if first oversight has not taken place of oneself? The preacher should take heed that the sermon is not voided by the preacher's own failure to partake of the grace of God (c.f., 1 Tim 4:16). "God has never saved any man for being a preacher; but because he was justified [and] sanctified."[18]

To be qualified to preach a sermon, the preacher must be in a state of grace:

> Preach to yourselves the sermons which you study, before you preach them to others . . . When your minds are in a holy frame, your people are likely to partake of the fruits of it. Your prayers and praises, and doctrine will be sweet and heavenly to them. They will likely feel when you have been much with God: that which is most on your hearts is likely to be most in their ears . . .

---

15. Ibid., 167f.
16. Ibid.
17. Quoted in Packer, *Redemption and Restoration*, 174.
18. Baxter, *The Reformed Pastor*, 53f.

When I let my heart grow cold, my preaching is cold; and when it is confused, my preaching is confused; and so I can oft observe also in the best of my hearers, that when I have grown cold in preaching, they have grown cold, too.[19]

Baxter believed the state of the preacher's heart is important and detectable to the hearers. Any failure to personally comprehend the message and allow it to rest in the preacher's heart will result in preaching to no avail. Robert Murray McCheyne was clearly influenced by this train of thought when he warned W. C. Burns in a letter dated March 22, 1839, "Take heed to thyself. Your own soul is your first and greatest care." Similarly, "the greatest need of my people is my personal holiness." And "a holy minister is an awful weapon in the hand of God."[20]

On diligent self-watch of the pastor's spiritual life, Baxter continues: "O brethren, watch therefore over your own hearts: keep out lusts and passions, and worldly inclinations; keep up the life of faith, and love, and zeal: be much at home, and be much with God. Above all be much in secret prayer and meditation. Thence you must fetch the heavenly fire that must kindle your sacrifices: remember, you cannot decline and neglect your duty, to your own hurt alone; many will be losers by it as well as you. For your people's sake, then, look into your own hearts."[21]

Another reason for self-watch is to guard oneself from pride and error. Error in preaching is serious (for thereby dangerous schism is caused), but for Baxter the particular besetting sin is spiritual pride. When this overtakes the preacher, this develops into false teaching that subsequently damages the body of Christ: "Error and vanity insinuate slyly. Apostasies usually have small beginnings." Going on, he said, "Maintain your innocency and walk without offence."[22]

Baxter gives a similar warning in the sermon preached at the funeral of Henry Stubbs: "Preach to yourselves, first, before you preach to the people, and with greater zeal. O Lord, save thy church from worldly pastors, that study and learn the art of Christianity, and ministry; but never had the Christian, divine nature, nor the vital principle which must difference them and their services from the dead."[23]

As evidenced in his writing, Baxter believed preaching to be a serious business that required the preparation of the self as well as the preparation of the

---

19. Ibid., 61.

20. Robert Murray McCheyne, *The Life and Remains, Letters, Lectures and Poems* (New York: Robert Carter, 1874).

21. Baxter, *The Reformed Pastor*, 62.

22. Ibid., 65.

23. Richard Baxter, "A sermon preached at the Funeral of Henry Stubbs" (1678) in *The Practical Works of Richard Baxter*, Vol. 4, 970–78.

text. The sermon is not merely to inform the mind, but it is to change the life of the hearers. Hence Baxter believed that it was also crucial that the preacher was himself the first to benefit from the sermon.

Sermons made up of Doctrine and Use

The goal of preaching is to instruct the mind and to move the will. The heart is moved by the head. Sermons should be marked by gravity and plainness, thus aiding the congregation in remembering what is said, and refraining from exalting the preacher toward pride. On this he said, "Men are dull of understanding . . . they are slow to grasp divine truth, not merely through natural stupidity but because their wills are fundamentally antipathetic towards it."[24]

Below, we will illustrate the way in which Baxter follows the typical Puritan expository method (as outlined in the *Westminster Directory for the Public Worship of God*) by preaching "doctrine" and "use." According to this Puritan method, "doctrines" might be implicit or explicit in the text, or may be general propositions about God, the world, or humanity. The preacher's task was to make the evidence plain for the hearer to grasp. The Puritans understood "use" to be more than application, but was really further instruction, amplification, and teasing-out the implications of the doctrine for an understanding of *how* to live the Christian life—the practical corollaries of theoretical principles. Packer notes that, rather like many other Puritans, Baxter "wrote far more on the 'uses' of doctrines than on the doctrines themselves." We will see this illustrated in the two sermons which we shall examine in a moment.[25]

Prayer and Application

Like other Puritans, Baxter spent much of his sermon time in application. For certain, there was a tendency for the Puritan preacher to over-apply every tiny aspect of the passage, which feels somewhat laborious to modern ears. However, we might also infer a key difference between preaching and teaching. The Puritan methodology advocated that if a sermon is not earthed in contemporary illustration and applied to the detail of day-to-day life, Baxter and his contemporaries would not consider that a sermon had been preached at all. Accordingly, their goal was evidenced in his statement, "Take heed to your studies to screw the truth into men's minds and Christ into their affections."[26] This intention toward application can be seen in the Westminster Confession of Faith, which outlines six types of application: instruction, confutation (refutation of error),

---

24. Packer, *Redemption and Restoration*, 162.
25. Ibid., 40–41.
26. Baxter, *The Reformed Pastor*, 65.

exhortation, dehortation (i.e., condemning and mortifying sin), comfort, and trial (calls for self-examination). The *Directory for the Public Worship of God,* which was the pastoral rulebook of the day, says the following on the importance of application in the section "Of the Preaching of the Word":

> [The Preacher] is not to rest in general doctrine, although never so much cleared and confirmed, but to bring it home to special use, by application to his hearers: which albeit it prove a work of great difficulty to himself, requiring much prudence, zeal and meditation, and to the natural and corrupt man will be very unpleasant; yet he is to endeavour to perform it in such a manner, that his auditors may feel the word of God to be quick and powerful, and a discerner of the thoughts and intents of the heart; and that, if any unbeliever or ignorant person be present, he may have the secrets of his heart made manifest and give glory to God.[27]

Part of the work of application is prayer for the people to whom the sermon is going to be preached. If this is combined with the type of one-to-one family contact which exemplified much of Baxter's practice, then one feels that the Word would have come home with force and relevance when preached from Baxter's pulpit. He challenged pastors saying, "What a tragedy it is, then, to hear a minister expand doctrines and yet let them die in his people's hands for the lack of a relevant and living application."[28] Thus, prayer is the means whereby the words of application truly hit home to the heart. "Prayer must carry our work as well as preaching; he preacheth not heartily to his people, that prayeth not earnestly for them. If we prevail not with God to give them faith and repentance, we shall never prevail with them to believe and repent."[29]

Baxter believed preaching to be a deeply spiritual work. The careful preparation of the sermon could only truly be effectual in the life of the believer if the preaching ministry was accompanied by "prevailing prayer."

METHODOLOGY FOR PREACHING

What follows is an analysis of Richard Baxter's preaching methodology, accomplished through a review of his farewell sermon. Short of being able to hear the man, *Baxter's Practical Works* give us the clearest insight as to how he preached.

---

27. *Westminster Confession of Faith* (Glasgow: Free Presbyterian Publications, 1994), 380.
28. Baxter, *The Reformed Pastor,* 69.
29. Ibid., 67.

As a result of the enforcing of "The Act of Confirming and Restoring of Ministers," Baxter was ejected from Kidderminster in the autumn of 1660 by the bishop of Worcester. The bishop made it very clear that, as far as he was concerned, Baxter would neither return to the parish nor preach within his diocese, not even with the lesser title of lecturer. Such was the hostility toward him that he was not even allowed to return and preach this sermon, as he had hoped, before his departure. He comments at the start of *Baxter's Practical Works*, that he thought he had thrown this sermon out with "the rubbish of my old papers" and that much of his "farewell to the world" is now written up in *My Dying Thoughts*. However, in 1683, this farewell sermon (based on John 16:22) was finally published.[30]

> I remembered the benefit I often received upon your prayers; and craving the continuance of them, till you hear of my dissolution, therewith I send this, as my special farewell to yourselves, whom I am bound to remember with more than ordinary love and thankfulness, while I am Richard Baxter.[31]

This sermon is marked by a sense of urgency:

> How earnestly do we now wish that we had done much more; that I had preached more fervently, and you had heard more diligently, and we had all obeyed God more strictly, and done more for the souls of the ignorant, careless, hardened sinners that were among us![32]

As he considers the impending separation from his flock, he is aware he has much more to say to them and eager for them to take heed to what he has already preached. He describes the goal of his preaching, "We have preached, taught and warned, that we might present you perfect in Christ Jesus" (Col 1:28). He looks back and laments his cold and lifeless sermons, and regrets the neglect of the duty of private instruction of families.

Approaching death, he affirms the certainty of joy, which comes from Christ, who emphasizes that their present state is one of sorrow, but that their future state will be one of joy. From his text, John 16:22, six doctrinal positions follow in his explanation. These doctrinal positions highlight how doctrine and use were interwoven in his preaching.

---

30. Prepared to have been preached at Kidderminster. See *The Practical Works of Richard Baxter*, 1013–27.
31. Ibid., 1013.
32. Ibid., 1014.

Doctrine 1: Sorrow precedes joy (but not a sinful sorrow); so learn God's way of using sorrows.[33]

Baxter unpacks the details of the verse, asking questions of it. He engages in his exegetical task, providing the substance for the exposition. Having outlined the doctrine, he follows this with several investigative questions, such as: "Tell me, then, who it is that you suffer by?"; "Do you not see that carnal pleasure is far more dangerous than all your sorrows?"; "Would not you follow your saviour, and rather be conformed to him and to his saints, than to the wicked that have their portion in this life?" This section of the sermon includes anticipating objections which might naturally arise in the minds of the congregation and responding to them.

Doctrine 2: Christ's death and departure was the cause of their sorrow.

There are three parts to the doctrine: (a) that their dear Lord will be taken from them, causing great sorrow; (b) that the manner of his death will increase their sorrows; and (c) that their sorrow is so much greater because they have little foresight of his resurrection and return.[34]

In the section on the "use" of this doctrine, Baxter makes the pastorally astute point that Jesus encouraged his disciples to grieve his absence, thereby showing that grieving God's absence, and lamenting, is part of the Christian's experience.[35]

Doctrine 3: The sorrow of his followers is but short.

There are four principal reasons for this: life is short; God's displeasure is short; our trial is short; the power of those who afflict God's servants is short-lived.

The "use" in this passage is based on the implications for the Christian's thinking once they have grasped the necessity of Christ's death: your sufferings don't last longer than your sins; your sufferings don't last longer than necessary; your sufferings are shorter than what they really deserve; your sorrows are shorter than the sorrows of the ungodly; your sorrows are not as long as the joys which will follow; even now these sorrows are mixed with joy. The "uses" of this doctrine are designed to encourage Baxter's congregation to have a wise and godly perspective on their current difficulties and to realize the joys that soon will be ahead of them.

---

33. It should be noted that not all parts of the sermon are divided into "doctrine" and "use." Some, as in this first section, include rhetorical questions: "What kind of sorrow is it that goeth before our joy?" Answer: "There is a sorrow positively sinful which doeth, but should not, go before our joy" with a shorter section on "use." See *The Practical Works of Richard Baxter,* 1015. On other occasions he moves from "doctrine" to supporting "reason."

34. Ibid., 1018.

35. Ibid., 1019.

Doctrine 4: Christ will again visit his sorrowful disciples.

Jesus has conquered the greatest enemy; he remains in close relationship with his followers; he has not in the least stopped loving us; he has not revoked any of his promises; he has invested in his people and takes an interest in them. His departure was in his followers' interest, so he will surely return. Thus, the "use" here is that the Christian should live expecting that Christ will return; He will return even to those who seem forsaken; "learn then, how to behave yourselves in the absence of your Lord, till his return"; don't be content with his absence (don't learn to live without him); keep your love warm; don't look for contentment anywhere else; don't use his absence as an excuse for sin.[36]

Doctrine 5: When he returns, sorrow will turn to joy.

Lament will turn to joy; his church too (as a whole) will be restored; that joy will be great when Christ returns in all his glory. "It is Christ himself that is the object of their joy."[37] Baxter exhorts his hearers to ensure that Christ is the chief focus of their hearts and urges them to long for the glory ahead when joy will be complete.

Doctrine 6: This joy cannot be taken away by any person;
it will be impregnable.

We should fear no human being and no one can deprive us of joy because Christ is not here; he is risen; the grave is empty. Here we see that the "use" is based on the steadfastness of our joy. Neither we ourselves, the devil, nor any other person can take this joy away from us; a firm grasp of this will rejoice the soul: "I will therefore take my farewell of you, in advising and charging you as from God, that you be not deceived by a flattering world, nor dejected by a frowning world; but place your hopes on those joys which no man can take from you."[38] He closes his sermon by thanking God for the privilege of serving them, for their warmth and hospitality to him, and that they have responded to his teaching and warning.

His final exhortation summarizes his desire that the dear congregation of Kidderminster will keep looking to Christ as the true source of love, hope, patience, and joy:

> I need not lengthen my counsels further to you now, having been called by the will and providence of God to leave behind me a multitude of books, which may remember you of what you have heard, and acquaint the world

---

36. *The Practical Works of Richard Baxter*, 1022.
37. Ibid., 1024.
38. Ibid., 1025.

what doctrine I have taught you; and if longer studies shall teach me to retract and amend any failing, in the writings or practice of my unripe and less experienced age, as it will be to myself as pleasing as the cure of bodily disease, I hope it will not seem strange or ungrateful to you: though we must hold fast the truth which we have received, both you and I are much to be blamed, if we grow not in knowledge, both in matter, words and method: the Lord grant that also we may grow in faith, obedience, patience, in hope, love and desire to be with Christ.[39]

CONTRIBUTIONS TO PREACHING

We have summarized these two examples from Baxter's preaching because they give us a flavor of Baxter the preacher. In many respects they are typical of the Puritan preaching methodology. He speaks meaningfully of the way in which the sermon he preached has been applied to his own heart, and illustrates that with "I" comments. He shows how "doctrine" precedes "use" (the indicative before the imperative). He exemplifies the Puritan belief that the light of the gospel needs to be clearly seen before the heart is warmed by the truth.

Baxter shows the necessity of going deep into the text; at times one feels that he has near exhausted the text. But the sustained focus on the Bible, feeding solid food to the congregation, is noteworthy. This clearly necessitates time spent in study and preparation—not just of an individual sermon, but something of a curriculum of Bible education for the whole parish. His application is pastoral and pertinent, including practical assistance for living the Christian life in a hostile culture.

Ultimately, Baxter saw pastoral ministry as a ministry of the Word that was carried out faithfully and regularly in the pulpit, taking up the Puritan challenge also to apply it faithfully and thoroughly to the lives of his hearers. We surely need this task to be well done in churches worldwide! But he did not stop there. He saw the house-to-house ministry as an extension of that Word ministry, looking for evidences of the Word's work in the homes and lives of his two thousand parishioners, not least by asking them questions and responding to their needs, praying with them in homes and seeing the Word do its work in the entire household. The great preacher Charles Spurgeon comments: "Richard Baxter is the most forceful of writers. If you want to know the art of pleading, read him, especially his sermon on 'Making Light of It,' and his *Reformed Pastor*."[40]

---

39. *The Practical Works of Richard Baxter*, 1027.

40. Quoted in Edward Donnelly, "Richard Baxter—A Corrective for Reformed Preachers," *The Banner of Truth Magazine*, no. 166–7 (Jul-Aug 1977), in lieu of page numbers a PDF version of this article can be found here, http://www.puritansermons.com/pdf/baxter15.pdf.

Baxter's ministry is summarized well with the words of Edward Donnelly: "This then is Richard Baxter of Kidderminster. A preacher who laboured to make plain the truth of God, who spoke from a burning heart as he pleaded with his people to close with Christ. A pastor who knew his sheep by name, who spoke to them personally about the great concerns of their souls. He is not merely a historical curiosity, a fossil to be marvelled at, but a stimulus, a rebuke, an encouragement."[41]

Great changes occurred in Kidderminster within a decade after Baxter's arrival. George Whitefield makes observations in his diary in 1743, of his visit to Kidderminster, which seem to indicate that nothing less than a lasting work of the Spirit of God had gone on in Kidderminster during that time: "I was greatly refreshed to find what a sweet savour of good Mr. Baxter's doctrine, works and discipline remained unto this day."[42] Seriousness, fervency, self-watch, as well as doctrinally applied, prayerful, and penetrating preaching were the hallmarks of this great man's preaching. I dare say that if the Church of England could raise up more men of his ilk, the parishes of our land would be greatly blessed.

Baxter's own advice is summarized below, and borne out in his own approach to preaching, outlined in the example above. This serves as a fitting conclusion to our observations on the Puritan style of preaching exemplified in Baxter's preaching.

Sermon Excerpt

From Chapter XIX "Directions for Profitable Hearing God's Word Preached"[43]

Titus 3: Directions for Holy Resolutions and Affections in Hearing

THE *understanding* and *memory* are but the passage to the *Heart*, and the *Practice* is but the *expression* of the *Heart:* therefore how to work upon the *Heart* is the principal business.

---

41. Edward Donnelly, quoted in Wallace Benn, "Preaching with a Pastor's Heart: Richard Baxter's 'The Reformed Pastor,'" in *Preach the Word*, eds. Leland Ryken and Todd Wilson (Wheaton, IL: Crossway, 2007), 139.

42. Quoted in J. Belcher, *George Whitefield: A Biography* (New York: American Tract Society, 1857), 248–49.

43. Richard Baxter, *The Practical Works of Richard Baxter: Essays on his Genius, Works and Times in four volumes*, vol. 1 (London: Virtue, 1838), 475–76.

Directions:

1. Live under the most convincing lively serious Preacher that possibly you can.
2. Remember that Ministers are the Messengers of Christ, and come to you on his business and in his name. Hear them therefore as his officers, and as men that have more to do with God himself than with the speaker.
3. Remember that this God is instructing you and warning you and treating with you, about no less than the saving of your souls: Come therefore to hear as for your salvation.
4. Remember that you have but a little time to hear in; and you know not, whether ever you shall hear again: Hear therefore as if it were your last.
5. Remember that all these days and Sermons must be reviewed, and you must answer for all that you have heard.
6. Make it your work with diligence to apply the Word as you are hearing it, and to work your own hearts to those suitable resolutions and affections which it bespeaketh.
7. Chew the Cud, and call up all when you come home in secret, and by Meditation Preach it over to your selves.
8. Pray it over all to God and there lament a stupid heart, and put up your complaints to Heaven against it.
9. Go to Christ by faith for the quickenings of his spirit.
10. Make Conscience of Teaching and provoking others. ♦

BIBLIOGRAPHY

Baxter, Richard. *The Reformed Pastor*. Edinburgh: Banner of Truth, 1989.

_____. *The Practical Works of Richard Baxter. Essays on his Genius, Works and Times in Four Volumes.* London: Virtue, 1838.

Beeke, Joel, and M. Jones. *A Puritan Theology: Doctrine for Life*. Grand Rapids: Reformation Heritage, 2012.

Belcher, J. *George Whitefield: A Biography*. New York: American Tract Society, 1857.

Benn, Wallace. *The Baxter Model: Guidelines for Pastoring Today*. Orthos 13 series. Blackpool, England: Fellowship of Word and Spirit, 2007.

_____. "Preaching with a Pastor's Heart: Richard Baxter's 'The Reformed Pastor.'" Pages 127–39 in *Preach the Word: Essays on Expository Preaching: In honor of R. Kent Hughes*. Edited by Leland Ryken and Todd Wilson. Wheaton, IL: Crossway, 2007.

Black, J. William. *Reformation Pastors*. Milton Keynes: Paternoster, 2004.

Bucer, Martin. *Concerning the True Care of Souls*. 1538; repr., Carlisle: Banner of Truth, 2009.

Packer, J. I. *Among God's Giants: The Puritan Vision of the Christian Life*. Eastbourne: Kingsway, 1991. (Published in USA under the title *A Quest for Godliness*. Wheaton, IL: Crossway, 1990).

_____. *The Redemption and Restoration of Man in the Thought of Richard Baxter*. Rev. ed. Carlisle: Paternoster, 2003.

John Owen

Preaching for the Glory of God

HENRY M. KNAPP

John Owen (1616–1683) is widely acknowledged as one of the most prominent and highly influential thinkers of the post-Reformation period. A prolific writer, both of theological and pastoral material, he was one of the ablest defenders of Puritan orthodoxy, a scholar of the highest ability, and universally respected by admirers and opponents alike. In an era where personal piety, an experiential communion with the divine, mastery of a rapidly expanding academic milieu, and dogmatic rigor in theological approach were valued and esteemed, Owen stands out as an exemplar among his peers.

HISTORICAL BACKGROUND

Born sometime in 1616 into a Puritan family,[1] Owen not only witnessed the momentous social, theological, and political upheavals of his day but was actively involved in many of the most significant cultural events in seventeenth-century England. Lifelong admirer J. I. Packer comments that Owen "is by common consent not the most versatile, but the greatest among Puritan theologians," and that he "was one of the greatest of English theologians. In an age of giants, he overtopped them all."[2] Owen was educated at Oxford and afterward served as a private chaplain and country pastor until moving to London during the Civil War, where his long association with Parliament, Oliver Cromwell, and the Commonwealth began. In the mid-1640s, his mild Presbyterianism had transformed

---

1. While the definition of "Puritan" is notoriously difficult to nail down, and some scholars have challenged if the label applies to Owen at all, we will follow the general consensus of identifying him with the Puritan movement. See, Carl Trueman, *John Owen: Reformed Catholic, Renaissance Man* (Burlington, VT: Ashgate, 2007), 5–12; Ryan McGraw, *A Heavenly Directory* (Göttingen: Vandenhoeck & Ruprecht, 2014), 13–20.

2. J. I. Packer, *A Quest for Godliness* (Wheaton, IL: Crossway, 1990), 81, 191. See the similar evaluation of Owen in Carl Trueman, *The Claims of Truth: John Owen's Trinitarian Theology* (Milton Keynes: Paternoster, 1998); Kelly Kapic, *Communion with God: The Divine and the Human in the Theology of John Owen* (Grand Rapids: Baker, 2007); Sinclair Ferguson, *John Owen on the Christian Faith* (Carlislie, PA: Banner of Truth, 1987).

to a firm Congregationalism which he stoutly defended throughout his life. In 1649, when Parliament sent Cromwell to suppress the rebellion in Ireland, and then again to Scotland, he invited Owen to accompany him as a chaplain; he also became Cromwell's chief adviser in ecclesiastical matters. This further led to his appointment as Dean of Christ Church, Oxford, and eventually as the university's Vice-Chancellor (1650s). However, Owen had a falling out with his benefactor when he opposed the plan to offer Cromwell the crown. Though he was one of the more prominent churchmen during the Civil War and the Commonwealth, Owen's political connections spared him the full brunt of royal displeasure which visited many other Puritan clergy following the Stuart Restoration. Nevertheless, he was ejected from his position at Oxford at the Restoration, and his ministry was further hampered by the Clarendon Code.[3] Owen continued to illegally lead a small house congregation until it finally merged with that of fellow Congregationalist Joseph Caryl, bringing the formal church membership to around two hundred individuals.

His second marriage (the first ending with the death of his wife) brought financial independence to the family and enabled Owen to focus on his writings. His latter years were marked by his continued efforts on behalf of nonconforming orthodox believers and the publication of his theological, exegetical, and pastoral works. Owen left behind no extant diary, and the biographical information in his correspondence is remarkably scant; consequently, little is known of his personal side or of his family affairs.

Given his extensive theological output and the many avenues of inquiry present there, it is not surprising that Owen's preaching and pastoral work have not received extensive attention in contemporary scholarship.[4] In his varied career, however, Owen spent a large amount of his time in the pulpit, and what happened there had an immense effect on his life and thought. Owen's crucial relationship with Oliver Cromwell and Parliament developed as a result of his preaching to that body—including preaching the day following the execution of Charles I. As military chaplain, Owen preached frequently to the troops and in the territories occupied by the army, where a strong interest in the evangelism of the Irish and opposition to Irish Catholicism were strong foci of his ministry. Though there were extensive administrative responsibilities at the university, Owen preached in

---

3. The Clarendon Code were four penal laws, named after Charles II's chief minister, the first Earl of Clarendon, aimed at suppressing nonconformist clergy following the Restoration. The impact of the Clarendon Code on Owen and the Puritan movement as a whole is well articulated in Owen's biographies, such as Peter Toon, *God's Stateman: The Life and Work of John Owen* (Exeter: Paternoster, 1971).

4. Owen's biographers make some mention of his preaching: Andrew Thomson, "Life of Dr. Owen," in *The Works of John Owen*, vol. 1 (Carlisle, PA: Banner of Truth Trust, 1991); William Orme, *Life of the Reverend John Owen* (1840; repr. Choteau, MT: Gospel Mission, 1981); Toon, *God's Statesman*.

and around Oxford on the Lord's Day and lectured regularly to the student body. Following his removal from the university, Owen's primary role was as a pastor and preacher during the final two decades of his life. Preaching God's Word to God's people dominated John Owen's life.

A portion of the many sermons Owen preached through the years are collected in two volumes of his corpus, and some of his Oxford addresses have also been published.[5] In addition, a number of Owen's more popular works originated as sermons and/or student lectures.[6] Although Owen himself once remarked wistfully to Charles II of trading his abilities for the power of John Bunyan's speaking, witnesses testified to the impact of Owen's preaching.[7] His efforts as a pastor were appreciated and admired at the time: William Goold, his nineteenth-century editor, noted, "The merits of Owen as a preacher have not been sufficiently appreciated. In this respect he seems to have stood higher in the estimation of his contemporaries than he has subsequently done."[8] One contemporary, Anthony Wood, assessed Owen's preaching this way: "His personage was proper and comely and he had a very graceful behavior in the pulpit, an eloquent elocution, a winning and insinuating deportment and could, by the persuasion of his oratory . . . move and win the affections of his admiring auditory almost as he pleased."[9] Owen's pulpit ministry is notable, not only for its contemporary impact, but also for many of those who through the years have benefited from the fruit of his labors.

THEOLOGY OF PREACHING

There are a number of good reasons to focus on the preaching ministry of John Owen, not the least of which is his great significance in the articulation and development of Reformed theology in England, a theology which is pervasive throughout his sermons. Described by contemporaries as "the Calvin of England" and "a pastor, a scholar, a divine of the first magnitude,"[10] Owen was steeped in Puritan Reformed thought, and his theological formulations represent the pinnacle of

---

5. *The Works of John Owen*, volumes 8 and 9; John Owen, *The Oxford Orations of John Owen*, ed. Peter Toon (Callington: Gospel Communication, 1971).

6. See, particularly, *On the Mortification of Sin, On Temptation*, and *On Indwelling Sin* in *The Works of John Owen*, vol. 6 (Carlisle, PA: Banner of Truth Trust, 1991).

7. Thomson, "Life of Dr. Owen," 1:xcii. Testimonies of those impacted by Owen's preaching are recorded in John Rogers, *Beth-shemesh*, vol. 3 (London, 1653), 6.

8. *The Works of John Owen*, vol. 8 (Carlisle, PA: Banner of Truth Trust, 1991), viii.

9. Anthony Wood, *Athenae Oxonienses*, 4 vols. (London, 1813), 4:Col.102.

10. Ambrose Barnes, *The Memoirs of the Life of Mr. Ambrose Barnes, late merchant and sometime alderman of Newcastle upon Tyne*, ed. William Longstaffe (Durham: Andrews & Co., 1867), 16; the latter quote is from David Clarkson's funeral sermon for Owen as printed in Orme, *Life of the Reverend John Owen*, 411.

Reformed orthodoxy in seventeenth-century England. He was knowledgeable, well-schooled, and conversant with the myriad of alternative theological movements of his era, but his embrace of the Reformed tradition saturates his work. By Owen's time, the Scripture's primacy in doctrinal formulations had long been part and parcel of the Protestant challenge to Rome's authoritative assertions, and the development and articulation of a distinctly Reformed understanding of the Bible—characteristically, the Reformed scholastic approach—was a key component of the high orthodox period. The distinctive Reformed emphases on the divine initiative in salvation, the centrality of Jesus Christ, his vicarious sacrifice, and their implications for worship and individual sanctification permeated Owen's writings.[11]

Regardless of whether John Owen perfectly fits some specific definition of "Puritan," his ministry and writings certainly demonstrate those qualities which are generally associated with the movement. Beyond his Calvinistic theology, Owen taught an experiential faith: the true Christian experienced a real and powerful communion with the triune God; doctrine was not simply an intellectual assent to propositions but ultimately for the reformation of the person; the believer sought the cultivation of personal godliness, piety, and holy worship. Coupled then with the Puritan emphasis on an experiential, scriptural Christian lifestyle, Owen's theologically rich, biblically-driven, and academic environment constituted the ministry framework in which he worked and preached.

This rich background underlies all that Owen produced, either written or proclaimed. Although he did not write a systematic theology per se, Owen's theological contribution to the church is immense.[12] Polemically, he was a vigorous defender of Reformed orthodoxy against Roman, Arminian, Socinian, and other heterodox views. Much of his writings were either attacks on, or a defense against, authors he felt were leading the faithful astray. Owen's attention to theological detail was not just an academic interest or scholastic exercise, for he recognized the dangerous nature of these alternative teachings not only in the academy, but first and foremost in the everyday lives of believers. Thus, Owen's sermons have considerable theological content and demand a lot from his listeners. Preaching was a necessary part of the godly transformation of the mind—negatively combatting erroneous beliefs and positively communicating orthodox truth.

Owen preached and wrote passionately on the person and work of Christ, encouraging the believer's communion with the Godhead, and his work on the

---

11. On Reformed Orthodoxy, see Richard A. Muller, *Post-Reformation Reformed Dogmatics*, 4 vols. (Grand Rapids: Baker, 2003).

12. The closest would be John Owen, *Theologoumena Pantodapa* (1661; repr. *Biblical Theology*, Pittsburgh: Soli Deo Gloria, 1994).

nature and operation of the Holy Spirit is masterful and has few equals. His care for his congregation was expressed through his development of a catechism for the education of the people, his preaching and teaching on sanctification, and his focus on the daily concerns of the Christian life. In light of the Anglican-Presbyterian-Congregationalist controversies of his time, and as a leader of the Independent movement, Owen was deeply concerned about the nature of the church and, consequently, about the duties of the pastor. And, most important for this study, Owen was immersed in the Scriptures, in their interpretation and exposition—something which is manifestly evident in his sermons.

Owen's preaching makes a good case study because he was so completely a product of his age. Owen is widely recognized as a superior theologian and scholar of his time, and his intellect was clearly substantial. However, what makes Owen so extraordinary as a pastor, exegete, and theologian is not that he was ahead (or outside) of his time, but that his thought and writings encompassed, all at once, all that was representative of his age; he was chief of his era—not because he represented something beyond his time, but because he represented the best *of* his era.[13]

By the seventeenth century, Renaissance humanism had shaped the academic and cultural landscape for over a century. Advances in linguistics, philosophy, the sciences, and more led to a vast shift in the approach and presentation of theological material. As is evident from his sermons and books, Owen had all the training, skills, and expertise of a highly educated humanist, and this background is inextricably woven into the fabric of his exegetical approach. Owen was a highly skilled linguist, quoting freely from the Greek and the unpointed Hebrew texts, referencing cognate languages, and noting specific grammatical and lexical issues in the text. His wide grasp of geography, history, and philosophy is also evident throughout his entire corpus. Rightly counted among the "Reformed scholastics," Owen nevertheless made use of rhetorical devices and argumentation normally associated with humanist authors. While Owen did not overwhelm his audience just to display his intellect, his academic abilities and interests are evident in the preparation and delivery of his material.

In contrast with his familiarity with humanism, Owen can also easily be (and often is) classified as a scholastic thinker, employing the techniques and methods of scholasticism throughout his work—including in his biblical exposition and proclamation. Like his scholastic brethren, Owen's sermons and pastoral work are filled with finely crafted definitions and distinctions, examples of rigorous logical

---

13. Trueman, *The Claims of Truth*; Trueman, *John Owen: Reformed Catholic, Renaissance Man*; Sebastian Rehnman, *Divine Discourse: The Thological Methodology of John Owen* (Grand Rapids: Baker, 2002); Muller, *Post-Reformation Reformed Dogmatics.*

and deductive reasoning, and a presentation of the material which reflects a clear pedagogical purpose. And as with other Reformation and post-Reformation authors, while he can speak rather disparagingly of the "schoolmen," Owen clearly was aware of and made use of the historical developments of religious thought throughout the church age. Owen shared in the presuppositions of other premodern biblical exegetes: the assumption that the Scripture was self-consistent and that orthodox doctrine grew faithfully from the Bible led to the application of the analogy of Scripture (that Scripture interprets Scripture) and the analogy of faith (that all accurate interpretation will be consistent with the overall sweep of the Christian faith) to the exposition of every biblical text. Owen, like other Puritan preachers, understood that the scriptural text was directed not only to its original hearers but ultimately for the continual benefit of the whole church; the "great end" of the Bible lies in its perpetual witness to modern believers. The goal of biblical interpretation and preaching is not to learn "the form of the doctrine of godliness, but to get the power of it implanted in our souls."[14] In these ways, Owen reflects his time's continuity with scholastic methods and the preachers of the past centuries.

Above all, Owen was a scholar. His writings exhibit a thorough knowledge of a wide variety of intellectual areas, and his academic abilities are evident from his time at Oxford and the respect of his colleagues. What Owen called, "my own small library," contained nearly three thousand works, many of them multivolume sets.[15] The auction catalog of his library in 1684 attests to the breadth of his intellectual interests and lists numerous classics: writings on philosophy, history, geography, and extensive philological works. Of course, the bulk of the catalog enumerates the vast collection of books on divinity—including the major authors of the patristic, medieval, Reformation, and contemporary periods. Thus, John Owen was a Reformed, scholastic, humanistic, academically remarkable theologian and exegete—which makes his biblical preaching important for this study.

METHODOLOGY FOR PREACHING

The Goal of Preaching

John Owen's approach to his preaching ministry was shaped in large part by his understanding of the purpose and goals of the sermon and his view of

---

14. John Owen, *Causes, Ways, and Means,* in *The Works of John Owen,* vol. 4 (Carlisle, PA: Banner of Truth Trust, 1991), 205.

15. John Owen, *Of the Death of Christ: The Price He Paid, and The Purchase He Made,* in *The Works of John Owen,* vol. 10 (Carlisle, PA: Banner of Truth Trust, 1991), 471; Edward Millington, ed., *Bibliotheca Oweniana, sive Catalogus librorum . . . Rev. Doct. Vir. D. Joan. Oweni . . .* (London, 1684).

the overall intent of worship. In various places throughout his writings, Owen expresses what the preacher is to strive for when speaking to the congregation. In his discussion on what it means to bless another in his commentary on Hebrews 7:7, Owen argues that the minister's role is to "bless the church in the dispensation and preaching of the word, to the conversion and edification of the souls of men."[16] Thus, the saving power of the gospel, communicated through the sermon, was a powerful motivation for Owen's preaching ministry. While in Ireland, his time was taken by "constant preaching to a numerous multitude of as thirsting a people after the gospel as ever yet I conversed withal."[17] A yearning for the spread of the gospel in Ireland and throughout England shaped much of Owen's ministry, and was expressed during his time in the pulpit. The sermon was one means whereby the Spirit might awaken the sinner and lead to a reformed, godly life.

The preacher also has responsibility to care for those already saved, to seek the "edification of the souls of men." Paraphrasing Jeremiah 3:15, "to feed the church with knowledge and understanding" is the duty of the pastor, and "he is no pastor who doth not feed his flock . . . by preaching of the gospel."[18] According to Owen, preaching is "the outward way and means whereby [God] ordinarily communicates" his divine love for his people.[19] The sermon was "food for our souls," leading to necessary "growth and strength"[20] and bringing joy and a sense of divine love to the believer. Citing Colossians 1:28 and Ephesians 4:8, Owen spoke of the "design" and "great end" of preaching: to warn and to teach every person in all wisdom for the edification and building up of the church.[21] This goal is readily seen in much of the doctrinal content of his sermons—communicating biblical truths to uplift and encourage the believer—as well as in the expressed application he provides—spurring on a life of faith for the listener.

Consistent with his Reformed tradition and Puritan background, Owen argued that "the chief end of believers is, the glory of God. This, I say, is so, or ought to be so. For this purpose they were made, redeemed to this purpose, and purchased to be a peculiar people."[22] For the minister, then, "the first and

---

16. Owen, *An Exposition of Hebrews*, in *The Works of John Owen*, vol. 21 (Carlisle, PA: Banner of Truth Trust, 1991), 373.

17. Owen, *Of the Death of Christ*, 10:479. Cf., John Owen, "A Vision of Unchangeable, Free Mercy," in *The Works of John Owen*, vol. 8 (Carlisle, PA: Banner of Truth Trust, 1991), 16–41, where he urges the evangelization of all peoples of the nation.

18. John Owen, "The Duty of a Pastor," in *The Works of John Owen*, vol. 9 (Carlisle, PA: Banner of Truth Trust, 1991), 453.

19. John Owen, *The Grace and Duty of Being Spiritually Minded* in *The Works of John Owen*, vol. 7 (Carlisle, PA: Banner of Truth Trust, 1991), 437.

20. Owen, *Being Spiritually Minded,* 7:440.

21. Owen, "The Duty of a Pastor," 9:452, 454.

22. John Owen, "Of Walking Humbly with God" in *The Works of John Owen*, vol. 9 (Carlisle, PA: Banner of Truth Trust, 1991), 122.

principal end" of preaching is "to ascribe and give to God the glory that is His due."[23] Real, biblical worship and glory are intimately tied; indeed, "the true worship of God is the height and excellency of all glory in the world."[24] While the sermon was necessarily to have an impact on the congregation, the entirety of the Christian life, including preaching and all worship, was to focus our praise and adoration on God.

Preaching the Word of God was a necessary element in the public worship of God's people[25]—an especially important element in the Reformed conception of worship in the post-Reformation era. A concern for, and a focus on, the proper worship of God was a dominant theme in Owen's writings, and he spoke of preaching from within this context. It is here that Owen makes a distinctive contribution to the intersection of Reformed theology, Puritan thought, and Christian worship—his stress on the believer's communion with God as central in worship.[26] Reflecting again his Puritan roots, public worship in Owen's mind was never merely a question of correct form or the performance of specific rites; rather, true worship is intertwined with the worshipper's experience of the divine. This is, Owen says, the glory, beauty, and excellency of gospel worship: "There is not the meanest believer but, with his most broken prayers and supplications, hath an immediate access unto God, and that as a Father; nor the most despised church of saints on the earth but it comes with its worship into the glorious presence of God himself."[27] True communion with the triune God—and, hence, communion with the divine Persons—is best expressed by his people in and through their worship together. The primary benefit of worship is the believer's communion with God, and this communion-in-worship goal directs true preaching.[28] True biblical preaching, as part of godly worship, is manifest in one's communion with God, and any preaching which does not foster this divine experience, no matter how rigorous or doctrinally attentive, is false worship—"men's attempting to worship God who are not interested in this privilege of access unto him, is the ground of all the superstitious idolatry that is in the world."[29]

---

23. Owen, *Being Spiritually Minded,* 7:444. See also, John Owen, "The Chamber of Imagery," in *The Works of John Owen,* vol. 8 (Carlisle, PA: Banner of Truth Trust, 1991), 556; Owen, *A Brief Instruction on Worship* in *The Works of John Owen,* vol. 15 (Carlisle, PA: Banner of Truth Trust, 1991), 447, 474.

24. Owen, "The Chamber of Imagery," 8:555.

25. Owen, *A Brief Instruction on Worship,* 15:477.

26. "Communion with the Trinity as expressed in public worship both permeates and ties together the entire corpus of his theology," McGraw, *A Heavenly Directory,* 12. Cf., Kapic, *Communion with God,* 27–29.

27. John Owen, "The Nature and Beauty of Gospel Worship," in *The Works of John Owen,* vol. 9 (Carlisle, PA: Banner of Truth Trust, 1991), 60. Cf., 9:56–57.

28. Owen, *Communion with God* in *The Works of John Owen,* vol. 2 (Carlisle, PA: Banner of Truth Trust, 1991), *passim*; especially, 2:268–69; Owen, "Nature and Beauty," 9:56–59.

29. Owen, "Nature and Beauty," 9:60.

The Calling of the Preacher

Who, then, is sufficient for such a task? If preaching aims at such lofty goals, what manner of person might rightfully take on this responsibility? The nature, structure, and governance of the church was a controversial issue in the seventeenth century, and as a leader for the Independents, Owen was at the forefront of this discussion. A significant portion of his writings deal, either directly or tangentially, with the question of church officers and the role of the pastor.[30] As one would expect, Owen began to answer this question by stressing the necessity of being called by God—ministry is a divine gift and only those given this gift should deem to attempt it.[31] Owen taught that the qualifications for a pastor paralleled Christ's own ministry—what made Christ a good pastor, indeed, the Good Shepherd, will also be required of his servant pastors: the faithful exercise of spiritual gifts, a real compassion and love for the flock, a continual watchfulness (to keep, preserve, feed, and lead the flock), an overriding zeal for the glory of God, and some measure of conformity to Christ's own holiness.[32]

While Owen recognized the manifold responsibilities of a pastor—he lists a number of duties at various points—he maintained that the primary and foremost concern of the pastor is "to preach the word diligently, dividing it aright," so as "to feed the church with knowledge and understanding."[33] Preaching is not just part of the pastor's duty, it is indispensable: "The first and principal duty of a pastor is to feed the flock by diligent preaching of the word . . . This feeding is of the essence of the office of a pastor, as unto the exercise of it; so that he who doth not, or can not, or will not feed the flock is no pastor, whatever outward call or work he may have in the church."[34] Preaching as feeding is not proclamation alone: the pastor is "not only to declare [the truth] in the preaching of the gospel; but to defend and preserve it against all opposition—to hold up the shield and buckler of faith against all opposers."[35]

To rightly preach the Word demands much from the pastor—"the most difficult ministration of any that a person can be called unto."[36] The duty of

30. Owen, "The Duty of a Pastor," 9:459; John Owen, "The Ministry The Gift of Christ," in *The Works of John Owen*, vol. 9 (Carlisle, PA: Banner of Truth Trust, 1991), 432–35; John Owen, *The Duty of Pastors and People Distinguished*, in *The Works of John Owen*, vol. 13 (Carlisle, PA: Banner of Truth Trust, 1991), 29–35; Owen, *A Brief Instruction on Worship*, 15:486–99; Owen, *Two Discourses*, in *The Works of John Owen*, vol. 4 (Carlisle, PA: Banner of Truth Trust, 1991), 486–98; John Owen, *The True Nature of a Gospel Church*, in *The Works of John Owen*, vol. 16 (Carlisle, PA: Banner of Truth Trust, 1991), 54–56.

31. Owen, "The Ministry," 9:431.

32. Owen, *True Nature of a Gospel Church*, 16:49–51.

33. Owen, *A Brief Instruction on Worship*, 15:499; Owen, "The Duty of a Pastor," 9:453.

34. Owen, *True Nature of a Gospel Church*, 16:74–75.

35. Owen, "The Duty of a Pastor," 9:458.

36. Owen, "Ministerial Endowments," in *The Works of John Owen*, vol. 9 (Carlisle, PA: Banner of Truth Trust, 1991), 451.

preaching requires: (1) spiritual wisdom to understand the mystery of the gospel so that one might preach the whole counsel of God; (2) an authority which comes from an unction or anointing of the gifts of the Spirit; (3) a personal experience of the truths which one proclaims; (4) the skill of rightly dividing the Word, (i.e., the practical wisdom of handling and communicating Scripture); (5) an awareness and knowledge of the spiritual state of the congregation (e.g., temptations, doubts, fears)—"he who doth not duly consider these things, never preaches aright unto them"; and (6) the motivation of the zeal for God's glory and the good of people's souls.[37] Given the daunting task and the demanding requirements, Owen followed the list above with the plea: "we have a great need to pray for ourselves, and that you should pray for us. Pray for your ministers."[38]

The importance of the power and presence of the Spirit dominates this description of the pastor, and it should not be surprising that the author who wrote so extensively on the Holy Spirit would place great stress on articulating his role in preaching. The Spirit grants spiritual gifts to the preacher which are necessary and indispensible: "the communication of the gifts of the Holy Ghost is the foundation of the ministry," for "whenever Jesus Christ calls and appoints a minister in his house, for the building work of it, he gives him spiritual abilities to do that work by the Holy Ghost."[39] There is a harmony between the Spirit's gifts, the role of the pastor, and the duties to the church: "The original of all church order and rule is in gifts; the exercise of those gifts is by office; the end of all those gifts and offices is, edification."[40] While natural abilities, effort, and skill are helpful in a pastor's job, the absence of the demonstration and manifestation of spiritual gifts is "sufficient evidence" that a ministry is "a degenerating apostasy," and "no outward call or order can constitute any man an evangelical pastor" who lacks those gifts.[41] While "spiritual gifts of themselves make no man actually a minister; yet no man can be made a minister according to the mind of Christ who is not partaker of them."[42]

The preacher is the first audience for the sermon, and the work of the Spirit through that preaching must reach to the pastor's own heart—"no man preaches that sermon well to others that doth not first preach it to his own heart."[43] This initial conviction empowers the preaching beyond the human abilities of the preacher:

---

37. Owen, "The Duty of a Pastor," 9:453.

38. Ibid., 456. Cf., Owen, *True Nature of a Gospel Church*, 16:75–77.

39. Owen, *A Brief Instruction on Worship*, 15:493; Owen, "Ministerial Endowments," 9:448. See also, Owen, *Two Discourses*, 4:498–508; McGraw, *A Heavenly Directory*, 201–4.

40. Owen, "The Duty of a Pastor," 9:453. Cf., Owen, *Two Discourses*, 4:509–12.

41. Owen, *Two Discourses*, 4:482; Owen, *True Nature of a Gospel Church*, 16:49. See also, Owen, "Ministerial Endowments," 9:448.

42. Ibid., 494. Cf., Owen, "The Ministry," 9:432.

43. Owen, "The Duty of a Pastor," 9:455.

It is an easier thing to bring our heads to preach than our hearts to preach. To bring our heads to preach, is but to fill our minds and memories with some notions of truth, of our own or other men, and speak them out to give satisfaction to ourselves and others: this is very easy. But to bring our hearts to preach, is to be transformed into the power of these truths; or to find the power of them . . . and to be acted with zeal for God and compassion to the souls of men. A man may preach every day in the week, and not have his heart engaged once. This hath lost us powerful preaching in the world.[44]

Therefore, a good sermon might result simply from the mental efforts of the preacher, but "he will never make a good minister of Jesus Christ whose heart and mind is not always in the work."[45]

SERMON PREPARATION AND CONTENT

The writings of John Owen are notoriously difficult for modern readers to follow, and, while his sermons are not as hard to read, they still remain a challenge for us today.[46] Owen's style did not differ significantly from his contemporaries, but to twenty-first-century ears, they can sound very dry, convoluted, and unnecessarily technical. Owen expected much of his listeners; his sermons rarely include summaries of his points, transitions from one idea to another are not clearly marked, key thoughts are not stressed (e.g., through repetition or emphasis), he rarely employs mnemonic aids, and the sermons often end abruptly and without a closing summation.[47] This is not to imply that his sermons lack structure; on the contrary, they are highly structured, frequently involving many intricate and nested arguments.[48] Illustrations are infrequent in Owen's preaching, and those that are present are almost never personal or taken from daily experience.

---

44. Ibid.

45. Ibid., 451.

46. George Hunsinger captures the unease of a modern reader: "No one has accused John Owen of making matters easy for his readers. Every sentence he wrote could be exhausting. A complex syntax, which constantly nested one relative clause within another, time after time within the same sentence, was compounded by his penchant for using three words in a row where one word would do." In "Justification and Mystical Union with Christ: Where Does Owen Stand?" in *John Owen's Theology*, eds. Kelly Kapic and Mark Jones (Burlington, VT: Ashgate, 2012), 204.

47. Consider, for example, the abrupt ending of the sermon, "Walking Humbly with God," 9:130.

48. A great example of this is found in "Walking Humbly with God," where Owen describes the idea of perfection through a series of increasingly intricate levels, 9:95–97. Owen's contemporary, Daniel Burgess, describes Owen's preaching as "most weighty and seasonable argument, with very judicious and methodical management." Owen, "Seasonable Words for English Protestants," in *The Works of John Owen*, vol. 9 (Carlisle, PA: Banner of Truth Trust, 1991), 2.

Occasionally, he will employ a metaphor or simile, but what minimal illustrations exist are mostly biblical, as in accordance with the Reformed belief in the analogy of Scripture.[49] Human interest stories did not seem to interest Owen (at least in his sermons)! Attentiveness and a skill in listening would have been necessary in Owen's congregation.

Given Owen's association with the Puritans and the Reformed orthodox, it is not surprising that his sermons are heavily content-laden. It was the pastor's responsibility to communicate the gospel in its fullness—and that requires the articulation and exposition of Christian doctrine, even on a detailed and technical level. Owen warned against the inclination to preach "novel opinions," saying, "Who would have thought that we should have come to an indifferency" as to the basic Christian beliefs? Failure to adhere to the truths of the faith risks all manner of evils.[50] This can, of course, result in arduous sermons which are not always well received. In response, Owen himself bemoaned the "reproachful scorn and contempt cast upon laborious preaching—that is, laboring in the word and doctrine."[51] Owen's systematic exposition of the doctrine of faith in his sermon, "The Strength of Faith," is an excellent example of his dogmatic style of preaching.[52]

This emphasis on dogmatic content does not mean Owen's preaching lacked passion or feeling. True, his sermons certainly do not contain sentimental stories nor are they written to capture the readers' (or hearers') emotions. However, Owen's own emotional commitment to what he was preaching is evident. At times he pleads with his congregation, at times speaking with what one can only assume is a strident tone, sometimes mocking, sometimes marveling, sometimes in sympathy, always seeking to inspire and motivate.[53] Owen often expressed his feelings and passion through hypothetical and probing questions: "Do you suppose you shall be accepted or that peace will be your latter end? I fear many that hear me this day may be in this condition. Pardon me if I am jealous with a godly jealousy. What means else that hatred of the power of godliness, that darkness in the mystery of the gospel, that cursed formality, that enmity to the Sprit of God—that hatred of reformation, that is found amongst us?"[54]

---

49. E.g., fire and plague metaphors, 9:327; a brief illustration from agriculture, 9:29. Biblical examples abound through his work, as, for instance, Owen, "Nature and Beauty," 9:55, where he "confirms" his point with various other Scriptures.

50. Owen, "The Duty of a Pastor," 9:459–60.

51. Owen, *True Nature of a Gospel Church,* 16:75.

52. In *The Works of John Owen,* vol. 9 (Carlisle, PA: Banner of Truth Trust, 1991), 21–28.

53. Some examples of Owen's passion in preaching: his pleading, 9:6; mocking, 9:65; marveling and awe, 9:83; motivating, 8:24.

54. Owen, "Walking Humbly with God," 9:92.

The Scriptural Text

For Owens, preaching is an act of worship, and for the Puritan, real worship was governed by Scripture: "In order that everything be performed duly and in order in His Church, according to the will of God, Christ ordained that His Word, the Scriptures, should be the standard of evangelical worship and the sole rule for judging all matters of faith, obedience, and worship. Anything added over and above His Word is done without His sanction."[55] Owen's understanding of preaching, then, was intertwined with the Reformed doctrine of Scripture, its sufficiency and authority; the text and its exposition dominated the sermon. What texts are used for the church's edification? Which particular doctrines are preached? This, Owen claimed, is one of the benefits of the pastor's intentional, focused prayer life—"In our prayers for our people, God will teach us what we shall preach unto them."[56]

This priority of the text is evident in the consistent sermon structure employed by John Owen: preaching began with the reading of a passage of Scripture, whereupon some exegetical and interpretive comments are given, followed by a more lengthy articulation and exploration of the theological doctrine(s) arising from the text (including, frequently, questions and answers), and ending with a "uses" section, where the text and doctrine are applied to the congregation. Owen's nineteenth-century editor, William Goold, describes Owen's two sermons, "Ebenezer: A Memorial of the Deliverance," in a way that captures his entire preaching corpus: "They take the shape of a running comment upon a very sublime passage of Scripture. The verses are expounded in order, and the author educes from them a series of general principles or observations, which he illustrates with tact and power. Exegetic statements are made the basis of important principles, and relieved by eloquent expressions, and maxims of practical wisdom. Though necessarily brief, some of the appeals interwoven with the details of exposition are specimens of close and urgent dealing with the conscience."[57]

Owen's sermons begin with a discussion of the selected scriptural text, usually, a single verse, and his exegesis reflects the best of the scholarship available at the time. As noted above, Owen was fully cognizant of, and adept at using, the contemporary developments in humanistic learning. This was evident even in his preaching, where developments in grammatical and lexical studies, knowledge of the biblical languages, the analysis of rhetorical usage, and other linguistic advances are manifest. When it was determined to be helpful and/or necessary

---

55. Owen, *Biblical Theology*, 657. See also, 434. Cf., Owen, *Brief Instruction on Worship*, where Owen expands on how true principles of worship grow out of the Reformed doctrine of Scripture; McGraw, *A Heavenly Directory*, 82–90.

56. Owen, "The Duty of a Pastor," 9:457.

57. In *The Works of John Owen*, vol. 8 (Carlisle, PA: Banner of Truth Trust, 1991), 72.

in exploring the meaning of the text, Owen would summarize, restate, or elaborate upon the pericope, usually examining its various parts and interconnections within the passage. He would cite and translate the Greek or Hebrew text, expound on the lexical meaning of a word or phrase, or examine details of the grammar of the text—yet not so much as to overwhelm his audience or simply to display his scholastic abilities.[58] He also provided the biblical and historical context of a text when needed "to give you the state of things here represented."[59]

The Doctrine of the Text

However, Owen did not try to educate his congregation on biblical nuance or religious history, but to expound upon the salvific doctrine revealed in the text. Thus, once he examined the verse in question, he then elucidated the Christian doctrine found therein. This would make up the bulk of his preaching—perhaps on average as much as three-quarters of the sermon. The post-Reformation period has been accused of proof-texting—finding random biblical texts and pulling them out of context so as to appear to support dogmatic assertions—a criticism that has been rebuffed in recent scholarship.[60] Owen's own attitude was that theology naturally arose from the Bible, so that preaching the text was preaching doctrine. "I shall go no farther than the text to prove it; for the opening the text and the proof of the doctrine will be one and the same."[61] After stating the doctrine in view, he then proceeded to defend it by referencing other Scriptures, to clarify it in light of other teachings, and to connect it to the overall body of Christian faith and practice. In this portion of the sermon, Owen would answer hypothetical objections, make "observations" concerning the doctrine's implications, and/or contrast this teaching with other ideas.

The Application of the Text

Finally, Owen concluded his sermons by identifying a series of "uses" or ways, numbering anywhere from one to ten, in which the doctrine in view may be applied

---

58. Good examples of Owen's "division" of the text into parts and his use of original languages can be found in "Perilous Times" in *The Works of John Owen*, vol. 9 (Carlisle, PA: Banner of Truth Trust, 1991), 320–22. In "The Duty of a Pastor," Owen looks at the semantic range of "labour" and "striving" from Colossians 1:29 (KJV) in terms of the effort of preaching, 9:454.

59. John Owen, "Christ's Pastoral Care," in *The Works of John Owen*, vol. 9 (Carlisle, PA: Banner of Truth Trust, 1991), 277, where Owen spends almost half the sermon providing the biblical context for his verse in question.

60. Richard A. Muller, "Biblical Interpretation in the 16th & 17th Centuries," in *Historical Handbook of Major Biblical Interpreters*, ed. Donald McKim (Downers Grove, IL: InterVarsity Press, 1998), 135–36. See also, Muller, *Post-Reformation Reformed Dogmatics*, 2:500–501; Henry M. Knapp, "Understanding the Mind of God: John Owen and Seventeenth Century Exegetical Methodology" (PhD diss., Calvin Theological Seminary, 2002).

61. Owen, "Christ's Pastoral Care," 9:277.

by the congregation.[62] It is here—where what has been implicit in Owen's preaching becomes explicit—the belief that Scripture is intended for the ongoing edification of God's people. The true meaning of all Scripture, while firmly tied to the grammar of the text, is ultimately orientated to the full life of the Church.[63] In his commentary on Hebrews, Owen stresses this universal purpose of the text: "Though this Epistle was written unto the Hebrews, and immediately for their use, yet it is left on record in the canon of the Scripture by the Holy Ghost, for the same general end with the other parts of Scripture, and the use of all believers therein to the end of the world."[64]

Thus, the task of the preacher demanded a contemporary exposition of the text to the present-day church. Owen recognized this step of application as a necessary part of the preacher's task: "I know not whether these things may be of concern and use unto you; they seem so to me, and I cannot but acquaint you with them."[65] Failing to apply the text, to identify how the text is important for the ongoing faith and life of the people of God, is a failure to properly handle the passage and one's duties as a pastor.

In his varied career, Owen preached to Parliament and at various other civic events, and these sermons naturally referenced contemporary national or local incidents.[66] Owen was not hesitant to express how the biblical passage and the doctrine addressed therein was to shape not only individual lives but the national state as well. It was part of his responsibilities as a pastor to speak to the contemporary situation of the church: "I have had a great persuasion that the clouds that are gathering will, at least in their first storm, fall upon the people of God. I must repeat it again and again; I have been warning you for some years, and telling you it would be so."[67] Elsewhere he said, "I have been warning of you continually of an approaching calamitous time, and considering the sins that have been the causes of it."[68] Usually, however, Owen directed his "uses" to his own flock, challenging them toward

---

62. For instance, in "Perilous Times": "One word of use, and I have done" is followed by six separate "uses," 9:331.

63. Richard A. Muller, "Biblical Interpretation in the Era of Reformation: The View of the Middle Ages" in *Biblical Interpretation in the Era of the Reformation,* eds. Richard Muller and John Thompson (Grand Rapids: Eerdmans, 1996), 11; Muller, *Post-Reformation Reformed Dogmatics,* 2:509; Knapp, "Understanding the Mind of God," 89–93.

64. Owen, *An Exposition of Hebrews,* 17:13–14. "The exposition of the text is attended with an improvement of *practical observations,* answering the great end from which the epistle was committed over to all generations for the use of the church." Owen, *An Exposition of Hebrews,* 17:9.

65. Owen, "Perilous Times," 9:326.

66. See, for instance, "Seasonable Words," 9.3, where Owen references the national disasters of the plague and the London fires, war with the Dutch, political intrigue, and treasonous plots. Many of the sermons in volume eight were delivered at public civic events.

67. John Owen, "The Use of Faith Under Reproaches and Persecutions," in *The Works of John Owen,* vol. 9 (Carlisle, PA: Banner of Truth Trust, 1991), 499.

68. John Owen, "The Use and Advantage of Faith," in *The Works of John Owen,* vol. 9 (Carlisle, PA: Banner of Truth Trust, 1991), 491.

greater holiness, repentance, or action. For instance, in his sermons "On Walking Humbly with God," Owen pleads for self-examination, encourages godliness and faith, and warns of an unbelieving life.[69] His "uses" would challenge his listeners in their behavior, in their beliefs, in their devotion. Believing the Scripture to be God's Word to the people of God in every generation, Owen's preaching applied the doctrine of the text to the contemporary lives of his nation and his congregation. It would have been near impossible to listen to Owen's preaching and not hear the God of the Bible directing the modern church toward greater faith and godliness.

CONTRIBUTIONS TO PREACHING

According to his twentieth-century biographer, Peter Toon, John Owen understood his task as a preacher to be "that of carefully expounding and explaining the nature of the biblical view of the Christian life and witness, exhorting his hearers zealously to obey and seek after God and to cultivate the grace of God in their hearts. He placed great stress not only upon sound doctrine but also upon the actual experience of God in Christian worship and in the soul of the believer."[70] This understanding and goal for his preaching is clearly reflected in the sermons published during and after his lifetime, and provides an excellent exemplar for contemporary preachers.

First, as in Owen's time, preaching today requires a merging of the biblical message with the contemporary church community. Owen's was a singular mind with immense theological insight, and yet his work unquestionably arose from his religious, political, and sociological context. An outspoken advocate of orthodox Reformed thought, immersed in the biblical, historical, and linguistic scholarship of his day, and committed to a heart-warming, experiential communion with his God, Owen's preaching wove together the most prevalent themes of his era. Led always by the Spirit, attentive to the needs of the flock, and beginning in his or her own heart and life, the pastor proclaims the Word in worship, for communion with the triune God and for his glory.

All too frequently, the desire for "relevance" eclipses the preacher's responsibility to the written Word. Scripture was central in the preaching of John Owen. The pastor's duty is to communicate the gospel message to their congregation, and that message comes through the Word. In and through the worship of the church, of which the proclamation of the Scripture is crucial, the people might commune with the triune God. Each of Owen's sermons began with a biblical passage, the text set in context and analyzed, and its connection to other Scriptures explored.

---

69. Owen, "Walking Humbly with God," 9:84–130.
70. Toon, *God's Statesman*, 157–58.

This led naturally to an exposition of the theological content of the passage. Owen recognized and lamented the tendency to avoid doctrine in preaching—something he saw as crucial and necessary to the pastor's calling. Preaching was an exposition of the Scripture—seeking to understand the mind of God expressed therein—and this was impossible to do faithfully without theology.[71]

Nevertheless, Owen's sermons were not dogmatic lectures; nor should be the sermons of today. Owen's preaching was marked by a relentless application of the biblical text to the contemporary community of God. His premodern hermeneutic stressed that the Bible was intended for the edification of God's church in every era. Thus, his sermons addressed the national concerns of his day: the doctrinal controversies threatening the church in England and the continent, and the common, daily Christian struggle for faithfulness. Owen's preaching was filled with points of application, where he would promote a particular belief or doctrine, encourage specific behavior, or inspire an active faith from his listeners—all for a deeper communion with God and the majesty of his glory.

CONCLUSION

Owen himself well expresses the goal for his whole life and ministry, and certainly for his preaching: "I hope I may own in sincerity that my heart's desire unto God, and the chief design of my life in the station wherein the good providence of God hath placed me, are, that mortification and universal holiness may be promoted in my own and in the hearts and ways of others, to the glory of God, that so the Gospel of our Lord and Savior Jesus Christ may be adorned in all things."[72]

Sermon Excerpt

Walking Humbly with God[73]

The aim of God, in general, is his own glory; he makes all things for himself, Prov.xvi.4; Rev.iv.11;—in particular, as to the business of our walking with him, it is the praise of his glorious grace, Eph.i.6.

Now, in this aim of God to exalt his glorious grace, two things are considerable:—First, That all which is to be looked for at the hand of God,

---

71. Owen, *Causes, Ways, and Means*, 4:*passim*.
72. Owen, *Mortification of Sin*, 6:4.
73. Owen, "Walking Humbly with God," 9:89–91.

is upon the account of mere grace and mercy, Tit.iii.4,5. God aims at the exalting of his glory in this,—that he may be known, believed, magnified, as a God pardoning iniquity and sin. And, secondly, That the enjoyment of himself, in this way of mercy and grace, is that great reward of him that walks with him. So God tells Abraham, when he calls him to walk before him, "I am thy shield, and thy exceeding great reward," Gen xv.1. The enjoyment of God in covenant, and the good things therein freely promised and bestowed by him, is the exceeding great reward of them that walk with God. This also, then, is required of him that will walk with God,—that he hath the same design in his so doing as God hath;—that he aims in all his obedience at the glory of God's grace; and the enjoyment of him as his exceeding great reward.

Now, according to what was before said of the design of God, this may be referred unto three heads:—

1. In general: that the design of the person be the glory of God. "Whatever we do," saith the apostle (that is, in our worship of God, and walking with him), "let all be done to his glory." Men who, in their obedience, have base, low, unworthy ends, walk as contrary to God in their obedience as in their sins. Some serve him for custom; some for an increase of corn, wine, or oil, or the satisfying of some low earthly end; some aim at self and reputation. All is lost;—it is not walking with God, but warring against him.
2. To exalt the glory of God's grace. This is one part of the ministry of the gospel,—that in obedience we should seek to exalt the glory of grace. The first natural tendency of obedience was, to exalt the glory of God's justice. The new covenant hath put another end upon our obedience: it is to exalt free grace;—grace given in Christ, enabling us to obey; grace accepting our obedience, being unworthy; grace constituting this way of walking with God; and grace crowning its performance.
3. Aiming at the enjoyment of God, as our reward. And this cuts off the obedience of many from being a walking with God. They preform duties, indeed; but what sincerity is there in their aims for the glory of God? Is it almost once taken into their thoughts? . . . Especially, how little is the glory of his grace aimed at! ♦

BIBLIOGRAPHY

Ferguson, Sinclair. *John Owen on the Christian Life*. Carlisle, PA: Banner of Truth, 1987.

Kapic, Kelly M. "John Owen (1616–1683)." Pages 795–99 in *Historical Dictionary of Major Biblical Interpreters*. Edited by Donald K. McKim. Downers Grove, IL.: InterVarsity Press, 2007.

_____. *Communion with God: The Divine and the Human in the Theology of John Owen*. Grand Rapids: Baker Academic, 2007.

Kapic, Kelly M., and Mark Jones, eds. *John Owen's Theology*. Burlington, VT: Ashgate, 2012.

McGraw, Ryan. *A Heavenly Directory*. Göttingen: Vandenhoeck & Ruprecht, 2014.

Oliver, Robert W., ed. *John Owen: The Man and His Theology*. Phillipsburg, NJ: P & R; Darlington, UK: Evangelical, 2002.

William Orme, *Life of the Reverend John Owen*. 1840; repr. Choteau, MT: Gospel Mission, 1981.

Owen, John. *The Works of John Owen*. 23 vols. Edited by William Goold. 1850–1855. Repr. Carlisle: Banner of Truth Trust, 1991.

_____. *The Correspondence of John Owen*. Edited by Peter Toon. Cambridge: Clarke, 1970.

_____. *The Oxford Orations of Dr. John Owen*. Edited by Peter Toon. Callington: Gospel Communication, 1971.

Packer, J. I. *A Quest for Godliness*. Wheaton, IL: Crossway, 1990.

Rehnman, Sebastian. *Divine Discourse: The Theological Methodology of John Owen*. Grand Rapids: Baker Academic, 2002.

Toon, Peter. *God's Statesman: The Life and Work of John Owen*. Exeter: Paternoster, 1971.

Trueman, Carl R. *John Owen: Reformed Catholic, Renaissance Man*. Great Theologians series. Burlington, VT: Ashgate, 2007.

_____. *The Claims of Truth: John Owen's Trinitarian Theology*. Milton Keynes: Paternoster, 1998.

John Bunyan
Preaching the Word from the Heart to the Heart

LARRY STEVEN MCDONALD

John Bunyan (1628–1688) experienced many of the same trials in life as the main character of his famous work, *Pilgrim's Progress*. He is an example of a preacher who took the Word of God directly to his own heart, wrestling with God about the meaning and application for his own life. It was out of his own heart and life that he taught the Word of God to others, aiming directly for their hearts. Perhaps his legacy is not so much in a preaching style or method, but in the life he lived. He faithfully persevered in preaching God's Word, regardless of his circumstances, whether in times of personal and family grief, in prison, or when the government opposed him.

HISTORICAL BACKGROUND

John Bunyan was born in 1628 in the agricultural midlands near Bedford, England, where he followed in the footsteps of his father, a tinker who made and mended household metal pots.[1] With this modest background, Bunyan was provided little formal education. At the age of sixteen, following his mother's and sister's death and his father's remarriage, he joined the continental army, where he was traumatized by the death of a soldier who had taken his place on the battlefield.

Although Bunyan attended an Anglican church during his formative years, at the age of twenty he was greatly influenced by two Puritan classics, *The Plain Man's Pathway to Heaven* (1601) by Arthur Dent[2] and *The Practice of Piety* (1612)

---

1. For more details, see W. R. Owens, "Chronology of Bunyan's Life and Times," in John Bunyan, *The Pilgrim's Progress*, Oxford World's Classics, ed., W. R. Owens (New York: Oxford University Press, 2003), xlv–lvi. For biographies of John Bunyan, see Richard Greaves, *Glimpses of Glory: John Bunyan and English Dissent* (Palo Alto, CA: Stanford University Press, 2002); Christopher Hill, *A Tinker and a Poor Man: John Bunyan and His Church, 1628–1688* (New York: Knopf, 1989); John Piper, *The Hidden Smile of God: The Fruit of Affliction in the Lives of John Bunyan, William Cowper, and David Brainerd*, vol. 2, *The Swans are not Silent* (Wheaton, IL: Crossway, 2001); William Y. Tindall, *John Bunyan: Mechanick Preacher*, Columbia University Studies in English and Comparative Literature (1934; repr., New York: Russell & Russell, 1964); and Ola E. Winslow, *John Bunyan* (New York: Macmillan, 1961).

2. Arthur Dent, *The Plain Man's Pathway to Heaven* (1601; repr., Morgan, PA: Soli Deo Gloria, 1997).

by Lewis Bayly.[3] Both were books his wife had brought into marriage as her only material possessions. Over time, he wrestled with his conversion, spurred on with the reading of these books, and continued, over the next few years, struggling deeply with spiritual turmoil and doubt. This battle was eventually replaced with peace and assurance of his salvation, however. He described this transformation saying,

> But one day, as I was passing in the field, and that too with dashes on my Conscience, fearing lest yet all was not right, suddenly this sentence fell upon my Soul, Thy righteousness is in Heaven; and methought withal, I saw with the eyes of my Soul Jesus Christ at God's right hand, there, I say, as my Righteousness; so that wherever I was, or whatever I was a doing, God could say of me, He wants my Righteousness, for that was just before him. I also saw moreover, that it was not my good frame of Heart that made my Righteousness better, nor yet my bad frame that made my Righteousness worse: for my Righteousness was Jesus Christ himself . . . Now did my chains fall off my Legs indeed, I was loosed from my affliction and irons, my temptations also fled away: so that from the time those dreadful Scriptures of God left off to trouble me; now went I also home rejoicing, for the grace and love of God.[4]

In addition, Bunyan was also encouraged by his reading of Martin Luther's *Commentary on Galatians*[5] and by the counsel of John Gillford, pastor of St. John's Church, an independent Baptist congregation in Bedford, where Bunyan eventually became a member, baptized by immersion in 1653. Under the tutelage of Gillford, Bunyan developed as a preacher, and within two years he was called to be a pastor. Since he had no formal training, this caused some in the church to question the decision.[6]

Although Bunyan was not educated, licensed, or ordained by the Church of England, he was encouraged to preach among the dissenters and became known as a lay preacher.[7] In 1657, he published his first work, a pamphlet entitled *Some*

3. Lewis Bayly, *The Practice of Piety* (1612; repr., Morgan, PA: Soli Deo Gloria, 1997).

4. John Bunyan, *Grace Abounding: With Other Spiritual Autobiographies*, Oxford World's Classics, eds. John Stachniewski and Anita Pacheco (New York: Oxford University Press, 2008), 65–66.

5. Bunyan stated, "I do prefer this Book of Mr. Luther upon the Galatians, (excepting the Holy Bible) before all the Books that ever I have seen, as most fit for a wounded Conscience." Ibid., 38.

6. See David L. Larsen, *The Company of Preachers: A History of Biblical Preaching from the Old Testament to the Modern Era* (Grand Rapids: Kregel, 1998), 274.

7. Daniel V. Runyan, "Introduction," in John Bunyan, *The Holy War: Annotated Companion to The Pilgrim's Progress*, ed. Daniel V. Runyan (Eugene, OR: Pickwick, 2012), xi.

Gospel-Truths Opened,[8] which dealt with a controversy pertaining to Quakers. A year later he wrote his first sermon treatise, *A Few Sighs from Hell.*[9]

MARRIAGE AND FAMILY

Bunyan's wife passed away in 1658. His wife and he had four children, one of whom was born blind. History has forgotten his wife's name, but her influence on Bunyan, both by her sharing of books and her Christlike example, has reverberated throughout history. He remarried a year later to Elizabeth, who was eighteen years old. Eventually, they had three children together, one of whom died soon after birth. As a result of the Act of Uniformity, a year after they married, Bunyan was arrested for illegal/unlicensed preaching and was sentenced to jail in Bedford. Although initially sentenced for three months, because of his refusal to stop preaching, he remained in jail for a total of twelve years. His imprisonment brought poverty and hardship on his family. Bunyan was unable to provide for them and was deeply concerned for their welfare and the care of his blind daughter, whom he said "lay nearer to my heart than all I had besides."[10] The most he could offer them was a little money he made by making lace.

Yet even in the midst of this suffering, Bunyan persevered in his passion to preach. When Justice Keelin instructed Bunyan to leave preaching, Bunyan responded, "I told him, as to this matter, I was at a point with him: For if I was out of prison today, I would preach the Gospel again tomorrow, by the help of God."[11] Judge Twisdon questioned Bunyan's wife, Elizabeth, wanting her to persuade Bunyan to stop preaching. Even though she survived on the charity of others as she raised their young children, she responded, "My Lord . . . he dares not leave preaching, as long as he can speak."[12] His family's commitment to him and his calling to preach are equally admirable.

A PILGRIM'S JOURNEY

Bunyan's imprisonment was also a time of literary productivity. He was additionally allowed to preach while in prison, both to prisoners and occasionally to those outside. After being released from prison in 1672, Bunyan assumed the post of

---

8. John Bunyan, *Some Gospel-Truths Opened* in *The Miscellaneous Works of John Bunyan*, vol. 1, ed. T. L. Underwood (Oxford: Oxford University Press, 1980).

9. John Bunyan, *A Few Sighs from Hell* in *The Miscellaneous Works of John Bunyan*, vol. 1, ed. T. L. Underwood (Oxford: Oxford University Press, 1980).

10. Bunyan, *Grace Abounding*, 89.

11. John Bunyan, "A Relation of the Imprisonment," in *Grace Abounding*, 110.

12. Ibid., 119.

pastor in Bedford. There he was pastor until his second imprisonment, where he wrote his famed allegory, *Pilgrim's Progress.*[13]

In all, Bunyan wrote over sixty books during his ministry. His most famous book, *Pilgrim's Progress,* is an allegorical and fictional story about a man named Christian who travels through life on his way to the Celestial Kingdom. Bunyan explains much about the Christian life through the experiences of this young pilgrim. The influence of this book has been so widely acclaimed that it is difficult to capture its effect in only a few words. D. L. Jeffrey states, *Pilgrim's Progress* is "one of the most influential works in all of English literature."[14] C. H. Spurgeon would say, "Next to the Bible, the book I value most is John Bunyan's 'Pilgrim's Progress.' I believe I have read it through at least a hundred times."[15] Spurgeon spoke eloquently about Bunyan by stating, "Why, this man is a living Bible! Prick him anywhere; and you will find that his blood is Bibline, the very essence of the Bible flows through him. He cannot speak without quoting a text, for his very soul is full of the Word of God."[16]

Despite the accolades stemming from Bunyan's writing, his preaching is often overlooked. However, for Bunyan "preaching the Word was second only to the importance of the Word itself."[17] In his estimation, his primary ministry was as a preacher, and while he was jailed he would do what he could to continue in the vestiges of his calling—and so he wrote and preached. It is said people would sit outside the jail so they could hear Bunyan preach. Charles II, King of England, once asked John Owen, the learned Puritan theologian, why he went to hear the preaching of the unlearned John Bunyan. Owen responded, "May it please your majesty, could I possess the tinker's abilities for preaching, I would willingly relinquish all my learning."[18] Later in his ministry Bunyan would detract slightly from Ames, Perkins, and Owens, pointing out what he considered to be excesses of Sabbatarians. Bunyan became difficult to label. He was like a Puritan but also favored pietism. He was a Baptist but did not insist on immersion as a requirement for church membership. He adopted covenant theology but adapted his position on federalism.[19] Yet throughout his ministry, Bunyan continued as pastor of the Bedford Church.

13. Larsen, *The Company of Preachers,* 274.

14. D. L. Jeffery, "Bunyan, John," in *Biographical Dictionary of Evangelicals,* ed. Timothy Larsen (Downers Grove, IL: InterVarsity Press, 2003), 99.

15. Charles H. Spurgeon, *Pictures from Pilgrim's Progress: A Commentary on Portions of John Bunyan's Immortal Allegory.* (1903; repr., Pasadena, TX: Pilgrim's Publication, 1992), 11

16. Charles H. Spurgeon, *C. H. Spurgeon's Autobiography* (London: Passmore & Alabaster, 1897), 4:268.

17. Jeffery, "Bunyan, John," 99.

18. Andrew Thomson, "Life of Dr. Owen," in *The Works of John Owen* (1850–1853; reprint, Carlisle, PA: Banner of Truth Trust, 1965–1968), 1:xcii.

19. Larsen, *A Company of Preachers,* 275.

In August 1688, Bunyan was on his way to preach in London when he was summoned to Reading to reconcile a family. Upon finishing this pastoral ministry to the family, Bunyan resumed his journey to London, only to be caught in a heavy rainstorm. Even though wet and exhausted, he insisted on preaching. He then developed a high fever and at the age of fifty-nine, Bunyan's life ended due to complications from pneumonia. He was buried in 1688 at Bunhill Fields, which was the "dissenters" graveyard of the community.[20] Harris states, "Thus Bunyan finished his course about the two matters closest to his heart, pastoring and preaching."[21]

METHODOLOGY FOR PREACHING

Bunyan's preaching has been characterized in many ways. Julie Coleman described Bunyan's language as homespun, natural, unpolluted, plain, and direct.[22] He adopted the "plain style" of his contemporary Puritan brothers, but added his giftedness in storying, which was flavored with folksy and colloquial rhetoric. He had an active imagination and had the tendency to allegorize Scripture.[23] Bunyan himself indicated that a sermon length should be one hour as he stated, "Ah friends! Time is precious, an hour's time to hear a sermon is precious; I have sometimes thought thus with myself."[24]

George Offor, editor of the nineteenth-century edition of *The Works of John Bunyan*, explained that Bunyan was unique in the way that his "preaching went to the heart, producing intense interest, and tears of contrition over the stubbornness of human nature."[25] John Harris agreed with this assessment as he believes Bunyan's preaching both moved and stirred the heart.[26] Joel Beeke has said that in the midst of sound Puritan preachers, Bunyan "stands among the highest, for he had the God-given ability to engage not only the mind but also the heart through his preaching."[27] David Parry described Bunyan's sermons as treatises that "intermingle logos and pathos, teaching and moving, methodical exposition

---

20. Ibid.

21. John Harris, "Moving the Heart: The Preaching of John Bunyan," in *Not by Might nor by Power*, Westminster Conference Paper, 1988 (London: Westminster Conference, 1989), 32.

22. Julie Coleman, "The Manufactured Homespun Style of John Bunyan's Prose," *Bunyan Studies* 18 (2014): 107.

23. Larsen, *A Company of Preachers*, 275.

24. Bunyan, *A Few Sighs from Hell*, 283.

25. George Offor, "Footnote," in John Bunyan, *Saved by Grace* in *The Works of John Bunyan*, ed. George Offor (1854; repr., Carlisle, PA: Banner of Truth Trust, 1991), 1:350.

26. Harris, "Moving the Heart," 32.

27. Joel R. Beeke, "John Bunyan's Preaching to the Heart," in *A Puritan Theology: Doctrine for Life*, eds. Joel R. Beeke and Mark Jones (Grand Rapids: Reformation Heritage, 2014), 712.

with passionate exhortation."[28] William Tindall picked up on this intermingling of logos and pathos as he believed Bunyan had two styles: "the popular for the immature; and the simple and direct for the knowing."[29] He saw Bunyan's two methods as "founded upon the practice of the Saviour, who, he said, had used parables to reach the emotions of the people, but had appealed by directness and simplicity to the understandings of the disciples."[30]

In Bunyan's *Grace Abounding,* a book Michael Davies described as "one of the greatest spiritual autobiographies in the English language,"[31] we find important details on Bunyan's thoughts on preaching. Here, Bunyan emphasized the priority of preaching in his own life as he stated, "I could not be content unless I was found in the exercise of my Gift."[32] He states that he exercised this gift "with great fear and trembling at the sight of my own weakness, did set upon the work, and did according to my Gift."[33] The gift he spoke of was to "preach that blessed Gospel that God had shewed me in the only Word of truth."[34] In exercising this gift Bunyan indicated that his countrymen "came in to hear the Word by hundreds"[35] as he believed that "God had called me to and stood by me in this Work."[36] This proved true. In London, he drew Sunday crowds of up to three thousand, and attracted up to 1,200 for 7:00 a.m. weekday sermons.[37]

Although Christopher Hill thinks "we know too little of Bunyan's preaching techniques,"[38] Graham Midgley believes "Bunyan was aware of some of the technicalities and the technical jargon of sermon style."[39] Midgley maintains that William Perkins's work *The Art of Prophesying* was the "most recommended and quoted authority among the dissenting sects"[40] and that it certainly influenced Bunyan's preaching. Perkins speaks of the importance of the Bible in preaching as he states "The Word of God is to be preached, in its perfection and inner

28. David Parry, "A Divine Kind of Rhetoric: Puritanism and Persuasion in Early Modern England Puritanism and Rhetoric," (PhD diss., Christ's College, University of Cambridge, 2011), 245.

29. William Y. Tindall, *John Bunyan: Mechanick Preacher,* Columbia University Studies in English and Comparative Literature (1934; repr., New York: Russell & Russell, 1964), 186.

30. Ibid., 187.

31. Michael Davies, "Grace Abounding to the Chief of Sinners: John Bunyan and Spiritual Autobiography," in *The Cambridge Companion to Bunyan,* ed. Anne Dunnan-Page (Cambridge: Cambridge University Press, 2010), 68.

32. Bunyan, *Grace Abounding,* 76.

33. Ibid., 77.

34. Ibid.

35. Ibid.

36. Ibid., 78.

37. Graham Midgley, "Introduction," in *The Miscellaneous Works of John Bunyan,* vol. 5, ed. Graham Midgley (Oxford: Oxford University Press, 1986), 5:xiv.

38. Hill, *A Tinker and a Poor Man,* 104.

39. Midgley, "Introduction," 5:xxvii.

40. Ibid. Roger Pooley also makes this connection in "Plain and Simple: Bunyan and Style," in *John Bunyan: Conventicle and Parnassus,* ed. N. H. Keeble (Oxford: Clarendon; Oxford University Press, 1988), 92.

consistency. Scripture is the exclusive subject of preaching, the only field in which the preacher is to labour."[41]

Midgley summarizes this approach as the "explication of the text, the collection and proof of doctrines from it, and the Application,"[42] which flows from doctrinal accuracy. He indicates that these dissenters "saw themselves in reaction against the preaching style of the earlier establishment, condemning it as over-elaborate in its rhetoric and figured pose."[43]

Beeke believes Bunyan had a "lively, experiential faith, which acquainted him with the full scope of religious troubles and affections."[44] He indicates that Bunyan "knew sin, conviction, temptation, doubt, fear, Satan, forgiveness, and grace."[45] Bunyan summarized this by stating, "When God shews a man the Sin he has committed, the Hell he has deserved, the Heaven he has lost; and yet that Christ, and Grace, and Pardon may be had; this will make him serious, this will make him melt, this will break his heart . . . and this is the man, whose Heart, whose Life, whose Conversation and All, will be ingaged [sic] in the matters of the Eternal Salvation of his Precious and Immortal Soul."[46] Beeke states, "Bunyan's experience was the life of his preaching . . . Bunyan preached as a man touched by God."[47] N. H. Keeble believed that Bunyan's authority did not lie in "academic distinction but in experiential authenticity and divine inspiration."[48]

It was out of Bunyan's personal walk with God that he preached to the heart of his listeners. Bunyan's experiential knowledge involved particulars that characterized this preaching to the heart.[49] Through participatory preaching Bunyan sought to move people beyond being spectators. He "usually addressed his hearers very personally . . . was very direct . . . was also illustrative and simple, so that even the common people heard him gladly."[50] Bunyan "passionately reasoned with his listeners to respond to the truth of sin and judgment as well as forgiveness and grace."[51] Bunyan's preaching to the heart was "pleading preaching," as Beeke indicates: "While Bunyan pleaded with people to see the severity of sin and hell, he also pleaded the mercies of God."[52]

41. William Perkins, *The Art of Prophesying* (1606; repr., Carlisle, PA: Banner of Truth Trust, 1996), 9.
42. Midgley, "Introduction," 5:xxviii.
43. Ibid., 5:xxx.
44. Beeke, "John Bunyan's Preaching to the Heart," 715.
45. Ibid., 717.
46. John Bunyan, *The Acceptable Sacrifice*, in *The Miscellaneous Works of John Bunyan*, vol. 12, ed. W. R. Owens (Oxford: Oxford University Press, 1994), 12:78–79.
47. Beeke, "John Bunyan's Preaching to the Heart," 717.
48. Keeble, "John Bunyan's Literary Life," 19.
49. The following two points are from Beeke, "John Bunyan's Preaching to the Heart," 718–23.
50. Beeke, "John Bunyan's Preaching to the Heart," 718.
51. Ibid., 719.
52. Ibid., 721.

Theology of Preaching

With Bunyan's lack of formal training, he never fully developed a theology of preaching. His preaching nevertheless clearly contains theological themes. In fact, his writings are saturated with concepts that articulate basic theological teachings of the Bible. Although it is beyond the scope of this chapter to consider all of these, three of his most prominent ones will be briefly considered.

Bunyan prioritized his preaching according to his study of the Bible. He emphasized that he preached the truth he felt and experienced. He states, "In my preaching of the Word, I took special notice of this one thing, namely, That the Lord did lead me to begin where his Word begins with Sinners, that is, to condemn all flesh, and to open and alledge [*sic*] that the curse of God by the Law doth belong to and lay hold on all men as they come into the World, because of sin . . . I preached what I felt, what I smartingly did feel, even that under which my poor Soul did groan and tremble in astonishment."[53]

Bunyan himself described this period of his preaching, "I went myself in chains to preach to them in chains."[54] For two years Bunyan continued to preach against people's sins and to warn of where those sins would take them. But then he described a change that took place. He stated, "The Lord came in upon my own Soul with some staid peace and comfort thorow [*sic*] Christ; for he did give me many sweet discoveries of his blessed Grace thorow [*sic*] him: wherefore now I altered in my preaching (for still I preached what I saw & felt); now therefore I did much labour to hold forth Jesus Christ in all his Offices, Relations, and Benefits unto the World."[55]

Parry described this transition by stating, "Thus Bunyan must first convince his hearers/readers that they are guilty and condemned by the Law, but must then persuade them to trust in the Gospel promises."[56]

Harris believes this is the "single most prominent theme of Bunyan's ministry."[57] Richard Greaves concurs, as he indicates of Bunyan, "through the spoken and printed word he made the workings of divine grace come alive."[58] Consider Bunyan's own words as they illustrate this best in his work *Saved by Grace*: "O grace! O amazing grace! To see a Prince entreat a Beggar to receive an Alms would be a strange sight; to see a King entreat the Traitor to accept of Mercy, would be a stranger sight than that; but to see God entreat a Sinner to hear Christ

---

53. Bunyan, *Grace Abounding*, 78.
54. Ibid.
55. Ibid.
56. Parry, "A Divine Kind of Rhetoric," 201.
57. Harris, "Moving the Heart," 41.
58. Richard Greaves, *John Bunyan*, vol. 2 of *Courtenay Studies in Reformation Theology* (Grand Rapids: Eerdmans, 1969), 2:160.

say I stand at the door and knock, with a heart-full, and a heaven-full of grace, to bestow upon him that opens; this is such a sight as dazzles the eyes of Angels. What saist thou now, Sinner, Is not this God rich in Mercy? Hath not this God great Love for Sinners?"[59]

And then in his work *Light for Them that Sit in Darkness*:

> It giveth us the best discovery of ourselves. Wouldest thou know Sinner, what thou art; look up to the Cross and behold a Weeping, Bleeding, Dying Jesus: nothing could do but that, nothing could save thee but his Blood; Angels could not, Saints could not, God could not, because he could not ly [*sic*]; because he could not deny himself. What a thing is Sin, that it should sink all that bear its burdens, yea, it sunk the Son of God himself into death and the Grave, and had also sunk him into Hell-fire for ever, had he not been the Son of God; had he not been able to take it on his Back and bear it away. O, this Lamb of God. Sinners are going to Hell, Christ was the Delight of his Father, and had a whole Heaven to himself; but that did not content him, Heaven could not hold him. He must come into the world to save sinners.[60]

In addition, Beeke emphasizes Bunyan's bringing together the grace of God with the fear of the Lord. He states, "John Bunyan delighted to fear the Lord . . . [He] feared God because He is God—the infinitely glorious Lord, beyond our comprehension. The only proper response to such a Being is awe and adoration."[61] Bunyan's own words bring together these thoughts as he states, "Thus you see what a weighty and great grace this grace of the holy fear of God is."[62]

Harry Poe believes Bunyan especially stressed the work of Christ, as Bunyan believed that the Quakers had spiritualized Christ out of the gospel. In fact, Poe thinks Bunyan "made the historical activity of Christ the primary focus of his preaching."[63] Beeke concurs, as he states, "the singular aim of a heart mastered by grace is to lift up and magnify Jesus Christ, both as the Christ revealed Word and the Christ of personal experience based on that Word . . . Bunyan excelled in both."[64]

---

59. John Bunyan, *Saved by Grace* in *The Miscellaneous Works of John Bunyan*, ed. Richard L. Greaves (Oxford: Oxford University Press, 1979), 8:202.

60. John Bunyan, *Light for Them that Sit in Darkness* in *The Miscellaneous Works of John Bunyan*, ed. Richard L. Greaves (Oxford: Oxford University Press, 1979), 8:151.

61. Joel R. Beeke and Paul M. Smalley, *John Bunyan and the Grace of Fearing God* (Phillipsburg, NJ: P & R, 2016), 131.

62. John Bunyan, *A Treatise of the Fear of God* in *The Miscellaneous Works of John Bunyan*, ed. Richard L. Greaves (Oxford: Oxford University Press, 1981), 9:62.

63. Harry L. Poe, "John Bunyan," in *Baptist Theologians*, eds. Timothy George and David S. Dockery (Nashville: Broadman & Holman, 1990), 31.

64. Beeke, "John Bunyan's Preaching to the Heart," 722.

Bunyan's own words reflect this priority of Christ in his preaching:

For I have been in my preaching, especially when I have been engaged in the doctrine of the life by Christ, without works, as if an angel of God had stood at my back to encourage me: O it hath been with such power and heavenly evidence upon my own soul, while I have been laboring to unfold it, to demonstrate it, and to fasten it upon the consciences of other, that I could not be contented with saying, I believe and am sure; methought I was more than sure, if it be lawful so to express myself, that those things which I then asserted, were true.[65]

Beeke emphasizes that Bunyan "focused on Christ and the riches of His grace, moving his listeners to exalt their Savior." In his sermon *Saved by Grace*, Bunyan preached: "O Son of God! Grace was in all thy tears, grace came bubbling out of thy side with thy blood, grace came forth with every word of thy sweet mouth. Grace came out where the whip smote thee, where the thorns pricked thee, where the nails and spear pierced thee. O blessed Son of God! Here is grace indeed! Unsearchable riches of grace! Grace enough to make angels wonder, grace to make sinners happy, grace to astonish devils."[66]

Harris believes Bunyan has "much to say to the man living the Christian life."[67] In his work *The Heavenly Footman*, Bunyan exhorts believers to run the race set before them. He states, "Arise man, be slothful no longer, set foot, and heart and all into the way of God, and run, the crown is at the end of the race; there also standeth the loving fore-runner, even Jesus, who hath prepared heavenly provision to make the soul welcome, and he will give it thee with a more willing heart than even thou canst desire it of him."[68]

According to Barry Horner, Bunyan's most famous work, *Pilgrim's Progress*, is "nearly 90% concerned with the progressive sanctification of Christian [the book's main character] through periods of both buffetings in the wilderness and of blessings experienced through Christian fellowship."[69] Horner sees *Pilgrim's Progress* as an "allegorical tract that focuses mainly upon the authentic life-journey of a bona fide Christian."[70] In addition, he sees Christian's journey

---

65. Bunyan, *Grace Abounding*, 79.

66. John Bunyan, *Saved by Grace* in *The Miscellaneous Works of John Bunyan* in *Works*, ed. Richard L. Greaves (Oxford: Oxford University Press, 1979), 8:191.

67. Harris, "Moving the Heart," 46.

68. John Bunyan, *The Heavenly Footman* in *The Miscellaneous Works of John Bunyan*, ed. Graham Midgley (Oxford: Oxford University Press, 1986), 5:140.

69. Barry E. Horner, *John Bunyan's Pilgrim's Progress: Themes and Issues* (Webster, NY: Evangelical, 2003), 146.

70. Ibid., 146–47.

toward the heavenly city as "a most graphic representation of the biblical pattern of encountering 'conflicts without' and 'fears within.'"[71]

In this race, spiritual exercises are extremely important for the Christian. Harris thinks that prayer is "the most important and yet the most difficult of the spiritual exercises."[72] Bunyan speaks to this, as he encourages believers through his own experience. He states,

> For, as for my heart, when I go to pray, I find it so loath to go to God, and when it is with him, so loath to stay with him, that many times I am forced in my prayers; first, to beg of God he would take mine heart and set it on himself in Christ, and when it is there, that he would keep it there . . . Oh the starting holes that the heart hath in the time of prayer! none knows how may by-ways the heart hath, and back-lains to slip away from the presence of God.[73]

Despite not fully developing a theology of preaching, prominent themes of theology typify Bunyan's writings. Beeke believes, "Bunyan's preaching was not only doctrinal in dealing with the weighty matters of the faith but it was also *doxological*, calling forth praise from awakened hearts."[74] Parry concurs, as he states, "Most of Bunyan's sermon treatises follow the doctrine and use structure, beginning with explication of a biblical text and then applying it to his hearers. However, though there are often identifiable 'doctrine' and 'use' sections of Bunyan's discourses, these are not sharply distinct, but intermingle. Likewise, Bunyan mingles methodical exposition and passionate exhortation throughout. Teaching and moving go hand in hand for Bunyan."[75]

Although Bunyan did not develop a formal theology of preaching, Bunyan had much to say about theology. As discussed, especially prominent in his sermons were the theological themes of the grace and fear of God, exaltation of Christ, and perseverance in the Christian life. Perhaps his legacy was not so much in a preaching style or method, but in the life he lived. He faithfully persevered in preaching God's Word, regardless of his circumstances, doing so even during time of personal and family grief, and when in prison, or when the government opposed him. He even communicated God's Word through the writing of books.

---

71. Ibid., 145.
72. Harris, *Moving the Heart*, 47.
73. John Bunyan, *I Will Pray with the Spirit* in *The Miscellaneous Works of John Bunyan*, ed. Richard L. Greaves (Oxford: Oxford University Press, 1976), 2:256–57.
74. Beeke, "John Bunyan's Preaching to the Heart," 722.
75. Parry, "A Divine Kind of Rhetoric," 214.

CONTRIBUTIONS TO PREACHING

What, then, is Bunyan's preaching legacy? It appears that Bunyan was a preacher who applied God's Word directly to his heart and to the heart of his listeners. This is similar to Ezra, "For Ezra had devoted himself to the *study* and *observance* of the Law of the LORD, and *to teaching its* decrees and laws in Israel" (Ezra 7:10, emphasis added). Such biblical and personal integrity largely explains why Bunyan's preaching was so greatly used by God. Beeke describes this by saying, "For Bunyan not only taught perseverance; he also persevered, through many sore trials, across many years . . . His life likewise reveals that such perseverance is not rooted in mere human strength, but results from God's mighty grace at work in us."[76] Parry summarized this by stating, "Bunyan is both a shepherd of his flock, who gives propositional instruction to keep them on the straight path, and a fisherman, who offers imaginative bait to lure sinners into the gospel net."[77]

Or in Bunyan's own words he stated, "When men do come to see the things of another world, what a God, what a Christ, what a heaven, and what an eternal glory there is to be enjoyed also, when they see that it is possible for them to have a share in it, I tell you it will make them run through thick and thin to enjoy it."[78]

Sermon Excerpt

On Praying in the Spirit[79]

[Prayer] is a sincere pouring out of the soul to God. Sincerity is such a grace as runs through all the graces of God in us, and through all the actings of a Christian, and hath the sway in them too, or else their actings are not anything regarded of God, and so of and in prayer, of which particularly David speaketh, when he mentions prayer, Psal. 66:17,18. I cried unto him, the Lord with my mouth, and he was extolled with my tongue. If I regard iniquity in my heart, the Lord will not hear my prayer, Psal. 17:1, 2 3, 4. Part of the exercise of prayer is sincerity, without which God looks not upon it as prayer in a good sense: Then shall you seek me and find me, when ye shall search for me with all your heart, Jer. 29:12,13.

---

76. Joel R. Beeke, "Bunyan's Perseverance," in *The Pure Flame of Devotion: The History of Christian Spirituality*, eds. G. Stephen Weaver Jr. and Ian H. Clary (Kitchener, Ontario: Joshua, 2013), 325.

77. Parry, "A Divine Kind of Rhetoric," 245.

78. Bunyan, *The Heavenly Footman*, 5:163.

79. Bunyan, *I Will Pray with the Spirit*, 2:236–37.

The want of this made the Lord reject their prayers in Hos. 7:14, where he saith, They have not cried unto me with their heart (that is, in sincerity) when they howled upon their beds. But for a pretence, for a show in hypocrisy, to be seen of men, and applauded for the same, they prayed.

Sincerity was that which Christ commended in Nathaniel, when he was under the fig tree; Behold, an Israelite indeed, in whom is no guile. Probably this good man was pouring out of his soul to God in prayer under the fig tree, and that in a sincere and unfainted spirit before the Lord. The prayer that hath this in it, as one of the principal ingredients, is the prayer that God looks at. Thus, The prayer of the upright is his delight, Prov. 15:8.

And why must sincerity be one of the essentials of prayer which is accepted of God, but because sincerity carries the soul in all simplicity to open its heart to God, and to tell him the case plainly without equivocation; to condemn itself plainly, without dissembling; to cry to God heartily, without complementing. I have surely heard Ephraim bemoaning himself thus; Thou has chastised me, and I was chastised, as a bullock unaccustomed to the yoak [sic], Jer. 31:18. Sincerity is the same in a corner alone as it is before the face of the world. It knows not how to wear two vizards, one for an appearance before men, and another for a short snatch in a corner; but it must have God, and be with him in the duty of prayer. It is not lip-labour that it doth regard, for it is the heart that God looks at, and that which sincerity looks at, and that which prayer comes from, if it be that prayer which is accompanied with sincerity. ◆

BIBLIOGRAPHY

Primary Sources

Bunyan, John. *Grace Abounding to the Chief of Sinners*. Edited by Roger Sharrock. Oxford: Oxford University Press, 1962.
_____. *Grace Abounding: With Other Spiritual Autobiographies*. Oxford World's Classics. Edited by John Stachniewski and Anita Pacheco. New York: Oxford University Press, 2008.
_____. *The Holy War*. Edited by Roger Sharrock and James Forrest. Oxford: Oxford University Press, 1980.
_____. *The Holy War: Annotated Companion to The Pilgrim's Progress*. Edited by Daniel V. Runyan. Eugene, OR: Pickwick, 2012.
_____. *The Life and Death of Mr. Badman*. Edited by James F. Forrest and Roger Sharrock. Oxford: Oxford University Press, 1988.
_____. *The Miscellaneous Works of John Bunyan: Volume 1: Some Gospel-Truths Opened, A Vindication of Some Gospel-Truths Opened, and, A Few Sighs from Hell*. Edited by T. L. Underwood. Oxford: Oxford University Press, 1980.
_____. *The Miscellaneous Works of John Bunyan: Volume 2: The Doctrine of the Law and Grace Unfolded, and, I Will Pray With the Spirit*. Edited by Richard L. Greaves. Oxford: Oxford University Press, 1976.

_____. *The Miscellaneous Works of John Bunyan: Volume 3: Christian Behaviour, The Holy City, The Resurrection of the Dead*. Edited by J. Sears McGee. Oxford: Oxford University Press, 1987.

_____. *The Miscellaneous Works of John Bunyan: Volume 4: A Defence of the Doctrine of Justification, A Confession of My Faith, Differences in Judgment About*. Edited by T. L. Underwood. Oxford: Oxford University Press, 1990.

_____. *The Miscellaneous Works of John Bunyan: Volume 5: Barren Fig-Tree; Strait Gate; Heavenly Footman*. Edited by Graham Midgley. Oxford: Oxford University Press, 1986.

_____. *The Miscellaneous Works of John Bunyan: Volume 6: The Poems*. Edited by Graham Midgley. Oxford: Oxford University Press, 1980.

_____. *The Miscellaneous Works of John Bunyan: Volume 7: Solomon's Temple Spiritualized, The House of the Forest of Lebanon, The Water of Life*. Edited by Roger Sharrock. Oxford: Oxford University Press, 1989.

_____. *The Miscellaneous Works of John Bunyan: Volume 8: Instruction for the Ignorant; Light for Them That Sit in Darkness; Saved by Grace; Come, & Welcome to Jesus Christ*. Edited by Richard L. Greaves. Oxford: Oxford University Press, 1979.

_____. *The Miscellaneous Works of John Bunyan: Volume 9: A Treatise of the Fear of God, The Greatness of the Soul, A Holy Life*. Edited by Richard L. Greaves. Oxford: Oxford University Press, 1981.

_____. *The Miscellaneous Works of John Bunyan: Volume 10: Seasonable Counsel and A Discourse upon the Pharisee and the Publicane*. Edited by Owen C. Watkins. Oxford: Oxford University Press, 1988.

_____. *The Miscellaneous Works of John Bunyan: Volume 11: Good News for the Vilest of Men; The Advocateship of Jesus Christ*. Edited by Richard L. Greaves. Oxford: Oxford University Press, 1985.

_____. *The Miscellaneous Works of John Bunyan: Volume 12: The Acceptable Sacrifice; Last Sermon; An Exposition of the Ten First Chapters of Genesis; Of. . .* Edited by W. R. Owens. Oxford: Oxford University Press, 1994.

_____. *The Miscellaneous Works of John Bunyan: Volume 13: Israel's Hope Encouraged; The Desire of the Righteous Granted; The Saints Privilege and Profit*. Edited by W. R. Owens. Oxford: Oxford University Press, 1994.

_____. *The Pilgrim's Progress: From this World to that Which is to Come*, 2nd ed. Edited by Roger Sharrock. Oxford: Oxford University Press, 1960.

_____. *The Pilgrim's Progress*. Oxford World's Classics. Edited by W. R. Owens. New York: Oxford University Press, 2003.

_____. *The Works of John Bunyan*. Edited by George Offor. 3 vols. 1854. Repr. Carlisle, PA: Banner of Truth Trust, 1991.

Biographies on John Bunyan

Jeffrey, D. L. "Bunyan, John." in *Biographical Dictionary of Evangelicals*. Edited by Timothy Larsen. Downers Grove, IL: InterVarsity Press, 2003.

Greaves, Richard. *Glimpses of Glory: John Bunyan and English Dissent*. Palo Alto, CA: Stanford University Press, 2002.

_____. *John Bunyan*. Vol. 2 of *Courtenay Studies in Reformation Theology*. Grand Rapids: Eerdmans, 1969.

Hill, Christopher. *A Tinker and a Poor Man: John Bunyan and His Church, 1628–1688*. New York: Knopf, 1989.

Larsen, David L. *The Company of Preachers: A History of Biblical Preaching from the Old Testament to the Modern Era*. Grand Rapids: Kregel, 1998.

Piper, John. *The Hidden Smile of God: The Fruit of Affliction in the Lives of John Bunyan, William Cowper, and David Brainerd*. Vol. 2 of *The Swans Are Not Silent*. Wheaton, IL: Crossway, 2001.

Poe, Harry L. "John Bunyan." Pages 26–48 in *Baptist Theologians*. Edited by Timothy George and David S. Dockery. Nashville: Broadman & Holman, 1990.

Rupp, Gordon. *Six Makers of English Religion: 1500–1700*. New York: Harper & Brothers, 1957.

Schwanda, Tom. "Bunyan, John (1628–1688)." Pages 324–25 in *Dictionary of Christian Spirituality*. Edited by Glen G. Scorgie. Grand Rapids: Zondervan, 2011.

Tindall, William Y. *John Bunyan: Mechanick Preacher*. Columbia University Studies in English and Comparative Literature. 1934. Repr. New York: Russell and Russell, 1964.

Winslow, Ola Elizabeth. *John Bunyan*. New York: Macmillan, 1961.

John Bunyan's Preaching

Batson, E. Beatrice. "The Artistry of John Bunyan's Sermons." *The Westminster Theological Review* (1976): 166–81.

Beeke, Joel R. "John Bunyan's Preaching to the Heart." Pages 711–24 in *A Puritan Theology: Doctrine for Life*. Edited by Joel R. Beeke and Mark Jones. Grand Rapids: Reformation Heritage, 2014.

Coleman, Julie. "The Manufactured Homespun Style of John Bunyan's Prose." *Bunyan Studies* 18 (2014): 107–37.

Harris, John. "Moving the Heart: The Preaching of John Bunyan." Pages 32–51 in *Not by Might nor by Power*. Westminster Conference Papers, 1988. London: Westminster Conference, 1989.

Pooley, Roger. "Plan and Simple: Bunyan and Style." Pages 91–110 in *John Bunyan: Conventicle and Parnassus: Tercentenary Essays*. Edited by N. H. Keeble. Oxford: Clarendon; Oxford University Press, 1988.

Preaching of the Puritans

Adlington, Hugh, Peter McCullough, and Emma Rhatigan, eds. *The Oxford Handbook of the Early Modern Sermon*. Oxford: Oxford University Press, 2011.

Carlson, Eric Josef. "The Boring of the Ear: Shaping the Pastoral Vision of Preaching in England." Pages 249–96 in *Preachers and People in the Reformations and Early Modern Period*. Edited by Larissa Taylor. Leiden: Brill, 2001.

Graham, Elspeth. "'Lewd, Profane Swaggers' and Charismatic Preachers: John Bunyan and George Fox." Pages 307–18 in *Sacred and Profane: Secular and Devotional Interplay in Early Modern British Literature*. Edited by Helen Wilcox, Richard Todd, and Alasdair MacDonald. Amsterdam: VU University Press, 1996.

Huges, Ann. "The Pulpit Guarded: Confrontations between Orthodox and Radicals in Revolutionary England." Pages 31–50 in *John Bunyan and His England, 1628–1688*. Edited by Anne Laurence, W. R. Owens, and Stuart Sim. London: Hambledon, 1990.

Hunt, Arnold. *The Art of Hearing: English Preachers and their Audiences, 1590–1640*. Cambridge: Cambridge University Press, 2010.

Keeble, N. H. *Literary Culture of Nonconformity in Later Seventeenth-Century England*. Athens, GA: University of Georgia Press; Leicester: Leicester University Press, 1987.

Parry, David. "A Divine Kind of Rhetoric: Puritanism and Persuasion in Early Modern England Puritanism and Rhetoric." PhD diss., Christ's College, University of Cambridge, 2011.

Patterson, W. B. *William Perkins and the Making of a Protestant England*. New York: Oxford University Press, 2014.

Perkins, William. *The Art of Prophesying* and *The Calling of the Ministry*. Edited by Sinclair B. Ferguson. 1606. Repr. Carlisle, PA: Banner of Truth Trust, 1996.

Swaim, Kathleen M. *Pilgrim's Progress, Puritan Progress: Discourses and Contexts*. Chicago: University of Illinois Press, 1993.

General Works on John Bunyan

Beeke, Joel R. "Bunyan's Perseverance." Pages 323–41 in *The Pure Flame of Devotion: The History of Christian Spirituality*. Edited by G. Stephen Weaver Jr. and Ian Hugh Clary. Kitchener, Ontario: Joshua, 2013.

Beeke, Joel R. and Paul M. Smalley. *John Bunyan and the Grace of Fearing God*. Phillipsburg, NJ: P & R, 2016.

Davies, Michael. *Graceful Reading: Theology and Narrative in the Works of John Bunyan*. New York: Oxford University Press, 2002.

_____, ed. *Oxford Handbook of John Bunyan*. Oxford: Oxford University Press, 2018.

Duke, Roger D., and Phil A. Newton. *Venture All for God: Piety in the Writings of John Bunyan*. Profiles in Reformed Spirituality. Grand Rapids: Reformation Heritage, 2011.

Dunan-Page, Anne, ed. *The Cambridge Companion to Bunyan*. Cambridge: Cambridge University Press, 2010.

Horner, Barry E. *John Bunyan's Pilgrim's Progress: Themes and Issues*. Webster, NY: Evangelical, 2003.

Kaufmann, U. Milo. *The Pilgrim's Progress and Traditions in Puritan Meditation*. Vol. 163 of *Yale Studies in English*. New Haven: Yale University Press, 1966.

Lewis, C. S. "The Vision of John Bunyan." Pages 146–53 in *Selected Literary Essays*. Edited by Walter Hooper. Cambridge: Cambridge University Press, 1969.

Najapfour, Brian G. *The Very Heart of Prayer: Reclaiming John Bunyan's Spirituality*. Memphis: Borderstone, 2012.

Packer, J. I. *A Quest for Godliness: The Puritan Vision of the Christian Life*. Wheaton, IL: Crossway, 1990.

Matthew Henry

Exegesis and Exposition for the Church and the Pulpit

WILLIAM C. WATSON
W. ROSS HASTINGS

Matthew Henry (1662–1714), although known most for his *Exposition of the Old and New Testaments*, was also a powerful preacher. His greatest contribution, however, has been the great influence he has had on some of the most renowned preachers over the past three hundred years. His *Exposition* has proven to be an invaluable guide for sermon preparation, expository preaching, promoting piety, and encouraging pastoral care. In addition to his exposition, his sermons exemplify the kind of exegetical exposition from the Scriptures which has come to characterize the Reformed tradition.

HISTORICAL BACKGROUND

Shortly after Matthew Henry's birth in Chester, England (1662), near the Welsh border, his Puritan father, Philip Henry, was ejected from the Established Church of England for refusing to comply with changes made in the Church at the Restoration of the Stuart monarchy. All worship now had to conform to the liturgy and prayer book of the Established Church. Those who did not comply were barred from holding political office (which included the pastoral office). The result was the ejection of approximately two thousand pastors from their ministry positions and churches. The expulsion extended beyond just their pulpits; they were not allowed within five miles of the towns in which they pastored.[1] At this time in England, no one could preach without a license, which was only issued by bishops who were appointed by the king. Many were imprisoned for preaching without a license, as was John Bunyan, a Baptist and author of *Pilgrim's Progress*. All unauthorized worship was outlawed, except for gatherings with less than five

---

1. "Charles II, 1665: An Act for restraining Non-Conformists from inhabiting in Corporations," in *Statutes of the Realm*, vol. 5: 1628–80 (Great Britain Record Commission, 1819), 575.

people who were not in the same family. Matthew Henry's father, Philip, was fined several times for leading illegal congregations and was twice imprisoned under accusations of conspiracy, until the Revolution of 1688 brought religious toleration to England.

Matthew Henry apparently began reading the Bible at the age of three.[2] He was converted at the age of ten after hearing one of his father's sermons on repentance. He was homeschooled and as a boy would mimic the preaching styles of other pastors, often repeating their sermons verbatim, to the amazement of others. Some feared that young Matthew was so good at this that he would be lifted up with pride, but his father replied, "Let him go on; he fears God and designs well, and I hope God will keep him and bless him."[3]

Nonconformists were also excluded from attending the universities, so at the age of eighteen, Matthew was sent by his father to London to attend a nonconformist academy, until it was forcibly closed by the government. He then studied law at the Inns of Court for a year before returning home to Chester to pursue his real passion, the ministry of preaching. In spite of persecution by the government and a year studying law, his "desire to 'make known the mystery of the gospel,' instead of being weakened, had increased; it was more intense, more enlightened."[4] Back in Chester he quickly became a popular preacher, and in 1687 was ordained into the Presbyterian ministry. Within a few decades the small church grew to nearly four hundred members, and he turned down at least five calls from much larger churches in London and Manchester.

Finally, in 1711, Matthew Henry accepted a call to pastor in east London. He decided it would provide "a much wider door of opportunity to do good,"[5] since he had begun to work on his multivolume commentary on the Bible, and it would give him access to book printers and research libraries. While at London he continued to experience "considerable demand as a preacher,"[6] which kept him from his life's goal of completing *The Exposition of the Old and New Testaments*. His four volumes of the Old Testament were published between 1707 and 1712, and the first volume of the New Testament on the Gospels and Acts of the Apostles was published in 1714. The first volume of his New Testament exposition had only been written through the Acts of the Apostles and was at the printers when he passed away at the age of fifty-two. The rest of his expositions were completed

---

2. Stanford E. Murrell, *A Man Worthy Of Remembrance: A Brief Biography Of Matthew Henry (1662–1714)*, http://www.sounddoctrine.net/LIBRARY/Bible%20Studies/MHenry-biography.htm.

3. Ibid.

4. J. B. Williams, *Memoirs of the Life, Character and Writings of the Rev. Matthew Henry* (Boston: 1830), 59.

5. "Matthew Henry" in *Oxford Dictionary of National Biography* (2004 edition), 26:582–84.

6. Ibid.

by a group of nonconforming ministers.[7] They did this primarily by referring to his own writings and from personal recollections based on his sermons.

THEOLOGY OF PREACHING

It has been observed that the great preaching ministry of George Whitefield shows a great measure of dependence on Matthew Henry's *Commentary on the Whole Bible*.[8] Henry's careful exegetical approach to Scripture bore fruit in the lucid and powerful expositions of this great Calvinistic Methodist. Given that theology has its primary source and ultimate authority in the Word of God (properly exegeted and interpreted), one can safely assume that Whitefield's theology in general, and his theology of preaching in particular, reflected that of his commentator. David Crump confirms this connection: "Puritan theology, passed on as it was through the writings of Matthew Henry, may well have enjoyed the period of its greatest influence during the ministry of George Whitefield. Certainly, Puritan concern for an evangelized England was largely fulfilled through this man's preaching, while Henry's in-depth, practical, Calvinistic and biblical exposition served as the educational backdrop for almost every one of Whitefield's sermons. Had Matthew Henry never been read by anyone other than George Whitefield, he still would have spoken to an audience of thousands."[9]

The more widely known theology of George Whitefield, inasmuch as it was influenced by Henry's commentary, provides a window into the specific theological bents of Henry. These include "Puritanism, not only in its theology but also in its method of evangelism."[10] This included Calvinistic "federalism," which derives from the Latin term for covenant (*foedus*). Soteriological federalism is a stream of Reformed thought which stressed the federal headship of Adam and then of the last Adam, Christ. Thus, each human, being represented by Adam, is, legally speaking, guilty before God as a consequence of Adam's primal sin, irrespective of his or her own individual sin, although corruption of all Adam's descendants made their own sin inevitable. Likewise, on this account, humanity in Christ is declared justified through the righteous act of Christ in his death for us. This was, of course, restricted to elect and redeemed humanity, who by the secret decree of God are brought into union with Christ in the eternal councils of God.

---

7. Ibid.

8. David Crump, "The Preaching of George Whitefield and His Use of Matthew Henry's Commentary," *Crux* 25, no. 3 (September 1989): 19–28.

9. Ibid., 24.

10. Ibid.

Interestingly, on examination of Henry's exposition of Romans 5, the core text on federalism, one finds a nuancing that reflects a balance on a number of issues. For example, on the matter of the adjoining of justification and sanctification, he seems clear and in line with Calvin, over against an excessive federalism. Thus, in his commentary on Romans 5:18–19, reflecting on the results of Christ's representative act of obedience for humanity, he states: "This free gift is to all believers, upon their believing, unto justification of life. It is not only a justification that frees from death, but that entitles to life." Furthermore, though he does clearly express that only the elect believer is the beneficiary of Christ's salvation, he nevertheless shares the gospel tones of invitation to all. Thus, he says,

> There is a free gift come upon all men, that is, it is made and offered promiscuously to all. The salvation wrought is a common salvation; the proposals are general, the tender free; whoever will may come, and take of these waters of life. . . . Much more the grace of God, and the gift by grace. God's goodness is, of all his attributes, in a special manner his glory, and it is that grace that is the root (his favour to us in Christ), and the gift is by grace. We know that God is rather inclined to show mercy; punishing is his strange work.[11]

These Calvinistic and modified federalistic foundations affected the preaching of the gospel by Henry and Whitefield in the following ways: (1) they were not afraid to preach that in Christ there was salvation *sufficient* for all; (2) they did not know who the elect were and therefore could preach grace to all, yet trusting that God, by the power of the Spirit, would draw those to him who would prove to be the elect; and (3) they knew the drawing power of the gospel of Christ and were confident in it over against the power of guilt and sin. On this latter point, Henry is eloquent in his Romans 5 exposition where he is comparing the efficacy of the condemning consequences of Adam's act with that of the justifying consequences of Christ's reconciling act. There he speaks of "the communication of grace and love by Christ" which "goes beyond the communication of guilt and wrath by Adam" and the "magnifying of Christ's love" and of the exceedingly greater "power and efficacy in the righteousness and grace of Christ . . . to justify and save us," compared with the power and efficacy of the first Adam's sin to condemn us. In Christ, the last Adam, "The stream of grace and righteousness is deeper and broader than the stream of guilt," he concludes.[12]

---

11. Matthew Henry, *Commentary on the Whole Bible*, ed. Leslie F. Church (Grand Rapids: Zondervan, 1961), 1765.

12. Ibid., 1765–66.

As a Calvinist, Matthew Henry also believed that prayer was crucial to preaching. The sovereignty of God and the responsibility to pray were somehow compatible. He said, "God's grace can save souls without our preaching, but our preaching cannot save them without God's grace, and that grace must be sought by prayer."[13] Prayer was a major emphasis of Matthew Henry's ministry; he believed it should not be taken lightly but with order and purpose. His work *A Method for Prayer* is currently experiencing renewed popularity among those interested in spiritual formation.[14] In his diary, Henry wrote: "I love prayer. It is that which buckles on all the Christian's armour."[15] In a list of eight things which become available to the Christian through prayer, number seven in Henry's list is: "strength ready for all their performances in doing work, fighting work. He is their *arm every morning* (Isa 33:2)."[16]

The way Whitefield, Henry's protégé, ended sermons is evidence of the influence of Henry's belief in the primary agency of the sovereignty of God in the human response to preaching. While he did call his audience to personal response, his closing plea was not like the altar call with which many are familiar, and which is inherited from more Arminian roots. Whitefield did not ask people to "respond immediately or publicly to his message." Rather they were exhorted to "search themselves, examine their condition before God, go home, diligently pray that God would apply his saving grace to their lives, and then continue in this condition until they 'knew' with[in] themselves that they had been made new by the Spirit."[17]

Commitment to Exegetical Preaching

Henry exhibited a high view of Scripture, always preaching "through the lens of Biblical primacy."[18] Instead of preaching to satisfy his own personal fancies, or those of his congregation, he methodically taught through the Bible in an expository method to emphasize what the Bible emphasized. According to one of his associates who wrote a memoir of Matthew Henry shortly after his death, "He shunned not to declare the whole counsel of God. He delighted in preaching Christ

---

13. *Matthew Henry's Commentary on the Whole Bible* (Old Tappan, NJ: Revell, 1900), Ezekiel 37:1–14, IV:966.

14. See, Matthew Henry, *A Method for Prayer and Directions for Daily Communion with God* (Eremitical Press, 2009). This renewed interest is evidenced by digital accessibility.

15. J. B. Williams, *The Lives of Philip and Matthew Henry* (Carlisle, PA: Banner of Truth Trust, 1974), 2:210.

16. Allan Harman, ed. *Matthew Henry's Unpublished Sermons on The Covenant of Grace* (Ross-shire, Scotland, UK: Christian Heritage, 2003), 200.

17. Crump, "The Preaching of George Whitefield and His Use of Matthew Henry's Commentary," 24.

18. John Hun Joo, *Matthew Henry: Pastoral Liturgy in Challenging Times* (Eugene, OR: Pickwick, 2014), xxi.

and the doctrines of free grace; but with a zeal he preached up holiness . . . saying, 'That they who believe God should be careful to maintain good works.'"[19] Since a primary emphasis of his preaching was personal morality, he was often accused of being too legalistic, but his reply was that "he was no more of a legalist than the Apostle James whom he knew well how to reconcile with the Apostle Paul."[20]

The Bible was certainly central to Matthew Henry's preaching. He considered Scripture reading during the worship service "not only an exhortation, but an adjuration by the LORD,"[21] a practice much neglected in many churches in our time. Henry insisted that "reading the scriptures in religious assemblies is an ordinance of God, whereby He is honored and his church edified."[22] Henry cited the example of Ezra and the Levites leading worship in Jerusalem after their return, "what they read they expounded, showed the intent and meaning of it, and what use was to be made of it; they gave the sense in other words, that they might cause the people to understand the meaning."[23] According to Henry, "reading is good, and preaching good, but expounding brings the reading and the preaching together, and makes the reading the more intelligible and the preaching the more convincing."[24]

In this regard, Henry was in fact simply expressing what was commonplace in his own Reformed tradition. He affirmed the Second Helvetic Confession of the Protestant Reformation which says, "The preaching of the Word of God is the Word of God."[25] In this confession is the notion that we ourselves have nothing of importance to say comparable with what God has said.[26]

Commitment to Evangelical, Gospel-Centric Preaching

It was said of Whitefield that he clothed the exegesis of Henry with real-world exhortation and that he increasingly perceived that the role of every text and every sermon was the proclamation of the good news. As Crump indicates, "It should, then, come as no surprise to learn that after 1739, no matter what the sermon text, no matter how expositional he may have begun, no matter how many of Henry's points he may or may not have incorporated into his own outline, Whitefield's messages always evolved into and concluded themselves as powerful offers of the

19. S. Palmer, "Memoirs of Matthew Henry," preface in *Matthew Henry's Commentary on the Whole Bible*, I:viii.

20. Ibid.

21. *Matthew Henry's Commentary*, 1 Thessalonians 5:27, VI, 791.

22. Ibid., Nehemiah 8:1–8, II:1094 in Joo, *Matthew Henry*, 87.

23. Ibid., Nehemiah 8:8, II:1095 in Joo, *Matthew Henry*, 87.

24. Ibid., Nehemiah 8:3–8, II:1094 in Joo, *Matthew Henry*, 87.

25. The Second Helvetic Confession, https://www.ccel.org/creeds/helvetic.htm, paragraph 4.

26. As Bryan Chapell has said, "When we speak, therefore, we design our messages to express the truths of the eternal Word so that the church may be the 'mouth house' of God that Martin Luther described" *Christ-Centered Preaching: Redeeming the Expository Sermon*, 2nd ed. (Grand Rapids: Baker, 2005), 32.

gospel of grace."[27] One might be tempted to say with Darrell Johnson, that he preached good news, not good advice.[28] Some of Whitefield's sermons seem to have been in the good advice category when he preached in churches, and certainly Henry offered much by way of good advice concerning holiness and morality in his preaching. Whether this was always ensconced in the gospel is a matter for debate. Henry has, as noted, been accused of legalism. The tone and ethos of exhortation in Puritan preaching can sometimes seem to lack full gospel immersion, such that repentance may sometimes seem legalistic as opposed to grace-driven. That is, in the words of James Torrance, the Scholastic Calvinist gospel sometimes feels more like contract rather than covenant. Torrance persistently critiques the law-gospel model of high Federal Calvinism. According to him its nature-grace interpretation, along with the *ordo salutis* (Man-Law-Sin-Repentance-Grace), are inconsistent with the New Testament God who is love in his innermost being, and therefore in his work and ways as Father, Son, and Holy Spirit.[29]

Commitment to Applicational Preaching

Crump states, "Whitefield was such a good preacher and evangelist, partly, because he gave such a prominent place to application. His sermons were never ethereal or theoretical. They were always firmly planted in the soil of the real world. This was his gift. He was able to take the points of exposition laid out by Henry and put clothes on them."[30] This seems to suggest a tendency in Matthew Henry to be somewhat more theological and distant from real experience than Whitefield. While this may have been true, one can celebrate the idiosyncratic nature of the teaching gifts in each. Henry's ministry was more of a steady and systematic teaching ministry in the context of the local church, while Whitefield's primary focus was evangelistic and in the fields. Henry's emphasis on the sovereignty of God in preaching may have led him to let the *implications* of the preaching be enough, allowing the Spirit to make specific application in the individual lives of the congregants.[31]

---

27. Crump, "The Preaching of George Whitefield and His Use of Matthew Henry's Commentary," 23.

28. Darrell Johnson, *The Glory of Preaching: Participating in God's Transformation of the World* (Downers Grove, IL: InterVarsity Press, 2009).

29. James B. Torrance, "Interpreting the Word by the Light of Christ or the Light of Nature? Calvin, Calvinism, and Barth," *CALVINIANA: Ideas and Influence of Jean Calvin*, ed. R. V. Schnucker (Kirksville, MO: Sixteenth Century Journal, 1988), Vol.X, 255–67; *Worship, Community And The Triune God Of Grace* (The Didsbury Lectures) (Milton Keynes: Paternoster, 1996); "Covenant or Contract? A Study of the Theological Background of Worship in Seventeenth-Century Scotland," *Scottish Journal of Theology* 23 (1970): 51–76; "Covenant or Contract? The Contribution of McLeod Campbell to Scottish Theology," *Scottish Journal of Theology* 26 (1973): 295–311; "The Incarnation and Limited Atonement," *Scottish Bulletin of Evangelical Theology* 2 (1984): 32–40; "The Doctrine of the Trinity in Our Contemporary Situation," *The Forgotten Trinity,* ed. Alasdair Heron (London: BCC/CCBI, 1991), 3. A Selection of Papers, 3–17.

30. Crump, "The Preaching of George Whitefield and His Use of Matthew Henry's Commentary," 23.

31. A contemporary preacher who speaks in support of the "implication" point of view is Darrell Johnson, who opines that it leaves greater room for the Spirit and gives less opportunity for any manipulative tendencies the preacher may have. See Johnson, *The Glory of Preaching,* 140–68.

METHODOLOGY FOR PREACHING

Henry's sermons were crafted around his exegesis and tended to be a point-by-point extraction of the text into the sermon. He eschewed the practice of eisegesis, refusing to concoct his own topic, creating unrelated tangents or superfluous stories. Instead, as one draws living water from a well, he drew out of God's Word what God would have for his people. Each of Matthew Henry's sermons was thus an exposition of the Scriptures with an elaborate argument around that text and numerous supporting points. He enumerated his sermons as if they were a legal brief, perhaps due to his training in law. Sometimes he would draw so much out of the text, especially during the application at the end, that it may have seemed to some that his sermons were topical rather than expository, but he always brought his hearers back to the Word of God.

Although Matthew Henry's sermons in Chester often followed a particular theme which could last for months, each of his sermons had a text that he exposited carefully. Instead of repeating sermons, he would have a different text and would approach his consistent theme with a different emphasis, always arriving at a similar conclusion. Most common was the importance of holiness.[32] Unfortunately, none of his early sermons survive. In his East London pulpit, Matthew Henry continued to exposit the Scriptures, but purposed to preach his way through the Bible. So he preached his first Sunday morning sermon on Genesis 1 and in the afternoon a sermon on Matthew 1.[33] He then proceeded in subsequent Sundays to preach this way through the entire Bible. Henry soon received numerous requests to preach in churches all around London, and "so ready he was to comply with them, that he sometimes appears in his diary to think that he needed an apology . . . he preached so often."[34] Wherever he preached, he always exposited a text in depth, rather than taking a topical approach.

CONTRIBUTIONS TO PREACHING

Matthew Henry's preaching style of expositing the Scriptures insured that "his hearers had particular advantage for improving in Scripture knowledge above those whose ministers discourse only upon short detached passages" so that "Mr. Henry's people in general greatly excelled in judgment and spiritual understanding."[35]

---

32. Palmer, "Memoirs of Matthew Henry," vii.
33. Ibid., xiii.
34. Ibid.
35. Ibid., viii.

According to church historian Philip Schaff, "Few exegetical works outlive their generation; those of Calvin are not likely to be superseded any more than [is] Matthew Henry's *Exposition* for devotional purposes and epigrammatic suggestions to preachers."[36] For three hundred years many great preachers have relied on Henry's *Exposition* in their own sermon preparation. Both George Whitefield and Charles Spurgeon were avid readers of Matthew Henry, Spurgeon placing him in a higher position than John Calvin, insisting that:

First among the mighty for general usefulness we are bound to mention the man whose name is a household word, MATTHEW HENRY. He is most pious and pithy, sound and sensible, suggestive and sober, terse and trustworthy. You will find him to be glittering with metaphors, rich in analogies, over-flowing with illustrations, superabundant in reflections. He delights in apposition and alliteration; he is usually plain, quaint, and full of pith; he sees right through a text directly; apparently he is not critical, but he quietly gives the result of an accurate critical knowledge of the original fully up to the best critics of his time. . . . he is deeply spiritual, heavenly, and profitable; finding good matter in every text, and from all deducing most practical and judicious lessons. . . . Every minister ought to read Matthew Henry entirely and carefully through once at least. I should recommend you to get through it in the next twelve months after you leave college. . . . You will acquire a vast store of sermons if you read with your notebook close at hand; and as for thoughts, they will swarm around you like twittering swallows around an old gable towards the close of autumn. If you publicly expound the chapter you have just been reading, your people will wonder at the novelty of your remarks and the depth of your thoughts, and then you may tell them what a treasure Henry is.[37]

Matthew Henry not only influenced Whitefield and Spurgeon, but a host of powerful preachers throughout the eighteenth, nineteenth, and twentieth centuries, including Jonathan Edwards, John Gill, J. Vernon McGee, Martyn Lloyd-Jones, John Stott, John MacArthur, and the Calvary Chapel movement.[38] All of them purposely preached through the Scriptures in an expository manner and utilized Matthew Henry's renowned *Exposition of the Old and New Testaments*.

---

36. Philip Schaff, *History of the Christian Church* (Grand Rapids: Eerdmans, 1910), viii, 525.

37. C. H. Spurgeon, *Commenting and Commentaries: Two Lectures addressed to the students of the Pastor's College, Metropolitan Tabernacle* (London: Passmore & Alabaster, 1876.

38. Stitzinger, "The History of Expository Preaching," *The Masters Seminary Journal* 3, no. 1, 3/1 (Spring 1992): 24, 27.

Another example of Henry's influence is instanced by Allan Harman, who reflects eloquently the reality that the writings of Philip and Matthew Henry "form an important link between puritan biblical exegesis and the evangelical revival" of the eighteenth century in the United Kingdom and in America. He adds, "No other commentary than Matthew Henry's was so widely available and used in the eighteenth century, and deservedly so."[39] Specifically, Harman highlights the influence of this commentary on John Wesley's preaching and writing (minus the Reformed doctrines of particular election and limited atonement) and on various hymns of Charles Wesley. Henry also influenced Scottish Christianity, where Reformed theology was prevalent. John Brown of Haddington "knew Matthew Henry's writings well, and used his exposition while working on his *Self-Interpreting Bible*. He characterized commentators by a single adjective: elegant Calvin, copious Gill, sensible Clarke, curt Bengel, and 'practical Henry.'"[40]

On the other side of the Atlantic, New England Puritan Jonathan Edwards, whose preaching was so influential in the Great Awakening, also reflects an appreciation of Matthew Henry's exegetical preaching that shaped his commentary.[41] There are fifty-two mentions of Henry in Edwards's Yale works.[42] The *Apocalyptic Writings*, for example, includes mention of Henry as a source of Edwards's writing on the book of Revelation (though it has to be said that Willliam Tong actually wrote the commentary on the book of Revelation in Henry's commentary, reflecting Henry's thought as faithfully as he could).[43] Stephen Stein, editor of the *Apocalyptic Writings,* adds that "Edwards drew heavily upon Henry's *Exposition* in the 'Scripture' and in the 'Blank Bible' suggesting that this popular commentator was more influential upon his ideas and interpretations of the Bible than the infrequent use in the 'Apocalypse' implies."[44] In his commentary on the *Notes on Scripture*, Stein again references Henry as a significant influence on Edwards's preaching and writing. He states: "Edwards shared the assumptions and strategies of the Protestant commentarial tradition (including the principle of *sola scriptura*) with a distinguished line of exegetes who set out to explain and interpret the Bible for their own instruction as well as the edification and nurture

---

39. Allan M. Harman, "The Impact of Matthew Henry's *Exposition* on Eighteenth-Century Christianity," *Evangelical Quarterly* 82.1 (2010): 14 (3–14).

40. Ibid., 12.

41. See for example, the influence of Henry's commentary on Proverbs on Edwards's meditation on Proverbs 4:23, as noted in Stephen J. Stein, "'Like Apples of Gold in Pictures of Silver': The Portrait of Wisdom in Jonathan Edwards's Commentary on the Book of Proverbs," in *Church History* 54, no. 3 (September 1985): 328 (324–37).

42. A link to reference all of them is as follows: http://edwards.yale.edu/archive?path=aHR0 cDovL2Vkd2FyZHMueWFsZS5lZHUvY2dpLWJpbi9uZXdadwaGls9zaG93cmVzdF8/Y29uYYy 42LjIuOTcwS4wLjUxLndqZZW8=

43. Jonathan Edwards [1723], *Apocalyptic Writings (WJE Online Vol. 5)*, ed. Stephen J. Stein, 062.

44. Ibid., 063.

of others."[45] Just as Whitefield, Wesley, and Edwards were all formed by the writings of Henry, so have many unknown and unnamed preachers throughout the history of the church. His legacy lives on in the preaching from these pulpits.[46]

Sermon Excerpt

Self-Consideration Necessary to Self-Preservation[47]

Solomon's Proverbs being generally designed to instruct us in our duty to God and man . . . by 'opening the ear to instruction,' . . . In this text Solomon in a few words gives such an account of those whom he found he could do no good upon, as makes their folly manifest before all men. . . . Solomon gives this short account of them . . . they refuse instruction, and in so doing they despise their own souls. We, that have the gospel preached among us . . . may truly say that . . . yet, as to multitudes, he stretcheth out his hand in vain . . . And what is the reason?

First, They refuse instruction. The fool in the text . . . is described to be one that refuseth instruction . . . The word for instruction the margin reads correction; for in our fallen state, when we are all wrong, that which instructs us must correct us. . . . 1. They refuse to hear instruction; they turn their backs upon the word, and will not come where it is preached . . . 2. They refuse to heed it; like the deaf adder, they—if they should come within hearing of it-stop their ears . . . 3. They refuse to comply with it; they will do as they have a mind, whatever they are told or taught to the contrary . . .

Secondly, They that refuse instruction thereby make it to appear, that they despise their own souls; they evidence that they have very low and mean thoughts of their souls. . . . There is a despising ourselves which is commendable and our duty, the same with denying ourselves . . . By giving us divine revelation for the enlightening and directing, the renewing

---

45. Jonathan Edwards [1722], *Notes on Scripture (WJE Online Vol. 15)*, ed. Stephen J. Stein, 6–7. Nearly half the references to Henry come from Edwards's *Catalogues of Books, Yale Works*, vol. 26.

46. On this impact Harman said, "The work of the Wesleys and Whitefield was indebted to Mathew Henry's commentary in particular, and it formed the foundation of biblical teaching from which many of their converts drew spiritual nourishment. No assessment of the evangelical revivial can neglect the impact of the writings of Mathew Henry of Chester and Hackney" "Impact of Matthew Henry's *Exposition*," 12.

47. *Self-Consideration Necessary to Self-Preservation: Or, The Folly of Despising our own Souls and our own Ways, Opened in Two Sermons to Young People* (London: J. Lawrence, 1713). His key text was Proverbs 15:32, which says "He that refuseth instruction despiseth his own soul."

and sanctifying of our souls, God has put the greatest honour imaginable upon us, has distinguished us, not only from the beasts of the earth . . . Now, if we regard not the dictates of divine revelation, we throw away this honour God has put upon our souls, and declare we do not value it. . . . If, therefore, we have any value for that part of their honour, we will receive that instruction.

III. For application. First, Let us see and bewail our folly in having had such low thoughts of our own souls, and that we have forgot their dignity, . . . Secondly, Let us learn for the future how to put a due value upon our own souls; not to magnify ourselves above our brethren—for they are not inferior to us—but to magnify ourselves above the brutes . . . Thirdly, Let us make it to appear that we do indeed value our own souls, and do nothing that looks like despising or undervaluing them. . . . Lastly, If we must not despise our own souls, we must not despise the souls of others: for if ours be precious, are theirs; . . . binds us to do all we can for the salvation of the souls of others, as for the salvation of our own. . . . Pity self-destroying sinners, that are damning their own souls, and if you can do anything . . . help them. ♦

BIBLIOGRAPHY

Henry, Matthew. *The Complete Works of the Rev. Matthew Henry (unfinished commentary excepted) being a collection of All His Treatises, Sermons, and Tracts.* 2 vols. 1855. Repr. Grand Rapids: Baker, 1979.
Matthew Henry's Commentary on the Whole Bible. Old Tappan, NJ: Revell, 1900.
Beeke, Joel R., and Mark Jones. *A Puritan Theology.* Grand Rapids: Reformation Heritage, 2012.
Joo, John Hun. *Matthew Henry: Pastoral Liturgy in Challenging Times.* Eugene, OR: Pickwick, 2014.
Palmer, S. "Memoirs of Matthew Henry." Preface in *Matthew Henry's Commentary.* Old Tappan, NJ: Revell, 1900.
Stitzinger, James. "The History of Expository Preaching." *The Masters Seminary Journal* 3, no. 1, 3/1 (Spring 1992): 5–32.
Summers, William T. *The Quotable Matthew Henry.* New York: Revell, 1962.
Williams, J. B. *Memoirs of the Life, Character and Writings of the Rev. Matthew Henry.* Boston, 1830.
Wykes, David L. "Matthew Henry." *Oxford Dictionary of National Biography* 26 (2004 edition): 582–84.

Published Sermons

Henry, Matthew. "A Church in the House: A Sermon Concerning Family Religion." 1704.
_____. "A Sermon Concerning the Right Management of Friendly Visits." 1704.
_____. "Great Britain's Present Joys and Hopes: Displayed in Two Sermons Preached in Chester."
_____. "Sermon Showing that The Christian Religion is not a Sect, Yet it is Everywhere Spoken Against." (n.d.)
_____. "Disputes Reviewed: In a Sermon, Preached . . . at Salter's Hall . . ." 1710.
_____. "A Sermon Concerning the Work and Success of the Ministry: Preached at Salter's Hall . . ." 1710.
_____. "Hope and Fear Balanced: A Sermon." 1711.
_____. "A Sermon Concerning the Forgiveness of Sin as a Debt." 1711.
_____. "Faith in Christ inferred from Faith in God, in a Sermon." 1711.

_____. Six Funeral Sermons for the Revs. James Owen, Samuel Benion, Frances Tallents, Samuel Lawrence, Richard Stretton, and Daniel Burgess. 1706, 1708, 1712. And for his own mother, Katherine Henry. 1707.

_____. Two Ordination Sermons for Mr. Atkinson and Samuel Clarke. 1713–14.

_____. A Sermon Preached to the Societies for Reformation of Manners, at Salter's Hall. 1712.

_____. "Christ's Favor to Little Children Displayed in a Sermon." 1713.

_____. "A Sermon on the Catechising of Youth." 1713.

_____. "A Memorial of the Fire of the Lord: In a Sermon . . . on the Day of Commemoration of the Burning of London in 1666." 1713.

_____. "Self-Consideration Necessary to Self-Preservation: Or, The Folly of Despising our own Souls and our own Ways, Opened in Two Sermons to Young People." 1713.

Additional Works

Henry, Matthew. *The Exposition of the Old and New Testaments* (Philadelphia, 1828), also known as his *Commentary*.

_____. *The Pleasantness of a Religious Life, Opened and Improved; and Recommended to the Consideration of All, Particularly Young People.* 1714.

_____. *Sober-Mindedness Pressed upon Young People, in a Discourse on Titus 2:6.* 1712.

_____. *Four Discourses against Vice and Profaneness: viz. I. Drunkenness. II. Uncleanness. III. Sabbath-Breaking. IV. Profane Speaking.* n.d.

_____. *Directions for Daily Communion with God, in Three Discourses: Showing I. How to Begin Every Day with God, II. How to Spend the Day with God, III. How to Close the Day with God.* 1712.

_____. *The Communicants' Companion: Or Instructions for the Right Receiving of the Lord's Supper.* 1704.

_____. *Family Hymns, Gathered Mostly out of the Translations of David's Psalms.* 1694.

_____. *A Treatise on Baptism.* n.d.

_____. *A Method for Prayer: With Scripture Expressions Proper to be Used Under Each Head.* 1710.

PART Five

Preaching among the Revivalists

The eighteenth century was a time of great upheaval in the church. While the Protestant Reformation had released people from the chains of church tradition and freed them to study the Scriptures alone for faith and practice, the increasing influence of philosophy on the study of theology caused a seismic shift in the study of religion. When Immanuel Kant bifurcated faith and reason, he also bifurcated the church into two distinct schools: theological liberalism and biblical orthodoxy.

Theological liberalism, as developed through German higher criticism, rejected the infallibility of Scripture and elevated reason over faith. Friedrich Schleiermacher was one of the early champions of a neo-orthodoxy, and he located biblical meaning not in authorial intention but in the mind of the reader. The result in many churches throughout Europe during this era was a rejection of the infallibility and authority of Scripture, and a corresponding embrace of human-centered theology.

Biblical orthodoxy, which built on the legacy of the Puritans, embraced the infallibility of Scripture and viewed faith and reason as partners in the pursuit of God's truth. John Owen, the famed Oxford theologian, repeatedly defended Calvinist doctrine and interpretation, and influenced the development of biblical orthodoxy in the Free Church traditions. The preaching of biblical orthodoxy during this era, which located the meaning of Scripture in authorial intention, continued to affirm Martin Luther's five *Solas* and placed a strong emphasis on the proclamation of the gospel. As a result, the concept of evangelistic meetings began to develop, which emphasized the need of people to experience personal conversion. Further, the corresponding development of oceanic travel made global proclamation of the gospel possible for the first time. There were many revivalist preachers, pastors, and priests during this time, but four are most notable for their enduring contributions to the history of the church.

In a very different locale and theological tradition, stood the French court preacher, **Francois Fénelon** (1651–1715). His ministry bridged the seventeenth and eighteenth centuries. As a Catholic priest, he stood outside the Protestant tradition. Yet he is acknowledged to be one of the greatest preachers in the history of the Catholic Church, and he was a noted rhetorician and student of homiletics. He was unique in his preaching, teaching, and writing styles, emphasizing the pursuit of an experiential relationship with God.

Jonathan Edwards (1703–1758) is the giant among this group, and he remains one of the most influential preachers in church history. While pastoring at Northampton, his preaching contributed to the First Great Awakening. He demonstrated a classic approach to Calvinistic evangelism, balancing both God's sovereignty and human responsibility. **John Wesley** (1703–1791) came from a long line of clergy in the Church of England, but his conversion to Christianity resulted in the development of an evangelistic movement called Methodism. Wesley rejected Calvinism and embraced instead the Arminian understanding of humanity's free will in the process of conversion. He, too, was instrumental in the First Great Awakening and the spread of Methodism in both Britain and the American colonies. **George Whitefield** (1714–1770), a collegiate and ministry contemporary of John Wesley, was a powerful evangelist during the First Great Awakening, making no less than seven preaching trips to America during his lifetime. He is deemed to be one of the greatest orators of the eighteenth century and perhaps one of the greatest orators in the entire history of the Christian church. He was an evangelistic Calvinist, which ultimately led to a schism in his relationship with John Wesley.

Each of these men uniquely shared the message of the gospel with an emphasis on the need for a personal experience with God. Their theologies included Calvinism, Arminianism, and Catholicism. The Great Awakening is indebted to Edwards, Wesley, and Whitefield, while the French Court experienced a fresh renewal of faith through the mysticism of Fénelon. These men stand as a testament to the power of the gospel to transform the lives of those who will receive it by faith.

François Fénelon
The Art of Eloquence

MARTIN I. KLAUBER

With the recent resurgence of interest in spiritual formation and its emphasis on personal solitude and devotion, there has developed a renewed interest in the writings of many among the seventeenth-century French Quietist movement. One of the most famous among the Quietists was also one of the greatest preachers of seventeenth-century France, François de Salignac de la Mothe-Fénelon (1651–1715). During his ministry he preached to the French Royal Court and while still in his twenties, he authored a seminal work on the subject of preaching entitled *Dialogues on Eloquence,* which sought to improve the quality of public oration.

HISTORICAL BACKGROUND

François Fénelon was born on August 6, 1651, the second of three children, to a noble family at the Fénelon Castle in Périgord, in the Aquitaine region, in the southwest of France. His father was Pons de Salignac, Comte de La Mothe-Fénelon and the family had significant connections in both church and state. His uncle Antoine was the bishop of nearby Sarlat and members of the La Mothe-Fénelon family had occupied that seat for fifteen generations. François's early education took place under the watchful eye of private tutors at the Château de Fénelon, as was the custom for members of the nobility. It consisted of the classic Jesuit method of education that emphasized not only mastery of the Latin language but also of the arts of rhetoric and philosophy. When Francois expressed interest in an ecclesiastical career and the study of theology, his uncle was able to help him get enrolled at the *Collège du Plessis* in Paris, where he displayed such an amazing oratorical ability that he was invited to deliver a public sermon at age fifteen. Having completed his education at the *Collège du Plessis* and then at the *Séminaire de Saint-Sulpice,* also in Paris, Fénelon attained the priesthood and began his preaching career. He quickly distinguished himself as a young preacher, and when he drew the attention of the local archbishop in 1679, he was named the head of the *Congregation des Nouvelles-Catholiques,* a school for recently converted young Huguenot girls.[1] While serving in this position, he gained the attention of the King Louis XIV. Louis commissioned him along with the famed court preacher Jacques Bénigne Bossuet to go to western France, which was the stronghold of French Protestantism, in the name of French Catholicism. Just after the Revocation of the Edict of Nantes in 1685, their task in the La Rochelle area was to ensure that those who had been forced to convert to Roman Catholicism would be sincere in their so-called new faith. Fénelon preached there for two years with minimal success, but he did win over support within the Roman Catholic hierarchy. He made a distinction between winning the intellectual debate and winning hearts, noting that it is much more important to win the heart. However, he was much more successful with the former than with the latter.[2]

After his stint in western France, he returned to the *Congregation des Nouvelles* and continued to gain experience in educating young women, which would help him later when the Duchesse de Beauvillier, who had eight daughters asked him for advice on how to educate them. He responded with his *Traité de l'education des filles* in which he argued that girls must be schooled because they would ultimately have the primary responsibility for raising and educating their own children. Her husband, the Duc de Beauvillier was in charge of the education of the king's grandsons and quickly signed up Fénelon for the task of tutoring the king's grandson, the *petit-dauphin*, thereby including Fénelon into the inner circle at the royal court. As the tutor to the Dauphin's eldest son, the seven-year old Duke of Burgundy, from 1689 to 1697 Fénelon composed for him his most famous work about adventures of the son of Ulysses, *Les Aventures de Télémaque* (1693–1694), a book mildly critical of divine right monarchy. In spite of this disparagement, the king then in 1694 named Fénelon as Abbot of Saint-Valéry, a lucrative position, and in 1696 named him Archbishop of Cambrai. While he was in the king's good favor for most of his career, Fénelon ran afoul of royal approval because of some of his religious views which seemed to many to be similar to those of the controversial Quietist movement and the teachings of the influential Mme Guyon. As a result, he was effectively banished from the court, and the king ordered him confined to his diocese.

THE QUIETIST CONTROVERSY

The goal of the Quietist movement was the attainment of pure love for God through the process of contemplation and at disregard for the self. The Spanish

---

1. The Huguenots were the French Protestants who followed the Reformed tradition. The origin of the term is at bit obscure but may have been derived from the German word *Eidgenossen*, which meant those confederates bound together by an oath.

2. Hughes Oliphant Old, *The Reading and Preaching of the Scriptures in the Worship of the Christian Church, Volume 4: The Age of the Reformation* (Grand Rapids: Eerdmans, 2002), 512.

mystic, Miguel de Molinos (1628–1696) had been condemned in 1687 by the Roman Catholic Church on suspicion of elevating contemplation over meditation, stillness over audible prayer, spiritual passivity over Christian action, with the goal of achieving union with God. In this union, it was believed, the individual could reach a sinless state.

Although Mme Guyon (1648–1717) never claimed to be a follower of Quietism, the similarities between her teachings in her book *A Short and Easy Method of Prayer* and those of the Quietists were unmistakable. Fénelon met Mme Guyon in 1688 when she was a part of the social circle of the Duchesse of Beauvillers. He was very impressed by her strong devotional life and encouraged her in her faith. When the Bishop of Chartres noticed the resemblance of her views with Quietism, he informed the king's wife, Mme de Maintenon, who requested an official inquiry into her views led by Fénelon's old friend Bossuet. Some of her views were condemned and Fénelon had to sign off on it. When Bossuet followed up with his *Instructions on the Method of Oration*, he requested that Fénelon sign off on that as well. Fénelon refused, arguing that Mme Guyon had already acquiesced to the original condemnation. He then wrote a rejoinder entitled *Explication des Maximes des Saints,* which was somewhat sympathetic to her views. Louis XIV was shocked that someone so close to the royal household could believe such things and removed Fénelon from his post and ordered him confined to his diocese of Cambrai. Things grew worse for Fénelon when Pope Innocent XII listed twenty-three propositions from Fénelon's book as heterodox. When Fénelon submitted to the pope's authority, the matter died down, but the damage to Fénelon's reputation had already been done.[3]

THEOLOGY OF PREACHING

Fénelon's theology combined traditional Roman Catholic doctrine with a strong emphasis on personal devotion to God. As one can see in his sermons and in his attempts to console the so-called *nouveau convertis*, he fully embraced doctrines such as transubstantiation and ridiculed the so-called Protestant heretics for what he believed was their overemphasis on Scripture, to the detriment to ecclesiastical traditions. In his discussion of the feast of Corpus Christi, he expressed wonder at the "Blessed Sacrament in which he conceals all the treasures of his love."[4] He went on to lament that one week was far too short to devote to the humility of Christ.

3. For more detail on the relationship between Fénelon and Mme Guyon, see: Ernest Antoine Aimé Léon Seillière, *Mme Guyon et Fénelon: précurseurs de Rousseau* (Paris: F. Alcan, 1918).

4. François Fénelon, *The Complete Fénelon*, trans. Robert J. Edmonson and Hal M. Helms (Brewster, MA: Paraclete, 2008), 274.

Christ's body is given to the church as a gift to feed upon to the point where the believer no longer desires anything else. One has to look, he argued, into the mystery of the sacrament where God's glory is hidden. Fénelon lamented that the true followers of Christ must lose themselves in him in order to become one with him.[5]

As discussed above, Fénelon was strongly influenced by the Quietist movement, which was a doctrine that sought to quiet the soul. In this approach to Christian mysticism, the soul becomes passive and allows God to fully control it. This leads to a kind of self-annihilation and an absorption of the soul wholly into the divine being. It makes sense that many believed that Fénelon and the Quietists were moving dangerously close to a form of pantheism. It is no wonder that many among the Roman Catholic elite of his day, such as Bossuet, were quite suspicious that his views were heterodox.[6]

In his discussion of All Souls' Day, November 2, Fénelon sounded like a contemporary preacher as he lamented the horrible state of humanity which was "falling into ruin" right in front of them. He went on to argue for the transitory nature of life and pointed to the idea that the future belongs to God. The entire world is an illusion in comparison to the greatness of God. He relished the thought that he as a man was nothing and looked forward to his own death when he would be united with the bridegroom. However, he went even further by saying that cherished death must take place during this life when the believer's life can become totally hidden in God.[7] One can clearly see the profound influence of Quietist ideas and his strong sense of the worthiness of God and the comparative worthlessness of humanity.

A RHETORICAL APPROACH TO PREACHING

Although Fénelon's *Dialogues on Eloquence*[8] was written in the late 1670s when he was still in his twenties, it was not published until after his death.[9] The *Dialogues* soon became recognized as a significant work; George Kennedy stated that it was "the greatest work on classical rhetoric in French and the finest statement of the philosophical strand of the tradition since antiquity."[10] Fénelon drew heavily on

---

5. Fénelon, *The Complete Fénelon*, 275–76.

6. For more on the Quietist controversy in seventeenth-century France, see: David C. Bellusci, *Amor Dei in the Sixteenth and Seventeenth Centuries* (Amsterdam: Editions Rodopi, 2013).

7. Fénelon, *The Complete Fénelon*, 287–88.

8. François Fénelon, *Dialogues on Eloquence*, trans. Wilbur Howell (Princeton: Princeton University Press, 1951).

9. Steven W. Smith, "Surrendered Communication: The Homiletic Theory of François Fénelon's *Dialogues on Eloquence*" (PhD diss., Regent University, 2003), 121.

10. George A. Kennedy, *Classical Rhetoric and its Christian and Secular Tradition from Ancient to Modern Times* (Chapel Hill: University of North Carolina Press, 1980), 166.

dialogues of the classical age, especially Plato's *Republic, Gorgias,* and *Phaedrus.* He also used Cicero's *De Oratore.*[11]

The goal of the *Dialogues* was to discover the nature of true eloquence. Emphasizing eloquence in the classical rhetorical style, Fénelon argued that the speaker must preach truth in such a way as to persuade the hearer without drawing excessive attention to one's own oratorical flair. He defined eloquence as the art of speaking well with an emphasis on its impact on the listener as opposed to the self-glorification of the speaker. The emphasis was therefore on simplicity rather than on adornment.[12]

Fénelon used the Platonic dialogue format as the organizational principle of the book with three characters listed as A, B, and C. Because of the format, the author never directly addresses the topic and the reader must glean his thoughts from the three protagonists. B serves as the initiator of the topics of discussion and considers himself representative of the ornateness typical of the preaching of the era. A, by contrast, represents the voice of reasonableness, and directs the conversation. C tends to reaffirm the opinions of A and helps to bring his thoughts to a helpful summary.[13]

The influence of Cicero is unmistakable, and an entire section in the first dialogue is devoted to a discussion of his *De Oratore.* Augustine, well-known for his extensive use of rhetoric, serves as his major Christian source, especially in the third dialogue where Fénelon refers extensively to his *On Christian Doctrine.*[14]

FIRST DIALOGUE

The first *Dialogue* begins with B returning from listening to an Ash Wednesday sermon which he found very captivating, yet he cannot remember what the speaker said. A replies that he would rather hear a sermon that he could remember than one that was more pleasing to the ear. Furthermore, when he presses B for some detail, he finds that the preacher completely took the biblical passage the sermon was based on out of context. In addition, the sermon revolved around a secular story told in puerile form, and it contained clever witticism designed to entertain the audience. Therefore, the preacher was speaking with the desire to please rather than to persuade.[15]

Person A goes on to discuss the importance of high moral standards for the speaker, whether from the pulpit or a secular setting. An immoral but eloquent

---

11. Smith, "Fénelon," 17.
12. Ibid., 157.
13. Wilbur S. Howell, "Introduction to the *Dialogues,"* in Fénelon, *Dialogues on Eloquence,* 4–6.
14. Smith, "Fénelon," 82.
15. Fénelon, *Dialogues,* 58–61.

speaker could potentially spread falsehood. Furthermore, speakers could become so enamored with themselves that they could become mere entertainers who use rhetoric for their own selfish purposes. The most excellent orator would be one who displays personal virtue and who lives a simple life. A argues that the main goal of eloquence is to persuade people of the truth and make them more virtuous. He rejects the view that eloquence is a neutral art that evildoers use to promote falsehood and injustice.[16]

B argues that sometimes public speakers do intend to improve their own reputations. This was the case even with Cicero, Isocrates, and Demosthenes. Even when they eulogized other great men, they were really seeking their own public glory. A takes exception to this view and seeks to disentangle it. First, he agrees that Isocrates was of especially low quality as an orator. He was a "lifeless speaker" intent on providing melodic elements without any significant content. He was also extremely slow to write and took ten to fifteen years to compose his Panegyric in support of Greece against the Persians. This speech took so long that it was of little practical use to the republic. Demosthenes, however, was really concerned more with the state of Greece than with his own welfare. He composed his speeches in a tight and urgent manner designed to move the reader in support of his deep and sincere reverence for the republic.[17]

B seems to have a hard time accepting A's negative comments about Isocrates, so A points to three possible aspects of true eloquence. The first would be where the speaker seeks to persuade people of the truth and make them more virtuous. The second is a more neutral approach that can either point one to falsehood and injustice or to justice and truth. The third is for selfish people who seek to provide mere pleasure for the listener in order to build themselves up in the eyes of the public.[18] Isocrates would be in the third category, a fact that B is forced to admit.[19]

The discussion then moves to the concept of one's professional occupation which both agree should strive toward the good of society. Any vocation which serves only to provide amusement rather than to improve the status of the soul would have limited usefulness. This leads to a discussion of the importance of the arts, which do amuse the hearers but they also serve to ennoble the heart and to inspire the listener to perform great deeds and to the pursuit of virtue.[20]

Pleasure, A continues, can lead to the extinguishment of wisdom. It should support the development of wisdom, but it is devious and can lead one astray to

---

16. Ibid., 65.
17. Fénelon, *Dialogues*, 62–65.
18. Ibid., 65.
19. Ibid., 66–67.
20. Ibid., 68–69.

seek pleasure for its own sake. B agrees, pointing out that one can find pleasure in a number of ways, so it would be better to seek it in serious matters rather than trivial ones. So they both would omit from their ideal society those idle people who seek mere amusement for its own sake.[21]

A asserts that when a speaker expounds on the virtues of so-called great people, they must do so in a way that leads the public to imitate such behavior. Excessive praise that carries no instruction to the hearer is of little value. A goes on to point to the *Iliad,* where Achilles is the main character, but Homer portrays him with all his faults in order to inspire the Greeks to the love of glory. Ulysses displayed a more consistent behavior due in part to his maturity and his wisdom. Homer uses his wisdom as a means of showing countless examples of moral guidance for specific situations. Likewise, Virgil in the *Aeneid* models his hero Aeneas, portraying him as more temperate and self-consistent as an example for his Roman hearers to emulate.[22]

At the end of the first book of the *Dialogues,* A cites Plato's *Gorgias* as an authority, in his attempt to thwart the problem of speaking falsehoods. The speaker should prepare themself both morally and intellectually to be qualified to deliver an oration. Careful preparation is therefore an essential element of good public speaking. One should also be aware of the nature of the audience and know their social, political, and intellectual circumstances in order to be able to communicate more effectively. This preparation mirrors that of the philosopher who is uniquely qualified as a communicator of truth. A agrees with Cicero that rhetoric should always be paired with philosophy.[23]

SECOND DIALOGUE

In the second book the interlocutors attempt to deal with the correct goals of the speaker. How can one persuade others to behave in an ethical and virtuous manner? One must be able to "touch" the listener in a similar way as the use of poetry can touch one's emotions and lead to an understanding and commitment to a higher truth. A person who establishes truth in a dry and uninspiring way would be a mere philosopher rather than an orator. However, he shuns the use of cheap humor such as puns or bad jokes as below the standards of proper speech. He also condemns rhetorical flourishes, which he compares to bad music of ornamentation, which he compares to Gothic architecture. Both are over the top and diminish the true value of public speech. He agrees with Cicero that philosophy

---

21. Fénelon, *Dialogues,* 70–71.
22. Ibid., 74–75.
23. Ibid., 83–87.

and eloquence must remain connected. Persuasion without wisdom and knowledge has limited or no value. Furthermore, Cicero claimed it was unusual for him to see a true speaker who can move the hearts and minds of the hearer. He rather heard many seemingly fluent talkers who fill their speech with charming flourishes but with minimal purpose.[24]

Cicero served as a shining example of true eloquence, especially in his mature years in the defense of the Republic. As a young speaker, Cicero seemed more concerned with his own reputation, which was common among the legal profession of the day. He reached his true brilliance when the foundations of society were threatened by Marc Anthony. Cicero was also able to portray his situation in such a clear way that the hearer could almost imagine themself in the same predicament. Virgil did the same in his description of the extreme grief of Dido at the departure of Aeneas. A points out that the imagery is so vivid that one could almost see the Trojan fleet sailing away and the lines of sadness on her face.[25]

A goes on to discuss the issue of gestures and facial expressions, arguing that they cannot be feigned in order to arouse a response for the audience; they have to be natural. If they match the words they might be acceptable, but the normal state would be a motionless exposition.[26]

Another issue A discusses is whether the orator should memorize his speech or speak extemporaneously. Since Fénelon published very few of his sermons, it seems as though he personally preferred the latter approach. A certainly cautions against over-preparation and memorization, as it diminishes the naturalness of the speaker and makes the speech seem too artificial. The skillful speaker who does not memorize their speech is able to adapt their approach to the specific effect that they notice from the audience. They are able to repeat major points in a more forceful way and with more poignant analogies. The orator who memorizes their speech is unable to adapt the content to the mood of the listeners. In a way, they are trapped within the confines of their own prepared remarks. This was the problem with Isocrates; his written speeches read better than when he recited them orally. The vocal inflections were forced and not natural, which diminished the impact on those listening and watching.[27]

A admits that Cicero praised the value of the speaker having a prodigious memory. Yet he denies that Cicero ever suggested that the entire speech be memorized. Cicero preferred that the orator remember the outline and important illustrations of their remarks while being ready to improvise when

---

24. Fénelon, *Dialogues*, 89–90.
25. Ibid., 92–93.
26. Ibid., 106–7.
27. Ibid., 108–9.

necessary.[28] On the other hand, A admits that most speakers who do not memorize their speeches also do not perform the hard work of adequate preparation. The result inevitably would be a poor oration that provides little or no value to the audience.[29]

In addition to proper preparation, one should not automatically divide the sermon into three points, which A believes to be arbitrary and based on artificial scholastic style. This makes it difficult for the speaker to unify the disjointed points into a coherent whole. He prefers what he calls a "sequence of proofs," by which each point follows its natural sequence and every subsequent section helps to strengthen those that come before. When the sequence is completed, the speaker is able to sum up more naturally and forcefully. Furthermore, Cicero often concealed his major point until the very end of his speech, thereby being able to bring his argument to a crescendo and drive his ideas more forcefully to maximize the effect on the listener.[30]

Not only is it important not to divide a speech into artificial divisions, a proper oration must be based on facts. For example, Xenophon in his *Cyropaedia* never directly stated that Cyrus was an admirable figure. That would be an opinion. However, by describing in detail his great deeds, he portrayed him as a heroic individual. At this point A criticizes what he calls the "stuffed shirts" of his own era, who say nothing without rhetorical flair to puff up the speaker and create false illusions of the subject. By contrast, Virgil provided exquisite detail about the Trojan fleet as they left the beaches of Africa or as they arrived at the coast of Italy. The detail provided, however, must be relevant to the point at hand. When expositing Scripture, the speaker often ignores relevant passages that do not lend themselves to oratorical flair. This is a mistake that the great orators such as Homer omitted. He was able to combine simplicity with exactitude, much as a painter should avoid limiting themselves to great examples of architecture that can eventually become tiresome. A great painter can also paint a rural landscape. A great chef knows how to prepare food with proper seasoning rather than dousing the entire dish with heaps of salt and pepper.[31]

THIRD DIALOGUE

The third section of the *Dialogues* makes greater use of Christian rather than classical sources. Here, Fénelon discussed preaching as an art form in the third

---

28. Fénelon, *Dialogues*, 109–10.
29. Ibid., 110–11.
30. Ibid., 112.
31. Ibid., 118–19.

book and based much of his method on Augustine's *On Christian Learning*.[32] One interesting aspect of his use of Augustine is that he did not view him as a Christian Cicero but as a pastor and a preacher who cared for his flock.[33] He also makes great use of the writing of Augustine's contemporary, Jerome. Here, Fénelon points to Scripture itself as the epitome of eloquence; so much so, that the preacher can simply let Scripture speak for itself.

A good preacher must be thoroughly familiar with the biblical text in its proper context and must be attuned to the ability of the congregation to understand. Technical terms, names, and places should be explained clearly. One must assume that the majority of people are rather uneducated in even the basics of Christian religion. So the preacher should explain doctrine simply, while at the same time not be condescending so as to offend the listeners. For example, when discussing the apostle Paul's comment that Christ is our Passover, the preacher needs to explain what the Passover meant to the Jews.[34]

The Role of Language in Preaching

Having shown the need to provide important biblical background, A goes on to discuss the importance of language. The apostles wrote in the common Greek language of their era, which was not as lofty as classical Greek. God, however, permitted the New Testament to be written in such a corrupted tongue. Paul was clear, however, in noting that he was renouncing eloquence in order to present doctrine clearly so all could understand. A admits that some of the church fathers such as Augustine, especially in his youth, disdained the quality of New Testament Greek compared to the classical form. However, as Augustine grew older and wiser, he recognized the beauty and sublimity of the apostle Paul. Here C objects, arguing that the apostle Paul deliberately shunned excellency of speech in order to know among them Jesus Christ and him crucified. It seems to C that Paul was arguing for the opposite of what A seems to be supporting.[35]

A then begins to explain that nothing is inherently wrong with simplicity in oratory and agrees with C that the nature of true eloquence is the art of moving the hearts of the listener.[36] In other places in his writings, the apostle Paul made more sophisticated arguments such as in his speech to the philosophers at Mars Hill or in his exposition of weighty doctrine in the Epistle to the Romans. Assuming that the apostle Paul also wrote the book of Hebrews, A points to

---

32. George A. Kennedy, *Classical Rhetoric and Its Christian and Secular Tradition from Ancient to Modern Times*, 2nd ed. (Chapel Hill: University of North Carolina Press, 1999), 268.

33. Old, *The Reading and the Preaching*, 513.

34. Fénelon, *Dialogues*, 121–22.

35. Ibid., 124–25.

36. Fénelon, *Dialogues*, 125.

the difficult language and provides a pretty heady doctrine comparing Christ as priest to the order of Melchizedek. It is obvious, then, that Paul did not totally disclaim the use of wisdom and eloquence.[37]

The difference between Paul and other famous orators according to A was that he spoke with divine wisdom with the goal of converting the entire world. He did not use human arguments or human persuasions, but rather those he received from on high. Therefore, he was both an excellent philosopher and an outstanding orator. God deliberately chose people who were weak and despised in order to show his own power. It was necessary that the gospels be presented in a simple way to show the power of God to the world. All of Paul's writings, therefore, were based not on the persuasion of human philosophy but on the influence of the Holy Spirit and the power of God.[38]

Spirituality for Preaching

A also points to the necessity that the preacher must rely wholly on their faith in God. Prayer is also essential, and one must arm oneself with the sword of the Word of God. The apostles were endowed with a special inspiration of the Spirit, but the contemporary speaker, not being inspired in the same way as the disciples, has to be thoroughly prepared and familiar with Scripture. They must avoid the vain display of words used by many who believe they are eloquent. And they must be sufficiently knowledgeable and prepared in humility.[39]

Expositional Foundations of Preaching

In addition to pointing out the importance of Scripture as the proper foundation of preaching, A argues that the Bible surpasses the great writings of Homer, Plato, and Xenophon in "simplicity, liveliness, and grandeur." The hymns of Moses, the poetry of the Psalms, and the tenderness of the prophet Jeremiah all surpass the excellence of Homer. Similarly, in the New Testament, the discourses of Christ project a grandeur that is completely natural to him. Furthermore, the writings of the apostles display an irregularity of style, yet everything they write displays noble character. Therefore, those who preach from Scripture can borrow its eloquence by preaching it in context and in its proper form.[40]

In addition, A disdains the practice of preaching through isolated passages. Preaching is better if it is exegetical, following the "consecutive" nature of the

---

37. Ibid., 125–26.
38. Fénelon, *Dialogues*, 127–29.
39. Ibid., 130.
40. Fénelon, *Dialogues*, 132–33.

Bible. Stringing together similar passages to prove a point fails to do justice to the sublimity of Scripture. It fails to capture its spirit or its style. It would not altogether be a bad idea to preach book after book rather than to opine on the prescribed text of the week. Such sermons would derive their authority from the Word of God rather than the reasonings of philosophers.[41]

The use of the Early Church Fathers can assist the preacher because they help explain the teachings of the Bible and the doctrines of the church. However, one must be careful in citing them, because, at times, they could stray from the proper interpretation of Scripture with their constant allegorizing. Furthermore, they were not consistent in their opinions. On the whole, A refers to the fathers as masters of the faith, with great minds and highly polished skills. They were also quite refined in their writing—that can help produce a profound effect on the Christian faith. C agrees, pointing out that they spoke out of an abundance of their hearts. He commends Augustine in particular, who did not memorize his sermons but prepared the general outline of his remarks in his mind.[42]

A takes issue with aspects of the teaching of Tertullian. He admits there are praiseworthy aspects of his writings but he used many false metaphors. Many preachers read him and copy his weaknesses. Many are enthralled by Tertullian's use of diction and they imitate his style. Cyprian also reflects the bombastic nature of the preaching of his era, yet his *Epistle to Donatus* is quite eloquent, so much so that even Augustine copied aspects of it, even though at times it is filled with unnecessary ornamentation. The fall of the western Empire naturally contributed to the slow destruction of literary style that began to make a bit of a recovery in the Renaissance.[43]

The western fathers suffered, according to A, from a decline of the Latin language. Their style was inferior to the grandeur of Scripture. The eastern fathers benefitted from a slower diminution of Greek style and Chrysostom in particular should be commended. He could be a bit wordy, but overall he rejected false ornamentation. Gregory of Nazianzus was less persuasive, but his style was more poetic and neat.[44]

A and C agree here that the best way to provide the truth of the faith is to explain it clearly. The truth of Scripture is self-authenticating and one only has to read it to recognize its sublimity. A sound preacher who grounds their sermons on sound doctrine and can explain the nature of the sacrament and traditions of

---

41. Ibid., 133–34.
42. Ibid., 139–40.
43. Ibid., 145–46.
44. Fénelon, *Dialogues*, 147–48.

the church can help to strengthen the believer to withstand the false teachings of the heretics.[45]

A concludes the third discourse with a quote from a letter of Jerome that quite nicely sums up the essence of the entire essay: "When you teach in the church, do not stir up applause; stir up lamentations in the people. Let the tears of your listeners be your praise. The discourses of a preacher must be full of the sacred Scripture. Don't be a declaimer, but a true teacher of the mysteries of God."[46]

CONTRIBUTIONS TO PREACHING

Hughes Oliphant Old places Fénelon as one of the most significant preachers during the age of Louis XIV and describes him as an evangelistic preacher. The evangelism was obviously directed toward the Huguenots. Furthermore, Fénelon went beyond the flowery court preachers of his age to add a pietistic flavor. This emphasis on personal holiness was significant and displayed some degree of similarity with pietistic Protestant preaching. He emphasized proper exposition of Scripture and disdained the topical approach that often ignored the context of the passage. He disdained oratory for oratory's sake alone and focused on the impact the sermon had on the hearer in order to direct the congregation toward proper worship of God. Old concludes that while we may find aspects of Fénelon's support of French royal absolutism to be a bit offensive to the modern sensibility, his portrayal of the faith is "more profound" than one would expect from a court preacher in the age of Louis XIV.[47]

As we can see in Fénelon's *Discourse on Eloquence* and in his sermons, Fénelon was an inspiring orator. He practiced what he preached by not writing down his sermons word for word. It likely made for a better oration, but left little for posterity to study and enjoy. His arguments are convincing but also full of great passion that can bring the congregation to its knees. One can see his emphasis on personal devotion not only to God but also to church and king. He served both the king and his parishioners well and pointed them to follow God and practice a virtuous life.

SERMON ANALYSIS

As a bishop, Fénelon took his preaching duties seriously and, like Bossuet, did not write out his sermons. We do have some of his notes and outlines, but only a few

---

45. Ibid., 141–42.
46. Ibid., 153.
47. Old, *The Reading and Preaching*, 514.

of his complete sermons have survived.[48] Old points out that many of Fénelon's Sunday sermons in his parish were informal conversations that resembled the style of the Pietists, with a major concern for personal holiness.[49]

One of Fénelon's most famous sermons was his message delivered on Epiphany, January 6, 1685, at the *Eglise des Missions Etrangères* in the presence of ambassadors from Siam. The text for the homily was Isaiah 60:1 "Arise, shine, for your light has come, and the glory of the LORD rises upon you." He paid special heed to his visitors from the east, comparing them favorably to the wise men who came to see the baby Jesus, calling them the new magi who can bring the gospel to the gentiles.[50] He begins the sermon, asking his hearers to rejoice in the Lord but with fear and trembling. The major theme is the preaching of the gospel to the gentiles. He goes on to praise the zeal of world missions, tracing its history from the era of the apostles and early church fathers, such as Irenaeus and Tertullian, who ministered in the midst of a pagan Roman Empire.[51] Throughout the centuries the gospel went forth to more and more peoples, even finally to the Americas, where it had already produced tremendous fruit. He singles out Louis IV for his support and also praises the work of Jesuit missionaries to Asia.[52] He praises the Lord Jesus, whose gospel was still fertile throughout all corners of the earth. He also gives thanks for the true church, which shines like a beacon to the pagan world.[53] Pivoting to a critique of contemporary French society, Fénelon excoriates the moral decadence and apathy of his generation, listing pride and vanity as the primary problems, encouraging his audience to return to their faith in God as the way out of such moral failure.[54] He laments the loss of the territories in England, the Netherlands, Germany, and Scandinavia to the Protestants, but praises God that he has replaced them with new followers throughout the world.[55]

What stands out in this sermon is its adherence to the standards outlined in the *Dialogues*. In contrast to the scholastic style of his contemporaries such as Louis Bourdaloue, the famous French Jesuit court preacher, Fénelon presents his sermon in a simple, unadorned style. The message is full of passion and inspiration in comparison to a dry, academic oration.[56]

A second extant sermon is his "Sermon for the Profession of a New Convert," addressed to Mlle De Peray, a Huguenot aristocrat, who converted to Roman

---

48. Ibid., 508; Marguerite Haillant, *Fénelon et la predication* (Paris: Editions Klincksieck, 1969), 11ff.
49. Old, *The Reading and Preaching*, 508.
50. François Fénelon, *Oeuvres diverses de Fénelon* (Paris: Lefèvre, 1824), 181–82.
51. Ibid., 185.
52. Ibid., 188–89.
53. Ibid., 192–93.
54. Ibid., 195–96.
55. Ibid., 202.
56. Old, *The Reading and Preaching*, 509–14.

Catholicism after the Revocation. She, as did many of her compatriots, faced a difficult choice. If she left the country to practice her religion, she would forfeit her entire estate. Or she could stay and convert. So she sought the counsel of Bossuet, who easily convinced her of the alleged errors of Protestantism. She then attended Fénelon's school, where she learned much about her new-found faith and was so convinced of it that she decided to join the Carmelite order. In the sermon, Fénelon pointed her toward the heavenly bridegroom who stood ready to welcome her into her eternal home. He encouraged her to embrace her role as the handmaid of the Lord and to glorify the Lord in her humility. Fénelon then calls on the Holy Spirit to ignite the flame of heavenly passion in the hearts of his hearers and concludes by leading in the recitation of the *Ave Maria*.[57]

Sermon Excerpt
For the Feast of Epiphany[58]

Gathered souls, fervent spirits, hasten to remain in the faith that so easily escapes you. You know that ten righteous people would have saved the abominable city of Sodom that the fire from heaven ultimately consumed. It is for you to bow unceasingly at the foot of the altar to pray for those who do not recognize their own sin. Therefore, oppose their iniquity and become the defender of Israel against the anger of the Lord . . .

O Lord, as you say in your Scriptures: "Can a woman forget her nursing child and have no compassion on the son of her womb? Even these may forget, but I will not forget you." (Isaiah 49:15) Do not turn your face from us. Let your word increase in the kingdoms where you send it; do not forget the former Churches which you have guided so skillfully with your hand to plant the faith among new people. Remember the seat of St. Peter, the solid foundation of your promises. Remember the Church of France, mother of the new churches in the east, on which your grace rests. Remember this house which belongs to you and the servants who worship there, and their tears and their prayers and their works. What will I say to you Lord on our behalf? Remember us in our weakness and in your mercy. Remember the blood of your Son which was shed for us, who intercedes to you on our behalf, and in whom alone do we trust. Although

---

57. Ibid., 509–10.
58. Fénelon, *Oeuvres diverses*, 206–7.

we were far away, he gathered us according to your righteousness, help us to increase this small amount of faith which still remains in us, purify our hearts, give us life in you. May your grace pierce the darkness; may it stifle all of our passions, may it correct all of our judgments in order that, having believed, we can be found eternally in your presence. ◆

BIBLIOGRAPHY

Fénelon, François. *The Complete Fénelon*. Trans. and edited by Robert J. Edmonson and Hal M. Helms. Brewster, MA: Paraclete, 2008.

Fénelon, François. *Dialogues on Eloquence*. Trans. by Wilbur Howell. Princeton: Princeton University Press, 1951.

Fénelon, François. *Dialogues sur l'éloquence en général et celle de la chair en particulier*. Amsterdam: Bernard, 1718.

Fénelon, François. *Oeuvres diverses de Fénelon*. Paris: Lefèvre, 1824.

Haillant, Marguerite. *Fénelon et la predication*. Paris: Editions Klincksieck, 1969.

Howell, Wilbur S. "Oratory and Poetry in Fénelon's Library." *The Quarterly Journal of Speech* 37 (1951): 1–10.

Kennedy, George A. *Classical Rhetoric and its Christian and Secular Tradition from Ancient to Modern Times*. Chapel Hill: University of North Carolina Press, 1980. 2nd ed. 1999.

Little, Katherine Day. *François de Fénelon: A Study in Personality*. New York: Harper, 1951.

Neff, Roger H. "Rhetorical Theory and Practice in Selected Works of Fénelon." PhD diss., Ohio State University, 1973.

Old, Hughes Oliphant, *The Reading and Preaching of the Scripture in History, Volume 4: The Age of the Reformation*. Grand Rapids: Eerdmans, 2002.

Smith, Steven W. "Surrendered Communication: The Homiletic Theory of François Fénelon's *Dialogues on Eloquence*." PhD diss., Regent University, 2003.

Warnick, Barbara. "Fénelon's Recommendations to the French Academy Concerning Rhetoric." *Communication Monographs* 45 (1978): 75–84.

Jonathan Edwards

Preaching the Beauty of Holiness

GERALD R. MCDERMOTT

Jonathan Edwards (1703–1758) was one of the greatest preachers of the Great Awakening (1740–41) and the greatest theologian in the history of the Americas. More than any other theologian in the history of Christian thought, he made aesthetics central to his vision of God. This theological aesthetic is a central feature of his preaching, and one of the chief reasons why preachers like D. Martin Lloyd-Jones, John Piper, and Tim Keller have used Edwards as a model.

HISTORICAL BACKGROUND[1]

After completing graduate studies at Yale, Edwards preached at an English Presbyterian congregation in New York City for eight months (August 1722—April 1723). At age twenty-three, he arrived at his grandfather Stoddard's church in Northampton, Massachusetts. Here he spent his next twenty-three years in what was the largest and most influential church outside Boston, preaching two sermons every Sunday in an academic gown and powdered periwig, and delivering a lecture on most Wednesdays. In 1729, two years after Edwards had been ordained at Northampton, Stoddard died and Edwards took over as senior pastor.

In 1734, Edwards revisited the theme of his master's *Questio* for a lecture that became his first published treatise, *Justification by Faith Alone.* This lecture on justification, which Edwards turned into two sermons, made a deep impression on the Northampton congregation, especially its young people. Before too long, the "Little Awakening" broke out, eventually culminating in a spiritual earthquake

---

1. A different version of part of this chapter was published in Hungary as an article: Gerald R. McDermott, "Words of Beauty and Power: Jonathan Edwards as Homiletical Artist," in Sára Tóth, ed., *The Power of Words: Papers in Honor of Tibor Fabiny's Sixtieth Birthday* (Budapest: Károli—L'Harmattan, 2015), 215–28. Adapted with permission.

that rocked not only Edwards's congregation but spread to other towns up and down the Connecticut River Valley.

A year after he delivered his *History of Redemption* (1739) series, the dam burst. Historians have referred to the resulting flood as the Great Awakening. The downpours of the Spirit were triggered by George Whitefield's preaching tour of the colonies in 1739, and fed by Edwards's famous sermon, "Sinners in the Hands of an Angry God." When Whitefield came to Northampton on Edwards's invitation in October of 1740, the church was entranced by the twenty-six-year-old celebrity from England; Edwards's wife, Sarah, wrote that all one could hear was muffled sobs. The following July, Edwards was asked by the Reverend Peter Reynolds at Enfield, Connecticut, to help prepare his congregation for awakening. Edwards delivered a sermon which he had previously preached at Northampton, but with no visible effect. This "Sinners" sermon emphasized God's holding back his wrath from deserving sinners. Edwards's images (an arrow pointed at one's heart and bow drawn, a spider held over a fire) were so effective this time that his Enfield listeners screamed and Edwards had to stop not once but several times. As far as we can tell, he was never able to finish.[2]

Although this revival boosted Edwards's prestige, neither the revival nor the preacher's reputation was to last. In 1750, New England was shocked when an overwhelming majority of voting members of the Northampton church voted to dismiss Edwards from the pastorate. Leaders of the church had been offended by his proposal in 1749 to change qualifications for communion—thus rejecting Stoddard's open communion policy—by restricting it to those who could tell him they hoped they were regenerate.

In the summer of 1751, Edwards moved into exile as a missionary to a small English congregation and 150 Mahican and Mohawk families in Stockbridge (western Massachusetts).

Troubles within and outside the mission did not prevent Edwards from applying himself assiduously to his missionary tasks. In addition, here Edwards wrote four of his greatest works: *Freedom of the Will* (1754), *Original Sin* (1758), *The End for Which God Created the World*, and *Nature of True Virtue* (published in tandem in 1765).

At the end of 1757, the trustees of the college of New Jersey (at Princeton) invited Edwards to become the college's new president. But shortly thereafter, smallpox broke out in a nearby town. The College trustees recommended vaccinations, and Edwards set an example by getting inoculated on February 23.

---

2. For historical context and analysis, see Wilson H. Kimnach, Caleb J. D. Maskell, and Kenneth P. Minkema, eds., *Jonathan Edwards's "Sinners in the Hands of an Angry God": A Casebook* (New Haven: Yale University Press, 2010).

Tragically, the serum was corrupted, and Edwards's throat became so swollen that he could not swallow the medicine he needed. Edwards died on March 22, 1758, at the age of fifty-four.

THEOLOGY OF PREACHING

Edwards considered preaching of paramount importance for the work of redemption, which was at the center of his ecclesiology and historical vision.[3] But his conception of the goal of preaching reflected his theology of religious experience: true religion is *seeing* the beauty of holiness. Since aesthetic perception goes beyond acceptance of doctrine or morality, preaching must make what is true become real in the perception of hearers or readers. Edwards had noticed that lack of spiritual experience and frequent repetition of religious maxims can obscure recognition of what is real. When he was only nineteen years old, he preached on the doctrine "When man dies, he is forever stripped of all earthly enjoyments." He told his hearers that while all the world "knows the *truth* of this doctrine perfectly well" it nevertheless "don't [sic] seem at all *real* to them."[4] Five years later he said two things are required in order for something to seem real to us: "believing the truth of it, and having a sensible idea or apprehension of it."[5] This was his classic notion of a simple idea imparted by a "divine and supernatural light," that makes what was previously a mere notion become a vivid reality by means of something like a sixth sense. In his private notebooks Edwards wrote that this is "a light cast upon the ideas of spiritual things . . . which makes them appear clear and real which before were but faint, obscure representations."[6] What was previously only thought, becomes seen, tasted, and felt. It takes on a tactile dimension that forever fixes its reality in the apprehension of the believer. Edwards believed this new seeing and tasting of the reality of divine things comes principally, if not exclusively, through preaching.

Although Edwards said the preacher's sermon must penetrate the affections of his listeners and not simply change their thinking, he was emphatic about the necessity of cognitive content. In a 1739 sermon on "the importance and advantage of a thorough knowledge of divine truth," he taught that Christians must not be content to remain babes in knowledge of divine things, or to be satisfied with spiritual experience alone. They must seek "not only a practical and

---

3. Helen Westra's *The Minister's Task and Calling in the Sermons of Jonathan Edwards* (Lewiston, NY: Mellen, 1986) is especially helpful on this score.

4. Jonathan Edwards, *The Works of Jonathan Edwards, Vol. 10: Sermons and Discourses, 1720–1723,* Wilson H. Kimnach, ed. (New Haven: Yale University Press, 1992), 10:405–6. (Henceforth WJE).

5. *WJE* 14:201.

6. *WJE* 13:470.

experimental, but also a doctrinal knowledge of the truths and mysteries of religion." He explained that there are two kinds of knowledge of divine things—the speculative or natural that pertains to the head, and the practical and spiritual that is sensed in the heart. While speculative knowledge without spiritual knowledge is worthless, speculative knowledge nevertheless is "of infinite importance" because "without it we can have no spiritual or practical knowledge." There is no other way we can benefit from means of grace except by knowledge. "Therefore the preaching of the gospel would be wholly to no purpose, if it conveyed no knowledge to the mind." This assertion was based on Edwards's understanding of the human person: "The heart cannot be set upon an object of which there is no idea in the understanding."[7] He would explicate this at much greater length in his *Religious Affections* seven years later, but here he summarized as follows: "Such is the nature of man, that nothing can come at the heart but through the door of the understanding: and there can be no spiritual knowledge of that of which there is not first a rational knowledge." The upshot was that the "sense of the heart" that is at the core of true religion is normally impossible without doctrinal understanding: "A man cannot see the wonderful excellency and love of Christ in doing such and such things for sinners, unless his understanding be first informed how those things were done. He cannot have a taste of the sweetness and divine excellency of such and such things contained in divinity, unless he first have a notion that there are such and such things." Hence the way to deeper spiritual experience was through greater cognitive understanding of divine things: "The more you have of a rational knowledge of the things of the gospel, the more opportunity will there be, when the Spirit shall be breathed into your heart, to see the excellency of these things, and to taste the sweetness of them." Therefore, the Christian preacher is obliged not only to preach but also to teach more and more of the infinite and unsearchable wonders of God and his redemption.[8]

Kimnach has observed that although Edwards was a homiletical artist and powerful logician, he nevertheless conceived of the perfect sermon as a vehicle of power more than reason or beauty.[9] He boasted in his preface to the five discourses that were delivered during the Little Awakening of 1734–35 that God had "smiled upon and bless[ed his] very plain, unfashionable way of preaching" even though he was "unable" to preach or write "politely."[10] The important thing

---

7. *WJE* 22:84, 87–89, 100.

8. *WJE* 2:266–91.

9. Kimnach, "Edwards as Preacher," in Stephen Stein, ed., *The Cambridge Companion to Jonathan Edwards* (Cambridge: Cambridge University Press, 2007), 105.

10. *WJE* 19:797.

was not aesthetic but effect, not prestige but power. Power was never guaranteed, of course, by simply preaching Scripture. It was necessary that the preacher beg God's Spirit to inspire his preparation and enliven his words, and for the minister to preach with pathos and fervency. Prayer was indispensable and an affective manner helpful. But the preacher need not display his learning or be especially eloquent. Power came from God's blessing, without which even labored preparation and enthusiastic delivery would produce no lasting results. Preachers should not be surprised if some of their listeners are "stupid and senseless as stones," whispering to their neighbors or sleeping or dreaming during sermons.[11] God is not frustrated because "he will see to it that his word shall not be in vain or without effect."[12] Those who refuse to hear the Word will pay attention in the next world and remember "that there ha[d] been a prophet among 'em."[13] Perhaps reflecting his own frustrations with the Northampton congregation he called "sermon-proof," he warned there would be "dark seasons" in the church when preachers would seem to "labor in vain."[14] They would sometimes fish all night, as it were, and bring up their nets empty time after time. But they must not give up or get discouraged, for God is faithful. So whether a sermon becomes a thing of power depends on God. The minister can only sow the seed of the Word, and leave the rest to sun, and rain, and the influences of heaven. One must wait patiently, like the hard-working farmer, for the harvest. But that means one should not be presumptuous by neglecting diligent study, especially in the Bible, and one must be "much in seeking God." In the end the minister can only be faithful and "leave the event with God."[15]

METHODOLOGY FOR PREACHING

Jonathan Edwards learned about preaching from the Calvinist Puritan tradition in which he was raised. Calvin himself said the preacher is a "trumpet of God" who should style his or her sermons after the nature of Scripture itself. So his sermons were generally expository, direct, and brief. Unlike Edwards, Calvin typically did not write his sermons out but preached nearly every day without notes and after studying the text. The most popular Calvinist preaching manuals in Edwards's era were by English Puritan William Perkins, English preacher John Edwards (no relation), and Boston's Cotton Mather. Perkins's *Art of Prophesying*

---

11. *WJE* 17:178, 179.
12. *WJE* 17:179.
13. *WJE* 4:386–88; "Preaching the Gospel," Richard Bailey and Gregory Wells, eds., *The Salvation of Souls: Nine Previously Published Sermons* (Wheaton, IL: Crossway, 2002) [hereafter BW], 153.
14. *WJE* 19:113; 24:965–66.
15. Sermon on Matt 13:3–4(a), *WJE* 56.

(1592) urged a "plain style" that opens a text simply without affectations of classical learning (frequently on display in Anglican sermons). John Edwards's *The
Preacher* (1703) recommended intense belief and feeling, and attention to application. Mather's *Manuductio ad Ministerium* (1726) dismissed rhetoric and logic in
favor of "natural reason and a cultivated personal style based upon emulation of
the actual practice of admired authors."[16] Edwards also learned from personal role
models. His father, Timothy, was a Harvard graduate who used a large number
of subheadings and biblical citations in his sermons and was also an animated
speaker who presided over revivals in his East Windsor, Connecticut, parish.
Jonathan's grandfather Solomon Stoddard, under whom Edwards served as assistant for twenty-seven months at Northampton, was a powerful revivalist who
declared that "when men don't Preach much about the danger of Damnation,
there is want of good Preaching." Stoddard enjoyed using rhetorical dialogue in
his sermons and urged preachers to "rebuke sharply" those who needed reproof.[17]

New England churches in Edwards's day were plain "meetinghouses" with
unpainted clapboard on the outside and seating around a pulpit or "desk" near
the center on the inside. In reaction against what they considered "graven images"
and "Catholic" ostentation in Anglican churches, Puritans eschewed crosses and
stained-glass windows, and sang mostly psalms without musical instruments.
Ministers preached in academic gowns to demonstrate they were learned but not
a sacred priesthood. They also wanted to hide class distinctions that might be
apparent in street dress. They delivered two sermons every Sunday—morning
and afternoon—and often a weekday lecture. In Northampton, Edwards followed this schedule with sermons of sixty to ninety minutes each. The principal Sunday service consisted of ten parts: (1) a biblical text as call to worship,
(2) corporate "prayer of approach," (3) Old Testament reading, with the minister
giving a short "sense of the text," (4) New Testament reading with a sense of the
text, (5) singing a psalm metrically, (6) prayer of confession and intercession, (7) a
sermon, (8) corporate prayer led by the minister which could last up to thirty
minutes, (9) another psalm, and then (10) the benediction. Every eight weeks
in Northampton, Edwards conducted a "sacrament" service (the Lord's Supper)
between the two regular Sunday services. Twice a year, there were fast days by
colonial decree, with special sermons. Thanksgiving days were also held at least

---

16. Wilson H. Kimnach's "Editor's Introduction," in WJE, 10:19. Kimnach's 254-page introduction is
the finest guide to Edwards's sermons ever published. See also Kimnach's introduction in John Gerstner, *The
Rational Biblical Theology of Jonathan Edwards* (Powhatan, VA: Berea, 1991), 1:481–6; Douglas A. Sweeney,
Jonathan Edwards and the Ministry of the Word (Downers Grove, IL: IVP Academic, 2009), 79–80; and
Kimnach, "The Sermons: Concept and Execution," in Sang H. Lee, ed., *The Princeton Companion to Jonathan
Edwards* (Princeton, NJ: Princeton University Press, 2005), 243–57.

17. *WJE* 10:14.

once a year, depending on circumstances, and each would feature a sermon. Edwards produced all these sermons for a parish of 1,300 people, with usually seven hundred present on Sundays, while receiving a steady stream of visitors at his home and regularly supervising pastoral interns.[18]

THREE PERIODS OF PREACHING

Wilson Kimnach, the unrivalled scholar of Edwards's homiletics, divides Edwards's thirty-seven-year preaching career into three periods. The first period, 1722–27, is what Kimnach calls his "apprenticeship," during which he preached in New York City, Bolton (Connecticut), and (after his tutorship at Yale) as an assistant under Stoddard. Kimnach says the young preacher's sermons were "as busy in [their] formal structure as the music of Johann Sebastian Bach." Edwards helped his note-taking hearers follow along by announcing new sections as they began. While he avoided strong rhetorical devices such as alliteration and rhythm, he piqued attention by using "the vigor of a vulgar idiom." For example, the apprentice described the unregenerate as one who "spends his days in groveling in the dirt, makes his mind much like a mole or muck worm, feeding on dirt and dung, and seldom lifts his mind any higher than the surface of the earth he treads on."[19]

From 1727 to 1742 Edwards used the sermon "primarily as an instrument of awakening and pastoral leadership." This was the period of "mastery" in which, especially starting in 1729, sermons became more complex, and parts were in outline form. When he offered pastoral guidance, the focus was less on sins of youthful flesh and more on the abuses of commerce. Edwards began to experiment with the shape of his sermons, gradually evolving his form to suit the production of theological treatises. So he preached more sermon series, dividing long discourses into preaching units only after most of the writing was done. Kimnach writes, "The sermon was dissolving under the pressure of long, long thoughts"— changing from a homily to an essay. The most famous sermons started to become tied to important occasions: "Sinners in the Hands of an Angry God" (1741) was the last sermon with renown that was not also the marker of an important event, such as the "Farewell Sermon" (1750). Yet while the sermons were developing toward longer productions, Edwards was not indifferent to style. Kimnach notes that when he took his sermons from the pulpit to print, he made sure to build a rising crescendo, saving the best arguments and most important points for last.

---

18. Sweeney, 25–26,57–8,63; *WJE* 17:16.
19. Kimnach, "Edwards as Preacher," in Stephen Stein, ed., *The Cambridge Companion to Jonathan Edwards* (Cambridge, UK: Cambridge University Press, 2007), 104; *WJE* 10:99.

Interestingly, during this period the maturing preacher worked on several sermons at once, "apparently stor[ing] some of his output in fruitful times against times of dearth."[20]

The last phase of Edwards's extraordinary sermonic production started in January 1742, when he drew a vertical line down the middle of his sermon booklet on Daniel 5:25, dividing it into double columns—a form he retained for most of his sermons until his death sixteen years later.[21] Kimnach thinks this was the result of watching George Whitefield preach without notes.[22] From there on out, Edwards made even more efforts to use his sermons to help him compose treatises. As he became more of an international intellectual, he turned from his earlier "personalist" focus on subjective religious experience to highlighting objective religious phenomena such as the work of redemption through the course of human history. His sermons were almost entirely outlines that grew to be "more and more like bare lists." According to Kimnach, this might have indicated a certain "indifference" to preaching, particularly as his own tenure at Northampton grew more tenuous. At the same time, his growing predilection for treatises and "things to be considered" instead of formal "doctrines" ironically paralleled the move by Boston's liberal ministers toward what would eventually become Emersonian essays.[23]

At Stockbridge, where he had been exiled after his dismissal from Northampton, the discouraged preacher had new audiences, and the Native Americans there seem to have inspired new enthusiasm. He preached more than 187 new sermons, and on another twenty occasions preached from earlier manuscripts. It is clear from the extant manuscripts that Edwards worked hard to adapt his rhetoric to the abilities of his hearers. As Rachel Wheeler has noted, the Stockbridge sermons tell more stories than the Northampton sermons; they are also simpler in presentation and employ more imagery derived from nature. But though he preached more simply to his uneducated Native American audience, the sermons were not simplistic. He did not restrict his aesthetic vision to learned adepts but told the Stockbridge Native Americans in his very first sermon there that they must have "their eyes opened to see how lovely [Christ] is," and in a communion lecture explained that a good person loves God "above all else for his own beauty." His outlines were less complex and his imagery earthier than in his sermons to the white congregation at Stockbridge, but the vision he tried to evoke was no less sublime.[24]

---

20. Kimnach, "Edwards as Preacher," 110; *WJE* 10.105,11–12,107n9.

21. There are approximately 1,200 extant sermons, with roughly 200 published in print.

22. It also enabled him to conserve paper—hard to come by in his day—since the outlined sermons took up less space.

23. *WJE* 10:119,122; *WJE* 25:45; *WJE* 10:123; *WJE* 25:46.

24. Rachel Wheeler, "'Friends to Your Souls': The Egalitarian Calvinism of Jonathan Edwards,"

THE ROLE OF IMAGERY IN PREACHING

Samuel Hopkins tells us that Edwards took "great pains" to compose his sermons, getting up earlier and studying Scripture more than his contemporaries. But his secret weapon was his unrivalled use of imagery.[25] Kimnach calls it his "armor-piercing device of sensational imagery."[26] Light was perhaps his favorite image, no doubt influenced in part by his age of Enlightenment. But though it was common among his contemporaries, "no one looked more intensely at the biblical meaning of light for his day than did Edwards." Marsden explains that for Edwards it was "the most powerful image of how God communicated his love to the creation. *Regeneration* meant to be given eyes to see the light of Christ in hearts that had been hopelessly darkened by sin."[27]

The fountain was another favorite. In his 1738 sermon series on love (*Charity and Its Fruits*) he declared that God is a fountain of love that pours out its "effusions of love" into the bosoms of the saints, whom he likened to "the flowers on the earth in a pleasant spring day" that "open their bosoms to the sun to be filled with his [sic] warmth and light, and to flourish in beauty and fragrancy by his rays." Every saint is a flower in God's garden, and "holy love is the fragrancy and sweet odor" that they all emit. In the same breath he said every saint is "as a note in a concert of music which sweetly harmonizes with every other note . . . and so all helping one another to their utmost to express their love of the whole society to the glorious Father and Head of it, and [to pour back] love into the fountain of love, whence they are supplied and filled with love and with glory."[28] The following spring he interrupted his series on the history of redemption with a sermon devoted entirely to comparing Christ to the sun. To believers, Christ's second coming will "be a thousand times more refreshing to them than ever was the sight of the rising sun to them that have wandered in a wilderness, through the longest and darkest night. The sight of [it] will fill their souls with unspeakable gladness and rejoicing. It will be a bright day to the saints. The beams of that glorious Sun that will then appear will make it bright." But for unbelievers, "every ray of that glory that Christ shall then appear in will be like

unpublished paper, used by permission, n.41; Wheeler, "'A Heathenish, Barbarous, Brutish Education': Jonathan Edwards and the Stockbridge Indians" (unpub. paper loaned by the author), 6; see also Gerald R. McDermott, "Missions and Native Americans," in Sang Hyun Lee, ed., *The Princeton Companion to Jonathan Edwards* (Princeton, NJ: Princeton University Press, 2005), 264–65.

25. Kristin Emery Saldine focuses on Edwards's landscape imagery in her "Preaching God Visible: Geo-Rhetoric and the Theological Appropriation of Landscape Imagery in the Sermons of Jonathan Edwards" (PhD diss., Princeton Theological Seminary, 2004).

26. *WJE* 10:171.

27. George M. Marsden, *Jonathan Edwards: A Life* (New Haven: Yale University Press, 2003), 55.

28. *WJE* 8:386.

a stream of scorching fire, and will pierce their hearts with a keener torment than a stream of fierce lightning . . . That day will burn as an oven indeed. That brightness that the light of Christ's glory shall fill the world with will be more terrible to them than if the world was filled with the fiercest flames." Edwards's words were rarely big and never obscure, but the pictures he painted with them were vivid and memorable.[29]

If his imagery made his sermons memorable, their clear and compelling logic left his auditors "little room to escape his web of arguments." Most New Englanders had "cut their eyeteeth on the logic of carefully-argued sermons," since educated eighteenth-century people were trained in and had great confidence in the power of logic to settle arguments. Edwards was a master of logical argument and used it to great effect in his sermons. In his golden years of sermon composition—the late 1720s through the early 1740s—he carefully assembled arguments and examples "both from Scripture and reason, as even to force the assent of every attentive hearer . . . His words were so full of ideas, set in such a plain and striking light, that few speakers have been able to command an audience as he." When logical skill was mixed with what Kimnach calls "the intensity of an inchworm," the result was remarkable intellectual focus: "Like an eagle Edwards circled over the context [of the biblical text]," observes Gerstner, "until he found his point and then descended deeply to snatch his homiletic prey and hold it up to the full view of all. For the next hour or more, Jonathan Edwards's only interest was to dissect the text, to analyze it, and to feed his hungry people."[30] Ten-year-old Nehemiah Strong sat in the Northampton pews during Edwards's 1739 series on the history of redemption. Years later he told Edwards's grandson Timothy Dwight that he became so entranced by Edwards's sermon on the second coming that "he expected without one thought to the contrary the awful scene to be unfolded on that day and in that place," and was "deeply disappointed when the day terminated and left the world in its usual state of tranquility."[31]

METHOD IN CONTEXT: THREE OF HIS BEST

Let us look very briefly at three of Edwards's finest sermons. Undoubtedly his most famous sermon, "Sinners in the Hands of an Angry God," was preached at the height of the Great Awakening in New England. Harry Stout calls it "arguably

---

29. *WJE* 22:60.
30. Gerstner, *The Rational Biblical Theology of Jonathan Edwards*, 1:486.
31. Timothy Dwight, *Travels in New England and New York*, 4 vols. (Cambridge: Harvard University Press, 1969), 4:230–31, quoted in Marsden, *Jonathan Edwards*, 195.

America's greatest sermon." In it, Edwards tried to compose the "perfect idea" of an awakening sermon by using "rhetorical dynamite" to produce "unprecedented terror." The core idea was "that one could get to life eternal only after first being scared to death." Curiously, Edwards preached it first in Northampton in June 1741, but with no discernible effect. Several weeks later he delivered it at Enfield, Connecticut, where, as Kimnach writes, "the congregation virtually rioted when the preacher had barely begun, so it is impossible to say that they actually heard the sermon." Uncounted scholars and students have studied Edwards's legendary employment of imagery in this sermon. His most striking images—the archer with the drawn bow, the loathsome spider, pent-up waters, unleashed lions—come from Scripture. Some bear repeating: sinners' righteousness would have no more power to keep them from hell "than a spider's web would have to stop a falling rock"; "there are black clouds of God's wrath now hanging directly over your heads, full of the dreadful storm, and big with thunder"; "the wrath of God is like great waters that are dammed for the present" but "they increase more and more, and rise higher and higher . . . the waters are continually rising and waxing more and more mighty"; the devils watching for sinners to fall into hell "stand waiting for them, like greedy hungry lions that see their prey, and expect to have it, but are for the present kept back."[32]

Marsden has observed that the sometimes-missed logic of the sermon is that "it is the weight of sinners' own sins that is dragging them toward the abyss." Edwards said they stand on slippery ground and need nothing but their "own weight to throw [them] down." Their own "hellish *principles*" would kindle and flame out into hellfire if God permitted them. "Your wickedness," Edwards warned, "makes you as it were heavy as lead." Another oft-missed theme is that *God* is keeping sinners from falling into hell. He "restrains" their wickedness; if not for his restraints, their souls would turn into fiery ovens. The fire pent up in their hearts is struggling to break out, but God's "forbearance" keeps it in check. Only God's "arbitrary will" preserves sinners from hell every moment. Only God's power and pleasure "holds you up"; only his hand keeps "you from falling into the fire every moment" and is the reason "why you han't [sic] gone to hell since you have sat here in the house of God." If these words did not make his hearers feel radically insecure, he had more: they were walking over the pit of hell on a rotten covering with innumerable places that could not bear their weight; there were unseen arrows of death that fly about, even at noonday; no one in hell

---

32. *WJE* 22:34, 31; Kimnach, "Edwards as Preacher," 116; Gerstner, *Rational, Biblical Theology*, 1:494; *WJE* 22:410, 406; Edward J. Gallagher says these images taken together deliver a "recurrent pulsation" that makes the sermon primarily an auditory experience. Gallagher, "'Sinners in the Hands of an Angry God': Some Unfinished Business," *New England Quarterly* 73 (2000): 202–21.

ever intended to go there, but all flattered themselves they would not wind up there; and there was nothing between them and hell "but the air." "You hang by a slender thread, with the flames of divine wrath flashing about it, and ready every moment to singe it, and burn it asunder." The true issue, as Kimnach writes, was not place but time. It was urgent that sinners not wait any longer. "How awful it is to be left behind at such a day ... God seems *now* to be hastily gathering in his elect ... [P]robably the bigger part of adult persons that ever shall be saved, will be brought in *now* in a little time ... The wrath of almighty God is *now* undoubtedly hanging over great part of this congregation." Modern readers may be surprised to learn that the original manuscript version was far more encouraging and mild than the later printed revision. Kimnach says the sermon given at Enfield "preserves a nice balance between the carrot and the stick," unlike the version most Americans have read.[33]

Edwards's "Farewell Sermon" was one of the few homiletic productions of his last period that were fully written out. In Kimnach's estimation, it was "as sustained and disciplined" as "Sinners," but "supplant[ed] fire with ice" in eleven pages of doctrine and thirteen pages of application. It was delivered on the first Sunday in July 1750 after his Northampton congregation had voted to eject him from their pulpit. With cool detachment Edwards defended his doctrine, "Ministers and the people that have been under their care, must meet one another, before Christ's tribunal, at the day of judgment." "We live in a world of change," he began, when those who seem most united suddenly become "most disunited." But even if they are removed to places distant from one another, they will meet again in the next world. Then there will be "clear, certain and infallible light" so that all "deceit and delusion shall vanish away." There will be no more debate and disagreement. When ministers meet their people now, and try to instruct and correct them on eternal matters, "all is often in vain." Despite everything their ministers say, many remain "stupid and unawakened." This does not mean that ministers are always right; in fact, they are not infallible in discerning the state of souls, and the "most skillful of them are liable to mistakes." But neither can the people know certainly the state of their minister or one another. "Very often" hypocrites are mistaken for "eminent saints," and "some of God's jewels" are censured and abused. Therefore, it is also "very often" that "great differences and controversies arise between ministers and the people that are under their care." People "are ready to judge

---

33. Marsden, *A Life*, 222; *WJE* 22:404,404,407, original emphasis, 409,412,407,410,412; Kimnach, "Edwards as Preacher," 116; *WJE* 22:417–8, emphasis added; *WJE* 10:114. The notion that God's "arbitrary will" keeps sinners out of hell every moment is underscored by Edwards's occasionalism—his idea that at every moment God recreates the world and wills what is. My thanks to Ken Minkema for this observation.

and censure one another . . . [and] are greatly mistaken in their judgment, and wrong one another in their censures." But on that future day in eternity when pastors and their people meet again, the secrets of every heart shall be made manifest, and no one will be careless or sleeping or "wandering [in] mind from the great concern of the meeting." The great Judge will "do justice between ministers and their people," and all will see that these affairs of the church were more important "than the temporal concerns of the greatest earthly monarchs, and their kingdoms or empires."[34]

In the application Edwards defended his ministry in Northampton. "I have not spared my feeble strength, but have exerted it for the good of your souls . . . I have spent the prime of my life and strength in labors for your eternal welfare." He said he was never lazy or ambitious for his own financial gain, but "have given myself to the work of the ministry, laboring in it night and day, rising early and applying myself to this great business to which Christ has appointed me." He declared that he had borne "heavy burdens," but God had strengthened him. "Although I have often been troubled on every side, I have not yet been distressed; perplexed, but not in despair; cast down, but not destroyed." Then came a stunning admission of failure: "But now . . . my work is finished . . . You have publicly rejected me." As if to deflect attention from his defeat, he turned again to that future meeting when "our hearts will be turned inside out" and all will see "whether I have been treated with that impartiality, candor and regard which the just Judge esteemed due." He concluded by addressing different groups within the congregation. To those "I leave in a Christless, graceless condition," he feared all his labors had only hardened them and prayed God would grant his Word to be "the fire and hammer that breaketh the rock [of their hearts] in pieces." To those "who are under some awakenings," he told them to "beware of backsliding" and turn to him "who is the infinite fountain of light" so their eyes would be opened and they could meet their minister "in joyful and glorious circumstances." He told the teenagers and twenty-somethings that out of love for themselves they ought not to reject the teaching he had given them. The younger children, he advised, should not imitate those who "cast off fear." "Remember that great day when you must appear before the judgment seat of Christ, and meet your minister there, who has so often counseled and warned you." Parents were admonished not to be like Eli, who failed to restrain his children. Everyone in the church was told to avoid contention, which was "one of the greatest burdens" he had labored under. He suggested they give themselves to "secret" prayer, and beware of hiring an Arminian for a minister.

---

34. *WJE* 25:457, 463, 468, 469, 471, 473.

After asking them to pray for him—even if they disagreed with him—he closed with a final exhortation to keep in mind their future meeting: "And let us all remember, and never forget our future solemn meeting, on that great day of the Lord; the day of infallible decision, and of the everlasting and unalterable sentence, Amen."[35]

"Heaven Is a World of Love" describes the world he thought believers would enjoy just after the final scene depicted in the "Farewell Sermon." It was the fifteenth and last in his 1738 series on Paul's paean to love in 1 Corinthians 13. In his explication of the text (vv. 8–10), he asserts that "other gifts of the Spirit" and "all common fruits of the Spirit" shall cease at the end of the church age, and that only charity or love will remain in heaven. His next eighteen pages in the Yale edition develop seven reasons to support the doctrine ("heaven is a world of love"), followed by eleven pages of application. The reasons start with the declaration that while God is everywhere, he is "more especially" in some places than others—such as his progressively greater presence in Israel, Jerusalem, the Temple, the Holy of Holies, and the mercy seat. But heaven is "his dwelling place above all other places in the universe." There sits the infinite fountain of love which is the "mutual holy energy" created by the infinite love of the Father for the Son and the infinite love of the Son for the Father. The Father's love flows to Christ the Head and through him to all his members. The saints are then secondarily subjects of love, just as planets give off reflected light from the sun. All the residents of heaven are perfectly lovely, and harmonize as so many notes "in a concert of music which sweetly [harmonize] with every other note." They are ranked differently according to their capacities for love, but there is no envy in those lower toward those higher because the highest in glory are also highest in holiness and humility and therefore have more love than others. All exist in "an eternal youth" with "perfect tranquility and joy." In heaven there is no fading beauty or decaying love or satiety in our faculty of enjoyment.[36]

In his application Edwards charged his listeners to beware of contention in families, for this especially causes people to "live without much of a comfortable sense of heavenly things, or any lively hope of it." He said saints are happy because they have seen and tasted that heavenly glory. But at the same time, they struggle after holiness, since love always struggles "for liberty" against sin. In his "use" for "awakening to sinners" he told them, "You are in danger. Hell is a world of hatred . . . [it] is, as it were, a vast den of poisonous, lusting

---

35. *WJE* 25:475–77, 480–1, 484, 488.
36. *WJE* 8:369, 386, 383–5.

serpents." Everything that is hateful in this universe "shall be gathered together in hell." Even those who were friends on earth will be enemies there. Everyone will hate one another and "to their utmost torment one another." Misery will not love company there. But "God gives men their choice." If sinners would choose heaven and persevere in well-doing, and love the path which leads to it, "it will certainly lead [them] to heaven at last." They can stay on the path by looking to Jesus, trusting in his mediation and blood—the price of heaven—and intercession for them, and then trusting to his strength to live by his Spirit sent from heaven. Finally, Edwards reassured the saints that to live a life of love to God and neighbor is a way of "inward peace and sweetness." This is the way to have "clear evidences of a title to heaven" because "heavenliness consists in love." So "if ever you arrive at heaven, faith and love must be the wings which must carry you there."[37]

CONTRIBUTIONS TO PREACHING

Edwards tutored many intern preachers in his home, and several generations of preachers modeled their preaching on that of the "New Divinity" of his theological epigones. Not all followed his model with precision, of course. But one can see in the next century of New England preaching, and that of the New Divinity who took Edwardseanism to the new western territories, a number of tendencies that reflect Edwards's preaching. In the following, I will isolate five.

First, Edwards always focused on doctrine. As we have seen, he followed his Puritan predecessors in using the word "doctrine" for a particular and specific teaching that became the assertion to be argued in each of his sermons. For example, his January 1740 sermon on Matthew 12:7 ("If ye had known what this meaneth, I will have mercy, and not sacrifice, ye would not have condemned the guiltless") used ten thousand words to prove the doctrine, "Moral duties towards men are a more important and essential part of religion than external acts of worship of God."[38] One of his Stockbridge sermons to the Native Americans was the repreaching of a Northampton sermon.[39] The new sermon was considerably shorter and used simpler language, but it was clearly devoted, like the earlier one, to "proving" the truth of the doctrine ("The fishermen that cast the net are ministers of the gospel whom Christ appoints to gather men into his church"). The application took the doctrine and pressed it home: "You have had the gospel preached to you. The net has been let down and many of you have

---

37. *WJE* 8:386, 389–91, 395–7.
38. *WJE* 22:115.
39. *WJE* 25:577–81.

been gathered in it . . . But remember, they that be gathered in the net are not all good."[40] The point is that Edwards always tried to leave his hearers with one proposition churning in their brains as they walked away. He was convinced that true religion was founded on knowing, and that knowing comes from the Bible. Preaching is to make true things real, but it must take one of the true things, identify it clearly and succinctly, show how it emerges from the Bible, and then challenge the audience to apply it in concrete ways.

Second, Edwards showed the connection in new ways between preaching and aesthetics, aesthetics and revival, and revival and human history. The ultimate goal of all preaching, he reiterated, is to provide material the Spirit can use to open the eyes of auditors to see the beauty of God. So the purpose of preaching is not only to *explain* one doctrine or proposition, but also to make that truth become *real* by seeing how it further unveils the beauty of holiness. Seeing that is the essence of true religious experience for Edwards. It is the chain reaction of whole communities seeing that beauty, triggered by revival, that propels human history. This is the thesis of Edwards's *History of the Work of Redemption*: revival is the engine of history. Each awakening is a communal combustion in which masses of souls come to see the divine beauty and are thereby transformed. Edwards wrote that revivals come principally by preaching, as ministers are empowered by the Spirit to declare the glorious gospel. Preaching, then, is integral to the history of redemption, which is the secret history driving all of what we call "external" history.

Third, Edwards taught that the important thing in preaching is not beauty but power. He didn't strain to use fancy language or to impress with literary allusions. He was happy instead with plain language and biblical imagery—which, because he was steeped in Scripture, came naturally and easily to him. He told young preachers not to strive for eloquence or cleverness, but to seek God while preparing a sermon, and to pray for the Holy Spirit's anointing. Perhaps he remembered that the first time he preached his legendary *Sinners in the Hands of an Angry God*, it went over like a lead balloon. It was in his home church. But months later, when he preached it in a church in the next colony (Connecticut), the congregation erupted in shrieks and groans. The difference could be attributed to a number of factors such as distance and expectancy, the latter caused by the congregation's internal dynamics and the preacher's reputation. But another factor was the movement of the Holy Spirit.

Fourth, Edwards rarely told stories from history or his own life. But he was a master at using biblical stories and bringing them to life. Many of his images

---

40. Ibid., 25:579.

were drawn directly from the Bible. In this day when preachers are tempted to rummage through handbooks or look on the internet for illustrations, Edwards would advise them to stick to the Bible, whose stories and images are far richer. Think of the beauty and pathos in such stories as the prodigal son, Mary and Martha, the raising of Lazarus, Jesus calling Peter to walk on the water, Abraham on Mount Moriah with Isaac, Jeremiah's bold words while being persecuted, or the Israelites' testings in the wilderness. Edwards used them all, and probed deeply into the actors and their feelings and motivations. This resulted in searching explorations of God's character and human nature.

Fifth, every Edwards sermon was deeply researched and well organized. It was said of Edwards by one of his parishioners that if you accepted the premise at the beginning of the sermon, you were led inexorably to his conclusions. This is not to say that Edwards's sermons were syllogistic treatises. Nor did they use big words. Invariably he used simple words and easily-understood concepts. He did not try to impress by name-dropping or using sophisticated theological terms. But his sermons moved logically from point to point. He used biblical doctrine and biblical stories to proceed in an order that was compelling because it was clear and logical. This combination of clarity and logic drew in both the barely-educated slave (sadly, he had some, and there were others in his congregations) and the educated well-to-do. All who tried to follow his thinking—and before he lost favor with the elite in the last few years at Northampton, most did—had little difficulty doing so. His sermons were living lessons to preachers to work long and hard to prepare biblical arguments that everyone can understand.

CONCLUSION

Edwards likened preaching to Elijah's building a water-soaked-altar at Mount Carmel. Elijah had to complete his work before God "could" do his. Elijah had to build and pray before God would be pleased to send down fire. Edwards of course believed that God acted in whatever way he so pleased. If he had chosen, he could have sent down fire and destroyed the prophets of Baal without Elijah's work of building and praying and slaying. But Edwards observed that it is "God's manner" to send his Spirit to inspire his ministers first to obey by preparing and studying and praying. Then those ministers were to pray some more, and beg God to send down his Spirit on the work they had prepared at his direction and by his leading. If they did their part, then they could trust that God would do his—open the eyes of his people to see more and more of the beauty of holiness. This should be the aim, he taught, of every good preacher and every good sermon.

Sermon Excerpt

Psalm 24:7–10[41]

When the Psalmist in this Psalm had inquired who shall ascend "the hill of the Lord," he makes answer: "he that has clean hands, and a pure heart." In one sense, all Christ's sincere disciples and followers are such. They are pure in heart and hands, with a purity of sincerity [and] universal obedience; but in another sense, Christ alone is so, who was perfectly free from all defilement of heart and hands. This Psalm treats of the ascension of both head and members of the church of Christ into heaven.

When Christ ascended into heaven after his sore battle or conflict with his enemies in his death and suffering, and his glorious victory over them in his resurrection, wherein he appeared to be the Lord strong and mighty, the Lord mighty in battle, the word was proclaimed to the gates of that eternal city and doors of that everlasting temple, that house not made with hands, eternal in the heavens, that they should be lift up, that the King of glory might come in: signifying with what joy and welcome Christ was received in heaven by his Father and all the heavenly inhabitants, when he returned thither after his victory over sin and Satan in his death. When Christ ascended to heaven, he ascended in triumph in a most joyful manner: as the Roman generals, when they had been forth on any expedition and had obtained any remarkable victory, when they returned to the city of Rome, whence they were sent forth by the supreme authority of that city, used to enter the gates of the city in triumph, the authority of the Roman state gladly opening the gates to 'em, and all the Roman people receiving them with shouting and the sound of the trumpet and with many such-like manifestations of joy, and their enemies that they conquered led in triumph at their chariot; which the Psalmist in the 47th Psalm, 5th verse, speaking of Christ's ascension, says, "God is gone up with a shout. The Lord with the sound of the trumpet."

And 'tis probable that the day of Christ's ascension into heaven, was the most joyful day that ever was seen there, when he ascended, as it were leading principalities and powers in triumph at his chariot, which [was] attended with a glorious retinue of angels, and many saints that rose and

---

41. Jonathan Edwards, "Who is this King of Glory?" edited and introduced by Oshea Davis (New Haven: Yale University, Jonathan Edwards Center, 2007–).

ascended with their bodies into heaven with him. When Christ thus joyfully ascended, this sight was beheld by the angels, and those holy ones that saw it, with great joy and admiration: and therefore, when that word was preached, "Lift up your heads, O ye gates," they upon it inquired, "Who is the King of glory," which is a note of their great admiration at the sight which they beheld. ✦

BIBLIOGRAPHY

Bailey, Richard, and Gregory Wells, eds., *The Salvation of Souls: Nine Previously Published Sermons on the Call of Ministry and the Gospel by Jonathon Edwards*. Wheaton, IL: Crossway, 2002.

Dwight, Timothy. *Travels in New England and New York*. Pages 230–31 in vol. 4. Cambridge: Harvard University Press, 1969.

Edwards, Jonathan. *The Works of Jonathan Edwards, Vol. 2: Religious Affections*. Edited by John E. Smith. New Haven: Yale University Press, 1959.

_____. *The Works of Jonathan Edwards, Vol. 4: The Great Awakening*. Edited by C. C. Goen. New Haven: Yale University Press, 1972.

_____. *The Works of Jonathan Edwards, Vol. 8: Ethical Writings*. Edited by Paul Ramsey. New Haven: Yale University Press, 1989.

_____. *The Works of Jonathan Edwards, Vol. 10: Sermons and Discourses, 1720–1723*. Edited by Wilson H. Kimnach. New Haven: Yale University Press, 1992.

_____. *The Works of Jonathan Edwards, Vol. 13: The "Miscellanies," a-500*. Edited by Thomas A. Schafer. New Haven: Yale University Press, 1994.

_____. *The Works of Jonathan Edwards, Vol. 14: Sermons and Discourses, 1723–1729*. Edited by Kenneth P. Minkema. New Haven: Yale University Press, 1997.

_____. *The Works of Jonathan Edwards, Vol. 17: Sermons and Discourse, 1730–1733*. Edited by Mark Valeri. New Haven: Yale University Press, 1999.

_____. *The Works of Jonathan Edwards, Vol. 19: Sermons and Discourse, 1734–1738*. Edited by M. X. Lesser. New Haven: Yale University Press, 2001.

_____. *The Works of Jonathan Edwards, Vol. 22: Sermons and Discourse, 1739–1742*. Edited by Harry S. Stout and Nathan O. Hatch with Kyle P. Farley. New Haven: Yale University Press, 2003.

_____. *The Works of Jonathan Edwards, Vol. 24: The Blank Bible*. Edited by Stephen Stein. New Haven: Yale University Press, 2006.

_____. *The Works of Jonathan Edwards, Vol. 25: Sermons and Discourses, 1743–1758*. New Haven: Yale University Press, 2006.

Gerstner, John. *The Rational Biblical Theology of Jonathan Edwards*. Powhatan, VA: Berea, 1991.

Kimnach, Wilson H. "Edwards as Preacher." Pages 103–24 in *The Cambridge Companion to Jonathan Edwards*. Edited by Stephen J. Stein. Cambridge: Cambridge University Press, 2007.

_____. "The Sermons: Concept and Execution." Pages 243–57 in *The Princeton Companion to Jonathan Edwards*. Edited by Sang Hyun Lee. Princeton: Princeton University Press, 2005.

Kimnach, Wilson H., Kenneth P. Minkema, and Douglas A. Sweeney, eds. *The Sermons of Jonathan Edwards: A Reader*. New Haven: Yale University Press, 1999.

Marsden, George M. *Jonathan Edwards: A Life*. New Haven: Yale University Press, 2003.

_____. *A Short Life of Jonathan Edwards*. Grand Rapids: Eerdmans, 2008.

McClymond, Michael J., and Gerald R. McDermott. *The Theology of Jonathan Edwards*. New York: Oxford University Press, 2012.

McDermott, Gerald R. *Jonathan Edwards Confronts the Gods: Christian Theology, Enlightenment Religion, and Non-Christian Faiths*. Oxford: Oxford University Press, 2000.

_____. "Missions and Native Americans." Pages 258–73 in *The Princeton Companion to Jonathan Edwards*. Edited by Sang Hyun Lee. Princeton: Princeton University Press, 2005.

_____. *One Holy and Happy Society: The Public Theology of Jonathan Edwards*. University Park: Pennsylvania State University Press, 1992.

_____. *Seeing God: Jonathan Edwards and Spiritual Discernment.* Vancouver: Regent College Publishing, 2000; first edn. Downers Grove, IL: InterVarsity Press, 1995.

_____. *Understanding Jonathan Edwards: Introducing America's Theologian.* Oxford: Oxford University Press, 2008.

McDermott, Gerald, and Ronald Story, eds. *The Other Jonathan Edwards: Selected Writings on Society, Love, and Justice.* Amherst, MA: University of Massachusetts Press, 2015.

Sweeney, Douglas A. *Jonathan Edwards and the Ministry of the Word.* Downers Grove, IL: InterVarsity Press, 2009.

Westra, Helen. *The Minister's Task and Calling in the Sermons of Jonathan Edwards.* Lewiston, NY: Mellen, 1986.

John Wesley
Homiletic Theologian

MICHAEL PASQUARELLO III

John Wesley (1703–1791) is often remembered for a way of preaching that produced significant results in both personal conversion and social change. However, a desire to emulate Wesley's presumably effective methods, and enthusiasm for replicating his impressive results, have often caused preachers to overlook the theological convictions, dispositions, and habits that oriented his life and ministry to the knowledge, love, and enjoyment of God. During more than sixty years of ministry and in excess of forty thousand sermons, Wesley's theology emerged from and fed into his preaching—a "homiletical theology" by which he sought to bear faithful witness to the gospel. It was not possible for Wesley to conceive of good preaching apart from the transformation of preachers by what is spoken or of proclaiming "scriptural holiness" apart from faith in Christ, which engenders love of God and neighbor through the gracious empowerments of the Spirit. Understanding Wesley as a preacher requires appreciation for the kind of doctrinal commitments and practical wisdom he shared with preaching theologians from earlier periods in Christian tradition.

HISTORICAL BACKGROUND

John Wesley was born in Epworth, England, to Samuel and Susanna Wesley. Samuel was a priest in the Church of England and, in tandem with Susanna, provided John and his siblings with a solid grounding in learning and religion. Being the son of an Anglican clergyman enabled Wesley to attend Charterhouse School in London (1713–1720), which was followed by his matriculation to Oxford University, where he received his BA in 1724 and an MA in 1727. Wesley's vocational interests oriented him toward pursuing ordination as a deacon and then as a priest in the Church of England (1725 and 1728), as well as a fellowship at Lincoln College, Oxford (1728).[1]

---

1. Here I am following the narratives in Kenneth J. Collins, "Wesley's Life and Ministry," in *The*

Wesley's long career as a preacher began during his student years in and around Oxford. During this time his convictions concerning the character and activity of preaching were deeply influenced by his participation with a group of Oxford students, including his brother Charles, in small societies that sought to promote "holy living." Holiness of heart and life would become the central focus of Wesley's preaching ministry during the next six decades. Moreover, his membership in what came to be called the "Holy Club" involved him in a way of living in fellowship with others that provided a particular ethos that would shape and characterize his faith, life, and ministry. Arguably, preaching would serve as an integrative focus for a particular way of thinking, believing, living, and speaking in what might best be described as the "preaching life."[2]

Participation in the Holy Club at Oxford was a deeply transformative experience for Wesley, comprising daily prayer, Scripture reading and meditation, study, fasting, self-examination, receiving the Lord's Supper, mutual encouragement, and works of mercy with the poor, the sick, the imprisoned, and the unschooled. Wesley's early homiletical theology, then, was oriented by a vision of personal and social holiness which placed primary emphasis on the necessity of continued education and personal edification as a minister of the Word. The study of theology, for Wesley, was thus a practical affair, or "practical divinity," which was oriented toward forming people in the life of faith, active in the love that is the Spirit's gift and empowerment.[3]

Wesley's preaching ministry took a significant turn after a period of mission work in the American colony of Georgia (1735–1738). The experience of preaching and evangelization was personally and pastorally disappointing for him. However, a providential encounter with German pietism pointed him toward a way of reconciling his High Church Anglican convictions with a deeply "heartfelt" faith, active in love, which would be expressed by Methodists as a form of "sacramental evangelicalism." Soon after his return to England in 1738, Wesley underwent a spiritual crisis that eventuated in a surprising renewal of his faith and vocation. The turn in Wesley's life and ministry was more personal and practical rather than doctrinal. He had longed for the assurance of faith, a desire he believed was providentially granted in May 1738, at a religious society meeting

---

Cambridge Companion to John Wesley, eds. Randy L. Maddox and Jason E. Vickers (Cambridge: Cambridge University Press, 2010), 43–59; Richard Heitzenrater, *Wesley and the People Called Methodists* (Nashville: Abingdon Press, 1995), 17–98.

2. For a fuller explication of Wesley and the integrative nature of his preaching, see Michael Pasquarello III, *John Wesley: A Preaching Life* (Nashville: Abingdon Press, 2011).

3. See here Rebekah L. Miles, "Happiness, Holiness, and the Moral Life in John Wesley" in *The Cambridge Companion to John Wesley*, eds. Randy L. Maddox and Jason E. Vickers (Cambridge: Cambridge University Press, 2010), 207–24.

on Aldersgate Street in Oxford. Faith, as confident trust in God's gracious initiative and action, became an experiential reality and not simply a conceptual idea.[4]

Wesley's startling experience challenged more than his theological opinions; it generated a joyful confession of living faith in Christ, *"Christus pro me"* (Christ for me), that reoriented his ministry. Wesley's receptivity to the Spirit's gift of assurance was not merely an intense feeling but was a deep conviction that the Spirit is the mysterious source of both inner assurance and outward fruits that together display the character of being and living by faith in Christ alone. In the months immediately following Aldersgate, Wesley was encouraged by George Whitefield to test the implications of the Spirit's prompting in his ministry of preaching. Whitefield had already established a strong ministry of evangelical preaching in both England and America. Following Whitefield's example, Wesley decided to take up field preaching, or "open air" preaching. This was a centuries-old evangelistic approach that brought the proclamation of the gospel to people, particularly large numbers of common folk, who did not attend services in the established churches.[5]

Although trained for the liturgical ministry of the Church of England, Wesley quickly adjusted to a new means of preaching the gospel that allowed him to address crowds numbering in the thousands. This eighteenth-century form of missional preaching was accompanied by surprising manifestations of God's power, as listeners were awakened and moved to vital faith by the work of the Spirit through the ministry of the Word. Wesley's vision for ministry was greatly expanded, no longer bound by Anglican parish protocol. Field preaching marked the beginnings of a "Wesleyan" evangelical movement, the scope of which was determined by God's prevenient, gracious leading. A significant aspect of Wesley's homiletical effectiveness was his adaptation of the formation of religious societies, a familiar practice within the Church of England. Following the pattern displayed in the book of Acts, Wesley saw such small groups as a necessary means of cultivating a faith active in love for God and love for neighbor—holiness of heart and life.[6]

By 1740, the Oxford-educated theologian had begun searching both within and beyond the Anglican tradition for a way of interpreting and proclaiming the gospel which would be able to unite faith in God's justifying grace through Christ with the sanctifying work of the Holy Spirit. The stage was set for Wesley's contributions to a remarkable evangelical revival, which spread beyond England and eventually became a global movement. The rise of modern evangelicalism

---

4. Collins, "Wesley's Life and Ministry," 47–48.
5. Heitzenrater, *Wesley and the People Called Methodists*, 94–103.
6. Ibid., 103–17.

was affected by and would also profoundly affect the ministry of preaching across doctrinal traditions and ecclesial boundaries. This movement of the Spirit was marked by robust proclamation of the gospel, evangelical conversion, enthusiastic testimony, and manifestations of renewed spiritual and moral vitality. In a very real sense, the end goal of Wesley's preaching was the formation of disciples who shared a common life through faith in Christ and the power of the Spirit in pursuing the "perfection of love."[7]

Preaching was arguably the defining activity of John Wesley's ministry (1703–1791). As he confessed, "I do indeed live by preaching."[8] He was convinced the proclamation of the Word of God was the Spirit's principle means of gathering converts into Christian communities and building them up into the life of holy love. Arguably, Wesley's whole life can be seen as oriented toward the vocation of preaching, in which pursuit he exceeded forty thousand sermons in popular and academic contexts, in Anglican churches and Methodist preaching chapels, and among large gatherings in open fields. A remarkable characteristic of Wesley's preaching was the exercise of practical wisdom, which enabled him to adjust his sermons to address listeners in diverse settings and changing circumstances, while continuing to be guided by what he would identify as the "scripture way of salvation."[9]

THEOLOGY OF PREACHING

Albert Outler has explained that in order to make sense of Wesley's life and ministry, one needs to view it in light of the larger ecclesial and theological tradition in which he stood. "Wesley has been invoked oftener than he has been read and usually has been read with a low-church anti-intellectual bias that celebrates his warm heart and worn saddlebags, unconcerned with his theology. But this very pathos could rescue the study of Wesley from the genetic fallacy that haunts most denominational histories. It is more important, I have come to believe, to study Wesley's theology in the light of his antecedents than his successors."[10]

Wesley insisted the faith of "Methodists" was the true religion of the Bible, interpreted by the Church of England through its *Book of Common Prayer*,

---

7. Heitzenrater, *Wesley and the People Called Methodists*, 74–98; Charles I. Wallace, "Wesley as Revivalist/ Renewal Leader," in *The Cambridge Companion to John Wesley*, 85–93.

8. John Wesley, *Journals and Diaries IV* (28 July 1757), eds. W. Reginald Ward and Richard P. Heitzenrater, vol. 21 in *The Works of John Wesley* (Nashville: Abingdon Press, 1988–2003), 118.

9. See here the good summary by Richard P. Heitzenrater, "Wesley, John" in the *Concise Encyclopedia of Preaching*, eds. William H. Willimon and Richard Lischer (Louisville: Westminster/John Knox Press, 1995), 500–502; William J. Abraham, "Wesley as Preacher" in *The Cambridge Companion to John Wesley*, 98–112.

10. Albert C. Outler, *The Wesleyan Theological Heritage: Essays of Albert C. Outler*. Thomas C. Oden and Leicester R. Longden, eds. (Grand Rapids: Zondervan, 1991), 53–54.

Articles of Religion, and official *Homilies,* which sought to fill the hearts and minds of its people with the knowledge and love of God. On numerous occasions, Wesley expressed this commitment, writing of the common life he shared with others according to the principles of the Church of England—as confirmed by its liturgy, homiletical theology, and doctrine—and congruent with the whole tenor of Scripture.[11] Accordingly, for Wesley,

> Methodism is the old religion, the religion of the Bible, the religion of the Primitive Church, the religion of the Church of England. This old religion . . . is none other than love, the love of God and of all mankind . . . This love is the great medicine of life . . . Wherever this is, there are virtue and happiness going hand in hand . . . This religion of love and joy and peace has its seat in the inmost soul; but is ever showing itself by its fruits . . . spreading virtue and happiness to all around it.[12]

A Trinitarian Theology for Preaching

For Wesley, preaching was attentive to and affected by the presence of Christ, who constitutes the church as his body through the work of the Holy Spirit as mediated by the witness of Scripture. The practical wisdom of preaching is engendered by divine grace, which works through the virtues of faith, hope, and love that enable judgment and discernment for faithful speaking. As Wesley writes: ". . . . the love of God and man not only filling my heart, but shining through my whole conversation."[13] In his sermon "The Circumcision of the Heart," Wesley writes of the particular kind of humility which is required to see reality clearly— with the eyes of the heart and understanding illumined by the "mind of Christ" which was embodied in loving obedience to the Father.

> In general, we may observe it is that habitual disposition of soul which in the Sacred Writings is termed "holiness," and which directly implies the being cleansed from sin, "from all filthiness of both flesh and spirit," and by consequence of being endued with those virtues which were also in Christ Jesus, the being so "renewed in the image of your mind" as to be "perfect, as our Father in heaven is perfect" . . . This is that lowliness of mind which they have learned of Christ who follow his example and tread in his steps.

---

11. Frank Baker, *John Wesley and the Church of England* (Nashville: Abingdon, 1970).
12. Cited in *The Wesleyan Theological Heritage: Essays of Albert C. Outler,* eds. Thomas C. Oden and Leicester R. Longden (Grand Rapids: Zondervan, 1991).
13. John Wesley, "An Address to the Clergy," in *The Works of John Wesley,* 3rd ed. (Grand Rapids: Baker, 1978), 485, 499.

And this knowledge of their disease, whereby they are more and more cleansed from one part of it, pride and vanity, disposes them to embrace a willing mind the second thing implied in "circumcision of the heart"—that faith which alone is able to make them whole, which is the one medicine given under heaven to heal their sickness.[14]

Wesley's preaching gives homiletic expression to the knowledge of faith that works through love within a tradition of shared beliefs and practices guided by the faith confessed in the creeds. Thus, the truth and goodness by which the Spirit orders the intellect and will to the fellowship of the Father and the Son is a necessary presupposition for preaching as an expression of "Scriptural Christianity." Geoffrey Wainwright comments on Wesley's Trinitarian hermeneutics: "Study of the Scriptures in the Spirit, by whom they were divinely written, conveys the incarnate Christ, who gives knowledge of the Father who sent him, so that we may love Him and thus be conformed to the Son and enjoy the holiness which the Spirit gives."[15]

For Wesley, reading Scripture is guided by a conviction that the truth and reality of the triune God is mediated by the testimony of the Spirit to Christ through the whole biblical canon. This is a participatory and transformative way of reading, which includes but also exceeds the historical, cultural, and linguistic matters related to the biblical text. Wesley's theological orientation did not exclude the historical and human dimensions of study, ministry, and preaching but rather sought their completion in love for God and neighbor.[16]

Preaching Christ and the Gospel

An example of Wesley's homiletical wisdom is evinced by a letter he wrote in December 1751, when the spread of evangelical revival was provoking both enthusiasm and resistance. Wesley wrote to an inquirer about "preaching Christ," presumably after pondering this matter for a period of several months.[17] His description of "preaching Christ" is both theological and pastoral in scope, providing a summary of God's mission—the love of God for sinners, demonstrated in the life, death, resurrection, and intercession of Christ and his blessings—and

---

14. *The Works of John Wesley: The Bicentennial Edition,* ed. Albert C. Outler (Nashville: Abingdon, 1984–) I., 405. Hereafter cited as *Works.*

15. Geoffrey Wainwright, "The Trinitarian Hermeneutic of John Wesley," in *Reading the Bible in Wesleyan Ways: Some Constructive Proposals,* eds. Barry L. Callen and Richard P. Thompson (Kansas City: Beacon Hill, 2004), 23.

16. Here I would recommend Wainwright, *Reading the Bible in Wesleyan Ways,* passim.

17. For the following description I am drawing from *The Works of John Wesley,* 3rd ed. (repr., Grand Rapids: Baker Book House, 1978) 11, 486–92.

the law setting forth the commands of Christ, in particular the Sermon on the Mount.

This practical vision was cultivated by Wesley's study of Scripture and intimate knowledge of the Christian life, thus uniting the Word and the work of God. Revealing his theological and pastoral understanding of the relation between law and gospel, his comments reflect the practical judgment which is required to address a wide range of spiritual and moral conditions, including that of sinners, the justified, the diligent, the proud, the careless, and the weak in understanding.[18]

Wesley directs particular attention to Methodist preacher John Wheatley, whom he describes as a "gospel preacher," that is, one who was "neither clear nor sound in the faith." According to Wesley, Wheatley's sermons had the sound of "an unconnected rhapsody of unmeaning words" and "Verses, smooth and soft as cream, in which was neither depth nor stream." Wesley was concerned with the effects of "gospel" preaching, which, its rhetorical finesse and popular appeal notwithstanding, lacked theological coherence and moral wisdom. Long on promises and short on commands, "gospel" preaching corrupted hearers, vitiated their taste, ruined their desire for sound teaching, and spoiled their spiritual appetites, feeding them "sweetmeats" until the genuine wine of the kingdom seemed insipid. Wesley concluded that while such popular "gospel preachers" were adept at attracting large crowds, their preaching was characterized by "cordial upon cordial" that eventually destroyed listeners' capacities for retaining and digesting the pure milk of the Word.[19]

On the other hand, the Methodist manner of preaching provided practical wisdom for interpreting both law and gospel in light of the truth of Christ, who by the work of the Spirit calls and creates a people in the knowledge and love of God. Wesley states,

> At our first beginning to preach at any place, after a general declaration of the love of God to sinners, and his willingness that they should be saved, to preach the law, in the strongest, the closest, the most searching manner possible; only intermixing the gospel here and there, and showing it, as it were, afar off. After more and more persons are convinced of sin, we may mix more and more of the gospel in order to "beget faith," to rein into

---

18. Ibid., 488–90.
19. Ibid., 489. John Wheatley was a Methodist itinerant preacher accused of moral indiscretions which led his to expulsion from the ministry by Wesley. Wheatley's preaching was sentimental but without the call to repentance and reform of faith and life. He was very popular and successful at drawing large crowds of listeners, a case which accentuated the need for Wesley's attention to examining, teaching, and disciplining his preachers. See Heitzenrater, *Wesley and the People Called Methodists,* 180–202.

spiritual life those whom the law hath slain; but is not to be done too hastily either.[20]

Preaching Salvation

Wesley sketches a brief order of salvation in which one is drawn, converted, and led by the teaching of the law to living faith in the saving activity of Christ through which the Spirit bears the fruit of good works and holiness. "God loves you; therefore, love and obey him. Christ died for you; therefore, die to sin. Christ is risen; therefore, rise in the image of God. Christ liveth forevermore; therefore, live to God, till you live with him in glory."[21] A sermon written in the same year, "The Law Established by Faith II," states this more fully:

> It is our part thus to "preach Christ" by preaching all things whatsoever he hath revealed. We may indeed, without blame, yea, and with a peculiar blessing from God, declare the love of our Lord Jesus Christ. We may speak in a more especial manner, of "the Lord our righteousness" [Jer 23:6], we may expatiate upon the grace of God "reconciling the world unto himself" [2 Cor 5:19]; we may, at proper opportunities, dwell upon his praise, as bearing the "iniquities of us all," as "wounded for our transgressions" and "bruised for our iniquities," that "by his stripes we might be healed" [Isa 53:4–5]. But still we should not preach Christ according to his Word if we would wholly confine ourselves to this. We are not ourselves clear before God, unless we proclaim him in all his offices. To preaching Christ as a workman that needeth not be ashamed [2 Tim 2:15] is to preach him not only as our great "High Priest, taken from among men, and ordained for men, in things pertaining to God" [Heb 5:1], as such "reconciling us by his blood" [Rom 5:9, 10], and "ever living to make intercession for us" [Heb 7:25], but likewise as the Prophet of the Lord, "who of God is made unto us wisdom" [1 Cor 1:30], who, by his word and his Spirit, "is with us always, guiding us into all truth" [John 16:13]; yea, and as remaining a King forever, as giving laws to all whom he has bought with his blood, as restoring those to the image of God whom he had first reinstated in his favor, as reigning in all believing hearts until he "subdued all things to himself" [Phil 3:21], until he hath utterly cast out all sin, and "brought in everlasting righteousness" [Dan 9:24].[22]

---

20. *The Works of John Wesley*, 491.
21. Ibid., 486, 492.
22. *Works*, II, 37–38.

Wesley's biblically-informed, evangelically-oriented preaching—"plain truth for plain people"—articulated the gospel as the wisdom and power of God. Such preaching evoked new conversions and fresh returnings, penitent responses to the promptings of the Spirit that were communicated by joyful witness to Christ and nurtured into disciplined love for God and neighbor within a common life of grace. The gift of living faith in love and the fruit of good works was evinced in a wide range of circumstances but especially among the poorest and most humble of circumstances and conditions into which God's generous love and abundant goodness were gladly received. Bearing witness to surprising manifestations of divine grace, such communal remembrances of God's redemptive work evoked robust, energetic outpourings of "wonder, love and praise" that called attention to their source and goal: the praise of the triune God, who forgives, reconciles, and restores human creatures to the divine image.[23]

Preaching That People May Know and Love God

These startling acts of conversion and social witness in eighteenth-century England were not seen as a result of choosing the right homiletic method or using the most effective evangelistic technique, but rather were viewed as forms of concrete, visible witness—in both their initial workings and maturing fruit— pointing to the joy of knowing and loving God, or "one thing needful." Wesley articulated this practical wisdom in his sermon, "The New Creation," demonstrating a proper relation between the goods of our created life and the final good, which is God.

> The one perfect good shall be your ultimate end. One thing shall ye desire for its own sake—the fruition of him who is all in all. One happiness ye shall propose to your souls, even a union with him that made them, the having fellowship with the Father and the Son, the being "joined to the Lord in one Spirit." One design ye are to pursue to the end of time—the enjoyment of God in time and eternity. Desire other things so far as they tend to this. Love the creature—as it leads to the Creator. But in every step you take be this, the glorious point that terminates your view. Let every affection, and desire or fear, whatever ye seek or shun, whatever ye think, speak, or do, be in order to your happiness in God, the sole end as well as the source of

---

23. See the discussion of Wesley, worship, and Methodism in "Worship, Evangelism, Ehics: On Eliminating the 'And,'" in Stanley Hauerwas, *A Better Hope: Resources for a Church Confronting Capitalism, Democracy, and Postmodernity* (Grand Rapids: Brazos, 2000), 155–62; Horton Davies, *Worship and Theology in England, Vol. II: From Watts and Wesley to Martineau, 1690–1900* (Grand Rapids: Eerdmans, 1996), 184–209.

your being. Have no end, no ultimate end, but God. Thus our Lord: "One thing needful."[24]

Wesley homiletic wisdom points to a "way" which is ordered by faith that unites knowledge and love.[25] Such practical wisdom entails a participation in Christ's human righteousness; having the "mind that was in Christ" through which the Spirit transforms and guides thinking, living, and speaking by the law of the gospel ruling in the mind and heart.[26] As he writes, "Prudence (or practical wisdom), properly so called, is not that offspring of hell which the world calls prudence, which is mere craft, cunning dissimulation; but . . . that 'wisdom from above' which our Lord peculiarly recommends to all who would promote his kingdom upon earth. . . . This wisdom will instruct you how to suit your words and whole behavior to the persons with whom you have to do, to the time, place, and all other circumstances."[27]

Preaching in and of the Power of the Spirit

Wesley's homiletic discourse was thoroughly Trinitarian in bearing witness to the cosmic scope of the new creation inaugurated by Christ through the power of the Spirit. This is the truth which the church receives, celebrates, embodies, and proclaims to the world through the illumination and empowerment of the Spirit. "[God] is already renewing the face of the earth. And we have strong reason to hope that the work he hath begun, he will carry on unto the day of the Lord Jesus; that he will never intermit this blessed work of his Spirit, until he has fulfilled all his promises; until he hath put a period to sin, and misery, and infirmity, and death; and re-established universal holiness and happiness, and caused all the inhabitants of the earth to sing together, 'Hallelujah, the Lord God omnipotent reigneth!'"[28]

Of all the genres in the Wesley corpus, the written sermons focus and expound a homiletic theology which springs from and points to the gospel he believed, lived, and proclaimed. Wesley describes this as the happiness of the Christian religion, a life that springs from the joy of knowing and loving God, the way of holiness which bears fruit in good works and words that witness the

---

24. See the sermons "On the Trinity" and "The New Creation" in *Works*, II: 373–86, 500–510; On Wesley and Christian conversion, see William H. Willimon, "Suddenly a Light from Heaven" in *Conversion and the Wesleyan Tradition*, eds. Kenneth J. Collins and John H. Tyson (Nashville: Abingdon, 2001), 240–50.

25. Randy Maddox, *Responsible Grace: John Wesley's Practical Theology* (Nashville: Abingdon, 1994), 26–47.

26. D. Stephen Long, *John Wesley's Moral Theology: The Quest for God and Goodness* (Nashville: Abingdon, 2005), 171–202.

27. *Works*, II, 318.

28. Ibid., 499.

love of God indwelling human life. The preface to the 1746 edition of *Sermons on Several Occasions* describes Wesley's desire to know, live, and communicate the way of holiness and happiness in God.

> I want to know one thing, the way to heaven—how to land safe on that happy shore. God himself has condescended to teach the way; for this very end he came down from heaven. He hath written it down in a book. O give me that book! Give me the Book of God! . . . I have according set down in the following sermons what I find in the Bible concerning the way to heaven . . . I have endeavored to describe the true, the scriptural, experimental religion, so as to omit nothing which is a real part thereof, and to add nothing thereto which is not.[29]

Springing from the personal knowledge and love of God, such happy preaching entails the transformation of the intellect, affections, and will, through the work of Christ and the Holy Spirit, which restores human beings to the divine image, the most definitive form of human receptivity to the Word. Through prayerful attentiveness to the divine realities revealed in Scripture, new habits of the heart and mind are received that enable a way of thinking, speaking, and living according to the wisdom and virtue of Christ.[30] Through the ministry of the Word, preachers are formed into a life of spiritual and moral excellence through the Spirit's gifts, virtues, and fruit, learning to love and advancing in hope, bearing witness to "a beauty, a love, a holiness."[31] Wesley writes of the joy of knowing God through living faith:

> We may learn hence . . . that this happy knowledge of the true God is only another name for religion; I mean Christian religion, which indeed is the only one that deserves the name. Religion, as to the nature or essence of it, does not lie in this or that set of notions, vulgarly called "faith"; nor in a round of duties, however carefully "reformed" from error and superstition. It does not consist in any number of outward actions. No; it properly and directly consists in the knowledge and love of God, as manifested in the Son of his love, through the eternal Spirit. And this naturally leads to every heavenly temper, and to every good word and work.[32]

---

29. *Works,* I. 106–7.
30. Eugene H. Peterson, *Under the Unpredictable Plant: An Exploration in Vocational Holiness* (Grand Rapids: Eerdmans; Leicester: Gracewing, 1992).
31. Ibid., 21.
32. *Works,* III, 99.

The Heart of a Wesleyan Theology of Preaching

The heart of Wesley's homiletic witness was oriented theologically for the church. It was a form of first order discourse which springs from and forms a common life of devotion, doctrine, and discipline in which the triune God is known and loved as the source and goal of all that is. For this reason, Wesley's homiletic witness is unintelligible apart from the ecclesial habits that gave shape to his faith, wisdom, and virtue as a lover of God and hearer of the Word. Or to put this differently, the renewal of the mind in God's image is enabled by the gifts of faith, hope, and love, through which the Spirit enables the return of the whole of one's life to God as a sacrifice of praise.

> This eternal life then commences when it pleases the Father to reveal the Son in our hearts; when we first know Christ, being enabled to "call him Lord by the Holy Ghost;" when we can testify, our conscience bearing us witness in the Holy Ghost, "the life I now live, I live by faith in the Son of God, who loved me, and gave himself for me." And then it is that happiness begins-real, solid, substantial. Then it is that heaven is opened in the soul, that the proper heavenly state commences, while the love of God, as loving us, is shed abroad in the heart, instantly producing love to all mankind; general pure benevolence, together with its genuine fruits, lowliness, meekness, patience, contentedness in every state; an entire, clear, full acquiescence in the whole will of God, enabling us to "rejoice evermore, and in everything give thanks."[33]

Although Wesley is well known as a popular preacher, he was not a typical popularizer who chose to omit aspects of the gospel to enable sermonizing that was adjusted to doing whatever "works." Transcending much of the popular wisdom of his day, Wesley's primary concern was both spiritual and moral, personal and social: that the credibility of living faith which bears visible, tangible fruit in a life of love, goodness, peace, and joy not be lost in such popular superficialities. Moreover, this commitment was sustained by a single-mindedness of devotion which was grounded in the truth of the scriptural witness, illumined by the church's Trinitarian faith, and nourished by the Spirit through the ecclesial means of grace.

Of primary importance for Wesley was that the ministry of "preaching Christ" entails openness and vulnerability to the witness of the Spirit, who

---

33. *Works*, III, 96.

awakens repentance, bestows living faith, and inspires a life of holiness and good works toward God, others, and all creatures. For Wesley, then, preaching is itself a discourse through which the self-communication of the Father in the Son is appropriated by the Spirit's gifts of faith, hope, and love into a way of thinking, living, and speaking, which is discerned with the "mind that was in Christ."[34]

Writing in response to an inquirer, Wesley described the intimate relation between the truth of doctrine, preaching, and Christian way of life engendered by the new law of the gospel ruling in the heart, mind, and speech.

> I do preach to as many as desire to hear, every night and morning. You ask; what would I do with them; I would make them virtuous and happy, easy in themselves and useful to others. Whither would I lead them? To heaven; to God the Judge, the lover of all, and to Jesus the Mediator of the new covenant. What religion do I preach? The religion of love; the law of kindness brought to light by the gospel. What is this good for? To make all who receive it enjoy God and themselves: to make them like God; lovers of all; contented in their lives; and crying out at their death, in calm assurance, "O grave, where is thy victory! Thanks be unto God."[35]

METHODOLOGY FOR PREACHING

Wesley did not have what some would consider a fully-orbed *methodology of preaching* like many pulpiteers of the church. Instead, what Wesley did have was a conviction that the holiness of the preacher was of prime importance, and that without such a life of holiness, great preaching (and methodology) would have no lasting value. Accordingly, the holiness of the preacher is inseparable from the identity of the church as a people called and formed by the self-giving of the Father, which is mediated by the Son through the work of the Spirit in the means of grace. This assumes, however, that homiletic excellence aims for congruence with the knowledge and love engendered by faith in the Word through whom the Spirit draws believers into the triune life. Prayer and preaching are inseparable, so that the language of preaching is to be tested by the church's primary vocation of worship, which is inseparable from works of piety and mercy.[36] In the following, we will briefly consider Wesley's instruction on

---

34. *Works*, II, 156–57.
35. Cited in W. L. Doughty, *John Wesley: Preacher* (London: Epworth, 1955), 194.
36. Stanley Hauerwas, "Carving Stone and Learning to Speak Christian" in *The State of the University: Academic Knowledge and the Knowledge of God* (Malden and Oxford: Blackwell, 2007), 121.

the need for spiritual and practical preparation for those pursuing a ministry of preaching.

The purpose of the official *Homilies* was to direct readers, especially preachers, to diligent study of Scripture, with assurance that God acts through the Holy Spirit to grant living faith in Christ which is energized by love.[37] Wesley discovered in the soteriology and homiletic wisdom of the Church of England a "grammar," or logic, for Methodist preaching, evangelization, and catechesis. Moreover, while the Bible was the chief source of the homilies, the liturgical ethos of Anglicanism was their home. Summoned by the truth and goodness of Christ announced in the gospel, gatherings of prayer, praise, and proclamation were occasions for grateful response to the astonishing overflow of the Father's pure, unbounded love in the ministry of the Son through the power of the Spirit. Wesley's preaching was thus guided by a Trinitarian vision of salvation.[38]

Anglican Foundations of Methodism

As a homiletic theologian, Wesley's life and vocation was defined by the gospel. As a preacher and teacher of preachers, his homiletic wisdom was nourished by the teaching of Scripture, with the guidance of the official *Book of Homilies* published in the sixteenth century during the reign of Edward VI and Elizabeth I—formularies to which Wesley was ever eager to confess his allegiance. During the latter years of his ministry, upon returning from a tour of Methodist societies throughout England and Ireland, Wesley spoke of the theological value of the homilies for preaching: "The book, which next to the Holy Scriptures was of greatest use to them in settling their judgment as to the grand point of justification by faith, is the book of *Homilies*. They were never clearly convinced that we are justified by faith alone till they carefully consulted these and compared them with the sacred writings [Holy Scripture]. And no minister of the Church can, with any decency, oppose these, seeing that at his ordination he subscribed to them in subscribing to the thirty-sixth article of the Church."[39]

Almost fifty years earlier, Wesley had provided a doctrinal summary for Methodist preaching by printing an extract of the *Doctrine of Salvation, Faith*

---

37. *The Journal of the Reverend John Wesley, A.M.*, ed. Nehemiah Curnock (London: Epworth, 1960), 2, 101.

38. Horton Davies, *Worship and Theology in England: From Watts and Wesley to Martineau, 1690–1900*, vol. 2 (Grand Rapids: Eerdmans, 1996), 194–97.

39. Cited in *Certain Sermons or Homilies (1547) and a Homily against Disobedience and Wilful Rebellion (1570)*, ed. Ronald B. Bond (Toronto: University of Toronto Press, 1987), 15–16.

and Good Works from the *Homilies of the Church of England.*[40] This tract defined a position from which he never wavered, proclaiming the gift of living faith in Christ that works through loving devotion and grateful obedience to God. He writes, "I began more narrowly to inquire what the doctrine of the Church of England is concerning the much-controverted point of justification by faith; and the sum of what I found in the homilies, I extracted and printed for the use of others."[41]

The Role of Spiritual Preparation for Preaching

In *An Address to the Clergy,* Wesley writes of a need for zeal in doing good and care in abstaining from evil. He describes the practical wisdom that is required for speaking, which guides others to a holy life by faith in Christ.

> Have I any knowledge of the world? Have I studied men (as well as books) and observed their tempers, maxims, and manners? Have I learned to be beware of men; to add the wisdom of the serpent to innocence of the dove? Has God given me by nature, or have I acquired, any measure of the discernment of spirits; or of its near ally, prudence, enabling me on all occasions to consider all circumstances, and to suit and vary my behavior according to the various combinations of them? . . . And do I omit no means which is in my power, and consistent with my character, of "pleasing all men" with whom I converse, "for their good to edification"?[42]

Preaching Christ is inseparable from the sense that a preacher's vocation consists in making the wisdom and virtue of Christ his or her own. This is not possible, however, unless the love of God is the controlling passion of one's life and ministry; a desire for the eyes of one's heart to be purified in order to see the beauty of God's holiness radiating in and through all things. Significantly, Wesley gives this practical wisdom a christological interpretation.

> Do all who have spiritual discernment take knowledge (judging of the tree by its fruits) that "the life which I now live, I live by faith in the Son of God"; and that in all "simplicity and godly sincerity I have my conversation in the world?" Am I exemplarily pure from all worldly desire, from all vile and vain affections? Is my life one continued labor of love, one tract of praising God and helping man? Do I in everything see "Him who is invisible, beholding

---

40. Albert C. Outler, ed., *John Wesley* (New York: Oxford University Press, 1964), 121–33.
41. Cited in Outler, *The Wesleyan Theological Heritage: Essays of Albert C. Outler,* 66.
42. Wesley, "An Address to the Clergy," 484.

with open face the glory of the Lord," am I "changed into the same image from glory to glory, by the Spirit of the Lord"?[43]

As an exemplary "homiletic theologian" or "preaching theologian," Wesley is still able to guide preachers to see that God matters in every aspect of preaching. Wesley's life and ministry demonstrates a steadfast commitment to reading, thinking, and speaking theologically, i.e., with the conviction that, as a means of grace, the use of Scripture in the life of the church mediates the reality of Christ through the work of the Holy Spirit. Although we do not possess a single book or treatise on preaching from Wesley, much of his work, especially his written sermons, can be read as a kind of *summa homiletica*—a summary of homiletic theology—for instructing preachers in the language and "grammar" of faith and holy living.[44] Thus, as a preacher and teacher of preachers, Wesley's work encourages and exemplifies a particular constancy in ministry that aimed to assist the Spirit's work of evangelizing and transforming listeners into the way, truth, and life of Jesus Christ.[45] His sermons summoned listeners to a life of repentance and devotion to God's kingdom in the life, death, and resurrection of Jesus, who reigns with the Father by the power of the Holy Spirit.[46] For Wesley, this occurs as by

. . . . the power of God attending his Word he brings these sinners to repentance: an entire inward as well as outward change, from all evil to all good. And this is in a sound sense to "cast out devils," out of the souls wherein they had hitherto dwelt. The strong one can no longer keep his house. A stronger one than he has come upon him, and hath cast him out, and taken possession for himself, and made it a habitation of God through his Spirit. Here then the energy of Satan ends, and the Son of God "destroys the works of the devil." The understanding of the sinner is now enlightened, and his heart sweetly drawn to God. His desires are refined, his affections purified; and being filled with the Holy Ghost he grows in grace till he is not only holy in heart, but in all manner of conversation.[47]

---

43. Ibid.

44. I have attempted to identify the "grammar" of preaching in Michael Pasquarello III, *We Speak Because We Have First Been Spoken: a 'Grammar' of the Preaching Life* (Grand Rapids: Eerdmans, 2011). My hope is that readers will look to Wesley as a mentor in the ministry of preaching the Gospel for the purpose of making Christians and nurturing them into the fullness of Christ: love for God and neighbor.

45. This is similar to the description given in Nicholas M. Healy, *Thomas Aquinas: Theologian of the Christian Life* (Aldershot: Ashgate Publishers, 2003), 33.

46. See the collection of essays situating Methodism within a larger ecumenical context by Geoffrey Wainwright, *Methodists in Dialog* (Nashville: Abingdon Press, 1995).

47. *Works*, II. 68.

The Role of Practical Preparation for Preaching

Wesley counsels ministers to become persons of sound learning, piety, and virtue.[48] He identifies the need for acquiring capacities of understanding, apprehension, judgment and reason in relation to a number of subjects: knowledge of the world and of human nature, character, dispositions and tempers; knowledge of the sciences, natural history, metaphysics, and philosophy; competence in thinking logically and speaking clearly; and possessing the virtue of courage for speaking the truth in love. To these he adds serious engagement with the fathers of the church, especially their interpretation of Scripture. Wesley gives strongest emphasis to knowing Scripture, which entails critical mastery of its original languages, grammar, and genres, as well as a grasp of its parts in relation to the whole canon—the analogy of faith—as the clue for unfolding its literal and spiritual senses for listeners. At the same time, only the wisdom of God, the Divine Teacher, is sufficient for bringing to completion these intellectual pursuits and tasks.

They [ministers] are assured of being assisted in all their labour by Him who teacheth man knowledge. And who teacheth like Him? Who, like Him, giveth wisdom to the simple? How easy is it for Him, (if we desire it, and believe that he is both able and willing to do this,) by the powerful, though secret, influences of the Spirit, to open and enlarge our understanding; to strengthen all our faculties; to bring to our remembrance whatsoever things are needful, and to fix and sharpen our attention to them; so that we may profit above all who wholly depend upon themselves, in whatever may qualify us for our Master's work.[49]

CONTRIBUTIONS TO PREACHING

The intelligibility of Wesleyan preaching was inseparable from the existence and formation of a holy people whose greatest desire is to know and love the truth and goodness of the Lord who is present in proclamation. For Wesley, preaching is ordered by the intellect, affections, and will, through which the Spirit illumines the mind and kindles the heart to bear the fruit of speaking the truth in love. The character of the "preaching life" is inseparable from the gifts of faith, hope, and love by which the truth of God in Christ is received, lived, and proclaimed.

---

48. Wesley, "An Address to the Clergy," 485–86.
49. Ibid.

As a means of grace, then, preaching Christ engenders and is engendered by true religion, or the power of godliness, the love of God indwelling and filling the life of preachers and people through the presence and work of the Spirit. This is "true religion, even the whole mind which was also in Christ Jesus." Wesley continues,

> There can be no doubt that but from this love to God and man a suitable conversation will follow. His "communication," that is, discourse, will "be always in grace, seasoned with salt," and meet to "minister grace to the hearers." He will always "open his mouth with wisdom," and there will be "in his tongue the law of kindness." Hence his affectionate words will "distil as the dew, and as the rain upon the tender herb." And men will know "it is not" he only "that speaks, but the Spirit of the Father that speaketh in him." His actions will spring from the same source as his words, even from the abundance of a loving heart.[50]

Such theologically-informed and spiritually-illumined practice makes Wesley a salutary exemplar of preaching that bears witness to the saving and sanctifying activity of the Father, Son, and Holy Spirit. Such humility makes possible the theological judgment required to discern that the activities of evangelism, worship, and preaching are not of greater importance than faith that comes by hearing and being formed by the Word into a common life of love for God and others.

For Wesley, evangelism not oriented toward transformation of the heart and life through participation in the righteousness of Christ would be seen as less than fully Christian. Left behind would be the convictions, habits, and dispositions which are cultivated through the reading of Scripture and proclamation, confessing the creeds, participation in the liturgy and Eucharist, adhering to the doctrine and discipline of the Anglican Church, and following the General Rules of Methodist Societies. As Outler comments, "The 'catholic substance' of Wesley's theology is the theme of participation—the idea that all is of grace and all grace is the mediation of Christ by the Holy Spirit."[51] Preaching, then, was the fruit of prayerful attention to God; preaching was public acclamations of praise for the extravagant love of the Father who sends the Son and Spirit to call, convert, and sanctify a people whose existence embodies the reality of God's mission in the world.

---

50. *Works*, IV, 70.
51. Outler, *The Wesleyan Theological Heritage*, 53.

An eighteenth-century observer described the character of Wesley's life and "conversation" in the following manner.

Today I learned for the first time to know Mr. John Wesley, so well-known here in England, and called the spiritual Father of the so-called Methodists. He arrived home from his summer journey to Ireland, where he visited his people. He preached today at the forenoon service in the Methodist Chapel in Spitafield for an audience of more than 4000 people. His text was Luke 1:68. The sermon was short but eminently evangelical. He has not great oratorical gifts, no outward appearance, but he speaks clear and pleasant. After the Holy Communion, which in all English Churches is held with closed doors at the end of the preaching service, when none but the Communicants are usually present, and which here was celebrated very orderly and pathetic. I went forward to shake hands with Mr. Wesley, who already . . . knew my name, and was received by him in his usual amiable and friendly way. He is a small, thin, old man, with his own and long and strait hair, and looks as the worst country curate in Sweden, but has learning as a Bishop and zeal for the glory of God which is quite extraordinary. His talk is very agreeable, and his mild face and pious manner secure him the love of all rightminded men. He is the personification of piety, and he seems to me as a living representation of the loving Apostle John. The old man Wesley is already 66 years, but very lively and exceedingly industrious.[52]

Accounts such as this could be dismissed as mere "hagiography." However, it does point to important elements of Wesley's life and work as a preacher that were exemplary and instructive. As a "preaching theologian," Wesley displayed a happy knowledge of God's justifying and sanctifying grace. Moreover, only God's abundant self-communication, mediated through the Son and the witness of the Spirit, is capable of engendering Christian speech characterized by faith, knowledge, love, understanding, and the discernment of grace.[53] Wesley's intention was that ministers would cultivate such practical wisdom for inviting others into the life of faith and holy living. "O how can these who themselves know nothing aright, impart knowledge to others? How to instruct them in all the variety of duty; to God, their neighbor, and themselves? How will they guide

---

52. Cited in William Abraham, "The End of Wesleyan Theology," in *Wesleyan Theological Journal*, 40, no. 1 (Spring 2005): 19.

53. Nicholas Lash, *Voices of Authority* (repr., Eugene: Wipf & Stock, 2005), 11–12.

them through the mazes of error, through all the entanglements of sin and temptation? How will he apprize them of the devices of Satan, and guard them against all the wisdom of the world?"[54]

Wesley's homiletic theology is unintelligible apart from his confident trust in and knowledge of the gracious initiative and providential action of the Spirit through the witness of Scripture in the ministry of preaching that conforms the lives of its participants to Christ.

CONCLUSION

The aim of this chapter has been to call attention to Wesley as a "preaching theologian," an exemplar of the practice of preaching in which the Holy Spirit awakens listeners to the joy of hearing God's Word. Such enjoyment is sheer gift, a noninstrumental, participative activity, with no purpose other than delighting in the extravagant outpouring of love through which the Father communicates his being and life to the Son, who through the work of the Spirit restores human creatures to the divine image.

Because Wesley believed the end of human life was conformance to the image of Christ through the gifts of justifying and sanctifying grace, he understood human actions—including preaching—as true and good when directed to God, who is known and loved for his own sake, rather than a means to achieving something else. At the heart of Wesley's vision is a conviction that humanity's true end is the joy and delight of communion with God and others, so that the witness of preaching springs from and leads back to doxology, the praise of God's glory. For Wesley, the activity of preaching and the goal of preaching are one: rendering faithful, public witness to the gospel of Jesus Christ through the presence and work of the Spirit in the worshiping life of the church.

For Wesley, then, speaking of God was the effect of a prior grace: the divine being, truth, and goodness communicated in the Word through the witness of the Spirit who engenders faith that comes by hearing. Guided by the law of the gospel through the witness of the Spirit, preaching seeks to imitate the manner of God's speaking in Jesus Christ as mediated by the whole of Scripture. Wesley thus saw sermons as a primary place for doing theology— homiletical theology—by which the witness of the Spirit generates living faith and holy living.

---

54. Wesley, "An Address to the Clergy," 488–89.

Sermon Excerpt

The Circumcision of the Heart[55]

I am first to inquire wherein that circumcision of the heart consists which will receive the praise of God. In general we may observe it is the habitual disposition of soul which in the Sacred Writings is termed "holiness," and which directly implies the being cleansed from sin, "from all filthiness both of flesh and spirit," and by consequence the being endued with those virtues which were also in Christ Jesus, the being so "renewed in the image of your mind," as to be "perfect as our Father in heaven is perfect" . . . At the same time we are convinced that we are not sufficient of ourselves to help ourselves; that without the Spirit of God we can do nothing but add to sin; that it is he alone "who worketh in us" by his almighty power, either "to will or do" that which is good—it being as impossible for us even to think a good thought without the supernatural assistance of his Spirit as to create ourselves, or to renew our whole souls in righteousness and true holiness.

Our gospel, as it knows no other foundation of good works than faith, or of faith than Christ, so it clearly informs us we are not his disciples while we either deny him to be the author or his Spirit to be the inspirer and perfecter both of our faith and works. "If any man have not the Spirit of Christ, he is none of this." He alone can quicken those who are dead unto God, can breathe into them the breath of Christian life, and so prevent, accompany, and follow them with his grace as to bring their good desires to good effect. And "as many as are thus led by the Spirit of God, they are the sons of God." This is God's short and plain account of true religion and virtue, and "other foundation can no man lay." ♦

BIBLIOGRAPHY

Abraham, William J. "Wesley as Preacher." Pages 98–112 in *The Cambridge Companion to John Wesley*. Edited by Randy L. Maddox and Jason E. Vickers. Cambridge: Cambridge University Press, 2010.

---

55. "The Circumcision of the Heart" in *The Works of John Wesley*, vol. 1, ed. Albert C. Outler (Nashville: Abingdon Press, 1984), 402, 411. Outler's introduction to the sermon shows the important place it held in Wesley's preaching ministry for more than forty years. As "landmark sermon," it was first preached in 1733 and on numerous occasions in the following decades of Wesley's work as an evangelist and pastor. Wesley himself expressed his approval of the sermon, placing it at the beginning of his standard sermons. As such, "The Circumcision of the Heart" provides an exemplary articulation of Wesley's fundamental convictions concerning soteriology. See Albert C. Outler, "An Introductory Comment," in *The Works of John Wesley*, vol. 1, 398–400.

Abraham, William J. "The End of Wesleyan Theology." *Wesleyan Theological Journal* 40, no. 1 (2005): 7–25. ATLA.

Baker, Frank. *John Wesley and the Church of England*. Nashville: Abingdon, 1970.

Bond, Ronald B., ed. *Certain Sermons or Homilies (1547) And a Homily against Disobedience and Willful Rebellion (1570)*. Toronto: University of Toronto Press, 1987.

Collins, Kenneth J. "Wesley's Life and Ministry." Pages 43–59 in *The Cambridge Companion to John Wesley*. Edited by Randy L. Maddox and Jason E. Vickers. Cambridge: Cambridge University Press, 2010.

Davies, Horton. *Worship and Theology in England: From Watts and Wesley to Martineau, 1690–1900*. 3 vols. Grand Rapids: Eerdmans, 1996.

Heitzenrater, Richard P. *Wesley and the People Called Methodists*. Nashville: Abingdon, 1995.

_____. "Wesley, John." Pages 500–502 in *Concise Encyclopedia of Preaching*. Edited by William H. Willimon and Richard Lischer. Louisville: Westminster John Knox, 1995.

Hauerwas, Stanley. *A Better Hope: Resources for a Church Confronting Capitalism, Democracy, and Postmodernity*. Grand Rapids: Brazos, 2000.

_____. *The State of the University: Academic Knowledge and the Knowledge of God*. Malden, MA: Blackwell, 2007.

Lash, Nicholas. *Voices of Authority*. 1976. Repr. Eugene, OR: Wipf & Stock, 2005.

Long, D. Stephen. *John Wesley's Moral Theology: The Quest for God and Goodness*. Nashville: Abingdon Press, 2005.

Maddox, Randy L. *Responsible Grace: John Wesley's Practical Theology*. Nashville: Abingdon, 1994.

Miles, Rebekah L. "Happiness, Holiness, and the Moral Life in John Wesley." Pages 207–24 in *The Cambridge Companion to John Wesley*. Edited by Randy L. Maddox and Jason E. Vickers. Cambridge: Cambridge University Press, 2010.

Outler, Albert C., ed. *John Wesley*. New York: Oxford University Press, 1964.

_____. *The Wesleyan Theological Heritage: Essays of Albert C. Outler*. Edited by Thomas C. Oden and Leicester R. Longden. Grand Rapids: Zondervan, 1991.

Pasquarello III, Michael. *John Wesley: A Preaching Life*. Nashville: Abingdon, 2011.

Wainwright, Geoffrey. "The Trinitarian Hermeneutic of John Wesley." Pages 17–38 in *Reading the Bible in Wesleyan Ways: Some Constructive Proposals*. Edited by Barry L. Callen and Richard P. Thompson. Kansas City: Beacon Hill, 2004.

Wallace, Charles. "Wesley as Revivalist/Renewal Leader." Pages 81–97 in *The Cambridge Companion to John Wesley*. Edited by Randy L. Maddox and Jason E. Vickers. Cambridge: Cambridge University Press, 2010.

Wesley, John. *The Journal of Reverend John Wesley, A.M.* Edited by Nehemiah Curnock. London: Epworth, 1960.

_____. "An Address to the Clergy." In *The Works of John Wesley*. 3rd ed. Grand Rapids: Baker, 1978.

_____. "The Circumcision of the Heart" in *The Works of John Wesley*. Vol. 1. Edited by Albert C. Outler. Nashville: Abingdon Press, 1984.

_____. *Journals and Diaries*. 7 vols. Edited by W. Reginald Ward and Richard P. Heitzenrater. In *The Works of John Wesley*. Nashville: Abingdon, 1988–2003.

_____. *Sermons*. 4 vols. Edited by Albert C. Outler. Nashville: Abingdon Press, 1984–1987.

Willimon, William H. "Suddenly a Light from Heaven." Pages 240–50 in *Conversion and the Wesleyan Tradition*. Edited by Kenneth J. Collins and John H. Tyson. Nashville: Abingdon, 2001.

George Whitefield
Calvinist Evangelist

BILL CURTIS
TIMOTHY MCKNIGHT

Few men in the history of preaching have had the type of global ministry enjoyed by George Whitefield (1714–1770). He became a follower of Christ as a young man, and God used him to shake the American colonies during the First Great Awakening. Admired by statesmen and enjoyed by commoners, Whitefield took Puritan preaching to new heights, in both content and delivery. Imbued by God with an amazing array of gifts, including a magnificent voice, he was as comfortable preaching in a hayfield as in a church. Whitefield, the first great evangelist of the post-Reformation church, provides an amazing example of the union of great preparation, doctrinal integrity, and dynamic delivery in the proclamation of the gospel; an example that still challenges preachers in our own day.

HISTORICAL BACKGROUND

George Whitefield was born to Thomas and Elizabeth Whitefield on December 16, 1714, in Gloucester, England. When Whitefield was merely two years of age, his father died suddenly. Elizabeth was left with seven children and the family's inn. When Whitefield turned ten, his mother married an ironmonger named Capel Longden; however, the marriage ended in a bitter divorce, leaving Elizabeth again with seven children and the inn.

At the age of twelve, Whitefield enrolled in the St. Mary de Crypt grammar school. In his early years at the school, he began to develop an interest in drama and public speaking. The decline of business at his mother's inn cut short his first years at school. Concerning Whitefield's decision to quit school, his biographer and friend John Gillies commented, "Before he was fifteen, he persuaded his mother to take him from school, saying that she could not place him at the university, and more learning would spoil him for a tradesman."[1] Having resigned to

---

1. John Gillies, *Memoirs of Rev. George Whitefield* (New Haven: Whitmore & Buckingham and H. Mansfield, 1834), 11.

the idea that he could not attend the university, Whitefield helped his mother by serving guests and cleaning the inn; however, a servitor from Pembroke College at Oxford interrupted his time away from school.[2] The young student informed Whitefield's mother that attending Oxford was possible for her son. Upon hearing the news, both son and mother agreed that he should finish grammar school and go to Oxford.

Eighteen-year-old George Whitefield arrived at Oxford possessing a deep interest in religion. He began to encounter Methodists and, impressed by their examples of piety, longed to be part of their group. In time, he met Charles and John Wesley, who invited him to attend their meetings. Shortly after his involvement with the Wesleys and the Methodists, Whitefield fell under deep conviction of sin and was converted at the age of twenty.

In 1736, the Church of England ordained Whitefield a deacon. After preaching his first sermon, Whitefield claimed "that a complaint had been made of the bishop, that I drove fifteen mad."[3] Following this sermon, his popularity grew to the point that thousands of Englishmen came to hear him that year in Bristol and London. In 1737, six of his sermons were published. Whitefield received many invitations to preach in towns around England; however, he felt the call to be a missionary in Georgia and did not allow his popularity to distract him from this endeavor.

On May 7, 1738, George Whitfield arrived in Savannah, Georgia. While in Georgia, Whitefield toured the land and met the leaders of the colony. He preached at every opportunity and visited in the homes of residents of Savannah and Frederica. It was during this first visit to Georgia that the young evangelist decided to build an orphanage in that colony.[4]

Whitefield returned to England in 1739 to raise funds for the orphanage and to gain approval for it from the trustees of Georgia. Whitefield was ordained a priest on January 11, 1739, while in England. Following his ordination, he set out to preach throughout England and to obtain contributions for his orphan house. After being refused access to several churches, Whitefield preached his first open air sermon to a group of miners in Kingswood, England. He continued to preach

---

2. The servitors were servants for the students from higher socioeconomic backgrounds. These servants cleaned rooms, polished shoes, ran errands, and washed clothes for their student employers. The servitors were not allowed to initiate conversations with students in higher positions. Special times for the partaking of the Sacrament were arranged so that servitors did not socialize with the rest of the student body. These servants were also required to wear particular clothes that distinguished them from the other students.

3. George Whitefield, *George Whitefield's Letters* (Carlisle, PA: The Banner of Truth Trust, 1976), 19.

4. Whitefield's self designation was "itinerant preacher." Throughout this chapter, the terms "evangelist" and "itinerant" will be used interchangeably when referring to Whitefield. Both terms refer to his efforts to share the gospel with as many persons as possible, so they might repent and place their faith in Christ for their salvation.

in fields throughout the English countryside. During this year in England, it was common for crowds of ten to twenty thousand people to gather in the fields to hear Whitefield preach.[5]

Whitefield, however, did not allow the crowds to take his focus away from his work in America. On August 14, 1739, he began his second voyage to the American colonies. The First Great Awakening began during this visit. Whitefield's preaching played a key role in this revival. He preached in towns and cities throughout the colonies from New York to Savannah. In Philadelphia, an audience of more than ten thousand came to hear him.[6] And in Boston, fifteen thousand people attended one of his messages.[7] It was unusual for Whitefield to have less than one thousand members in his audience at any given time when he preached near a colonial town or city. Besides preaching, he also formed relationships with American clergymen such as Jonathan Edwards, Gilbert Tennent, and William Tennent. Some of these clergy conducted follow-up on Whitefield's evangelistic efforts after he left the colonies.

Whitefield returned to England in March of 1741. There, he encountered a hostile reception from groups whom John Wesley, his close friend and fellow evangelist, incited against Calvinism through published criticisms and sermons. In response to Wesley's sermon "Free Grace," Whitefield published a letter that refuted each point of his argument.[8] Ultimately, this theological dispute damaged the ministry relationship between the Wesleys and Whitefield, but they never lost their love or respect for one another. Whitefield stayed three years in his native land, despite this opposition from both friends and foes. Toward the end of this visit to England, the evangelist married Elizabeth James on November 14, 1741; he determined not to allow the marriage to interrupt his travels or his preaching schedule, however.

Less than eight months after the loss of their four-month-old son, John, the Whitefield's left for America. During this third trip to the colonies (1745–1748), Whitefield discovered that the opposition against him was not confined to England. Critics scorned Whitefield for appealing to people's passions, emphasizing the New Birth, dividing the clergy, and preaching in towns without the approval of local clergy. The itinerant wrote responses to his critics and continued

---

5. Joseph Belcher, *George Whitefield: A Biography* (New York: American Tract Society, 1857), 468.

6. George Whitefield, *George Whitefield's Journals* (London: The Banner of Truth Trust, 1960), 359.

7. Ibid., 460.

8. For Wesley's sermon and Whitefield's response, see John Wesley, "Free Grace," in *The SAGE Digital Library* [CD-ROM] (Albany, OR: Ages Software, 1996), 415–28; George Whitefield, "A Letter to the Reverend Mr. John Wesley: in Answer to His Sermon, Entituled *Free-Grace*," in *The Works of the Reverend George Whitefield* (London: Printed for Edward and Charles Dilly, in the Poultry; and Messrs. Kincaid and Bell, at Edinburgh, 1771–1772), 4:52–73.

to preach to large audiences; however, the third trip witnessed the detrimental effect preaching had on his health. At the suggestion of his doctor, the Whitefields left for Bermuda in 1748.

The orphanage Whitefield founded in Georgia was in precarious financial condition, and this cut short his fourth visit to the colonies (1751–1752). During Whitefield's fifth trip (1754–1755), he returned to find that his orphanage had prospered in his absence. Throughout this trip, he generally preached twice a day. Any further specifics about this fifth journey are difficult to reconstruct because of the lack of letters from Whitefield describing this season of his life.

During his sixth voyage to America (1763–1765), the itinerant's ill health became more apparent than in his previous trips to the colonies (he suffered from severe asthma and angina). Rather than preaching twice a day, sickness confined him to preaching only twice a week at times. Concerning the people's reaction to Whitefield's ill health, Arnold Dallimore wrote, "The people, however, had heard earlier of his invalided condition, and it is evident that now, seeing him so changed and so weak, they looked upon him as indeed a dying man, and more than ever they held him in affection. Realizing they might have but few further opportunities, they came in still greater earnestness to hear him preach."[9] He did not disappoint them; he preached whenever his strength would allow him to stand.

Whitefield's wife, Elizabeth, died of fever shortly before he was to embark on his seventh voyage to the colonies. The aging evangelist wrote concerning his loss, "I feel the loss of my right hand daily; but right hands and right eyes must be parted with for Him, who ordereth all things well."[10] True to the devotion to God that he exemplified throughout his life, Whitefield did not allow his personal loss to prevent his passage to America. Gillies noted,

Between 1738 and 1770, George Whitefield conducted seven evangelistic tours of the American colonies. His preaching and evangelistic efforts played a pivotal role in the movement of God commonly known as the First Great Awakening.[11] During his itinerant ministry in America, he preached throughout the colonies and towns including New York, Philadelphia,

9. Arnold A. Dallimore, *George Whitefield: The Life and Times of the Great Evangelist of the Eighteenth Century Revival* (Carlisle, PA: The Banner of Truth Trust, 1970–1980), 2:426.

10. George Whitefield, "Letter MCCCCVI," in *Works of the Rev. George Whitefield*, 3:382.

11. Throughout this chapter, the term "awakening" means a movement of the Holy Spirit in which spiritually dead individuals are converted from death to life through repentance and faith in Jesus Christ. Such an awakening may occur within the life of a single individual or may involve multitudes of individuals over wide geographic spans. The term "revival" means a movement of the Holy Spirit in which believers are convicted to live lives that reflect greater holiness and commitment to Christ and his gospel. Revivals also result in believers becoming more involved in evangelism. For a discussion regarding the meaning of the terms

Boston, Charleston, Savannah, Trent Town, Newport, Lewis Town, and Williamsburg. Thousands of Americans, approximately 80 percent of the population, came to hear him preach.[12] In Philadelphia and Boston, Whitefield preached to audiences of ten and fifteen thousand.[13] Before his death on September 30, 1770, the "Great Itinerant" had preached at least eighteen thousand times.[14]

THEOLOGY OF PREACHING

Regarding Whitefield's theology, many Christian scholars, church historians, and biographers agree that George Whitefield was a Calvinist.[15] In his biography of Whitefield, Harry S. Stout wrote, "From first to last he was a Calvinist who believed that God chose him for salvation and not the reverse."[16] Describing Whitefield's ministry, Stout stated it was characterized by "an all-inclusive ecumenicity that was explicitly 'Calvinist' in theology and opposed to all forms of 'Arminianism.'"[17] He also noted that, in a letter to scholars at Harvard, Whitefield described himself as a Calvinist and stated that he would preach no other doctrines but Calvinism.[18]

Another biographer, Frank Lambert, identified Whitefield as a Calvinist. He noted that Whitefield wrote a letter replying to critics who claimed he was a newcomer to Calvinism. In the letter, the English evangelist contended that he preached on the doctrine of election even before he left for America

---

"awakening" and "revival," see Errol Hulse, *Give Him No Rest* (Durham, UK: Evangelical, 1991), 10–11; and J. Edwin Orr, *The Event of the Century* (Wheaton, IL: International Awakening, 1989), xi–xvi.

12. Kevin A. Miller, "Did You Know?" *Christian History* 38, no.2 (1993): 2.

13. Whitefield, *Journals*, 284.

14. Gillies, *Memoirs*, 284.

15. For this chapter, the term Calvinism refers to the five points of Calvinism as outlined and explained by the Synod of Dort in 1618. While the five points of Calvinism do not exhaust every aspect involved in the theological system known as Calvinism, they do represent the Calvinist's understanding of soteriology and the gospel.

In his preface to John Owen's work entitled *The Death of Death in the Death of Christ*, J. I. Packer writes of the five points of Calvinism, "They stem from a very different principle—the biblical principle that 'salvation is of the Lord;' and they may be summarized thus: (1.) Fallen man in his natural state lacks all power to believe the gospel, just as he lacks all power to believe the law, despite all external inducements that may be extended to him. (2.) God's election is a free, sovereign, unconditional choice of sinners, as sinners, to be redeemed by Christ, given faith and brought to glory. (3.) The redeeming work of Christ had as its end and goal the salvation of the elect. (4.) The work of the Holy Spirit in bringing men to faith never fails to achieve its object. (5.) Believers are kept in faith and grace by the unconquerable power of God till they come to glory. These five points are conveniently denoted by the mnemonic TULIP: Total depravity, Unconditional election, Limited atonement, Irresistible grace, Preservation of the saints." J. I. Packer, "Introductory Essay," in *The Death of Death in the Death of Christ*, John Owen (Carlisle, PA: The Banner of Truth Trust, 1995), 4.

16. Harry S. Stout, *The Divine Dramatist: George Whitefield and the Rise of Modern Evangelicalism* (Grand Rapids: Eerdmans, 1991), xxiii.

17. Ibid., 95.

18. Ibid., 192.

in 1739.[19] Regarding the theological content of Whitefield's sermons, Lambert wrote, "Although Whitefield preached Calvinist tenets throughout his ministry, his was an evangelical Calvinism, one that emphasized the universal need for preaching."[20] This author also cited Whitefield's Calvinism as a reason for his success in the American colonies. Lambert asserted, "He was particularly appealing to colonial revivalists. His Calvinism linked him theologically to New England Congregationalists and Middle Colony Presbyterians."[21]

Two of the most comprehensive biographies of Whitefield echo Stout and Lambert's claims identifying Whitefield as a Calvinist. Luke Tyerman, in his two-volume biography of Whitefield, repeatedly designated George Whitefield a Calvinist. Like Lambert, Tyerman mentioned Whitefield's Calvinism as a reason for his warm reception and success in New England. He asserted, "As to the creed of these miscellaneous religionists, there cannot be a doubt that, speaking generally, it was Calvinistic, and quite in harmony with those views of election and final perseverance which Whitefield had embraced. In such a colony, Wesley would have been branded as a heretic; whereas Whitefield was warmly welcomed as a friend, whose faith was gloriously orthodox."[22]

Regarding the strong differences in theology between the Wesleys and George Whitefield, Tyerman noted, "Charles Wesley regarded Whitefield's Calvinism with abhorrence; and Whitefield regarded some of Wesley's doctrines as pernicious heresy."[23]

In another two-volume biography of Whitefield, Arnold Dallimore also mentioned Whitefield's Calvinism. Regarding the reason for Whitefield's warm reception in Scotland, Dallimore explained, "Ever since his first rise to fame he had appeared a heroic figure in the minds of Gospel-loving people everywhere, and to many in Scotland he seemed very much an embodiment of their ideals: he too was a Calvinist, yet his Calvinism was not mere theory, but, as advocated by *The Marrow*, it was doctrine aglow with evangelistic fire."[24] Describing Whitefield's theological understanding shortly before he was ordained a deacon in 1736, Dallimore asserted,

> Certainly the terms "free grace" and "justified by faith only" did not, at this early time, have the immense meaning for him which, as we shall see, he

---

19. Frank Lambert, *Pedlar in Divinity: George Whitefield and the Transatlantic Revivals, 1737–1770* (Princeton: Princeton University Press, 1994), 72.

20. Ibid., 227.

21. Frank Lambert, *Inventing the "Great Awakening"* (Princeton: Princeton University Press, 1999), 105.

22. Luke Tyerman, *The Life of the Reverend George Whitefield*, vol. 1 (London: Hodder & Stoughton, 1876–1877; Repr. Azle, TX: Need of the Times Publishers, 1995), 407–8.

23. Ibid., 479.

24. Dallimore, *George Whitefield*, 2:87.

enunciated with clarity and conviction in 1739. Nevertheless, it is evident that he had grasped certain fundamental truths: he knew salvation was a Divine work—the placing of the "life of God in the soul of man"—and that it was an eternal work. These truths were already a foundation upon which, he was, from this time forth, to build a steadily increasing understanding and finally a system of theology. This was the beginning of his lifelong adherence to what he called "the doctrines of grace"—the system commonly known as Calvinism.[25]

Besides Dallimore and Tyerman, authors of numerous essays and journal articles on Whitefield have noted the English evangelist's Calvinism. Church historian Mark Noll wrote, "Unlike later revivalists, Whitefield was a Calvinist."[26] In an essay entitled "John Calvin and George Whitefield," D. M. Lloyd-Jones said, "George Whitefield was a follower of the teaching of Calvin. He was a truly Reformed man in his doctrine, whereas Wesley was Arminian."[27] Addressing Whitefield's Reformed theology, J. I. Packer identified Whitefield as "an Anglican Calvinist of the Puritan type."[28] Packer also designated Whitefield a Calvinist in his essay entitled "A Calvinist—and an Evangelist."[29]

Christian scholars, church historians, and biographers also agree that George Whitefield was a passionate evangelist. Numerous testimonies throughout church history praise this itinerant preacher's zeal for evangelism.[30] In a sermon preached on the occasion of Whitefield's death, John Wesley queried, "Have we read or heard of any person since the apostles, who testified the gospel of the grace of God, through so widely extended a space, through so large a part of the habitable world? Have we read or heard of any person, who called so many thousands, so many myriads of sinners to repentance? Above all, have we read or heard of any, who has been a blessed instrument in his hand of *bringing* so many sinners from *darkness to light, and from the power of Satan unto God*?"[31]

---

25. Dallimore, *George Whitefield,* 1:85.

26. Mark Noll, *A History of Christianity in the United States and Canada* (Grand Rapids: Eerdmans, 1992), 91.

27. D. M. Lloyd-Jones, "John Calvin and George Whitefield," in *The Puritans: Their Origins and Successors* (Carlisle, PA: The Banner of Truth Trust, 1996), 103.

28. J. I. Packer, "The Spirit with the Word: The Reformational Revivalism of George Whitefield," in *The Bible, the Reformation, and the Church,* ed. W. P. Stephens (Sheffield: Sheffield Academic, 1995), 174.

29. J. I. Packer, "A Calvinist—and an Evangelist," in *Serving the People of God* (Milton Keynes: Paternoster, 1998), 2:205–10.

30. This chapter will use the term "evangelism" to refer to sharing the gospel, through the power of the Holy Spirit, with the hope that individuals repent of their sins, place their faith in the righteousness of Christ for their salvation, and display evidence of true faith through their obedience to Christ in doing good works.

31. John Wesley, *A Sermon on the Death of the Rev. Mr. George Whitefield. Preached at the Chapel in Tottenham-Court-Road, and at the Tabernacle Near the Moorfields, on Sunday, November 18, 1770* (London: J. & W. Oliver, 1770; repr., Atlanta: The Library of Emory University, 1953), 14–15.

Whitefield's biographers affirm his evangelistic efforts. Tyerman wrote, "George Whitefield was pre-eminently the outdoor preacher, evangelist extraordinaire who pioneered open-air preaching; the most popular evangelist of the age; a roving revivalist, who, with unequalled eloquence and power, spent above thirty years testifying to enormous crowds, in Great Britain and America, the gospel of the grace of God."[32] J. C. Ryle claimed that Whitefield "seemed to live only for two objects—the glory of God and the salvation of souls."[33] In his history of preaching, Edwin Charles Dargan asserted, "The history of preaching since the apostles does not contain a greater worthier name than that of George Whitefield (1714–1770)."[34] Dallimore contended that "Whitefield was superbly equipped for the work to which God had called him—'the work of an evangelist.' . . . God has had His great and good men in all ages, but there can be little doubt Whitefield deserves the primacy often accorded him: 'The greatest evangelist since Paul.'"[35] D. M. Lloyd-Jones said of Whitefield, "Here is the greatest evangelist England had ever produced and he was a Calvinist."[36]

METHODOLOGY FOR PREACHING

A number of scholars describe the preaching of the First Great Awakening as topical and lump most of the preachers of that era into that category.[37] James Stitzinger wrote, "As the Puritan era gave way to the preaching of the Evangelical

---

32. Tyerman, *The Life of the Reverend George Whitefield*, 1:iii–iv.

33. J. C. Ryle, "George Whitefield and His Ministry," in *Select Sermons of George Whitefield* (Carlisle, PA: The Banner of Truth Trust, 1997), 41.

34. Edwin C. Dargan, *A History of Preaching* (Grand Rapids: Baker, 1954), 2:307.

35. Dallimore, *George Whitefield*, 2:536.

36. Lloyd-Jones, "John Calvin and George Whitefield," 126.

37. Topical preaching, as it developed in the last half of the seventeenth century, is credited primarily to John Wilkins, who wrote *Ecclesiastes; or, The Gift of Preaching* in 1646, and John Tillotson, who later became the Archbishop of Canterbury. Tillotson became famous by developing Wilkins's topical approach to preaching. This approach was developed in response to the "logic-chopping exegesis of the Puritans." It was characterized by plain, nonemotional speech. Tillotson would "begin a sermon with a short introduction that raised the issues he planned to discuss and showed their importance. Then he listed the divisions into which his subject fell and went on to discuss the issues thus raised like a woodsman methodically chopping a log into stove-sized pieces. At the end there was no stirring peroration, no emotional appeal. When he finished presenting his case, he left it to stand on its own merits." This approach became extremely popular in England. Yet, after him, English preaching seems to have degenerated into moral essays delivered orally. William H. Willimon and Richard Lischer, eds., "John Tillotson," in *Concise Encyclopedia of Preaching* (Louisville: Westminster John Knox, 1995), 489–91. Charles Dargan said of Tillotson, "He introduced a new mode of sermon composition, which not only affected the subsequent development of the English pulpit, but was strongly influential in Holland and elsewhere in Europe." Edwin Charles Dargan, *A History of Preaching*, vol. 2 (Grand Rapids: Baker, 1954), 166. Whitefield would later say of him, "The Archbishop knew no more of true Christianity than Mahomet [*sic*]." Arnold A. Dallimore, *George Whitefield: God's Anointed Servant in the Great Revival of the Eighteenth Century* (Wheaton, IL: Crossway, 1990), 83. Whitefield would also say about a woman who once admired Bishop Tillotson that, "Having her eyes now opened, to discern spiritual things, [she] can no longer take up with such husks." Whitefield, *Journals*, 438. In light of this evidence, it is unlikely that Whitefield was a topical preacher after the school of Tillotson.

Awakening, preaching that was generally topical, such as that of Wesley and Whitfield [*sic*], replaced exposition."[38] F. R. Webber concurred with this view: "The preachers of the Evangelical Awakening had been trained in an age when expository preaching was a low ebb. Wesley, Whitefield, and their fellow laborers grew up in an age when the art of exposition was not understood, hence their sermons are generally topical."[39] Dargan characterized English preaching, and by extension English preachers, in a similar way. While he did acknowledge the impact of Whitefield's preaching, he concurred with the view that the preaching of this period was primarily topical. He noted, "The topical method of composing sermons remained the dominant method in the eighteenth century."[40] John A. Broadus said, "During the first half of the eighteenth century, English preaching did not rise above mediocrity."[41]

As noted above, support for the view that Whitefield was a topical preacher is often defended on the basis that he, like other preachers in that era, was not adequately trained in the art of expository preaching and could not, therefore, be an expository preacher. Further, scholars support this view by pointing to the itinerant nature of his ministry. They conclude that he did not have the time to develop expository sermons.[42]

That said, those years were not devoid of expository preaching. "Some major Puritan preachers who demonstrated ability as expositors were Joseph Hall (1574–1656), Thomas Goodwin (1600–1680), Richard Baxter (1615–1691), and John Owen (1616–1680). Other significant Puritan expositors were Thomas Manton (1620–1677), John Bunyan (1628–1688), and Stephen Charnock (1628–1680). . . . All of these were diligent students of the Word, seeking to explain the truths of Scripture clearly to others."[43] As the seventeenth century gave way to the eighteenth century, another group of men continued the tradition of expository preaching. "The most notable were John Gill (1697–1771) . . . and Matthew Henry (1662–1714)."[44]

---

38. James F. Stitzinger, "The History of Expository Preaching," *The Master's Seminary Journal* 3, no. 1 (Spring 1992): 24.

39. F. R. Webber, *A History of Preaching, part one* (Milwaukee: Northwestern, 1952), 325–26.

40. Dargan, *A History of Preaching*, vol. 2, 293.

41. John A. Broadus, *History of Preaching* (New York: A. C. Armstrong & Son, 1891), 221.

42. It is true that Whitefield preached so often that his time to study was limited while he was on preaching tours. His journeys included multiple trips to Scotland, Ireland, and America. He often spent months at sea traveling from place to place, and these trips provided him ample time for Bible study, the study of Matthew Henry, and sermon development. It was at these times that he developed his new sermons. Once on shore, he simply reused the sermons he had already developed, much like any itinerant evangelist. Thus, to say that he had no time to develop expository sermons is a faulty assumption.

43. Stitzinger, "The History of Expository Preaching," 23–24.

44. Ibid., 24. Stitzinger lists other significant eighteenth-century expositors: Andrew Fuller (1754–1815), Robert Hall (1764–1831), John Brown (1784–1858), and Alexander Carson (1776–1858).

Following his conversion, George Whitefield began a systematic study of the Scriptures. "He made use of several works of the Reformers and the Puritans, and these books served towards giving him a solid doctrinal understanding."[45] Perhaps the most beneficial extra-biblical work for Whitefield was Matthew Henry's *Commentary on the Whole Bible*.[46] Clearly, this was one of the resources that guided Whitefield into Calvin's theology. Whitefield wrote, "How sweetly did my hours in private glide away in reading and praying over Mr. Henry's comment upon the Scriptures."[47] It is said that Whitefield studied his Bible, the Greek New Testament, and Henry's commentary for hours on end.[48] In fact, he would read Henry's commentary four times over the course of his life. Consequently, Matthew Henry made a significant impact on Whitefield's life and preaching. "In fact, Whitefield in the pulpit was but a reflection of Whitefield in the study ... So fully had he drunk of the wells of Biblical exposition in Matthew Henry that much of his public utterance was little more than the thought of the great commentator—thought that had become assimilated in his own mind and soul, and poured forth spontaneously both as he prepared and as he preached his sermons."[49]

There is little doubt that Henry's commentary helped shape Whitefield's understanding of theology and sermon development.[50]

Matthew Henry was not the only Puritan expositor that influenced George Whitefield, however. Whitefield "was particularly fond of Puritan literature."[51] He read the writings of the Puritan Solomon Stoddard, the grandfather of Jonathan Edwards, and recommended that college students read them.[52] He was fond of the Puritan expositor Bishop Joseph Hall. He said of Hall, "Though weak, I often spent two hours in my evening retirements, and prayed over my Greek Testament, and Bishop Hall's most excellent Contemplations, every hour that my health would permit."[53] Another Puritan he enjoyed reading was Richard Baxter; Whitefield read Baxter's *Call to the Unconverted*.[54] These are just a few of the

---

45. Dallimore, *George Whitefield: God's Anointed*, 22.

46. "He especially wanted to own Matthew Henry's Commentary, but since he was too poor to purchase it, Gabriel Harris, a book dealer, let him take it and pay for it later." Dallimore, *George Whitefield*, 22.

47. Whitefield, *Journals*, 78.

48. Arnold A. Dallimore, *George Whitefield: The Life and Times of the Great Evangelist of the Eighteenth-Century Revival*, vol. 1 (Great Britain: Billing & Sons, 1970), 126.

49. Ibid., 128.

50. George Whitefield called Matthew Henry his "favorite commentator." George Whitefield, *Sermons*, (London: Thomas Tegg & Son, 1838), 220.

51. David Crump, "The Preaching of George Whitefield and His Use of Matthew Henry's Commentary," *Crux* 25, no. 3 (September 1989): 19–28.

52. Dallimore, *George Whitefield: The Life and Times*, 1:551.

53. Whitefield, *Journals*, 57.

54. Dallimore, *George Whitefield: The Life and Times*, 1:82.

Puritan works with which Whitefield was familiar. He also advocated the study of Jonathan Edwards, Joseph Alleine, John Bunyan, and John Owen.[55] Based on Whitefield's own usage and recommendation of these sources, it becomes apparent that their theology and principles of exposition were familiar to him.

It has been said that describing the preaching of Whitefield is an "impossible task."[56] Perhaps it is better to call it a formidable task. As noted earlier, the place to begin is with an awareness and understanding of the impact of Matthew Henry on his preaching. David Crump believed that Whitefield used Henry as the primary source for many of his sermons. Crump said, "Henry's in-depth, practical, Calvinistic and biblical exposition served as the educational backdrop for almost every one of Whitefield's sermons."[57]

Unlike Henry, however, "Whitefield's goal was not the thorough exposition of Scripture but the exposition of the gospel."[58] This is not to say that Whitefield was not an expositor; it simply means he didn't attempt a systematic exposition of Scripture in the same way as Matthew Henry. Rather, he incorporated elements of expository preaching to communicate the gospel.[59] Crump cited no less than nine sermons in which Whitefield demonstrated a dependence on Henry in support of his premise of Matthew Henry's primacy in his preaching.[60] This dependence on Henry lends credibility to the belief that Whitefield practiced exposition on occasion and that he learned much of his exposition and interpretation skills from his study of Matthew Henry's commentary. Another element that makes the describing of Whitefield's preaching a formidable task is the relatively small amount of Whitefield's sermons that are extant. Arnold Dallimore noted, "Whitefield's authentic sermons (including seventeen which were published without his knowledge or consent) number sixty-three, forty-six of which he produced before he was twenty-five years of age."[61] Because so few of Whitefield's sermons survive, some discount their quality. In spite of these concerns, however,

---

55. Ibid., 2:492–93.

56. Marion D. Aldridge, "George Whitefield: The Necessary Interdependence of Preaching Style and Sermon Content to Effect Revival," *Journal of the Evangelical Theological Society* 23, no. 1 (March 1980): 55–64.

57. Crump, "The Preaching of George Whitefield and His Use of Matthew Henry's Commentary," 24.

58. Ibid., 23–24.

59. This article supports the contention that Whitefield's success in evangelism was not simply the result of his prowess in the pulpit.

60. Crump, "The Preaching of George Whitefield and His Use of Matthew Henry's Commentary," 24. Crump cites similarity of outline, common proof texts, the use of key phrases, common illustrations, and similar development of thought not explicitly suggested by the text alone.

61. Dallimore, *George Whitefield: The Life and Times,* 1:128. This fact does not mean that his surviving sermons are inferior to those sermons delivered during his prime. After all, he is said to have made fifteen people go "mad" during the first sermon he ever preached! Flarvius Leslie Conrad Jr. claims there are seventy-eight of Whitefield's sermons extant. Flarvius Leslie Conrad Jr., *"The Preaching of George Whitefield, with special reference to the American Colonies: A Study of His Published Sermons"* (PhD diss., Temple University, 1959), 91.

they do provide one's only opportunity to examine the method that Whitefield used to craft his sermons.

The sermon, "Walking with God," will provide evidence that George Whitefield often used elements of exposition in his sermon development.[62]

"Walking with God"

William Perkins's first principle for an expository sermon was "to read the text distinctly out of the canonical Scriptures." Whitefield used Genesis 5:24 as his text for this sermon and quotes it in its entirety and context during the message.[63]

William Perkins's second principle for an expository sermon was "to give the sense and understanding of it, being read, by the Scripture itself." Whitefield provided a brief overview of this passage by sharing information about Enoch, and he used Hebrews 11:5 to supplement this information. He discussed Enoch's influence on his world as a person of public character and a preacher of righteousness, and demonstrated Enoch's importance to the Jews' future understanding of the translation of Jesus into heaven following his resurrection.[64]

William Perkins's third principle for an expository sermon was "to collect a few and profitable points of doctrine out of the natural sense." Whitefield listed four prerequisites for walking with God. First, walking with God implies that God has begun the process of drawing one to himself. Second, it implies that one has actually experienced the new birth through faith in Jesus Christ. Third, it implies a depth in one's relationship with God. Fourth, it implies a growing walk with God on a daily basis. From these examples Whitefield demonstrated that walking with God is rooted in the doctrine of salvation (Whitefield used this part of his sermons to explain the doctrine of salvation from a Calvinistic perspective. God's unconditional election made salvation possible for the elect, but they must turn to God in repentance and confession to be saved.)

William Perkins's fourth principle for an expository sermon was "to apply the doctrines, rightly collected, to the life and manner of men in a simple and plain speech." At this point of the sermon, Whitefield applied how true salvation demonstrated itself in the life of a person who was "walking with God." First, believers walk with God by reading his Word. Second, they walk with God by secret prayer. Third, they walk with God by meditation on the Word of God. Fourth, they walk with God by observing his providential work in the

---

62. Each sermon will be examined in light of William Perkins's model for expository preaching. Perkins's main points will be mentioned and evidence from Whitefield's sermons will be offered in support.

63. Whitefield, *Sermons*, 46.

64. Ibid., 46–47.

circumstances of their lives. Fifth, they walk with God by watching the work of the Spirit in their hearts. Sixth, they walk with God through consistent worship. Seventh, and finally, they walk with God through consistent fellowship with other believers. Whitefield concluded the sermon by elucidating the benefits of walking with God: it is an honorable, pleasing, and profitable thing to do.[65]

If one looked at nothing but the title of this sermon and the accompanying Scripture references, it would be easy to suppose it to be a topical sermon. And certainly, it deals with a specific topic concerning elements involved in walking with God. Yet, when one applies William Perkins's model of expository preaching, it becomes apparent that Whitefield was following a similar pattern.

CONCLUSION

Despite the prevailing view that Whitefield was simply another topical preacher of the eighteenth century, the evidence in this chapter suggests he was more heavily influenced by Puritan expositors like Matthew Henry than anything else. After reassessing his sermons with the expository preaching method of William Perkins, the evidence further suggests that Whitefield regularly used elements of an expository method of sermon development. Certainly, it is unfair to assess Whitefield's preaching in light of today's advanced expository models. Yet it is clear he did not subscribe to the popular, topical approach of his day. Instead, he was a careful and consistent exegete who used expository preaching elements to enhance his ability as a gospel preacher.

As one examines the impact of Whitefield's evangelistic preaching on the eighteenth century, it is impossible to attribute his success to any one factor. The content of his message, presented through dynamic oration, faithfully proclaimed through expository preaching, and accompanied by the power of the Holy Spirit, was the source of his success as an evangelist.

That said, his theology of preaching and preaching methodology provide helpful insights for the preacher today. First, Whitefield demonstrates that evangelistic preaching may be expository in its approach, if the message is derived from a particular text of Scripture that is carefully exegeted. The gospel will never suffer under the guardianship of biblical exposition. Second, Whitefield demonstrates that extemporaneous sermon delivery (well practiced but with limited notes) is one of the best ways to connect with one's audience. Whitefield's dynamic orations were a departure from the cold, disconnected manuscript preaching of his age, and it captivated his listeners. Whitefield reminds us there is never a good

---

65. Ibid., 50–57.

reason to bore one's listeners. Third, and finally, in our contemporary context where evangelical Arminianism and Calvinism remain at odds, Whitefield joins men like C. H. Spurgeon and John A. Broadus to remind us that Calvinism and evangelism are not at odds with one another. Many of the greatest preachers and evangelists who ever lived were Calvinists, as is also true with modern preachers. Remember, when there is a disconnect between Calvinism and evangelism, the problem is always with the preacher not the Scriptures. George Whitefield never lost that balance, and he shook the world for Christ.

Sermon Excerpt
The Lord Our Righteousness from Jeremiah 23:6[66]

And that is, in one word, by imputation. For it pleased GOD after he had made all things by the word of his power, to create man after his own image. And so infinite was the condescension of the high and lofty One who inhabiteth eternity, that although he might have insisted on the everlasting obedience of him and his posterity; yet he was pleased to oblige himself, by a covenant, or agreement, made with his own creatures, upon condition of an unsinning obedience, to give them immortality and eternal life. For when it is said, "The day thou eatest thereof, thou shalt surely die;" we may fairly infer, so long as he continued obedient, and did not eat thereof, he should surely live. The 3rd of Genesis gives us a full, but mournful account, how our first parents broke this covenant, and thereby stood in need of a better righteousness than their own, in order to procure their future acceptance with GOD. For what must they do? They were as much under a covenant of works as ever. And though, after their disobedience, they were without strength; yet they were obliged not only to do, but to continue to do all things, and that too in the most perfect manner, which the LORD had required of them: and not only so, but to make satisfaction to GOD'S infinitely offended justice for the breach they had already been guilty of. Here then opens the amazing scene of divine philanthropy; I mean, GOD'S love to man: For, behold, what man could not do, JESUS CHRIST, the Son of his Father's love, undertakes to do for him. And that GOD might be just in justifying the ungodly, though

---

66. George Whitefield, "The Lord Our Righteousness," in *The Works of the Reverend George Whitefield* (London: Printed for Edward and Charles Dilly, in the Poultry; and Messrs. Kincaid and Bell, at Edinburgh, 1771–1772), 5:216–34.

"he was in the form of GOD, and therefore thought it no robbery to be equal with GOD; yet he took upon him the form of a servant," even human nature. In that nature he obeyed, and thereby fulfilled the whole moral law in our stead; and also died a painful death upon the cross, and thereby became a curse for, or instead of, those whom the Father had given to him. As GOD, he satisfied, at the same time that he obeyed and suffered as man; and being GOD and man in one person, he wrought out a full, perfect, and sufficient righteousness for all to whom it was to be imputed. ◆

BIBLIOGRAPHY

Aldridge, Marion D. "George Whitefield: The Necessary Interdependence of Preaching Style and Sermon Content to Effect Revival." *Journal of the Evangelical Theological Society* 23/1 (March 1980): 55–64.

Belcher, Joseph. *George Whitefield: A Biography.* New York: American Tract Society, 1857.

Belden, Albert D. "What America Owes to George Whitefield." *Religion in Life* 20, no. 3 (Summer 1951): 445–49.

Broadus, John A. *History of Preaching.* New York: A. C. Armstrong & Son, 1891.

Crump, David. "The Preaching of George Whitefield and His Use of Matthew Henry's Commentary." *Crux* 25/3 (September 1989): 19–28.

Dallimore, Arnold A. *George Whitefield: The Life and Times of the Great Evangelist of the Eighteenth-Century Revival.* 2 vols. Carlisle, PA: Banner of Truth Trust, 1970–1980.

_____. *George Whitefield: God's Anointed Servant in the Great Revival of the Eighteenth Century.* Wheaton, IL: Crossway, 1990.

Dargan, Edwin C. *A History of Preaching, Vol. 2.* Grand Rapids: Baker, 1954.

Franklin, Benjamin. *The Life of Benjamin Franklin.* Auburn, NY: Miller, Orton & Mulligan, 1854.

Gillies, John. *Memoirs of Rev. George Whitefield.* New Haven: Whitmore & Buckingham and H. Mansfield, 1834.

Hulse, Erroll. *Give Him No Rest.* Durham, UK: Evangelical, 1991.

Lambert, Frank. *Inventing the "Great Awakening."* Princeton: Princeton University Press, 1999.

_____. *Pedlar in Divinity: George Whitefield and the Transatlantic Revivals, 1737—1770.* Princeton: Princeton University Press, 1994.

Lloyd-Jones, D. M. *The Puritans: Their Origins and Successors.* Carlisle, PA: The Banner of Truth Trust, 1996.

Miller, Kevin A. "Did You Know?" *Christian History* 38, no. 2 (1993): 2.

Noll, Mark. *A History of Christianity in the United States and Canada.* Grand Rapids: Eerdmans, 1992.

Orr, J. Edwin. *The Event of the Century.* Wheaton, IL: International Awakening, 1989.

Packer, J. I. "A Calvinist—and an Evangelist." Pages 205–10 in *Serving the People of God, Vol. 2.* Milton Keynes: Paternoster, 1998.

_____. "Introductory Essay." Pages 1–25 in *The Death of Death in the Death of Christ.* By John Owen. Carlisle, PA: The Banner of Truth Trust, 1995.

_____. "The Spirit with the Word: The Reformational Revivalism of George Whitefield." Pages 166–89 in *The Bible, the Reformation and the Church.* Edited by W. P. Stephens. Sheffield: Sheffield Academic, 1995.

Stitzinger, James F. "The History of Expository Preaching." *The Master's Seminary Journal* 3/1 (Spring 1992): 5–32.

Stout, Harry. *The Divine Dramatist: George Whitefield and the Rise of Modern Evangelicalism.* Grand Rapids: Eerdmans, 1991.

Tyerman, Luke. *The Life of the Reverend George Whitefield.* 2 vols. London: Hodder & Stoughton, 1876–1877; Repr. Azle, TX: Need of the Times Publishers, 1995.

Webber, F. R. *A History of Preaching.* Part One. Milwaukee: Northwestern, 1952.

Wesley, John. "Free Grace." Pages 415–28 in *The SAGE Digital Library* [CD ROM]. Albany, OR: Ages Software, 1996.

_____. *A Sermon on the Death of the Rev. Mr. George Whitefield. Preached at the Chapel in Tottenham-Court-Road, and at the Tabernacle Near Moorfields, on Sunday, November 18, 1770.* London: J. and W. Oliver, 1770. Repr., Atlanta: The Library of Emory University, 1953.

Whitefield, George. *George Whitefield's Journals.* London: The Banner of Truth Trust, 1960.

_____. *George Whitefield's Letters.* Carlisle, PA: The Banner of Truth Trust, 1976.

_____. *Sermons.* London: Thomas Tegg & Son, 1838.

_____. *Select Sermons of George Whitefield.* Edited by J. C. Ryle. Carlisle, PA: The Banner of Truth Trust, 1997.

_____. *The Works of the Reverend George Whitefield.* 6 vols. London: Printed for Edward and Charles Dilly, in the Poultry, and Messrs. Kincaid and Bell, at Edinburgh, 1771–1772.

Scripture Index

Old Testament

New Testament

Apocrypha

Subject Index